ISBN 978-1-332-28017-9
PIBN 10308382

RESTRUCTURING THE FEDERAL SCIENTIFIC ESTABLISHMENT: FUTURE MISSIONS AND GOVERNANCE FOR THE DEPARTMENT OF ENERGY (DOE) NATIONAL LABS

HEARING

BEFORE THE

SUBCOMMITTEE ON BASIC RESEARCH

AND THE

SUBCOMMITTEE ON ENERGY AND ENVIRONMENT

OF THE

COMMITTEE ON SCIENCE

U.S. HOUSE OF REPRESENTATIVES

ONE HUNDRED FOURTH CONGRESS

FIRST SESSION

ON

H.R. 87, H.R. 1510, H.R. 1993 (Title II), and H.R. 2142

SEPTEMBER 7, 1995

[No. 30]

Printed for the use of the Committee on Science

RESTRUCTURING THE FEDERAL SCIENTIFIC ESTABLISHMENT: FUTURE MISSIONS AND GOVERNANCE FOR THE DEPARTMENT OF ENERGY (DOE) NATIONAL LABS

JOINT HEARING

BEFORE THE

SUBCOMMITTEE ON BASIC RESEARCH

AND THE

SUBCOMMITTEE ON ENERGY AND ENVIRONMENT

OF THE

COMMITTEE ON SCIENCE

U.S. HOUSE OF REPRESENTATIVES

ONE HUNDRED FOURTH CONGRESS

FIRST SESSION

ON

H.R. 87, H.R. 1510, H.R. 1993 (Title II), and H.R. 2142

SEPTEMBER 7, 1995

[No. 30]

Printed for the use of the Committee on Science

U.S. GOVERNMENT PRINTING OFFICE

22–056CC WASHINGTON : 1996

For sale by the U.S. Government Printing Office
Superintendent of Documents, Congressional Sales Office, Washington, DC 20402
ISBN 0-16-052849-6

COMMITTEE ON SCIENCE

ROBERT S. WALKER, Pennsylvania, *Chairman*

F. JAMES SENSENBRENNER, JR., Wisconsin
SHERWOOD L. BOEHLERT, New York
HARRIS W. FAWELL, Illinois
CONSTANCE A. MORELLA, Maryland
CURT WELDON, Pennsylvania
DANA ROHRABACHER, California
STEVEN H. SCHIFF, New Mexico
JOE BARTON, Texas
KEN CALVERT, California
BILL BAKER, California
ROSCOE G. BARTLETT, Maryland
VERNON J. EHLERS, Michigan**
ZACH WAMP, Tennessee
DAVE WELDON, Florida
LINDSEY O. GRAHAM, South Carolina
MATT SALMON, Arizona
THOMAS M. DAVIS, Virginia
STEVE STOCKMAN, Texas
GIL GUTKNECHT, Minnesota
ANDREA H. SEASTRAND, California
TODD TIAHRT, Kansas
STEVE LARGENT, Oklahoma
VAN HILLEARY, Tennessee
BARBARA CUBIN, Wyoming
MARK ADAM FOLEY, Florida
SUE MYRICK, North Carolina

GEORGE E. BROWN, JR., California RMM*
RALPH M. HALL, Texas
JAMES A. TRAFICANT, JR., Ohio
JAMES A. HAYES, Louisiana
JOHN S. TANNER, Tennessee
PETE GEREN, Texas
TIM ROEMER, Indiana
ROBERT E. (Bud) CRAMER, JR., Alabama
JAMES A. BARCIA, Michigan
PAUL McHALE, Pennsylvania
JANE HARMAN, California
EDDIE BERNICE JOHNSON, Texas
DAVID MINGE, Minnesota
JOHN W. OLVER, Massachusetts
ALCEE L. HASTINGS, Florida
LYNN N. RIVERS, Michigan
KAREN McCARTHY, Missouri
MIKE WARD, Kentucky
ZOE LOFGREN, California
LLOYD DOGGETT, Texas
MICHAEL F. DOYLE, Pennsylvania
SHEILA JACKSON LEE, Texas
WILLIAM P. LUTHER, Minnesota

DAVID D. CLEMENT, *Chief of Staff and Chief Counsel*
BARRY BERINGER, *General Counsel*
TISH SCHWARTZ, *Chief Clerk and Administrator*
ROBERT E. PALMER, *Democratic Staff Director*

SUBCOMMITTEE ON BASIC RESEARCH

STEVEN SCHIFF, New Mexico, *Chairman*

JOE BARTON, Texas
BILL BAKER, California
VERNON J. Ehlers, Michigan
GIL GUTKNECHT, Minnesota
CONSTANCE A. MORELLA, Maryland
CURT WELDON, Pennsylvania
ROSCOE G. BARTLETT, Maryland
ZACH WAMP, Tennessee
DAVE WELDON, Florida
LINDSEY O. GRAHAM, South Carolina
VAN HILLEARY, Tennessee
SUE MYRICK, North Carolina

PETE GEREN, Texas
ALCEE L. HASTINGS, Florida
LYNN N. RIVERS, Michigan
LLOYD DOGGETT, Texas
WILLIAM P. LUTHER, Minnesota
JOHN W. OLVER, Massachusetts
ZOE LOFGREN, California
MICHAEL F. DOYLE, Pennsylvania
SHEILA JACKSON LEE, Texas
(Vacancy)
(Vacancy)

*Ranking Minority Member
**Vice Chairman

SUBCOMMITTEE ON ENERGY AND ENVIRONMENT

DANA ROHRABACHER, California, *Chairman*

HARRIS W. FAWELL, Illinois
CURT WELDON, Pennsylvania
ROSCOE G. BARTLETT, Maryland
ZACH WAMP, Tennessee
LINDSEY O. GRAHAM, South Carolina
MATT SALMON, Arizona
THOMAS M. DAVIS, Virginia
STEVE LARGENT, Oklahoma
BARBARA CUBIN, Wyoming
MARK ADAM FOLEY, Florida
STEVEN H. SCHIFF, New Mexico
BILL BAKER, California
VERNON J. EHLERS, Michigan
STEVE STOCKMAN, Texas

JAMES A. HAYES, Lousiana
DAVID MINGE, Minnesota
JOHN W. OLVER, Massachusetts
MIKE WARD, Kentucky
MICHAEL F. DOYLE, Pennsylvania
TIM ROEMER, Indiana
ROBERT E. (Bud) CRAMER, JR., Alabama
JAMES A. BARCIA, Michigan
PAUL McHALE, Pennsylvania
EDDIE BERNICE JOHNSON, Texas
LYNN N. RIVERS, Michigan
KAREN McCARTHY, Missouri

CONTENTS

BILLS

WITNESSES

APPENDIX

Hearing on Restructuring the Federal Scientific Establishment: Future Missions and Governance for The Department of Energy [DOE] National Laboratories

---

THURSDAY, SEPTEMBER 7, 1995

U.S. House of Representatives,
Committee on Science,
Subcommittee on Basic Research, and
Subcommittee On Energy and Environment,
Washington, DC.

The Subcommittees met at 9:38 a.m., in Room 2318 of the Rayburn House Office Building, the Honorable Steven H. Schiff, Chairman of the Subcommittee on Basic Research, presiding.

Mr. Schiff. I'd like to welcome everyone here to this legislative hearing.

Chairman Dana Rohrabacher of the Subcommittee on Energy and Environment, and I, the Chairman of the Basic Research Subcommittee, are jointly holding this hearing on four bills which have been introduced in Congress which will, if enacted, affect the Department of Energy and our national laboratories.

I want to say that Chairman Rohrabacher was gracious enough to allow me to preside over this hearing. It is, however, a joint hearing of our two subcommittees.

I would, in exchange, like to recognize Chairman Rohrabacher first for an opening statement.

Mr. Rohrabacher. I thank my friend from New Mexico, who has shouldered many serious responsibilities in the 104th Congress. I also thank him for the time and effort that he's put in to help arrange this hearing.

This is a reflection of the high priority that he places on the future of our national labs. And this hearing also reflects the priority that this whole Committee places on the future of the labs.

I am pleased that we will be able to consider a variety of proposals at this hearing. And I agree with the Galvin Commission Report that our national labs provide America with, and I quote, "essential fundamental cornerstone for continuing leadership" in science and technology.

I also agree with the same report that "the existing lab system is oversized due to management inefficiencies, excess capacity, and political considerations."

It is essential, then, that we consolidate and downsize the enormous laboratory structure that served our needs during the cold war because the cold war is over. Reform and restructuring is the responsible order of the day. Maintaining the status quo is unaffordable.

Now we have under consideration a number of pieces of thoughtful legislation dealing with the national labs. They propose defining the missions, fitting out the personnel, and setting up a BRAC-style commission to consolidate and to reconfigure these national assets.

Each of these bills have strong and weak points. All are well motivated. It is fitting that we move forward with open minds and open discussion, but not necessarily open pocketbooks.

This hearing will give us an opportunity to look at the management structure of our national labs. Is DOE's unique system of government-owned, contractor-operated labs the most efficient and effective system of operation?

That's a good question.

Is privatization or corporatization of the labs a practical alternative? Another question.

I look forward to hearing the views of these issues from our distinguished witnesses today, just as I look forward to visiting the display next door, which I understand is based on the best PR advice that money can buy.

In particular, however, on another issue, I would like to welcome the participation of our new interim provost from the University of California, Dr. C. Judson King, who will give us the perspective of both a major contractor for the DOE and a major academic institution as well.

Mr. Chairman, I look forward to this hearing. I would like to apologize beforehand that I will be here most of the time. But, as usual, we have scheduled three important events at exactly the same time that I will have to be participating in. So I will be here for most of the hearing, but at some moments, I will have to ease out and then come back in. But I will be paying close attention to all the testimony because I will read that which I am not here to hear.

Thank you.

Mr. SCHIFF. Mr. Chairman, again, thank you for joining me in calling this hearing. I know that we disagree on some points, but I'm glad that we're working together to bring out all the facts through expert witnesses.

I have a brief opening statement I would like to read, and then I'll do some recognition for other opening statements before going to the first witnesses.

I would like to say, however, just to make the point up front, that I believe that the national laboratories, the Department of Energy, and every other agency or project sponsored by the United States government, certainly has to do its share in terms of contributing to efficiency and balancing the budget.

The point of my bill, which is one of the four bills that's introduced here today, is that we should first establish missions for the national laboratories and then build that productivity design around what the missions are.

I think that is the logical way to proceed.

Over the past decade, several government advisory groups have emphasized the need for the Department of Energy to clarify the role of the laboratories and their missions.

Earlier this year, our two subcommittees held another joint hearing on two studies: "National Laboratories Need Clearer Missions and Better Management," that's the report to the Secretary of Energy by the United States General Accounting Office, dated January, 1995, and "Alternative Futures for the Department of Energy National Laboratories," the Secretary of Energy Advisory Board, Task Force on Alternative Futures for the Department of Energy National Laboratories, which is also known as the Galvin Task Force Report of February, 1995. Both studies emphasized the need for changes within the Department of Energy governance infrastructure and with the departmental laboratories' missions and management.

Through their unique historical missions, the Department of Energy's National Laboratories have developed core competencies and scientific capabilities that have contributed and continue to contribute technology to ensure the maintenance of the nuclear deterrent and other elements of our national security. These laboratories collectively represent an extensive science and technology resource of people, facilities, and equipment.

The national laboratories have established successful collaborative relationships with other federal agencies, universities, and private industry that have allowed each partner to share and leverage their capabilities. Their contributions to energy-related and basic science, and environmental restoration and waste management, and other emerging scientific fields, are internationally significant.

Over the years, however, the missions of the national laboratories have become diffuse. Congress is now in the process of rethinking the infrastructure which supports research by the federal scientific establishment.

There are those who believe that in this process, we should close down the Department of Energy and some of the labs.

I do not. I believe it is vital that the laboratories' pre-eminence as research facilities and their contributions to the nation's overall national security, scientific and industrial well-being be recognized, defined and focused.

Whatever the final form of the Department of Energy in our federal research support infrastructure, the national laboratories will continue to play a prominent role. That is why we have separated the two issues—the future of the Department of Energy and the future of the national laboratories—at this hearing.

And I want to take a moment to emphasize that point.

As you all know, there are proposals before the Congress to dissolve the Department of Energy. I do not personally support those proposals. But others do.

The point, however, is that the national laboratories, even under those proposals, would continue to exist, although perhaps assigned to a different department. And the focus of this hearing is the national laboratories.

This rethinking has led to the introduction of several pieces of legislation. Each proposal has a different emphasis, reflecting the views of the author. But each proposal directs that some action be taken concerning the national laboratories. And so it's our intention to hear from those who have expertise in this area and from those who may be affected by these proposed changes.

The purpose of this hearing, therefore, is to receive testimony from the Department of Energy, from government-affiliated and public witnesses, and the Department of Energy contractors and directors of the national laboratories on the four pending pieces of legislation.

The sponsors of these four bills are all Members of the Science Committee. I introduced H.R. 2142, the Department of Energy Laboratory Missions Act, and will briefly summarize it before recognizing the Ranking Member of our subcommittees. And then I intend to recognize Congressman Bartlett, Congressman Roemer, and Congressman Tiahrt to explain their legislative proposals, which are also the subject of this hearing.

[The prepared statement of Mr. Schiff follows:]

OPENING STATEMENT

JOINT HEARING

SUBCOMMITTEES ON BASIC RESEARCH AND ENERGY & ENVIRONMENT

HONORABLE STEVE SCHIFF

CHAIRMAN, SUBCOMMITTEE ON BASIC RESEARCH

SEPTEMBER 7, 1995

Good morning, ladies and gentlemen. I would like to welcome you to this legislative hearing.

Chairman Rohrabacher of the Subcommittee on Energy and Environment and I are holding this joint hearing on four bills which have been introduced in this Congress which will, if enacted, affect the Department of Energy and our National Laboratories. Since both subcommittees have jurisdiction over these bills we felt that it would be more productive to hold this legislative hearing together.

Over the past decade, several government advisory groups have emphasized the need for DOE to clarify the role of the laboratories and their missions. Earlier this year our two subcommittees held another joint hearing on two studies: "National Laboratories Need Clearer Missions and Better Management," Report to the Secretary of Energy, U.S. General Accounting Office, January 1995; and, "Alternative Futures for the Department of Energy National Laboratories," Secretary of Energy Advisory Board, Task Force on Alternative Futures for the Department of Energy National Laboratories, (also known as the Galvin Task Force Report), February 1995. Both studies emphasized the need for changes within the DOE governance infrastructure and with the departmental laboratories' missions and management.

Through their unique historical missions, DOE's National Laboratories have developed core competencies and scientific capabilities that have contributed, and continue to contribute, technology to ensure the maintenance of the nuclear deterrent and other elements of our national security. These laboratories collectively represent an extensive science and technology resource of people, facilities, and equipment. The national laboratories have established successful collaborative relationships with other Federal agencies, universities, and private industry that have allowed each partner to share and leverage their capabilities. Their contributions to energy-related and basic science, environmental restoration and waste management, and other emerging scientific fields are internationally significant.

Over the years, however, the missions of the national laboratories have become diffuse. Congress is now in the process of rethinking the infrastructure which supports research by the Federal scientific establishment. There are those who believe that in this process we should close down the Department of Energy and some of the labs. I do not. I believe that it is vital that the laboratories' preeminence as research facilities and their contributions to the Nation's overall national security, scientific and industrial wellbeing be recognized, defined and focused. Whatever the final form of the Department of Energy in our Federal research support infrastructure, the national laboratories will continue to play a prominent role. That is why we have separated the two issues—the future of DOE and the future of the national labs—at this hearing.

This rethinking has led to the introduction of several pieces of legislation. Each proposal has a different emphasis, reflecting the views of the author. But each proposal directs that some action be taken concerning the national laboratories and so it is our intention to hear from those who have some expertise in this area and from those who may be affected by these proposed changes.

The purpose of this hearing, therefore, is to receive testimony from the Department of Energy, government affiliated and public witnesses, and the DOE contractors and directors of the National Laboratories on the four pending pieces of legislation. The sponsors of these four bills are all Members of the Science Committee. I introduced H.R. 2142, the "Department of Energy Laboratory Missions Act" and will briefly summarize it before recognizing Chairman Rohrabacher and the Ranking Members of our subcommittees. I will then recognize Mr. Bartlett, Mr. Roemer, and Mr. Tiahrt to explain their legislative proposals.

The bill, H.R. 2142, the "Department of Energy Laboratories Missions Act," defines a three step public process by which the Secretary of Energy, working with the interested parties, including Congress, first defines the appropriate missions for the laboratories. These missions include: maintaining our national security; helping to ensure our Nation's energy supply; conducting basic research in energy-related science and technology; and, to carry out research and development for the purpose of minimizing the environmental impacts of hazardous and radioactive waste. The bill then sets out the criteria for the Secretary of Energy to assign those missions, streamlining the labs, if necessary, to carry out those missions.

Additionally, H.R. 2142 would direct DOE to cease internal health, safety and environmental regulation of the departmental labs and to transfer those responsibilities to other appropriate Federal and state regulatory agencies, which are already responsible for these areas. Recent reports to the Secretary of Energy on this issue of governance indicate this would substantially improve management of the labs and release scarce resources to accomplish the laboratories' missions.

[Copies of the four bills follow:]

104TH CONGRESS
1ST SESSION

H. R. 87

To establish the Department of Energy Laboratory Facilities Commission, and for other purposes.

IN THE HOUSE OF REPRESENTATIVES

JANUARY 4, 1995

Mr. BARTLETT of Maryland introduced the following bill; which was referred to the Committee on Science and, in addition, to the Committees on National Security and Rules, for a period to be subsequently determined by the Speaker, in each case for consideration of such provisions as fall within the jurisdiction of the committee concerned

---

A BILL

To establish the Department of Energy Laboratory Facilities Commission, and for other purposes.

Be it enacted by the Senate and House of Representatives of the United States of America in Congress assembled,

SECTION 1. SHORT TITLE.

This Act may be cited as the "Department of Energy Laboratory Facilities Act of 1995".

SEC. 2. DEPARTMENT OF ENERGY LABORATORY FACILITIES COMMISSION.

(a) ESTABLISHMENT.—There is established an independent commission to be known as the "Department of Energy Laboratory Facilities Commission".

(b) DUTIES.—The Commission shall carry out the duties specified for the Commission in this Act.

(c) APPOINTMENT.—

(1) IN GENERAL.—The Commission shall be composed of 7 members appointed by the President, by and with the advise and consent of the Senate. The President shall transmit to the Senate the nominations for appointment to the Commission not later than 3 months after the date of the enactment of this Act.

(2) CONSULTATION.—In selecting individuals for nominations for appointments to the Commission, the President should consult with—

(A) the Speaker of the House of Representatives concerning the appointment of 1 member;

(B) the majority leader of the Senate concerning the appointment of 1 member;

(C) the minority leader of the House of Representatives concerning the appointment of 1 member; and

(D) the minority leader of the Senate concerning the appointment of 1 member.

(3) CHAIRPERSON.—At the time the President nominates individuals for appointment to the Commission, the President shall designate one such individual who shall serve as Chairperson of the Commission.

(d) TERMS.—Each member of the Commission shall serve until the termination of the Commission under subsection (l).

(e) MEETINGS.—Each meeting of the Commission, other than meetings in which classified information is to be discussed, shall be open to the public.

(f) VACANCIES.—A vacancy in the Commission shall be filled in the same manner as the original appointment, but the individual appointed to fill the vacancy shall serve only for the unexpired portion of the term for which the individual's predecessor was appointed.

(g) PAY AND TRAVEL EXPENSES.—

(1) IN GENERAL.—

(A) BASIC PAY.—Each member, other than the Chairperson, shall be paid at a rate equal to the daily equivalent of the minimum annual rate of basic pay payable for level IV of the Executive Schedule under section 5315 of title 5,

United States Code, for each day (including travel time) during which the member is engaged in the actual performance of duties vested in the Commission.

(B) PAY OF CHAIRPERSON.—The Chairperson shall be paid for each day referred to in subparagraph (A) at a rate equal to the daily equivalent of the minimum annual rate of basic pay payable for level III of the Executive Schedule under section 5314 of title 5, United States Code.

(2) TRAVEL EXPENSES.—Members shall receive travel expenses, including per diem in lieu of subsistence, in accordance with sections 5702 and 5703 of title 5, United States Code.

(h) DIRECTOR.—

(1) IN GENERAL.—The Commission shall, without regard to section 5311(b) of title 5, United States Code, appoint a Director who—

(A) has not served as a civilian employee of the Department of Energy during the one-year period preceding the date of such appointment;

(B) has not been an employee of a departmental laboratory during the 5-year period preceding the date of such appointment; and

(C) has not been an employee of a contractor operating a departmental laboratory during the 5-year period preceding the date of such appointment.

(2) PAY.—The Director shall be paid at the rate of basic pay payable for level IV of the Executive Schedule under section 5315 of title 5, United States Code.

(i) STAFF.—

(1) APPOINTMENT BY DIRECTOR.—Subject to subparagraphs (B) and (C), the Director, with the approval of the Commission, may appoint and fix the pay of additional personnel.

(2) APPLICABILITY OF CERTAIN CIVIL SERVICE LAWS.—The Director may make such appointments without regard to the provisions of title 5, United States Code, governing appointments in the competitive service, and any personnel so appointed may be paid without regard to the provisions of chapter 51 and subchapter III of chapter 53 of that title relating to classification and General Schedule pay rates, except that an individual so appointed may not re-

ceive pay in excess of the annual rate of basic pay payable for level IV of the Executive Schedule under section 5315 of title 5, United States Code.

(3) LIMITATIONS.—Not more than one-third of the personnel employed by or detailed to the Commission may be on detail from the Department of Energy. No employee of a departmental laboratory, or of a contractor who operates a departmental laboratory, may be detailed to the Commission.

(4) SUPPORT FROM OTHER AGENCIES.—Upon request of the Director, the head of a Federal agency may detail any of the personnel of that agency to the Commission to assist the Commission in carrying out its duties under this section.

(5) SUPPORT FROM COMPTROLLER GENERAL.—The Comptroller General of the United States shall provide assistance, including the detailing of employees, to the Commission in accordance with an agreement entered into with the Commission.

(j) OTHER AUTHORITY.—

(1) TEMPORARY AND INTERMITTENT SERVICES.—The Commission may procure by contract, to the extent funds are available, the temporary or intermittent services of experts or consultants pursuant to section 3109 of title 5, United States Code.

(2) AUTHORITY TO LEASE SPACE AND ACQUIRE CERTAIN PROPERTY.—The Commission may lease space and acquire personal property to the extent funds are available. To the extent practicable, the Commission shall use suitable real property available under the most recent inventory of real property assets published by the Resolution Trust Corporation under section 21A(b)(11)(F) of the Federal Home Loan Bank Act (12 U.S.C. 1441a(b)(12)(F)).

(k) FUNDING.—There are authorized to be appropriated to the Commission such funds as are necessary to carry out its duties under this section. Such funds shall remain available until expended.

(l) TERMINATION.—The Commission shall terminate not later than 20 months after the date of the enactment of this Act.

SEC. 3. PROCEDURE FOR MAKING RECOMMENDATIONS FOR LABORATORY FACILITIES.

(a) SELECTION CRITERIA.—

(1) IN GENERAL.—Not later than 3 months after the date of the enactment of this Act, the Secretary of Energy shall publish in the Federal Register and transmit to the congressional energy committees the criteria proposed to be used by the Secretary in making recommendations for the closure or

reconfiguration of departmental laboratories resulting in cost savings for the overall budget for such laboratories. The Secretary shall provide an opportunity for public comment on the proposed criteria for a period of at least 30 days and shall include notice of that opportunity in the publication required under this paragraph. In developing the criteria, the Secretary shall consider—

(A) the program costs and program distributions on a State and county basis, including real and personal property costs associated with each departmental laboratory considered;

(B) the number of participants in programs conducted through a departmental laboratory and staff resources involved;

(C) duplication of effort by departmental laboratories and overhead costs as a proportion of program benefits distributed through a departmental laboratory;

(D) cost savings and increases that would accrue through the reconfiguration of departmental laboratories;

(E) changes in the roles and missions of each departmental laboratory; and

(F) the privatization of the laboratories as an alternative to closure or reconfiguration.

(2) FINAL CRITERIA.—Not later than 5 months after the date of the enactment of this Act, the Secretary shall publish in the Federal Register and transmit to the congressional energy committees the final criteria to be used in making recommendations for the closure or reconfiguration of departmental laboratories under this section.

(b) SECRETARY'S RECOMMENDATIONS.—

(1) PUBLICATION IN FEDERAL REGISTER.—Not later than 1 year after the date of the enactment of this Act, the Secretary shall publish in the Federal Register and transmit to the congressional energy committees and to the Commission a list of the departmental laboratories that the Secretary recommends for closure or reconfiguration on the basis of the final criteria referred to in subsection (a).

(2) SUMMARY OF SELECTION PROCESS.—The Secretary shall include, with the list of recommendations published and transmitted pursuant to paragraph (1), a summary of the selection process that resulted in the recommendation for each departmental laboratory, including a justification for each recommendation.

(c) EQUAL CONSIDERATION OF LABORATORIES.—In considering departmental laboratories for closure or reconfiguration, the Secretary shall consider all such laboratories equally without regard to whether a laboratory has been previously considered or proposed for closure or reconfiguration by the Secretary.

(d) AVAILABILITY OF INFORMATION.—The Secretary shall make available to the Commission and the Comptroller General of the United States all information used by the Secretary in making recommendations to the Commission for closures and reconfiguration.

(e) REVIEW AND RECOMMENDATIONS BY THE COMMISSION.—

(1) PUBLIC HEARINGS.—After receiving the recommendations from the Secretary pursuant to subsection (b), the Commission shall conduct public hearings on the recommendations.

(2) REPORT.—Not later than 18 months after the date of the enactment of this Act, the Commission shall transmit to the President and the congressional energy committees a report containing the Commission's findings and conclusions based on a review and analysis of the recommendations made by the Secretary, together with the Commission's recommendations for closures and reconfigurations of

departmental laboratories. In conducting such review and analysis, the Commission shall consider all departmental laboratories.

(3) DEVIATION FROM SECRETARY'S RECOMMENDATIONS.—In making its recommendations, the Commission may make changes in any of the recommendations made by the Secretary if the Commission determines that the Secretary deviated substantially from the final criteria referred to in subsection (a) in making recommendations. The Commission shall explain and justify in the report any recommendation made by the Commission that is different from the recommendations made by the Secretary.

(4) PROVISION OF CERTAIN INFORMATION.—After transmitting the report, the Commission shall promptly provide, upon request, to any Member of Congress information used by the Commission in making its recommendations.

(f) ASSISTANCE FROM COMPTROLLER GENERAL.—The Comptroller General of the United States shall—

(1) assist the Commission, to the extent requested, in the Commission's review and analysis of the recommendations made by the Secretary pursuant to subsection (b); and

(2) not later than 15 months after the date of the enactment of this Act, transmit to the congressional energy committees and to the Commission a report containing a detailed analysis of the Secretary's recommendations and selection process.

(g) REVIEW BY THE PRESIDENT.—

(1) IN GENERAL.—Not later than 19 months after the date of the enactment of this Act, the President shall transmit to the Commission and to the congressional energy committees a report containing the President's approval or disapproval of the Commission's recommendations.

(2) PRESIDENTIAL APPROVAL.—If the President approves all of the recommendations of the Commission, the President shall transmit a copy of such recommendations to the congressional energy committees together with a certification of such approval.

(3) PRESIDENTIAL DISAPPROVAL.—If the President disapproves the recommendations of the Commission, in whole or in part, the President shall transmit to the Commission and the congressional energy committees the reasons for that disapproval. The Commission shall then transmit to the President, not later than 20 months after the date of the

enactment of this Act, a revised list of recommendations for the closure and reconfiguration of departmental laboratories resulting in cost savings for the overall budget for such departmental laboratories.

(4) CERTIFICATION.—If the President approves all of the revised recommendations of the Commission transmitted to the President under paragraph (3), the President shall transmit a copy of such revised recommendations to the congressional energy committees, together with a certification of such approval.

(5) FAILURE TO CERTIFY.—If the President does not transmit to the congressional energy committees an approval and certification described in paragraph (2) or (4) by 21 months after the date of the enactment of this Act, the process by which departmental laboratories may be selected for closure or reconfiguration under this section shall be terminated.

SEC. 4. CLOSURE AND RECONFIGURATION OF DEPARTMENTAL LABORATORIES.

(a) IN GENERAL.—Subject to subsection (b), the Secretary shall—

(1) close all departmental laboratories recommended for closure by the Commission in the re-

port transmitted to the congressional energy committees by the President pursuant to section 3(g);

(2) reconfigure all such laboratories recommended for reconfiguration by the Commission in the report; and

(3) complete the closures and reconfigurations not later than the end of the 6-year period beginning on the date on which the President transmits the report pursuant to section 3(g).

(b) CONGRESSIONAL DISAPPROVAL.—

(1) IN GENERAL.—The Secretary may not carry out any closure or reconfiguration of a departmental laboratory recommended by the Commission in the report transmitted from the President pursuant to section 3(g) if a joint resolution is enacted, in accordance with the provisions of section 8, disapproving the recommendations of the Commission before the earlier of—

(A) the end of the 45-day period beginning on the date on which the President transmits the report; or

(B) the adjournment of Congress sine die for the session during which the report is transmitted.

(2) For purposes of paragraph (1) of this subsection and subsections (a) and (c) of section (8), the days on which either House of Congress is not in session because of an adjournment of more than three days to a day certain shall be excluded in the computation of a period.

SEC. 5. IMPLEMENTATION OF CLOSURE AND RECONFIGURATION ACTIONS.

(a) ACTIONS OF THE SECRETARY.—In closing or reconfiguring a departmental laboratory under this Act, the Secretary shall—

(1) take such actions as may be necessary to close or reconfigure the departmental laboratory;

(2) provide outplacement assistance to any employees employed by the Department of Energy at the office whose employment is being terminated, and may use for such purpose funds in the Account or funds appropriated to the Department of Energy for outplacement assistance to employees;

(3) take such steps as may be necessary to ensure the safe keeping of all records stored at the departmental laboratory; and

(4) reimburse other Federal agencies for actions performed at the request of the Secretary with respect to any such closure or reconfiguration, and

may use for such purpose funds in the Account or funds appropriated to the Department of Energy and available for such purpose.

(b) MANAGEMENT AND DISPOSAL OF PROPERTY.—

(1) IN GENERAL.—The Administrator of General Services shall delegate to the Secretary of Energy, with respect to excess and surplus real property and facilities located at a departmental laboratory closed or reconfigured under this Act—

(A) the authority of the Administrator to utilize excess property under section 202 of the Federal Property and Administrative Services Act of 1949 (40 U.S.C. 483);

(B) the authority of the Administrator to dispose of surplus property under section 203 of that Act (40 U.S.C. 484);

(C) the authority of the Administrator to grant approvals and make determinations under section 13(g) of the Surplus Property Act of 1944 (50 U.S.C. App. 1622(g)); and

(D) the authority of the Administrator to determine the availability of excess or surplus real property for wildlife conservation purposes in accordance with the Act of May 19, 1948 (16 U.S.C. 667b).

(2) EXERCISE OF AUTHORITY.—

(A) IN GENERAL.—Subject to subparagraph (C), the Secretary shall exercise the authority delegated to the Secretary pursuant to paragraph (1) in accordance with—

(i) all regulations in effect on the date of the enactment of this Act governing the utilization of excess property and the disposal of surplus property under the Federal Property and Administrative Services Act of 1949; and

(ii) all regulations in effect on the date of the enactment of this Act governing the conveyance and disposal of property under section 13(g) of the Surplus Property Act of 1944 (50 U.S.C. App. 1622(g)).

(B) REGULATIONS.—The Secretary, after consulting with the Administrator of General Services, may issue regulations that are necessary to carry out the delegation of authority required by paragraph (1).

(C) LIMITATION.—The authority required to be delegated by paragraph (1) to the Secretary by the Administrator of General Services shall not include the authority to prescribe general policies and methods for utilizing excess property and disposing of surplus property.

(c) WAIVER.—The Secretary may close or reconfigure departmental laboratories under this Act without regard to any provision of law restricting the use of funds for closing or reconfiguring such departmental laboratories included in any appropriations or authorization Act.

SEC. 6. ACCOUNT.

(a) ESTABLISHMENT.—There is hereby established on the books of the Treasury an account to be known as the "Department of Energy Laboratory Facility Closure Account" which shall be administered by the Secretary as a single account.

(b) CONTENT OF ACCOUNT.—There shall be deposited into the Account—

(1) funds authorized for and appropriated to the Account;

(2) any funds that the Secretary may, subject to approval in an appropriation Act, transfer to the Account from funds appropriated to the Department of Energy for any purpose, except that such funds may be transferred only after the date on which the Secretary transmits written notice of, and justifica-

tion for, such transfer to the congressional energy committees; and

(3) proceeds received from the transfer or disposal of any property at an office closed or reconfigured under this section.

(c) USE OF FUNDS.—The Secretary may use the funds in the Account only for the purposes described in section 5(a).

(d) REPORTS.—

(1) IN GENERAL.—Not later than 60 days after the end of each fiscal year in which the Secretary carries out activities under this Act, the Secretary shall transmit a report to the congressional energy committees of the amount and nature of the deposits into, and the expenditures from, the Account during such fiscal year and of the amount and nature of other expenditures made pursuant to section 5(a) during such fiscal year.

(2) UNOBLIGATED FUNDS.—Unobligated funds which remain in the Account after the termination of the Commission shall be held in the Account until transferred by law after the congressional energy committees receive the report transmitted under paragraph (3).

(3) ACCOUNTING REPORT.—Not later than 60 days after the termination of the Commission, the Secretary shall transmit to the congressional energy committees a report containing an accounting of—

(A) all the funds deposited into and expended from the Account or otherwise expended under this section; and

(B) any amount remaining in the Account.

SEC. 7. REPORTS ON IMPLEMENTATION.

As part of the budget request for each fiscal year in which the Secretary will carry out activities under this Act, the Secretary shall transmit to the congressional energy committees—

(1) a schedule of the closure and reconfiguration actions to be carried out under this Act in the fiscal year for which the request is made and an estimate of the total expenditures required and cost savings to be achieved by each such closure and reconfiguration and of the time period in which these savings are to be achieved in each case; and

(2) a description of the departmental laboratories, including those under construction and those planned for construction, to which functions are to be transferred as a result of such closures and reconfigurations.

SEC. 8. CONGRESSIONAL CONSIDERATION OF COMMISSION REPORT.

(a) TERMS OF THE RESOLUTION.—For purposes of section 4(b), the term "joint resolution" means only a joint resolution which is introduced within the 10-day period beginning on the date on which the President transmits the report to the Congress under section 3(g), and—

(1) which does not have a preamble;

(2) the matter after the resolving clause of which is as follows: "That Congress disapproves the recommendations of the Department of Energy Laboratory Facilities Commission as submitted by the President on ______", the blank space being filled in with the appropriate date; and

(3) the title of which is as follows: "Joint resolution disapproving the recommendations of the Department of Energy Laboratory Facilities Commission.".

(b) REFERRAL.—A resolution described in subsection (a) that is introduced in the House of Representatives shall be referred to the Committee on National Security and the Committee on Science of the House of Representatives. A resolution described in subsection (a) introduced in the Senate shall be referred to the Committee on Armed Services and the Committee on Energy and Natural Resources of the Senate.

(c) DISCHARGE.—If the committee to which a resolution described in subsection (a) is referred has not reported such resolution (or an identical resolution) by the end of the 20-day period beginning on the date on which the President transmits the report to the Congress under section 3(g), such committee shall be, at the end of such period, discharged from further consideration of such resolution, and such resolution shall be placed on the appropriate calendar of the House involved.

(d) CONSIDERATION.—

(1) IN GENERAL.—On or after the third day after the date on which the committee to which such a resolution is referred has reported, or has been discharged (under subsection (c)) from further consideration of, such a resolution, it is in order (even though a previous motion to the same effect has been disagreed to) for any Member of the respective House to move to proceed to the consideration of the resolution (but only on the day after the calendar day on which such Member announces to the House concerned the Member's intention to do so). All points of order against the resolution (and against consideration of the resolution) are waived. The motion is highly privileged in the House of Representatives and is privileged in the Senate and is not de-

batable. The motion is not subject to amendment, or to a motion to postpone, or to a motion to proceed to the consideration of other business. A motion to reconsider the vote by which the motion is agreed to or disagreed to shall not be in order. If a motion to proceed to the consideration of the resolution is agreed to, the respective House shall immediately proceed to consideration of the joint resolution without intervening motion, order, or other business, and the resolution shall remain the unfinished business of the respective House until disposed of.

(2) DEBATE.—Debate on the resolution, and on all debatable motions and appeals in connection therewith, shall be limited to not more than 2 hours, which shall be divided equally between those favoring and those opposing the resolution. An amendment to the resolution is not in order. A motion further to limit debate is in order and not debatable. A motion to postpone, or a motion to proceed to the consideration of other business, or a motion to recommit the resolution is not in order. A motion to reconsider the vote by which the resolution is agreed to or disagreed to is not in order.

(3) QUORUM CALL.—Immediately following the conclusion of the debate on a resolution described in

subsection (a) and a single quorum call at the conclusion of the debate if requested in accordance with the rules of the appropriate House, the vote on final passage of the resolution shall occur.

(4) APPEALS FROM DECISION OF CHAIR.—Appeals from the decisions of the Chair relating to the application of the rules of the Senate or the House of Representatives, as the case may be, to the procedure relating to a resolution described in subsection (a) shall be decided without debate.

(e) CONSIDERATION BY OTHER HOUSE.—

(1) If, before the passage by one House of a resolution of that House described in subsection (a), that House receives from the other House a resolution described in subsection (a), then the following procedures shall apply:

(A) The resolution of the other House shall not be referred to a committee and may not be considered in the House receiving it except in the case of final passage as provided in subparagraph (B)(ii).

(B) With respect to a resolution described in paragraph (1) of the House receiving the resolution—

(i) the procedure in that House shall be the same as if no resolution had been received from the other House; but

(ii) the vote on final passage shall be on the resolution of the other House.

(2) CONSIDERATION AFTER DISPOSITION BY OTHER HOUSE.—Upon disposition of the resolution received from the other House, it shall no longer be in order to consider the resolution that originated in the receiving House.

(f) RULES OF THE SENATE AND HOUSE.—This subsection is enacted by Congress—

(1) as an exercise of the rulemaking power of the Senate and House of Representatives, respectively, and as such it is deemed a part of the rules of each House, respectively, but applicable only with respect to the procedure to be followed in that House in the case of a resolution described in subsection (a), and it supersedes other rules only to the extent that it is inconsistent with such rules; and

(2) with full recognition of the constitutional right of either House to change the rules (so far as relating to the procedure of that House) at any time, in the same manner, and to the same extent as in the case of any other rule of that House.

SEC. 9. DEFINITIONS.

For purposes of this Act:

(1) The term "Account" means the Department of Energy Laboratory Facility Closure Account established in section 6(a).

(2) The term "Commission" means the Department of Energy Laboratory Facilities Closure and Reconfiguration Commission.

(3) The term "congressional energy committees" means the Committee on Armed Services of the Senate, the Committee on National Security of the House of Representatives, the Committee on Science of the House of Representatives, and the Committee on Energy and Natural Resources of the Senate.

(4) The term "departmental laboratory" means a Federal laboratory, or any other laboratory or facility designated by the Secretary, operated by or on behalf of the Department of Energy.

(5) The term "Federal laboratory" has the meaning given the term "laboratory" in section 12(d)(2) of the Stevenson-Wydler Technology Innovation Act of 1980 (15 U.S.C. 3710a(d)(2)).

(6) The term "Secretary" means the Secretary of Energy.

○

104TH CONGRESS
1ST SESSION

H. R. 1510

To prohibit the Department of Energy from acting as the agency of implementation, with respect to nondefense Department of Energy laboratories, for certain environmental, safety, and health regulations, and to require reduction in personnel at such laboratories.

IN THE HOUSE OF REPRESENTATIVES

APRIL 7, 1995

Mr. ROEMER (for himself, Mr. DOYLE, Mr. JACOBS, and Mr. KLUG) introduced the following bill; which was referred to the Committee on Science

---

A BILL

To prohibit the Department of Energy from acting as the agency of implementation, with respect to nondefense Department of Energy laboratories, for certain environmental, safety, and health regulations, and to require reduction in personnel at such laboratories.

Be it enacted by the Senate and House of Representatives of the United States of America in Congress assembled,

SECTION 1. SHORT TITLE.

This Act may be cited as the "Department of Energy Laboratories Efficiency Improvement Act".

SEC. 2. ELIMINATION OF SELF-REGULATION.

Notwithstanding any other provision of law, the Department of Energy shall not be the agency of implementation, with respect to departmental laboratories, other than departmental defense laboratories, of Federal, State, and local environmental, safety, and health rules, regulations, orders, and standards.

SEC. 3. PERSONNEL REDUCTIONS.

(a) REQUIREMENTS.—The aggregate number of individuals employed at all government-owned, contractor-operated departmental laboratories, other than departmental defense laboratories, shall be reduced, within 10 years after the date of the enactment of this Act, by at least one-third from the number so employed as of such date of enactment. At least 1 percent of such reduction shall be accomplished within 1 year, at least 3 percent within 2 years, at least 6 percent within 3 years, at least 10 percent within 4 years, and at least 15 percent within 5 years.

(b) OBJECTIVES.—The Secretary of Energy shall ensure that the personnel reductions required by subsection (a) are made consistent with, to the extent feasible, the following objectives:

(1) Termination of departmental laboratory research and development facilities that are not the most advanced and the most relevant to the pro-

grammatic objectives of the Department, when compared with other facilities in the United States.

(2) Termination of facilities that provide research opportunities duplicating those afforded by other facilities in the United States, or in foreign countries when United States scientists are provided access to such facilities to the extent necessary to accomplish the programmatic objectives of the Department.

(3) Relocation and consolidation of departmental laboratory research and development activities, consistent with the programmatic objectives of the Department, within laboratories with major facilities or demonstrable concentrations of expertise appropriate for performing such research and development activities.

(4) Reduction of management inefficiencies within the Department and the departmental laboratories.

(5) Reduction of physical infrastructure needs.

(6) Utilization of other resources for performing Department of Energy funded research and development activities, including universities, industrial laboratories, and others.

SEC. 4. REPORTS TO CONGRESS.

(a) INITIAL REPORT.—Within 1 year after the date of the enactment of this Act, the Secretary of Energy shall transmit a report to the Congress that—

(1) identifies the extent to which Department of Energy and departmental laboratory staffs have been reduced as a result of the implementation of section 2 of this Act; and

(2) explains the extent to which reductions required by section 3(a) have been made consistent with the objectives set forth in section 3(b).

(b) ANNUAL REPORTS.—The Secretary of Energy shall transmit to the Congress, along with each of the President's annual budget submissions occurring—

(1) after the report under subsection (a) is transmitted; and

(2) before the full personnel reduction requirement under section 3 is accomplished,

a report containing the explanation described in subsection (a)(2) of this section.

SEC. 5. DEFINITIONS.

For purposes of this Act—

(1) the term "departmental laboratory" means a Federal laboratory, or any other laboratory or facility designated by the Secretary of Energy, operated by or on behalf of the Department of Energy;

(2) the term "departmental defense laboratories" means the Lawrence Livermore National Laboratory, the Los Alamos National Laboratory, and the Sandia National Laboratories;

(3) the term "Federal laboratory" has the meaning given the term "laboratory" in section 12(d)(2) of the Stevenson-Wydler Technology Innovation Act of 1980 (15 U.S.C. 3710a(d)(2)); and

(4) the term "programmatic objectives of the Department" means the goals and milestones of the Department of Energy, as set forth in departmental strategic planning documents and the President's annual budget requests.

○

104TH CONGRESS
1ST SESSION

H. R. 1993

To abolish the Department of Energy.

IN THE HOUSE OF REPRESENTATIVES

JUNE 30, 1995

Mr. TIAHRT (for himself, Mr. BROWNBACK, Mr. BASS, Mr. BARTLETT of Maryland, Mr. COBURN, Mr. CREMEANS, Mr. FOLEY, Mr. SHADEGG, Mr. ARMEY, Mr. DELAY, Mr. BOEHNER, Mr. KASICH, Mr. SOLOMON, Mr. SCARBOROUGH, Mr. NEUMANN, Mr. HOSTETTLER, Mr. EWING, Mrs. WALDHOLTZ, Mrs. MYRICK, Mr. SMITH of Michigan, Mr. PACKARD, Mr. PARKER, Mr. CHRISTENSEN, Mr. CRANE, Mr. DORNAN, Mr. LOBIONDO, Mr. STOCKMAN, Mr. HANCOCK, Mr. HOEKSTRA, Mr. WICKER, Mrs. SEASTRAND, Mr. ROYCE, Mr. GUTKNECHT, Mr. CHRYSLER, Mrs. LOWEY, Mr. MILLER of Florida, Mr. HUTCHINSON, Mr. KLUG, Mr. FUNDERBURK, Mr. LINDER, Mr. HOKE, Ms. DUNN of Washington, Mr. TATE, Mr. WHITE, Mr. NETHERCUTT, Mr. METCALF, Mrs. CUBIN, Mrs. CHENOWETH, Mr. SAM JOHNSON of Texas, and Mrs. SMITH of Washington) introduced the following bill; which was referred to the Committee on Commerce, and in addition to the Committees on National Security, Science, Resources, Rules, and Government Reform and Oversight, for a period to be subsequently determined by the Speaker, in each case for consideration of such provisions as fall within the jurisdiction of the committee concerned

---

A BILL

To abolish the Department of Energy.

Be it enacted by the Senate and House of Representatives of the United States of America in Congress assembled,

SECTION 1. SHORT TITLE.

This Act may be cited as the "Department of Energy Abolishment Act".

SEC. 2. TABLE OF CONTENTS.

The table of contents for this Act is as follows:

TITLE V—NATIONAL SECURITY AND ENVIRONMENTAL MANAGEMENT PROGRAMS

Subtitle A—Defense Nuclear Programs Agency

Subtitle B—Environmental Restoration Activities at Defense Nuclear Facilities

TITLE VI—DISPOSITION OF MISCELANEOUS PARTICULAR PROGRAMS, FUNCTIONS, AND AGENCIES OF DEPARTMENT

TITLE VII—CIVILIAN RADIOACTIVE WASTE MANAGEMENT

TITLE VIII—MISCELLANEOUS PROVISIONS

TITLE I—ABOLISHMENT OF DEPARTMENT OF ENERGY

SEC. 101. REESTABLISHMENT OF DEPARTMENT AS ENERGY PROGRAMS RESOLUTION AGENCY.

(a) REESTABLISHMENT.—The Department of Energy is hereby redesignated as the Energy Programs Resolution Agency, which shall be an independent agency in the executive branch of the Government.

(b) ADMINISTRATOR.—

(1) IN GENERAL.—There shall be at the head of the Agency an Administrator of the Agency, who shall be appointed by the President, by and with the advice and consent of the Senate. The Agency shall be administered under the supervision and direction of the Administrator. The Administrator shall receive compensation at the rate prescribed for level II of the Executive Schedule under section 5313 of title 5, United States Code.

(2) INITIAL APPOINTMENT OF ADMINISTRATOR.—Notwithstanding any other provision of this Act or any other law, the President may, at any time after the date of the enactment of this Act, appoint an individual to serve as Administrator of the Energy Programs Resolution Agency (who may be the Secretary of Energy), as such position is estab-

lished under paragraph (1). An appointment under this paragraph may not be construed to affect the position of Secretary of Energy or the authority of the Secretary before the effective date specified in section 109(a).

(c) DUTIES.—The Administrator shall be responsible for—

(1) the administration and wind-up, during the wind-up period, of all functions of the Administrator pursuant to section 102 and the other provisions of this Act;

(2) the administration and wind-up, during the wind-up period, of any outstanding obligations of the Federal Government under any programs terminated or repealed by this Act; and

(3) taking such other actions as may be necessary, before the termination date, to wind up any outstanding affairs of the Department of Energy.

SEC. 102. FUNCTIONS.

Except as otherwise provided in this Act, the Administrator shall perform all functions that, immediately before the effective date of this section, were functions of the Department of Energy (or any office of the Department) or were performed by the Secretary of Energy or any other officer or employee of the Department in the capacity as such officer or employee.

SEC. 103. DEPUTY ADMINISTRATOR.

The Agency shall have a Deputy Administrator, who shall—

(1) be appointed by and report to the Administrator; and

(2) shall perform such functions as may be delegated by the Administrator.

SEC. 104. CONTINUATION OF SERVICE OF DEPARTMENT OFFICERS.

(a) CONTINUATION OF SERVICE OF SECRETARY.—The individual serving on the effective date specified in section 109(a) as the Secretary of Energy may serve and act as Administrator until the date an individual is appointed under this title to the position of Administrator, or until the end of the 120-day period provided for in section 3348 of title 5, United States Code (relating to limitations on the period of time a vacancy may be filled temporarily), whichever is earlier.

(b) CONTINUATION OF SERVICE OF OTHER OFFICERS.—An individual serving on the effective date specified in section 109(a) as an officer of the Department of Energy other than the Secretary of Energy may continue to serve and act in an equivalent capacity in the Agency until the date an individual is appointed under this title to the position of Administrator, or until the end of the 120-day period provided for in section 3348 of title 5, United States Code (relating to limitations on the period of time a vacancy may be filled temporarily) with respect to that appointment, whichever is earlier.

(c) COMPENSATION FOR CONTINUED SERVICE.—Any person—

(1) who acts as the Administrator under subsection (a), or

(2) who serves under subsection (b),

after the effective date specified in section 109(a) and before the first appointment of a person as Administrator shall continue to be compensated for so serving at the rate at which such person was compensated before such effective date.

SEC. 105. REORGANIZATION.

The Administrator may allocate or reallocate any function of the Agency pursuant to this Act among the officers of the Agency, and may establish, consolidate, alter, or discontinue in the Energy Programs Resolution Agency any organizational entities that were entities of the Department of Energy, as the Administrator considers necessary or appropriate.

SEC. 106. ABOLISHMENT OF ENERGY PROGRAMS RESOLUTION AGENCY.

(a) IN GENERAL.—Effective on the termination date under subsection (d), the Energy Programs Resolution Agency is abolished.

(b) ABOLITION OF FUNCTIONS.—Except for functions transferred or otherwise continued by this Act, all functions that, immediately before the termination date, were functions of the Energy Programs Resolution Agency are abolished effective on the termination date.

(c) PLAN FOR WINDING UP AFFAIRS.—Not later than the effective date specified in section 109(a), the President shall submit to the Congress a plan for winding up the affairs of the Agency in accordance with this Act and not by later than the termination date under subsection (d).

(d) TERMINATION DATE.—The termination date under this subsection is the date that is 3 years after the date of the enactment of this Act.

SEC. 107. GAO REPORT.

Not later than 180 days after the date of enactment of this Act, the Comptroller General of the United States shall submit to the Congress a report which shall include recommendations for the most efficient means of achieving, in accordance with this Act—

(1) the complete abolishment of the Department of Energy; and

(2) the termination or transfer or other continuation of the functions of the Department of Energy.

SEC. 108. CONFORMING AMENDMENTS.

(a) PRESIDENTIAL SUCCESSION.—Section 19(d)(1) of title 3, United States Code, is amended by striking "Secretary of Energy,".

(b) EXECUTIVE DEPARTMENTS.—Section 101 of title 5, United States Code, is amended by striking the following item:

"The Department of Energy.".

(c) SECRETARY'S COMPENSATION.—Section 5312 of title 5, United States Code, is amended by striking the following item:

"Secretary of Energy.".

(d) DEPUTY SECRETARY'S COMPENSATION.—Section 5313 of title 5, United States Code, is amended by striking the following item:

"Deputy Secretary of Energy.".

(e) UNDER SECRETARY'S COMPENSATION.—Section 5314 of title 5, United States Code, is amended by striking the following item:

"Under Secretary, Department of Energy.".

(f) MISCELLANEOUS OFFICERS' COMPENSATION.—Section 5315 of title 5, United States Code, is amended—

(1) by striking the following items:

"Assistant Secretaries of Energy (8).

"General Counsel of the Department of Energy.

"Administrator, Economic Regulatory Administration, Department of Energy.

"Administrator, Energy Information Administration, Department of Energy.

"Inspector General, Department of Energy.

"Director, Office of Energy Research, Department of Energy."; and

(2) by striking the following item:

"Chief Financial Officer, Department of Energy.".

(g) INSPECTOR GENERAL ACT OF 1978.—The Inspector General Act of 1978 (5 U.S.C. App.) is amended—

(1) in section 9(a)(1), by striking subparagraph (E);

(2) in section 11(1), by striking "Energy,";

(3) in section 11(2), by striking "Energy,";

(h) DEPARTMENT OF ENERGY ORGANIZATION ACT.—Effective on the termination date, the following provisions of the Department of Energy Organization Act (42 U.S.C. 7101 et seq.) are repealed:

(1) Sections 1 and 2.

(2) Titles I, II, and III.

SEC. 109. EFFECTIVE DATE.

(a) IN GENERAL.—Except as provided in subsection (b), this title shall take effect on the date that is 6 months after the date of the enactment of this Act.

(b) PROVISIONS EFFECTIVE ON DATE OF ENACTMENT.—The following provisions of this title shall take effect on the date of the enactment of this Act:

(1) Section 101(b).

(2) Section 106(c).

(3) Section 107.

TITLE II—ENERGY LABORATORY FACILITIES

SEC. 201. ENERGY LABORATORY FACILITIES COMMISSION.

(a) ESTABLISHMENT.—There is established an independent commission to be known as the "Energy Laboratory Facilities Commission", for the purpose of reducing the number of energy laboratories and programs at those laboratories, through reconfiguration, privatization, and closure, while preserving the traditional role the energy laboratories have contributed to the national defense.

(b) DUTIES.—The Commission shall carry out the duties specified for the Commission in this title.

(c) APPOINTMENT.—

(1) IN GENERAL.—The Commission shall be composed of 7 members appointed by the President, by and with the advice and consent of the Senate. The President shall transmit to the Senate the nominations for appointment to the Commission not later than 3 months after the date of the enactment of this Act.

(2) CONSULTATION.—In selecting individuals for nominations for appointments to the Commission, the President should consult with—

(A) the Speaker of the House of Representatives concerning the appointment of 2 members; and

(B) the majority leader of the Senate concerning the appointment of 2 members.

(3) CHAIRPERSON.—At the time the President nominates individuals for appointment to the Commission, the President shall designate one such individual who shall serve as Chairperson of the Commission.

(d) TERMS.—The term of each member of the Commission shall expire on the termination of the Commission under subsection (l).

(e) MEETINGS.—Each meeting of the Commission, other than meetings in which classified information is to be discussed, shall be open to the public.

(f) VACANCIES.—A vacancy in the Commission shall be filled in the same manner as the original appointment.

(g) PAY AND TRAVEL EXPENSES.—

(1) BASIC PAY.—

(A) PAY OF MEMBERS.—Each member, other than the Chairperson, shall be paid at a rate equal to the daily equivalent of the minimum annual rate of basic pay payable for level IV of the Executive Schedule under section 5315 of title 5, United States Code, for each day (including travel time) during which the member is engaged in the actual performance of duties vested in the Commission.

(B) PAY OF CHAIRPERSON.—The Chairperson shall be paid for each day referred to in subparagraph (A) at a rate equal to the daily equivalent of the minimum annual rate of basic pay payable for level III of the Executive

Schedule under section 5314 of title 5, United States Code.

(2) TRAVEL EXPENSES.—Members shall receive travel expenses, including per diem in lieu of subsistence, in accordance with sections 5702 and 5703 of title 5, United States Code.

(h) DIRECTOR.—

(1) IN GENERAL.—The Commission shall, without regard to section 5311(b) of title 5, United States Code, appoint a Director who—

(A) has not served as a civilian employee of the Department of Energy during the 2-year period preceding the date of such appointment;

(B) has not been an employee of an energy laboratory during the 5-year period preceding the date of such appointment; and

(C) has not been an employee of a contractor operating an energy laboratory during the 5-year period preceding the date of such appointment.

(2) PAY.—The Director shall be paid at the rate of basic pay payable for level IV of the Executive Schedule under section 5315 of title 5, United States Code.

(i) STAFF.—

(1) APPOINTMENT BY DIRECTOR.—Subject to paragraphs (2) and (3), the Director, with the approval of the Commission, may appoint and fix the pay of additional personnel.

(2) APPLICABILITY OF CERTAIN CIVIL SERVICE LAWS.—The Director may make such appointments without regard to the provisions of title 5, United States Code, governing appointments in the competitive service, and any personnel so appointed may be paid without regard to the provisions of chapter 51 and subchapter III of chapter 53 of that title relating to classification and General Schedule pay rates, except that an individual so appointed may not receive pay in excess of the annual rate of basic pay payable for level IV of the Executive Schedule under section 5315 of title 5, United States Code.

(3) LIMITATIONS.—Not more than one-third of the personnel employed by or detailed to the Commission shall be individuals employed by the Department of Energy on the day before the date of the enactment of this Act. No employee of an energy laboratory, or of a contractor who operates an energy laboratory, may be detailed to the Commission.

(4) SUPPORT FROM OTHER AGENCIES.—Upon request of the Director, the head of a Federal agen-

cy may detail any of the personnel of that agency to the Commission to assist the Commission in carrying out its duties under this title.

(5) SUPPORT FROM COMPTROLLER GENERAL.—The Comptroller General of the United States shall provide assistance, including the detailing of employees, to the Commission in accordance with an agreement entered into with the Commission.

(j) OTHER AUTHORITY.—

(1) TEMPORARY AND INTERMITTENT SERVICES.—The Commission may procure by contract, to the extent funds are available, the temporary or intermittent services of experts or consultants pursuant to section 3109 of title 5, United States Code.

(2) AUTHORITY TO LEASE SPACE AND ACQUIRE CERTAIN PROPERTY.—The Commission may lease space and acquire personal property to the extent funds are available. To the extent practicable, the Commission shall use suitable real property available under the most recent inventory of real property assets published by the Resolution Trust Corporation under section 21A(b)(11)(F) of the Federal Home Loan Bank Act (12 U.S.C. 1441a(b)(12)(F)).

(k) FUNDING.—There are authorized to be appropriated to the Commission such funds as are necessary to carry out its duties under this title. Such funds shall remain available until expended.

(l) TERMINATION.—The Commission shall terminate not later than 30 days after the date on which it transmits its final recommendations under section 202(f)(4).

SEC. 202. PROCEDURE FOR MAKING RECOMMENDATIONS FOR LABORATORY FACILITIES.

(a) SELECTION CRITERIA.—In making recommendations for the reconfiguration, privatization, and closure of energy laboratories and termination of programs at such laboratories under this section, the Secretary or the Administrator, as appropriate, and the Commission shall—

(1) give strong consideration to the closure or reconfiguration of energy laboratories;

(2) eliminate duplication of effort by energy laboratories and reduce overhead costs as a proportion of program benefits distributed through an energy laboratory;

(3) seek to achieve cost savings for the overall budget for such laboratories;

(4) define appropriate missions for each energy laboratory, and ensure that the activities of each such laboratory are focused on its mission or missions;

(5) consider the program costs and program distributions on a State and county basis, including real and personal property costs associated with each energy laboratory considered;

(6) consider the number of participants in programs conducted through an energy laboratory and staff resources involved;

(7) estimate the cost savings and increases that would accrue through the reconfiguration of energy laboratories;

(8) consider the potential of each energy laboratory to generate revenues or to offset costs;

(9) consider the transfer of energy laboratories to other Federal agencies;

(10) consider the privatization of the energy laboratories as an alternative to closure or reconfiguration; and

(11) be subject to the requirements of section 601 of this Act.

(b) RECOMMENDATIONS.—

(1) PUBLICATION AND TRANSMITTAL.—Not later than 3 months after the date of the enactment of this Act, the Secretary or the Administrator, as appropriate, shall publish in the Federal Register and transmit to the congressional energy committees

and to the Commission a list of the energy laboratories that the Secretary or the Administrator, as appropriate, recommends for reconfiguration, privatization, and closure.

(2) SUMMARY OF SELECTION PROCESS.—The Secretary or the Administrator, as appropriate, shall include, with the list of recommendations published and transmitted pursuant to paragraph (1), a summary of the selection process that resulted in the recommendation for each energy laboratory, including a justification for each recommendation.

(c) EQUAL CONSIDERATION OF LABORATORIES.—In considering energy laboratories for reconfiguration, privatization, and closure, the Secretary or the Administrator, as appropriate, shall consider all such laboratories equally without regard to whether a laboratory has been previously considered or proposed for reconfiguration, privatization, or closure by the Secretary of Energy.

(d) AVAILABILITY OF INFORMATION.—The Secretary or the Administrator, as appropriate, shall make available to the Commission and the Comptroller General of the United States all information used by the Secretary or the Administrator, as appropriate, in making recommendations under this section.

(e) INDEPENDENT AUDIT.—(1) Within 30 days after the date of the enactment of this Act, the Director of the Office of Management and Budget shall issue a request for proposals for the performance of an audit under paragraph (3).

(2) Within 60 days after the date of the enactment of this Act, proposals shall be due in response to the request under paragraph (1).

(3) Within 90 days after the date of the enactment of this Act, the Director of the Office of Management and Budget shall enter into a contract with an independent financial consulting firm for an audit of the energy laboratories and their programs, facilities, and assets. Such audit shall assess the commercial potential of the energy labs and their programs and make recommendations on how the Government could best realize such potential. The audit shall be completed and transmitted to the Commission, the Secretary or the Administrator, as appropriate, and the congressional energy committees within 6 months after the contract is entered into under this subsection.

(f) REVIEW AND RECOMMENDATIONS BY THE COMMISSION.—

(1) PUBLIC HEARINGS.—After receiving the recommendations from the Secretary or the Administrator, as appropriate, pursuant to subsection (b),

the Commission shall provide an opportunity for public comment on the recommendations for a 30-day period.

(2) INITIAL REPORT.—Not later than 1 year after the date of the enactment of this Act, the Commission shall publish in the Federal Register an initial report containing the Commission's findings and conclusions based on a review and analysis of the recommendations made by the Secretary or the Administrator, as appropriate, and the audit conducted pursuant to subsection (e), together with the Commission's recommendations for reconfiguration, privatization, and closure of energy laboratories. In conducting such review and analysis, the Commission shall consider all energy laboratories.

(3) DEVIATION FROM RECOMMENDATIONS.—In making its recommendations, the Commission may make changes in any of the recommendations made by the Secretary or the Administrator, as appropriate, if the Commission determines that the Secretary or the Administrator, as appropriate, deviated substantially from the criteria described in subsection (a) in making recommendations. The Commission shall explain and justify in the report any recommendation made by the Commission that is

different from the recommendations made by the Secretary or the Administrator, as appropriate.

(4) FINAL REPORT.—After providing a 30-day period for public comment following publication of the initial report under paragraph (2), and after full consideration of such public comments, the Commission shall, within 15 months after the date of the enactment of this Act, transmit to the Secretary or the Administrator, as appropriate, and the congressional energy committees a final report containing the recommendations of the Commission.

(5) PROVISION OF CERTAIN INFORMATION.—After transmitting the final report under paragraph (4), the Commission shall promptly provide, upon request, to any Member of Congress information used by the Commission in making its recommendations.

(g) ASSISTANCE FROM COMPTROLLER GENERAL.—The Comptroller General of the United States shall—

(1) assist the Commission, to the extent requested, in the Commission's review and analysis of the recommendations made by the Secretary or the Administrator, as appropriate, pursuant to subsection (b); and

(2) not later than 6 months after the date of the enactment of this Act, transmit to the congres-

sional energy committees and to the Commission a report containing a detailed analysis of the recommendations of the Secretary or the Administrator, as appropriate, and the selection process.

SEC. 203. RECONFIGURATION, PRIVATIZATION, AND CLOSURE OF ENERGY LABORATORIES.

(a) IN GENERAL.—Subject to subsection (b), the Secretary or the Administrator, as appropriate, shall—

(1) reconfigure, within 1 year after the date of the transmittal of the final report under section 202(f)(4), all energy laboratories recommended for reconfiguration by the Commission in such report;

(2) provide for and complete the privatization, within 18 months after the date of the transmittal of the final report under section 202(f)(4), of all energy laboratories recommended for privatization by the Commission in such report; and

(3) except as necessary to achieve the privatization of an energy laboratory under paragraph (2), close, within 1 year after the date of the transmittal of the final report under section 202(f)(4), all energy laboratories recommended for closure by the Commission in such report.

(b) CONGRESSIONAL DISAPPROVAL.—

(1) IN GENERAL.—The Secretary or the Administrator, as appropriate, may not carry out any reconfiguration, privatization, or closure of an energy laboratory recommended by the Commission in the report transmitted pursuant to section 202(f)(4) if a joint resolution is enacted, in accordance with the provisions of section 207, disapproving the recommendations of the Commission before the earlier of—

(A) the end of the 45-day period beginning on the date on which the Commission transmits the report; or

(B) the adjournment of Congress sine die for the session during which the report is transmitted.

(2) For purposes of paragraph (1) of this subsection and subsections (a) and (c) of section 207, the days on which either House of Congress is not in session because of an adjournment of more than three days to a day certain shall be excluded in the computation of a period.

SEC. 204. IMPLEMENTATION OF RECONFIGURATION, PRIVATIZATION, AND CLOSURE ACTIONS.

(a) IMPLEMENTATION.—In reconfiguring, privatizing, or closing an energy laboratory under this title, the Secretary or the Administrator, as appropriate, shall—

(1) take such actions as may be necessary to reconfigure, privatize, or close the energy laboratory;

(2) take such steps as may be necessary to ensure the safe keeping of all records stored at the energy laboratory; and

(3) reimburse other Federal agencies for actions performed at the request of the Secretary or the Administrator, as appropriate, with respect to any such reconfiguration, privatization, or closure, and may use for such purpose funds in the Account or funds appropriated to the Department of Energy and available for such purpose.

(b) MANAGEMENT AND DISPOSAL OF PROPERTY.—

(1) IN GENERAL.—The Administrator of General Services shall delegate to the Secretary or the Administrator, as appropriate, with respect to excess and surplus real property and facilities located at an energy laboratory reconfigured, privatized, or closed under this title—

(A) the authority of the Secretary or the Administrator, as appropriate, to utilize excess property under section 202 of the Federal

Property and Administrative Services Act of 1949 (40 U.S.C. 483);

(B) the authority of the Secretary or the Administrator, as appropriate, to dispose of surplus property under section 203 of that Act (40 U.S.C. 484);

(C) the authority of the Secretary or the Administrator, as appropriate, to grant approvals and make determinations under section 13(g) of the Surplus Property Act of 1944 (50 U.S.C. App. 1622(g)); and

(D) the authority of the Secretary or the Administrator, as appropriate, to determine the availability of excess or surplus real property for wildlife conservation purposes in accordance with the Act of May 19, 1948 (16 U.S.C. 667b).

(2) EXERCISE OF AUTHORITY.—

(A) IN GENERAL.—Subject to subparagraph (C), the Secretary or the Administrator, as appropriate, shall exercise the authority delegated to the Secretary or the Administrator, as appropriate, pursuant to paragraph (1) in accordance with—

(i) all regulations in effect on the date of the enactment of this Act governing the utilization of excess property and the disposal of surplus property under the Federal Property and Administrative Services Act of 1949; and

(ii) all regulations in effect on the date of the enactment of this Act governing the conveyance and disposal of property under section 13(g) of the Surplus Property Act of 1944 (50 U.S.C. App. 1622(g)).

(B) REGULATIONS.—The Secretary or the Administrator, as appropriate, after consulting with the Administrator of General Services, may issue regulations that are necessary to carry out the delegation of authority required by paragraph (1).

(C) LIMITATION.—The authority required to be delegated by paragraph (1) to the Secretary or the Administrator, as appropriate, by the Administrator of General Services shall not include the authority to prescribe general policies and methods for utilizing excess property and disposing of surplus property.

(c) WAIVER.—The Secretary or the Administrator, as appropriate, may reconfigure, privatize, or close energy laboratories under this title without regard to any provision of law restricting the use of funds for reconfiguring, privatizing, or closing such energy laboratories included in any appropriations or authorization Act.

SEC. 205. ACCOUNT.

(a) ESTABLISHMENT.—There is hereby established on the books of the Treasury an account to be known as the "Energy Laboratory Facility Closure Account" which shall be administered by the Secretary or the Administrator, as appropriate, as a single account.

(b) CONTENT OF ACCOUNT.—There shall be deposited into the Account—

(1) funds authorized for and appropriated to the Account;

(2) any funds that the Secretary or the Administrator, as appropriate, may, subject to approval in an appropriation Act, transfer to the Account from funds appropriated to the Department of Energy for any purpose, except that such funds may be transferred only after the date on which the Secretary or the Administrator, as appropriate, transmits written notice of, and justification for, such transfer to the congressional energy committees; and

(3) proceeds received from the transfer or disposal of any property at an office reconfigured, privatized, or closed under this section.

(c) USE OF FUNDS.—The Secretary or the Administrator, as appropriate, may use the funds in the Account only for the purposes described in section 204(a).

(d) REPORTS.—

(1) IN GENERAL.—Not later than 60 days after the end of each fiscal year in which the Secretary or the Administrator, as appropriate, carries out activities under this title, the Secretary or the Administrator, as appropriate, shall transmit a report to the congressional energy committees of the amount and nature of the deposits into, and the expenditures from, the Account during such fiscal year and of the amount and nature of other expenditures made pursuant to section 204(a) during such fiscal year.

(2) UNOBLIGATED FUNDS.—Unobligated funds shall be held in the Account until transferred by law.

SEC. 206. REPORTS ON IMPLEMENTATION.

As part of the budget request for each fiscal year in which the Secretary or the Administrator, as appropriate, is authorized to carry out activities under this title, the Secretary or the Administrator, as appropriate, shall transmit to the congressional energy committees—

(1) a schedule of the reconfiguration, privatization, and closure actions to be carried out under this title in the fiscal year for which the request is made and an estimate of the total expenditures required and cost savings to be achieved by each such reconfiguration, privatization, or closure and of the time period in which these savings are to be achieved in each case; and

(2) a description of the energy laboratories to which functions are to be transferred as a result of such reconfigurations, privatizations, and closures.

SEC. 207. CONGRESSIONAL CONSIDERATION OF COMMISSION REPORT.

(a) TERMS OF THE RESOLUTION.—For purposes of section 203(b), the term "joint resolution" means only a joint resolution which is introduced within the 10-day period beginning on the date on which the Commission transmits the report to the Congress under section 202(f)(4), and—

(1) which does not have a preamble;

(2) the matter after the resolving clause of which is as follows: "That Congress disapproves the recommendations of the Energy Laboratory Facilities Commission as submitted on ______", the blank space being filled in with the appropriate date; and

(3) the title of which is as follows: "Joint resolution disapproving the recommendations of the Energy Laboratory Facilities Commission.".

(b) REFERRAL.—A resolution described in subsection (a) that is introduced in the House of Representatives shall be referred to the Committee on National Security and the Committee on Science of the House of Representatives. A resolution described in subsection (a) introduced in the Senate shall be referred to the Committee on Armed Services and the Committee on Energy and Natural Resources of the Senate.

(c) DISCHARGE.—If the committee to which a resolution described in subsection (a) is referred has not reported such resolution (or an identical resolution) by the end of the 20-day period beginning on the date on which the Commission transmits the report to the Congress under section 202(f)(4), such committee shall be, at the end of such period, discharged from further consideration of such resolution, and such resolution shall be placed on the appropriate calendar of the House involved.

(d) CONSIDERATION.—

(1) IN GENERAL.—On or after the third day after the date on which the committee to which such a resolution is referred has reported, or has been discharged (under subsection (c)) from further con-

sideration of, such a resolution, it is in order (even though a previous motion to the same effect has been disagreed to) for any Member of the respective House to move to proceed to the consideration of the resolution (but only on the day after the calendar day on which such Member announces to the House concerned the Member's intention to do so). All points of order against the resolution (and against consideration of the resolution) are waived. The motion is highly privileged in the House of Representatives and is privileged in the Senate and is not debatable. The motion is not subject to amendment, or to a motion to postpone, or to a motion to proceed to the consideration of other business. A motion to reconsider the vote by which the motion is agreed to or disagreed to shall not be in order. If a motion to proceed to the consideration of the resolution is agreed to, the respective House shall immediately proceed to consideration of the joint resolution without intervening motion, order, or other business, and the resolution shall remain the unfinished business of the respective House until disposed of.

(2) DEBATE.—Debate on the resolution, and on all debatable motions and appeals in connection therewith, shall be limited to not more than 2 hours,

which shall be divided equally between those favoring and those opposing the resolution. An amendment to the resolution is not in order. A motion further to limit debate is in order and not debatable. A motion to postpone, or a motion to proceed to the consideration of other business, or a motion to recommit the resolution is not in order. A motion to reconsider the vote by which the resolution is agreed to or disagreed to is not in order.

(3) QUORUM CALL.—Immediately following the conclusion of the debate on a resolution described in subsection (a) and a single quorum call at the conclusion of the debate if requested in accordance with the rules of the appropriate House, the vote on final passage of the resolution shall occur.

(4) APPEALS FROM DECISION OF CHAIR.—Appeals from the decisions of the Chair relating to the application of the rules of the Senate or the House of Representatives, as the case may be, to the procedure relating to a resolution described in subsection (a) shall be decided without debate.

(e) CONSIDERATION BY OTHER HOUSE.—

(1) IN GENERAL.—If, before the passage by one House of a resolution of that House described in subsection (a), that House receives from the other

House a resolution described in subsection (a), then the following procedures shall apply:

(A) The resolution of the other House shall not be referred to a committee and may not be considered in the House receiving it except in the case of final passage as provided in subparagraph (B)(ii).

(B) With respect to a resolution described in paragraph (1) of the House receiving the resolution—

(i) the procedure in that House shall be the same as if no resolution had been received from the other House; but

(ii) the vote on final passage shall be on the resolution of the other House.

(2) CONSIDERATION AFTER DISPOSITION BY OTHER HOUSE.—Upon disposition of the resolution received from the other House, it shall no longer be in order to consider the resolution that originated in the receiving House.

(f) RULES OF THE SENATE AND HOUSE.—This section is enacted by Congress—

(1) as an exercise of the rulemaking power of the Senate and House of Representatives, respectively, and as such it is deemed a part of the rules

of each House, respectively, but applicable only with respect to the procedure to be followed in that House in the case of a resolution described in subsection (a), and it supersedes other rules only to the extent that it is inconsistent with such rules; and

(2) with full recognition of the constitutional right of either House to change the rules (so far as relating to the procedure of that House) at any time, in the same manner, and to the same extent as in the case of any other rule of that House.

SEC. 208. DEFINITIONS.

For purposes of this title:

(1) The term "Account" means the Energy Laboratory Facility Closure Account established in section 205(a).

(2) The term "Administrator" has the meaning given such term in section 809(1) of this Act.

(3) The term "Commission" means the Energy Laboratory Facilities Commission.

(4) The term "congressional energy committees" means the Committee on Armed Services of the Senate, the Committee on National Security of the House of Representatives, the Committee on Science of the House of Representatives, and the

Committee on Energy and Natural Resources of the Senate.

(5) The term "energy laboratory" means the Lawrence Livermore National Laboratory, the Los Alamos National Laboratory, the Sandia National Laboratories, the Argonne National Laboratory, the Brookhaven National Laboratory, the Idaho National Engineering Laboratory, the Lawrence Berkeley Laboratory, the Oak Ridge National Laboratory, the Pacific Northwest Laboratory, the National Renewable Energy Laboratory, the Ames Laboratory, the Bates Linear Accelerator Laboratory, the Bettis Atomic Power Laboratory, the Continuous Electron Beam Accelerator Facility, the Energy Technology Engineering Center, the Environmental Measurements Laboratory, the Fermi National Accelerator Laboratory, the Inhalation Toxicology Research Institute, the Knolls Atomic Power Laboratory, the Laboratory of Radiobiology and Environmental Health, the Morgantown Energy Technology Center, the National Renewable Energy Laboratory, the New Brunswick Laboratory, the Oak Ridge Institute for Science and Education, the Pittsburgh Energy Technology Center, the Princeton Plasma Physics Laboratory, the Savannah River Ecology Labora-

tory, the Savannah River Technology Center, the Specific Manufacturing Capability Facility, or the Stanford Linear Accelerator Facility.

(6) The term "the Secretary or the Administrator, as appropriate" means the Secretary of Energy, or, after the effective date stated in section 109(a), the Administrator.

TITLE III—PRIVATIZATION OF FEDERAL POWER MARKETING ADMINISTRATIONS

SEC. 301. SHORT TITLE.

This title may be cited as the "Federal Power Asset Privatization Act of 1995".

SEC. 302. FINDINGS.

The Congress finds that:

(1) the Federal Power Marketing Administrations, over the years, have served to help bring electricity to many areas in the Nation;

(2) they have done so with the investment of the American taxpayer;

(3) the necessity of federally owned power generation and transmission facilities has passed and halting this practice is in the best national interest of the United States;

(4) in fairness to the longtime consumers of Federal Power Marketing Administrations, any process of sale should be open to them;

(5) the taxpayers, through investing in the construction and operation, have established equity in the facilities; and

(6) this equity entitles the American taxpayer to expect the highest possible return in the sale process.

SEC. 303. SALE OF ASSETS.

(a) SALE OF ASSETS.—The Secretary is authorized and directed to take such steps as necessary to sell all electric power generation facilities and transmission facilities, that are currently owned and operated by Federal departments and agencies under the supervision of, or coordination with, the Federal Power Marketing Administrations other than the Bonneville Power Administration. No foreign person or corporation may purchase any such facilities; such facilities may be sold only to a United States citizen or to a corporation or partnership organized under the laws of a State. After such sales are completed the Secretary shall terminate the operations of the Federal Power Marketing Administrations other than the Bonneville Power Administration. The heads of other affected Federal departments and agencies shall assist the Secretary of Energy in implementing the sales authorized by this section.

(b) PRICE; STRUCTURE OF SALE.—

(1) PRICE.—The Secretary shall obtain the highest possible price for such facilities. In determining the highest possible price, the value of future tax revenues shall be included.

(2) RETENTION OF FINANCIAL ADVISOR.—In order to conduct the sales authorized by this section in such manner as will produce the highest possible price for the facilities to be sold consistent with this title, within 30 days of enactment of this section, the Secretary shall, through a competitive bidding process, retain an experienced private sector firm to serve as financial advisor to the Secretary with respect to such sales.

(3) FINANCIAL ADVISOR'S REPORT.—Within 90 days of being retained by the Secretary, the financial advisor shall provide to the Secretary a report containing—

(A) a description of those assets described in subsection (a) which, in the opinion of the financial advisor, can be successfully transferred to private sector ownership or operation;

(B) the value of each such asset, calculated on the basis of the valuation method or methods which the financial advisor deems most appropriate to a particular asset;

(C) the appropriate alternative transactional methods for transferring each such asset to private sector ownership or operation;

(D) the amount of proceeds which the financial advisor estimates would be paid to the United States Government as a result of such transaction, including the present value of future revenue from taxes and any other future payments to be made to the United States Government; and

(E) an estimate of the average market rate for wholesale electric power sales within each region served by a Federal Power Marketing Administration.

(c) TIME OF SALE.—Sales of facilities under this section shall be conducted in accordance with the time of sale schedule set forth in section 304. At least one year before the date of any sale specified in such schedule, the Secretary, in consultation with the Secretary of the Army and the Secretary of the Interior, and based on the recommendations of the financial advisor, shall select the facilities or groups of facilities to be sold and establish the terms and conditions of the sale.

(d) FORMER EMPLOYEES OF PMAS.—It is the sense of the Congress that the purchaser of any such facilities should offer to employ, where possible, former employees of the Federal Power Marketing Administrations in connection with the operation of the facilities following their purchase.

(e) PROCEEDS.—The Secretary of Energy shall deposit sale proceeds in the Treasury of the United States to the credit of miscellaneous receipts.

(f) PREPARATION.—The Secretary of Energy is authorized to use funds appropriated to the Department of Energy for the Federal Power Marketing Administrations and funds otherwise appropriated to other Federal agencies for power generation and related activities in order to prepare these assets for sale and conveyance. Such preparation shall provide sufficient title to ensure the beneficial use, enjoyment, and occupancy to the purchasers of the assets to be sold and shall include identification of all associated laws and regulations to be amended for the purpose of these sales. The Secretary of Energy shall undertake a study of the effect of sales of facilities under this title on existing contracts for the sale of electric power generated at such facilities.

(g) REPORTING OF SALES.—Not later than one year after the sale of the assets of each Federal Power Marketing Administration (other than the Bonneville Power Administration) in accordance with this title, the Secretary of Energy shall—

(1) complete the business of, and close out, such administration; and

(2) prepare and submit to Congress a report documenting the sales.

(h) TREATMENT OF SALES FOR PURPOSES OF CERTAIN LAWS.—The sales of assets under this title shall not be considered a disposal of Federal surplus property under the following provisions of law:

(1) Section 203 of the Federal Property and Administrative Services Act of 1949 (40 U.S.C. 484).

(2) Section 13 of the Surplus Property Act of 1944 (50 U.S.C. App. 1622).

SEC. 304. TIME OF SALES.

(a) SCHEDULE.—During the next 5 years, the Secretary of Energy shall complete the sale of the electric power generation and transmission assets referred to in section 303 in accordance with the following schedule:

Power Administration	Sale Completion Date
Alaska	Before September 30, 1996
Southeastern	Before September 30, 1997

Power Administration	Sale Completion Date
Southwestern	Before September 30, 1998
Western Area	Before September 30, 1999

(b) UNEXPENDED BALANCES.—Following the sale of the assets of each of the Federal Power Marketing Administrations and their associated power generation facilities, the Secretary of Energy shall return the unexpended balances of funds appropriated for that administration to the Treasury of the United States.

SEC. 305. RATE STABILIZATION FOR AFFECTED CONSUMERS.

So that the affected consumers of the Federal Power Marketing Administrations are not impacted by severe rate increases, each purchaser of electric power generation facilities providing electric power to customers within any region shall be required, as part of the agreement to purchase such facilities, to insure that the price at which electric power is sold to such consumers does not increase above the baseline price at a rate greater than 10 percent annually. For purposes of this section, the term "baseline price" means the price for the sale of electric power to a consumer that is in effect on the date of the sale of the facility. The preceding sentence shall cease to apply when the price at which electric power is sold to a consumer is at least equal to the average market rate for wholesale electric power sales within the region concerned, as determined by the Financial Advisor.

SEC. 306. LICENSING OF PROJECTS TO PRESERVE CURRENT OPERATING CONDITIONS.

(a) ORIGINAL LICENSE.—Simultaneously with the sale of hydroelectric generation facility under this title, the Federal Energy Regulatory Commission shall issue an original license under part 1 of the Federal Power Act (16 U.S.C. 791a–823b) to the purchaser for the construction, operation, and maintenance of such facility. Such license shall expire on the date 10 years after the date of the sale of the facility and shall contain standard terms and conditions for hydroelectric power licenses issued under part 1 of such Act for facilities installed at Federal water projects, together with such additional terms and conditions as the Commission deems necessary, in consultation with the department or agency which operates such water project, to further the project purposes and insure that the project will continue operations in the same manner and subject to the same procedures, contracts, and other requirements as were applicable prior to the sale. The Commission shall publish such license terms and conditions for each facility to be sold under this title as promptly as practicable after the date of the enactment of this Act but not later than one year prior to the date established for the sale of the facility.

(b) LICENSE REQUIRED.—Notwithstanding any other provision of law, the Federal Energy Regulatory Commission shall have jursidiction under part 1 of the Federal Power Act over any hydroelectric generation facility sold under this title.

SEC. 307. ENABLING FEDERAL STUDIES.

Section 505 of the Energy and Water Development Appropriations Act of 1993 (Public Law 102–377) is hereby repealed.

SEC. 308. BONNEVILLE POWER ADMINISTRATION.

(a) TRANSFER OF FUNCTIONS.—There are hereby transferred to the Secretary of the Interior all functions performed by the Department of Energy with respect to the Bonneville Power Administration (BPA) on the day before the effective date of this section.

(b) STUDY REGARDING FUTURE OF BONNEVILLE POWER ADMINISTRATION.—The Secretary of the Interior shall conduct a study, taking into consideration any relevant factor, including debt, statutory or treaty obligations, to determine which option regarding the future disposition of BPA represents the most cost-effective option for both the Pacific Northwest and United States as a whole.

(c) REPORT REGARDING STUDY.—The Secretary shall submit to Congress a report describing the results of the study and containing such recommendations as consistent with the findings of the report within 1 year after the enactment of this Act.

SEC. 309. DEFINITIONS.

For purposes of this title:

(1) The term "power generation facility" means a facility used for the generation of electric energy. If any portion of a structure or other facility is used for flood control, water supply or other purposes in addition to the generation of electric energy, such term refers only to that portion of the structure or facility used exclusively for the generation of electric energy, including turbines, generators, controls, substations, and primary lines used for transmitting electric energy therefrom to the point of juncture with the interconnected primary transmission system. Such term shall not include any portion of a facility used for navigation, flood control, irrigation, water supply, or recreation.

(2) The term "Secretary" means the Secretary of Energy or any successor agency. If any such agency terminates prior to the complete execution of all duties vested in the Secretary of Energy under

this title, such duties shall be vested in the Secretary of the Interior.

TITLE IV—TRANSFER AND DISPOSAL OF RESERVES

SEC. 401. STRATEGIC PETROLEUM RESERVE.

(a) TRANSFER OF FUNCTIONS.—There are hereby transferred to the Secretary of the Interior all functions performed by the Department of Energy with respect to the Strategic Petroleum Reserve on the day before the effective date of this section.

(b) SALE OF CERTAIN RESERVES.—Notwithstanding section 161 of the Energy Policy and Conservation Act, the Secretary of the Interior shall sell the reserves held at Weeks Island, Louisiana, in a manner that provides for minimal disruption of petroleum markets.

(c) ADVISORY BOARD.—(1) The Secretary of the Interior shall appoint an advisory board, consisting of 3 individuals with experience in oil markets and production and international relations, which shall—

(A) monitor the sale of reserves under subsection (b) and its effects on petroleum markets; and

(B) within 60 days after the completion of such sale, submit to the Congress a report containing recommendations as described in paragraph (2).

(2) The advisory board shall make recommendations on whether the United States should maintain or dispose of the Strategic Petroleum Reserve, based on information obtained pursuant to paragraph (1)(A) and any other relevant information the advisory board obtains. If the advisory board recommends maintaining the Strategic Petroleum Reserve, it shall include recommendations for administering the Reserve, and if it recommends disposing of the Reserve, it shall include recommendations for procedures for carrying out such disposal.

(3) Notwithstanding section 14 of the Federal Advisory Committee Act, the advisory board established under this subsection shall terminate within 30 days after it submits a report under paragraph (1)(B).

(d) EFFECTIVE DATE.—This section shall take effect on the effective date stated in section 109(a).

SEC. 402. TRANSFER OF NAVAL PETROLEUM RESERVES TO DEPARTMENT OF THE INTERIOR; SALE OF NAVAL PETROLEUM RESERVE NUMBERED 1 (ELK HILLS).

(a) TRANSFER OF JURISDICTION.—The Secretary of Energy shall transfer the naval petroleum reserves (as defined in section 7420(2) of title 10, United States Code) from the jurisdiction and control of the Department of Energy to the jurisdiction and control of the Department of the Interior. The transfer required by this subsection shall be made without compensation or reimbursement.

(b) TIME FOR TRANSFER.—The transfer required by subsection (a) shall be made as soon as possible after the date of the enactment of this Act, but in no case later than one year after that date.

(c) SALE OF ELK HILLS UNIT REQUIRED.—Chapter 641 of title 10, United States Code, is amended by inserting after section 7421 the following new section:

"§ 7421a. Sale of Naval Petroleum Reserve Numbered 1 (Elk Hills)

"(a) SALE REQUIRED.—(1) Notwithstanding any other provision of this chapter, the Secretary shall sell all right, title, and interest of the United States in and to lands owned or controlled by the United States inside Naval Petroleum Reserve Numbered 1, commonly referred to as the Elk Hills Unit, located in Kern County, California, and established by Executive order of the President, dated September 2, 1912. Within one year after the effective date, the Secretary shall enter into one or more contracts for the sale of all of the interest of the United States in the reserve.

"(2) In this section:

"(A) The term 'reserve' means Naval Petroleum Reserve Numbered 1.

"(B) The term 'unit plan contract' means the unit plan contract between equity owners of the lands within the boundaries of Naval Petroleum Reserve Numbered 1 entered into on June 19, 1944.

"(C) The term 'effective date' means the date of the enactment of the Department of Energy Abolishment Act.

"(b) EQUITY FINALIZATION.—(1) Not later than five months after the effective date, the Secretary shall finalize equity interests of the known oil and gas zones in Naval Petroleum Reserve Numbered 1 in the manner provided by this subsection.

"(2) The Secretary shall retain the services of an independent petroleum engineer, mutually acceptable to the equity owners, who shall prepare a recommendation on final equity figures. The Secretary may accept the recommendation of the independent petroleum engineer for final equity in each known oil and gas zone and establish final equity interest in the Naval Petroleum Reserve Numbered 1 in accordance with such recommendation, or the Secretary may use such other method to establish final equity interest in the reserve as the Secretary considers appropriate.

"(3) If, on the effective date, there is an ongoing equity redetermination dispute between the equity owners under section 9(b) of the unit plan contract, such dispute shall be resolved in the manner provided in the unit plan contract within five months after the effective date. Such resolution shall be considered final for all purposes under this section.

"(c) TIMING AND ADMINISTRATION OF SALE.—(1) Not later than two months after the effective date, the Secretary shall retain the services of five independent experts in the valuation of oil and gas fields to conduct separate assessments, in a manner consistent with commercial practices, of the fair market value of the interest of the United States in Naval Petroleum Reserve Numbered 1. In making their assessments, the independent experts shall consider (among other factors) all equipment and facilities to be included in the sale, the net present value of the reserve, and the net present value of the anticipated revenue stream that the Secretary determines the Treasury would receive from the reserve if the reserve were not sold, adjusted for any anticipated increases in tax revenues that would result if the reserve were sold. The independent experts shall complete their assessments within five months after the effective date. In setting the minimum acceptable price for the reserve, the Secretary shall consider the average of the five assessments or, if more advantageous to the Government, the average of three assessments after excluding the high and low assessments.

"(2) Not later than two months after the effective date, the Secretary shall retain the services of an investment banker to independently administer, in a manner consistent with commercial practices and in a manner that maximizes sale proceeds to the Government, the sale of Naval Petroleum Reserve Numbered 1 under this section.

"(3) Not later than five months after the effective date, the sales administrator selected under paragraph (2) shall complete a draft contract for the sale of Naval Petroleum Reserve Numbered 1, which shall accompany the invitation for bids and describe the terms and provisions of the sale of the interest of the United States in the reserve. The draft contract shall identify all equipment and facilities to be included in the sale. The draft contract, including the terms and provisions of the sale of the interest of the United States in the reserve, shall be subject to review and approval by the Secretary, the Secretary of the Treasury, and the Director of the Office of Management and Budget.

"(4) Not later than six months after the effective date, the Secretary shall publish an invitation for bids for the purchase of the reserve.

"(5) Not later than nine months after the effective date, the Secretary shall accept the highest responsible offer for purchase of the interest of the United States in Naval Petroleum Reserve Numbered 1 that meets or exceeds the minimum acceptable price determined under paragraph (1).

"(d) FUTURE LIABILITIES.—The United States shall hold harmless and fully indemnify the purchaser of the interest of the United States in Naval Petroleum Reserve Numbered 1 from and against any claim or liability as a result of ownership in the reserve by the United States.

"(e) TREATMENT OF STATE OF CALIFORNIA CLAIM.—(1) All claims against the United States by the State of California or the Teachers' Retirement Fund of the State of California with respect to land within the Naval Petroleum Reserve Numbered 1 or production or proceeds of sale from the reserve shall be resolved only as follows:

"(A) A payment from funds provided for this purpose in advance in appropriation Acts.

"(B) A grant of nonrevenue generating land in lieu of such a payment pursuant to sections 2275 and 2276 of the Revised Statutes of the United States (43 U.S.C. 851 and 852).

"(C) Any other means that would not be inconsistent with the Congressional Budget Act of 1974 (2 U.S.C. 621 et seq.).

"(D) Any combination of subparagraphs (A), (B), and (C).

"(2) The value of any payment, grant, or means (or combination thereof) under paragraph (1) may not exceed an amount equal to seven percent of the proceeds from the sale of the reserve, after deducting the costs incurred to conduct the sale.

"(f) PRODUCTION ALLOCATION FOR SALE.—(1) As part of the contract for purchase of Naval Petroleum Reserve Numbered 1, the purchaser of the interest of the United States in the reserve shall agree to make up to 25 percent of the purchaser's share of annual petroleum production from the purchased lands available for sale to small refiners, which do not have their own adequate sources of supply of petroleum, for processing or use only in their own refineries. None of the reserved production sold to small refiners may be resold in kind. The purchaser of the reserve may reduce the quantity of petroleum reserved under this subsection in the event of an insufficient number of qualified bids. The seller of this petroleum production has the right to refuse bids that are less than the prevailing market price of comparable oil.

"(2) The purchaser of the reserve shall also agree to ensure that the terms of every sale of the purchaser's share of annual petroleum production from the purchased lands shall be so structured as to give full and equal opportunity for the acquisition of petroleum by all interested persons, including major and independent oil producers and refiners alike.

"(g) MAINTAINING ELK HILLS UNIT PRODUCTION.—Until the sale of Naval Petroleum Reserve Numbered 1 is completed under this section, the Secretary shall continue to produce the reserve at the maximum daily oil or gas rate from a reservoir, which will permit maximum economic development of the reservoir consistent with sound oil field engineering practices in accordance with section 3 of the unit plan contract. The definition of maximum efficient rate in section 7420(6) of this title shall not apply to the reserve.

"(h) EFFECT ON EXISTING CONTRACTS.—(1) In the case of any contract, in effect on the effective date, for the purchase of production from any part of the United States' share of Naval Petroleum Reserve Numbered 1, the sale of the interest of the United States in the reserve shall be subject to the contract for a period of three months after the closing date of the sale or until termination of the contract, whichever occurs first. The term of any contract entered into after the effective date for the purchase of such production shall not exceed the anticipated closing date for the sale of the reserve.

"(2) The Secretary shall exercise the termination procedures provided in the contract between the United States and Bechtel Petroleum Operation, Inc., Contract Number DE–ACO1–85FE60520 so that the contract terminates not later than the date of closing of the sale of Naval Petroleum Reserve Numbered 1 under subsection (c).

"(3) The Secretary shall exercise the termination procedures provided in the unit plan contract so that the unit plan contract terminates not later than the date of closing of the sale of reserve under subsection (c).

"(i) EFFECT ON ANTITRUST LAWS.—Nothing in this section shall be construed to alter the application of the antitrust laws of the United States to the purchaser of Naval Petroleum Reserve Numbered 1 or to the lands in the reserve subject to sale under this section upon the completion of the sale.

"(j) PRESERVATION OF PRIVATE RIGHT, TITLE, AND INTEREST.—Nothing in this section shall be construed to adversely affect the ownership interest of any other entity having any right, title, and interest in and to lands within the boundaries of Naval Petroleum Reserve Numbered 1 and which are subject to the unit plan contract.

"(k) CONGRESSIONAL NOTIFICATION.—Section 7431 of this title shall not apply to the sale of Naval Petroleum Reserve Numbered 1 under this section. However, the Secretary may not enter into a contract for the sale of the reserve until the end of the 31-day period beginning on the date on which the Secretary notifies the Committee on Armed Services of the Senate and the Committee on National Security and the Committee on Commerce of the House of Representatives of the proposed sale.".

(b) CLERICAL AMENDMENT.—The table of sections at the beginning of such chapter is amended by inserting after the item relating to section 7421 the following new item:

"7421a. Sale of Naval Petroleum Reserve Numbered 1 (Elk Hills).".

(c) CONFORMING AMENDMENTS TO TITLE 10, UNITED STATES CODE.—

(1) REFERENCES REGARDING ADMINISTRATION OF RESERVES.—Chapter 641 of title 10, United States Code, is amended—

(A) in section 7420(4), by striking "Secretary of Energy" and inserting "Secretary of the Interior";

(B) in section 7427, by striking "of the Interior";

(C) in section 7430(d), by striking ", in consultation with the Secretary of the Interior,"; and

(D) in section 7430(j), by striking "he, or the Secretary of the Interior where the authority extends to him,".

(2) TRANSITION.—Until such time as the Secretary of Energy transfers administration of the naval petroleum reserves to the Secretary of the Interior, as required by subsection (a), the Secretary of Energy shall continue to be responsible for administering the reserves.

SEC. 403. STUDY REGARDING FUTURE OF NAVAL PETROLEUM RESERVES (OTHER THAN NAVAL PETROLEUM RESERVE NUMBERED 1).

(a) STUDY REQUIRED.—The Secretary of the Interior shall conduct a study to determine which of the following options regarding the naval petroleum reserves represents the most cost-effective option for the United States:

(1) Retention and operation of the naval petroleum reserves under chapter 641 of title 10, United States Code.

(2) Transfer of all or a part of the naval petroleum reserves to the jurisdiction of another Federal agency.

(3) Lease of the naval petroleum reserves.

(4) Sale of the interest of the United States in the naval petroleum reserves.

(b) CONDUCT OF STUDY.—The Secretary shall retain an independent petroleum consultant to conduct the study.

(c) CONSIDERATIONS UNDER STUDY.—An examination of the benefits to be derived by the United States from the sale of the naval petroleum reserves shall include an assessment and estimate, in a manner consistent with commercial practices, of the fair market value of the interest of the United States in the naval petroleum reserves. An examination of the benefits to be derived by the United States from the lease of the naval petroleum reserves shall consider full exploration, development, and production of petroleum products in the naval petroleum reserves, with a royalty payment to the United States.

(d) REPORT REGARDING STUDY.—Not later than December 31, 1995, the Secretary shall submit to Congress a report describing the results of the study and containing such recommendations as the Secretary considers necessary to implement the most cost-effective option identified in the study.

(e) Naval Petroleum Reserves Defined.—For purposes of this section, the term "naval petroleum reserves" has the meaning given that term in section 7420(2) of title 10, United States Code, except that such term does not include Naval Petroleum Reserve Numbered 1.

TITLE V—NATIONAL SECURITY AND ENVIRONMENTAL MANAGEMENT PROGRAMS

Subtitle A—Defense Nuclear Programs Agency

SEC. 501. DEFINITIONS.

In this subtitle:

(1) The term "defense nuclear programs matters" means matters related to the military use of nuclear energy and nuclear weapons, including all such matters that were under the jurisdiction of the following entities on the day before the date of the enactment of this Act:

(A) The Department of Energy.

(B) The Defense Nuclear Agency of the Department of Defense.

(C) The Defense Nuclear Facilities Safety Board.

(2) The term "Under Secretary" means the Under Secretary of Defense for Defense Nuclear Programs.

(3) The term "Agency" means the Defense Nuclear Programs Agency.

SEC. 502. ESTABLISHMENT AND ORGANIZATION OF DEFENSE NUCLEAR PROGRAMS AGENCY.

(a) ESTABLISHMENT OF DEFENSE NUCLEAR PROGRAMS AGENCY.—There is established an agency in the Department of Defense to be known as the Defense Nuclear Programs Agency.

(b) UNDER SECRETARY.—The Agency shall be headed by an Under Secretary for Defense Nuclear Programs, who shall serve as the principal adviser to the President and the Secretary of Defense on defense nuclear programs matters. In carrying out his duties under this Act, the Under Secretary for Defense Nuclear Programs shall, subject to the authority, direction, and control of of the Secretary of Defense, have primary responsibility within the Government for defense nuclear programs matters. The Under Secretary shall be appointed by the President, by and with the advice and consent of the Senate. A commissioned officer of the Armed Forces serving on active duty may not be appointed Under Secretary. The Under Secretary shall be compensated at the rate provided for level

II of the Executive Schedule under section 5313 of title 5, United States Code.

(c) DEPUTY UNDER SECRETARY.—A Deputy Under Secretary for Defense Nuclear Programs shall be appointed by the President, by and with the advice and consent of the Senate. The Deputy Under Secretary shall perform such duties and exercise such powers as the Under Secretary for Defense Nuclear Programs may prescribe. The Deputy Under Secretary shall act for, and exercise the powers of, the Under Secretary during the Under Secretary's absence or disability or during a vacancy in such office. A commissioned officer of the Armed Forces serving on active duty may not be appointed Deputy Under Secretary. The Deputy Under Secretary shall be compensated at the rate provided for level III of the Executive Schedule under section 5314 of title 5, United States Code.

(d) ASSISTANT SECRETARIES.—(1) Four Assistant Secretaries of the Agency shall be appointed by the President, by and with the advice and consent of the Senate. They shall perform such duties and exercise such powers as the Under Secretary may prescribe.

(2) One of the Assistant Secretaries shall have as his principal duty the overall supervision of environmental restoration of defense nuclear weapons facilities.

(3) One of the Assistant Secretaries shall have as his principal duty the overall supervision of the oversight of the defense and nondefense functions and budgets of the Sandia National Laboratories, the Los Alamos National Laboratory, and the Lawrence Livermore National Laboratory (or whatever laboratories (or portions of laboratories) carrying out the functions of such laboratories remain after reconfiguration, privatization, or closure (if any) pursuant to title II).

(4) Each Assistant Secretary shall be compensated at the rate provided for level IV of the Executive Schedule under section 5315 of title 5, United States Code.

(e) INSPECTOR GENERAL.—There shall be an Inspector General of the Agency, who shall be appointed as provided in section 3 of the Inspector General Act of 1978 (5 U.S.C. App. 3). The Inspector General shall perform the duties, have the responsibilities, and exercise the powers specified in the Inspector General Act of 1978 (5 U.S.C. App. 3).

(f) GENERAL COUNSEL.—There shall be a General Counsel of the Agency, who shall be appointed by the Under Secretary. The General Counsel shall be the chief legal officer for all legal matters arising from the conduct of the functions of the Agency. The General Counsel shall be compensated at the rate provided for level V of the Executive Schedule under section 5316 of title 5, United States Code.

SEC. 503. FUNCTIONS OF DEFENSE NUCLEAR PROGRAMS AGENCY.

(a) IN GENERAL.—The Under Secretary for Defense Nuclear Programs shall be responsible for the exercise of all powers and the discharge of all duties of the Agency.

(b) TRANSFERRED FUNCTIONS.—The Under Secretary for Defense Nuclear Programs shall carry out all functions transferred to the Under Secretary pursuant to section 504.

(c) STAFF DIRECTOR OF NUCLEAR WEAPONS COUNCIL.—Paragraph (2) of section 179(c) of title 10, United States Code, is amended to read as follows:

"(2) The Under Secretary for Defense Nuclear Programs shall be the Staff Director of the Council.".

SEC. 504. TRANSFERS OF FUNCTIONS.

(a) DEPARTMENT OF ENERGY.—(1) There are hereby transferred to the Under Secretary for Defense Nuclear Programs all functions performed by the Department of Energy on the day before the date of the enactment of this Act relating to the national security functions of the Department, including defense, nonproliferation, and defense-related environmental management programs.

(2) There are hereby transferred to the Under Secretary for Defense Nuclear Programs all functions performed by the Department of Energy on the day before the date of the enactment of this Act relating to the oversight of the defense and nondefense functions and budgets of the following laboratories:

(A) Sandia National Laboratories, Albuquerque, New Mexico, and Livermore, California.

(B) Los Alamos National Laboratory, Los Alamos, New Mexico.

(C) Lawrence Livermore National Laboratory, California.

(b) DEFENSE NUCLEAR AGENCY.—There are hereby transferred to the Under Secretary for Defense Nuclear Programs all functions performed by the Defense Nuclear Agency of the Department of Defense on the day before the date of the enactment of this Act relating to nuclear weapons systems.

(c) DEFENSE NUCLEAR FACILITIES SAFETY BOARD.—There are hereby transferred to the Under Secretary for Defense Nuclear Programs all functions performed by the Defense Nuclear Facilities Safety Board on the day before the date of the enactment of this Act.

(d) OTHER NUCLEAR WEAPONS-RELATED FUNCTIONS.—The Secretary of Defense may transfer to the

Under Secretary for Defense Nuclear Programs such other functions performed in the Department of Defense on the day before the date of the enactment of this Act relating to nuclear weapons as the Secretary considers appropriate.

(e) CONFORMING REPEALS.—

(1) ASSISTANT TO THE SECRETARY OF DEFENSE FOR ATOMIC ENERGY.—Section 141 of title 10, United States Code, is hereby repealed. The table of sections at the beginning of chapter 4 of such title is amended by striking out the item relating to such section.

(2) DEFENSE NUCLEAR FACILITIES SAFETY BOARD.—Chapter 21 of the Atomic Energy Act of 1954 (42 U.S.C. 2286) is hereby repealed.

(3) REFERENCES.—Any reference to the Assistant Secretary of Defense for Atomic Energy or the Defense Nuclear Facilities Safety Board in any provision of law or in any rule, regulation, or other paper of the United States shall be treated as referring to the Under Secretary for Defense Nuclear Programs.

SEC. 505. LIMITATION ON TRANSFERS OF FUNDS.

No amount appropriated to the Agency may be transferred to any other account (other than another account of the Agency) unless the transfer of such amount to such account is specifically authorized by law. No amount appropriated to the Department of Defense or another department or agency may be transferred to the Under Secretary for Defense Nuclear Programs or to an account for the Agency unless the transfer of such amount to such account is specifically authorized by law.

SEC. 506. TRANSITION PROVISIONS.

(a) EXERCISE OF AUTHORITIES.—Except as otherwise provided by law, the Under Secretary for Defense Nuclear Programs may, for purposes of performing a function that is transferred to the Under Secretary by this Act, exercise all authorities under any other provision of law that were available with respect to the performance of that function to the official responsible for the performance of that function on the day before the date of the enactment of this Act.

(b) AUTHORITIES TO WIND UP AFFAIRS.—

(1) IN GENERAL.—(A) The Director of the Office of Management and Budget may take such actions as the Director considers necessary to wind up any outstanding affairs of the Department of Energy associated with the functions that are transferred pursuant to section 504(a).

(B) The Secretary of Defense may take such actions as the Secretary considers necessary to wind up any outstanding affairs of the Defense Nuclear Agency associated with the functions that are transferred pursuant to section 504(b), any outstanding affairs of the Department of Defense associated with any functions that may be transferred pursuant to section 504(d), and any outstanding affairs of the Assistant to the Secretary of Defense for Atomic Energy.

(C) The Secretary of the Navy may take such actions as the Secretary considers necessary to wind up any outstanding affairs of the Strategic Systems Programs of the Department of the Navy associated with the functions that are transferred pursuant to section 504(c).

(D) The Director of the Office of Management and Budget may take such actions as the Director considers necessary to wind up any outstanding affairs of the Defense Nuclear Facilities Safety Board.

(2) TRANSFER OF ASSETS.—So much of the personnel, property, records, and unexpended balances of appropriations, allocations, and other funds employed, used, held, available, or to be made available in connection with a function transferred to the

Under Secretary for Defense Nuclear Programs by this Act are transferred to the Under Secretary for use in connection with the functions transferred.

(3) FURTHER MEASURES AND DISPOSITIONS.—Such further measures and dispositions as the President considers necessary to effectuate the transfers referred to in subsection (b) shall be carried out in such manner as the President directs and by the heads of such agencies as the President designates.

SEC. 507. TECHNICAL AND CONFORMING AMENDMENTS.

(a) INSPECTOR GENERAL ACT OF 1978.—Section 11 of the Inspector General Act of 1978 (5 U.S.C. App.) is amended—

(1) in paragraph (1), by inserting after "International Development," the following: "the Defense Nuclear Programs Agency,"; and

(2) in paragraph (2), by striking out "or the Social Security Administration;" and inserting in lieu thereof "the Social Security Administration, or the Defense Nuclear Programs Agency;".

(b) EXECUTIVE SCHEDULE.—(1) Section 5313 of title 5, United States Code, is amended by adding at the end the following:

"Under Secretary for Defense Nuclear Programs.".

(2) Section 5314 of title 5, United States Code, is amended by adding at the end the following:

"Deputy Under Secretary for Defense Nuclear Programs.".

(3) Section 5315 of title 5, United States Code, is amended by adding at the end the following:

"Assistant Secretaries, Defense Nuclear Programs Agency (4).

"Inspector General, Defense Nuclear Programs Agency.".

(4) Section 5316 of title 5, United States Code, is amended by adding at the end the following:

"General Counsel, Defense Nuclear Programs Agency.".

SEC. 508. EFFECTIVE DATE AND TRANSITION PERIOD.

(a) EFFECTIVE DATE.—Except as provided in subsection (b), this title shall take effect on the date of the enactment of this Act.

(b) DELAYED EFFECTIVE DATE FOR ESTABLISHMENT OF AGENCY AND TRANSFERS OF FUNCTIONS.—Section 502(a) and section 504 of this Act shall take effect one year after the date of the enactment of this Act.

(c) TRANSITION PERIOD.—The Secretary of Defense, the Secretary of Energy, the Assistant to the Secretary of Defense for Atomic Energy, and the Defense Nuclear

Facilities Safety Board shall, beginning as soon as practicable after the date of the enactment of this Act, plan for the orderly establishment of, and transfer of functions to, the Agency pursuant to this Act.

(d) APPOINTMENT AUTHORITY.—The President may make appointments under section 2 notwithstanding the delayed effective date under subsection (b) for the establishment of the Agency.

Subtitle B—Environmental Restoration Activities at Defense Nuclear Facilities

SEC. 521. ENVIRONMENTAL RESTORATION ACTIVITIES AT DEFENSE NUCLEAR FACILITIES.

The Comprehensive Environmental Response, Compensation, and Liability Act of 1980 (42 U.S.C. 9601 et seq.) is amended by adding at the end the following new title:

"TITLE IV—ENVIRONMENTAL RESTORATION ACTIVITIES AT DEFENSE NUCLEAR FACILITIES

"Subtitle A—General Provisions

"SEC. 401. APPLICABILITY.

"Notwithstanding section 120, the provisions of this title shall apply with respect to selection of remedial actions at defense nuclear facilities.

"SEC. 402. DEFINITIONS.

"For purposes of this title:

"(1) The term "defense nuclear facility" means—

"(A) a production facility or utilization facility (as those terms are defined in section 11 of the Atomic Energy Act of 1954 (42 U.S.C. 2014)) that is under the control or jurisdiction of the Under Secretary of Defense for Defense Nuclear Programs and that is operated for national security purposes (including the tritium loading facility at Savannah River, South Carolina, the 236 H facility at Savannah River, South Carolina; and the Mound Laboratory, Ohio), but the term does not include any facility that does not conduct atomic energy defense activities and does not include any facility or activity covered by Executive Order Number

12344, dated February 1, 1982, pertaining to the naval nuclear propulsion program;

"(B) a nuclear waste storage or disposal facility that is under the control or jurisdiction of the Under Secretary of Defense for Defense Nuclear Programs;

"(C) a testing and assembly facility that is under the control or jurisdiction of the Under Secretary of Defense for Defense Nuclear Programs and that is operated for national security purposes (including the Nevada Test Site, Nevada; the Pinnellas Plant, Florida; and the Pantex facility, Texas);

"(D) an atomic weapons research facility that is under the control or jurisdiction of the Under Secretary of Defense for Defense Nuclear Programs (including the Lawrence Livermore, Los Alamos, and Sandia National Laboratories); or

"(E) any facility described in paragraphs (1) through (4) that—

"(i) is no longer in operation;

"(ii) was under the control or jurisdiction of the Department of Defense, the Atomic Energy Commission, the Energy

Research and Development Administration, or the Department of Energy; and

"(iii) was operated for national security purposes.

"(2) The term 'Under Secretary' means the Under Secretary of Defense for Defense Nuclear Programs.

"(3) The term 'Administrator' means the Administrator of the Environmental Protection Agency.

"Subtitle B—Selection of Remedial Action

"SEC. 411. REVIEW OF ONGOING AND PLANNED REMEDIAL ACTIONS.

"REVIEW OF ONGOING AND PLANNED ACTIVITIES.—(1) Not later than one year after the date of the enactment of this title, the Under Secretary shall review each remedial action described in paragraph (2) for purposes of determining whether the remedial action was selected in a manner consistent with the requirements of this subtitle. If the Under Secretary determines the selection was not consistent with the requirements of this subtitle, the Under Secretary shall modify the remedial action in a manner consistent with the requirements of this subtitle. The Under Secretary shall, to the maximum extent practicable, ensure the minimization of any delays in the performance of the remedial action that result from the Under Secretary's activities under this paragraph.

"(2) Paragraph (1) applies to any remedial action at a defense nuclear facility—

"(A) which is ongoing as of the date of the enactment of this title, including a facility for which construction is ongoing or has been completed as of such date; or

"(B) for which construction is planned but has not yet commenced as of such date of enactment.

"SEC. 412. SELECTION OF REMEDIAL ACTION.

"(a) IN GENERAL.—The Under Secretary shall select a remedial action for a defense nuclear facility based upon consideration of a site-specific risk assessment conducted in accordance with section 413 and an analysis of risk reduction benefits and costs conducted in accordance with section 414.

"(b) REQUIREMENT FOR LOWEST COST ACTION.—In selecting a remedial action, the Under Secretary shall select the lowest cost action which achieves a residual risk that is within the risk range goal established by the National Contingency Plan for protection of public health and the environment, unless—

"(1) the incremental benefits of a more expensive remedial action justify incurring the incremental costs of the more expensive remedy, as set forth in the analysis of risk reductions cost and benefits for the remedial action pursuant to section 414, in which case a more expensive remedy may be selected, or

"(2) the benefits of the lowest cost remedy which achieves a residual risk level within the risk range goal are not reasonably related to the costs of such remedy, in which case a less expensive remedy may be selected.

"(c) CONSULTATION.—Before selection of a remedial action and before public comment under subsection (d), the Under Secretary shall consult with the Administrator, officials of State, local, or tribal governments having jurisdiction over the property or, in the case of property which is exclusively under Federal jurisdiction, having jurisdiction over the surrounding areas. Such consultation shall include discussion of, at a minimum, current area demographics, land and water uses, and currently planned land and water uses, the determination of which shall remain the sole purview of the appropriate State, local, or tribal government with jurisdiction.

"(d) PUBLIC COMMENT.—Before selection of a remedial action, the Under Secretary shall provide a period of not less than 30 days for public comment on the remedial action.

"(e) CERTIFICATION.—The Under Secretary shall certify the following when selecting a remedial action:

"(1) That the analysis of risk reduction benefits and costs for the remedial action pursuant to section 414 is based on objective and unbiased scientific and economic evaluations of all significant and relevant information and on risk assessments provided to the agency by interested parties relating to the costs, risks, and risk reduction and other benefits of the remedial action selected.

"(2) That the incremental risk reduction or other benefits of the remedial action will be likely to justify, and be reasonably related to, the incremental costs incurred by the Federal Government, by State, local, and tribal governments, and other public and private entities.

"(3) That other alternative remedial actions identified or considered by the agency were found to be less cost-effective at achieving a substantially equivalent reduction in risk.

"(f) ADMINISTRATIVE RECORD.—All documents considered by the Under Secretary shall be made part of the administrative record for purposes of judicial review.

"SEC. 413. SITE-SPECIFIC RISK ASSESSMENT.

"(a) In General.—(1) A site-specific risk assessment shall be performed in accordance with this section before the selection of a remedial action at a defense nuclear facility. The Under Secretary shall apply the principles set forth in subsection (b) in order to ensure that a site-specific risk assessment—

"(A) distinguishes scientific findings from other considerations;

"(B) is, to the extent feasible, scientifically objective, unbiased, and inclusive of all relevant data; and

"(C) relies, to the extent available and practicable, on factual site-specific data.

"(2) Discussions or explanations required under this section need not be repeated in each risk assessment document as long as there is a reference to the relevant discussions or explanation in another agency document which is available to the public.

"(b) Principles.—The principles to be applied in conducting a site-specific risk assessment are as follows:

"(1) When discussing human health risks, a site-specific risk assessment shall contain a discussion of both relevant laboratory and relevant epidemiologic data of sufficient quality which finds, or fails to find, a correlation between health risks and a potential toxin or activity. Where conflicts among such data appear to exist, or where animal data is used as a basis to assess human health, the site-specific risk assessment shall, to the extent feasible and appropriate, include discussion of possible reconciliation of conflicting information, and, as relevant, differences in study designs, comparative physiology, routes of exposure, bioavailability, pharmacokinetics, and any other relevant factor, including the sufficiency of basic data for review. The discussion of possible reconciliation should indicate whether there is a biological basis to assume a resulting harm in humans. Animal data shall be reviewed with regard to its relevancy to humans.

"(2) Where a site-specific risk assessment involves selection of any significant default value, assumption, inference, or model, the risk assessment document shall, to the extent feasible—

"(A) present a representative list and explanation of plausible and alternative assumptions, inferences, or models;

"(B) explain the basis for any choices;

"(C) identify any policy or value judgments;

"(D) fully describe any model used in the risk assessment and make explicit the assumptions incorporated in the model; and

"(E) indicate the extent to which any significant model has been validated by, or conflicts with, empirical data.

"(3) The site-specific risk assessment shall meet each of the following requirements regarding risk characterization and communication:

"(A) The risk characterization shall describe the populations or natural resources which are the subject of the risk characterization. If a numerical estimate of risk is provided, the agency shall, to the extent feasible, provide—

"(i) the best estimate or estimates for the specific populations or natural resources which are the subject to the characterization (based on the information available to the Federal agency); and

"(ii) a statement of the reasonable range of scientific uncertainties.

In addition to such best estimate or estimates, the risk characterization document may present plausible upper-bound or conservative estimates in conjunction with plausible lower-bound estimates. Where appropriate, the risk characterization document may present, in lieu of a single best estimate, multiple best estimates based on assumptions, inferences, or models which are equally plausible, given current scientific understanding. To the extent practicable and appropriate, the document shall provide descriptions of the distribution and probability of risk estimates to reflect differences in exposure variability or sensitivity in populations and attendance uncertainties. Sensitive subpopulations or highly exposed subpopulations include, where relevant and appropriate, children, the elderly, pregnant women, and disabled persons.

"(B) Exposure scenarios shall be based on actual exposure pathways and currently planned future land and water uses as established by any local governmental authorities with jurisdiction over the property and shall consider the availability of alternative water supplies. To the extent feasible, the site-specific risk assessment shall include a statement of the size of the population at risk under any proposed exposure scenario and the likelihood of such scenario.

Exposure scenarios shall explicitly identify those exposure scenarios which result in plausible completed exposure pathways.

"(C) A site-specific risk assessment shall contain a statement that places the magnitude of risks to human health, safety, or the environment in context. Such statement shall, to the extent feasible, provide comparisons with estimates of greater, lesser, and substantially equivalent risks that are familiar to and routinely encountered by the general public as well as other risks, and where appropriate and meaningful, comparisons of those risks with other similar risks regulated by the Federal agency resulting from comparable activities and exposure pathways. Such comparisons should consider relevant distinctions among risks, such as the voluntary or involuntary nature of risks and the preventability or nonpreventability of risks.

"(D) Each site-specific risk assessment shall include a statement of any significant substitution risks to human health, where information on such risks has been provided to the Under Secretary.

"(E) If a commenter provides the Under Secretary with a relevant risk assessment and a summary thereof in a timely fashion and the risk assessment is consistent with the principles and the guidance provided under this section, the Under Secretary shall, to the extent feasible, present such summary in connection with the presentation of the site-specific risk assessment. Nothing in this paragraph shall be construed to limit the inclusion of any comments or material supplied by any person to the administrative record of any proceeding.

"(4) A site-specific risk assessment may satisfy the requirements of subparagraph (C), (D), or (E) of paragraph (3) by reference to information or material otherwise available to the public if the document provides a brief summary of such information or material.

"SEC. 414. ANALYSIS OF RISK REDUCTION BENEFITS AND COSTS.

"(a) IN GENERAL.—The Under Secretary shall prepare an analysis of risk reduction benefits and costs in accordance with this section before the selection of a remedial action at a defense nuclear facility.

"(b) CONTENTS OF ANALYSIS.—An analysis of risk reduction benefits and costs for a remedial action shall contain the following:

"(1) An identification of reasonable alternative strategies, including strategies that are proposed during a public comment period.

"(2) An analysis of the incremental costs and incremental risk reduction or other benefits associated with each alternative remedial action identified or considered. Costs and benefits shall be quantified to the extent feasible and appropriate and may otherwise be qualitatively described.

"(3) A statement that places in context the nature and magnitude of the risks to be addressed and the residual risks likely to remain for each alternative strategy identified or considered by the Under Secretary. Such statement shall, to the extent feasible, provide comparisons with estimates of greater, lesser, and substantially equivalent risks that are familiar to and routinely encountered by the general public as well as other risks and, where appropriate and meaningful, comparisons of those risks with other similar risks regulated by the Federal Government resulting from comparable activities and exposure pathways. Such comparisons should consider relevant distinctions among risks, such as the voluntary or involuntary nature of risks and the preventability or nonpreventability of risks.

"(4) An analysis of whether the identified benefits of the remedial action are likely to exceed the identified costs of the remedial action.".

SEC. 522. CONFORMING AMENDMENT.

Section 120(a)(3) of the Comprehensive Environmental Response, Compensation, and Liability Act of 1980 (42 U.S.C. 9620(a)(3)) is amended by inserting after the second sentence the following: "This subsection also shall not apply to the extent otherwise provided in title IV with respect to selection of remedial actions at defense nuclear facilities.".

SEC. 523. RENEGOTIATION OF COMPLIANCE AGREEMENTS.

(a) REQUIREMENT.—For each defense nuclear facility with respect to which a compliance agreement has been entered into by the Secretary of Energy, the Environmental Protection Agency, and a State as of the date of the enactment of this Act, the Under Secretary of Defense for Defense Nuclear Programs shall enter into negotiations with the Environmental Protection Agency and the State concerned to renegotiate the terms of the compliance agreement to reflect title IV of the Comprehensive Environmental Response, Compensation, and Liability Act of 1980, as added by section 521.

(b) DEADLINE.—The Under Secretary of Defense for Defense Nuclear Programs shall complete renegotiation of compliance agreements as required by subsection (a) not later than one year after the date of the enactment of this Act.

TITLE VI—DISPOSITION OF MISCELANEOUS PARTICULAR PROGRAMS, FUNCTIONS, AND AGENCIES OF DEPARTMENT

SEC. 601. ENERGY RESEARCH AND DEVELOPMENT.

(a) AUTHORIZATION.—

(1) LIMITATIONS.—The amount which may be appropriated for Energy Supply Research and Development activities of the Department of Energy, including Basic Energy Sciences, Magnetic Fusion Energy, Solar and Renewable Energy, Nuclear Fission, and Biological and Environmental Sciences research and development, and all other research and development activities of the Department of Energy other than General Science and Research activities, shall not exceed—

(A) for fiscal year 1996, 75 percent of the budget authority available for such purposes for fiscal year 1995;

(B) for fiscal year 1997, 50 percent of the budget authority available for such purposes for fiscal year 1995;

(C) for fiscal year 1998, 50 percent of the budget authority available for such purposes for fiscal year 1995;

(D) for fiscal year 1999, 50 percent of the budget authority available for such purposes for fiscal year 1995; and

(E) for fiscal year 2000, 50 percent of the budget authority available for such purposes for fiscal year 1995.

(2) DEFINITION.—For purposes of this subsection, the term "budget authority" has the meaning given such term in section 3(2) of the Congressional Budget Act of 1974.

(b) RECOMMENDATIONS.—Within 1 year of the date of the enactment of this Act, the Energy Laboratory Facilities Commission established under section 201(a) of this Act shall identify in a report to Congress all research and development activities of the Department of Energy carried out at energy laboratories (as such term is defined in section 208(5) of this Act) or at institutions of higher education, that perform a critical research function of importance to the long-term economic wellbeing of the United States. Such report shall include recommendations for the transfer of such activities to appropriate Federal agencies.

(c) TERMINATION OF PROGRAMS.—

(1) CLEAN COAL TECHNOLOGY.—The Secretary of Energy shall terminate all clean coal technology research and development activities of the Department of Energy.

(2) FOSSIL ENERGY AND ENERGY CONSERVATION.—There are authorized to be appropriated to the Secretary of Energy—

(A) for fossil energy research and development activities of the Department of Energy—

(i) $150,000,000 for fiscal year 1996;

(ii) $135,000,000 for fiscal year 1997; and

(iii) $120,000,000 for fiscal year 1998; and

(B) for energy conservation research and development activities of the Department of Energy—

(i) $427,000,000 for fiscal year 1996;

(ii) $412,000,000 for fiscal year 1997; and

(iii) $397,000,000 for fiscal year 1998.

The fossil energy and energy conservation research and development activities of the Department of Energy shall be terminated at the end of fiscal year 1998.

(d) TRANSFER OF PROGRAMS.—The following activities of the Department of Energy shall, no later than 60 days after the date of the enactment of this Act, be transferred to the Department of Defense:

(1) All activities described under the category "Weapons Activities" in the annual budget request of the President for fiscal year 1996, including weapons stockpile stewardship and management.

(2) All activities described under the category "Materials Support and Other Defense Programs" in the annual budget request of the President for fiscal year 1996.

(e) PROGRESS REPORTS.—The Secretary of Energy shall, every 90 days after the date of the enactment of this Act until the completion of the execution of subsections (c) and (d), transmit to the Congress a report on the progress made toward such execution.

SEC. 602. ENERGY INFORMATION ADMINISTRATION.

There are hereby transferred to the Department of the Treasury all functions performed by the Energy Information Administration on the day before the effective date of this section. There are authorized to be appropriated for carrying out the activities of the Energy Information Administration $40,000,000 for each of the fiscal years 1996 through 2000.

SEC. 603. ENERGY REGULATORY ADMINISTRATION.

There are hereby transferred to the Attorney General all functions performed by the Energy Regulatory Administration on the day before the effective date of this section.

SEC. 604. EFFECTIVE DATE.

(a) GENERAL RULE.—Except as provided in subsection (b), this title shall take effect on the date specified in section 109(a) of this Act.

(b) EXCEPTIONS.—Section 601(c), (d), and (e), shall take effect on the date of the enactment of this Act.

TITLE VII—CIVILIAN RADIOACTIVE WASTE MANAGEMENT

SEC. 701. NUCLEAR WASTE REPOSITORY.

Effective upon the expiration of the 3rd calendar month beginning after the date of the enactment of this Act section 304 of the Nuclear Waste Policy Act of 1982 (42 U.S.C. 10224) is amended to read as follows:

"ARMY CORPS OF ENGINEERS

"SEC. 304. (a) TRANSFER.—The Office of Civilian Radioactive Waste Management (referred to in this section as the 'office') is terminated and the authority and assets of the office with respect to its activities under title I respecting a repository for radioactive waste and spent nuclear fuel is transferred to the Army Corps of Engineers (referred to in this section as the 'Corps'. In connection with the transfer, the Corps shall assume all contracts and other obligations of the office with respect to the Yucca Mountain site and the permits from the State of Nevada for the site shall be reissued for the Corps.

"(b) YUCCA MOUNTAIN SITE.—The Corps shall review the characterization plan of, and the work undertaken by, the office for the Yucca Mountain site. Effective 6 months after the transfer under subsection (a), the Corps shall prepare its own site characterization plan in accordance with section 113. The plan shall be submitted to the Nuclear Waste Technical Review Board for its review and comments. If the Yucca Mountain site is found to be suitable, the Corps shall be responsible for managing the design and construction of the site. Once completed, the site shall be operated by the Corps in accordance with this Act. The Corps shall provide benefits to the State of Nevada in accordance with subtitle F of title I.

"(c) OTHER SITE.—If the Yucca Mountain site is found to be unsuitable, the Corps shall undertake a site characterization plan for another site.".

TITLE VIII—MISCELLANEOUS PROVISIONS

SEC. 801. REFERENCES.

Any reference in any other Federal law, Executive order, rule, regulation, or delegation of authority, or any document of or pertaining to an office from which a function is transferred by this Act—

(1) to the Secretary of Energy or an officer of the Department of Energy, is deemed to refer to the head of the department or office to which such function is transferred; or

(2) to the Department of Energy is deemed to refer to the department or office to which such function is transferred.

SEC. 802. EXERCISE OF AUTHORITIES.

Except as otherwise provided by law, a Federal official to whom a function is transferred by this Act may, for purposes of performing the function, exercise all authorities under any other provision of law that were available with respect to the performance of that function to the official responsible for the performance of the function immediately before the effective date of the transfer of the function under this Act.

SEC. 803. SAVINGS PROVISIONS.

(a) LEGAL DOCUMENTS.—All orders, determinations, rules, regulations, permits, grants, loans, contracts, agreements, certificates, licenses, and privileges—

(1) that have been issued, made, granted, or allowed to become effective by the President, the Secretary of Energy, any officer or employee of any office transferred by this Act, or any other Government official, or by a court of competent jurisdiction, in the performance of any function that is transferred by this Act, and

(2) that are in effect on the effective date of such transfer (or become effective after such date pursuant to their terms as in effect on such effective date),

shall continue in effect according to their terms until modified, terminated, superseded, set aside, or revoked in accordance with law by the President, any other authorized official, a court of competent jurisdiction, or operation of law.

(b) PROCEEDINGS.—This Act shall not affect any proceedings or any application for any benefits, service, license, permit, certificate, or financial assistance pending on the date of the enactment of this Act before an office transferred by this Act, but such proceedings and applications shall be continued. Orders shall be issued in such proceedings, appeals shall be taken therefrom, and payments shall be made pursuant to such orders, as if this Act had not been enacted, and orders issued in any such proceeding shall continue in effect until modified, terminated, superseded, or revoked by a duly authorized official, by a court of competent jurisdiction, or by operation of law. Nothing in this subsection shall be considered to prohibit the discontinuance or modification of any such proceeding under the same terms and conditions and to the same extent that such proceeding could have been discontinued or modified if this Act had not been enacted.

(c) SUITS.—This Act shall not affect suits commenced before the date of the enactment of this Act, and in all such suits, proceeding shall be had, appeals taken, and judgments rendered in the same manner and with the same effect as if this Act had not been enacted.

(d) NONABATEMENT OF ACTIONS.—No suit, action, or other proceeding commenced by or against the Department of Energy or the Secretary of Energy, or by or against any individual in the official capacity of such individual as an officer or employee of an office transferred by this Act, shall abate by reason of the enactment of this Act.

(e) CONTINUANCE OF SUITS.—If any officer of the Department of Energy or the Energy Programs Resolution Agency in the official capacity of such officer is party to a suit with respect to a function of the officer, and under this Act such function is transferred to any other officer or office, then such suit shall be continued with the other officer or the head of such other office, as applicable, substituted or added as a party.

SEC. 804. TRANSFER OF ASSETS.

Except as otherwise provided in this Act, so much of the personnel, property, records, and unexpended balances of appropriations, allocations, and other funds employed, used, held, available, or to be made available in connection with a function transferred to an official by this Act shall be available to the official at such time or times as the Director of the Office of Management and Budget directs for use in connection with the functions transferred.

SEC. 805. DELEGATION AND ASSIGNMENT.

Except as otherwise expressly prohibited by law or otherwise provided in this Act, an official to whom functions are transferred under this Act (including the head of any office to which functions are transferred under this

Act) may delegate any of the functions so transferred to such officers and employees of the office of the official as the official may designate, and may authorize successive redelegations of such functions as may be necessary or appropriate. No delegation of functions under this section or under any other provision of this Act shall relieve the official to whom a function is transferred under this Act of responsibility for the administration of the function.

SEC. 806. AUTHORITY OF OFFICE OF MANAGEMENT AND BUDGET WITH RESPECT TO FUNCTIONS TRANSFERRED.

(a) DETERMINATIONS.—If necessary, the Office of Management and Budget shall make any determination of the functions that are transferred under this Act.

(b) INCIDENTAL TRANSFERS.—The Director of the Office of Management and Budget, at such time or times as the Director shall provide, may make such determinations as may be necessary with regard to the functions transferred by this Act, and to make such additional incidental dispositions of personnel, assets, liabilities, grants, contracts, property, records, and unexpended balances of appropriations, authorizations, allocations, and other funds held, used, arising from, available to, or to be made available in connection with such functions, as may be necessary to carry out the provisions of this Act. The Director of the Office of Management and Budget shall provide for the termination of the affairs of all entities terminated by this Act and for such further measures and dispositions as may be necessary to effectuate the purposes of this Act.

SEC. 807. PROPOSED CHANGES IN LAW.

Not later than one year after the date of the enactment of this Act, the Director of the Office of Management and Budget shall submit to the Congress a description of any changes in Federal law necessary to reflect abolishments, transfers, terminations, and disposals under this Act.

SEC. 808. CERTAIN VESTING OF FUNCTIONS CONSIDERED TRANSFER.

For purposes of this title, the vesting of a function in a department or office pursuant to reestablishment of an office shall be considered to be the transfer of the function.

SEC. 809. DEFINITIONS.

Except as otherwise provided in this Act, for purposes of this Act the following definitions apply:

(1) ADMINISTRATOR.—The term "Administrator" means the Administrator of the Energy Programs Resolution Agency.

(2) AGENCY.—The term "Agency" means the Energy Programs Resolution Agency.

(3) FUNCTION.—The term "function" includes any duty, obligation, power, authority, responsibility, right, privilege, activity, or program.

(4) OFFICE.—The term "office" includes any office, administration, agency, institute, council, unit, organizational entity, or component thereof.

(5) TERMINATION DATE.—The term "termination date" means the termination date under section 106(d).

(6) WIND-UP PERIOD.—The term "wind-up period" means the period beginning on the effective date specified in section 109(a) and ending on the termination date.

○

104TH CONGRESS
1ST SESSION

H. R. 2142

To promote the scientific, technological, and the national security interests and industrial wellbeing of the United States through establishing missions for and streamlining Department of Energy laboratories, and for other purposes.

IN THE HOUSE OF REPRESENTATIVES

JULY 31, 1995

Mr. SCHIFF (for himself, Mr. PETE GEREN of Texas, Mr. FAWELL, Mr. HASTERT, Mr. WAMP, Mr. BAKER of California, and Mrs. MORELLA) introduced the following bill; which was referred to the Committee on Science, and in addition to the Committee on National Security, for a period to be subsequently determined by the Speaker, in each case for consideration of such provisions as fall within the jurisdiction of the committee concerned

---

A BILL

To promote the scientific, technological, and the national security interests and industrial wellbeing of the United States through establishing missions for and streamlining Department of Energy laboratories, and for other purposes.

Be it enacted by the Senate and House of Representatives of the United States of America in Congress assembled,

SECTION 1. SHORT TITLE.

This Act may be cited as the "Department of Energy Laboratory Missions Act".

SEC. 2. DEFINITIONS.

For purposes of this Act—

(1) the term "departmental laboratory" means a Federal laboratory, or any other laboratory or facility designated by the Secretary, operated by or on behalf of the Department of Energy;

(2) the term "Federal laboratory" has the meaning given the term "laboratory" in section 12(d)(2) of the Stevenson-Wydler Technology Innovation Act of 1980 (15 U.S.C. 3710a(d)(2));

(3) the term "relevant congressional committees" means the Committee on Armed Services of the Senate, the Committee on National Security of the House of Representatives, the Committee on Science of the House of Representatives, and the Committee on Energy and Natural Resources of the Senate; and

(4) the term "Secretary" means the Secretary of Energy.

TITLE I—MISSION ASSIGNMENT

SEC. 101. FINDINGS.

The Congress finds that—

(1) through their unique historical missions, the departmental laboratories have developed core competencies and technical capabilities that strategically

position them to contribute to the scientific and technological wellbeing of the Nation;

(2) the departmental laboratories have contributed and continue to contribute technology to ensure the maintenance of the nuclear deterrent and other elements of the national security;

(3) through their contributions to the national security in the production of nuclear and conventional weapons, the departmental laboratories have helped deter the repetition of the global conflicts of the past, and have helped maintain the relative peace which the United States enjoys;

(4) the departmental laboratories collectively represent an extensive science and technology resource of people, facilities, and equipment that contribute to the achievement of national technology goals;

(5) in carrying out their Department of Energy mission responsibilities, the departmental laboratories have established successful collaborative relationships with other Federal agencies, universities, and other federally funded laboratories that allow each of the partners to share and leverage their unique capabilities;

(6) collaboration in partnerships among the departmental laboratories, other Federal agencies, universities, and private industry, especially through cooperative research and development agreements, should be encouraged to enable the departmental laboratories to ensure the maximum return on the taxpayer's investment; and

(7) the departmental laboratories need well defined and assigned missions to continue to successfully contribute to the scientific, technological, and national security interests of the United States.

SEC. 102. MISSIONS.

The Department of Energy may maintain departmental laboratories for the purpose of advancing, and shall carry out research and development activities which are essential to support and perform, the following core missions:

(1) To maintain national security, as follows:

(A) To provide for the Nation's nuclear weapons requirements, to be stewards of the Nation's nuclear weapons stockpile, and to meet other national security requirements as determined by the President.

(B) To reduce the threat of nuclear war, by assisting with the dismantlement of nuclear weapons, working to curb the proliferation of weapons of mass destruction, including nuclear, chemical, and biological weapons, supporting efforts to counter the proliferation of weapons of mass destruction, including nuclear, chemical, and biological weapons, and their delivery systems, and conducting research on and the development of technologies needed for the effective verification of international arms control agreements, including prospective international arms control agreements, which may include the production and dissemination of foreign intelligence pertinent to the Department's missions.

(C) To provide for the advancement of science and technology in the development of nuclear and conventional weaponry for national security purposes.

(2) To ensure the Nation's energy supply and to reduce the Nation's reliance on imported energy sources through research and development on generic, precompetitive technologies that enhance energy supply and improve the efficiency of energy end uses, with an emphasis on long-term, high-risk research.

(3) To conduct basic research in energy-related science and technology, in the fundamental understanding of matter, and in emerging scientific fields, including construction and operation of unique scientific instruments and facilities for use by the Federal Government, academia, industry, and other appropriate non-Federal institutions.

(4) To carry out research and development for the purpose of minimizing the environmental impacts of the production and use of energy, nuclear weapons, and materials, including the development of technologies for the safe disposal and cleanup of hazardous and radioactive wastes.

(5) To carry out such additional missions as are assigned to the Department of Energy by the President.

In furthering the core missions of the departmental laboratories, the Secretary and the departmental laboratories may establish mutually beneficial collaborative, mission-oriented research and development relationships with other agencies of the Federal Government, academia, and other appropriate non-Federal institutions, providing for the mutual sharing of nonproprietary and unclassified information.

SEC. 103. PROCEDURE FOR MAKING PROPOSALS FOR LABORATORY MISSION ASSIGNMENTS AND STREAMLINING.

(a) MISSION ASSIGNMENT AND STREAMLINING CRITERIA.—

(1) IN GENERAL.—Not later than 3 months after the date of the enactment of this Act, the Secretary shall publish in the Federal Register and transmit to the relevant congressional committees the criteria proposed to be used by the Secretary in making proposals for the assignment of a mission or missions to, and the streamlining, if necessary, of, departmental laboratories. The Secretary shall provide an opportunity for public comment on the proposed criteria for a period of at least 30 days and shall include notice of that opportunity in the publication required under this paragraph. In developing the criteria, the Secretary shall consider—

(A) the unique technical and experimental capabilities which exist at each of the departmental laboratories, including the critical infrastructure needed for nuclear weapons systems development, production, and maintenance;

(B) unnecessary duplication of effort by departmental laboratories and overhead costs as a proportion of program benefits distributed through a departmental laboratory;

(C) cost savings and increases that would accrue through the streamlining of departmental laboratories;

(D) the potential and appropriateness of the performance of research and other missions of the departmental laboratories by other entities such as academic, private industry, and other Federal facilities; and

(E) expert advice from appropriate outside individuals.

(2) FINAL CRITERIA.—Not later than 5 months after the date of the enactment of this Act, the Secretary shall publish in the Federal Register and transmit to the relevant congressional committees the final criteria to be used in making proposals for the assignment of a mission or missions to, and the streamlining of, departmental laboratories under this section.

(b) SECRETARY'S PROPOSALS.—

(1) PUBLICATION IN FEDERAL REGISTER.—Not later than 1 year after the date of the enactment of this Act, the Secretary shall publish in the Federal Register and transmit to the relevant congressional

committees the Secretary's proposals for mission assignments and streamlining for the departmental laboratories, on the basis of the final criteria published under subsection (a)(2) and the statement of missions contained in section 3. In formulating those proposals, the Secretary shall solicit the advice of appropriate outside expert individuals.

(2) SUMMARY OF PROCESS.—The Secretary shall include, with the proposals published and transmitted pursuant to paragraph (1), a summary of the process that resulted in the proposals for each departmental laboratory, including a justification for each proposal.

(c) AVAILABILITY OF INFORMATION.—The Secretary shall make available to the Comptroller General of the United States all information used by the Secretary in making proposals under subsection (b).

(d) COMPTROLLER GENERAL REPORT.—The Comptroller General of the United States shall, not later than 15 months after the date of the enactment of this Act, transmit to the relevant congressional committees a report containing a detailed analysis of the Secretary's proposals and procedures.

SEC. 104. ASSIGNMENT OF MISSIONS TO, AND STREAMLINING OF, DEPARTMENTAL LABORATORIES.

The Secretary shall—

(1) assign a mission or missions to all departmental laboratories as proposed in the report transmitted to the relevant congressional committees pursuant to section 103(b)(1);

(2) streamline all such laboratories proposed for streamlining in such report; and

(3) complete the mission assignments and streamlining not later than the end of the 4-year period beginning on the date on which such report is transmitted.

SEC. 105. REPORTS ON IMPLEMENTATION.

As part of the budget request for each fiscal year in which the Secretary will carry out activities under this Act, the Secretary shall transmit to the relevant congressional committees—

(1) a schedule of the mission assignment and streamlining actions to be carried out under this Act in the fiscal year for which the request is made and an estimate of the total expenditures required and cost savings to be achieved by each such mission assignment and streamlining, and of the time period in which these savings are to be achieved in each case; and

(2) a description of the departmental laboratories, including those under construction and those planned for construction, to which functions are to be transferred as a result of mission assignments and streamlining.

TITLE II—GOVERNANCE

SEC. 201. FINDINGS.

The Congress finds that—

(1) there is an inordinate internal focus at every level of the Department of Energy and the departmental laboratories on compliance issues and questions of management processes, which takes a major toll on research performance;

(2) there has been a growing emphasis at the Department on administrative and support organizations and their oversight and compliance roles;

(3) the costs of dealing with review groups significantly interferes with research operations at the department laboratories;

(4) far too much influence has been ceded by the Department to nonregulatory advisory boards, and such organizations generate recommendations with no apparent cost/benefit analysis, which results in significant unnecessary expenditures and productivity losses; and

(5) enforcement of environmental, safety, and health rules, regulations, orders, and standards is a function of government agencies other than the Department of Energy.

SEC. 202. ELIMINATION OF SELF-REGULATION.

Notwithstanding any other provision of law, the Department of Energy shall implement, but shall not be the agency of enforcement of, Federal, State, and local environmental, safety, and health rules, regulations, orders, and standards at departmental laboratories, unless the Secretary certifies that a particular action is unique to the activities of the Department and is necessary to maintain human health and safety.

SEC. 203. EFFECTIVE DATE.

This title shall take effect on October 1, 1996.

○

Mr. SCHIFF. The bill, H.R. 2142, the Department of Energy Laboratories Mission Act, defines a three-step public process by which the Secretary of Energy, working with the interested parties, including Congress, first defines the appropriate missions for the laboratories. These missions include: maintaining our national security; helping to ensure our nation's energy supply; conducting basic research in energy-related science and technology; and, to carry out research and development for the purpose of minimizing the environmental impacts of hazardous and radioactive waste.

The bill then sets out the criteria for the Secretary of Energy to assign those missions, streamlining the labs, if necessary, to carry out those missions.

Additionally, H.R. 2142 would direct the Department of Energy to cease internal health, safety and environmental regulation of the departmental laboratories and to transfer those responsibilities to other appropriate federal and state regulatory agencies, which are already responsible for these areas.

Recent reports to the Secretary of Energy on this issue of governance indicate this would substantially improve management of the labs and release scarce resources to accomplish the laboratories' missions.

At this point, I would like to recognize the Ranking Member of the Full Science Committee, Congressman Brown of California, for any remarks he might like to make.

Mr. BROWN OF CALIFORNIA. Thank you very much, Mr. Chairman.

I'm sitting in for the two Ranking Members who I hope will be here later during the course of the hearing.

First, let me compliment you and Congressman Rohrabacher for jointly sponsoring this hearing today, which I consider to be of the very highest priority.

We are at a critical juncture which requires that we reanalyze all of the functions of government. The Department of Energy is one of those agencies which, perhaps because it's relatively new, will be the subject of intense scrutiny.

For some period of time, I kept on my desk down the hall here a stack of reports over the past couple of decades purporting to review and reanalyze the functions of the Department of Energy and how to improve on them.

I finally had to give up that task because it posed certain structural hazards to the safety of the office.

[Laughter.]

And at no time during that period of time while we were collecting these studies did we actually do very much in terms of reorganization, partly because the time wasn't appropriate or maybe because those free-spending Democrats didn't want to do anything.

[Laughter.]

But, in any event, today, the time is appropriate and we are going to have to do something.

Now, Chairman Schiff I think has very well stated what the primary functions of the Department should be and it's included in his legislation. And while I do not agree 100 percent with everything that's in that bill, I have a great deal of confidence that bill, as far as the functions are concerned, is on the right track and that we can develop a set of mission statements that will be highly appropriate.

I'm also of the belief that any agency of government can be cut probably by at least a third without seriously impairing the overall results, if it's done in a proper way. And I think that we ought to be willing to do that.

I make these remarks only for the purpose of emphasizing the high priority I attach to these hearings. The defense function is not going to go away. The energy R&D function is not going to go away.

In fact, I would say that as long as we have a continuing need to import oil at the rate of $40 or $50 billion a year, and we have as large a balance of payments deficit as we have overall, that it's critical to our economic future that we do more to secure energy independence and the Department of Energy is in a position to make a contribution to that.

So for all of these reasons, I commend you and I ask unanimous consent to put the full text of my statement in the record at this point.

Mr. SCHIFF. I thank you for your remarks. And without objection, your full statement will be made part of the record. And without objection, my statement and all Members' statements will be made part of the record.

[The prepared statement of Mr. Brown follows:]

PREPARED STATEMENT OF HON. GEORGE E. BROWN, JR.

Mr. Chairman, the Subcommittees will consider today several approaches to laboratory management and alternative goals for the future of the national energy laboratory system. I commend you for this hearing; it will produce a timely discussion as the cuts that Congress will impose on the energy R&D budget will dramatically affect the laboratories, along with other performers of energy R&D.

For many years and on both sides of the aisle, lawmakers and the Executive Branch have wrestled with questions concerning the size, scope, and capabilities of the national laboratory system. Numerous panels and commissions, both inside and outside of the Department of Energy, have looked at the laboratories. The most recent report, from the Galvin Commission, made suggestions that DOE has embraced and begun to implement effectively across the laboratory system. Some questions remain, however, concerning whether these reforms go far enough.

The laboratories are very quick to do what they do best—research and cooperative ventures with industry—and we applaud them vigorously for that. However, public administration of the laboratories slows the pace of administrative change and the closure of out-dated facilities. Through no fault of their own, the labs are run by their contractors, the Department of Energy, and 535 Members of Congress each of whom feel that they know what is best for the national laboratory system.

Today, we will discuss several competing proposals for the future of the laboratories and try to develop some consensus. In our deliberations, I believe that we need to stress balance in the broad base of energy R&D performers to maximize competition and quality. This base should include universities, industrial research performers, independent researchers, as well as the laboratories. We also need to consider present and future changes in energy R&D funding and the missions of the laboratories.

If the Majority succeeds in its plans to dramatically reduce Federal energy R&D funding, a severe reduction in our national research effort will ensue. While some may seek to protect research infrastructure in the laboratories, perhaps hoping for a better day, that approach may not be what is best for the Nation. Other research performers have important roles to play in the development of energy R&D, and the bureaucratic fact that it is easier to cut external research performers must not be allowed to unduly influence the management of energy R&D. I have confidence in the Department that it will choose a wise path toward downsizing; however, I am concerned that DOE may need some help from Congress to provide the appropriate momentum to accomplish this task. I hope that this Committee will be helpful toward that end and exert its influence to ensure maximum benefit for the Nation.

To date, Science Committee Members have produced four proposals concerning the national laboratory system, H.R.'s 87, 1510, 1993, and 2142. I find merit in each of them; also, I note that in many provisions they agree and in others they are not mutually exclusive. I hope that this Committee will approach each of these proposals with an open mind and seek to combine their strengths and craft the best legislation possible.

I look forward to the process of developing this legislation, and I thank our witnesses for helping us begin this process with the best foot forward. Since I may not get the chance later, I would like to extend a personal greeting and express appreciation to each of the witnesses for taking time out of their busy lives to be with us today. Thank you.

Mr. SCHIFF. I'd like to now recognize the Chairman of our Full Committee, Congressman Walker from Pennsylvania, for any remarks he might like to make.

Mr. WALKER. Thank you, Mr. Chairman. I, too, congratulate you and Mr. Rohrabacher for the hearing today. It's a badly needed hearing.

We had an interesting experience during the recess where some of us from the Committee went out on an investigative visit looking at some of the labs. It was a very, very useful visit.

I thought it was interesting that as we came into some of the communities that have labs, the local press was reporting that we were there to make judgments as to whether or not this lab was going to be closed or not.

Well, absolutely nothing of the kind was happening. We were out simply seeing what goes on at the laboratories so that this Committee would have a better understanding of what real work is being accomplished there.

And as some of the people who will testify here today know, I've generally gone out and done a good bit of that throughout my career on this Committee. I think it's an important part. But it also tells you something about kind of the attitude that is out there at the present time amongst some of the public, within the media, about the nature of the federal laboratories.

It's extremely important that we do the right things here.

I believe that the national labs are a national asset. On the other hand, there is no doubt that their role has changed as a result of the end of the cold war. And so we now have to find out the proper way to structure the laboratories to see to it that they fit into a national mission over the years ahead.

This hearing is a part of gleaning that kind of information. There have been a number of important reports done in recent months with regard to the lab. We certainly want to examine those. We want to look at the legislation that has been introduced by a number of Members of this Committee and others in the Congress that bears on this subject matter.

But, above all, we want to, in the end, find a way to structure national laboratory activities so that they both meet the national need, but at the same time, do so in an efficient and effective manner that befits the taxpayers' commitment.

And Mr. Chairman, I certainly congratulate you for the hearing that we are having today.

Mr. SCHIFF. Thank you, Mr. Chairman. I want to say that I consider it an honor that both you, Mr. Chairman, and our Ranking Member, Chairman Brown, have both come here this morning.

In the order that the other three bills that are also consideration today were introduced—the first is H.R. 87. It was introduced by Congressman Bartlett of Maryland—Congressman, you're recognized for an opening statement about your bill.

Mr. BARTLETT. Thank you very much. And I would first like to thank Chairman Rohrabacher and Chairman Schiff for holding this hearing today. I believe this is long overdue and am excited at the possibility of legislation such as H.R. 87 and Title II of H.R. 1993, receiving a hearing.

As you may know, I am a scientist and have deeply held convictions about the need to pursue scientific knowledge to assure our future national security, our economic competitiveness, and the quality of our environment. And I believe my first-hand experience in the scientific community serves as an asset to the Committee.

Additionally, I take very seriously our national debt of $5 trillion and my responsibility to eliminate out-of-control spending.

During the 103rd Congress, I introduced a bill very similar to H.R. 87 and Title II of H.R. 1993. I believe the only certain way to ensure the labs are run as efficiently as possible is to establish an independent commission to examine the labs and make recommendations that Congress must act on, either up or down, but cannot change.

You're all aware of this process as it is modelled after the BRAC procedure.

I have first-hand knowledge how painful the BRAC process can be for an area, but it is the only way to assure that objectivity prevails and to depoliticize the decision-making process.

Many of the witnesses today who will testify have direct interest in the future of the labs, and many of my colleagues who serve on thi Committee also have a vested interest in the future of the labs.

I think this in itself is the reason that it is crystal clear why any decisions need to be made independent of the political process. Until we take the politics out of the decision-making process of the labs, we are truly jeopardizing the future of this country and the integrity of every science project.

Please make no mistake. I strongly support our national labs. I want them strengthened and made more efficient. That is why it is essential to pass a bill which independently examines them and makes recommendations so we continue to receive their benefits.

Obviously, I support H.R. 87. But even more strongly, I support Title II of H.R. 1993, as it takes H.R. 87 and it expands it to include more labs, which I believe is a positive addition to H.R. 87.

I was honored to work on this bill, 1993, with Representative Todd Tiahrt, and appreciate all of his efforts and time putting together the bill to eliminate the Department of Energy and to strengthen our national laboratory systems.

Again, thank you very much for holding these important hearings.

Mr. SCHIFF. Thank you, Congressman Bartlett. And we're grateful for your contribution to these hearings.

The second bill introduced that we're going to consider is H.R. 1510, by our colleague, Mr. Roemer.

Mr. Roemer, you're recognized for an opening statement.

Mr. ROEMER. Thank you, Mr. Chairman. I, too, would like to join in the chorus of people commending you and Mr. Rohrabacher for having this hearing, for Mr. Brown and Mr. Walker to attend such an important hearing at such an important time in our nation's history.

I want to remind our Committee and our viewers and our participants in today's panel that the environment that we're having this debate in is certainly a critical one. The environment is one where a number of people in the United States Congress want to completely abolish the Department of Energy, want to get rid of our resources, our genius, our scientists, our national laboratories, and many of these national laboratories throughout the country that have contributed so much to the heritage, the rich and copious heritage of this country.

And on the other hand, we have some people that don't want to do anything. They want to protect the parochial interests of their constituencies or their states or let the status quo sit firmly where it is.

Now many people on this Committee want to take a common sense and balanced approach, to move our national laboratories into the new millennium, to meet the challenges that these national laboratories have met through the years in more efficient ways, with better resources, but also require of our national laboratories that they too must contribute to reducing the deficit.

Nobody should be excluded from that contribution.

Now in that context, I think Daniel Bornstein said it best in "The Discoverers." He noticed the rich contribution that scientists make to this country. He dialogued those. He categorized them. He indexed those people that have made these rich contributions. And I think that's something that we have to keep firmly in mind with this legislation, that we must keep and utilize our scientists and our genius in these national laboratories.

But we also must reform and restructure these laboratories. Why? Here is what the General Accounting Office said about the current structure of our Department of Energy laboratories.

They said the DOE labs do not have a clearly-defined ozone mission to focus their considerable resources. The GAO report said that program-to-program management style has been costly and inefficient.

These said, three key changes in the nation's agenda create a necessity for a new DOE mission. Dramatic changes in the nuclear arms race. Secondly, the demand for technology to solve massive environmental programs. And thirdly, the growing international competition facing the United States, industry from other countries.

Taxpayers have heavily invested in the labs and DOE has a responsibility to extend proper focus on national priorities.

Finally, the GAO said, administrative oversight requirements from DOE have resulted in an avalanche of paperwork reporting requirements, as many as 400 reviews a year at some labs, forcing management to spend huge amounts of time processing oversight paperwork and therefore, not leading science and energy researchers towards achieving stated goals.

What we have tried to do on this Committee, working in a bipartisan way with other Members, is put a bill together that is balanced, that does have common sense, that does utilize the great resources that we have at the national laboratories. It accomplishes basically three things—or hopefully accomplishes three things.

One, it downsizes the full-time employees by one-third at the national laboratories. They will make a contribution to the deficit.

Secondly, it terminates duplicative research and seeks to make better use of our universities and colleges and the private sector.

Thirdly, it makes fundamental changes in the self-regulatory functions that the DOE currently undertakes, thereby freeing up many resources for science and for innovation and for cultivating this genius, rather than going the route of creating new layers of bureaucracy in Washington, D.C., to self-regulate.

I am very proud of what the national laboratories have been able to do, from discoveries in energy efficiencies to helping us with solar technologies and power production, to protecting us through better resources and national security, to even coming up with better ways to extract natural gas.

Certainly, we must protect this ability in our national laboratories to enhance this ability as the United States of America moves into a new millennium.

I think that this bill achieves the balanced approach by, as the Chairman said, defining a mission for our laboratories. Secondly, improving the management and eliminating redundancies and duplication. Thirdly, contributing to the deficit. And fourth, lastly, and maybe most importantly, not eliminating the Department of Energy, but keeping these vital teams of scientists together, some of whom have been working together for decades, utilizing this genius and moving this country forward into a new and exciting century.

With that, Mr. Chairman, I look forward to working with you and other people on this Committee towards the goals that I think all of us are concerned with, with the jurisdiction of this Committee.

[The prepared statement of Mr. Roemer follows:]

PREPARED STATEMENT OF HON. TIM ROEMER, A REPRESENTATIVE IN CONGRESS FROM THE STATE OF INDIANA

Mr. Chairman, I want to thank both Mr. Schiff and Mr. Rohrabacher as well as Mr. Hayes and Mr. Brown who is sitting in for Mr. Geren for convening this hearing today, and for this opportunity for me to explain my legislation, H.R. 1510.

This legislation will require the non-defense DOE labs to downsize the level of Full Time Employees by one-third over a period of 10 years, with the first 15% in reductions in the first 5 years.

The result will be either that each lab accomplishes its current mission more efficiently, or it will narrow its focus to more closely meet its original mission.

This bill requires the DOE lab structure to terminate research and facilities that duplicate work being done in the private sector, to cease activity that is not relevant to its programmatic objectives, and to use, whenever feasible, universities or other private sector facilities to complete its objectives.

The bill allows, but does not require, closing or scaling back of labs to meet these objectives.

The bill also requires fundamental changes in how the DOE labs follow health and safety regulations.

Currently, the DOE labs are required to follow Federal, state and local environmental regulations. The bill does not change this. However, DOE currently uses an intricate and cumbersome internal system of regulation to meet these requirements. The bill requires termination of this practice, known as "self-regulation." Instead, the Labs will follow such requirements directly, as any business would do. This will eliminate a large bureaucratic layer of the DOE, and should result in downsizing of a sector of the DOE Washington headquarters.

The bill also contains requirements that the Secretary report on the progress of implementing this legislation to Congress.

I believe that this is a balanced approach that will preserve an important national asset—while realizing the requirements of the current fiscal environment and our need to downsize government. Much as the Galvin Commission reported earlier this year, the DOE labs have an important place in both our governmental and scientific infrastructure, but the labs must become more focused, more efficient, and more closely aligned with national needs.

Much like the days of the Manhattan Project, the DOE labs can and should be the centerpiece of a critical national effort to stay on the cutting edge of fundamental research in power production, defense and national security, and environmental management.

The DOE labs contributed greatly to the development of our nuclear stockpile. They now must function to oversee the care and maintenance of this stockpile, and probably the dismantling of a large portion. This is a true national concern.

The DOE labs must generate stronger links between energy production and environmental concerns. The GAO offers one good example: electric vehicles reduce emissions, but create a battery disposal hazard. Nuclear power reduces emissions but requires cutting-edge waste storage. The labs are equipped to deal with such problems.

I believe that my bill is a good way to begin accomplishing these goals, and I am pleased to be here today to discuss these important issues.

Mr. SCHIFF. Thank you, Mr. Roemer. And I just want to add a quick word.

I served on both of these subcommittees during the previous six years as a minority Member of Congress. And I want to say very emphatically that Chairwoman Lloyd and Chairman Boucher both treated me and I think the other Members of the Subcommittee, all the Members of the Subcommittee, as equals. They never distinguished between majority and minority Members on the Subcommittee.

We all had equal input.

And I'm doing my very best, and I know Chairman Rohrabacher is, to continue that tradition and that courtesy they showed us.

The fourth bill we are considering today is H.R. 1993, introduced by our colleague, Congressman Tiahrt, from Kansas.

Congressman, you are recognized to discuss your bill.

Mr. TIAHRT. Chairman Schiff, Chairman Rohrabacher, and distinguished Members of the Subcommittee, thank you for the opportunity of this joint hearing and to share my views regarding the future of the Department of Energy National Laboratory complex.

I want to commend both the Chairmen for their continuing willingness and interest in wanting to both streamline the current DOE lab complex and set forth new and specific missions which match up our nation's 21st century needs and budget realities.

I'm looking forward to what I hope will be an open and candid discussion regarding the DOE national laboratory missions.

Let me start by saying that while I realize that the focus of this hearing is on DOE's national laboratory missions, its current government structure, I believe it is a fundamental note that the problems which plague the DOE lab complex are problems that are somewhat systematic throughout the Department of Energy.

Specifically, while recognizing the multi-purpose labs have made a vital contribution to our nation's defense, to science, and to technological efforts, the labs are now largely programs in search of rationale, having lacked for years a coherent and definable mission, and suffering greatly from a lack of focus from the DOE.

As you know, one of the DOE's loudest critics has been the GAO, which has recently released the two reports as noted by Chairman Schiff on the Department of Energy, one entitled, "National Laboratories: Needing Clear Missions and Better Management," and another report released last month entitled, "A Framework for Restructuring the DOE and Its Missions."

I wish to include both of these reports, along with my statement, as part of today's record.

Mr. SCHIFF. Without objection, both reports will be introduced in the record, along with your statement.

Mr. TIAHRT. Both reports detail the type of problems I alluded to earlier regarding poor management and lack of defined missions.

The GAO has stated the "DOE is not an effective or successful Cabinet Department" and cited several problems, including the inability of the DOE leadership to overcome management weakness, the burden of mission overload, lack of any credibility, an eroding public support and diminished sense of purpose.

I would recommend including testimony of representatives of the GAO and any additional hearings that you may have on this matter. The GAO has an intimate understanding of the Department of Energy and would offer a unique and valuable perspective of this discussion.

Today, the Committee has asked me to speak regarding H.R. 1993, and in particular, Title II. Here, I want to thank Congressman Bartlett, who is a Member of the DOE Task Force and helped put this legislation together, and for his efforts and expertise, I am grateful.

H.R. 1993 was introduced this past June and currently enjoys the support of over 50 cosponsors, including eight Members of these joint committees.

Let me summarize what the legislation would do.

Title II would establish an Energy Laboratory Facilities Commission for the stated purpose of consolidating the number of DOE laboratories and research programs through reconfiguration, privatization, and closure, while preserving the traditional role of the laboratories that have contributed to the national defense.

The Commission, which is similar in purpose and operation to the Military Base Closure Commission, would consist of seven individuals appointed by the President. The DOE Task Force endorsed this plan in a constructive way to examine the vast DOE laboratory and research complex.

The Commission would be provided with 12 selection criteria in making recommendations to Congress. The criteria would include a mandate to define appropriate missions for each energy laboratory. The new mission would focus the laboratories while maintaining a competitive bid process for lab work.

The commission would be required to file a final report to Congress within 15 months after enactment of the legislation. This report would include the Commission's recommendations for reconfigation, privatization, or closure of the laboratories, and unless ongress rejected the Commission's report, the plan would be imemented.

While H.R. 1993 may not present the first time a BRAC-like mmission has been proposed to help streamline the DOE lab mplex, it does represent the first time a comprehensive and reonsible effort has been made which both recognizes the value of e DOE laboratories, while understanding that the DOE lab comlex is oversized and inefficient.

These points were validated in the 1995 Galvin Report, which as the product of a distinguished corporate and academic Task orce appointed by Secretary O'Leary.

Let me mention that I have had the fortunate opportunity to eet with Bob Galvin during my work with the DOE Task Force d I look forward to hearing what insights he has to offer on this ıbject.

In conclusion, let me say that I believe each of these four bills hich are the focus of today's hearings have something positive to fer to this discussion. And while the different bills take separate aths, there is a common thread which runs through each of them. d that is the understanding that the current Department of Enrgy lab complex must be improved.

As such, I'm hopeful that we can reach an accord which will be oth beneficial to the American taxpayer and to the future of our ation's defense, and our scientific/technological base.

Again, Chairman Schiff and Rohrabacher, I thank you for the oportunity to make a statement today regarding H.R. 1993, and I look forward to the testimony.

[The reports referred to by Hon. Todd Tiahrt follow:]

United States General Accounting Office

GAO

Report to the Congress

August 1995

DEPARTMENT OF ENERGY

A Framework for Restructuring DOE and Its Missions

GAO/RCED-95-197

United States
General Accounting Office
Washington, D.C. 20548

Resources, Community, and
Economic Development Division

B-261382

August 21, 1995

To the President of the Senate and the
Speaker of the House of Representatives

This report on the need to reevaluate the missions of the U.S. Department of Energy is the final report in a series of GAO management reviews of the Department. The series of reports assessed the Department's management, analyzed problems and determined their underlying causes, and identified ways in which departmental management processes and structures could be improved. This final report discusses GAO's overall observations and emphasizes the Congress's important role, with the Secretary of Energy, in fundamentally reevaluating DOE's missions and alternatives.

We are sending copies of this report to the Secretary of Energy; the Director, Office of Management and Budget; interested congressional committees and subcommittees; individual Members of Congress, and others. Copies are available upon request.

This work was performed under the direction of Victor S. Rezendes, Director of Energy and Science Issues, who can be reached at (202) 512-3841. Other major contributors are listed in appendix IV.

Keith O. Fultz
Assistant Comptroller General

Executive Summary

Purpose

The U.S. Department of Energy (DOE) is at a critical juncture in its history. The Department's original core missions—to develop and test nuclear weapons, conduct basic energy research, and set national energy policy—are being replaced by major new challenges in environmental cleanup and the commercial applications of science. However, because of organizational structures and processes inherited from its emphasis on producing nuclear weapons during the Cold War, DOE faces a highly uncertain future as the Congress moves to reevaluate the Department as an institution—both its missions and its capacity to manage them effectively.

GAO has issued a series of reports on DOE that (1) analyzed underlying causes for the Department's management problems and (2) identified ways to improve organizational structures, management systems, and strategies for the Department's changing priorities. Building on those earlier reports, this report presents GAO's overall observations about DOE and its missions.

Background

Created in 1977 from several diverse agencies, DOE manages the nation's nuclear weapons production complex and conducts research and development on both energy and basic science. DOE operates an elaborate network of facilities, its core being the nuclear weapons complex—a collection of 17 major facilities in 13 states that design, develop, test, produce, and now dismantle the nation's vast nuclear arsenal. About half of DOE's resources are devoted to the nuclear weapons complex, an allocation that reflects both the buildup of these weapons through the 1980s and, more recently, the rapidly escalating cost of nuclear waste management and environmental restoration. DOE also maintains one of the world's largest networks of scientific laboratories, comprising nearly 30 sophisticated laboratories valued at over $100 billion. Budgeted at $17.5 billion for fiscal year 1995, DOE has nearly 20,000 federal employees and 140,000 contract workers.

Results in Brief

With the recent dramatic changes in national priorities, now is an ideal time to reevaluate DOE and its missions. DOE has begun to modify its Cold War organizational structures and processes to meet newer responsibilities, from environmental cleanup to industrial competitiveness. However, until a more fundamental reevaluation of DOE's missions and alternatives is undertaken—including opportunities to restructure and privatize operations—it is not clear if the Department and its missions are still needed in their present form or could be implemented more effectively elsewhere in the public or private sectors.

Although DOE has begun several reinvention efforts, such as contract reform and a "Strategic Alignment and Downsizing Initiative" to improve long-standing management weaknesses, the Department has assumed that existing missions are still valid and are best managed by it. For some missions, such as those of the civilian nuclear waste program, experts have argued that DOE is not the best place to conduct them. For other missions, such as those of the power-marketing administrations (e.g., Bonneville and Alaska), petroleum reserves, and the national laboratories, changing conditions have led many policymakers (including the Congress) to seriously consider alternatives to DOE's management.

As a first step in reevaluating DOE, each mission should be assessed to determine if it fulfills an inherently governmental role and what alternatives are available in the federal government or private sector to accomplish it most effectively. Criteria developed by a former DOE advisory panel can be used to evaluate the best organizational structure for each Departmental mission according to such factors as stability, cost-effectiveness, flexibility, responsiveness, and accountability. Experts GAO consulted, including former Energy Secretaries, offered many suggestions for restructuring DOE. Most urged that the Department be streamlined around fewer missions; a minority recommended eliminating DOE as a Cabinet department; and none argued for DOE's remaining the same.

Principal Findings

DOE's Changing Priorities

With the end of the Cold War, DOE's missions have dramatically changed. Today, DOE is

- converting its massive nuclear weapons complex from producing weapons to cleaning up the environmental consequences;
- deciding on the appropriate weapons complex configuration in the post-Cold War era;
- expanding activities for its multibillion-dollar national laboratories, which are seeking new uses for their defense-oriented facilities;

- attempting to find a way to honor the long-delayed legislative mandate to develop and operate a civilian nuclear waste repository;
- developing a National Energy Policy Plan; and
- continuing traditional core responsibilities in energy policy, information, and research while defining new roles for itself in industrial competitiveness and science education.

Responding to these changing missions and new priorities within existing organizational structures is a daunting task. For example, DOE's contract management approach, which it is only now changing, was first put in place during the World War II Manhattan Project. In contrast to the past practice of allowing private contractors to manage and operate billion-dollar facilities with minimal direct federal oversight (yet reimbursing them for all costs regardless of their actual achievements), DOE now needs to impose modern standards for accountability and performance. Also, because management and information systems were never adequate, DOE has been prevented from exercising effective contractor oversight. In addition, DOE's elaborate and highly decentralized field structure is slow to respond to changing conditions and priorities, fraught with communication problems, and poorly positioned to tackle difficult issues requiring a high degree of cross-cutting coordination.

DOE's Reforms Do Not Resolve Fundamental Issues of Core Missions

DOE is grappling with its long-standing internal management problems while at the same time realigning itself for changing missions and priorities among these missions. The Department has launched an aggressive effort to define its core missions around five "business lines": industrial competitiveness, energy resources, science and technology, national security, and environmental quality. DOE is also identifying ways to reduce overlap and duplication in policy and administrative functions through its Strategic Alignment and Downsizing Initiative. In addition, the Secretary has a total quality management initiative and is increasing stakeholders' participation in decision-making. These and other reinvention efforts to modify its management structure, processes, and policies to pursue changing missions and new priorities reflect a strong commitment by leadership to improve and will likely strengthen DOE's capacity to better manage its responsibilities.

However, resolving internal issues without first evaluating and achieving consensus on missions is not the best approach to restructuring DOE. For example, although DOE's reinvention efforts have assumed that existing missions are still valid government responsibilities and are still best implemented by the Department, some experts have argued that DOE is not the best place to manage the civilian nuclear waste mission, which has struggled to meet its goals under DOE. Some experts have also questioned whether DOE is the best place to manage the cleanup of defense nuclear waste. Responsibilities in science education and industrial competitiveness have raised additional questions among experts about their placement in the Department.

Once agreement is reached on which missions are appropriate to the government, a practical set of criteria, such as those developed by a former DOE advisory panel, can be used to evaluate the best organizational structure for each mission. These criteria allow for rating each alternative structure according to its ability to promote cost-effective practices, attract technical talent, be flexible to changing conditions, and be accountable to stakeholders. These criteria could help identify more effective ways to implement DOE's missions, particularly those that might be privatized or reconfigured under alternative government organizations. In addition, a panel convened by the National Academy of Public Administration developed criteria that could be used to determine if DOE should remain a Cabinet-level department. These criteria center on such questions as the following: "Is there a sufficiently broad national purpose for the Department?" "Are Cabinet-level planning, executive attention, and strategic focus necessary to achieve the goals of DOE's missions?" "Would a non-Cabinet-level agency be able to recruit and retain sufficient technical talent to implement DOE's missions?"

Many experts GAO consulted—including four former Energy Secretaries, business leaders, and specialists on DOE's issues—believed that redefining DOE's missions to focus on essential energy activities was the best way to help the Department achieve future success. Experts had wide-ranging opinions about the Department's missions. Most favored streamlining missions, and some suggested major realignments to other agencies or to new public-private entities. None of the experts wanted DOE to remain the same, although most preferred that it continue as a Cabinet-level department. Overwhelmingly, former DOE executives and energy experts recommended retaining the following four responsibilities within DOE: energy policy-making, energy information, the Strategic Petroleum Reserve, and research and development to increase energy supplies. Most considered moving weapons-related functions to the Department of Defense and environmental cleanup to other agencies or a new structure and sharing the national laboratories with other federal agencies or perhaps privatizing them.

Because transferring missions and their related statutory requirements from DOE to other agencies has broad effects, reevaluating DOE (including proposals to dismantle it) should be considered as part of an overall governmentwide restructuring effort. It is imperative that the Congress and the administration form an effective working relationship on restructuring initiatives.

Recommendations

Because the Congress is actively examining DOE and its missions, GAO is not making any recommendations at this time. In other reports in this series, GAO has made several recommendations to strengthen DOE's management—for contracting, environmental cleanup, financial and information management, and the national laboratories.

Agency Comments

DOE commented that it would have welcomed a thoughtful and timely analysis of options for change within the Department. DOE also commented that many of its reform efforts were not adequately recognized by GAO and that the survey of former DOE executives and other experts reflected outdated opinions.

GAO's intent was to show how changing missions and priorities over time require a fundamental reassessment of missions and alternatives. GAO did not set out to develop specific options for DOE. Resolving internal issues without first evaluating and achieving consensus on missions is not, in GAO's opinion, the best approach to restructure DOE. This report provides a framework—drawn from a former DOE advisory panel—to assess alternatives and points to the need for a governmentwide approach to restructuring. GAO's purpose in surveying former DOE executives and experts—all of whom have substantial knowledge of DOE's operations either as contractors, advisers, or long-time observers of the Department's performance—was to focus on fundamental issues related to the Department's missions and structures. GAO believes that resurveying the experts would serve little useful purpose because DOE is essentially the same now as it was when that survey was conducted; its missions and structures have not changed.

The report has been updated to include the additional reforms mentioned by DOE, specifically the initiatives by the Galvin Task Force and the Yergin Task Force on Strategic Energy Research and Development.

Contents

Abbreviations

DOD	Department of Defense
DOE	Department of Energy
EPA	Environmental Protection Agency
ERDA	Energy Research and Development Administration
GAO	General Accounting Office
M&O	management and operating
NAPA	National Academy of Public Administration
PMA	power marketing administration
R&D	research and development

Chapter 1

DOE's Changing Missions and Priorities

Today's DOE bears little resemblance to the Department that the Congress created in 1977. Established from many diverse agencies, DOE manages the nation's nuclear weapons complex and funds research and development on both energy and basic science through its multibillion-dollar national laboratories. It manages the five power marketing administrations (hydroelectric producers, such as Bonneville) and maintains petroleum reserves for military and civilian use. To perform these missions, DOE was authorized to spend $17.5 billion in fiscal year 1995 and has nearly 20,000 federal employees and 140,000 contract workers.

The Evolution of DOE

The end of the Cold War has dramatically altered DOE's missions and priorities. Making nuclear weapons, which dominated DOE's budget for years, has largely given way to environmental cleanup The national laboratories are now highly diversified. Furthermore, DOE has new or expanded missions in industrial competitiveness, science education; environment, safety, and health, and nuclear arms control and nonproliferation.

Table 1.1: Comparison of DOE'S Traditional and New and Emerging Missions

DOE's traditional missions[a]	DOE's new and emerging missions
Nuclear weapons production	Dismantling nuclear weapons
Energy and technology research	Environmental cleanup
Energy policy development	Industrial competitiveness
Civilian nuclear waste	Environment, safety, and health
	Nuclear arms control and nonproliferation
	Science education

[a]DOE also has nominal responsibilities for the Navy's nuclear reactor program and in the Federal Energy Regulatory Commission

Almost from the time of its creation in 1977, DOE has been in transition. For its first 3 years, DOE's programs emphasized research and initiatives to cope with a global energy crisis that disrupted U.S. and world markets and economies. By the mid-1980s, accelerating nuclear weapons production and expanding space-based defense research dominated DOE's budget resources. Since the late 1980s, DOE's budget has reflected a growing emphasis on solving a half-century's environmental and safety problems caused by the nuclear weapons and research activities of DOE and its predecessors.

With the end of the Cold War, DOE's missions and priorities have changed dramatically. Today, DOE is

- converting its massive nuclear weapons complex from producing weapons to cleaning up the environmental consequences;
- deciding on the appropriate weapons complex configuration in the post-Cold War era;
- expanding activities for its multibillion-dollar national laboratories, which are seeking new uses for their defense-oriented facilities;
- attempting to find a way to honor the long-delayed legislative mandate to develop and operate a civilian nuclear waste repository;
- developing a National Energy Policy Plan; and
- continuing traditional core responsibilities in energy policy, information, and research while defining new roles for itself in industrial competitiveness and science education.

Since 1978, DOE's budget priorities have gradually shifted from energy policy to defense, and since 1989 they have rapidly shifted from defense to the environment. (See fig. 1.1) We defined "missions" as the responsibilities the Department is expected to perform. We considered DOE's "priorities" as those missions receiving the highest levels of funding: at first such programs as energy conservation and renewable resources, more recently environmental waste and restoration projects. Changes within DOE's budget have also been notable. For example, weapons production has given way to dismantling nuclear warheads and explosive testing of nuclear weapons has ceased.

Figure 1.1: DOE's Changing Budget Priorities

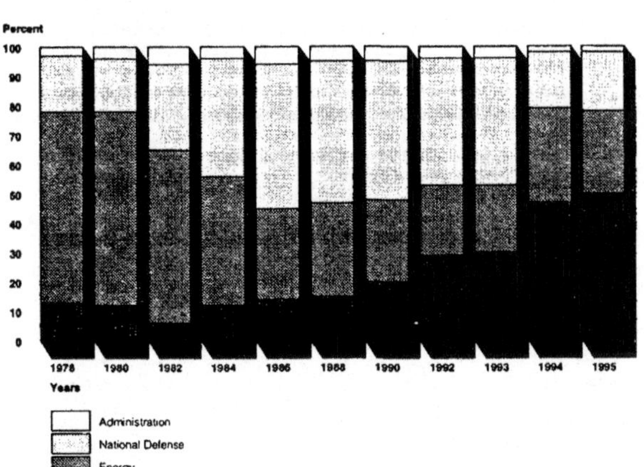

Note Percentages from 1992 to 1995 are presented in 1-year increments to more clearly show recent trends

Objectives, Scope, and Methodology

This is one in a series of reports that identify ways in which DOE can make and sustain management improvements that will clarify and meet the Department's fundamental missions. (See the list of related GAO products at the end of this report.) This report presents overall observations on DOE's major activities and evolution, including its missions, changing priorities, and management initiatives.

This report draws on the results of our past, as well as ongoing, work on various aspects of DOE's operations. Over the past 3 years, GAO conducted hundreds of interviews with DOE staff in its headquarters, field offices, and national laboratories. GAO also interviewed many contractors and policy experts in both the public and private sectors.

For this report, GAO studied DOE's current management reforms, particularly contracting and strategic alignment and downsizing activities. To gain a perspective on DOE and its missions, GAO surveyed nearly 40 former DOE officials (including four former DOE Secretaries) and energy and science policy experts from the public, academic, and private sectors. (See app. I for a list of the experts we consulted.) This survey was completed by mid-1994, before the current debate about whether to abolish the Department.

We obtained comments on a draft of this report from DOE. DOE's comments and our response to them appear in appendix III and are discussed, as relevant, at the end of chapters 2 and 3.

We conducted our work from December 1993 through June 1995. Our work was performed in accordance with generally accepted government auditing standards.

DOE's Reforms Are Based on Existing Missions

Recognizing that the Energy Department needs to change, current leadership has set a course to manage DOE's missions more efficiently and effectively. DOE's Strategic Plan and Strategic Alignment and Downsizing Initiative, as well as new efforts in contract reform, are the foundation of the current leadership's vision to improve the Department. Although these efforts are important and much needed, they are based on the assumption that existing missions are still valid in their present form and that DOE is the best place to manage them.

Strategic Plan and Strategic Alignment and Downsizing Initiative

The need to better match resources to missions and build a more integrated department led DOE to publish its Strategic Plan in April 1994. This Plan cited five "business lines" that DOE's leaders consider the Department's principal missions: industrial competitiveness, energy resources, science and technology, national security, and environmental quality. These five missions could succeed, DOE maintained, only if four critical factors were integrated with them: communication and trust; human resources; environment, safety, and health; and management practices.

After the Strategic Plan's release in April 1994, DOE launched a Strategic Alignment and Downsizing Initiative, which was designed to reorient the Department's resources and functions around the Strategic Plan's concepts as well as to streamline operations and find ways to reduce its budget. (As part of this initiative, DOE renamed "industrial competitiveness" as "economic productivity" and "environmental quality" as "weapons site cleanup.") In late 1994, DOE's Deputy Secretary said that the Strategic Alignment and Downsizing Initiative promised to "fundamentally alter how we look and how we conduct business...."[1] On May 3, 1995, the Secretary announced a variety of actions, such as the following, that resulted from this initiative:

- reducing DOE employment,
- consolidating functions,
- closing several small offices,
- selling surplus materials,
- removing the Federal Energy Regulatory Commission from the Department, and
- privatizing the power marketing administrations (PMA), as well as the Naval Petroleum and Oil Shale Reserves.

[1]Memorandum from William H. White, Deputy Secretary of Energy, to Heads of Department Elements, Nov 4, 1994.

The Energy Secretary stated that the alignment and downsizing actions, excluding privatization of the PMAS and Naval Petroleum and Oil Shale Reserves, would save $1.7 billion over 5 years. Sale of the PMAS and Oil Shale Reserves would bring an additional $5.3 billion, with other reforms underway providing the balance of $14.1 billion in savings over 5 years.

Contract Reform

In 1994, DOE's Contract Reform Team,[2] which was created to identify basic contracting weaknesses and determine fundamental improvements, reported that DOE needs to make major changes to its unique contracting system to accomplish its changing missions. The Team's basic premise was that DOE's contracting suffers from an over-reliance on cost-based contracts, a lack of well-defined performance criteria and measures, and weaknesses in oversight. To correct these conditions, the Team set goals calling for

- more flexibility in contracting by increasing competition and making wider use of performance measures,
- wider use of financial incentives for contractors in return for having them assume greater risks, and
- a willingness to experiment with new types of contracts and contractors.

The Team made more than 45 recommendations, including a call for more performance-based management contracts. The Team recommended new incentives to reduce costs, increased use of fixed-price contracts, and more objective performance criteria by which DOE's administrators could judge results. The Team also urged that contracts be competed more frequently. DOE has started to implement most of these recommendations and reports that some savings have already been achieved.

We believe these measures will give DOE a stronger basis for selecting and evaluating its contractors when deciding and budgeting its mission needs. The major question surrounding the contract reform's success will be how effectively the Department will be able to administer them.

[2] Making Contracting Work Better and Cost Less, Report of the Contract Reform Team, U.S. Department of Energy (Feb. 1994).

Refocusing Research and the National Laboratories

DOE created a task force to examine options for the future of the national laboratories.[3] The Task Force's basic findings—that the laboratories' missions should be redefined and their management should be improved—are largely consistent with the results of our work.[4] DOE believes that adopting the Task Force's recommendations could save up to $1.4 billion.

Perhaps the most far-reaching recommendation made by the Task Force is to create one or more nonprofit corporations to operate these laboratories under the direction of a board of trustees that would channel funding to various laboratories to meet the needs of both government and nongovernment entities. DOE disagreed with this recommendation, choosing instead to rely on a board of experts for advice.

To assess DOE's research and development (R&D) program, the Department also created what is known as the "Yergin Task Force."[5] Although its June 13, 1995, report advised against cutting R&D deeply, it concluded that DOE could reduce costs by 15 percent through management improvements and the application of "best practices."

Conclusions

DOE has many ambitious programs, and the current leadership has expended considerable effort toward achieving its new priorities. Especially noteworthy activities are now under way for contract reform and strategic alignment, two important areas in which marked improvements could greatly increase DOE's ability to better manage its diverse missions more effectively. Even with these improvements under way, however, DOE has little assurance that its proposed reforms are the best approach for implementing its missions.

Agency Comments and Our Evaluation

In commenting on a draft of this report, DOE stated that GAO had little appreciation for the many reforms undertaken over the past 2 years. Our earlier reports and the draft of this report discussed DOE's major reforms,

[3]The Secretary of Energy asked Robert Galvin to chair a task force to analyze the national laboratories. Its report was officially titled Alternative Futures for the Department of Energy National Laboratories, Secretary of Energy Advisory Board, Task Force on Alternative Futures for the Department of Energy National Laboratories (Feb. 1995)

[4]Department of Energy: National Laboratories Need Clearer Missions and Better Management (GAO/RCED-95-10, Jan. 27, 1995).

[5]Energy R&D: Shaping Our Nation's Future in a Competitive World, Final Report of the Task Force on Strategic Energy Research and Development, chaired by Daniel Yergin, President of Cambridge Energy Research Associates (June 1995).

except for the report from the Yergin Task Force, which was not released until after our draft was prepared. We have expanded our discussion of the work of the Galvin Task Force in this report, which also was the subject of our testimony before the Congress in March 1995.[6] We have also expanded our discussion of DOE's reform efforts to better recognize DOE's actions to date.

This report focuses on the Strategic Plan and Strategic Alignment and Downsizing Initiative because these had been promoted by DOE to fundamentally change the Department's way of doing business. While we believe these efforts are important and much needed, we have concluded that neither effort was preceded by a fundamental rethinking of the Department's missions and that neither one made a case that DOE is the best place to accomplish them.

[6] Department of Energy: Alternatives for Clearer Missions and Better Management at the National Laboratories (GAO/T-RCED-95-128, Mar. 9, 1995).

Reevaluation of DOE's Missions

While DOE's 1994 Strategic Plan and 1995 Strategic Alignment and Downsizing Initiative—as well as other reinvention activities—may lead to a more efficient Department, DOE did not thoroughly reevaluate its missions. A basic tenet of reinvention is determining which missions still make sense and where each should be implemented.

Reevaluating missions would help ensure that DOE's Strategic Plan and Strategic Alignment and Downsizing Initiative (as well as other reforms) meet the challenges that will face the Department and its missions. Because a major restructuring of DOE's missions would affect other agencies and institutions—to the extent they would gain these missions—reevaluating DOE should ideally be part of a governmentwide restructuring effort with the Congress and the administration working together to achieve consensus on DOE's missions.

The following two questions form an essential framework for evaluating DOE's missions:

- Which missions should be eliminated because they are no longer a valid government function?
- For those missions that are governmental, what is the best organizational placement of responsibilities?

DOE Needs to Change

DOE's structures, systems, and processes are not well matched with its changing missions and new priorities, as the following examples show:

- DOE's highly decentralized field network, established to manage nuclear weapons production during the Cold War, has changed little in terms of contractors or their staffs, even though mission objectives have shifted dramatically. DOE still employs many contractors—often the same organizations for decades, despite changing skill requirements.
- Attempts to establish direct accountability among program offices at headquarters, administrative units, field offices, and the national laboratories have been especially difficult. Reporting relationships changed often and sometimes have been confusing.
- The emergence of important new missions with cross-cutting responsibilities, such as those in environment, safety, and health matters, has resulted in additional redundancies that further complicate DOE's structures and add to communication and oversight confusion while causing organizational tensions.

- Begun under the Manhattan Project's wartime conditions as an expedient way to build the world's first nuclear weapons, management and operating (M&O) contracts have survived for more than half a century and still persist as DOE's principal way to conduct its missions. But the Department's M&O contracts have proven to be both difficult to administer and unsuited to changing conditions. Decades of relying heavily on contractors to conduct most of DOE's work, often in strict secrecy and under minimal oversight, has hampered the Department's ability to quickly and decisively redirect itself toward new priorities and new ways to conduct its business.
- Management information systems, particularly financial systems to support contracting oversight, have only recently received serious attention from DOE's leadership. In addition, the Department's internal directives have long been characterized as costly, inefficient, and onerous in their implementation.

DOE has launched many initiatives to resolve some of these issues, including those aimed at improving its management systems and internal directives. Of all these efforts, the Strategic Alignment and Downsizing Initiative, and contracting reform hold the most potential to influence DOE's future.

Evaluating DOE's Missions

Clearly, many of DOE's present functions and programs are activities that only the government can perform, such as stewardship over the nuclear weapons stockpile. Other activities may qualify as functions and programs with debatable relevance to inherently governmental missions.

Even without a complete restructuring, some dismantling has already occurred within DOE, and additional actions such as the following have been proposed:

- Under the Energy Policy Act of 1992, the federal uranium enrichment program was transferred to the United States Enrichment Corporation, a government corporation, with the expectation that it will be privatized later.
- As early as 1989, the Congress held hearings on whether to create a separate environmental cleanup commission that would be responsible for DOE's facilities.
- The congressional Office of Technology Assessment has developed cleanup options, including a separate commission to regulate and enforce cleanup of federal radioactive contamination at federal facilities. This idea is similar to one supported by DOE's previous environmental administrator.

- A RAND study sponsored by the Defense Department recommended consolidating within DOD all activities related to U.S. nuclear weapons.[7]
- Because of DOE's inability to manage waste storage effectively, state regulators have called for a separate civilian nuclear waste agency.
- DOE's own study of the future of the national laboratories by the Galvin Task Force has suggested creating private or federal-private corporations to manage most or all of them.

Without responding to these and other basic mission issues in a systematic manner, DOE has little assurance that its current Strategic Plan and Strategic Alignment and Downsizing Initiative are the best ways to accomplish its missions. DOE alone cannot make these determinations. They require a cooperative effort among all stakeholders with the Congress and the administration responsible for deciding which missions are needed and how best to implement them.

Those missions that should continue should be analyzed to determine which public and private sector alternatives would best achieve them. For example, although over a decade has passed since the Congress established the repository program for disposing of civilian nuclear waste and several billion dollars have been spent, siting a repository seems no closer than when that program was first started. Last year, 39 Members of Congress called for a presidential commission to review the nuclear waste program; others have proposed legislation to change the program; and some experts, including a former DOE internal advisory panel, have called for moving the entire program out of the Department.[8]

Various types of alternative organizations for administering a particular mission might include

- the present DOE cabinet structure,
- another federal subcabinet office,
- an independent federal commission,
- a mixed government-private corporation, or
- a private corporation.

[7] An Assessment of Defense Nuclear Agency Functions: Pathways Toward a New Nuclear Infrastructure for the Nation, National Defense Research Institute, RAND (MR-442-OSD, 1994)

[8] Managing Nuclear Waste—A Better Idea: A Report to the U.S. Secretary of Energy, Advisory Panel on Alternative Means of Financing and Managing Radioactive Waste Facilities (Dec. 1984).

DOE Criteria for Evaluating Alternative Institutions

Each of these organizational alternatives has variations that could be defined more precisely to meet particular needs. The following criteria, adapted from a former advisory panel that examined DOE's civilian nuclear waste program, offers a useful framework for evaluating alternative ways to manage the Department's missions:

- Mission orientation and focus: Will the institution be able to focus on its mission(s) or will it be encumbered by other priorities? Which organizational structure will provide the greatest focus on its mission(s)?
- Credibility: Will the organizational structure be credible, thus gaining public support for its actions?
- Stability and continuity: Will the institution be able to plan for its own future without undue concern for its survival?
- Programmatic authority: Will the institution be free to exercise needed authority to accomplish its missions without excessive oversight and control from external sources?
- Accessibility: Will stakeholders (both federal and state overseers as well as the public) have easy access to senior management?
- Responsiveness: Will the institution be structured to be responsive to all its stakeholders?
- Internal flexibility: Will the institution be able to change its internal systems, organization, and style to adapt to changing conditions?
- Political accountability: How accountable will the institution be to political sources, principally the Congress and the President?
- Immunity from political interference: Will the institution be sufficiently free from excessive and destructive political forces?
- Ability to stimulate cost-effectiveness: How well will the institution be able to encourage cost-effective solutions?
- Technical excellence: Will the institution attract highly competent people?
- Ease of transition: What will be the costs (both financial and psychological) of changing to a different institution?

GAO's Observations on Using Evaluation Criteria

Deciding the best place to manage specific DOE missions involves assessing the advantages and disadvantages of each alternative institution on the basis of its potential to achieve that mission and improve efficiency. Potential efficiency gains (or losses) that might result from transferring a part of DOE to another agency need to be balanced against the policy reasons that first led to placing that mission in DOE. While the substantial short-term costs of a transfer may be offset by long-term gains in efficiency, in some cases shifting a mission would likely become a contentious exercise, especially with DOE's major responsibilities for the nuclear weapons complex and its cleanup. For example, transferring the nuclear weapons complex to the Defense Department would require carefully considering many management and policy issues. Because of the apparently declining strategic role of nuclear weapons, some experts argue that in the long term consolidating all nuclear weapons activities within DOD is the best option for maintaining the infrastructure for nuclear weapons. Others argue, however, that civilian agency control over nuclear weapons has functioned well and should continue. Some experts advocate creating a new federal agency for weapons production.

Similarly, moving the responsibility for cleaning up DOE's defense facilities to another agency or to a new institution, as proposed by some experts, requires close scrutiny. For example, a new agency concentrating its focus on cleanup exclusively would not need to allocate its resources for competing programs. Furthermore, such an agency could maximize federal research and development investments by achieving economies of scale in technology. On the other hand, separating cleanup responsibility from the agency that created the waste may limit its incentives to reduce waste and to promote other environmentally sensitive approaches. In addition, considerable startup time and costs would accompany a new agency, at a time when the Congress is interested in reducing the federal government. Shifting responsibility to an existing agency, such as the EPA or DOD, also raises complications from the effects of assuming new responsibilities.

Need for a Governmentwide Perspective

Because transferring missions and their related statutory requirements from DOE to other agencies will have far-reaching effects, any proposal to dismantle DOE should be considered as part of an overall governmentwide restructuring effort. It is imperative that the Congress and the administration form an effective working relationship on restructuring initiatives.[9]

DOE's Future as a Cabinet-level Department

Streamlining DOE's missions raises the question of whether, in a reduced form, it should remain a Cabinet-level department. To help answer this question, a NAPA panel has developed 14 criteria for determining if an

[9]The Comptroller General of the United States recently testified on the need for an integrated approach to government reorganization. See Government Reorganization: Issues and Principles (GAO/T-GGD/AIMD-95-166, May 17, 1995).

agency is appropriate for Cabinet status.[10] The following three criteria directly apply to any decision that might be made about today's DOE.

- Is there a sufficiently broad national purpose for the Department? Integrating national energy policy was the dominant reason for creating DOE in 1977 and remains a core mission that would become critical in the event of another oil supply disruption. As much as any other Cabinet-level issue, energy policy directly affects all Americans and the U.S. economy.
- Are Cabinet-level planning, executive attention, and strategic focus necessary to achieve DOE's missions? We have previously recommended that DOE develop a strategic approach to managing its changing missions and believe this is essential to its future success.[11] The federal role in both energy policy and environmental restoration of the nuclear weapons complex will likely continue to be long-term national priorities.
- Would a non-cabinet-level agency be able to recruit and retain sufficient technical talent to implement DOE's missions? Most of DOE's technical work is performed by contractors, and this source of talent is unlikely to be lost to any federal management entity. Cabinet status provides only marginal benefits for recruiting these specialists.

Expert Opinions on DOE's Missions

To gain perspective on DOE and its missions, we asked experts on energy policy and former DOE executives about the need and proper place for the Department's missions. We received responses from 35 individuals. Although 12 respondents had DOE experience (including four former Energy Secretaries), there was little difference between their responses and those from the others. In addition, two other individuals offered opinions on their views about DOE's future and its missions. Former President Jimmy Carter, under whose administration DOE was created, also sent comments on the Department and its development.

All respondents agreed that DOE needs to change, beyond simply streamlining operations, and no one believed that the Department should remain as it is today. A majority also believed that DOE should remain a Cabinet department but with attention refocused on its original core missions, which were identified by most respondents as energy policy-making; energy information; energy-supply research and

[10]Evaluation of Proposals to Establish a Department of Veterans Affairs, National Academy of Public Administration (Mar. 1988). See app. II for a complete list of these criteria.

[11]Department of Energy: Management Problems Require a Long-Term Commitment to Change (GAO/RCED-93-72, Aug. 31, 1993).

development; and operation of the Strategic Petroleum Reserve as an instrument of energy policy.

Our respondents were divided about evenly over whether to keep certain missions within the Department, move them elsewhere, or sell them to private administrators. (See fig. 3.1.) For example, the power marketing administrations now within the Department could be managed by other institutions. But a clear majority favored moving the remaining nonenergy missions from DOE or sharing a few of them with other departments and agencies. A decisive majority favored shifting DOE's new mission to improve U.S. industrial competitiveness to the Commerce Department—especially its National Institute of Standards and Technology.

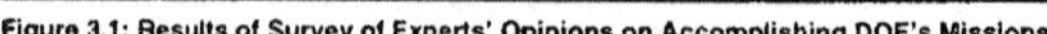

Figure 3.1: Results of Survey of Experts' Opinions on Accomplishing DOE's Missions

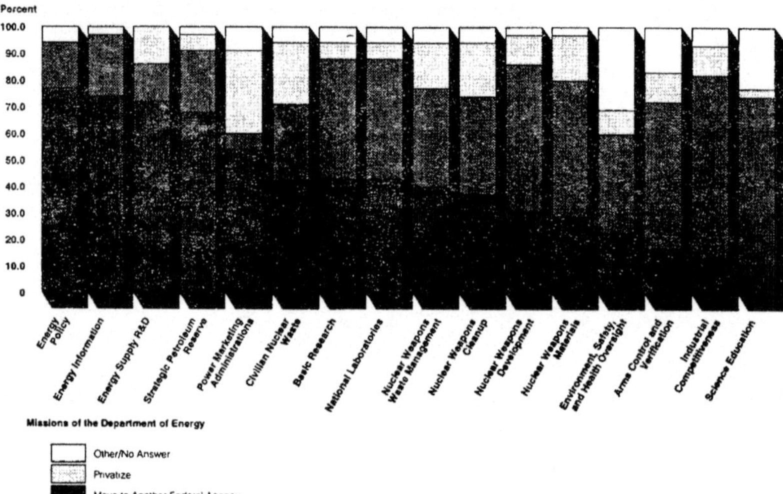

There was no clear consensus on where to locate the various basic research functions now performed by the national laboratories. About half of our respondents favored retaining these functions within DOE but with the laboratories restructured along clearer mission lines. Others expected more direction and focus if many basic research functions were moved to the National Science Foundation or divided among different non-DOE agencies. The majority of respondents indicated that science education and some basic research functions now performed by the national laboratories should be moved from DOE to the National Science Foundation.

- The majority of respondents also preferred that nuclear weapons cleanup and waste management for active nuclear weapons sites should be moved from DOE to the Defense Department or to a new federal agency. "The Energy Department should get out of the weapons and weapons cleanup business," said one respondent. "DOD has many program managers familiar with handling large programs. DOE has none. The weapons were made for DOD—they should now handle the cleanup." But other respondents favored DOE's continued role in cleanup because of its traditional expertise. For civilian nuclear waste, some favored DOE's continued management, but more preferred to place these facilities under other federal or federal-private institutions.

Conclusions

Now is an ideal time to fundamentally reevaluate DOE and its missions. While current reform efforts will strengthen DOE's management capacity, such efforts will not likely make DOE an effective, integrated department because of the problems inherent in managing so many disparate missions. None of the former DOE executives or energy experts we surveyed favored keeping the Energy Department as it is today.

According to our survey of experts' opinions and other reports we have recently issued in this series, many of DOE's missions could be performed either by private institutions or by other government agencies. To the extent some of DOE's missions might best be transferred to other federal entities, a careful evaluation of the costs and effects of such changes would have to be made, including the effects on the gaining agency. For this reason, a major restructuring of DOE should ideally be part of a governmentwide restructuring effort.

Agency Comments and Our Evaluation

DOE commented that it would have welcomed a thoughtful and timely analysis of options for changing DOE, that our survey of former DOE executives and other experts reflected outdated opinions, and that DOE is still the best institution to fulfill its current missions. Our intent has been to show how changing missions and priorities over time now require a fundamental reassessment of DOE's missions and alternatives to achieve them. Resolving internal issues without first evaluating and achieving consensus on missions is not, in our opinion, the best approach to restructuring DOE. While not providing specific options for DOE, the report does offer a framework to assess alternatives (drawn substantially from a former DOE advisory panel) and points to the need for a governmentwide approach to restructuring. Reevaluating DOE is an effort that involves the Congress and the administration working together to achieve consensus on what the Department should be in the future and where its missions should best be accomplished.

Our purpose in surveying former DOE executives and experts was to focus on fundamental issues related to the Department's missions and structures. Most or all of the survey respondents had substantial knowledge of DOE operations, either as contractors, advisers, or long-time observers of DOE's performance. Resurveying the experts would serve little useful purpose because DOE is essentially the same now as it was when we conducted our survey—its missions and structures have not changed, nor have its major reforms been substantially implemented.

We are unaware of any evidence to support DOE's contention that it can perform inherent government responsibilities "better than through any alternative organizational arrangement."

Appendix I

Experts Consulted by GAO

Current and Former Government Officials	Research and Academic Institutions	Other Private Sector
Jimmy Carter Former President of the United States	John Ahearne Former Nuclear Regulatory Commission Chairman Exec Dir., Sigma Xi	Harold Finger, consultant, former nuclear industry executive
John S Herrington Former Secretary of Energy	Lewis Branscomb Professor Harvard University-J F Kennedy School	Glenn Schleede New England Energy Inc
James D. Watkins Former Secretary of Energy	Jacob Scherr National Resources Defense Council	David Packard Hewlett-Packard Co
Donald Hodel Former Secretary of Energy	Roger Noll Professor Stanford University	Alex Radin Radin Assoc. Former President, American Public Power Association
James Edwards Former Secretary of Energy	Elihu Bergman Americans for Energy Independence	J. Robinson West Petroleum Finance Co
Henry Lee Professor Harvard University-J.F. Kennedy School	Alan Dean National Academy of Public Administration	Alvin Alm Science Applications International Corp
Richard Farmer Congressional Research Service	Edward Teller Hoover Institution	William Carey Carnegie Corp
Jan Mares Former DOE executive	Phillip Verleger Institute for International Economics	Charles Ebinger International Resources Group
Leo Duffy Former DOE Assistant Secretary	Howard Ris Union of Concerned Scientists	Wil Lepkowski Chemical & Engineering News
Alan Crane Office of Technology Assessment U S Congress	John Deutch Professor, Massachusetts Institute of Technology	Mason Willrich Pacific Gas & Electric Co
Lew Allen, Jr Jet Propulsion Laboratory	Malcolm Weiss Massachusetts Institute of Technology	Terry Lash consultant
	Robert Fri Resources for the Future	Theodore Taylor consultant
	R E. Balzhiser Electric Power Research Institute	William Perkins Potomac Communications Group

Note The experts' affiliations represent those at the time they completed our survey in July, 1994

Appendix II

Criteria for Evaluating Cabinet-Level Status

The following criteria were developed by a panel of the National Academy of Public Administration as an aid to deciding whether a government organization should function as a Cabinet department.

1. Does the agency or set of programs serve a broad national goal or purpose not exclusively identified with a single class, occupation, discipline, region, or sector of society?

2. Are there significant issues in the subject area that are not now adequately recognized or addressed by the existing organization, the President, or the Congress that would be better assessed or met by elevating the agency to a Cabinet department?

3. Is there evidence of impending changes in the type and number of pressures on the institution that would be better addressed if it were made a Cabinet department? Are these changes expected to continue into the future?

4. Would a Cabinet department increase the visibility and thereby substantially strengthen the active political and public support for actions and programs to enhance the existing organization's goals?

5. Is there evidence that becoming a Cabinet department would provide better analysis, expression, and advocacy of the needs and programs that constitute the agency's responsibilities?

6. Is there evidence that becoming a Cabinet department would improve the accomplishment of the existing agency's goals?

7. Is a Cabinet department required to better coordinate or consolidate programs and functions that are now scattered throughout other agencies in the executive branch?

8. Is there evidence that a Cabinet department (with the increased political authority of a centralized Secretary's office) would result in a more effective balance within the agency, between integrated central strategic planning and resource allocation, and the direct participation in management decisions by the line officers who are responsible for directing and managing agency programs?

9. Is there evidence of significant structural, managerial, or operational weaknesses in the existing organization that could be corrected by elevation to a Cabinet department?

10. Is there evidence that there are external barriers and impediments to timely decision-making and executive action that could be detrimental to improving the efficiency of the existing agency's programs? Would elevation to a Cabinet department remove or mitigate these impediments?

11. Would elevation to a Cabinet department help recruit and retain better qualified leadership within the existing organization?

12. Would elevation to a Cabinet department promote more uniform achievement of broad, cross-cutting national policy goals?

13. Would elevation to a Cabinet department strengthen the Cabinet and the Executive Office of the President as policy and management aids for the President?

14. Would elevation to a Cabinet department have a beneficial or detrimental effect upon the oversight and accountability of the agency to the President and the Congress?

Appendix III

Comments From the Department of Energy

Note: GAO comments supplementing those in the report text appear at the end of this appendix.

Department of Energy
Washington, DC 20585

June 22, 1995

Victor S. Rezendes
Director, Energy Issues
U.S. General Accounting Office
Washington, D.C. 20548

Dear Mr. Rezendes:

See comment 1

The Department has reviewed the draft report by the General Accounting Office (GAO) which examines the missions and management of the Department of Energy (DOE). During this fertile period for assessing how to make the government work better and cost less, the Department would have welcomed a thoughtful and timely analysis of options for change at DOE. Unfortunately, your draft report, Department of Energy: A Framework for Restructuring DOE and its Missions, provides an outdated understanding of the Department, with little appreciation for the reforms that have been put in place over the past two years. Given how long this report has been in development, we anticipated a much more significant product--especially in light of the many pathbreaking studies that GAO has produced in the past concerning DOE programs.

A fundamental flaw in your report is its methodology. The report is built upon the results of a survey of 38 "experts," who are cited as such on 30 occasions in the report. These individuals are referenced as the source for a range of options for restructuring and reforming the Department. However, the overwhelming majority of these individuals are conversant only with energy policy issues and would not, we are sure, profess to have expertise with the national security, environmental cleanup, or fundamental science functions of the Department --which together comprise more than 80 percent of our budget. The methodology of your report accords these survey respondents with expertise across all DOE mission areas, which we believe is a disservice to these individuals. It is not surprising that energy experts would suggest that the Pentagon would be a better manager for nuclear weapons development or environmental cleanup, but this is not a very convincing approach to a complex set of issues. Yet the methodology used in your report attempts to validate just such an approach.

Of greater concern is that the GAO has constructed a report around the opinions of survey respondents who could not possibly have known very much about the reforms that have been underway at DOE over the past two years. With all due respect for the historical knowledge of the individuals selected for your survey, we must point out that their knowledge about the Department is just that: historical. Less than one third of your respondents ever worked at the Department of Energy, and only three (including the previous Secretary) worked here at any point in the past five years. At the time your survey was conducted, we are certain that few, if any, of the respondents were familiar with the Department's strategic planning process or contract reform initiative--two major efforts that are reshaping the Department's management practices, mission focus, and contracting activities, while reducing costs.

Moreover, because the survey was completed one year ago, none of the respondents was familiar with the results of the Task Force on Alternative Futures for the Department of Energy Laboratories (completed February 1995), the Strategic Alignment and Downsizing Initiative (completed May 1995), or the Task Force on Strategic Energy Research and Development (completed June 1995). Your report states that "none of the experts wanted DOE to remain the same," and neither do we--as demonstrated by our comprehensive set of initiatives aimed at transforming the Department.

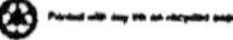

Your report's begrudging acknowledgment of the reforms underway at the Department is surprising. We note the following:

- In both this and previous reports, GAO concludes that DOE needs to develop a better consensus on its missions. Yet the draft report barely acknowledges the Department's unprecedented strategic planning effort during 1993 and 1994, which involved hundreds of employees from all levels of the organization and resulted in a tightly focussed Departmental view of our missions.

- In previous reports, GAO has called for reform of our contracting practices. We are in the process of instituting the most significant contract reform initiatives in the history of the Department, including many specific changes that GAO has previously supported (e.g. shifting to performance-based contracting).

- In prior reports, GAO has called for more focused mission assignments for the DOE laboratories. As part of our response to the Galvin Task Force, we now are developing a strategic mission framework for the laboratories that responds to this concern.

- In both this and previous reports, GAO expresses concern about potentially duplicative and inefficient organizational structures in the Department. Your draft report provides essentially no discussion, however, of our Strategic Alignment and Downsizing Initiative, which will reduce DOE employment by 27 percent through elimination of redundancies, consolidation of organizations, and re-engineering of processes so as to reduce layers of management and improve performance.

See comment 2.

Rather than commending these efforts, the report states that even with these initiatives "DOE has little assurance that its proposed reforms are the best approach for implementing its missions." While this is a truism—we have no assurance—we know that no alternative approach can provide that assurance either. Certainly a random sampling of 38 individuals on selective issues, such as presented in your report, cannot possibly yield stronger assurances about the best method for performing the Department's missions. The Department's reforms have emerged from a rigorous, two-year effort that has involved the following:

- Our Strategic Alignment and Downsizing Initiative rests upon a foundation of more than 2,000 survey responses and hundreds of interviews of employees who were asked how to make the Department work better and cost less.

- Our Contract Reform Initiative was the result of thousands of hours of intense focus on contracting practices of the Department and options for reform.

- Our review of the DOE laboratories was the result of a year-long study during which members of the Task Force, headed by Bob Galvin of Motorola, Inc., received over 100 detailed briefings and conducted more than three dozen visits to the DOE labs.

- The report of the Task Force on Strategic Energy R&D--including its two volumes of detailed assessments of each major DOE energy program and technology area--is perhaps the most comprehensive assessment of DOE's energy R&D programs ever, completed by more than 30 of the most senior energy experts in the nation, under the Chairmanship of Daniel Yergin, president of Cambridge Energy Research Associates.

See comment 1

Commenting on these major undertakings to fundamentally improve the efficiency and effectiveness of the Department, your study states that "Although DOE has begun several reinvention efforts...to improve longstanding management weaknesses, the Department assumes that existing missions are still valid and are best managed by DOE." This is simply not correct; we have made no such assumptions. Indeed, the Department has led the debate about privatizing DOE functions and consolidating the focus of our work.

See comment 3

Although your report states that "many lawmakers" are seriously considering alternative management for functions such as the Power Marketing Administrations (PMAs), we would point out that:

- It was the Department that proposed privatizing three of the PMAs and creating a government corporation to run the Bonneville Power Administration, and it was this Administration that submitted the legislation to Congress to implement these actions;
- It was the Department that proposed privatizing the Naval Petroleum and Oil Shale Reserves; and
- It was the Department that proposed severing the Federal Energy Regulatory Commission from DOE.

See comment 4

These and other reform actions initiated during the past two years will result in $14.1 billion in savings by the year 2000, while enhancing the strategic focus of the Department and improving the performance of our missions. Assuming the Congress acts on the legislation which we have submitted to privatize and restructure several functions that presently are within the Department, by the year 2000 our employment levels will have dropped from the current level of approximately 20,600 to 10,100.

Collectively, the Department's reform initiatives have put DOE on a completely different budgetary and management trajectory than existed at the beginning of this Administration. The final budget of the Bush Administration projected that DOE spending would reach $22.3 billion in FY 1998. Today, the Clinton Administration is projecting an FY 1998 budget for DOE of $15.2 billion--a reduction of $7.1 billion from the Bush Administration estimates. Between 1995 and 1998 alone, our Administration plans to spend $18.3 billion less on the DOE budget than was projected by the Bush Administration.

See comment 1

These savings are the result of intensive management attention aimed at reinventing how we do our business, as is being demonstrated through major productivity improvements and cost-cutting in our Environmental Management program. We have not assumed that DOE is the best location in government to perform our national security, energy research, environmental cleanup, and basic science missions. Rather, we believe that we have shown that we can perform these inherent government responsibilities better than through any alternative organizational arrangement. While we welcome constructive proposals on how these missions could be performed better, we have not yet seen a plan that would meet such a goal.

See comment 5

Finally, we are concerned about the misleading and inaccurate descriptions of the DOE missions that are found throughout your report. The listings of past and current missions and priorities of the Department convey only a rudimentary understanding of the scope of activities underway within our mission areas. The report states that "science education" is a new mission at the Department. While science education may be an important derivative activity to our enormous R&D investments, it certainly is not a new activity, and at only 0.3 percent of the Department's budget, we question how this could be considered a "mission." The Department's waste cleanup mission is referred to in the report as Environment, Safety and Health, yet these are very different functions: the former involves addressing the cleanup legacy of weapons production; the latter involves worker and public health and safety. Particularly enigmatic is the report's statement that the Department is defining new roles for itself in "science policy," as if this were a mission activity.

Again, we regret that the draft report does not offer a more sophisticated and substantive analysis. Although the document purports to provide a framework for restructuring DOE and its missions, the random sampling of opinion leaders (mostly from the energy field), the failure to take adequate account of reforms currently underway at the Department, and the simplistic and incomplete description of DOE missions weaken the value of this report as a framework for additional changes at the Department.

See comment 5.

We strongly recommend that you address these deficiencies before the report is issued in its final form. If the report retains a heavy reliance on the opinions of a select group of individuals, then we recommend that you re-survey these individuals--since your current data is more than one year old. In addition, we believe these individuals should be asked about their familiarity with the many reforms that have been instituted at the Department over the past two years, and that they be asked to address in their entirety the complex trade-offs and policy issues that necessarily accompany any reorganizational plan for the Department. Without such information, random opinions concerning the possible transfer of DOE functions to other agencies are not of much value.

Sincerely,

Joseph F. Vivona
Chief Financial Officer

The following are GAO's comments on the Department of Energy's letter dated June 22, 1995.

GAO Comments

1. Our intent in this report is to show how DOE's changing missions and priorities over time require a fundamental reassessment of its missions and structure. We did not set out to develop specific options for DOE. Resolving internal issues without first evaluating and achieving consensus on missions is not the best approach to restructuring DOE. This report provides a framework to assess alternatives—drawn substantially from a former DOE advisory panel—and points to the need for a governmentwide approach to restructuring DOE.

Our purpose in surveying former DOE executives and experts was to focus on fundamental issues related to missions and structure. Almost all of our respondents had substantial knowledge of DOE's operations, either as contractors, advisers, or long-time observers of DOE's performance. We did not ask respondents to comment on the Department's management reforms.

Officials directly responsible for the conduct of DOE's Strategic Alignment and Downsizing Initiative—the Department's major restructuring reform effort—advised us that they assumed existing DOE missions were still valid. They did not, as part of the analysis conducted for the Initiative, fundamentally reassess missions or evaluate alternatives to accomplish them. Furthermore, we are aware of no evidence to support DOE's contention that it can perform inherent government responsibilities "better than through any alternative organizational arrangement."

2. We agree that reforms underway at DOE are important and impressive efforts. The draft report that DOE reviewed discussed these reforms. We described some of DOE's reforms as "important areas where marked improvements could greatly increase DOE's ability to better manage its diverse missions more effectively."

We have updated our report to include the additional reforms DOE mentions, specifically the Galvin Task Force on the national laboratories and the Yergin Task Force on Strategic Energy R&D (which was completed after our draft was prepared).

We agree with DOE's characterization of these reforms for what they are: "major undertakings to fundamentally improve the efficiency and effectiveness of the Department." However, according to our examination of the reform efforts, although they were designed to improve operations, they did not entail a fundamental reevaluation of DOE's missions.

3. DOE correctly points to proposals it initiated for privatizing power marketing administrations, the Naval Petroleum and Oil Shale Reserves, and separating the Federal Energy Regulatory Commission from DOE. However, these proposals were products of the Strategic Alignment and Downsizing Initiative, whose activities appeared to center on streamlining existing operations. Senior advisers to the Secretary and officials directly responsible for the leadership of this Initiative told us that as part of the Initiative, they did not fundamentally reassess missions or evaluate alternatives to accomplish them. More importantly, as we pointed out, while the reforms are useful and needed, they do not address fundamental decisions about DOE's missions. Only the Congress working with the administration can decide which missions are still needed and how best to implement them.

4. DOE's plan to reduce its staff by 27 percent while simultaneously achieving billions in productivity savings is a very ambitious undertaking. We certainly applaud these and other efforts at budgetary savings and reform. However, the impact of dramatic changes in the budgets of its missions, especially reduced staff, is highly uncertain. According to the information contained in DOE's Strategic Alignment and Downsizing Initiative and other sources, it is unclear whether DOE will be truly managing its missions with fewer resources or performing fewer missions to achieve its budgetary goals.

5. We use "missions" to describe the many diverse activities conducted by DOE. While "science education" is an activity that receives a small budget, DOE lists it as one of five "goals" in its Science and Technology business line. DOE engages in many important activities not necessarily associated with large budgetary amounts—energy policy being but one.

In our budgetary chart (see fig. 1.1), we included the cleanup of nuclear waste within environment, safety, and health activities to limit the list to broad categories. We have corrected the reference to "science policy" as "science education."

6. Resurveying the experts would serve little useful purpose because DOE is essentially the same now as it was when we conducted our survey. Its

missions and structures have not changed nor have its major reforms been substantially implemented.

Appendix IV

Major Contributors to This Report

Resources, Community, and Economic Development Division Washington, D.C.

Bernice Steinhardt, Associate Director
Gary R. Boss, Assistant Director
William Lanouette, Evaluator-in-Charge
Diane Raynes, Senior Evaluator
Fran A. Featherston, Survey Researcher

Related GAO Products

Department of Energy: Alternatives for Clearer Missions and Better Management at the National Laboratories (GAO/T-RCED-95-128, Mar. 9, 1995).

Nuclear Weapons Complex: Establishing a National Risk-Based Strategy for Cleanup (GAO/T-RCED-95-120, Mar. 6, 1995).

Department of Energy: National Priorities Needed for Meeting Environmental Agreements (GAO/RCED-95-1, Mar. 3, 1995).

Department of Energy: Research and Agency Missions Need Reevaluating (GAO/T-RCED-95-105, Feb. 13, 1995).

Department of Energy: National Laboratories Need Clearer Missions and Better Management (GAO/RCED-95-10, Jan. 27, 1995).

Department of Energy: Need to Reevaluate Its Role and Missions (GAO/T-RCED-95-85, Jan. 18, 1995).

Department of Energy: Management Changes Needed to Expand Use of Innovative Cleanup Technologies (GAO/RCED-94-205, Aug. 10, 1994).

Department of Energy: Challenges to Implementing Contract Reform (GAO/RCED-94-150, Mar. 24, 1994).

DOE's National Laboratories: Adopting New Missions and Managing Effectively Pose Significant Challenges (GAO/T-RCED-94-113, Feb. 3, 1994).

Financial Management: Energy's Material Financial Management Weaknesses Require Corrective Action (GAO/AIMD-93-29, Sept. 30, 1993).

Department of Energy: Management Problems Require a Long-Term Commitment to Change (GAO/RCED-93-72, Aug. 31, 1993).

Energy Policy: Changes Needed to Make National Energy Planning More Useful (GAO/RCED-93-29, Apr. 27, 1993).

Energy Management: High-Risk Area Requires Fundamental Change (GAO/T-RCED-93-7, Feb. 17, 1993).

Nuclear Weapons Complex: Issues Surrounding Consolidating Los Alamos and Livermore National Laboratories (GAO/T-RCED-92-98, Sept. 24, 1992).

Department of Energy: Better Information Resources Management Needed to Accomplish Missions (GAO/IMTEC-92-53, Sept. 29, 1992).

High-Risk Series: Department of Energy Contract Management (GAO/HR-93-9, Dec. 1992).

Ordering Information

The first copy of each GAO report and testimony is free. Additional copies are $2 each. Orders should be sent to the following address, accompanied by a check or money order made out to the Superintendent of Documents, when necessary. Orders for 100 or more copies to be mailed to a single address are discounted 25 percent.

Orders by mail:

U.S. General Accounting Office
P.O. Box 6015
Gaithersburg, MD 20884-6015

or visit:

Room 1100
700 4th St. NW (corner of 4th and G Sts. NW)
U.S. General Accounting Office
Washington, DC

Orders may also be placed by calling (202) 512-6000
or by using fax number (301) 258-4066, or TDD (301) 413-0006.

Each day, GAO issues a list of newly available reports and testimony. To receive facsimile copies of the daily list or any list from the past 30 days, please call (301) 258-4097 using a touchtone phone. A recorded menu will provide information on how to obtain these lists.

For information on how to access GAO reports on the INTERNET, send an e-mail message with "info" in the body to:

info@www.gao.gov

PRINTED ON RECYCLED PAPER

United States General Accounting Office

GAO

Report to the Secretary of Energy

January 1995

DEPARTMENT OF ENERGY

National Laboratories Need Clearer Missions and Better Management

GAO/RCED-95-10

United States
General Accounting Office
Washington, D.C. 20548

Resources, Community, and
Economic Development Division

B-170004

January 27, 1995

The Honorable Hazel R. O'Leary
The Secretary of Energy

Dear Madam Secretary:

This review of the national laboratories is part of our general management review of the Department of Energy. The purpose of this review is to assess the Department's management, analyze problems and determine their underlying causes, and identify ways of improving departmental management processes and structures.

This report contains recommendations to you for improving the effectiveness of the Department's multiprogram national laboratories. As you know, 31 U.S.C. 720 requires the head of a federal agency to submit a written statement of the actions taken on our recommendations to the Senate Committee on Governmental Affairs and the House Committee on Government Reform and Oversight not later than 60 days after the date of this letter and to the House and Senate Committees on Appropriations with the agency's first request for appropriations made more than 60 days after the date of this letter.

We are sending copies of this report to interested congressional committees and subcommittees; individual Members of Congress; and other interested parties. We will also make copies available to others upon request.

Please contact me on (202) 512-3841 if you have any questions. Major contributors to this report are listed in appendix IV.

Sincerely yours,

Victor S. Rezendes
Director, Energy and
Science Issues

Executive Summary

Purpose

The Department of Energy's (DOE) multiprogram national laboratories have made vital contributions to the nation's defense and civilian science and technology efforts. Now, these laboratories face many changes as the nation redefines its defense requirements at the end of the Cold War and encounters increasing global competition in technology. These changes have raised questions about whether the laboratories are focusing their resources on the most important national priorities and are managed as effectively as possible.

As part of a general management review of DOE, GAO, with assistance from a panel of experts, assessed the laboratories' current and future missions and DOE's management of the laboratories.

Background

DOE's laboratories have combined annual budgets of about $6 billion and over 50,000 employees. DOE estimates that it has invested over $100 billion in the laboratories over the past 20 years. Most of the laboratories were established during or just after World War II as part of the Manhattan Project, which developed the world's first atomic bombs. The laboratories have since expanded their missions to encompass civilian research and development in many disciplines—from high-energy physics to advanced computing—at facilities located throughout the nation. The laboratories support DOE programs and address national needs in science and technology. DOE owns the laboratories but contracts with universities and private-sector organizations for their management and operation.

Results in Brief

DOE's laboratories do not have clearly defined missions that focus their considerable resources on accomplishing the Department's changing objectives and national priorities. As the manager of this important research and technology network, DOE has not coordinated these laboratories' efforts to solve national problems but has managed each laboratory on a program-by-program basis. As a result, DOE has underutilized the laboratories' special talents to tackle complex, cross-cutting issues, and the laboratories may not be prepared to meet future expectations. Although government advisory groups have recommended in the past that DOE redefine the laboratories' missions to meet changes in conditions and national priorities, DOE has not acted on these recommendations. DOE recently developed a Strategic Plan intended to integrate its missions and programs in five major areas, but questions remain about the Department's ability to lead the laboratories into the future.

DOE's day-to-day management of the laboratories—perceived as costly and inefficient by laboratory managers—inhibits the achievement of a productive working relationship between the laboratories and DOE that is necessary if the laboratories are to move successfully into new mission areas. Both laboratory and DOE managers believe that more realistic and consistent priorities are needed to accomplish the growing oversight and administrative requirements placed on the laboratories in recent years.

Principal Findings

Laboratories Need Clear and Coordinated Missions

Over the past decade, several government advisory groups have emphasized the need for DOE to clarify the laboratories' missions. Recent events—including dramatic changes in the nuclear arms race, the demand for technology to solve massive environmental problems, and the growing international competition facing U.S. industry—have brought this need into even sharper focus. Taxpayers have invested heavily in the laboratories, and DOE is responsible for ensuring that this investment is properly focused on national priorities.

The laboratories' missions are set forth as broad goals and activity statements rather than as a coordinated set of objectives with specific implementation strategies for bringing together the individual and collective strengths of the laboratories to meet departmental and national priorities. Faced with a "loss of coherence and focus" at the laboratories, as a 1992 energy advisory group reported, DOE has failed to develop a coordinated and shared "vision" for them. Laboratory managers fear that the lack of proper departmental direction is compromising both their effectiveness in meeting traditional missions and their ability to achieve new national priorities.

Part of the problem is that while DOE manages the laboratories program by program, it does not also manage them as a diversified research system. This approach prevents the laboratories from fully capitalizing on one of their great strengths—combining multidisciplinary talents to solve complex, cross-cutting issues. For example, research on preventing weapons proliferation requires combining expertise in nonproliferation and weapons design—activities that are carried out by different laboratories and managed by different assistant secretaries. The laboratories believe that better linkages are also needed among the energy conservation, fossil fuel, and nuclear energy research areas.

The need for a mechanism to facilitate cross-program coordination has been cited by past advisory groups and by GAO. DOE did create the Office of Laboratory Management to coordinate the interests of the various program offices that interact with the laboratories. However, the change was not implemented, and the existing office lacks the authority to resolve disputes among program offices and reports through two chains of command below the Secretary—an arrangement that does not promote effective interaction between DOE and the laboratories.

DOE created an Advisory Board Task Force on Alternative Futures for the National Laboratories, giving the Secretary another opportunity to chart a course for the future of the laboratories. The task force, whose report is due in February 1995, could set the foundation for developing clear and coordinated missions for the laboratory network. The success of the task force's efforts will depend, in large measure, on the extent to which DOE's leaders are now able—as they have been unable in the past—to achieve consensus among the laboratories, DOE, and the Congress on future missions for the national laboratories.

DOE's Management Inhibits Accomplishment of the Laboratories' Missions

Laboratory managers view DOE's day-to-day management as costly and unproductive in meeting the laboratories' missions. Tensions between laboratory and DOE executives may also be impeding progress toward reaching a shared vision of the laboratories' future. Laboratory managers have characterized DOE as a micromanager in many areas, especially in overseeing the laboratories' compliance with expanding administrative requirements.

Coping with the new requirements that have accompanied DOE's growing oversight responsibilities is, according to many of the laboratory managers we contacted, a major burden that not only increases the costs of research but also diverts attention from it. Although laboratory managers recognize the importance of meeting environmental, safety, and health goals, they expect DOE to set priorities for their administrative activities and to help them "balance" their responsibilities in the areas of research and administration.

DOE and other agencies conduct as many as 400 reviews annually at some laboratories, according to laboratory sources. One laboratory manager calculated that there was more than one oversight review a day in his program. Laboratory managers are concerned about the time required to prepare for oversight reviews and the loss of the best researchers' time during reviews. Another manager told GAO that he spends as much as 40 percent of his working time on oversight matters. Many laboratory managers expressed concern because they are held accountable for requirements that do not apply to research laboratories and do not differentiate between generic and specific problems.

Laboratory managers also worry that rising research costs—fueled by the growing costs of complying with administrative requirements—may be limiting the ability of the laboratories to compete for opportunities to conduct research sponsored by industry and other government agencies. This limitation could, in turn, diminish the ability of the laboratories to build partnerships with industry—the key to the success of their commercial technology mission.

DOE has begun to institute contract reform efforts. DOE believes that these efforts, especially the planned use of performance measures to guide and evaluate laboratory activities, will form a basis for a more productive management approach that better integrates the laboratories' mission goals with administrative requirements.

Recommendations

GAO recommends that the Secretary of Energy, on the basis of the management issues raised in this report, evaluate alternatives for managing the laboratories that more fully support the achievement of clear and coordinated missions, including strengthening the Department's Office of Laboratory Management.

Matter for Congressional Consideration

If DOE is unable to refocus the laboratories' missions and develop a management approach consistent with these new missions, the Congress may wish to consider alternatives to the present DOE-laboratory relationship. Such alternatives might include placing the laboratories under the control of different agencies or creating a separate structure for the sole purpose of developing a consensus on the laboratories' missions.

Agency Comments

DOE believes that the new strategic planning process that it put in place in 1994, together with the task force's upcoming report on the future of the laboratories, will address many of the issues raised in this report. The agency also believes that its new contract reform efforts, emphasizing the use of performance measures to evaluate the laboratories, will result in a more balanced management approach. DOE commented that these initiatives should be better reflected in GAO's report. GAO believes that the initiatives, when implemented, have the potential to substantially strengthen the agency's overall management capabilities. However, GAO also notes that past DOE reforms—including calls by previous task forces for clarifying the laboratories' missions and prior efforts at contract reform—have not always led to significant change. GAO has updated its report to reflect the agency's initiatives.

Contents

Contents

Appendixes

Table

Abbreviations

DOE	Department of Energy
GAO	General Accounting Office
R&D	research and development

Introduction

The Department of Energy (DOE) is responsible for some of the nation's largest and most impressive scientific facilities. The agency's nine national multiprogram laboratories employ more than 50,000 people and have annual operating budgets that exceed $6 billion. DOE estimates that more than $100 billion has been invested in the laboratories over the past 20 years.[1] The laboratories' work covers many scientific areas—from high-energy physics to advanced computing—at facilities located throughout the nation. Although DOE owns the laboratories, it contracts with universities and private-sector organizations for their management and operation—a practice that has made the laboratories more attractive to scientists and engineers. The laboratory contractors and DOE form unique partnerships at each site, but the Department remains responsible for providing the laboratories with their missions and overall direction, as well as for giving them specific direction to meet both program and administrative goals.

Laboratories Provide Unique Research and Development Capabilities

The laboratories provide the nation with unique research and development (R&D) capabilities. Specifically, the laboratories

- enable researchers to work on complex, interdisciplinary problems that dominate current science and technology;
- permit the study of large-scale, high-risk problems that would be difficult for industry or universities to undertake; and
- provide unique research facilities for universities and industry to use while serving as focal points for research consortia.

DOE's laboratories have made wide-ranging contributions to defense and civilian technologies. For example, the laboratories have long produced and applied nuclear isotopes now used in thousands of diagnostic medical procedures daily. Safer cars and planes have evolved using computer crash simulation software developed at one laboratory. In 1994, the laboratories' technological achievements received 25 of the 100 prestigious "R&D 100 Awards" given annually by R&D Magazine for the year's most technologically significant products. Appendix I contains information on the staffing and funding, as well as the contractor and programmatic emphases, at each laboratory.

[1] DOE is also responsible for several "single purpose" laboratories. These facilities concentrate in a particular program area or were created to pursue a single issue. Although these smaller laboratories are part of DOE's national laboratory network, we focused our attention on the nine multiprogram laboratories that dominate DOE's science and technology activities and budget resources.

Laboratories' Missions Have Evolved

When DOE was created in 1977, it inherited the national laboratories with a management structure that had evolved from the World War II "Manhattan Project," whose mission was to design and build the world's first atomic bombs. From this national security mission, the laboratories generated expertise that initially developed nuclear power as an energy source. The laboratories' missions broadened in 1967, when the Congress recognized their role in conducting environmental as well as public health and safety-related research and development. In 1971, the Congress again expanded the laboratories' role, permitting them to conduct nonnuclear energy research and development. During the 1980s, the Congress enacted laws to stimulate the transfer of technology from the laboratories to U.S. industry. DOE estimates that over the past 20 years, the nation has invested more than $100 billion in the laboratories.

The 1990s have brought the most dramatic changes affecting the multiprogram laboratories, including the following.

- The Soviet Union's collapse has reduced the nuclear arms race, raising questions about the need to maintain three separate weapons laboratories.
- The weapons laboratories, facing reduced funding in nuclear weapons research, have diversified their work in order to maintain their preeminent talent and facilities.
- Expectations are growing that all laboratories can and should help improve the nation's economic competitiveness by working with industry to develop commercial technologies.
- As the laboratories have aged, concerns have arisen about their ability to maintain their skills in weapons programs. Major investments will be needed to provide up-to-date facilities and attract younger scientists.
- In light of the general budget austerity facing the federal government, a stable funding environment is no longer guaranteed, and the laboratories will increasingly need to show useful results.

These and other forces have accelerated the laboratories' diversification from defense and nuclear research. For example, the nuclear weapons laboratories—Los Alamos, Sandia, and Lawrence Livermore—although created to design, develop, and test nuclear weapons, now devote less than half of their budgets to work on nuclear weapons. While these laboratories have been affected most dramatically by recent geopolitical changes, all DOE laboratories have been influenced by recent events and are redirecting their priorities.

The federal government owns the facilities and grounds of the laboratories and funds the work but has relied on contractors to manage and operate them. These contracts generally run for 5 years; however, some of the laboratories have been run by the same contractor for decades, even since their inception in the early 1940s. The laboratories' history of relative autonomy in daily research and operational management has led to concerns about their business practices as well as their attention to environmental, safety, and health issues.

Objectives, Scope, and Methodology

The objective of this report was to identify and examine the principal issues affecting the laboratories' missions and DOE's approach to laboratory management. The Congress has expressed considerable interest in these topics over the years, and our prior work at the laboratories, as well as other studies, has demonstrated that the laboratories' missions and management are key concerns. This work was carried out as part of our general management review of the Department of Energy.

Our work focused on DOE's nine multiprogram laboratories because of their size and importance as national science and technology resources. We selected laboratory staff to interview by asking each laboratory to identify five programs that best represented its current contributions and future capabilities. (App. II contains the list of programs the laboratories identified.) From these programs, we selected three for assessment. This approach allowed us to examine both the strengths as well as the weaknesses of the laboratories. When collecting information, we strove to identify and assess mission and management issues from the experience of the laboratory managers responsible for directing the programs we had selected. Our work also focused on each laboratory's technology transfer activities because of the increased national emphasis on using the laboratories to enhance U.S. technological competitiveness.

We collected information about the laboratories' missions and management from multiple sources with direct knowledge of these issues. At the laboratories, we interviewed managers who were responsible for the research programs we had chosen. We also held discussions with laboratory directors, senior officials responsible for technology transfer activities, and contractor representatives. At DOE, we interviewed program managers—Washington-based executives responsible for the research programs we had selected at the laboratories—and DOE field office managers, who oversee the Department's contractors at the laboratories.

To validate and refine our findings, we conducted two focus groups. The first group, which met with our staff in Chicago, consisted of one program manager from each of the nine laboratories. A second group, comprising program managers from DOE headquarters, met with our staff in Washington, D.C.

To obtain independent views about the laboratories' missions and management, we interviewed experts and industry representatives who were not associated with the laboratories. In addition, the National Academy of Public Administration assisted us in convening a panel of experts with backgrounds in (1) managing research in government and industry and (2) science and technology policy. Table 1 lists the panelists and their relevant professional experience.

Table 1: GAO's Panel of Energy Experts

Lewis Branscomb, Chair	Albert Pratt Public Service Professor, John F. Kennedy School of Government, Harvard University, Director, Science, Technology, and Public Policy Program Formerly: Vice President and Chief Scientist, IBM, Director, National Bureau of Standards; Chairman, National Science Board.
Erich Bloch	Distinguished Fellow, Council on Competitiveness Formerly: Director, National Science Foundation; Member, Committee on Computers in Automated Manufacturing; Vice President, Technical Personnel Development, IBM; Vice President and General Manager, IBM, East Fishkill, N.Y
Sydney Drell	Deputy Director, Stanford Linear Accelerator Formerly: Co-Director, Stanford University Center for International Security and Arms Control; Executive Head, Department of Theoretical Physics, Stanford University
Harry Finger	Consultant. Formerly. President and CEO, U.S. Council for Energy Awareness; Vice President for Strategic Planning and Development Operations, and General Manager, Center for Energy Systems, General Electric Company; Assistant Secretary for Research and Technology, U.S. Department of Housing and Urban Development; Associate Administrator for Management and Director, Space Power and Nuclear Systems, National Aeronautics and Space Administration.
Donald Kerr	Executive Vice President, Science Applications International Corporation. Formerly: President, EG&G, Director, Los Alamos National Laboratory; Assistant Secretary for Energy Programs, Department of Defense
Roland Schmitt	Consultant. Formerly: President, Rensselaer Polytechnic Institute, Senior Vice President, Science and Technology, General Electric; Senior Vice President, Corporate Research and Development, General Electric.
Robert White	President, National Academy of Engineering; Vice Chairman, National Research Council. Formerly: President, University Corporation for Atmospheric Research; Administrator, National Oceanic and Atmospheric Administration, Chief, U.S Weather Bureau.

We also reviewed information and analyses from the laboratories, DOE, the Congress, industry, and independent experts, as well as legislative proposals and testimony, DOE documents, budget materials, and previous studies conducted by government and private organizations.

In analyzing information, we compared and contrasted views about laboratory mission and management issues. We found considerable agreement among all types of respondents on both topics. To give the reader concrete illustrations of how mission and management issues were viewed, we have used quotations from sources we interviewed throughout this report.

We obtained written comments on a draft of this report from DOE. The agency's comments and our evaluation are presented in appendix III and at the end of chapter 5.

We conducted our work from July 1992 through December 1994 in accordance with generally accepted government auditing standards.

The Laboratories Need Their Missions Clarified

As the manager of the laboratories, DOE has not clarified how the laboratory system can and should meet national priorities. Although research programs set laboratory priorities to meet their own goals, DOE has not used the laboratories as a coordinated network of talent and facilities to meet missions that cut across programs. This approach not only inhibits the development of clear and coordinated missions for the multiprogram laboratories but also fails to draw upon the laboratories' expertise in multiple disciplines to solve complex, cross-cutting problems in science and technology.

These concerns are not new. In the past, many advisory groups emphasized the need to clarify and redefine the laboratories' missions. Although DOE recently developed a Strategic Plan and processes intended to integrate the Department's missions and programs in five major areas, questions remain about DOE's overall capacity to lead the national laboratories into new mission areas.

Laboratories' Missions Are Unclear

DOE's multiprogram laboratory system, as well as the individual laboratories, needs missions that are clear and coordinated with DOE's overall program goals in order to organize the system's efforts as effectively as possible. The clearer the mission, experts believe, the better the performance will be. In 1992, the Advisory Board to the former Secretary of Energy expressed the importance of clear missions as follows:

> Each national laboratory must have clearly defined, specific missions which support the over-arching missions of DOE to ensure the best technical and management performance and the greatest value to the nation [2]

Only with clear missions, experts believe, can implementation strategies or "road maps" be developed that describe how each mission will be accomplished and guide each organization's day-to-day operations.

We found that the multiprogram laboratories—both individually and as a group—do not have either clearly defined missions or specific implementation strategies that bring together laboratory resources to focus on accomplishing departmental objectives and national goals. Although current mission statements for the laboratories describe their ability to conduct research in defense, energy, and environmental cleanup;

[2] Secretary of Energy Advisory Board Task Force on the Department of Energy's National Laboratories, final report, July 1992.

to transfer technology to industry; and to perform basic research, these activities have not been translated into overall missions for the laboratory system and specific missions for each laboratory. For example, one laboratory manager expressed concern to us that all laboratories have "generic" mission statements that tend to look remarkably similar. Laboratory managers frequently made comments to us such as "we don't really have a mission . . ." and "The laboratories must have a vision and goal toward which they can work." An expert we consulted expressed the current situation as follows:

> [We] have not seen crisp, specific mission statements from individual laboratories, nor specific mission statements that would cover all DOE's laboratories. Furthermore, DOE has not been able to describe the mission of the laboratories, nor are the laboratories' missions defined in any piece of legislation. . . It is not possible to run a $6 billion organization without specific mission statements.

Laboratory managers we spoke with were also concerned that the Congress, DOE, and the laboratories do not share a "common vision" of the laboratories' missions. Such a common vision among the key "stakeholders" is crucial if the laboratories are to use their resources most effectively to support departmental programs and national goals—the main purpose of the laboratories' existence. Developing clear and more coordinated missions is particularly important, given the growing expectation that the laboratories will work together toward achieving national security, energy, environmental, and commercial technology goals. (Ch. 4 contains the opinions of our panel of experts on suitable missions for the national laboratories.)

The responsibility for developing the common vision rests with DOE. However, laboratory managers believed that DOE headquarters and operations offices have divergent views of the laboratories and their goals, and DOE has not been able to develop a consensus with the Congress on the future of the laboratories.

Clear and Coordinated Missions Would Help the Laboratories Address Cross-Cutting Issues

Without a coordinated set of laboratory missions, DOE is unable to address issues that require cooperation and coordination across its many mission areas. This not only inhibits cooperation among research programs but also keeps DOE from using its laboratories to achieve departmental missions.

Laboratory and DOE managers are concerned that DOE has not built on its individual programs to encourage valuable cross-program and cross-laboratory interactions, which are essential to meeting both current and future missions. Both laboratory and DOE program managers describe DOE's management as "fractured" and not particularly adept at combining the expertise of various program areas to tackle cross-disciplinary problems. Laboratory managers cited difficulties DOE has in establishing bridges between its basic science programs and applied science groups. Developing clear and coordinated missions—and strategies to implement them—would provide the necessary bridges between and among the laboratories on cross-cutting projects, according to many laboratory and independent experts.

Many laboratory managers believe that DOE and its laboratories lack effective coordinating mechanisms—among the most serious challenges facing the Department as an organization. One manager described as a "horrible problem" the limited emphasis on cross-program coordination.

To illustrate the difficulties in combining expertise from different programs to achieve core missions, several laboratory managers cited the fragmented research on preventing the proliferation of nuclear weapons. Although solutions to proliferation problems require expertise in identifying the effects of weapons, the nonproliferation and weapons missions are carried out in different laboratories and are managed by different assistant secretaries. Laboratory managers also cited weak links among the energy conservation, fossil fuel, and nuclear energy research programs as having limited DOE's progress in commercializing energy technologies.

When DOE and the laboratories have successfully combined their multidisciplinary resources, impressive results have occurred. For example, laboratory managers attributed the rapid progress toward a coordinated understanding of global environmental change in DOE's Global Studies Program to the use of nine laboratories' diverse capabilities. According to another laboratory manager, cross-laboratory cooperation in the fusion energy program is leading to a long-range strategy to guide research. These examples illustrate the potential for greater collaboration on technical issues that require multidisciplinary talent.

Mission Uncertainty Is a Persistent Problem

Concerns about the need to update and clarify the laboratories' missions are long-standing. Past studies and reviews of the laboratories have all reached the same conclusion, as the following examples show:

- In 1983, the White House Science Council Federal Laboratory Review Panel issued a report (commonly known as the Packard Report) addressing all federal laboratories.[3] The report found that while some of the laboratories, particularly DOE's, had clearly defined missions for parts of their work, most activities were fragmented and unrelated to the laboratories' main responsibilities. This report recommended that all parent agencies review and redefine the missions of their laboratories.
- In 1992, a DOE Secretary of Energy Advisory Board found that the broad missions the laboratories were addressing, coupled with rapidly changing world events, ". . . ha[d] caused a loss of coherence and focus at the laboratories, thereby reducing their overall effectiveness in responding to their traditional missions as well as new national initiatives. . . ." The Board identified the most important cause of the stress between DOE and its laboratories as ". . . the lack of a common vision as to the missions of the laboratories. . . ."[4]
- A 1993 report of an internal DOE task force on laboratory missions reported that the missions "must be updated to support DOE's new directions and to respond to new national imperatives. . . ."[5]

None of these past studies and reviews has resulted in overall consensus about the future missions of the multiprogram laboratory system, raising questions about DOE's capacity to provide a vision for this system. A 1982 DOE Energy Research Advisory Board task force provided some insights into this question.[6] The Advisory Board acknowledged the impressive nature of the research and development conducted throughout the system but noted that certain weaknesses prevented the laboratories from achieving their full potential. The Advisory Board found, for example, that structural problems and fragmented programs required the laboratories to interact with DOE on an excessive number of levels. The Advisory Board recommended that DOE designate a high-level official to focus solely on the laboratories. DOE did not follow the Advisory Board's recommendations. In

[3] Report of the White House Science Council, Federal Laboratory Review Panel, Office of Science and Technology Policy, May 15, 1983.

[4] Secretary of Energy Advisory Board, Final Report, 1992.

[5] Changes and Challenges at the Department of Energy Laboratories, Final Draft Report of the Missions of the Laboratories Priority Team, 1993.

[6] The Department of Energy Multiprogram Laboratories, A report of the Energy Research Advisory Board to the Department of Energy, Sept. 1982.

early 1993, however, DOE created an Office of Laboratory Management whose purpose was, in part, to coordinate the interests of the various DOE program offices that interact with the laboratories on a program-by-program basis. However, according to DOE officials, the plan was not implemented, and the existing office does not coordinate laboratory activities for all program offices and does not report directly to the Secretary.

We called attention to the limitations of DOE's program-by-program approach to directing its laboratories as early as 1978, after reviewing the laboratories' contributions to nonnuclear energy, a critical policy issue at that time.[7] The laboratories' activities in this area were limited by several factors. First, DOE's organizational alignment created obstacles; specifically, the laboratories reported to three different senior officials. This arrangement focused the efforts of the laboratories on particular programs and eroded their abilities to pursue research on topics cutting across several areas, such as nonnuclear energy. Second, the roles of the laboratories were determined in a piecemeal way so that each laboratory was given small, fragmented responsibilities. We recommended that DOE align the laboratories under a separate high-level office that was not responsible for specific programs.

In the absence of an overall mission strategy for the laboratories, individual research program goals are emphasized, sometimes at the expense of broader DOE and laboratory missions. One laboratory manager noted:

> Most of what we do is determined from the bottom-up . . . in other words, the program level in DOE—and DOE program managers don't [care] about what the [laboratory's] missions are. They want to know where the talent is, and they want to know where the capability is, and that's where they put their work.

A DOE operations office manager said that the Department's program-oriented approach toward the laboratories fails to recognize DOE's "corporate" responsibility for them. Another manager cited the need for DOE to develop a strategic approach to the laboratories. Laboratory managers pointed out that DOE's approach to the laboratories through individual research programs has not effectively linked the laboratory system's collective resources to DOE's missions. A laboratory manager described DOE as increasingly focused on individual programs; its

[7] The Multiprogram Laboratories: A National Resource for Nonnuclear Energy Research, Development and Demonstration (EMD-78-62, Mar. 22, 1978).

management is concentrated at the assistant secretary level, even though many projects do not fall within any one assistant secretary's program responsibilities.

Debate on Developing Missions for the Laboratories Is Growing

How best to develop missions for the laboratories—and how best to manage them—is the subject of growing debate in the scientific community and was discussed by our panel of experts. For example, proposals suggested or debated during our review included the following.

- Convert some laboratories, particularly those working closely with the private sector, into independent entities.
- Transfer the responsibility for one or more laboratories to another agency, whose responsibilities and mission are closely aligned with a particular DOE laboratory.
- Create a "lead lab" arrangement, under which one laboratory is given a leadership role in a mission or technology area and other laboratories are selected to work in that area.
- Consolidate the responsibility for research, development, and testing on nuclear weapons within a single laboratory.

While we have not analyzed these alternatives, each has advantages and disadvantages and needs to be evaluated in light of the laboratories' capabilities for designing nuclear weapons and pursuing other missions of national and strategic importance. Furthermore, the government may still need facilities dedicated to national and defense missions, a factor that would heavily influence any future organizational decisions. Important budgetary considerations also accompany each alternative.

An expert panelist advised caution in restructuring the laboratories, expressing concern that decades of national investment in these facilities have produced important assets that, if dispersed, could take many years and billions of dollars to reassemble.

The Previous Congress Took Some Action on Laboratory Mission and Management Issues

The previous Congress was also active in the debate on the laboratories' missions. For example, a House bill introduced in 1993 defined future missions for DOE's laboratories and suggested methods for measuring progress toward goals, along with incentives for improving the overall quality of research at the laboratories. This proposed legislation also sought to require more rigorous evaluation of the laboratories, articulated several missions for them (such as advancing nuclear science and technology for national security purposes), and advocated that they work with private industry to develop environmental technology and technology transfer activities. A bill passed by the Senate in 1993 contained similar provisions and was designed to sharpen the laboratories' focus on technology transfer and cooperative research agreements. This bill would have required the laboratories to allocate 20 percent of their budgets to partnerships with industry and academia.

Further Efforts Are Under Way to Clarify the Laboratories' Missions

Recognizing the important role that the multiprogram laboratories should play in accomplishing departmental goals and national priorities, DOE is making another attempt to define the laboratories' missions. In February 1994, the Secretary commissioned an independent task force to address the appropriate roles of DOE's laboratories. Chaired by the former chief executive officer of Motorola Corporation, this task force—the Secretary of Energy Advisory Board Task Force on Alternative Futures for the Department of Energy National Laboratories—is charged with, among other things, examining "alternative scenarios for future utilization of these laboratories for meeting national missions." The task force's charter encompasses examining the future roles and responsibilities of the national laboratories, including questions about their accountability and consolidation. The task force's report to the Secretary is expected by February 1995.

DOE has also initiated a strategic planning process that it believes will form a framework for coordinating the laboratories' missions with the agency's goals and objectives.[8] DOE's Strategic Plan will focus the agency's efforts on five main areas: preserving national security, conserving energy resources, promoting environmental protection, applying science and technology to national needs, and encouraging industrial competitiveness. Strategic plans have also been developed for each of these areas. In addition, DOE has begun a major reorganization effort, which is designed to follow the structure of its new Strategic Plan. Reorienting existing programs and the laboratories to best address these areas remains the Department's challenge.

[8]Strategic Plan. Fueling a Competitive Economy U S. Department of Energy, DOE/0108, Apr 1994.

A More Effective Management Approach Will Promote Mission Success

Laboratory managers see DOE's management of the multiprogram laboratories as costly and inefficient, creating tensions that impede the development of clear and coordinated missions for the laboratories and action steps that lead toward achieving these missions. According to laboratory managers, DOE micromanages the laboratories, particularly in overseeing their compliance with growing numbers of administrative requirements. Laboratory managers fault DOE for failing to set priorities or provide guidance about how to satisfy both research goals and administrative requirements.

Experts we consulted, as well as many laboratory and DOE managers, expressed concern that without a more effective management relationship between DOE and the laboratories, rising research costs may price the laboratories out of collaborative research with industry—a new mission area in which the laboratories are expected to make major contributions.

DOE does Not Balance Research and Administrative Objectives

In addition to meeting their research and technology objectives, laboratory managers are responsible for satisfying a wide variety of administrative requirements in areas such as procurement; travel; human resources; and environment, safety, and health. Prompted by criticism of its business practices and past inattention to environment, safety, and health issues, DOE has greatly increased its oversight of the laboratories during recent years.

Coping with the new requirements that have accompanied DOE's expanded oversight is, according to a consensus of laboratory managers, a major burden that not only increases research costs but also diverts attention from basic research. Although laboratory managers recognize the importance of meeting administrative goals—particularly in the area of environment, safety, and health—they want DOE to set priorities for their administrative activities and help them balance research and administration.

Administrative Requirements Have Proliferated

Administrative requirements increased under the former Secretary of Energy, largely in response to the well-publicized call for greater attention to the environment, safety, and health throughout the nuclear weapons complex. Thus, over 70 percent of the requirements listed in DOE's 1993 Directives Checklist are new or have been revised since 1989. A DOE operations office manager estimated that DOE has about 8,400 environment, safety, and health requirements. Directives define required actions to meet certain objectives; these actions range from preparing reports to conducting inspections. Both laboratory and DOE operations office managers who administer directives told us they were "numb" from the proliferation of requirements. According to a consensus of both laboratory and DOE managers, the laboratories have been overwhelmed, not only by the volume of new requirements but also by their detail and by inconsistent guidance for implementing them.

Closely related to the proliferation of administrative requirements has been the equally aggressive expansion of oversight activity. Oversight—or the assessment of how well managers handle the programs and requirements for which they are accountable—is critical to the operation of federal programs and is a key management responsibility. Despite its vital role, laboratory managers, the experts on our panel, and DOE managers agreed that sharply increased oversight in recent years has not been an effective management approach for DOE.

DOE and other agencies conduct as many as 400 reviews annually at each laboratory. One laboratory manager calculated that his program was reviewed more than once a day in 1992. Laboratory managers deplored the enormous amount of time required to prepare for oversight reviews, adding that the impact of losing the best researchers' time during reviews is difficult to quantify. Many scientists have become discouraged by administrative chores. One manager complained that administrative oversight consumed as much as 40 percent of his working time, and many managers questioned whether DOE's expanded oversight has produced benefits commensurate with its costs.

Oversight reviews of the laboratories have been particularly burdensome because they have been inconsistent. Laboratory managers deal with three large bureaucracies—DOE headquarters, DOE operations offices, and contractors. Each interprets DOE's oversight requirements, which, in turn, sometimes conflict. One manager expressed the problem this way:

> There are myriad rules and regulations that require a substantial amount of interpretation. In the absence of a single environment, safety, and health oversight organization, every laboratory will have a different level of compliance because each field office has a different interpretation of environment, safety, and health rules.

Requirements Do Not Reflect Laboratory Conditions

Both laboratory and DOE managers say they are held accountable for requirements that do not reflect problems in research laboratories or do not differentiate between general and isolated problems. According to the managers, many environment, safety, and health requirements are appropriate for problems and operations at weapons production facilities, not at laboratories. A laboratory manager explained the effect of inappropriate requirements on research:

> We end up treating very simple chemical experiments as if people were working with commercial nuclear reactors... our costs have gone right through the roof and our staff's ability to turn out the volume has decreased dramatically.

Many laboratory managers also said that they had been held accountable for problems that occurred at another location—experiencing what a DOE operations office manager described as "battalion punishment." For example, frozen pipes at one facility resulted in a directive to all laboratories, including those in warm climates. A laboratory manager explained:

> If lab A screws up—say environmental health or quality assurance—[DOE] headquarters decides that everybody's guilty and we're then overrun with sieges and inspections. Instead of going back to that laboratory and trying to understand why that went bad, we're all condemned by the same punishment.

Meeting all of these responsibilities presents a significant challenge, especially as budgets decline. Yet laboratory managers maintained that DOE has provided little guidance or assistance in setting priorities to help them balance their responsibilities.

Part of the problem, according to many laboratory managers, stems from the existence within DOE of parallel research and administrative reporting and oversight systems. Decisions are made about requirements in one area without assessing their impact on the other, and research and administrative compliance programs each have different reward structures. A laboratory manager also noted that no one takes responsibility for resolving conflicts between the two systems. As one senior laboratory manager explained to us:

> There is a split in DOE between the people who run programs and those who issue regulations....Funds tend to come in at the bottom to scientists, while regulations tend to come in at the top of the organization... often the scientists do not understand the rationale for regulations.

Costs Present a Major Issue

Managers at the laboratories, in DOE programs, and at DOE operations offices were troubled by the costs associated with achieving the

Department's administrative goals. Although little information or analysis has been completed on this issue, DOE's administrative compliance approach has had two results, according to both DOE and laboratory managers. First, it has been costly. Second, it has raised research costs and reduced the laboratories' ability to compete with universities for research sponsored by industry and other government agencies.

For example, a laboratory manager told us that operating a reactor costs significantly more under DOE's safety regulations than under the Nuclear Regulatory Commission's regulations for non-DOE reactors. A DOE operations office manager added that it would cost billions more than is currently spent to be in full compliance with all rules and regulations at several laboratories, even though these laboratories have lower-priority problems. Laboratory and DOE managers agreed that DOE has not provided the funding required to achieve compliance, particularly with environment, safety, and health regulations. A DOE operations office manager noted that no additional funds had been received at one laboratory where expenditures of more than $1 billion would be required to correct environment, safety, and health problems.

Managers also expressed considerable concern that DOE's administrative compliance approach has raised research costs, limiting the laboratories' ability to compete for research funded by industry and other government agencies. For example, one research organization reported that renewing its contract with a laboratory would cost up to 3 times more than its previous contract. Laboratory and DOE managers and experts agreed that universities—the laboratories' main competitors for research—need not meet many of the requirements that DOE imposes. An expert expressed concern that increases in the costs of research could adversely affect the laboratories' commercial technology mission, pointing out that

> There is a trend toward imposing the full range of government procurement requirements on the laboratories, and thus could kill government-industry cooperation. . . .For industry to find cooperative research agreements with laboratories a viable option, laboratory costs must be fully competitive.

Laboratory and DOE managers and an expert on our panel believe that administrative programs should be cost-effective and have priorities for compliance so that resources can be concentrated on the most significant risks. However, DOE has not systematically set priorities for its administrative requirements, and cost-benefit analyses have not been used to assess risks.

DOE Has Begun to Address Oversight Issues

DOE has begun to streamline the directives system and correct other oversight problems. Also, the Department is now seeking to avoid duplicative or unnecessary oversight reviews and is more careful about overloading laboratories with such reviews. In addition, DOE has begun to implement "total quality management" and is developing performance measures to guide its evaluation of the laboratories' management. DOE believes that these efforts should help both it and the laboratories balance their research and administrative goals more effectively in the future.

DOE's Contractual Relationships Inhibit Change

DOE's "management and operating" contracts with the academic institutions that operate most of the multiprogram laboratories pose a further stumbling block both to a more favorable relationship between the Department and the laboratories and to a reduction in DOE's oversight. Under these contracts, a contractor assumes responsibility for managing and operating a facility but incurs only limited liability. DOE pays virtually all of the contractor's costs except those resulting from willful misconduct or bad faith by top management or those designated as unallowable. Furthermore, under its contracts with the laboratory contractors, most of which are nonprofit or academic institutions, DOE has limited financial incentives for influencing the contractor's actions: It cannot adjust the fee that it pays to these contractors because it has historically negotiated a fixed fee with them that is not tied to their performance. In contrast, DOE pays its for-profit contractors a fee, called an "award fee," that is based on its assessment of their performance. The tensions created by the arrangements between DOE and its nonprofit contractors have raised questions about whether DOE's current contracting approach is effective for managing the laboratories. DOE and various oversight groups, including GAO, have expressed concerns about the laboratories' past business practices and have called for changes in contracts that better reflect the needs of the laboratories and the requirements of DOE.

DOE is changing its relationship with contractors. Under its contract reform initiative, contractors will be evaluated on the basis of performance measures—a process that DOE believes will better enable it to hold contractors accountable for results.[9] In addition, according to DOE staff, the use of performance measures will lead to a more rational, risk-based approach toward compliance with the increased number of requirements placed on the laboratories in recent years.

[9] We have reported on performance-based contracting in Department of Energy: Challenges to Implementing Contract Reform (GAO/RCED-94-150, Mar. 21, 1994).

We support DOE's contract reform efforts and believe that, once implemented, they offer opportunities for substantially improving the way the agency does business with its contractors, including its laboratory contractors. We are concerned, however, that the scope of DOE's current contract reform may not address all the major management problems that characterize the agency's relationship with the laboratories. For example, it is uncertain how contract reform will resolve the proliferation of laboratory oversight activities, which poses a major problem for laboratory managers. Furthermore, it could take many years for contract reform to take effect, given the multiyear time frame for existing contracts.

Chapter 4

Experts See Future Missions as Extensions of Current Missions

Our panel of experts and other experts believe that, with proper mission focus and management direction, the multiprogram laboratories can make vital contributions in many areas important to DOE and the nation. According to the panel, the highest-priority missions for the laboratories are national defense, energy, the environment, and commercial technology. While the laboratories have already made contributions in these areas—such as effective weapons systems, energy conservation programs, environmental cleanup techniques, and commercialized technologies—our panel concluded that clarifying and, in some cases, redefining the current missions for the laboratory system as a whole would enhance the value of the laboratories.

National Security Work Will Continue to Be Important

Our panel of experts agreed that the laboratories' national security work will continue to be important. Until the Department of Defense has decided whether to support defense work at the laboratories and DOE's missions are clear, the defense roles of Los Alamos, Sandia, and Lawrence Livermore are unclear. However, several panelists anticipated a defense mission with new and continuing objectives that would use these three laboratories' nuclear weapons competence and other laboratories' experience.

In nuclear weapons technologies, several of the experts on our panel predicted that the laboratories' missions would continue to shift from designing weapons to overseeing and dismantling the nuclear stockpile, verifying international nuclear treaties, and conducting research on nonproliferation. Because the Department is substantially responsible for overseeing the weapons stockpile, it will require the laboratories' unique competencies. Ensuring that stockpiled nuclear weapons are reliable and safe is a major responsibility that will persist as long as the nation needs to sustain a nuclear stockpile, a panelist pointed out.

The defense mission also makes the laboratories responsible for overseeing the dismantling of nuclear weapons in accordance with the nation's international treaty obligations—a task that will take decades to complete at the current pace, a laboratory director pointed out. According to a laboratory director, the United States and Russia each estimate that they can dismantle only 2,000 weapons a year. The current U.S. stockpile contains many thousands of weapons.

The proliferation of nuclear technology and materials will be an increasingly important national concern. As a DOE manager noted, a growing number of nations are now able to make nuclear weapons, and more have the political will to develop them. Our panel of experts concurred that the laboratories have unique knowledge to address these issues. For example, the laboratories already have experience in detecting clandestine nuclear weapons programs, locating terrorists' weapons, responding to nuclear weapons emergencies, and identifying the origin of nuclear materials and weapons.

Links Between Energy and Environmental Missions Are Needed

Energy and the environment are areas in which the laboratories have already made useful contributions. However, our panel of experts suggested that the laboratories could enhance their contributions by linking their missions in these areas to focus on energy-related environmental problems—an increasingly important issue, according to a DOE secretarial advisory board. Thus linkage would demonstrate the effect of research in one area on work in another, an important consideration because energy development and use underlie most of the nation's serious environmental problems. For example, the use of electric vehicles would reduce emissions of hydrocarbons but create problems in disposing of batteries. Similarly, the production of commercial nuclear power reduces some air quality problems but creates a need for technologies to dispose of radioactive wastes. As a panelist pointed out, linking energy and environmental research would draw upon the laboratories' ability to address cross-disciplinary problems. This linkage would benefit research in both areas and enhance the ability of DOE and the laboratories to set research and policy priorities.

Our panel of experts agreed that the laboratories have an important energy research mission. One panelist described it as perhaps their principal mission because developing energy sources and efficient uses of energy is vital to the nation's economy. However, another panelist maintained that although the laboratories' energy mission is broad, it has become fuzzy. Panelists also noted that despite substantial investment, the laboratories' energy research has been disappointing. One panelist noted that the nation has been unable to decide on an energy policy to guide the laboratories' work. DOE has produced several different national energy strategies over the years, each with different priorities, making long-term planning for the laboratories difficult. Despite these conditions, however, panelists agreed that a redirected energy mission would serve the United States very well and provide opportunities for large-scale interactions between industry and government. One panelist urged DOE to consider the laboratories' experience, encourage closer laboratory-industry interactions to define priorities, and focus on path-breaking, high-risk, cross-industry research with the potential for major payback in 10 to 20 years.

The laboratories' environmental mission has been more implicit than explicit, according to one panelist. Although the laboratories have been developing environmental technologies, the scope of their environmental mission has not been clear. However, several of the panelists envisioned that the laboratories could make unique contributions, particularly in environmental technology—an area where other federal agencies have limited experience—and in nuclear waste disposal. Significant contributions may also stem from the laboratories' ability to model environmental impacts with their advanced computing facilities. Several panelists believed that greater coordination between DOE and the Environmental Protection Agency would be needed to maximize the value of this type of laboratory work.

A laboratory director emphasized to us that through their basic research competencies the laboratories can make a major contribution to solving environmental challenges, but their strengths have been underutilized. According to the director, "Waste remediation cannot continue on its present course without 'bankrupting the country' because it is being done without a knowledge base."

As a laboratory manager noted, developing a basic understanding of underlying problems before developing waste cleanup technologies is important. If the basic science is not understood, environmental remediation problems may elude solution, just as efforts to cure cancer during the 1970s were unsuccessful because not enough was then known about basic cancer virology.

Laboratories Can Contribute to Commercial Technology Mission

Our panel of experts agreed that a commercial technology mission for the laboratories is legitimate and important. However, several panelists and other experts we consulted maintained that this mission should be broadly conceived—that is, it should emphasize research and development that can benefit all U.S. industries and should be integrated with other laboratory missions rather than become a central mission.

According to panelists, the principal reason for enlisting the laboratories in improving the nation's global competitive position is that they are building the intellectual foundation that allows the nation's economy to prosper. A laboratory director pointed out that U.S. industry has sometimes been at a disadvantage because public-private research is better coordinated in other countries.

There was considerable agreement among both the experts on our panel and other experts we consulted about the need to change the laboratories' current focus on transferring existing technology to industry on a project-by-project basis. Industry, expert, and government sources concurred that the technology mission would be more productive if it supported

- nonproprietary research that could help all industries compete;
- technology research as an integral part of the national security, energy, and environmental missions;
- long-term cooperative research relationships between the laboratories and industry; and
- training in science for future progress in technology.

According to a panelist, nonproprietary research that can benefit all industries is important but has been underfunded and conducted without focus. The panelist emphasized that the government can usefully and appropriately support research that underpins a broad array of specific technology applications in many different industries, stopping short of supporting proprietary technology that companies themselves should fund. For example, experts noted that laboratory research to improve the U.S. transportation system could enhance U.S. manufacturers' ability to compete. Similarly, a panelist noted that laboratory work on advanced computer-aided design tools could improve productivity throughout the U.S. manufacturing sector.

Although a commercial technology mission is important, laboratory managers, industry representatives, and experts cautioned that developing technology should not become the laboratories' primary mission or reason for existence. The officials described the challenge as defining a broad technology mission that supports long-term relationships between the laboratories and industry while sustaining the laboratories' other missions and abilities. For example, the laboratories develop technology through other missions that have technological needs of their own. Sustaining the laboratories' basic research is also important. Laboratory managers observed that a balance is needed between basic and applied research in order to avoid "eating the seed corn" that leads to new technologies. In addition, not all programs—such as high-energy physics—lend themselves to cooperation with industry. A laboratory manager said that with only a technology transfer mission, the laboratories would be out of business in 5 years.

Several of the experts on our panel encouraged laboratories and industry to develop long-term cooperative research relationships that can allow each party to better understand the other's needs and increase the potential for results.

Panelists and other experts we consulted agreed that training in science and mathematics is essential to the nation's future competitiveness in high-technology products and services and that helping train students is important to a commercial technology mission. Several panelists also urged that, to enhance industry's ability to produce marketable innovations, the laboratories expand their training programs to include mid-career technical retraining for industry personnel.

Implementing a Commercial Technology Mission Poses Special Problems

Working with industry on a commercial technology mission at the laboratories presents special challenges for DOE and laboratory management. Although some laboratories have considerable experience in working with industry, broad-scale cooperation represents a new venture for the laboratories. DOE has begun to work with the laboratories and industry to develop a strategic plan for technology partnerships. However, successful implementation of this new mission requires clearly defined roles for the laboratories and DOE, realistic expectations about the laboratories' potential to improve U.S. competitiveness, encouragement to experiment, well-defined mission objectives, and closer links between the laboratories and industry to ensure that the laboratories' work reflects the market's needs.

Chapter 5

Conclusions and Recommendations

U.S. taxpayers have a significant investment in the national laboratory network. DOE has a major responsibility to ensure that work at the laboratories is properly focused and intelligently managed so that the laboratories can make maximum contributions to national priorities. Achieving these goals requires two efforts: First, senior leadership needs to develop clear missions and implementation strategies that treat the laboratories as a coordinated set of facilities; second, DOE needs to adopt a management approach that supports the laboratories' achievement of their research missions and administrative responsibilities.

DOE has not been able to develop a consensus among laboratory and government leaders on appropriate missions for the national laboratories, even though past studies and special task forces have called for such action. Furthermore, the Department's management approach impedes progress toward current goals, raising questions about DOE's overall capacity to achieve these important objectives.

The results from the Secretary's Advisory Board Task Force on Alternative Futures for the National Laboratories could set the foundation for developing clear and coordinated missions for the national laboratory network. The success of these results can best be measured by the extent to which they help shape a consensus among key stakeholders: the Congress, DOE, and the laboratories. Such a consensus on the future missions for the national laboratories has not resulted from past advisory board recommendations.

DOE's ongoing contract reform efforts—especially the planned use of performance measures to guide and evaluate the laboratories' activities—could form a solid basis for an improved management approach that supports the laboratories' mission goals and administrative requirements. These goals will be difficult to achieve, however, given current management practices and the contracting constraints under which both DOE and the laboratories operate. For these and other reasons, experts are beginning to question where alternative forms of laboratory management should be considered.

As public debate on the future of the laboratories grows—for example, the Congress, in a previous session, proposed legislation setting specific missions for the laboratories—DOE's leaders cannot afford to delay efforts to define clear and coordinated missions and to implement a management approach that supports these missions.

Indeed, if the laboratories do not begin to function more as a system, it may be necessary to consider alternatives to the present DOE-laboratory relationship. Above all, strong DOE leadership is needed to establish a shared vision about the laboratories' expected contributions. DOE leadership is especially important to implementing the new commercial technology mission. There are encouraging signs that DOE is committed to involving industry in this implementation and improving its access to the laboratories.

Recommendations

We recommend that the Secretary of Energy evaluate alternatives for managing the laboratories that more fully support clear missions, achieve results by linking the laboratories' activities to DOE's missions, and maximize the laboratories' resources. Such a strategy could start by addressing the many management issues raised in this report and should be consistent with DOE's major efforts to reform contract management. The strategy must also support goals for DOE and the laboratories to comply with environment, safety, and health initiatives. To help achieve this goal, the Secretary should strengthen the Office of Laboratory Management by providing it with sufficient resources and authority to facilitate cooperation with the laboratories and resolution of management issues across all DOE program areas.

Matter for Congressional Consideration

If DOE is unable to refocus the laboratories' missions and develop a management approach consistent with these new missions, the Congress may wish to consider alternatives to the present DOE-laboratory relationship. Such alternatives might include placing the laboratories under the control of different agencies or creating a separate structure for the sole purpose of developing a consensus on the laboratories' missions.

Agency Comments and Our Evaluation

DOE officials believe that they are taking a number of actions that address our concern about DOE's leadership in providing mission focus for the national laboratories. Specifically, in its letter to GAO, and in discussions with us, DOE cited its new strategic planning process, which resulted in a Strategic Plan that, in turn, is supported by five separate plans covering each of the Department's core "business lines." DOE anticipates that this process, together with the upcoming report expected from the Secretary's Energy Advisory Board Task Force on Alternative Futures for the Laboratories, will provide the means through which the Department will exercise new leadership for its national laboratories.

GAO is encouraged by these initiatives. Coupled with the Department's contract reform efforts, they should, once fully in place, strengthen DOE's ability to improve its own management as well as provide a foundation for refocusing the laboratories' missions. The outcome of these efforts bears close monitoring by the Congress. Our optimism is tempered, however, by DOE's having reorganized before and having had planning efforts in the past. Furthermore, DOE has not used the recommendations of past advisory groups to refocus the laboratories or improve its management of them.

DOE expressed concern that our report would force "tight mission-driven parameters" for the laboratories, which would inhibit the laboratories' flexibility in conducting fundamental research. We are not suggesting that DOE narrow the laboratories' missions. Instead, we believe that DOE should clarify mission-focused research and development within its laboratories and coordinate these activities among them. The need to clarify and focus the laboratories' missions reflected a widespread consensus among the laboratory and DOE managers, as well as among the experts, with whom we spoke.

Appendix I

Profiles of DOE's National Laboratories

Dollars in millions

Laboratory/location	Actual budget (FY 1994)	Staff (FY 1994)	Program emphases	Contractor
Argonne/ Argonne, Illinois	$614	5,083	Basic energy sciences, nuclear engineering, environmental science and technology	University of Chicago
Brookhaven/ Upton, New York	$408	3,417	High-energy and nuclear physics, basic energy sciences	Associated Universities, Inc.
Idaho Engineering/ Idaho Falls, Idaho	$911	7,823	Reactors, environmental restoration, waste management	Lockheed Idaho Technologies Company
Lawrence Berkeley/ Berkeley, California	$282	3,129	Basic energy sciences, nuclear and high-energy physics, biological and environmental research	University of California
Lawrence Livermore/ Livermore, California	$965	7,321	Defense, energy, high-performance computing, lasers	University of California
Los Alamos/ Los Alamos, New Mexico	$1,075	7,024	Defense, applied research in nuclear deterrence and security	University of California
Oak Ridge/ Oak Ridge, Tennessee	$577	4,714	Basic energy sciences, conservation, renewable energy	Martin Marietta Energy Systems
Pacific Northwest/ Richland, Washington	$532	4,383	Environmental restoration, waste management, energy research	Battelle Memorial Institute
Sandia/ Albuquerque, New Mexico	$1,304	8,494	Defense, nuclear weapons and safety	Martin Marietta Corporation

Note The information for this appendix was supplied by DOE operations offices and the national laboratories.

Appendix II

Laboratory Programs We Reviewed

Laboratory	Programs submitted by laboratory
Argonne	•Integral Fast Reactor[a] •Operation and Research at the Tandem Linac Accelerator System •Electrochemical Dezincing of Scrap Galvanized Steel •Atmospheric Radiation Measurement[a] •Advanced Photon Source[a]
Brookhaven	•High-Energy Physics[a] •National Synchrotron Light Source[a] •Relativistic Heavy Ion Physics •Structural Biology[a] •High Flux Beam Reactor
Idaho National Engineering Laboratory	•Buried Waste Integrated Demonstration Program[a] •ICPP Spent Fuel and Waste Management Technology Development[a] •Power Reactors[a] •Biotechnology •Space Nuclear Power and Propulsion
Lawrence Berkeley	•Advanced Light Source[a] •Advanced Battery Consortium[a] •Solenoidal Tracker at RHIC •Human Genome Center •Center for Advanced Materials[a]
Lawrence Livermore	•Nuclear Weapons Research, Development, and Testing[a] •Nonproliferation, Arms Control, and International Security[a] •Fusion[a] •AVLIS •Environmental Technologies
Los Alamos	•Waste Treatment •Above Ground Experiments[a] •Human Genome Center[a] •High Temperature Superconductors •High Performance Computing and Communications[a]
Oak Ridge	•Basic Energy Sciences[a] •Conservation and Renewables[a] •Fusion[a] •Biology and Environmental Research •Advanced Neutron Source
Pacific Northwest	•Environmental Restoration and Waste Management[a] •National Security and Defense Technology[a] •Energy •Scientific Research[a] •Technology Transfer

(continued)

Laboratory	Programs submitted by laboratory
Sandia	•Complex 21 •Nonproliferation and Verification[a] •Microelectronics and Photonics Center[a] •Environmental Programs[a] •Combustion Research

[a]We discussed these programs with managers and staff. We selected these programs from those that each laboratory identified as best representing its future direction.

Appendix III

Comments From the Department of Energy

Note: GAO comments supplementing those in the report text appear at the end of this appendix.

Department of Energy
Washington, DC 20585

January 24, 1995

Mr. Victor Rezendes
Director, Energy and Sciences Issues
Resources, Community, and Economic
Development Division
U.S. General Accounting Office
Washington, D.C. 20585

Dear Mr. Rezendes:

See comment 1

Thank you for the opportunity to comment on your draft report entitled Department of Energy: Clear Missions and More Effective DOE Management Can Enhance the Value of the National Laboratories (GAO/RCED-95-10).

The primary finding of your report is that the Department of Energy has not delineated specific missions for its laboratories, and that a more precise allocation and integration of missions across the DOE laboratory system would enhance the contributions of these institutions. Your report correctly observes that previous reports on the DOE laboratories have contained similar conclusions, yet your draft fails to recognize the historic actions which the Department is undertaking to reduce costs, reform business practices, and redirect its resources--including the DOE laboratories--toward the major areas of national need within the DOE mission areas. These actions, described below, demonstrate the Clinton Administration's seriousness in reinventing government organizations and services.

One prior report on the DOE laboratories to which your draft refers, the July 1992 Secretary of Energy Advisory Board (SEAB) Report on the DOE National Laboratories, contained a fundamental truism:

> "A strategic vision of the future missions of the national laboratories cannot be developed until the Department and Nation have developed a similarly clear vision of their role in the future multipolar world."

The 1992 SEAB report recommended that the Department and the national laboratories do their part in addressing this problem by developing a strategic plan which would serve as a guide for decisions regarding the missions of both the Department and the laboratories.

During her first few months in office, Secretary O'Leary and senior departmental officials responded to this recommendation by initiating the development of a strategic plan for the Department. Through a lengthy and unprecedented process involving hundreds of DOE and laboratory employees, a strategic plan was developed which establishes priorities and a strategic vision for the Department in five areas: energy, environment, national security, science and technology, and industrial competitiveness.

Once the strategic plan was finalized, the Department had a tool which could be used to better focus Departmental resources, including the DOE laboratories. As the DOE strategic plan was being completed in early 1994, the Secretary established an independent task force–the Task Force on Alternative Futures for the Department of Energy National Laboratories, chaired by Robert Galvin, Chairman of the Motorola Executive Board–to provide recommendations on how best to align the DOE national laboratories with the energy, environmental, national security, scientific, and economic needs of the nation. The first meeting of the Task Force involved a briefing on the Department's strategic plan.

Over the past year, the Galvin Task Force has examined the capabilities of the DOE national laboratories in light of the DOE strategic plan. The Department appropriately has not instituted any drastic restructuring actions within the laboratory system, pending completion of the Galvin Task Force report. However, the Department in December 1994 announced its Strategic Alignment initiative as the means by which it would achieve alignment of the Department with the strategic plan and as one mechanism for implementing recommendations of the Galvin Task Force.

The Strategic Alignment project represents Phase-II of our strategic planning process, and is expected to result in the most dramatic changes in the way the Department conducts its business since the DOE was established in 1977. This intensive 120-day effort will culminate in recommendations on how to eliminate management inefficiencies, restructure the Department, and reduce the cost of DOE programs.

Throughout the past two years, the Department also has been working with Congress to adopt legislation that would clarify the missions for the DOE laboratories. In addition, we have pursued a major contract reform initiative which has been aimed, in part, at implementing performance-based contracts for the DOE's management and operations contractors. The contract reform initiative is expected to secure $2 billion in savings over a five year period.

We also have adopted a new institutional planning process for the laboratories which, for the first time, presents each laboratory's activities within the context of the five core business areas of the DOE strategic plan. More specifically, the defense-related R&D activities of the DOE weapons laboratories have been tightly linked with the specific requirements of our science-based stockpile stewardship program.

See comment 2

Your draft report is essentially silent on all of these initiatives, yet collectively they represent dramatic departures from the past and the basis for historic change in the future. In addition, we believe that your report's treatment of the question of laboratory missions misses some extremely important points.

The Department shares your observation that there is value to be gained from enhanced strategic focus at each of the DOE laboratories. However, we must note that it is important not to oversimplify this approach to laboratory management or to overestimate the potential benefits. For DOE's program-dedicated laboratories, the development of focussed missions is not an issue. For DOE's nine multi-program laboratories, however, the problem is far more complex. The distinctive value of these institutions stems to a significant degree from their multi-program, multi-disciplinary character. Forcing these labs to focus only within tight mission-driven parameters could sacrifice the unique versatility of these institutions to address large, complex problems in a way that more narrowly-focussed institutions cannot. Additionally, it is important to recognize the difficulty in trying to impose goal-oriented missions to areas of fundamental research--which is one of the major areas of DOE laboratory activity. In areas of fundamental science, new insights and discoveries cannot be predicted or scheduled according to a mission statement.

In summary, we believe that the Department of Energy has taken enormous strides in addressing problems--and symptoms of problems--identified in your report, and we feel that your report should have provided more direct attention to these actions.

Development of a new national consensus regarding the focus and management of the DOE national laboratories is a major challenge. Following the release of both your report and that of the Galvin Task Force, we hope to discuss further with you the inherent complexities in coordinating scientific and technical work over the very diverse set of R&D areas with which the Department and its laboratories operate.

Sincerely,

Joseph F. Vivona
Chief Financial Officer

The following are GAO's comments on the Department of Energy's letter dated January 24, 1995.

GAO's Comments

1. While we discussed most of these initiatives in the draft report, we updated the final report to reflect DOE's progress in these areas. We generally agree that DOE's initiatives, especially those in strategic planning and contract reform, will strengthen the Department's capacity to manage. We also agree that the initiatives have potential for helping DOE refocus the missions and improve the management of its laboratories. However, these initiatives have not yet been implemented. Furthermore, many of the contract reforms will take years to be fully implemented. Thus, the outcome of the initiatives, while promising, is very uncertain. We also caution that DOE has had planning systems in the past, has reorganized many times, and has tried to institute reforms in prior years—all without significant success. Additionally, as we discussed extensively in the report, prior advisory groups recommended that DOE refocus its laboratory missions and improve its management of them, yet DOE failed to take significant action.

2. We agree that one of the strengths of the multiprogram laboratories is their ability, as discussed in our report, to combine their multidisciplinary talents toward tackling large, complex problems. Our discussion of the need for more clarity in mission focus aims to facilitate, not hinder, more laboratory interactions in complex activities. We are not suggesting "forcing" the laboratories into "tight mission-driven parameters." Rather, we urge that DOE improve and expand its ability to integrate mission-focused research and development within and among its laboratories. The need for more mission clarity and focus reflected a widespread consensus among laboratory and DOE managers, as well as experts with whom we consulted.

Appendix IV

Major Contributors to This Report

Bernice Steinhardt, Associate Director
Gary R. Boss, Assistant Director
Allison Ingram, Assignment Manager
Libby Halperin, Evaluator-in-Charge
William J. Lanouette, Senior Evaluator
John Richter, Senior Evaluator
Leigh Nachowicz, Evaluator

Ordering Information

The first copy of each GAO report and testimony is free. Additional copies are $2 each. Orders should be sent to the following address, accompanied by a check or money order made out to the Superintendent of Documents, when necessary. Orders for 100 or more copies to be mailed to a single address are discounted 25 percent.

Orders by mail:

U.S. General Accounting Office
P.O. Box 6015
Gaithersburg, MD 20884-6015

or visit:

Room 1100
700 4th St. NW (corner of 4th and G Sts. NW)
U.S. General Accounting Office
Washington, DC

Orders may also be placed by calling (202) 512-6000
or by using fax number (301) 258-4066, or TDD (301) 413-0006.

Each day, GAO issues a list of newly available reports and testimony. To receive facsimile copies of the daily list or any list from the past 30 days, please call (301) 258-4097 using a touchtone phone. A recorded menu will provide information on how to obtain these lists.

PRINTED ON RECYCLED PAPER

Testimony of Donald Paul Hodel
Former Secretary of Energy
Before the
Subcommittee on
Government Management, Information, and Technology
May 23, 1995

Thank you for this opportunity to appear before this committee and discuss the future of the U.S. Department of Energy. In my opinion the Department of Energy should be terminated.

Please recognize that I have been away from the Department for more than a decade. Therefore, many details have changed, and as to those I am not commenting. Certainly, however, others have not, and it is to those I will direct my attention.

First, the very existence of a Department of "Energy" is undesirable. It suggests that the U.S. government is doing or is going to do something about energy beyond what it is capable of doing and beyond what I believe government should do. In many countries the government owns, operates or controls national energy companies: oil, gas, electric. In my experience when those countries deal with the U.S. government they assume that the U.S. government does the same, in part because of the existence of a "Department of Energy."

One of the frequent requests from OPEC countries during my tenure as Secretary of Energy was to hold a "producer-consumer" dialogue, that is, bring together consuming nations such as the U.S., European countries, Japan, etc., and producing nations, such as members of OPEC. The purpose was to "stabilize" world oil prices (by which was meant "reach an agreement on fixing world oil prices"). The U.S. resisted for a number of reasons, but an important one was that, even if we had held such a meeting and even if we had agreed that some fixed price level was appropriate, the Secretary of Energy had (and has) no authority to fix energy prices in the U.S. Further, the Secretary should not have such authority. DOE has no authority to order increases or decreases in price or production, and it should not. Yet, other energy ministers seemed not to understand that fact and continued to seek such a meeting.

On another occasion a major contract for the purchase of LNG from Algeria for delivery to the U.S. was abrogated unilaterally by the U.S. company after a sharp decline in natural gas prices. The Energy Minister from Algeria telephoned me and insisted that I order the U.S. company to honor the contract. I tried to persuade him that I had no such authority, but when the conversation finally ended I was convinced that he simply did not believe that the U.S. Secretary of Energy could not direct the company to perform.

Both of these anecdotes illustrate the importance of not sending the wrong signal to foreign countries about the role of the Department.

Finally, so long as there is a DOE there is temptation on the part of the Congress, the Administration and the American people to assume that DOE has the ability and the authority to solve any energy problems that arise—a false and misleading assumption which can lead to inappropriate and unproductive actions, as the history of energy price fixing and allocation clearly shows. That history emphasizes that the one thing Congress and the Administration must resist in the event of an "energy crisis" is imposing price controls and allocation of energy supplies.

Second, DOE has little beneficial impact on energy in the U.S. It is, unfortunately, and "energy" department without an energy mission. The closest it comes is in conducting or funding research. However none of those research projects requires a separate, cabinet-level department to administer the funding.

Third, as for the biennial publication of an Energy Policy, it is nearly meaningless in that DOE has no authority to implement it, and no other cabinet department pays any attention to it except when the policy can be quoted in support of something that department otherwise wants to do. I can recall no occasion where anyone in the energy industry has paid any attention to the national energy policy statement from DOE except to criticize it.

This function, if it were to be continued, could easily be housed in the Department of the Interior. From any practical standpoint, the Department of the Interior has much more to say about energy production issues than DOE because of its leasing responsibilities for the federal lands, its Minerals Management Service royalty collection, the Bureau of Mines, OSM, USGS, etc. The Department of the Interior has in recent years become a major obstacle to U.S. domestic energy production regardless of what DOE may publish as an Energy Policy. The statement of energy policy might as well come from DOI. It could even be beneficial, if DOI would take seriously the language in the policy which states that the U.S. government ought to assist in making federal energy resources available for domestic production—the one area where an energy policy ought to be applicable.

Fourth, if it were my decision, I would terminate or disperse the remaining elements of the DOE among other departments, probably as follows:

The Federal Energy Regulatory Commission, although organizationally housed by statute within DOE, is and ought to be an independent agency as was its predecessor, the Federal Power Commission.

The Defense portion of DOE has, unfortunately, become largely an environmental clean-up division. There is no benefit to having two agencies pursuing very similar programs.

One possibility which would probably be followed if this were not a governmental situation is that a separate division (entity) would be established to be responsible for clean-up. However, because this is government it is probably better that the clean-up budget be required to compete for money with the line activities of the agencies.

An alternative approach would be for clean-up for both DOD and the defense portion of DOE to be done as part of the DOD so that all defense clean-up projects are within one department and the priorities are consistently applied, rather than having two departments competing for funds and, very likely, misallocating those funds. There should be administrative savings in a consolidation. As a part of this process the clean-up standards must be revised. The present system is concerned not with health and safety but with environmental purity which can be achieved only at a horrendous cost—a cost so high that it is, in fact, not reasonably achievable. Real safety can be achieved much sooner at a much lower cost by allowing containment and stabilization of wastes until further experience, research, and technological successes provide better clean-up options. U.S. government research on clean-up should be restricted to hazardous waste streams unique to the government. The private sector has incentives to research clean-up on others.

If the day ever comes when weapons production recommences, that activity could continue in DOD. The "civilian control" issue could be dealt with by appropriate procedures at that time since it is more form than reality, even now. Certainly, although there was nominal civilian control of the process with weapons production housed in DOE, practically speaking, the military significantly controlled the nuclear weapons decision process. It should be remembered in discussions of civilian "control" of nuclear weapon production that it is only the production which is under nominal civilian control. Once the weapons are made and operational they are turned over to the military.

The Strategic Petroleum Reserve is a tempting target for those seeking revenues. I have been told that the facilities need upgrading before they could deliver the specified level of output, and there may be some technical problems with which I am not adequately familiar. I believe, however, that, properly utilized, the SPR can still be important and useful. Unfortunately, the chances of proper utilization are slim. When I was Secretary of Energy, we went through elaborate analyses of how SPR should be used. The only sound basis is to offer for sale on a bid basis a number of barrels per day equal to the anticipated shortfall *to the United States* from an interruption of supply. I dealt with this in much greater detail in my book, *Crisis in the Oil Patch.* I believe that the analysis is sound. However, unless sound bases for SPR's use can be codified in some binding way, SPR constitutes an enormous opportunity for mismanagement and governmental interference in the domestic market and might be better sold to the highest bidders (phased over time so as to minimize adverse market consequences).

The Power Marketing Administrations are attractive targets for privatization. From 1972 to 1978 I served as Administrator of the Bonneville Power Administration. During that time I often considered this question. I concluded that the balance of power among the constituencies of BPA (and, I suspected, among those of the other PMAs) was such that there was no practical way to accomplish a "spin-off." Public power fears that the investor-owned utilities would control BPA and they would lose their preference power. Investor-owned utilities fear that the public power systems would control BPA and use it as an economic weapon against them. Each will support the status quo before it will risk a change which might work to its disadvantage. I explored this question when I was Secretary of Energy and concluded that the politics simply made it infeasible to try at that time

It was clear to me then, and it is still clear to me that DOE is not necessary or even very helpful to the PMAs. They have been housed administratively for almost 18 years in DOE. It is hard to identify any particular benefits from that relationship. There are thousands of public and private electric utilities in the U.S. which get along just fine without help from the Secretary of Energy.

I am encouraged that the present atmosphere within the administration and Congress is such that the opportunity is much greater. If the administration and Congress followed the example of the U.K. in the privatization of its electric sector and simply mandated that by a given date it must happen and that the government would accept the highest and best bid(s) for these agencies. The industry would find a way to accomplish the objective. It would be extremely helpful in that case for an anti-trust exemption to be provided so that public and private utilities could join together for a combined bid for regional portions of particular PMAs. I do not believe that the DOE or the administration can significantly aid this process because by their very nature they are subject to multiple political pressures. I understand there is a proposal to establish an independent quasi-federal entity called The Forrestal Corporation to facilitate the use of private sources of energy on military bases. This corporation would, also, act as a broker for the federal government in the sale of existing military power facilities. Perhaps, this concept or even this corporation could be charged with the responsibility for obtaining the substantial benefits of divesting the PMAs.

The time has clearly come where PMA transmission can and should be separated from generation and privatized in line with the FERC and Congressional action (in the Energy Policy Act of 1992) of encouraging regional transmission groups in order to facilitate competition and efficient use of resources. Conceptually, generation could be similarly privatized.

Even if privatization is not feasible for federal generation, however, the PMAs, particularly BPA, ought to be relieved of the enormously expensive "social engineering" and environmental subsidies which they are required to provide and, in return, they ought to be required to charge rates sufficient to operate and maintain their systems and repay their federal debt on schedule. This would have a beneficial effect upon the federal budget, and it would require that those hidden subsidies to non-power purposes would have to compete in the federal budget against other worthwhile and useful projects.

The National Laboratories are a great national resource. The best that can be said for DOE, however, is that even after 18 years it has no peculiar expertise or role in managing them, and the labs do more than energy research, as well they should. The justification for the national labs, begun for military purposes, is shifting radically to the commercial side as they try to find a mission and a source of funds. This is a partial or de facto privatization which should be encouraged. The primarily defense-related labs should be shifted to DOD. The others could be privatized by sale or transfer to non-federal entities, such as universities, foundations, or the like. Government research needs could be accomplished through research contracts with these and other research laboratories.

Research and development grants ought to be restricted in some similar fashion. Any scientific entity, such as NSF, could handle grant programs. Research budgets of DOE have been highly politicized in the past so that projects could not be judged on the merits but rather were kept alive by key Senators or Congressmen as a means of aiding the local economy in some state or congressional district. Note, particularly, in this regard, magnetohydrodynamics and the clean coal technology program. Research and development expenditures require continuity. Changes of Administrations, Cabinet Secretaries, Assistant Secretaries and so on, disrupt that continuity and cause wasteful expenditures.

The government is ill-suited to develop anything entrepreneurial. When the U.S. government needed supercomputers, it developed the specifications for what it needed and then offered to buy *from the private sector* computers which met those specs. As a result the U.S. took the lead in supercomputers. This is not unlike the time 100 years ago when America wanted railroads to cross America. Instead of the government trying to build them (in which case they would still be under construction and significantly over budget), incentives were created for private capital to do so. It worked.

EIA, should be abolished. Any of its services with value to the economy could and would be done by the private sector, as they were before, if the government stopped doing them for "free." Any which would not be done by the private sector are probably not of value.

ERA should be abolished forthwith. I understand that some of the entitlement cases are still unresolved after 15 years! If that is true, it is outrageous and wasteful. It ought to be an embarrassment to anyone still connected with the process. If there are any matters of merit remaining after all these years of paying lawyers to pursue them, they should be transferred to the Department of Justice for final disposition.

Policy, International Affairs, and Emergency Response are activities which, as I have tried to show in my earlier discussion, do not serve an essential function which would require the retention of a Department of Energy to fulfill.

I suspect there are other parts of DOE which I have not covered, but none that could not be dealt with in similar fashion. The elimination of some of its functions and dispersal of others to other departments and the termination of the Department of Energy would send the right signal to our citizens and the world.

I wish you every success in your efforts to reduce the size and improve the operations of the U.S. government.

-o-

COMMITTEE ON GOVERNMENT REFORM AND OVERSIGHT
SUBCOMMITTEE ON GOVERNMENT MANAGEMENT,
INFORMATION AND TECHNOLOGY

PREPARED STATEMENT

JOHN S. HERRINGTON

Date Submitted
May 23, 1995

COMMITTEE ON GOVERNMENT REFORM AND OVERSIGHT
SUBCOMMITTEE ON GOVERNMENT MANAGEMENT,
INFORMATION AND TECHNOLOGY
STATEMENT OF JOHN S. HERRINGTON

MR. CHAIRMAN, IT IS A PRIVILEGE TO APPEAR BEFORE THIS COMMITTEE AND SUBMIT MY COMMENTS ON THE PROPOSAL TO ELIMINATE THE DEPARTMENT OF ENERGY.

IN 1979 AND 1980, RONALD REAGAN CAMPAIGNED ON THE UNIQUE IDEA THAT THE DEPARTMENTS OF EDUCATION AND ENERGY SHOULD BE CLOSED. AT THAT TIME, IT WAS UNHEARD OF FOR A PRESIDENT OF THE UNITED STATES TO PROPOSE THE ELIMINATION OF WHOLE DEPARTMENTS OF THE FEDERAL GOVERNMENT. DURING HIS ADMINISTRATION, MANY ATTEMPTS AT CARRYING OUT THIS PROMISE WERE MADE AND WERE FRUSTRATED AGAIN AND AGAIN BY THE DEMOCRATIC LEADERSHIP IN CONGRESS. ONCE AGAIN RONALD REAGAN WAS AHEAD OF HIS TIME, FOR HERE WE ARE FIFTEEN YEARS LATER FINALLY GIVING SERIOUS STUDY TO THIS PROPOSITION. BEFORE I BEGIN MY REMARKS, I WOULD LIKE TO SAY THAT DURING THE TIME I WAS SECRETARY OF THE DEPARTMENT OF ENERGY, I HAD THE GOOD FORTUNE TO WORK WITH SOME OF THE FINEST MEN AND WOMEN IN WASHINGTON AND IN GOVERNMENT. THEY WENT THROUGH THE OIL SHOCKS OF THE 1970'S. THEY EXECUTED THE REAGAN ERA BUILD-UP. THEY ENDURED THE BUSH ADMINISTRATION WITCH HUNTS FOR ENVIRONMENTAL LAW BREAKERS, AND THEY ARE SURVIVING THE POLITICAL CORRECTNESS OF THE CLINTON ADMINISTRATION. THEY ARE TRUE PUBLIC SERVANTS WHO

ALWAYS TRIED TO DO WHAT CONGRESS AND THE EXECUTIVE BRANCH WANTED THEM TO. THE COUNTRY OWES THEM A DEBT OF GRATITUDE. I STILL COUNT MANY OF THEM AMONG MY FRIENDS. MY COMMENTS TODAY ARE AIMED NOT AT THEM, BUT AT THE DEPARTMENT AND ITS MISSION, AND HOW WE MIGHT TOGETHER ACHIEVE MORE EFFECTIVE GOVERNMENT AT LESS COST TO THE TAXPAYERS.

THE DEPARTMENT OF ENERGY IS THE ONLY DEPARTMENT OF THE FEDERAL GOVERNMENT THAT CAN BE DESCRIBED AS RESEMBLING A LARGE INDUSTRIAL COMPLEX; IT ENRICHES URANIUM, BUILDS SUBMARINES, SPY SATELLITES, ELECTRIC CARS, ATOMIC REACTORS, WARHEADS FOR NUCLEAR BOMBS, AND HANDS OUT MONEY TO THE POOR TO HELP THEM MAKE THEIR HOMES MORE ENERGY EFFICIENT; IT BUYS AND SELLS OIL, RUNS THE LARGEST LABORATORY COMPLEX IN THE WORLD, GATHERS INFORMATION AND ENGAGES IN HUNDREDS MORE ACTIVITIES.

PRESIDENT CARTER ESTABLISHED THE DEPARTMENT BY BRINGING TOGETHER MANY URGENT PROGRAMS OF THE FEDERAL GOVERNMENT. HE TOLD THE AMERICAN PEOPLE IN A FAMOUS SPEECH THAT THIS WAS "THE MORAL EQUIVALENT OF WAR" WITH THE NOBLE GOAL OF MAKING AMERICA ENERGY INDEPENDENT. THEREAFTER, BILLIONS AND BILLIONS OF TAXPAYER DOLLARS WERE SPENT BY THE DEPARTMENT OF ENERGY IN THE NAME OF ENERGY INDEPENDENCE. MOST OF THE TIME, THE RESULTS HAVE BEEN MIXED AT BEST. BY FAR THE LARGEST EXAMPLE OF THIS WAS THE SIXTY-SIX BILLION DOLLAR SYNTHETIC FUELS CORPORATION. IN THAT

PROGRAM, THE GREATEST FAILURE WAS THE GREAT PLAINS COAL GASIFICATION PLANT. BUILT BY THE GOVERNMENT AT A COST OF TWO BILLION DOLLARS FOR THE PURPOSE OF TURNING LIGNITE COAL INTO NATURAL GAS, THE FACILITY OPERATED BEAUTIFULLY AND WAS AN ENGINEERING MARVEL. THE PROBLEM WAS THAT THE GAS HAD TO BE SOLD AT OVER $6.00 PER M.C.F. TO BE PROFITABLE. THE MARKET AT THAT TIME WAS UNDER $1.50. TYPICAL OF GOVERNMENT, THE PROPOSED SOLUTION WAS FEDERAL PRICE SUPPORTS FOR THE GAS TO KEEP THE PLANT RUNNING. THIS RESULTED IN THE LARGEST FORECLOSURE ON THE COURTHOUSE STEPS IN THE HISTORY OF THE FEDERAL GOVERNMENT.

THERE WERE MANY, MANY OTHER EXAMPLES OF THE SAME KIND. DOE BUILT WIND MACHINES, EXPERIMENTED WITH WAVE AND SUN POWER, DEVELOPED BATTERIES AND FUELS, AND GAVE GRANTS TO ALMOST ANYONE WITH A NEW IDEA, OR AN OLD ONE FOR THAT MATTER. NOT SURPRISINGLY, DOE WAS SOON CONSTRUCTING HIGHWAYS IN SPECIFIC STATES AND BUILDINGS AT FAVORED UNIVERSITIES. PROJECTS THAT FAILED AND WERE LOCATED IN APPROPRIATE CONGRESSIONAL DISTRICTS, CONTINUED TO RECEIVE LONG-TERM FUNDING. FOR EXAMPLE, A CLEAN COAL TECHNOLOGY CALLED MHD WAS RANKED AT THE BOTTOM OF THE LIST BY ALMOST EVERY EXPERT IN THE COUNTRY, BUT IT CONTINUED TO BE FUNDED AT THE RATE OF TWENTY OR THIRTY MILLION A YEAR FOR YEARS AFTER THIS INFORMATION WAS KNOWN. IT WAS A DISGUISED SUBSIDY FOR A SMALL UTILITY IN THE NORTHWEST.

WHILE THE DEPARTMENT OF ENERGY HAS UNDER ITS JURISDICTION MANY VITAL AND NECESSARY ACTIVITIES OF THE FEDERAL GOVERNMENT, IT IS PERFECTLY POSITIONED FOR DOWNSIZING, STREAMLINING, OR TOTAL ELIMINATION IN THIS ERA OF SMALLER, MORE EFFICIENT GOVERNMENT. I WOULD LIKE TO GIVE YOU SOME EXAMPLES:

URANIUM ENRICHMENT: THE FORMATION OF THE U.S. ENRICHMENT CORPORATION WAS UNDER DISCUSSION IN 1980, AND HAS BEEN EVER SINCE. THE DOE HAS EXPERIMENTED WITH THREE TYPES OF ENRICHMENT TECHNOLOGIES AND HAS SPENT HUNDREDS OF MILLIONS OF DOLLARS ON DEVELOPMENT. THE GAS CENTRIFUGE ALONE COST BILLIONS AND NEVER WAS OPERATIONAL. WHERE THE FEDERAL GOVERNMENT AND CONGRESS ARE CONCERNED, THE CONCEPTS OF CAPITAL INVESTMENT, COST OF PRODUCTION AND PRICE ARE USUALLY UNRELATED. ANY MOVEMENT TOWARD PRIVATIZATION WOULD BENEFIT TAX PAYERS. THIS ACTIVITY IS A BUSINESS AND NEEDS TO OPERATE LIKE ONE.

NAVAL PETROLEUM RESERVES (NPR): ESTABLISHED NEAR THE FIRST WORLD WAR WITH AN IDEA THAT OIL FIRED NAVY SHIPS NEEDED A RESERVE OF CRUDE OIL, IT HAS SERVED THE COUNTRY WELL, BUT IT IS NO LONGER NECESSARY AND THE ACTIVITY NEEDS TO END. THE NPR, AND ASSETS LIKE IT, SHOULD BE SOLD.

POWER MARKETING AGENCIES: BORN IN THE 1930'S WITH THE HELP OF 2% LOANS FROM THE FEDERAL GOVERNMENT, POWER MARKETING AGENCIES HAVE SERVED THE COUNTRY WELL, BUT THEY HAVE ALSO

BECOME VICTIMS OF POLITICS. IT IS NO ACCIDENT THAT DURING THE 1980'S WE SAW UTILITY BILLS IN CERTAIN COUNTIES OF WASHINGTON STATE COSTING $34, WHILE THE SAME BILL IN TEXAS OR NEW YORK WOULD COST $234. THESE AGENCIES SHOULD BE PRIVATIZED, OR SOLD TO UTILITIES. THEY ARE DISTORTING THE MARKET. ALTHOUGH IT IS NOT A PART OF THE DEPARTMENT OF ENERGY, THERE ARE SIMILAR PROBLEMS WITH THE TENNESSEE VALLEY AUTHORITY WHICH NEED TO BE ADDRESSED.

I WOULD LIKE TO SAY A FEW THINGS ABOUT DEFENSE PROGRAMS AND THE NATIONAL LABORATORIES. DEFENSE PROGRAMS AMOUNT TO TWO-THIRDS OF THE DEPARTMENTAL BUDGET, A FACT THAT FEW AMERICANS KNOW. THESE PROGRAMS FIND THEIR ROOTS IN THE ATOMIC ENERGY COMMISSION, AND THE OLD "ATOMS FOR PEACE" PROJECT OF 1952. THEY HAVE SERVED US WELL AND THE SCIENTISTS WHO PARTICIPATED INCLUDE SOME OF THE GREATEST NAMES IN AMERICAN SCIENTIFIC HISTORY. AS WE MOVE INTO THE 21ST CENTURY, NUCLEAR PROLIFERATION WILL BE ONE OF THE PRINCIPAL THREATS TO THE SECURITY OF OUR PEOPLE AND THE WORLD. WE SEE THE BEGINNING OF IT TODAY. THE COUNTRY REQUIRES A STRONG, VIABLE PROGRAM FOR DEVELOPMENT OF WEAPONS AND WEAPONS DEFENSE. THE PROGRAM INCLUDES TESTING, VERIFICATION AND EXPERIMENTATION. IT IS AMAZING TO ME THAT AT A TIME WHEN WE ARE HAVING A NATIONAL DEBATE ON GUN CONTROL AND THE RIGHT OF CITIZENS TO BEAR ARMS, IN MANY WAYS A HEALTHY DEBATE, WE ARE AT THE SAME TIME UNILATERALLY SHUTTING DOWN THE NUCLEAR WEAPONS PROGRAM

AND DISARMING THE COUNTRY WITHOUT A DEBATE ON THIS IMPORTANT ISSUE. WE HAVE SERVED AS THE WORLD'S POLICEMAN, AND WE ARE IN THE PROCESS OF DISARMING OUR POLICE FORCE AT A CRITICAL TIME, WITHOUT EVEN A MENTION OR A DISCUSSION. THE CURRENT ADMINISTRATION, AND ESPECIALLY OFFICIALS AT THE ENERGY DEPARTMENT, ARE RELICS FROM THE N.R.D.C, AND HAVE LITTLE INTEREST IN KEEPING THE WEAPONS PROGRAM HEALTHY. THEY DON'T BELIEVE IN IT. THE CENTER FOR SECURITY POLICY RECENTLY PUBLISHED A DECISION BRIEF CITING THE RADICAL DENUCLEARIZATION AGENDA OF DAN REICHER, SECRETARY O'LEARY'S DEPUTY CHIEF OF STAFF AND OTHER AVOWED ANTI-NUCLEAR ACTIVISTS AMONG THE DEPARTMENT'S SENIOR MANAGEMENT. THE DEFENSE PROGRAM'S FUNCTION OF THE ENERGY DEPARTMENT COULD AND SHOULD BE TRANSFERRED TO THE DEPARTMENT OF DEFENSE

AS TO ENVIRONMENTAL CLEANUP, THE GAO HAS NOTED THAT "DOE HAS RECEIVED ABOUT $23 BILLION FOR ENVIRONMENTAL MANAGEMENT SINCE 1889 . . . AND LITTLE CLEANUP HAS RESULTED." THIS PROGRAM HAS BEEN BADLY MISMANAGED. IT TOO COULD BE EASILY TRANSFERRED TO THE DEPARTMENT OF DEFENSE.

FINALLY, THE NATIONAL LABORATORIES ARE SCRAMBLING TO FIND WORK BECAUSE THEY HAVE BEEN TAKEN OUT OF THE WEAPONS BUSINESS. THEY WANT SOMETHING TO DO SO THEY WON'T LOSE FUNDING. IN MY HOME STATE, THE UNIVERSITY OF CALIFORNIA, MANAGERS OF LIVERMORE AND LOS ALAMOS, HAVE, FOR YEARS, BEEN TRYING TO GET OUT OF THE

WEAPONS BUSINESS. THE CLINTON ADMINISTRATION IS PLAYING RIGHT INTO THEIR HANDS. IF THERE HAS IN FACT BEEN A NATIONAL DECISION TO TAKE THE LABORATORIES OUT OF THE WEAPONS BUSINESS, AND I DO NOT THINK THERE HAS BEEN, THEN THE SOLUTION SHOULD BE TO PRIVATIZE THE LABORATORIES. IN THIS WAY THEY WILL BECOME MORE EFFICIENT, AND ONE OF THE TRADITIONAL SHORTCOMINGS OF THE EXISTING SYSTEM, TECHNOLOGY TRANSFER, WILL BE IMPROVED.

I THANK YOU FOR THE OPPORTUNITY TO TESTIFY AND WILL BE PLEASED TO ANSWER ANY QUESTIONS.

Mr. SCHIFF. Thank you, Congressman Tiahrt, and I join you in hoping we can reach an accord after hearings and further consideration.

Again, let me say any Member's opening statement will be made, by unanimous consent, a part of this report. But I will recognize any Member who seeks recognition at this time for an opening statement who has not been recognized.

I don't see any requests.

I have just two other administrative matters—I beg your pardon. Congressman Doyle, please.

Mr. DOYLE. Thank you, Mr. Chairman.

[The prepared statement of Mr. Doyle follows:]

OPENING STATEMENT OF HON. MICHAEL F. DOYLE, A REPRESENTATIVE IN CONGRESS FROM THE STATE OF PENNSYLVANIA

Mr. Chairman, I welcome the opportunity to participate in today's hearing. One of my greatest concerns as to how we are approaching the challenge of deficit reduction is the apparent willingness of some members of the majority to neglect our intellectual resources. This hearing is valuable because our approach to reforming the National Labs is a telling reflection of our attitudes towards how our nation should approach the 21st Century.

Do we opt for political expediency and relinquish our responsibility as elected officials? The people of Pittsburgh elected me to make difficult decisions, not to engage in a political shell game of taking credit for cutting spending, but not taking responsibility for prioritizing. If we were to adopt the approach embodied in H.R. 87 and in H.R. 1993, it would be an admission that this Committee does not possess the expertise to oversee the programs in our jurisdiction.

I disagree with this attitude. In assessing our National Labs, we are talking about roughly 20 facilities, depending on the parameters set for where we are seeking to reform. This is a far less imposing task than we faced in the BRAC process, which was dealing with hundreds of facilities and military groupings.

I go into this hearing with the belief that Mr. Roemer's bill, H.R. 1510, is the best alternative before us. By requiring a reduction in civilian lab employees, we are putting real pressure on DOE to streamline its operations. Also, this bill takes long overdue action to remove DOE's unique allowance for self-regulation.

I believe that it is possible for DOE to act decisively, especially when Congress is clear in its support of such action. This has been the case in the consolidation that is taking place in DOE's fossil energy program. Three facilities are being consolidated into two, and three separate management structures are being merged into one. I think there is much the Committee can learn from this example as we examine how to achieve more efficient National Labs.

Finally, I want to express my concern about the fate of the Naval Nuclear Propulsion Program. This program has been extremely successful, due in large part to its unique autonomy from the Department of Defense command structure. The two labs that are responsible for this program, Bettis and Knolls, should not be considered in the same light as the civilian labs. The Committee has endorsed this view by unanimously accepting my amendment to the text of H.R. 1510, when it was offered as an amendment to H.R. 1816, the DOE Civilian R&D Authorization Act. My amendment clarified the definition of what constitutes a National Lab to conform with the language of the Stevenson-Wydler Act.

I am grateful for these hearings, especially since we have actual legislation to review and are not just relying on a conceptual discussion before marking-up legislation. I hope that this precedent holds true for the remainder of the 104th Congress.

Mr. DOYLE. I just want to also submit for the record a statement by the distinguished Chairman of the Rules Committee, Mr. Solomon, on the restructuring of the DOE laboratories for the record.

Mr. SCHIFF. Without objection, it will be made part of the record. Thank you for offering it.

[The prepared statement of Mr. Solomon follows:]

CONGRESSMAN GERALD B. SOLOMON STATEMENT FOR SCIENCE COMMITTEE HEARINGS ON RESTRUCTURING D.O.E. LABORATORIES

I am pleased to have the opportunity to address this committee concerning the missions and regulation of the various Department of Energy laboratories. There is definitely a need to evaluate the goals and structure of the Department of Energy and its facilities. To that end, I wholeheartedly support your efforts to contribute to this review process. In my opinion, there are a great deal of suspect programs which place an unnecessary burden on the American taxpayer and contributes to the overwhelming mountain of debt which is suffocating the future of our nation. Such duplicative and trivial programs deserve to be restructured or eliminated.

However, I want to take this opportunity to highlight what I believe to be a positive example within the Department of Energy, a program with a proven track record. The program I am referring to is the Naval Nuclear Propulsion Program which deserves our favorable consideration. Having one of the Program's key facilities in my district, the Knolls Atomic Power Laboratory, I have witnessed first-hand the extraordinary accomplishments of this Program and have come to appreciate its unique organization as being critical to its impressive record.

The Naval Nuclear Propulsion Program, a dual agency arrangement of the Navy and Department of Energy, has demonstrated over its history the ability to efficiently integrate technological innovations with practical applications. The Program has made substantial contributions to the scientific community due to the relevance of its work to both civilian and military applications. Besides nuclear propulsion plants for the Navy's ships, almost half of which are now nuclear powered, the Program developed the first commercial nuclear power station, demonstrating their ongoing contribution to the commercial power industry. Even more importantly, with the future of commercial nuclear power generation up in the air, the Naval Nuclear Propulsion Program is the only organization reducing new nuclear power generating ideas to practice. The Program has done so while demonstrating technological excellence, an unequaled four decade safety record, and unfailing fiscal responsibility. Today, the Program is responsible for the cyperation of over 130 nuclear reactors and is developing new ones for the Navy.

The Naval Nuclear Propulsion Program exercises the authority provided the Department of Energy by the Atomic Energy Act to regulate nuclear propulsion activities of the Navy and the DOE. The Program's dual agency arrangement allows an arms length relationship with the Navy and Defense Department—at both an engineering and operating level—which is crucial to ensuring reactor safety. This arrangement, coupled with having facilities working solely for the Program, also has proven to be crucial when assuring the public and host countries of the safety of nuclear powered ships operating worldwide. In addressing concerns about oversight and regulation of the DOE, Congress repeatedly has recognized the Program as an exceptionally responsible regulator—we do not need to alter this regulatory arrangement. Moreover, the research and engineering accomplishments of the Program, principally achieved under its DOE "hat," and the operational record of the Navy's nuclear powered warships are a testament to the logic which led to establishing the unique joint agency Naval nuclear propulsion program.

With regard to the future relevance of the Department of Energy's programs and facilities, the Naval Nuclear Propulsion Program's significance remains clear—to continue the safe application of nuclear power for the propulsion of our current and future Naval warships. The Navy's dependence on nuclear propulsion affirms the need for this crucial program—over 40% of major combatants are nuclear powered, including all our strategic deterrent and attack submarines and the majority of our aircraft carriers. Moreover, the Program continues to carry out its mission while dealing with today's financial crisis by taking significant strides to further increase efficiency without compromising safety or performance. Unlike the general purpose nature of most Department of Energy laboratories, the Program's two laboratories, the Knolls and Bettis Atomic Power Laboratories, exist for a single purpose, to do nuclear propulsion work. They are an integral part of the Program under the organizational arrangement noted above, and have been highly successful with each making unique, important contributions. Given the crucial mission of the Naval Nuclear Propulsion Program, these dedicated facilities will remain essential.

Consequently, I believe we must provide for continuance of the Knolls and Bettis Atomic Power Laboratories under their current organizational and regulatory relationship within the Naval Nuclear Propulsion Program. Moreover, with their clearly defined and continuing mission, a review of these facilities would certainly prove counter-productive. Their structure and performance provides a standard for what can be accomplished given a consistent, focused mission and strong, effective leadership.

Mr. SCHIFF. Two more administrative matters. Thank you for bearing with us, Mr. Deputy Secretary.

The first is, down the hall, in Room 2325, there is an exhibit of various projects that are winners of the most recent prestigious R&D awards for research and development.

As you are probably familiar with, these are peer review awarded awards. They actually come through the private sector. The exhibit is of winners of those awards of research that were conducted at the national laboratories.

And I want to add, to the best of my knowledge, all of them, but certainly most of them, were joint research projects between the national laboratories and private enterprise, which I consider another important issue that we should consider with the mission of the national laboratories.

And you are all invited between now and 3:00 to visit and look at the exhibits. I think you'll find them most interesting and informative.

Unfortunately, because of votes, I'm sure there will be breaks in the testimony for you to have that opportunity.

Finally, I just want to say for anyone who has not attended a congressional hearing before, our comings and goings may be a little bit disconcerting to you if you haven't seen it before. Some Members will be here during some portion of the testimony, others will come during other portions, and still other Members are tied up elsewhere. But they have staff here in the room who are watching us and making notes.

The most important person probably at any congressional hearing is the gentleman quietly seated at the side of the front table, who is making the record of everything said here today. That record will be made available to every Member of Congress in due course so that they'll have this information as we consider legislation.

With that stated, I would like to personally welcome our first witness, the Deputy Secretary of Energy, the Honorable Charles Curtis.

Thank you for being with us today. You know the subject matter of the hearing today, so I invite you to proceed. Without objection, your formal written statement and all formal written statements of witnesses will be made a part of the record.

Secretary Curtis?

STATEMENT OF THE HONORABLE CHARLES B. CURTIS, ACTING DEPUTY SECRETARY, THE DEPARTMENT OF ENERGY

Secretary CURTIS. Thank you, Mr. Chairman. It's a pleasure to be here today to discuss the Department of Energy's national laboratories.

Let me first assure you that the department agrees that reducing federal spending and lowering the deficit is one of the most important issues facing this nation and it is essential for this nation's future economic health.

Those of us involved in the process in the Congress and the Executive Branch have a common duty to deliver on this responsibility to future generations.

The federal government's research and development expenditures, like every other part of the budget, will be, and should be, subject to severe scrutiny.

We need to dispel the almost mystical faith in constant expansion in research and development expenditure discussed in earlier proceedings in this room. But we also need to acknowledge that public investment in research and development is our nation's investment in its own future.

To borrow the words of our Task Force on Strategic Energy Research and Development: Just as our duty for fiscal discipline is rooted in our obligation to future generations, so too is our responsibility to assure for future generations that our nation's capacity to shape the future through scientific research and technological innovation is continually renewed. It is our most important renewable resource investment.

Striking the right balance between these mutual obligations to future generations will require our collective best judgment and wisdom or, as Chairman Walker more succinctly observed, it is extremely important we do the right thing here.

As one ponders the futures of these laboratories, it is also important to be mindful of their record of scientific excellence. In the past year alone, we identified the Top Quark that had alluded physicists for nearly 20 years. We've identified genes responsible for breast and colon cancer. We've developed a bendable, high-temperature, super-conducting wire that eventually could save American consumers billions of dollars in reduced electricity transmission losses.

And once again, one of our former colleagues, Cliff Shull, a former employee at Oak Ridge National Laboratory, received a Nobel Prize for his work in neutron-scattering physics.

Over the years, more than 60 Nobel Prize winners have been associated with the Department of Energy and its laboratories.

It is natural that some of this science should result in technology. And in fact, the department and its laboratories regularly receive the lion's share of the awards given annually by independent panels sponsored by the R&D Magazine.

The R&D 100 awards are given to the 100 most significant technological developments of the year. I am proud, the department is proud, that in 1995, DOE and its laboratories will be presented 32 of these 100 awards at a ceremony in Chicago later this month.

Among federal agencies, NASA achieved the second highest number—six, six compared to 32.

DOE has received more than the combined top four private-sector companies, and that has been our history throughout the period in which these awards have been given.

As the Chairman has noted, a few of these winning technologies are now on display down the hall in Room 2325. I do urge you to stop by there sometime today because it gives tangible evidence to the investment that you and we have made in science and innovation.

These innovations are not the result of one-year's budget. They are the result of the capabilities that were built with sustained bipartisan investment over decades.

The Congress can take credit and be proud of these accomplishments.

However, we also know there are problems. As Members know, in February of 1994, the department established the Task Force on Alternative Futures for the DOE national labs, under the guidance of Motorola chairman Bob Galvin. Essentially, the Task Force affirmed that the labs were an extraordinary national asset, but concluded that their management system needed repair.

We agree, and have set out on a far-reaching and detailed plan to cut costs and streamline management.

I believe it is essential that the Congress and the department work shoulder to shoulder on this endeavor, with a shared understanding of the problems and their possible solutions.

Six months ago, Secretary O'Leary presented to this Committee the department's implementation plan responding to the Galvin Task Force recommendations.

Today, I'd like to describe the status of our efforts, which may not be glamorous, but they are essential.

Our senior managers, working closely with our lab directors, are now eliminating most of the nonvalue-adding activities and requirements that have hampered the effectiveness of the laboratories.

I have often argued that government regulation of itself is the most pernicious form of government regulation because it has gone totally unchecked by a private-sector response.

The short truth of the Galvin Task Force findings is that we have overregulated our laboratories and we have crippled their capacity for effectiveness in the process, and we are addressing that.

Let me describe what we are doing.

First, we are reforming and dramatically cutting back DOE's directives. This is the system that DOE has used to establish formal requirements for the conduct of work by its federal and contractor employees. We are committed to cut these directives by 50 percent by December, and we are well on the path to that goal.

Second, we have established a new procedure called the Necessary and Sufficient Process for establishing safety standards for protecting the public, our workers, and the environment near our laboratories and other facilities. This will increase protection while reducing cost.

The key is to match the requirements to the specific work, be it decontaminating a facility or operating a particle accelerator.

Our facilities vary widely and require different procedures. The savings come from integrating environment, safety and health standards with the planning of work, including the analysis of hazards.

Today, we have nine pilot projects underway at Argonne, Fermilab, Los Alamos, Lawrence Berkeley, and Lawrence Livermore laboratories. The response has been enthusiastic and especially welcomed by our laboratories.

Third, we are taking steps to shift the department to external regulation of its activities, as several Members on this Committee have suggested.

We've appointed an advisory committee on external regulation, cochaired by John Ahearne, former NRC Chairman, and Gerald

Scannell, president of the National Safety Council and a former Assistant Secretary of Labor for Occupation Health and Safety.

They are scheduled to report by the end of this year. Your Committee has been given a copy of their August 14 interim report.

Fourth, a significant cost driver at the laboratories, as Mr. Roemer has noted, has been the persistent appraisals and audits conducted by DOE, GAO, the Congress, and state regulatory bodies.

Several labs have complained of a ten-fold or greater increase in audits over the past decade.

To rectify this, we've imposed a moratorium on DOE-directed business reviews, replacing them with a once-a-year review. Instead of 315 reviews a year—these are DOE-self-initiated reviews—we expect to do only 19 integrated ones. The cost will be cut by more than half, with 60 percent fewer people involved.

Two other pilot projects are underway. One will consolidate and simplify the technical reviews of the laboratories conducted by our program offices. The other will consolidate the 20 to 30 annual environmental safety and health reviews done by line management into just one appraisal per fiscal year per laboratory.

The pilot program with the companion-ordered moratorium on DOE program self-initiated environmental health and safety reviews was put in place last week. The pilot projects for reforming the technical reviews will be implemented next year.

Fifth, we are changing completely how we evaluate the procurement activities of our contractors. They were becoming increasingly bureaucratic. We have this week placed into effect a rule change permitting our laboratories to use best commercial practices instead of coercing adherence to a federal norm of procurement procedure.

We will reward performance, not bureaucratic procedure. Again, our laboratories have cheered this initiative.

Ensuring the success of these reforms will require persistent management attention over successive administrations and a paradigm shift in how the department regards and manages its laboratories.

To this end, we have named a laboratory operations board with eight senior DOE officials and eight private-sector members. I chair the board and John McTague, Ford's technical affairs vice president and former acting science advisor to President Reagan, serves as our vice chair.

The board will provide advice on micromanagement, reducing cost, developing a mission framework for the labs, better integrating DOE's various research programs, and improving collaboration among the laboratories, academia, industry, and other agencies.

This board will serve as an insistent set of advisors, a conscience, if you will, to keep the Department of Energy focused on achieving a more productive, mission-focused and cost-effective laboratory system.

Finally, we've established the internal research and development council to produce better integration among the department's basic and applied R&D programs. And here, too, by appointing the senior career deputies to the council, we intend to assure greater continuity over successive administrations.

Let me now briefly address the challenge of developing a clear mission framework for these laboratories, the lack of which has been a perennial concern of blue ribbon panels, the General Accounting Office, and others.

The department has historically resisted suggestions to force each of its laboratories into tightly defined missions. First, it is argued that if the laboratories' missions were to be drawn too narrowly, it would endanger what makes these laboratories so unique—their versatile approach to problem-solving in ways that narrowly-focused institutions cannot do.

Insights from research cannot be scheduled in advance to fit a particular mission. A precisely circumscribed mission could prevent individual labs from pursuing scientific results wherever they lead, curtailing innovation and limiting the capacity to contribute to other missions of the department.

Second, it is pointed out that it is difficult to strictly define a laboratory's mission.

The Department of Energy's national security mission, for example, involves six different components with over 215 separate, identifiable tasks and subtasks.

In mission specificity, it has been asked repeatedly, where and how do you draw the line?

These arguments seem cogent to me and should serve as an appropriate caution on becoming too specific in mission assignment or definition. But surely the department can and must do more to sharpen the mission responsibilities of its laboratories, and we are committed to do so.

While legitimate concern about the DOE labs is often couched in terms of lack of a clear mission, the issue really boils down to whether we believe that taxpayer funds are being spent cost-effectively among the laboratories, universities and industry to accomplish missions of public value.

We recognize it is our duty to demonstrate to the satisfaction of the Congress and these committees that we have developed more tightly focused mission allocations for our laboratories, stripped out redundancies, and prudently invested our research dollars.

By December of this year, we'll develop a strategic mission plan that will show how Department of Energy's missions are performed through programs across the department and the role each laboratory has in each of the Department of Energy's missions.

From that base, we intend to build a means to size and streamline our laboratories, identify areas of excellence and provide the Congress with the means, through structured oversight and budgetary control, to ensure that our funds are properly administered.

Let me now briefly comment on the pending legislation before your Committee.

We believe that H.R. 2142 is consistent with the efforts that I have just described. However, I should observe that we believe that these objectives could equally well be met through a disciplined and structured oversight process, one that I would commend to the Committee's consideration.

Nevertheless, we find this legislation consistent with our efforts and with what we consider good sense in this area. However, we do recommend against legislating in the area of external regulation until our advisory committee completes its work in December.

Regarding H.R. 1510, we cannot support its mandated reduction of DOE lab personnel by one third over a ten-year period.

It appears to us that this is the equivalent to what business consultant, Peter Drucker, has so sensibly and forcibly warned against—amputation in advance of diagnosis.

Rather than sizing the laboratories based on the national need for the valuable work of these institutions, regrettably, this bill would seem to determine how much work could be done by arbitrarily constricting the employment, regardless of the nation's need for the work.

Moreover, many of our laboratories receive ten to 20 percent of their work from other federal agencies, state governments and U.S. industry. These groups invest in the laboratories because they are the most effective place and often the only place to accomplish their goals.

We like the fact that other agencies, the Department of Defense, Justice, NIH, EPA, NASA and others, invest their funds in DOE laboratories. In some regards, it is the final exam and market test. If other agencies during these times of fiscal stringency are willing to invest in our laboratories, then you know full well that that's where the best science and capability resides.

We have worked hard to make these world-class resources available to the entire nation, not just the DOE missions. Arbitrarily mandated personnel reductions we believe would make it increasingly harder for our national laboratories to collaborate with others with no discernible benefit to the taxpayer.

Finally, regarding H.R. 87 and Title II of H.R. 1993, the Department does not agree with the presumption that there should be a broad closure effort of DOE laboratories. Nor do we agree that the proposed method is appropriate.

In the case of military bases from which this method is drawn, there was widespread agreement that there was excess capacity, only a lack of political will to deal with it.

In the case of R&D, there is no such consensus, at least yet established.

In fact, both parties have long recognized the importance of R&D to the future security interest and economic well-being of our country.

Moreover, the laboratories are not simple commodities that can be closed at will while their assets are moved elsewhere. This would seriously affect their capability to continue producing results.

In certain instances, closures may in fact be desirable. However, I think they should occur as a consequence of a carefully considered management decision rather than from a process controlled by people who may not have a long-term experience with these laboratories, that has as its main objective to close facilities.

In short, size should be a question of function. It is sensible and prudent to first decide what we want these laboratories to do and only then downsize or streamline accordingly.

This is the approach that is taken in H.R. 2142. It is also the approach we are taking at the department. We think it is the correct way to proceed.

In conclusion, I believe we have initiated the most intense and ambitious management actions ever undertaken to improve the productivity and to lower the cost to the DOE national labs. We're encouraged by our progress. But we know that correcting the deficiencies of several decades will take a sustained effort.

We will need your patience and assistance in solving these problems.

But the goal was well worth the candle. The recurring theme that runs throughout the many studies of the national laboratories, even including the ones that are critical, is that they are enormously impressive institutions that have contributed greatly to our nation.

But they are fragile institutions. If they are destroyed as a practical matter, it will be impossible to reconstitute them, or to reassemble the talent that makes them work.

All the more reason to suggest some caution in our approach.

So I return to where I begin. We need to cut spending and we need to protect our public investment in research and development.

Our goal, that of the Congress and the department, should be a common one—to reduce spending in a way that ensures that the proud legacy of these labs continues and that future generations of Americans are well served, as we have been in the past. Thank you, Mr. Chairman.

[The prepared statement of Secretary Curtis follows.]

STATEMENT OF

CHARLES B. CURTIS

DEPUTY SECRETARY

U.S. DEPARTMENT OF ENERGY

BEFORE THE

SUBCOMMITTEES ON BASIC RESEARCH

AND ENERGY AND ENVIRONMENT

COMMITTEE ON SCIENCE

U.S. HOUSE OF REPRESENTATIVES

SEPTEMBER 7, 1995

Mr. Chairmen, Members of the Committee, I appreciate the opportunity to appear before you today to discuss the Department of Energy (DOE) National Laboratories, the initiatives we are pursuing to enhance the productivity of these institutions, and proposed legislation that has been referred to your Committee for possible action. My testimony includes an attachment that addresses the seven questions raised in your letter of invitation (Attachment A).

Today we are faced with the challenge of resolving two conflicting obligations we hold to future generations. On the one hand, we have an obligation to control the Federal budget deficit. On the other hand, however, we have an obligation to make investments today in areas, especially research and development, that will lay the groundwork for future security and prosperity. Striking the right balance between cutting federal spending and protecting long-term federal investments is a challenge that will require our best judgment and wisdom.

It is this balance we are trying to achieve with our National Laboratories. Bringing down costs while enhancing R&D efficiency and performance at the National Laboratories has been a major focus for the Department and its laboratories, and has also been the subject of major reviews by independent groups such as the Task Force on Alternative Futures for the DOE National Laboratories (also known as the Galvin Task Force). These examinations have been productive, and the changes that we are implementing as a result hold the prospect of serving the needs of contributing to deficit reduction while also addressing major scientific and technical challenges that will affect the position of our Nation in the next century.

As we make these changes, we are mindful of what is at stake. The DOE National Laboratories are a key part of the nation's science and technology enterprise, and, as this Administration frequently asserts, scientific knowledge is the key to the future and technology is the engine of economic growth. The laboratories are unique in their combination of scientific excellence and their ability to address large complex problems of national importance. But the environment that produces R&D excellence can be fragile. If the labs were damaged, they would be extremely hard to rebuild. For these reasons, it is prudent for us -- meaning both the Congress and the Administration -- to make changes with caution, mindful of our role as stewards for future generations.

In prior hearings before this Committee, the Department's testimony has provided detailed descriptions of the research and the record of accomplishments of the DOE laboratories, and I will not repeat this here. But before discussing our efforts to improve the laboratory system and our view of pending legislation, I would like to spend a few minutes to illustrate the value of the laboratories.

There is little dispute about the laboratories' scientific excellence. In the past year we have identified and characterized the elusive Top Quark; we have broken our own world's record for sustained fusion energy; we have identified genes for breast and colon cancer; and we have seen our investment in scientific excellence rewarded with yet another Nobel Prize in Physics. (Dr. Clifford Shull, a former Oak Ridge National Laboratory employee who has been supported throughout his career by DOE. The prize is for his work in neutron scattering, which is a field predominately supported by DOE.) Over the years, more than 60 Nobel prize winners have been associated with the Department and its laboratories.

Less recognized, however, is the extent to which the laboratories create promising and practical technologies while pursuing their missions in energy, national security, environment, and fundamental science. In the Committee's other hearing room there is an exhibit of some of the Department's winners of this year's R&D 100 Awards. These awards -- the leading awards for innovation -- are given each year to the 100 most technologically significant products selected by an independent panel of judges under the sponsorship of R&D Magazine. Past R&D 100 Award winners include the flashcube, the digital wristwatch, antilock brakes, liquid crystal displays, the halogen lamp, and the fax machine. This year 32 of the R&D 100 Award-winning technologies came from DOE-sponsored research, most of which was conducted at our National Laboratories. Among Federal agencies, NASA received the second largest number -- six. Although private sector entities have received a majority of these awards since their beginning in 1963, the DOE National Laboratories have received more awards than all other federal agencies combined and more than the top four private sector companies combined.

One DOE winner this year is the Solar 1000 microwave sulphur light, for which the award went to the Department, Fusion Lighting Inc. and Lawrence Berkeley National Laboratory. At DOE headquarters, two prototype sulphur lights replaced 240 200-watt mercury lamps. The Sulphur light is brighter, many times more energy efficient, and environmentally more benign than the lights it replaces. Other DOE award-winning technologies will help redure the cost of synthetic gas production, enable new methods of materials processing, and help trouble-shoot integrated circuits.

These award-winning technologies epitomize the quality, creativity, and excellence present across the laboratory system. There are many other equally significant technologies emerging from our laboratories.

This year our labs were in the news for treating patients with the novel Boron-Neutron Capture Therapy. Many people are unaware that the entire field of nuclear medicine owes its existence to work growing out of DOE, and DOE is a major producer of medical isotopes. Technology developed by DOE is used to detect small lesions in the body, measure organ function, and treat cancer. Technetium-99m-labeled pharmaceuticals, for example, are routinely used in 35,000 medical procedures daily in the United States.

There are many other examples. A new breakthrough at Los Alamos laboratory may make possible the first practical high temperature superconducting wires.

This year, Lawrence Livermore National Laboratory invented a "radar on a chip" that is expected to have wide-ranging applications from collision avoidance systems for cars to construction studfinders.

These innovations are not the result of a single year's budget, but are the result of research capabilities arising out of sustained investment over decades. The Congress should feel proud of these accomplishments, because Congress, with strong help from this Committee, has been responsible along with the Department and its laboratories for creating and maintaining this extraordinary capacity for innovation.

Just as Congress and the Department can take satisfaction from the accomplishments of the laboratories, we share responsibility for their problems. In February of 1994, the Department established the Task Force on Alternative Futures for the DOE National Laboratories under the leadership of Robert Galvin, Chairman of the Executive Committee for Motorola, Inc. This task force issued its report in February 1995. Boiled down to its essentials, the Task Force report found that the laboratories are an extraordinary national asset, but that the management system of the laboratories is broken. The Task Force attributed the current problems to both the Department and the Congress. We agree that the system is broken and that we need your help to repair it. It is essential that the Congress and the Department work together with a common understanding of these problems and possible solutions.

Six months ago, on March 9, 1995, the Secretary presented to this Committee the Department's implementation plan in response to recommendations of the

Galvin Task Force. Today, I would like to describe in some detail the status of the our implementation efforts. These actions are not glamorous and may seem tedious, but they are essential.

Response to the Galvin Task Force Report

We call our framework to implement the Galvin Task Force recommendations our "Management Improvement Roadmap." It consists of a series of actions to help the Department and the laboratories remove the encrustation of cumbersome, inefficient, and non value-adding activities and requirements that have grown up over the past several decades and jeopardize the long-term quality and effectiveness of the laboratories. These actions were developed with the participation of both senior managers of the Department and the laboratories.

This is what we have set out to accomplish:

1. Create a more productive, mission-focused, and cost-effective Department and Laboratory system.

2. Adopt best business practices throughout the system.

3. Require performance-based, results-oriented contractor accountability.

4. Work aggressively to achieve credible external regulation and oversight.

5. Shift the balance of focus at the laboratories away from process compliance and toward mission success and results.

We believe that we are making progress toward meeting all of these goals, as demonstrated by actions to-date (Attachment B). We acknowledge, however, that we have considerable work yet to do to enhance the Department's stewardship of the laboratories. I ask you to support these management improvements and to help provide continuity across Administrations to stay the course.

Reforming and Reducing DOE Directives

The Department's current system of directives is not working as an effective management tool. Directives are the means by which the Department establishes formal requirements and guidance for the conduct of work by employees of the Department and its contractor workforce. We committed to reduce by 50 percent the number of DOE directives by the end of 1995, and committed to rewrite the "26 most burdensome" directives. As a result of initiatives championed by Marcia Morris of our Office of Human Resources and guided by Robert Nordhaus, our General Counsel, DOE directives have been reduced from 312 to 224, a 28 percent reduction. We are on track for meeting our goal of 156 by the end of the year.

The 26 most burdensome directives have been rewritten, and we expect most of these 26 to be issued in their new form by September 30, following meetings this month of the Directives Management Board, which I chair. This process will eliminate unnecessary requirements, simplify the directives, and reduce the burden of these requirements on the laboratories and other DOE management and operating contractors. This will result in cost savings in administrative areas through reduced reporting and reduced control by headquarters.

The effort to overhaul our directives is an intense, serious, long-term process. Each of the revised directives contains a sunset provision so that after two years the directive must be reaffirmed, revised, or allowed to lapse. Though perhaps a small step for mankind, this is a giant step for the Department. Other giant steps will be required to complete the process of streamlining our directives. The most important of these is the "Necessary and Sufficient Process."

Necessary and Sufficient Process

We are putting in place a new approach, called the "Necessary and Sufficient Process," to establish standards for protection of the safety and health of the workers, the public, and the environment near DOE laboratories and other facilities. This process holds the promise of significantly improving our ability to safeguard against workplace hazards and environmental damage, while reducing unnecessary paperwork and assuring accountability. The purpose of the Necessary and Sufficient Process is to match requirements with the specific work to be done --- whether that work be decontaminating or decommissioning a building, or operating a particle accelerator laboratory. The process integrates environment, safety and health standards with planning of work, including the analysis of hazards and setting of hazard controls.

Decisions are delegated to the lowest management level that is feasible, or as close to the work as possible.

While in the short term there may be some increased costs due to startup and implementation of the system throughout the DOE complex, we expect that in the long term it will result in improved efficiencies, higher levels of safety, and ultimately significant cost savings. We currently have nine pilot projects underway, including ones at Argonne, Fermilab, Los Alamos, Lawrence Berkeley, and Lawrence Livermore laboratories, and are receiving an enthusiastic response from the laboratories. We hope to begin to institutionalize the Necessary and Sufficient Process across DOE by early 1996.

Advisory Committee on External Regulation

The Department's existing complex system of self-regulation emerged from the Manhattan Project, the Atomic Energy Commission, and Congressional actions related to the urgency of the nuclear weapons mission and the need for secrecy at the weapons production complex. These facilities handle high-risk materials and their operations involve significant workplace hazards. Indeed, DOE facilities harbor some of the largest inventories of hazardous materials outside of Russia. On February 16, 1995, the Secretary announced formation of an Advisory Committee on External Regulation of Department of Energy Nuclear Safety. Headed by John Ahearne, former Chairman of the Nuclear Regulatory Commission, and Gerard Scannell, former Assistant Secretary of Labor for Occupational Safety and Health, this Committee was given the assignment of providing recommendations regarding external regulation by the end of the year.

An interim report of the co-chairs was completed August 14, a copy of which has been provided to the Committee. This report identifies options for external regulation of the DOE complex. These options range from transferring regulatory responsibility to existing external regulators to creating a new, independent external regulator for all aspects of safety at DOE nuclear facilities. The Advisory Committee has identified specific criteria that will be needed in an effective, comprehensive external regulatory scheme for the entire DOE complex. The co-chairs point out that a transition to external regulation will not be easy or quick. In particular, it is necessary to ensure that health and safety conditions do not deteriorate during any transition and that agencies to which responsibilities are transferred have adequate funds to exercise effective oversight. In our view, this concern becomes particularly acute in light of Congressional actions, which could cut OSHA's budget for enforcement by more than 35 percent. The co-chair's report cites a number of activities now underway at the Department such as the Necessary and Sufficient Process for setting safety and health standards, that will be helpful if they are well managed to completion. We expect that the Committee's final report will be the most comprehensive treatment of these complex issues, and we look forward to transmitting it to the Congress.

Reform Audits/Appraisals

A significant cost-driver at the laboratories has been the persistent audits and appraisals conducted by the Department and other review groups, including the Congressional General Accounting Office, and state regulatory bodies. Several laboratories have reported a ten-fold or more increase in the number of audits and appraisals over the past ten years. These have consumed literally thousands of hours of time of both the auditors/appraisers and the programs and offices being reviewed.

In response to the proliferation of uncoordinated, burdensome reviews, the Department committed to impose an immediate moratorium on business practice reviews (e.g. procurement, information systems, personal property, facilities management) and to begin a pilot project to conduct an integrated business practice review once a year at each laboratory. This effort is being led by Don Pearman, our Associate Deputy Secretary for Field Management. The commitment has been honored, and the results are impressive. During the pilot period of April 1995 through April 1996, a total of 19 integrated business practice reviews will be conducted at the labs, which compares with 315 such reviews during FY 1994. We expect to cut the cost of conducting these reviews by more than 50 percent, and to reduce the number of federal and laboratory personnel involved in the reviews by nearly 60 percent. The pilot project was recently extended to include all sites and contractors, not just the laboratories.

We have also committed to establishing similar pilot projects for internal environmental, safety and health self-assessments, and technical program reviews conducted by the program offices. The pilot project to simplify and consolidate technical reviews is being led by Dr. Martha Krebs, our Director of Energy Research. A draft report proposing ways to improve the review process was prepared in August, was circulated for comments, and is being revised.

Last week we issued a memorandum establishing pilot projects for environmental, safety and health self-assessments at Los Alamos, Lawrence Livermore, Lawrence Berkeley, Sandia, and Oak Ridge National Laboratories. This project is led by Dr. Everet Beckner, our Principal Deputy Assistant Secretary for Defense Programs. On the basis of this pilot project, I have put into effect an immediate moratorium, subject to exception only for cause, on all line management environmental, safety and health reviews at these laboratories. Under this pilot, 20 to 30 reviews per year at a given lab will be replaced with a single consolidated appraisal. The moratorium will not affect independent reviews done by the Office of Environment, Safety, and Health.

We have also made much progress in our efforts to streamline and improve the effectiveness of our independent oversight office. This office provides the Congress, the Secretary, and DOE managers with an independent and unbiased view of how well DOE line managers are performing in managing for environment, health and safety and safeguards and security. With the creation of this office in 1994, previously separate and overlapping oversight assessments conducted by separate organizations in areas such as nuclear safety, occupational safety, occupational medicine, safeguards and security were united in a single office reporting to the Assistant Secretary for Environment, Safety and Health. This has significantly reduced costs and burdens on our field sites. We have been able to reduce the number of contractors used in independent oversight assessments from 34 in 1994 to 9 today, and the number of contract personnel has been cut from 363 in 1994 to 91 today, representing a cost saving of nearly $14 million.

Procurement Reform

Another element of our Management Improvement Roadmap for the laboratories involves a commitment to revise completely the way we evaluate the procurement activities of our management and operating (M&O) contractors. Unlike other federal contractors, the Department's M&O contractors have been expected to adhere to what is called the "federal norm" in procurement practices. This concept has been a vague and evolving standard. Although the M&O's are not required to adhere to Federal Acquisition Regulations, per se, they were expected to conform to federal purchasing principles and practices. As a result, contractor purchasing has, over the years, become increasingly more like Federal practices and less like efficient and effective commercial practices. We announced that we would abandon this system and replace it with a system based on the use of best commercial practices. Led by our Deputy Assistant Secretary for Procurement and Assistance Management, Richard Hopf, we have done this, and published the final rule in the June 2 Federal Register. Representatives of the Department's M&O contractors are working together to benchmark best commercial business practices, and we have established a "best practices" bulletin board. In addition, we are leading a complex-wide effort to re-engineer purchasing to reduce overhead, eliminate non-value added activities, and develop more effective purchasing strategies. We expect this effort to result in reduced cost, greater efficiency, and improved performance. In a related action, we are transforming our oversight practices to place greater emphasis on results.

Providing Independent and Sustained Management Attention

While each of the initiatives mentioned above holds the promise of removing unnecessary costs and non-value added activities from the Department and its laboratories, we know that the task we face will require persistent management attention--involving top managers of the Department and extending through changes of Administrations. To help address this requirement, we have established a Laboratory Operations Board to provide focused attention to issues facing the Department's laboratory complex.

The Laboratory Operations Board is comprised of eight senior DOE officials and eight external members. I serve as the Chairman of the board, and one of the external members, Dr. John McTague, Vice President for Technical Affairs, Ford Motor Company, and formerly Acting Science Advisor to President Reagan, serves as the Vice Chair. Responsibilities of this board include:

- providing strategic direction for the laboratories, including validation of strategic plans, cross-cutting programmatic and management issues, and coordination of the laboratories as a system;

- developing a mission framework for the laboratories which delineates the distinctive expertise and areas of strength for each lab within the Department's overall mission assignments;

- assisting efforts to enhance integration among the Department's basic and applied research programs, and between the laboratory system and other R&D performers in academia, industry and other government agencies;

- recommending ways to contain costs, including ensuring application of best practices and addressing resource impacts of administrative and regulatory requirements; and

- providing advice on management improvement initiatives aimed at eliminating micro-management, reducing the burden of oversight, clarifying lines of control and securing higher levels of R&D performance at lower cost.

We have sought experienced external experts to serve on this Board (Attachment C), for we strongly believe that it will play a vital role in providing a continuity of purpose behind the Department's current effort to reform management practices of the labs and to enhance their contributions to the Nation.

This continuity of purpose is essential. Similar governance and management concerns have been voiced in reports over the past 20 years. For example, a 1975 independent study of the then Energy Research and Development Administration (ERDA) laboratories expressed strong concerns about the "bureaucratic clutter and red tape...that serves no real purpose."[1] Similarly, a 1982 study of the DOE labs concluded that "The laboratories have become grossly overburdened with detailed reporting and other paperwork requirements, the utility of which frequently is not apparent and which unnecessarily divert resources from their research and development mission."[2] Each of these reports was followed by a busy period of action, but management attention then lapsed due to changes of Administrations, turn-over of top Departmental officials, or a determination that nobody was watching any longer so the intensity of focus could be abandoned.

The Laboratory Operations Board is intended to address this problem through its inclusion of external members with staggered, six year terms. Their role is to serve as a conscience and an insistent set of advisors that will keep the Department focused on the challenge of creating a more productive, mission-focused, and cost-effective Department and laboratory system. They will help ensure that the Galvin Task Force report will not suffer the fate of many previous examinations of the DOE laboratories.

---

[1] Report of the Field and Laboratory Utilization Study Group, December 1975.

[2] The Department of Energy Multiprogram Laboratories, A Report of the Energy Research Advisory Board, U.S. Department of Energy, September 1982.

One of the immediate tasks which the Laboratory Operations Board is addressing involves meeting the Department's commitment to find $1.4 billion in cost savings through reductions in overhead costs at the laboratories. To address this challenge, we have established a Management and R&D Efficiency Subcommittee, Chaired by Dr. Alexander MacLachlan, our Deputy Under Secretary for R&D Management, who had led a similar effort as a Senior Vice President at Dupont. This Subcommittee has been focusing on management improvement initiatives at all of our laboratories. Pacific Northwest Laboratory, National Renewable Energy Lab, and Los Alamos National Laboratory have led the way in this effort. Each of these labs, as well as others, have taken significant actions recently to cut administrative costs and increase the productivity of their institutions. Preliminary indications are that the laboratories will be able meet these commitments through savings from reduced costs in complying with DOE orders, more efficient procurement, and reengineering.

These reforms will not take place without pain. For example, Los Alamos National Laboratory plans to go from a ratio of researchers to support staff of .94 to 1 to a ratio of 1.3 to 1 by fiscal year 1997. This change will require a reduction of support personnel of over 1300 full time equivalent positions. Pacific Northwest Laboratory, through a combination of cuts in overhead and in R&D, expects to reduce personnel by about 850 in fiscal year 1996.

A second, related mechanism that we have established to apply sustained attention to management issues is the R&D Council. The main function of this Council is to achieve greater integration among basic and applied R&D, among different areas of energy R&D, and among energy and environmental R&D in the Department, as recommended by both the Galvin report and the Department's Strategic Alignment Initiative. The Council will also serve as an internal arm to coordinate Departmental actions needed to support the Laboratory Operations Board. The Council is chaired by Dr. Alexander MacLachlan and has as its members the political leadership and senior career Deputies of the Department's major R&D programs. The participation of the senior career Deputies is especially important in order to provide continuity across Administrations. The Council will provide me with recommendations in October 1995, on how to improve the integration of basic and applied R&D in the Department.

Another major challenge facing the Laboratory Operations Board is the creation of a framework for characterizing the mission activities of the DOE laboratories, an effort which is consistent with the thrust of one of the pieces of legislation before this committee, The Department of Energy Laboratory Missions Act (H.R. 2142).

The Challenges of Developing a Mission Framework for the Labs

The lack of clear missions for the Department of Energy (DOE) laboratories has been a perennial concern over the years of blue ribbon panels, Members of

Congress, and oversight groups such as the General Accounting Office. For example:

- The 1983 Packard Commission report recommended that all federal agencies re-examine the missions of their laboratories and redefine them so that they are "sufficiently clear and specific as to guide the agency and the laboratories in setting goals against which the laboratories' performance can be evaluated."

- The Galvin Task Force concluded that "the multi-program laboratories currently have self-generated mission descriptions which are so broad and generalized that they are essentially indistinguishable. As such, it appears that each laboratory is attempting to keep its options open in all fields of science and technology, which is compounding the problems of effective management."

- Similarly, the General Accounting Office concluded earlier this year that "DOE's laboratories do not have clearly defined missions that focus their considerable resources on accomplishing the Department's changing objectives and national priorities...

Although government advisory groups have recommended in the past that DOE redefine the laboratories' missions to meet changes in conditions and national priorities, DOE has not acted on these recommendations. "[3]

While it is generally correct to state that the Department has not forced its nine multi-program laboratories into tightly defined missions, it is important to understand the reasons why. First, requiring these labs to focus only within tight mission-driven parameters could sacrifice what is truly unique about the DOE multi-program laboratories, which is their versatility in addressing large, complex problems in a way that more narrowly-focused institutions cannot. Second, it is difficult to impose a goal-oriented mission in many areas of DOE's fundamental research, because new insights and discoveries emerging from fundamental research cannot be scheduled in advance according to a performance-driven mission statement. And finally, there is uncertainty over what constitutes a mission.

At the highest level of aggregation, the DOE National Laboratories historically have been involved in four basic mission areas: National Security, Energy R&D, Basic Science, and Environmental Science and Technology. These were the Department's (and hence the DOE Laboratories') major missions in 1978, they are the same today, and likely will be the same in the future. If defined at a high level such as this, it is not clear that more detailed mission descriptions for the labs would be useful.

---

[3] Department of Energy National Laboratories Need Clearer Missions and Better Management, General Accounting Office, January 1996.

Within each of these mission areas, however, there exists a broad range of R&D problems that are being addressed through various DOE programs, and within each program exists a range of research priorities. The Department's National Security mission, for example, consists of six major components: Stockpile Stewardship, Stockpile Management, Verification and Control Technology, Nuclear Safeguards and Security, Fissile Materials Disposition, and Naval Reactors Technology. Each of these programs has subprograms. For example, Verification and Control Technology has subprograms in Nonproliferation and Verification R&D, Arms Control, and Intelligence. Each of these subprograms is broken down into tasks and subtasks. The Department's R&D programs break down to approximately 215 different pieces at the task or subtask level. Within this array, how many pieces comprise a "mission" area? How many missions should each laboratory have? What are the implications for excellent R&D work at a laboratory that doesn't fit within the lab's mission description?

While concern about the DOE Laboratories often is couched in terms of their lack of clear mission descriptions, it appears that what observers of the Laboratories actually are looking for is confidence that the Department is allocating the taxpayers funds among its laboratories, universities, and industry in the most cost-effective way to accomplish its missions. Observers want to know how and why the Department uses its laboratories vis-a-vis academia and industry. This information would help provide understanding that can lead to a strategic plan for using the laboratories, based on an explanation of the distinctive strengths of each laboratory in relation to

DOE's missions and programs, and would also help delineate roles and responsibilities across the DOE laboratories and among the labs, industry, and academia.

We have committed to develop a Strategic Laboratory Mission Plan by December of this year that will describe, in a fashion that we have not done before, how the Department's missions are performed through specific programs according to a particular distribution of funds across multiple R&D providers. This plan will serve as a management tool by the Department to help manage the laboratories more as a system, and will illustrate the role each DOE laboratory has in the missions of the Department.

This plan also will help us size the laboratories according to the scope of each of the federal missions performed at these institutions. For our national security mission, with our Science Based Stockpile Stewardship Program, we have in place a strategic plan with specific goals that determine the size of the necessary laboratory R&D effort. We are pursuing a similar approach with respect to the our energy R&D and our environmental science and technology missions.

With this Strategic Lab Mission Plan, we believe that the Congress will have an additional and valuable means of providing systematic, structured oversight of the Department and its laboratories. Specifically, we believe that this plan will help the Department and the Congress address the complex issue of eliminating redundancies within the National Laboratory system without eliminating either the complementary skills or the diversity needed to stimulate innovation.

Pending Legislation

This brings me to the issue of pending legislation before your Committee. In the previous Congress, legislation was introduced that was similar to the Department of Energy Laboratory Missions Act (H.R. 2142). The Administration supported that legislation. We feel that H.R. 2142 would be consistent with the efforts that I have just described aimed at creating a refined mission framework for the National Laboratories. However, we do have concerns with Sec. 202 of the bill. We strongly recommend against legislating in the area of external regulation for the Department of Energy until the Advisory Committee on External Regulation of Department of Energy Nuclear Safety, whose important work I described previously, has concluded its work in December of this year. In light on the fact that this effort is near completion, it is important not to preempt the Advisory Committee's work by legislating external regulation to only a portion of DOE.

Regarding the Department of Energy Laboratories Efficiency Improvement Act (H.R. 1510), we cannot support the bill's mandated reduction of DOE laboratory personnel by one-third over a 10 year period. While the Department shares the concern of the bill's sponsor regarding the importance of maintaining balance among various R&D providers during a period of budget cutbacks, we believe mandated personnel reductions approach the issue from the wrong direction. Rather than sizing the nation's laboratories and personnel levels based on determinations of the National need for the work of these institutions, H.R. 1510 would dictate how much work could be performed at the DOE labs through a steady constriction of their employment rolls.

To illustrate the flaw of this approach, consider that many of our laboratories receive ten to twenty percent of their work from sources other than DOE, including other Federal agencies, state governments, and private companies. These organizations invest money in the DOE laboratories because they are the most effective place -- and often the only place -- to accomplish their goals.

We believe it is a strong validation of capabilities of the laboratories that other agencies, including the Department of Defense and Department of Justice, invest their money in our laboratories. We have worked hard to make the laboratories available as resources for the whole nation, not just the Department of Energy. Toward that end we have entered into Memoranda of Understanding with many agencies, including the Department of Commerce, the Environmental Protection Agency, the National Institutes of Health, and others to facilitate their use of the laboratories.

As we reduce the overhead costs at the laboratories, it is likely that the demand for this work will increase. Mandated personnel reductions would likely prevent our laboratories from doing much work for other organizations, hurting the effectiveness of these organizations, with no benefits for the taxpayer.

H.R. 1510 states that the Secretary of Energy shall be guided by an objective of terminating departmental laboratory facilities that are not "the most advanced and the most relevant to the programmatic objectives." Such absolute determinations are extremely difficult to make. The Secretary also is to be guided by the objective of "terminating facilities that provide research opportunities duplicating those afforded by other facilities in the United States." By this approach, even user facilities for which there are long waiting lists, and for which this Committee supported increased access to, could be a candidates for termination. Section 2 of H.R. 1510 would legislate external regulation for the Department's laboratories and facilities. As mentioned above, we believe legislation should await the results of the Advisory Committee focusing on these issues.

Finally, regarding the Department of Energy Laboratory Facilities Act (H.R. 87) and Title II of the Department of Energy Abolishment Act (H.R. 1993), the Department opposes both the presumption that there should be a broad closure effort for DOE's laboratories and the proposed method for addressing opportunities for consolidation and restructuring. These pieces of legislation are modeled after the Base Realignment and Closure process, but there are major differences between military bases and research laboratories. In the case of military bases, there existed a broad political consensus that the nation had excess capacity but lacked the political means of taking action. In the case of federally-supported R&D, there exists no such consensus. Both political parties recognize the importance of R&D to the long-term security and economic interests of our nation. An arbitrary mandate to closing National Laboratories without a careful, scientific assessment would be counter to this recognition.

Moreover, the DOE National laboratories are not like military bases which can be closed and their principal assets (military personnel, mobile military equipment and transport vehicles) moved to other locations. Rather, a decision to close any one of these laboratories would require termination of a broad array of research projects involving highly trained scientists and engineers who are conducting their work largely through the use of sophisticated laboratory-based equipment. The prospects for relocating either the personnel or the equipment (e.g. research reactors, particle accelerators, materials laboratories) would be small.

In February 1994, the Department specifically asked the Galvin Task Force on Alternative Futures for the Department of Energy National Laboratories to examine opportunities for the redirection, restructuring, and closure of DOE laboratories. After a year of intensive examination, the Task Force did not recommend the closure of any of the National Laboratories, although it did conclude that the labs, in the aggregate, should be downsized. Such downsizing currently is underway as a result of management initiatives aimed at reducing unnecessary overhead expenses at the laboratories, as I have described in this testimony. Further reductions will occur at the laboratories as a result of programmatic budget reductions in FY 1996 and follow-on years. In the context of actions already underway to enhance budgetary discipline, improve R&D productivity, and remove costs from the laboratory system, we do not believe that a Lab Closure Commission is either necessary or advisable.

We will be pleased to provide the Committee with detailed technical comments on each bill for the record.

Conclusion

In this testimony I have described our efforts to meet our obligations to reduce the Federal deficit while continuing to support the science and technology needed for our country's future. I believe these are the most ambitious management actions ever taken to improve the productivity and lower the costs of the DOE National laboratories. We are encouraged by the progress made thus far, but acknowledge that correcting the inefficiencies and patterns of management oversight that have built up over several decades will take a sustained effort. We will need your patience and assistance in solving these problems.

In closing, let me make one point that puts purpose behind our actions. Although I have referenced many studies of the DOE laboratories over the years, and have cited concerns expressed therein of management problems, the one common theme that runs throughout these reviews is the observation that the DOE Laboratories are enormously impressive facilities that have contributed greatly to this nation. If they are destroyed, it will be nearly impossible to reconstitute the facilities or the collection of great minds that makes them work. Our goal is to ensure that the proud legacy of the laboratories continues and that future generations are served.

Attachment A

Answers to Advance Hearing Questions
Charles B. Curtis
Deputy Secretary
U.S. Department of Energy

1. What is the future role of the DOE National Laboratories in the context of the overall Federally-funded scientific establishment?

The Task Force on Alternative Futures for the DOE National Laboratories concluded that "the national laboratories serve a distinctive role in conducting long-term, often high-risk R&D, frequently through the utilization of capital intensive facilities which are beyond the financial reach of industry and academia, and generally through the application of multidisciplinary teams of scientists and engineers." The Task Force stated that the laboratories are uniquely qualified for work requiring multidisciplinary teams using sophisticated instruments and tools, and noted that the importance of this type of work justifies the existence of the DOE laboratories. Because science and technology continues to increase in complexity, the Department believes that this type of work, for which the National Laboratories are uniquely qualified, will continue to be of value to the nation. Consequently, we expect the laboratories to continue to be a major element of the overall Federally-funded scientific establishment.

The contributions that will flow from the DOE National Laboratories in the future will be the product of the distinctive characteristics and expertise that have been developed at these institutions as a result of their mission activities in national defense, energy R&D, basic science, and environmental science and technology. Through mission activities in these areas, the DOE Laboratory system has developed core technical capabilities in nine major areas:

- Advanced Materials, Synthesis and Characterization
- Advanced Computing, Modeling and Simulation
- Advanced Manufacturing and Processing Technology
- Bioscience and Biotechnology
- Nuclear Science and Technology
- High Energy and Nuclear Physics
- Environmental Science and Remediation Technology
- Integrated Defense Science and Technology

Each of these core technical capabilities depends upon multi-disciplinary skills drawn from the workforce of the laboratories. Collectively, these capabilities provide the means by which the laboratories address complex problems assigned by the Department; respond to new challenges and requests for assistance from other government agencies, academia, and the private sector; and generally move ideas from concept to reality--either through the generation of experimental data or development of new technologies and operational systems.

Although government, university, and private sector laboratories each have distinctive strengths which will determine their future roles within the overall Federally-funded scientific establishment, the nature of R&D increasingly has brought researchers from these three sectors together. Enhanced integration and collaboration among the DOE National Laboratories, industry and academia results in an acceleration of innovation through teaming of complementary strengths and collaboration toward shared goals. These collaborations strongly serve the National interests in advancing science and technology and enhancing its prospects for application and commercialization.

"The United States can no longer afford the luxury of isolating its government laboratories from university and industry laboratories," is how the Federal Laboratory Report to the White House Science Council, Chaired by David Packard, expressed the importance of these partnerships in 1983. Since then, major strides have been made to achieve broad engagement of the talents of the DOE National Laboratories with researchers in academia and the private sector.

More than 16,000 industry, university, and government sponsored scientists conduct their research at our scientific user facilities. With the scientific facilities initiative, included in the President's FY 1996 request that number would jump to nearly 20,000. The Office of Energy Research alone supports more than 2200 graduate students at the National Laboratories and more than 1200 post-doctorate researchers. In the last four years we have entered into more than 1400 cooperative R&D agreements with the private sector, representing a total investment of over $2.5 billion. These collaborations bring ideas, manpower and technology to DOE's laboratories and mission activities, and provide similar benefits to our collaborators.

These collaborations should continue to contribute the overall Federally-funded scientific establishment.

2. **What should be the criteria for developing future missions for the DOE National Laboratories?**

The answer to this question depends in part on how one defines the word "mission." At the highest level of aggregation, the DOE National Laboratories historically have been involved in four basic mission areas: National Security, Energy R&D, Basic Science, and Environmental Science and Technology. These were the Department's (and hence the DOE Laboratories) major missions in 1978, they are the same today, and likely will be the same in the future. If defined at a high level such as this, it seems unnecessary to develop criteria for developing future missions for the DOE National Laboratories, since most conceivable R&D would fit within these categories.

Within each of these mission areas, however, research priorities have changed considerably over the years and there are significant issues to be addressed regarding when individual DOE Laboratories, or the system as a whole, should be involved in specific research areas.

If missions are synonymous with much smaller categories of research priorities and R&D program areas, then a number of criteria seem appropriate for the purpose of determining whether the work should be done at a federal lab, at a university, or in industry. The foremost consideration should be an objective assessment of where the work can best be done based on considerations such as established expertise, record of performance, and likelihood of success. More specifically, R&D programs or missions would seem to be appropriately placed at DOE laboratories when such work:

- Takes advantage of multi-disciplinary skills, integration capabilities, and unique facilities, available at the laboratories;

- Is consistent with the Government's desire to maintain control of the R&D activity, as is the case with work involving nuclear weapons, non-proliferation, and disposition of fissionable materials; or

- Involves applied R&D beyond the general capability of universities and will not be performed by the private sector because the economic benefits are either sufficiently uncertain or so far in the future that industry chooses not to risk its own resources.

New missions or programs developed at DOE laboratories should not result in competition between the laboratories and industry and should emerge from distinctive expertise necessary to perform the missions or programs.

3. **Within the projected budgets for DOE and its strategic realignment implementation, is there a need for explicit size and personnel limits for the DOE National Laboratories?**

The Strategic Alignment Initiative announced on May 3 includes organizational reforms, legislative proposals, and cost-cutting measures that will contribute more than $1.7 billion in savings toward the Department's commitment, announced in December 1994, to reduce the Department's budget by $14.1 billion over five years. The Strategic Alignment Initiative primarily is aimed at reducing layers of management within the Department, eliminating organizational redundancies, re-engineering processes, and cutting unnecessary overhead costs. The overall federal workforce of the Department will be reduced by 3,788 (27 percent) over five years. If legislative permission is given to privatize (sell) the Power Marketing Administrations and the Naval

Petroleum Reserves administered by the Department, the savings and force reductions will be even greater.

While the Department does not believe that explicit size and personnel limits are necessary for the Laboratories as part of our Strategic Alignment or budget planning efforts, we do anticipate that these efforts will affect the size and personnel levels of the labs. As the Department streamlines its oversight procedures of the Laboratories, the Labs will be able to eliminate employees and simplify internal systems of operation in a fashion that provides companion savings. Within the Strategic Alignment Initiative we have set a goal of a 10 percent reduction in contractor employees at the Department's Laboratories over the next five years. This would result in a cut of approximately 5,900 employees from a FY 1994 workforce base of approximately 59,000. Some workforce reductions at the labs will be the direct result of cuts in programmatic funding. As cuts are made in R&D program areas, the Department will work to ensure that the impacts are distributed fairly among all three of the major R&D providers--labs, academia, and industry--which perform DOE missions.

While we are committed to meeting the 10 percent personnel reduction, we do not feel that explicit personnel targets for each lab will be necessary. We have set a specific goal of $1.4 billion in savings at the Laboratories through implementation of recommendations from the Galvin Task Force report. These savings and the 10 percent personnel reduction goal are being tracked by the Deputy Under Secretary for

Research Management, Al MacLachlan, who has extensive experience with downsizing and cost-cutting efforts from his years as a Vice President at Dupont. These efforts are on schedule and give us reason to believe that explicit targets for each lab will not be necessary. In general, we believe that it would be an additional act of micromanagement for the Department to be dictating to our contractors how many people they may employ to get the job done which we have funded them to do. The better approach, and the one we have adopted, is to work with the labs to ensure that best practices are adopted in their management systems to enable the reduction of overhead and administrative staff, while ensuring that R&D program cuts have a balanced impact across the many institutions which perform mission activities for the Department.

4. **Within the projected budgets for DOE and its strategic alignment implementation, will there be the need for consolidation or closure of the DOE National Laboratories? If so, should this occur after mission definition, or concurrently?**

Unless drastic reductions in R&D and in the Department's budget are adopted by the Congress, the Department does not anticipate that any of its National Laboratories -- a term which usually refers to our nine multi-program laboratories -- would be closed in the near term. However, we do anticipate some consolidation of programs and our own reviews could lead us to closing some of the smaller DOE laboratories.

The nine multi-program laboratories which are considered to be National Laboratories are as follows:

Argonne National Laboratory
Brookhaven National Laboratory
Idaho National Engineering Laboratory
Lawrence Berkeley National Laboratory
Lawrence Livermore National Laboratory
Los Alamos National Laboratory
Oak Ridge National Laboratory
Pacific Northwest Laboratory
Sandia National Laboratory

These laboratories are engaged in a broad range of research in the areas of national security, energy, environmental science and technology, and fundamental science. The Department of Energy National Labs house some of the most advanced scientific facilities and instrumentation in the world. The collective investment that has been made by the nation in these laboratories over the past several decades measures in the many tens of billions of dollars. These laboratories are not like military bases which can be closed and their principal assets (military personnel, mobile military equipment and transport vehicles) moved to other locations. Rather, a decision to close any one of these laboratories would require termination of a broad array of research projects involving highly trained scientists and engineers who are conducting their work largely through the use of sophisticated laboratory-based equipment. The prospects for relocating either the personnel or the equipment (e.g. research reactors, particle accelerators, materials laboratories) would be small.

Nonetheless, in February 1994, we specifically asked the Task Force on Alternative Futures for the Department of Energy National Laboratories, Chaired by Bob Galvin, to examine opportunities for the redirection, restructuring, and closure of DOE laboratories. The Galvin Task Force did not recommend the closure of any of the National Laboratories, although it did conclude that the labs, in aggregate, should be downsized. Such downsizing currently is underway as a result of management initiatives aimed at reducing unnecessary overhead expenses at the laboratories, and also as a result of programmatic budget reductions.

If it were determined that budget reductions required the closure of major federal research institutions, such as one or more National Laboratories managed by the Department of Energy, then it would appear that among the criteria used to determining which labs might be closed would be the following: impact on performance of National R&D missions in national security, energy, fundamental science and environmental science and technology; quality of R&D performed at the lab; anticipated impacts resulting from lab closure, including impact to U.S. position in R&D fields supported by the lab; prospects for transfer of sponsorship

and governance of the lab (or portions thereof) to a private sector entity or university; and value of the federal investment in instrumentation and facilities that would be lost due to lab closure.

5. **Does DOE believe that the present system of government-owned, contractor-operated national laboratories provides the best and most efficient system of management?**

It is difficult to conclude in absolute terms what the "best and most efficient system of management" of the National Laboratories might be. The Galvin Task Force determined that the existing system of management of the laboratories contains major inefficiencies. We agree. Some of these inefficiencies relate to the Department's functions in administering contracts of the laboratories; some are the result of Congressional actions, as implemented by the Department; and some are the function of the contract mechanisms themselves. We believe that the advantages of the current system of government-owned, contractor-operated (GOCO) laboratories are sufficiently important, and other management arrangements seem sufficiently less desirable, that our preference is to make improvements in the existing framework.

The GOCO approach to laboratory management began in the 1940's to meet pressing wartime needs. Through this mechanism of contracting, private contractors are selected from industry, academia, and university consortia to serve as the management and operating contractors of the laboratories. This approach provides flexibility in the assignment of resources and facilitates quick responses to a wide variety of program needs. It also enables private sector and university-based R&D management experience to be brought to bear on government work. One of the major benefits of the GOCO system has been its ability to attract and retain world-class scientists who have provided the means of scientific excellence and world-class R&D performance in the Department's mission areas--which are the most important objectives of the National Laboratories.

The Department recognizes that the GOCO system has been the subject of significant concerns regarding administrative and business management issues. In response to such concerns, the Department in 1993 launched a major contract reform initiative aimed at preserving the attributes of GOCO management, increasing competition within contracting, and institutionalizing a performance-based framework for the GOCO contracts, while addressing acknowledged deficiencies. Although the GOCO system of managing DOE's laboratories and facilities has received increased scrutiny in recent years, there also has been a growing recognition that the GOCO approach utilized by the Department of Energy has resulted in generally superior technical performance than is found at government-owned government-operated (GOGO) facilities. For example, the Defense Science Board in 1987 proposed that some of the Department of Defense laboratories be converted from government-owned, government-operated (GOGO) labs to GOCOs. The Office of Technology Assessment and National Academy of Sciences also have made recommendations that the GOCO model be seriously considered for DOD's laboratories.

6. **Are there other governance structures, such as corporatization or privatization, which may better suit the future management of the DOE National Laboratories? What are the advantages/disadvantages of such proposals?**

As noted in response to Question 5 above, the Department shares the view expressed by the Galvin Task Force that there exist major inefficiencies and counterproductive practices within the existing structure of governance of the National Laboratories. The Department has not ruled out the possibility that at some point in the future, an entirely new governance structure might be developed that would meet the needs of the National Laboratories and the Nation in a fashion superior to the existing structure. However, to-date, we have not been convinced that a plan to "corporatize" the labs--as proposed in the Galvin Task Force report--is either workable or achievable in the near-term.

Although some proponents of dismantlement of the Department of Energy have recommended privatization of the National Labs in the process of dismembering DOE, we believe that such an effort would be a certain failure. The National Laboratories are not now, nor have they ever meant to be, revenue-generating facilities. No private sector entity would be interested in procuring a National Laboratory unless there were the prospect of recovering the costs of the investment, and then making a profit. Only if the National Laboratories--which often are described as "crown jewels" within the Federal R&D infrastructure--were offered in a fire sale would a private sector entity be interested in making a deal. In such a case, privatization almost certainly would force these institutions into becoming job shops which perform routine R&D services on a reimbursable basis from paying customers. The long-term, high-risk R&D which is performed at the National Laboratories would be sacrificed and the enormous investment that the American public has made in these facilities would be squandered.

Because we cannot at present envision another viable governance structure for the National Laboratories that would provide clear advantages over the present system, our focus will remain on fixing what is not working in the present system.

7. **If DOE implemented, but was not the agency of enforcement of Federal, State, and local environmental, safety, and health rules, regulations, orders, and standards at departmental laboratories, what statutory and administrative changes would be necessary? What is the status of the Advisory Committee on External Regulation of DOE Nuclear Safety's analyses and recommendations?**

Specific statutory changes would depend on the intent of the Congress regarding external regulation of DOE laboratories. The language cited above is not clear in its intent. Currently, the departmental laboratories must comply with applicable environmental, health, and safety requirements established by DOE through an extensive system of directives and regulations required by the Atomic Energy Act of 1954, as amended. In addition, the departmental laboratories are subject to enforcement activities of other Federal and State agencies under certain environmental laws, such as the Clean Air Act, and of nuclear health and safety requirements specifically provided for in various legislation, for example, the Nuclear Waste Policy Act of 1982, as amended and the Energy Reorganization Act. To the extent that the authority of external regulatory agencies would be expanded to departmental laboratory operations beyond this extent, now-applicable DOE directives and regulations would be preempted and the laboratories would be held to the standards and requirements of such external regulatory agencies. In many instances, the extension of external enforcement to the departmental laboratories would require amendment of the respective regulators' existing authorities and their development of regulatory frameworks, including standards, applicable to departmental-laboratory operations. DOE facilities that are not within the definition of a "departmental laboratory" would continue to be governed by applicable DOE directives and regulations.

The Advisory Committee on External Regulation of DOE Nuclear Safety was formed in February 1995 in response to a 1994 commitment by then-Under Secretary of Energy Charles Curtis in testimony before the House of Representatives Subcommittee on Energy and Mineral Resources. The Under Secretary stated that the matter of external regulation deserved extended consideration and proposed that DOE convene a Federal advisory committee to conduct a detailed examination of the issues involved.

The Committee is made up of 25 members drawn from the public, Federal, State, industry and academic backgrounds. The members represent a variety of public health, worker and facility safety, environmental and regulatory backgrounds. It is co-chaired by John Ahearne, former Chairman of the NRC and Executive Director of Sigma Xi, the Scientific Research Society, and Gerard F. Scannell, President of the National Safety Council and former Assistant Secretary of Labor for Occupational Safety and Health. DOE is represented by Dr. Tara O'Toole, Assistant Secretary for Environment, Safety and Health and Bruce Twining, Manager of the Albuquerque Operations Office

The Committee's first meeting was held in March 1995. There have been five two-day meetings and an additional two are scheduled before the Committee presents its final report at the end of the year. Meetings have been held around the country at facilities representative of the range of DOE facilities. The Advisory Committee is now actively formulating options which it will present to the Secretary of Energy and the Council on Environmental Quality.

The Co-Chairs issued a status report on August 14. The final report will be complete by the end of the calendar year.

Attachment B

Management Improvement Roadmap
Status Report

Roadmap	Implementation Timeline	Status To-Date
1. Rules of the Road	Immediate Implementation	Distributed to Labs
2. Reform and Reduce Directives		
a. **50% reduction in # of orders**	Complete by 12/31/95	25% reduction already complete
b. **26 most burdensome reissued**	Complete by 7/31/95	Revisions complete; reissuance by Sept. 30
c. **Necessary & Sufficient process**	Field Pilots 3/95-9/95 Implementation fall 1995	Necessary and Sufficient Demonstration projects have been established at:
		Oak Ridge: Cost effective comparison of compliance-based vs necessary and sufficient
		Kansas City: Occupational medicine program
		Fermilab: Establishing ES&H standards
		Los Alamos: Radiation protection program
		Lawrence Berkeley Lab: National Tritium Labeling system
		Savannah River Site: Groundwater Remediation
		Rocky Flats: Draining Plutonium from Bldg 371
		Livermore: Radioactive waste handling
3. Committee on External Regulation	Interim report 8/95; final report 12/95	Interim Report submitted Aug. 14, 1995
	Pilot projects during 1995	Pilot site being identified

4. Reform Audits/Appraisals	Immediate moratorium on business practice reviews; implementation within 60 days for integrated business practice review; 90 days for simplified line program ES&H reviews; 180 days for simplified program reviews	Moratorium on business practice reviews in place; plan for Integrated Business Plan reviews has been established; implementation began April 3, 1995; during one-year pilot, Ops Offices will conduct only one integrated business review per site. Plans for simplified line ES&H and program reviews on schedule.
5. Procurement Reform	Notice of Rulemaking to eliminate "federal norm" sent to Federal Register 2/28/95; 60-day public comment; final rule summer 1995	Notice of proposed Rulemaking published March 2, 1995, Federal Register; Final Rule published June 2, 1995.
6. DOE Lab Operating Board	Charter finalized by 3/31/95; Standing Panel of Secretary of Energy Advisory Board established by 4/15/95; first meeting tentatively May 1995.	Charter finalized, membership selected, first meeting held June 29, 1995; next meeting September 22, 1995
7. Enhanced Mission Focus for labs; development of Strategic Lab Mission Plan as framework for strategic direction and lab sizing.	As major agenda item of DOE Lab Operations Board, this will be addressed during first meeting of the Board. Strategic Laboratory Mission Plan due in interim form 7/95 and final 12/95.	Draft framework completed 7/95 and on track for presentation at Sept. 22 meeting of Lab Operations Board; on track for completion in 12/95

Attachment C

EXTERNAL MEMBERS OF THE LABORATORY OPERATIONS BOARD

JOHN P. McTAGUE (Vice Chair)

Dr. McTague is Vice President for Technical Affairs of the Ford Motor Company, Dearborn, MI. Formerly, Dr. McTague served as Deputy Director of the Office of Science and Technology Policy, Office of the President and later as Acting Science Advisor to the President in the Executive Office of the President. He also was an adjunct professor of chemistry at Columbia University.
Dr. McTague was an Alfred P. Sloan Research fellow, a NATO senior fellow, and a John Simon Guggenheim Memorial fellow. He is a member of the President's Council of Advisors on Science and Technology, a fellow of the American Physical Society, and a member of the American Chemical Society, the American Association for the Advancement of Science, the Society of Automotive Engineers, the Engineering Society of Detroit, and Sigma Xi.

ROBERT P. BRINGER

Dr. Robert P. Bringer recently retired as the Staff Vice-President, Environmental Technology and Services, for 3M, located in St. Paul, Minn. He was responsible for the global environmental activities of this $15 billion sales, multinational company. Dr. Bringer received his Ph.D. and B.S. Degrees in chemical engineering from Purdue University. Most of his career has been spent in research and development functions. He was named Staff Vice-President, Environmental Technology and Services for 3M in 1994 and has been active in several trade and professional organizations. He is past chairman of the Corporate Conservation Council of the National Wildlife Federation and past chairman of the Environmental Council of the Conference Board. He currently serves as chairman of the Solid and Hazardous Waste Task Group, National Association of Manufacturers. In 1989, he was named an Outstanding Chemical Engineering alumnus of Purdue University.

RICHARD CELESTE

Governor Richard F. Celeste served as two-term Governor of Ohio (1983-1991), a tenure marked by a focus on helping Ohio companies in the global marketplace. He shaped an aggressive program to promote international trade and investment using Ohio's trade offices in Brussels, Tokyo, and Lagos, representatives in The People's Republic of China and India, and new offices in Hong Kong and Toronto. He led 10 trade missions abroad, resulting in new global links for over 75 Ohio firms. During his tenure, Ohio moved from dead last among the 50 states in job creation to one of the top five generators of new jobs. Celeste has been actively involved in fostering science and technology as a key to economic development. Ohio's Thomas Edison Centers, where government, universities and industry cooperate are supported by the National Academy of Sciences and the National Science Foundation. He has served a Special Advisory to Project California, a public-private effort geared toward identifying key clusters of business in the advanced transportation field which will create new high-wage jobs in that state. He is a member of the Board of Directors of Health South Rehabilitation Corporation, Navistar International Corporation, Habitat for Humanity International, Youth Service America, and AFS Intercultural Programs. He serves as Chair of the Pacific Northwest Laboratory Advisory Committee, and is a member of the Advisory Board of BP America, Inc., Oak Ridge National Laboratory, and The Leadership Institute at the University of Southern California. He is a member of the Board of Trustees of Carnegie Corporation of New York. Celeste chaired the National Health Care Campaign for President Clinton. He now operates Celeste & Sabety Ltd., a small consulting firm that specializes in public policy in science and technology, international trade, and health care.

EDWARD A. FRIEMAN

Dr. Frieman is Director of the Scripps Institution of Oceanography, La Jolla, California, and Vice Chancellor of Marine Sciences at the University of California, San Diego. Formerly, he was Director of Energy Research for the U.S. Department of Energy. Dr. Frieman is a recipient of the Distinguished Service Medal from the Department of Energy, the Distinguished Alumni award from Polytechnic Institute of Brooklyn, and the Richtmyer award from the American Physics Society. He was a National Science Foundation senior postdoctoral fellow and a Guggenheim fellow. He is former member of the Defense Science Board and has served as Vice-Chairman of the White House Science Council and Chairman of the Supercollider Site Evaluation Committee for the National Academy of Sciences. He is a member of the National Academy of Sciences, a fellow of the American Physical Society, and a member of the American Association for the Advancement of Science.

PAUL GILMAN

Dr. Gilman is Executive Director of the Commission on Life Sciences of the National Research Council of the National Academy of Sciences. He received his Ph.D. from John Hopkins University in ecology and environmental biology. As a Congressional Science Fellow of the American Association for the Advancement of Science, he served on the staff of Senator Pete V. Domenici. After completing his fellowship, he remained at the Senate, initially as staff Director of the Subcommittee on Energy Research and Development of the Senate Energy and Natural Resource Committee. Later, he served as Chief of Staff for Senator Domenici. Dr. Gilman also served as executive assistant and technical advisor to Secretary of Energy, James D. Watkins. Prior to joining the Academy in 1993, Dr. Gilman served in the Executive Office of the President as Associate Director of the Office of Management and Budget for Natural Resources, Energy, and Science. His responsibilities included budget formulation and oversight for the Environmental Protection Agency, Department of Interior, National Science Foundation, Department of Agriculture, and the Department of Energy, among other agencies.

PAUL A. FLEURY

Dr. Fleury is currently Director of Materials and Processing Research Laboratory at AT&T Bell Laboratories in Murry Hill, New Jersey. His current responsibilities include research in solid state chemistry and physics, organic and inorganic materials synthesis, processing chemistry and chemical engineering, as well as prototyping research for flat panel displays and advanced electronic packaging and miniaturization. Previously, Dr. Fleury was Vice President of research and Exploratory Technology at Sandia National Laboratories, where he was responsible for SNL core competencies and research and technology programs in physical sciences, high performance computing, engineering sciences, pulsed power, microelectronics, photonics, materials and process science and engineering, and computer networking. Dr. Fleury spent the latter half of 1978 at Oxford University on a Senior Research Fellowship from the British Science Research Council. He was also a visiting Fellow at St. John's College, Oxford. He holds five patents and has authored more than 120 scientific publications.

M.R.C. GREENWOOD

Dr. M.R.C. Greenwood serves as Dean of Graduate Studies and Professor of Nutrition and Internal Medicine at the University of California at Davis. Her research interests are in developmental cell biology, genetics, physiology and nutrition. She came to UC Davis from Vassar College where she was the John Guy Vassar Professor of Natural Sciences, Chair of the Department of Biology, and Director of the Undergraduate Research Summer Institute. Dr. Greenwood was appointed to the position of Associate Director for Science at the Office of Science and Technology Policy (OSTP) in the Executive Office of the President. She served in that position until May 1995. She supervised the Science Division of OSTP. Her responsibilities in OSTP included providing authoritative advice on a broad array of scientific areas to the OSTP Director in support of the President and his objectives, such as budget development for the multibillion dollar fundamental science national effort, and development of science policy documents, e.g., *Science in the National Interest*. In addition, she was responsible for interagencey coordination of science, and co-chaired two National Science and Technology Council (NSTC) Committees; the Fundamental Science Committee and the Committee on Health, Safety, and Food. She was an active principal in the NSTC Committee on Education and Training.

ROBERT H. WERTHEIM

From 1977 until 1980 Rear Admiral Robert H. Wertheim was Director of Navy Strategic Systems Projects, responsible for the research, development and production of the Navy's fleet ballistic missile system, which included Polaris, Poseidon and Trident missiles. He was elected Lockheed Corporation's Senior Vice President-Science and Engineering in March 1981, and remained in that position until his retirement in January 1988. He is currently a private consultant on national security related programs and related issues.
Admiral Wertheim was graduated from the U. S. Naval Academy at Annapolis in 1945 with a bachelor of science degree. Following World War II service, Admiral Wertheim participated in the Navy's first special (nuclear) weapons

assembly team at Sandia Base, New Mexico, managed and organized development of the re-entry system for the Polaris missile, and conceived and aided in development of the Chaparral surface-to-air missile. Admiral Wertheim's contributions to national defense have been recognized with the Distinguished Service Medal (two awards), the Legion of Merit, the 1972 Gold Medal of the American Society of Naval Engineers, and the Rear Admiral William S. Parsons Award of the Navy League of the United States.

Mr. SCHIFF. Thank you very much, Secretary Curtis.

Let me say to the Members of the Subcommittees, in a moment, I am going to recognize Members, including the Chair, for subcommittee Members to question.

I'm going to encourage Members to stay in the five-minute rule, just because of the number of witnesses that we have in the course of today. But I would not prevent any Member from going over or having a brief second round if there's something pressing that they wanted to ask.

And before calling on either myself or any other Members of the Subcommittees, I'm going to recognize without time limit, the Chairman of the Full Committee and then the Ranking Member of the Full Committee, for their questions.

Chairman Walker?

Mr. WALKER. Thank you, Mr. Chairman.

We appreciate your testimony, Secretary Curtis.

Let me ask you, you've given us, I think, a very detailed outline of what you're doing to respond to the Galvin Report.

In your view, is the Department being completely responsive to the Galvin Report recommendations?

Secretary CURTIS. I think it's fair to say, Mr. Chairman, that it remains to be seen.

We have put in place a structured plan to take cost and inefficiencies out of the Department of Energy's management of these laboratories and in circumstances appropriate, worked to the external regulation of these laboratories.

The implementation of those plans will be carried out in the next year and a half with most of the more important steps taken by the end of this year.

I believe that we have made significant progress. We have, I think, a sensible approach, certainly good intentions. But we have the obligation to demonstrate our capacity to deliver on this.

Mr. WALKER. But there are some phases of the Galvin Report that you have specifically decided not to implement.

Is that right?

Secretary CURTIS. Maybe you could help me by calling my attention to what you're referring to.

Mr. WALKER. Well, for example, I notice that in the prepared responses that you gave to questions that were asked, Question No. 6 at the back of your testimony, you say that the Department has specifically decided that a plan to corporatize the labs, as proposed in the Galvin Task Force report, is neither workable or achievable in the near term.

Secretary CURTIS. Yes, sir. The Galvin Report in its principal recommendation did recommend a corporatization, so described, of the management of the laboratories.

The report also noted that if this was not considered achievable, that it laid out in appendix B what it considered the obligation to manage the laboratories or to deal with these issues in the existing framework of the department.

We are operating on appendix B. We have not excluded new forms of management of these laboratories. We have not been able to discern at the present moment quite how to do that within a practical political framework.

So we are doing what we can do within our existing legal capacity, without waiting for studies and refinements on different governance models.

But we haven't excluded consideration of them, Mr. Chairman.

Mr. WALKER. Okay. But that's a fairly fundamental decision that you've made. I mean, it seems to me the primary recommendation of the Galvin Report was to move to the corporatization. And it's my understanding that one of the reasons for doing that is they believe the labs are administratively top-heavy, and that you can in fact reduce the administrative structure of the labs substantially, maybe up to 50 percent, and still manage the labs in a proper way if you manage them under corporate kinds of policies.

Now if I understand your testimony before the Committee today, you're not coming here with a recommendation as to how we should implement that particular phase of the Galvin Report. You're coming here testifying that what you're doing is implementing a secondary strategy that the Galvin Report gave and asking this Committee essentially to endorse your decision not to pursue the main option.

Am I mistaken?

Secretary CURTIS. No, that's fairly said and certainly true.

We don't think the corporatization model laid out in the Galvin Report will work. We don't think it will work for several reasons.

One, the corporatization model laid out in the Galvin Report contemplates that the laboratories would, in essence, be freed from any sponsoring agency or mission agency and serve only as a national capacity for the Department of Energy as a primary sponsor and others who may use those resources.

We are concerned that will evolve the laboratories into the job shop with no sponsor for the very considerable infrastructure investment that must be maintained to maintain their core competencies. Indeed, their capacity for scientific excellence.

So it is our judgment that is not an appropriate path to take.

Mr. WALKER. So just to clarify, you specifically have rejected the fundamental recommendation of the Galvin Report and are in fact moving to implement a secondary recommendation of the Galvin Report.

Secretary CURTIS. We think it's a more secure path to achieving the Galvin Report's objectives, yes.

Mr. WALKER. Okay. The answer is, yes, you rejected the fundamental recommendation of the Galvin Report and are moving to another option.

Secretary CURTIS. We certainly rejected that recommendation, yes. But we haven't precluded consideration of different governance models if we can figure out one that makes sense.

We don't think that one makes sense.

Mr. WALKER. And let me understand why. We rejected it in part. You've laid out in some detail why you feel that that's not an appropriate course of action to take with regard to the future of the labs. But I also think I heard you say that you rejected it because you do not have the authority to act as a department on the fundamental recommendation.

Secretary CURTIS. No. What I intended to say, in any case, is that we are operating within the existing legal framework that we have. The Galvin proposal would require a change in law.

Mr. WALKER. Okay. So, in other words——

Secretary CURTIS. We do not believe it an advisable change in law.

Mr. WALKER. Okay. So this Committee could in fact change the law and move us in the direction of implementing the fundamental recommendation of the Galvin Report.

You are not suggesting that we should do that.

Secretary CURTIS. That's correct.

Mr. WALKER. But that is in fact something where we would have to act in order to give you the authority to do it.

Is that correct?

Secretary CURTIS. You certainly would have to act. The Galvin Task Force—let me be very precise about this. The Galvin Task Force report on corporatization, and they have not laid out in great detail specifically a plan for doing that or what is meant by it, but in its essence, contemplates that the laboratories would be administered by an independent board of trustees and that the Congress would appropriate monies to the laboratories with a great deal of self-direction.

Now, it is our judgment that in political terms, especially in the reality of the fiscal problems that this Congress is wrestling with, that the Congress will simply not turn over large parts of the federal fisc to laboratories, undirected as to what they should do with the money.

The department believes that decoupling mission from science and technology is not a good idea.

Mr. WALKER. Thank you, Mr. Chairman.

Mr. SCHIFF. Thank you, Chairman Walker.

Mr. Brown, you're recognized for such time as you wish to consume.

Mr. BROWN OF CALIFORNIA. Thank you very much, Chairman Schiff.

Mr. Curtis, to pursue briefly the line that Mr. Walker is pursuing in his questions, you observed in the Galvin Report a substantial number of criticisms involving the structure and operations of the Department, many of which revolved around overdirection from the central office and perhaps some degree of unnecessary infrastructure at the labs, perhaps generated by the overregulation from the central office, to some degree, and other kinds of bureaucratic developments which are common to almost all government structures.

And you are trying to respond to those criticisms, but not going to the degree of corporatization or privatization that was one of the alternative methodologies suggested by Galvin.

Secretary CURTIS. Yes, sir.

Mr. BROWN OF CALIFORNIA. Is that a correct interpretation?

Secretary CURTIS. Yes.

Mr. BROWN OF CALIFORNIA. And you believe that you would be impeded from a legal standpoint in doing so because of the present structure of the laws governing the Department.

Secretary CURTIS. That's correct.

Mr. BROWN OF CALIFORNIA. Is it your view that you will be able to substantially achieve the corrections of the administrative problems through following the course that you are following which you've described in some detail of reducing administrative regulation, providing for external regulatory review, and other methods of that sort?

Secretary CURTIS. I believe we can and will be successful here. But I would add two caveats to it.

One, it will require the cooperation of the Congress to help us be successful here because much of the management, as the Galvin Report stated, much of the excessive management is the response to various demands that the Congress has made over the years.

And also, I believe that it is essential that this discipline be carried on from administration to administration.

It is my most serious concern whether we can carry these disciplines, this management process, from one administration into the next.

And so, I'd have to say, I think we can do it. I believe we will do it. But the jury is still out and we have to fairly acknowledge that.

Mr. BROWN OF CALIFORNIA. And have you figured out some effective way of disciplining the Congress, Mr. Curtis?

[Laughter.]

Secretary CURTIS. I've always felt the Congress responds to good reasoned explanation and I hope for that in the future.

Mr. BROWN OF CALIFORNIA. Well, I would just like to point out in conclusion that there is a sense that the Congress may be rushing down the road toward achieving certain kinds of goals, some of which include privatization or corporatization, for example, without the necessary insight or reflection and study that might guide this more properly.

I consider these hearings are in part, at least, aimed at providing us with the background and the wisdom to make the kind of judgments which are necessary in this rather complex situation.

And I think your testimony has contributed a great deal to that and I thank you for it.

Secretary CURTIS. Thank you.

Mr. SCHIFF. Thank you, Mr. Brown.

The Chair is now going to ask all Members, including the Chair, to try to abide by the five-minute rule, at least as the general goal here, because of the number of witnesses.

Mr. Curtis, I want to say first that the subject has been discussed now at some length of that portion of the Galvin Task Force report that recommends corporatization as an alternative management for the laboratories.

And of course, we're honored that Mr. Galvin is here personally and will be able to talk further about this directly following your testimony.

But I want to say that although I find a great deal of value in the Galvin Task Force report, I think it is a significant contribution to this very discussion of the future of the national laboratories.

I have my doubts about how corporatization would work in this particular case.

I may be unduly optimistic here, but the four bills that are under consideration in this hearing have been kind of portrayed as three against one in terms of their direction. Three bills have been characterized as sort of anti-national laboratory, in the sense of a closure commission or mandatory downsizing. And my bill has been promoted as promoting the laboratories.

But as I listen to the Members describe their bills, as I describe my own, the three sponsors of the bills that are called in some quarters anti-laboratory in some form, went out of their way to emphasize their confidence in the national laboratories and their belief the laboratories should continue, but their additional belief that there have to be changes in how they operate.

I personally, in promoting the laboratories, agree that the laboratories and the Department of Energy have to look at better ways of management to create a more efficient operation.

And so, I am hopeful that the four of us actually may be saying things that are very close to each other, when you come right down to it.

On top of that, we've had your testimony, which seems one additional voice along these same lines. In other words, you're talking about promoting the national laboratories, but the Department of Energy is looking at different ways of management.

And what I'd like to ask is, in the Department of Energy's current plan, in your current thinking, where do you think we'll be as a bottom line in this year, year and a half, two years, whatever it might take, in terms of—well, in terms of staffing of the national laboratories?

Do you see a reduction in the staff of the national laboratories as a bottom line here? And if so, how much?

Secretary CURTIS. First of all, we are managing a cost-reduction process in the national laboratories that has as a goal taking $1.4 billion over five years out of the national laboratory cost of operations.

We have set a ten-percent employment reduction over that five-year period.

Let me make clear in my comments on Mr. Roemer's bill that we think it is a useful management tool to manage against goals. It's the rigidity of a statutory process that would elevate those goals over our capacity to manage, to function, to national purpose in our science and technology investment that we object to.

The short answer is we're going to take $1.4 billion out. We already have a plan to take more than $1.4 billion out. That will be at least a staff reduction of ten percent in the national laboratories over the next five years.

Let me take this opportunity to add, if I can.

I think the bills are all commonly purposed. These bills all recognize the importance of science and technology to the nation's future, and they all recognize that in the post-cold war environment, that we need to examine our laboratories, make sure that we have properly focused the missions in our laboratories, rationalized the investment of laboratories against investments in universities and in the private sector, and deliver on our dual responsibility to both reduce the deficit and manage fiscal spending at the federal level and preserve this nation's capacity for research and science in the future.

So there is a common purpose here. It's a dispute about means.

Mr. SCHIFF. I would like to think that's the case and I think we'll know further as we proceed through these hearings and continue to discuss it.

But I want to emphasize that I understand your distinction between a goal and a statute that makes changes mandatory. But your estimate is that your own plans may reduce national laboratory employment by at least ten percent.

Secretary CURTIS. That's correct.

Mr. SCHIFF. One other matter I'd like to ask you about, Mr. Secretary.

The Galvin Task Force Report made great emphasis in terms of micromanagement of the laboratories. The Department of Energy has meeting now its own advisory committee on external regulation of energy and nuclear safety.

Could you briefly state when you expect that Task Force to complete its report? And what actions you would expect the Department of Energy to take at that time.

Secretary CURTIS. The Task Force will complete its report at the end of the year. We have submitted an interim report to the Committee, which reports on their progress.

It is—let me re-emphasize, that as a goal, the Department of Energy believes that we should work towards the external regulation of our laboratories and, indeed, of our M&O contractors that are employed throughout the conduct of our mission, environmental clean-up and other of our activities.

But this is a very complicated thing to do and it involves—it will involve changing the law in some respects. It will involve equipping federal and state agencies with resources and capabilities that they did not today possess.

So it's a complicated piece of business and you will have the report at the end of the year. It is why we are recommending caution in legislating external regulation.

It will need to be done very carefully.

Mr. SCHIFF. Thank you, Mr. Secretary. My time has expired.

Chairman Rohrabacher, you are recognized for five minutes.

Mr. ROHRABACHER. Again, let me apologize that I've had to be in and out of this hearing. So the question I ask may have been covered, but I don't believe so.

Just from what you have just stated, about a ten-percent reduction versus a one-third reduction that is basically being asked for by Mr. Roemer. I live in Orange County and there's something that most people know about Orange County these days. Not only is the weather good, but we're bankrupt out there.

I can tell you, it's pulling teeth to get these people on the board of supervisors to sell any of their assets. They'd rather just raise taxes, which the people don't want them to do. They want them to sell off the golf courses and the parking garages and the yacht harbors that the county owns rather than raise taxes.

It seems to me that when you say that you're looking for a ten-percent reduction, compared to Mr. Roemer who is suggesting one-third, a 33-percent reduction over ten years, what you're really talking about is maintaining the status quo. And what Mr. Roemer is really talking about is something that will force the labs to have dramatic reconfiguration and restructuring and some real fundamental reform.

But at ten percent, I think you guys can get by without any reform at all.

Secretary CURTIS. Right. I think it's a fair observation, but let me make two points.

I believe Mr. Roemer's bill is a one-third cut over ten years. We're talking about a goal of ten percent over the next five years.

First, it's simply a goal. I actually believe that the force reductions are going to be much more significant than that. Our first-cut planning, by the way, of this has already exceeded the $1.4 billion commitment over five years.

But we're not simply going to manage the ten-percent goal or the $1.4 billion goal and then try to convince you to congratulate us.

We're going to take the unnecessary cost out of the management system. These are costs that are laboratory costs and federal employment costs.

I believe the cuts will be greater than that.

Mr. ROHRABACHER. But let me note, Mr. Curtis, the last thing that anybody up here wants you to do is to basically leave a shell in place that costs a lot of money, but isn't able to accomplish anything.

Secretary CURTIS. Right.

Mr. ROHRABACHER. And sometimes it's better to have a smaller operation and get rid of the funds that way, but have a smaller operation that functions, rather than a big shell that can't get anything done.

Secretary CURTIS. Sure. May I make one observation?

We're taking, we're using best practices to re-engineer processes at our laboratories—Pacific Northwest, Los Alamos and others. Los Alamos I want to cite as an example. Sieg Hecker, the director of the laboratory is here. He'll be a witness later on in the proceedings.

Just to change the ratio from administrative worker to science and engineer, from 0.94 to 1.3, will involve employment reductions of almost 1300 people.

In the private sector, that ratio is one to over two something, administrative, support personnel, to scientist and engineer.

We've got a crazy system in place. We need to take it apart. We are committed to take it apart.

I think that's going to produce much larger savings than we would measure by a ten-percent goal or $1.4 billion, but we've got to do it one step at the time.

Mr. ROHRABACHER. Okay. One last question, and that is, and it goes directly to the heart of how you go about this restructuring.

These labs came about—really, what we're talking about is a national asset that was developed during the cold war.

Secretary CURTIS. Right.

Mr. ROHRABACHER. This is when this great asset was developed. It was developed for a purpose and it served its purpose very well during the cold war.

And now that the needs of the country have changed dramatically, the cold war has been over for a few years now. We're trying to restructure our system for a post-cold war world.

Isn't there any room for the closure of even one lab?

Secretary CURTIS. Sure. I think that through a combination of budget constraint and as we examine and develop our mission statement for the laboratories and a sharper focus to those laboratories, that we may find in the complex of the Department's 30 laboratories that we should close labs, and if we find that, we will do so.

And I'm sure we will have constructive guidance from the Congress in that respect.

Mr. ROHRABACHER. Well, you will. Obviously, there are people protecting labs and there are other people here who are protecting other projects on the Science Committee.

But the bottom line is we need this system, this asset, to function.

Secretary CURTIS. Absolutely.

Mr. ROHRABACHER. To maintain the asset's ability to function and provide a service for this country, it means a smaller number or a fewer number of labs. Perhaps that's the way we should go.

And I'd just like to offer that as a suggestion.

Secretary CURTIS. Right. Mr. Chairman, I don't want to be perceived as defending the national laboratories. I hope that what I should be perceived as is defending the prudent investment in science and technology for our future and for the conduct of the department's missions.

We may do that with fewer laboratories, consolidation of laboratories and some closed laboratories. We may in fact privatize some of these laboratories if we can give them over to universities in appropriate context.

All of that we are going to go through very carefully and I hope with these committees in structured and periodic oversight so that you have gained the necessary confidence which you need to have, and the prudence in what we're doing.

Mr. ROHRABACHER. Thank you, Mr. Curtis. Thank you, Mr. Chairman.

Mr. SCHIFF. Thank you. Mr. Roemer, you are recognized for five minutes.

Mr. ROEMER. Thank you, Mr. Chairman. I'm delighted to get into this debate since there has been so much interpretation over the intent of H.R. 1510.

Let me just say that there's an old Chinese proverb that goes something like, a thousand-mile journey begins with a single step.

I think what my bill is trying to do is ensure that you take some steps towards reform, and not to simply say, go ahead and do it any way you want and we wish and hope and pray that you're going to do some things, but we'll sit around and wait for a while for you to do it.

Our purpose as a Congress, the semantics here are important. It is not simply, sir, to say to you that goals are necessary. We do pass statutes and laws.

I just want to get something clear. On page 23 and 24 of your testimony, you say, and I quote: "We believe mandated personnel reductions approach the issue from the wrong direction," in criticism of H.R. 1510.

Yet, on page 7 of your testimony, you say: "Within the strategic alignment initiative, we have set a goal of ten-percent reduction in contractor employees at the department's laboratories over the next five years."

You go on to state goals of $1.4 billion in savings.

So I don't think that we're disagreeing with much, other than I think you're disagreeing with the magnitude and some of the semantics here.

Is that not correct?

Secretary CURTIS. Well, we're certainly disagreeing with legislating a requirement that is built simply on a body count at the laboratories.

We are using a goal of ten percent. But it is a focused goal on the administrative cost in those laboratories that are the product of a management system we have studied and know to be requiring correction.

When we talk more broadly, step back, you're talking about taking a third of the total employees—scientists, engineers, as well as administrative personnel—out of the laboratories over ten years.

That may happen as a product of sizing to function. But we think that the responsible thing to do is first to sharpen the mission focus of these laboratories, develop a system plan, and then we will have the capacity to size and streamline these laboratories to function.

We hope to have that in place by the end of this year. That will give you the capacity and give us the capacity to identify what needs to be done to size these laboratories to their contemporary missions.

Mr. ROEMER. Well, again, I think this is a difference on semantics because you do the same body count that I supposedly do in my legislation.

You outline that there are going to be 5900 people in your testimony that would be gone from the work place, from the work force.

I certainly think that part of our job as a Congress is to work with your department, and I hope to be able to do that with my legislation and with the Chairman's legislation.

But I certainly think that moving toward a statute and moving toward a higher level than ten percent over five years is a fair and reasonable and logical set of circumstances to shoot for.

Let me ask you another question.

In terms of adjusting this personnel reduction that you've set in your testimony, have you made any kind of further adjustments for that in light of the R&D cuts, the massive R&D cuts that this Congress is in the process of imposing on DOE?

And if not, are you going to do that?

Secretary CURTIS. We have not. Obviously, if the Congress follows through on the cuts in R&D that are contained in various parts of the authorizing or appropriating process, it will require reductions across the complex.

Mr. ROEMER. What are your estimates or projections on that? You've done some modelling on that?

Secretary CURTIS. There's still a considerable variety to the proposals that are before the Congress. But Mr. Brown has asked the Department for tables that would try to estimate those reductions by laboratory throughout the complex and that has been recently provided to him.

I'd be happy to provide it to the Committee.

Mr. ROEMER. You would share that with the Committee?

Secretary CURTIS. Of course.

Mr. ROEMER. Thank you, Mr. Curtis.

Finally, in your advisory committee report of August 14th, 1995, and the conclusion on page 11, you state that, in addressing some of the options on external regulation, that one of them is the creation of a newly independent external regulator for all aspects of safety at DOE nuclear facilities.

Now, that would create a different branch of more regulation for only nuclear facilities. And you might have a proclivity or a tendency to go toward what for the rest of the facilities, then?

Secretary CURTIS. Let me first put in context what the problem is.

The Department of Energy, over the years, because of its very sensitive nuclear weapons mission, has been a self-regulator of its activities. So it has functionally developed its own EPA, its own Occupational Health and Safety Commission, its own Nuclear Regulatory Commission to, in essence, give the Congress and the public assurance that workers and the public and the environment are safe from those activities.

The system hasn't worked very well. The public trust in the Department's capacity for self-regulation is very low.

And in some circumstances, in the case of our laboratories, they are subject to EPA and state environment regulation, in any case.

So what we're talking about is working toward a system of external regulation that would substitute for the system of internal self-regulation in order to take some of the cost of that system out, as well as rebuild public trust in the conduct of the Department's activities.

In the area of nuclear safety, the Congress has created the Defense Nuclear Facilities Safety Board to review the nuclear safety at the Department's facilities. It does not have mandatory authority of an external regulator. It makes recommendations. We respond to the recommendations.

What the advisory committee is signalling in what you just read to the Committee is that in the case of the NRC, which regulates civilian facilities, they get their fees by charging those civilian facilities and they have, obviously, great experience and expertise with civilian reactors. They don't have comparable experience with the types of things that the Department of Energy has involved.

So it may be necessary and it may be the appropriate path to create a new body with regulatory powers, a new external regulator for safety at our nuclear facilities, with broad regulatory powers.

That is one of the things that the advisory committee is examining and will be expected to report on at the end of the year.

But it shouldn't be understood that we are enthusiastic to create a new federal agency in this environment.

Mr. ROEMER. Thank you, Mr. Curtis.

Thank you, Mr. Chairman.

Mr. SCHIFF. So that Members might know the order they'll be called on, we're calling on the order in which Members arrived at the hearing.

Mr. Bartlett, you're recognized for five minutes.

Mr. BARTLETT. Thank you very much.

Mr. Curtis, I'm a little perplexed. On page 25 of your prepared statement, you say that the department opposes H.R. 87 and H.R. 1993, because you find in both of them—that is, Title II of 1993—you find in both of them, and I quote: "the presumption that there should be a broad closure effort for DOE's laboratories."

Where, sir, did you find that presumption in those two bills?

Secretary CURTIS. I think, Mr. Bartlett, both by the language of the bill and process.

First of all, borrowing, as it does, from the base closure process. And I believe in your remarks in describing the bill this morning, that you indicated that the purpose of that procedure is, in essence, to create an independent process, taking it out of the political process, which would be resistant to closures and downsizing.

The very purpose, therefore, I implied from your remarks, and I think from this bill, is that the objective of this commission would be to close laboratories, that the political process would not otherwise have the will to close.

Am I incorrect in that?

Mr. BARTLETT. You're both correct and incorrect.

Secretary CURTIS. Okay.

Mr. BARTLETT. You are correct in the presumption that we thought it very desirable to depoliticize the process.

You're incorrect if you conclude that we in any way had a presumption that laboratories should be closed.

Whether they should be restructured or closed or privatized or corporatized was not prejudged in either of these bills.

I am a very strong supporter of the national labs. I don't have any hesitancy in saying that I'm a strong supporter of the labs. Because I'm a strong supporter of the labs, I want them to be as good as they can be and as efficient as they can be.

And I think that when we obviously are faced with the necessity of re-evaluating the mission of the labs and the size of the labs because, as has been stated by so many people, including yourself, much of this capability was developed during the cold war. We are now in a post-cold war era.

That doesn't mean we don't need national laboratories. It may simply mean we need a refocusing of some of the activities of these laboratories.

I was the author of these bills and I in no way wanted a presumption that these bills were going to mandate broad closure of the laboratories. That was not at all the intent.

The real intent of the bill was to depoliticize the process so that we could get a recommendation for the Congress that was independent of the political arena, that we then vote up or down—now, this was only patterned after the BRAC process in the depoliticizing portion of that, not in the closure.

There is no broad-based study that says whether we should or should not close any of these national laboratories.

You stated I think correctly that there was a presumption that we had an excess of infrastructure for the military. Without a broad-based study looking at our laboratories, which is what we propose to do in this legislation, one could not say whether there is or is not a surplus of national laboratories.

There was no intent in these two bills of any presumption that there would be any mass closure of these laboratories.

Secretary CURTIS. Mr. Bartlett, let me make a couple observations, if I may.

Obviously, I take at face value your statement, and if I made the wrong assumption as both the process and procedure, then that is a mistake.

But we have had independent review of our laboratories. Indeed, just the Galvin Task Force on alternative futures of the laboratories primary purpose was to do just that. It was an independent body, genuinely independent, as you might observe from some of its recommendations. But it was an independent body that did not, specifically did not conclude that the laboratories or any one of them should be closed.

They did say that they were oversized and could be and should be downsized.

We believe that we can administer that charge subject to the oversight of this Committee. And in fact, I believe the political process must stay involved in this, just as the political process, you have a responsibility with us to deliver to future generations a fiscal discipline to cut our deficit and cut spending.

We have a political responsibility to future generations to preserve its scientific and technological capacity for innovation. And I would oppose removing political responsibility for the judgments made with respect to that.

Mr. BARTLETT. Our bill does not remove that responsibility. It simply gives the Congress an opportunity to act after a recommendation.

The ultimate responsibility is clearly the Congress's responsibility.

Mr. ROHRABACHER [presiding]. I think that's the proper note to go on to our next questioner.

Mr. BARTLETT. Thank you.

Mr. ROHRABACHER. Thank you, Mr. Bartlett. Mr. Olver from Massachusetts?

Mr. OLVER. Thank you, Mr. Chairman.

Mr. Curtis, I notice in your statements here that you early on point out that the environment that produces R&D excellence can be fragile, and if the labs are damaged, they would be extremely hard to rebuild.

I think I agree very much with that. You also give rather a long litany of the major advances in the scientific world leading on to the technological world, certainly, that have come out of the laboratories.

It seems to me that it should have been obvious perhaps to everybody that the situation that you describe of far too many directives, which you've chosen a very simple—there's nothing like an attention-getting number change to focus on that.

Now we don't know whether the directives that are going to be reduced from 312 to 156 represents a reduction by half of the impact of the directives or whether they're just going to become more complicated along the way in perhaps the usual way that bureaucracies function.

But that cannot have produced a very good atmosphere. You point out the number of reviews. You're reducing 20 or 30 reviews of a particular kind to one per year, which seems to make sense. A lot of that is going on.

The actions moving toward that go back—later in your testimony, you point out that in 1975 already, there were independent studies, and again in 1982, pointing out some of the overburden of all of these thing.

None of this can have been too beneficial to the atmosphere for producing research and development.

Is it only the matter of hitting this department or the Congress one way with the directives that come down here with a two-by-four in the middle of the forehead that the final attention to these things has been coming?

They're obviously bad things for getting good R&D results.

Secretary CURTIS. I truly can't explain why the Department has failed to manage the laboratories more effectively in the past.

Mr. OLVER. You would agree, I take it, that the management system is pretty broken, but maybe not agree with the Galvin Commission's precise options.

Secretary CURTIS. Yes. I agree that it's badly broken and greatly in need of repair.

I think the Galvin Task Force doubts that the Department is capable of fixing it because of the natural constraints of bureaucracy and congressional influence on that bureaucracy.

And that's why the more, as Bob Galvin would describe it, bold approach for corporatization.

I believe it can be fixed and we will fix it.

Mr. OLVER. Let me ask you. One of the other testifiers in another panel will make the comment that a balanced national R&D system includes four primary performers—research universities, industrial establishments, federal laboratories, and independent research institutions.

We're talking about the federal laboratories in this particular set of areas.

Balance means all of those being in some proper balance. Do you think we have a balanced—I think I agree with that comment. Do you think we now have a balanced system of where R&D is being done in those groups?

Secretary CURTIS. I think we need to—and this is probably a constant and continuing responsibility—that we need to re-examine the relationships between our laboratories, universities, and private industry to assure that the innovation process which is increasingly the product of a collaboration among the three is properly balanced and distributed.

Each have specific strengths that they bring to research and development and to the innovation model.

We are engaged in a process which we will conclude by the end of the year that will trace out how we manage our missions by program, showing how that investment is made in the laboratories, in universities, and the private sector.

That's never been done before.

Once that database is constructed, you and we will have the capacity to make the judgment whether we properly struck that balance.

Mr. OLVER. Well, the Galvin Report apparently makes the comments which you included in your testimony that, at least for the nine major labs, that their missions are so broad and generalized, that they're essentially indistinguishable, and it appears that they're attempting to keep options open in all fields.

Does that lead to any kind of efficiency? Does that serve the purpose of balanced and efficient research and development capacity over the whole of this group of agencies that should do their own thing, but also should collaborate to do things appropriately where that is valuable?

Secretary CURTIS. One of the great strengths of the national laboratories is their multi-disciplinary approach to problem-solving and their capacity to integrate those multi-disciplines to problem-solving.

So I think it is natural when you look at the multi-purpose laboratories, that you will see core competencies that at the surface will look like redundancies—high-performance computing. A great integrating national laboratory must have high-performance computing, for example.

Mr. OLVER. But these are service functions within the overall scientific function.

Secretary CURTIS. These are service functions, exactly right.

What Galvin has asked for and what we think most appropriate and are committed to do is to sharpen the mission focus of these laboratories, identify centers of excellence.

Mr. OLVER. Do you think it's better to have single-purpose ones? The smaller ones are largely single-purpose kinds of laboratories. Should they all be single-purpose?

Secretary CURTIS. I think there's probably room for both single-purpose and multi-purpose laboratories. But to too narrowly define a laboratory's mission in terms of single-purpose loses a multi-disciplinary approach to the science at that laboratory.

That's one of the great strengths of our national laboratories. We don't think you should go down that path.

Mr. ROHRABACHER. I hesitate to interrupt my colleague's enlightening line of questioning, but we must move on now to Mr. Wamp from Tennessee.

Mr. WAMP. Thank you, Mr. Chairman.

If I may make a short innocent observation and ask one question. Secretary Curtis, based on your comments thus far and my deep understanding that Secretary O'Leary had the instincts to preempt some of the new budget winds in Washington and propose her own reductions and your statements today in fact that you are cutting the budget and aggressively cutting the budget, and, quite honestly, my honest support for the Department of Energy in those initiatives.

And I just want to point out that, based on some of the press releases that worked their way into my district this summer from not only the Department of Energy, but also from the Ranking Member of the full Science Committee, you would think that the Republicans are the only ones proposing reductions in the Department of Energy work force.

I think you honestly can't have your cake and eat it, too.

I would respectfully request that we do try to be more bipartisan in spirit and that there is an effort, an honest effort on both sides, to reduce spending efficiently and effectively and that we are not all Attila the Huns and that you are not all Mary Poppinses.

And I think it's important to take that attitude, especially, Mr. Schiff, in my district where we've been outspoken advocates for science and energy research investment and I've supported openly before this very Committee those initiatives.

So let's try to be as fair as possible.

And I do think that the labs must play a critical role in international competitiveness, the creation of good jobs in this country, and the advancement of higher education.

And I want to reference in the form of a question the fact that about five weeks ago, Speaker Gingrich and I spent a weekend together. We were at the Temkin research facility in Canton, Ohio, and Tim Temkin shared with us that, through their best-practices efforts there, that research from 30-year-old MIT hot-shots, I think he called them, is leading their competitiveness internationally now.

And that reminded us there, hands on, that our higher educational institutions are going to give birth to advantages for our nation.

And I just want you to share with us a little of what you referenced earlier, your best-practices efforts, where DOE is going with regard to this, and how many partnerships can we develop between our institutions of higher learning and our national laboratory system, so as we look to higher education to lead the world competitively in technology and research and science, can we expect more and more partnerships, and how?

Secretary CURTIS. Well, first, Mr. Wamp, I appreciate your comments. I think this Committee has over the years operated at a high-level of bipartisanship in the investment in this nation's science and research capabilities, and I believe that we should try to maintain a high degree of bipartisanship and tone of respect in our discussion of these matters.

I'm sure you will respect that we must speak up when we think that actions are considered or about to be taken that we believe will severely damage that capability.

What I said in response to Mr. Olver is that we do need to constantly re-evaluate the investment in our laboratories and our collaborations with universities and the private sector to assure that we are taking advantage of the institutional strengths of each sector of the innovation establishment.

But let me point out that our department already contributes significantly to university research and academy and this should not be seen as a trade-off between the health of universities and jobs at our laboratories.

We administer over $600 million in grants to universities. We operate user facilities at which 16,000 researchers a year from academia and other government agencies and industry conduct research.

With the scientific facilities initiative that we propose, that will increase by another 20,000.

Our energy research program itself supports 1200 post-docs and over 2200 graduate students.

So the Department of Energy should be seen as a science agency that is supporting science and going to the best available source for that science.

Have we got it balanced right? I can't tell you that because we don't have the information base at present to explain it. But we will by the end of the year.

Mr. ROHRABACHER. Thank you, Mr. Curtis. Thank you, Mr. Wamp.

My California colleague, Ms. Lofgren?

Ms. LOFGREN. Thank you, Mr. Chairman.

I think all of us are aware that whatever we do with the labs, we need to be very thoughtful and careful because they provide something that is of enormous importance to our country and our country's future in terms of repository of some of the smartest people in the country who are thinking up the stuff that's going to make us prosperous in the next century.

And so I do think this hearing is very important. I come to this hearing without pre-conceived notions on what we can do.

However, as I've listened to the testimony and read through the written statements, it occurs to me that some of the bills before us seem to assume that if we defined our missions more clearly and shed the excess, that there would be substantial savings as a result.

I'm wondering how much of the current activity in the labs, in your judgment, is outside of the missions outlined, for example, in the Galvin Report?

Do you think that that assumption of shedding missions is likely to yield savings if we use the Galvin Report as a guide?

Secretary CURTIS. I think it depends on how one defines missions.

The missions of national security, energy research, environmental quality, and science and technology laid out in the Galvin Report at the highest level, are very, very broad categories. And you could fit almost any research and development——

Ms. LOFGREN. So you'd say basically everything we're doing fits within those broad categories.

Secretary CURTIS. Exactly so. But I think what the Galvin Committee report rather eloquently said is that these missions have genuine contemporary value. It is a mistake to get too caught up with the notion that we're in a post-cold war environment and therefore, this great capacity for innovation can be somehow dismantled very quickly.

Ms. LOFGREN. Oh, no, and I certainly do not argue that. If I may, our mission now is to compete effectively economically with the rest of the world. It's slightly different than it was in the cold war.

I'm wondering, you said earlier in response to another question that you had reservations about the management recommendations in the Galvin Report, or actually did not support them, if I quoted you correctly.

Secretary CURTIS. That's correct. We support those recommendations.

Ms. LOFGREN. I'm sorry?

Secretary CURTIS. We support the management recommendations in the Galvin Report. We do not support the recommendations for governance, that's correct.

Ms. LOFGREN. Now let me ask you this. Compared to laying off a third of the employees and staff in the labs, which do you think is preferable—the Galvin governance structure or closing a third of the personnel?

Secretary CURTIS. Well, you have to look forward and see at least where we think the Galvin governance structure goes.

It is my belief, and let me personalize this, my belief that to set the national laboratories apart, to fend for themselves on a work-for-others basis in essence with even a sponsoring agency such as the Department of Energy and other agencies, will radically result in downsizing that capacity.

That, incidentally, is the experience that the British had when they privatized their laboratories. They shrunk dramatically.

And you have to ask whether you, given Mr. Olver's concern, shared concern about the reconstitution capability of these laboratories, that you could ever rebuild the system if it were lost.

Ms. LOFGREN. No, it would be a disaster. I guess what I'm searching for is a way—all of the criticism I have heard stems to administrative practices, bureaucracy, that are really driven by this Congress and by the full dead weight of the federal rules.

I haven't heard a lot of complaints, frankly, about the individual on-site managers of labs who are trying to struggle within this morass of bureaucracy.

I haven't heard complaints about the universities. I haven't really heard complaints about the scientists.

So I'm searching for a way to pull that dead mass of bureaucracy and paperwork that stifles innovation away from these labs to allow them to move forward.

And in my years of government service at every level, I've never seen the government accomplish that unless you change the way you're doing business.

And I'm wondering, do you have a recommendation that could, other than what you've got in your written report, best management practices and I commend you for trying to do it. I don't believe it's going to accomplish what we both want.

Is there still another alternative that we should consider in terms of governance that could avoid the downsize that Britain saw and yet, get rid of the problem that everyone seems to agree upon?

Secretary CURTIS. I think it's fair to be skeptical whether the department is capable of delivering on what we all know needs to happen.

There may be other governance models that can give us more certainty in this path. I don't know what they are. But, as I said in my answer in my formal statement, is that we remain open to discussion of different governance models to see if we can get there.

One thing we're doing at the department is to create this laboratory operations board where we're bringing in eight outsiders from industry and academia and those who have had prior government experience to help us manage the laboratories to be our conscience and our constant disciplinarian in this effort and to carry this effort from one administration to another.

So we're open to talk about it. We just haven't found one yet.

Mr. ROHRABACHER. Thank you, Mr. Curtis. Now we have Mr. Tiahrt from Kansas.

Mr. TIAHRT. Thank you, Mr. Chairman.

I want to start off by quoting from Galvin Report. It says, that there have been many studies of the Department of Energy laboratories. As one reads these reports, one recognizes that the items which were recommended in previous reports are, for the most part, recommended in most subsequent reports.

As each past study has taken place, people of good intention do make sincere efforts to fine-tune the system. However, the department and the Congress should recognize that there has been little fundamental improvement as a function of the past studies.

I think that kind of captures the frustration that Congress has and many of these people have made in reports that see problems. They're reported in the GAO reports and other reports and there's no progress.

Secretary CURTIS. Right.

Mr. TIAHRT. And I think the four current bills under consideration are a reflection of the lack of progress and the concern.

I want to give you four data points and then ask you a question.

Quoting earlier from Ranking Minority Member Brown, he said that almost any government agency can be cut a third without seriously impairing the function of that agency, 33 percent.

The Galvin Report says that 20 percent can be saved from annual operating costs in the departmental laboratory complex.

The third data point would be from the Ergon report, which is the Secretary of Energy advisory board to the U.S. Department of Energy, Energy R&D—Shaping Our Nation's Future in a Competitive World.

This report recommends a 15-percent reduction over a period of one year.

And then if I look at what the Department of Energy and you're recommending is a four-percent reduction, or $1.5 billion over the next five years, four percent compared to 33, 15, 20, somewhere in that range.

Taking into consideration that most major corporations in the United States have downsized between 20 and 15 percent, somewhere in that range, 10 to 20 percent we'll say, and you're looking at a four percent.

Do you consider that aggressive enough to satisfy Congress in the light of the new wind that's blowing through Washington these days?

Secretary CURTIS. I think what we have here is a problem of comparisons.

The department is doing many more things than just taking the $1.4 billion out for Galvin. It is also reducing its federal work force by 27 percent, 33 percent of that being in Washington itself. And we're going to do two-thirds of that over the next two years.

We are going to reduce our applied research budget by $1.2 billion.

So none of that has been captured in my remarks this morning, although it appears in answer to one of the advance questions.

So I don't think you have apples and apples—I think you have apples and oranges. You don't have apples to apples together.

Obviously, if we are only talking about taking cost out of the system, ten percent over the next five years, that's an inadequate response. The Department is doing many, many more things than that. And I think we will get much more cost out of the system and deliver on a more rational—our commitment to deliver on a more rational management system.

The costs are very, very significant to our laboratories and to federal employment.

Mr. TIAHRT. Well, many of us who are strong advocates of research and development and see the national labs as a tremendous asset hate to see things going to waste, hate to see our resources going to waste because it adds to the pressure.

Secretary CURTIS. Right.

Mr. TIAHRT. And coming out of aerospace myself and knowing what type of ratios are involved, there is, from the casual observer, an excess in overhead and you have reflected that you're going to try and focus on that and I appreciate the efforts.

But I want you to keep in mind how aggressive this Congress has been and that if there is going to be some satisfaction, it's going to have to be on an aggressive note.

And I yield back the balance of my time.

Secretary CURTIS. I appreciate that.

Mr. SCHIFF [presiding]. Mr. Cramer, you're recognized for five minutes.

Mr. CRAMER. Mr. Chairman, since I came in late, I'll pass at this point.

Thank you.

Mr. SCHIFF. Mr. Cramer reserves his time.

Mr. Ehlers volunteers to be our next questioner. Mr. Ehlers, you are recognized for five minutes.

Mr. EHLERS. Thank you, Mr. Chairman. I never thought I'd be old enough to talk about the good old days, but I'm afraid I've reached that point.

I'm probably unique on this panel. I don't have any DOE facilities in my district, but I've worked at three of them and visited a number of others.

And I'm reminded of the history of Lawrence Berkeley laboratory, which started out with E.O. Lawrence building a cyclotron which could sit on a kitchen chair and he did some rather good experiments with that, in fact, won a Nobel Prize for him.

I was at Lawrence Berkeley lab in the '50s and we got a tremendous amount of research done at minimal cost with very little administrative work.

Over the years, I've watched that shift. First of all, the first sign of danger was when physicists hired engineers to design the equipment.

[Laughter.]

And they did a fine job. It's a beautiful job, probably the first time cyclotrons and other equipment ever got painted and color-coded for different things. But this all added to the overhead.

And that was not such a bad step.

The next step I noticed was the increased administrative overburden. Everyone talks about the bureaucracy. These are all incremental steps. They were well-intentioned. They went just bit by bit. Every one fulfilled an important purpose. But the net effect is that more and more resources were diverted away from the basic purpose of the laboratories, and that was research. And more and more got diverted into ancillary functions.

I haven't seen that trend change. It's still there. It's still a problem. We still talk about it. I'm not particularly enamored of any of these bills because I'm not sure that any of them specifically get at the problem.

But what is needed, I believe, is a very aggressive approach both by the Congress and the DOE.

Number one, I think we have to sort out the good science and the good projects from those that are less worthy and simply concentrate on the good ones.

I think it's also very important for us to get rid of both congressional and DOE micromanagement of the laboratories. And I'm willing to indict Congress as much as the DOE on that score.

A third item I would suggest is that we have to get more university involvement, affiliation, partnership, name it what you will, with the national laboratories, because that is a very fruitful, synergistic way to approach this. And it's worked very well at those laboratories that have it.

So I think if we set those three things as our objectives, sort the good science from the less worthy, get rid of the micromanagement, and I'm saying really cut deeply on that score because most scientists don't need that kind of micromanagement. They are self-starters. If they're good scientists, they're self-starters. They know what needs to be done. They'll do it. They'll get it done, and with very minimal fuss, muss, and bother.

And increase the university participation in this.

If we can come up with legislation or administrative action that does those three, I would be very pleased and I think everyone here would be pleased with the result.

Now to my question. What role do you think the Department of Energy can play in this? What can you do administratively on this score? What do you have planned?

And I'm talking about serious, deep introspection and action. And what specific authority would you need from Congress to implement such things?

Secretary CURTIS. Let me take the last first.

I don't think we need authority of the Congress. We need its cooperation and its patience and its participation in this process.

I think the three principles you laid out are sound principles. I suspect we will see a greater dependence, for example, on university research as a participant in the collaboration with the laboratories in the future.

I believe the Congress, these Subcommittees might consider, as I noted earlier, some very structured oversight of the department's administration of its responsibilities here because we do share common goals.

If, for example, on a six-month basis, we were in a reporting process to these committees on these very things, taking the micromanagement out of the laboratory, developing a mission plan for the laboratories, a sharpened focus of their missions, to identify how we carry out our missions programmatically within the laboratories and universities and in the private sector, identify centers of excellence and, in essence, streamline and sweep away that which is not excellent and therefore, not contributing value to the science and technology resource of this nation, that we will accomplish a great deal.

But there's just no substitute for hard work here. I think we can work at it together. I really don't see a legislative solution. It's the hardest part of the work of the Congress, its oversight and its insistence on its will through that process.

Mr. SCHIFF. Congressman Fawell, you're recognize for five minutes.

Mr. FAWELL. I was no. able to listen to the testimony. I'll pass at this time.

Mr. SCHIFF. Mr. Salmon, you're recognized for five minutes.

Mr. SALMON. Pass.

Mr. SCHIFF. We've now recognized all the Members of the Subcommittees.

I would ask, does any Member have a pressing question that they did not have the opportunity to ask that they'd like to be recognized for at the present time?

[No response.]

I don't see any requests, so let me say, Secretary Curtis, we thank you very much for your being here today, for your testimony, for your response to the questions.

Again, we appreciate your being here.

Secretary CURTIS. Thank you, Mr. Chairman.

Mr. SCHIFF. Let me say that the good news is that there is so much congressional interest in this subject, that we have spent about two-and-a-half hours almost with our first witness.

The bad news is there is so much congressional interest in the subject, that we spent about two-and-a-half hours with one witness. [Laughter.]

And I think that leads me to believe that our next panels will be equally well received in terms of interest. And I think, therefore, that it would behoove us to take a break now, and I don't mean to inconvenience people who are waiting to testify. But I think that what we've just seen is we went several hours without a break.

So I am going to call a recess until 12:30. And I would really like to bang the gavel back at 12:30, and would ask everyone to be back, if they possibly can, witnesses and Members.

And just one reminder, please, if I may. This would be a good time to stop by Room 2325 and to see the exhibit of R&D award winners from the national laboratories.

The Subcommittees are in recess until 12:30.

[Whereupon, at 11:45 a.m., the Subcommittees recessed, to reconvene at 12:30 p.m. of the same day.]

AFTERNOON SESSION

Mr. SCHIFF. I'd like to invite everyone to resume their seats please. The hearing is reconvened. Invite the panel of witnesses to take the witness table.

And, as they say, timing is everything. I think before we begin, I think we will recess for this vote, and we will proceed. I just work here too, you know. Give me one second.

[Pause.]

Mr. SCHIFF. You know, when we set these times for hearings, we don't know when that's going to happen. I think that rather than interrupting this panel in the middle of their presentations, I ask the panel of witnesses for their indulgence, apologize for this, but I think it's best that Members just go vote, and we will reconvene as quickly as possible after this vote ends.

The Committee will be in recess again.

[Recess.]

Mr. SCHIFF. I'd like to invite everyone again to take their seats and the witnesses to come forward. I don't think we're going to have a vote for a little while here, although we never know for sure. But thank you again for that indulgence.

I want to again say I think, most likely, those of you who are here now that were here this morning, that once again, if you've never seen a Congressional hearing, even though Members will come back over a period of time because they are occupied with other matters, the record goes on and a complete record is made of this hearing for all Members of Congress.

With that, I'd like to welcome our panel, our first panel. And the members of this panel include:

Robert W. Galvin, who is Chairman of the Executive Committee of Motorola, and of course chaired the Galvin Task Force on the national laboratories, that we've already referred to in great detail.

Erich Bloch, who is Acting President and Distinguished Fellow of the Council on Competitiveness.

Dr. Charles M. Vest, President of Massachusetts Institute of Technology.

Mr. Sherman McCorkle who is President of Technology Ventures Corporation.

And Dr. Bruce L.R. Smith, who is Senior Staff of the Brookings Institution.

Let me say that we are honored to have such a distinguished panel. We have your written statements and, without objection, they will be made a part of this record.

And I would invite you to proceed any way you wish, but I would encourage you to try to summarize your main points in five minutes, so that we can proceed with questions.

But with that, I'll recognize first Mr. Galvin. Welcome back.

STATEMENT OF ROBERT W. GALVIN, CHAIRMAN OF THE EXECUTIVE COMMITTEE, MOTOROLA

Mr. GALVIN. I will be focused, I will be brief. I presume to aggregate all of the four pieces of legislative proposals. Their virtual commonalities lead to my one fundamental proposal that follows these seven short paragraphs.

First. All of the acts proposed intend reduced costs at the laboratories, I emphasize at the laboratories. That may or may not be the right focus.

Second. Some acts intend some reduced costs at the Department of Energy, including a particular recommendation to abolish the Department.

All of your acts call for some mission and/or governance and/or reconfiguration and/or closure of the labs.

Forgive my over-simplification. I have aggregated all of my synthesis in those three paragraphs.

My fourth comment is that no act, as proposed, features the giant savings potential of a broad policy change by the Congress regarding accountability and the self-evident, obsessive micromanagement that it, the Congress, has bred. The report of the Task Force that I chaired for the Department of Energy in 1994 made it clear that Congressional policy is the first order cost driver of the system cost of our Department of Energy laboratories. You are a big part of the problem.

Five.

Mr. SCHIFF. I assume that's a "you" plural?

[Laughter.]

Mr. GALVIN. Both of you.

[Laughter.]

Mr. SCHIFF. How about all three of us?

[Laughter.]

Mr. GALVIN. Five. No act features the savings potential of a follow on policy that would call for the Department of Energy or any alternate identity you might legislate, also being relieved of virtually all accountability and management authorities, thus making possible the elimination of most Department personnel. There's a gigantic savings.

Six. No act features the savings potential in the laboratories, once they are allowed to then operate to world-class, private sector cost efficiencies, vis-a-vis working as a corporation. As hard as you in the Congress or the Department may try, and I do see good efforts, you and they cannot optimize the organizational environment in which private sector class cost efficiencies can be achieved. These efficiencies are over and above the micromanagement induced overhead costs of interfacing with the federal redundant overseers.

Seven. No act anticipates the high potential for retaining all or more than the current science and technology output, while retaining all qualified science and technology personnel, while still achieving an aggregate cost savings in the system, from my fourth, fifth, and sixth paragraph, at least as promising as any of the proposed legislative initiatives which are the subject of this hearing.

Thus, I propose corporatizing the labs, radically downsizing the Department, keeping all labs as divisions in a single corporation operating as a system under a board of trustees composed of our finest private sector and professional leaders who would guide it to its most productive and accountable configurations.

That is my oral testimony and I simply take note of the fact that a paper that defines and justifies the conversion of the governance system to corporatization from the current Department, which is the dominated gold coast system, is included in my document, which, incidentally, will be published in Issues Magazine this fall that relates, among others, to the various science communities.

Secondly, there is a short statement in my filed material referencing the precedent for the approach to and the modeling of a federal corporatization change on behalf of the laboratories, and you and your staff know all about how that kind of thing can be done, and further elucidation is available.

C] There is a short paper, and I would suggest this short paper be referred to, regarding the far-reaching values foreseeable in just the next decade or two, if we have an enlightened, aggressive approach encouraging a major step function by the energy industry in investments for energy generation throughout the rest of the world.

This will multiply markets that will help that industry and all American industry thrive as it never has before. It will create wealth at home and abroad while providing even greater public resources from a broader tax base, all of which promises an improved quality of life.

Science and more technology is the key to that. The national laboratories are a critical key holder to unlock the door to these achievable opportunities.

Thank you for hearing again my proposal.

[The prepared statement of Mr. Galvin follows:]

Testimony To

Subcommittee on Basic Research

and

Subcommittee on Energy and Environment

House Committee on Science

September 7, 1995

by

Robert W. Galvin

Chief Executive Officer, Motorola Inc., 1959-1990
Chairman, Executive Committee, Motorola Inc., 1990-
Co-Chairman, Commission on the Future, NFS, 1992
Chairman, Secretary of Energy Task Force on
Alternate Futures of (ten) Laboratories, 1994

CORPORATIZING THE DOE LABS

The U.S. Department of Energy produces an incredible array of products and services vital to this country. It provides a secure and reliable nuclear stockpile and methods for the cleanup and decommissioning of nuclear facilities. It develops research and technology that enhance our long-term energy supplies, protect the environment, and stimulate industry. The 20,000 scientists and engineers at DOE's laboratories have generated dozens of Nobel prizes, numerous commercial technologies, and discoveries in areas as diverse as atmospheric science and the human genome.

And yet, the DOE laboratory system is broken. It is grievously mismanaged from the top--that is, from Congress and the department itself. Micromanagement, oppressive oversight, compounding regulations, contradictory directives, audits upon audits, layers of bureaucracy, and isolated stovepipes of authority are suffocating the labs. The result is excessive overhead, poor morale, and gross inefficiencies.

That is not just my opinion; it is the major finding of an intensive year-long study by a special committee of 23 high-level professionals appointed by the secretary of energy--the Task Force on Alternative Futures for the DOE Labs, which I chaired. When the task force reported its findings in February, the secretary, lab directors, and many members of Congress acknowledged these problems and admitted significant change had to take place.

Incremental improvements within the existing DOE framework, as proposed by Energy Secretary Hazel O'Leary, will never counteract the enormous waste already in the system. Privatizing the labs--selling them outright--as has been proposed by some members of Congress, is politically untenable at this time. Besides, there are no likely buyers. Congress has quickly shot down the idea of dismantling DOE, once when it was suggested by the White House two years ago and recently when it was proposed again by freshmen representatives. This would also be a mistake, because there is a major near-term opportunity to export huge quantities of energy-generating technologies as developing countries attempt to accelerate their growth.

Closing some labs to save money--under a proposed congressional lab-closing commission--misses the point altogether. The bureaucratic system is the problem; it won't be solved by shuttering a lab or two.

The best solution, the task force concluded, is to corporatize the labs. The government would continue to own DOE's facilities, but the labs would be overseen by a board of trustees composed of industry and academic leaders.

My intention, here, is to go beyond the task force's bold recommendation--to explain not only why corporatizing the labs is the best solution, but how to implement the change, why the objections to it are weak, and why DOE and the nation will gain by taking swift action.

Bloated Bureaucracy

DOE has become bloated after 25 years of operation because each new set of government actors has added more governance to the department in the name of adding value. Wanting to be sure to be more than compliant, each energy secretary and staff person responsible for interpreting these directives has protected himself or herself by adding even more. As a consequence, micromanagement and excessive auditing has become the ingrained practice.

In order to survive this downward pressure, each lab has had to create a structure, and a set of people, to interface with the micromanagers and auditors. Lab directors have added safeguards of their own to prevent even the appearance of being the slightest bit unresponsive.

In the last decade, political fad has complicated the mix further. Political appointees have felt a need to prove that they are converting the labs into job-creating stimulators. This additional mission is denied by DOE officials, yet our task force found hundreds of people in the department and at the labs scurrying around trying to find a way to justify that what they were working on would help create a given set of jobs--and near-term, to boot.

This snowballing of wasted effort is not the labs' fault. Responsibility rests first with Congress, and second with the department. Congress has mandated too much of the "what to do" and too much of the "how to do." It has intimidated the department into imposing oppressive accountability requirements upon the labs. And the department has blithely succumbed.

Incrementalism Isn't Enough

Having acknowledged the problem, Congress favors reduced funding. People in the department are diligently examining how to save money and restructure. Shortly they will determine that enough has been done and the system will settle back to the "federal norm."

Indeed, in March Secretary O'Leary submitted to Congress her detailed reaction to the task force's 29 recommendations. She agreed with 25, and explained that the department was already making substantial progress on many of them. She claimed that DOE will save $10 billion by 1999 by streamlining operations. Among the four items she opposed was the recommendation to corporatize the labs, stating that the goals established by the task force could be accomplished within the existing government-owned, contractor-operated (GOCO) model.

Despite the rubric, DOE has become government-owned and government-operated. Continuation of the GOCO system is a license for meddling and interference. The system is so obfuscated with incorrect congressional and departmental policies that fine-tuning what is fundamentally wrong will insufficiently change the laboratory system. It amounts to rearranging the deck chairs on the Titanic.

Each institution in the United States government should be continually challenged to renew. This is not the natural talent of government. Therefore, the government must be substantially taken out of the operation of the system. Private sector experts will be required to do the job of leading (not governing or dictating to) DOE's labs so they become efficient enterprises--and remain that way.

The Payoff of Corporatizing

Thus the choice comes down to either privatize or corporatize the DOE labs. Privatize means that the private sector would own the labs' assets and largely fund lab work. That is not necessary to fix the problem, nor can industry presently afford ownership.

Corporatize means the labs would take the form of a federal corporation. The government would retain title to the sophisticated, complex physical assets of the laboratories. It would continue to fund the labs as well as university research at near-current levels. But the labs would be operated by the private sector. In form and function, each lab would be transformed to parallel that of a Baldrige-quality, commercial company.

DOE would remain the sponsor of the labs and the federal government would continue to be the labs' principle customer. The labs would also serve university and corporate clients. This dual role would be successfully carried out just as it is at such notable organizations as Bell Labs. Neither Congress nor DOE, however, would audit or direct the labs; world-class customers do not have to audit world-class suppliers.

The payoff would be swift and sweeping. This simplification would lead directly to a 75 percent reduction in DOE's cadre of personnel who interface with the labs. As a result, hundreds of millions of dollars would be saved annually from the federal personnel and support budgets. The labs, in turn, would be able to eliminate hundreds of people who now have to stand by to deal with the many Washington and field-office compliance checkers. (It is possible, too, that as the corporation eliminates redundancy, one of the labs could eventually be closed.)

What's more, the labs would finally be able to reach a high level of productivity, made possible by private-sector-type quality management systems. When these principles are applied at commercial companies, output is raised, and operating costs are typically reduced by a minimum of 20 percent (and 40 to 50 percent in pockets of activity).

The labs are good, but they do not approach modern quality management levels. Under the federal norm they never will. For years now, my company, Motorola, has used the latest quality management principles to continually reduce cost and price, increase volume, accomplish more tasks, and quicken R&D cycle times. Similar accomplishments are possible in the labs if government will get out of the way, just as top management in private companies has had to get out of the way! Quality systems are only productive if the doers are allowed to do what they do unhampered.

Operating Corporatized Labs

DOE's labs can be successfully operated in a corporatized manner if three issues are addressed: creation of a board of trustees, an altered funding protocol, and changes to several laws.

The policy and congressional intent underpinning this new nonprofit corporation will be carried out by a corporate board of trustees. The board would comprise private citizens--no government employees. Most would have business and science credentials and a record of private and civic service that demonstrates high achievement in enterprise leadership and integrity. As trustees, they would be trusted. Trust must be infused into the system if technology output and value are to grow.

Board members could be appointed by the President or through other responsible means. They would serve for modest or no compensation. Their work would be a privilege, conducted to show how new levels of scientific output, economy, and integrity can be achieved. The board would select a chief executive of the organization. He or she would be a full-time, well-paid top executive with an impressive and appropriate record, such as a former chief of Bell Labs or an outstanding head of one of DOE's current labs.

Lab directors would have the stature of laboratory presidents and would report to the chief executive. The central staff would be minimal--in the scores of people, not the thousands that are in DOE now. Would there be accountability? Of course. Just as there is in top-flight corporations. Accountability without profit motive? Of course. Trusted, dedicated leaders of science institutions have many qualitative and quantitative metrics they can use to measure and control while motivating and inspiring.

And public accounting firms, the Occupational Safety and Health Administration, the Environmental Protection Agency, and the like would certainly be able to hold the labs to high standards.

Funding of the corporation would be established in congressional line items in the DOE budget, in each of four mission areas: national defense, energy, basic research, and environment. There would be a fifth line item for "other programs," which would include health, facility improvement, global ecology, economic betterment, and so on. Each mission would contain funds that could be used across the full R&D spectrum, from basic research to development and technology demonstration. The budget would be for some multiple of years, with a decline built in over a five-year period. Renewal of funding would be subject to congressional approval.

Allocation of funds among the labs would be made by the corporation. The management of the corporation would consult with the traditional agencies for which the work is done to refine allocations. Micromanagement or earmarking of these allocations by Congress or DOE would not be allowed.

Legislation would be required to transfer the labs to private operation. However, there is considerable legal precedent to support an act of Congress to institutionalize a nonprofit corporation that encompasses the labs. Under the Government Corporations Control Act, Congress has set up such wholly owned companies as the Export-Import Bank of the United States, the Saint Lawrence Seaway Development Corp., and the Tennessee Valley Authority. It has also formed mixed-ownership government corporations, including Amtrak, the Federal Deposit Insurance Corp., and the Resolution Trust Co.

The authorizing legislation could include exemptions from existing laws that might impede progress. All the necessary changes could be provided in one piece of legislation, together with a statement of policy and a structure for policymaking decisions. This structure could include (but is not limited to) the following conditions

- DOE will carry out a revised role
- The corporation will be subject only to "normal" federal and state control of commercial companies.
- The federal government will continue to bear preexisting liabilities associated with the labs.
- Annual reports must document the presence of internal accounting and control systems.
- Audit reports will be submitted to Congress.
- The corporation has the authority to make financial commitments without fiscal year limitations.
- The corporation will not have to hire people from within the civil service system.
- A transitional planning mechanism will be put into place.

A major policy question is whether to include DOE's three national defense labs in the conversion. Several members of the task force raised concerns over security, safety, and the defense labs' tight linkage to national policies.

As the strongest task force advocate for corporatizing, I envision no insurmountable problem in operating the defense labs in a private sector mode. Highly sensitive and complex weapons responsibilities have been handled by corporations since the beginning of defense procurement. Eventually, procurement would have to be overhauled if the defense labs were to fully benefit from corporatization, but there is movement already underway in Congress to improve the procurement system.

However, because an important goal of corporatization is to run a serious experiment in governance, there is nothing fundamentally wrong with first corporatizing the seven major nondefense labs and later merging the three defense labs into the corporation.

Bias and Accountability

Since the task force's report, several legislators have raised objections to corporatizing the DOE labs. Let me address them here.

Much of the objection stems from a natural bias of government people to retain the governance system they already have. People who assume the role of public official often presume that they know better. They consider themselves the neutral broker between the taxpayer and the "doer" of tax-supported functions.

Furthermore, many public officials subliminally or overtly crave command and control, which they can exert through the powers of the purse. They, and DOE officials, also often rate the importance of their job based on the number of people they control. Finally, congressional and department people, even the top lab directors, are comfortable dealing with what and whom they know. Change can seem threatening.

These biases have surfaced in the form of claims that a board of trustees would not know what is technologically best for the nation, that they would not be neutral with taxpayer money (as if politicians are), that power of the purse is the only sure way to lead an institution, and that government is best changed gradually from within.

Each one of these objections is weak. Trustees would be selected based on their proven record of quality thinking and doing regarding fundamental scientific research and engineering. They would be the nation's best executive and academic leaders. As such, they would be far more qualified to decide what can be done with America's scientific resources than people who happen to be elected or appointed as political officials.

These kind of trustees would be just as neutral and trustable as any politician. Their incentive for being so is even greater, because their entire professional record will be on the line and judged according to how they perform in this experiment.

Governance by power of the purse is yesterday's demotivating management principle. All enlightened organization leaders now recognize there has to be a trusting, participative, empowering, and quality-based dynamic if an institution is to produce results. The examples in industry are legion. Corporatizing would create a structure in which this environment can flourish.

The United States cannot afford any extra overhead. The nation is demanding great reductions in the number of people who serve in government. Corporatizing preserves all the good work at the labs while cutting deeply into an enormous and unnecessary bureaucracy.

Finally, talented people must be ready to change, in service to the public instead of self-service. Science professionals should not have to maneuver within a restrictive cocoon woven by political motivations. As often happens in industry, when critical change is imposed upon an organization, its people discover, as they reluctantly but rapidly adapt, how much more effective they can be at doing their jobs.

Other, specific objections have also been raised. Again, there is little cause for concern.

Some members of Congress worry about accountability. They believe they have the best consciences, are the best managers of funds, and are the best overseers of compliance with regulations. However, they are also deeply concerned about avoiding negative publicity. Certain legislative aides interviewed by the task force emphasized that their member would not give up anything having to do with accountability, for fear of reading about some ensuing accusation or cynicism in the Washington Post. In these politicians' minds, according to the aides, it was worth spending as much as $100 to save the embarrassment of a presumption of a misexpenditure of $1. The real scandal that should be the subject of public scrutiny is this extraordinary waste of tax dollars, which gains nothing. The price of this exaggerated accountability as much as doubles the actual cost of the protected service or activity. Where is the accountability for that?!

The cost of today's accountability at DOE, which includes the majority of its staff, is many times the cost of what might be an occasional mismanaged expense. All institutions will at times manifest a discrepancy. But public officials have got to learn that on balance, they will save the taxpayer immensely more if they allow credentialed specialists to oversee the labs than if they continue to micromanage and immobilize the labs.

Other officials are concerned about what would in effect be block grants to the corporation through the budgeting process. They feel the spending of tax money should not be left to nongovernment officials. Of course, that would also preserve their ability to fund political plums. In addition, they claim the authorizing and appropriations responsibility of Congress has rarely allowed for too much elective appointment. In short, they believe they must be hands-on.

Just because we have used the same authorizing and appropriations methods in the past does not mean they are the best ones to lead the United States into the 21st Century. Block grants leave the decisions on specific allocations to the people best able to make those decisions--experienced science and engineering professionals. The simpler the federal process, the more effective it will be, and the more technology the public will gain from their taxes.

Finally, DOE itself, and its supporters in Congress, maintain that it should be allowed to correct itself. First of all, it cannot, because it cannot change Congress's stronghold on it. Second, in DOE's plan to incrementally save money, its expectations are too low and too slow. Furthermore, the distribution of its proposed savings is too evenly focused on the science budgets of the labs instead of where it belongs--on the wasteful administration of the DOE itself. Anyone in Congress who supports this incrementalism is misguided if he or she believes the public will tolerate support for the labs at all if they don't measure up to the new private sector norms, which are only possible through corporatizing. Micromanagement has continually made the labs less efficient; taxpayers are losing their patience with investing money in such costly pursuits and will substantially decrease their tolerance for most labs. A new system is essential to justify continued taxpayer support.

Critical Experiment

The political likelihood of near-term adoption of this proposal is small. Some members of Congress have spoken against it, claiming that an experiment with such a large organization is too risky. Others have publicly supported the task force's recommendation to corporatize, saying a bold initiative is needed. They have informed Secretary O'Leary that they do not intend for the task force's report to gather dust. In August, at this writing, several influential members of Congress told me that corporatizing is the only solution that will work. Further committee hearings on the topic were scheduled for September.

Government takes time to change and that alone may prevent corporatizing from occurring right away. But the common sense proposal's time will come. There are two emerging conditions that will inevitably impact organizations like government departments and laboratories: funding constraints and a global move toward privatization.

The tough decision about what to do with the DOE labs will have to be based on the lowest cost way to deliver the most science to the nation. Private enterprise is the incontestable choice. It's even called the American Way. Other industrialized nations are already choosing a new "private norm." The principle that private sector productivity is better than government productivity will take hold in the United States, for reasons of affordability alone. Well-conditioned federal folks may not want to believe this is needed today, but they will have to face the coming reality.

That is why I suggest an experiment: Corporatize the DOE labs. It would be a manageable trial. DOE's lab activity represents about $6 billion of work. To put that in perspective, it is only one-fourth the size of Motorola, a science-based organization. A board of trustees could certainly get its arms around the labs' activity.

Corporatizing the DOE labs is an experiment worth conducting. If nothing else, it will improve the labs' performance, and Americans will have been well served.

The nation stands to gain much more, however. If the experiment succeeds, it has the potential to lead to a new national environment in which pseudo-government, pseudo-private entities like the distinguished DOE laboratories can operate free of an outmoded, counterproductive federal norm, reaching a highly productive and less-costly private norm. The laboratories have languished in government acquiescence for decades, and government clearly has not been able to limit its own intrusion nor help the labs reach their greater potential.

Corporatizing, now, is also a prudent step toward what many political scholars maintain is the undeniable trend for the next century: privatizing certain parts of government. In only 15 years it is likely that the United States will have a goodly number of multi-hundred-billion-dollar high-technology corporations. One of DOE's smaller labs, generating $500 million in science projects, would represent less than 5 percent of such a corporation's R&D budget. Purchasing a lab will certainly be possible.

However, should the federal government want to sell some or all of DOE's labs, it will not find buyers if the labs are languishing in yesterday's underproductive culture. To set the stage for a sale, it will be necessary to enhance a lab's attractiveness, so it matches the operational quality and culture of the potential buyer. Corporatizing the labs will put them in just that state.

The experiment really entails no risk. If we were to find in 15 years that the labs were not markedly improved, we could simply reapply the old governance principles. Washington will still be practicing them, so we will not have lost the recipe. But there is great probability that this experiment will teach us how government and the private sector can work together to maximize efficiency.

Robert W. Galvin, Chairman of the Executive Committee of Motorola Inc., chaired the Task Force on Alternative Futures for the Department of Energy National Laboratories.

Recommended Reading

Supplement B

Precedent for Corporatizing

There is legal precedent to support an Act of Congress to institutionalize corporatization of the DOE Laboratories pursuant to the Government Corporations Control Act.

There is no need for the repeal or modification of existing laws to establish the Corporation. The legislation authorizing the creation of the Corporation could specifically provide an exemption from existing laws which may be perceived as impeding the achievement of the goals of efficient and productive laboratories. Each government corporation has only those powers set forth in its enacting charter and is only subject to the conditions prescribed by the enacting charter. All of the steps necessary to implement the Proposal can be provided for in the same legislation, together with a statement of legislative policy and a structure for policy-making decisions.

The Energy Policy Act for the United States Enrichment Corporation is a model close in some respects to the proposed Corporation.

Supplement C

Step Function Economic Development from Enlightened Aggressive High Technology Energy Investments World Wide

The opportunities in energy sciences set the stage for domestic and worldwide economic opportunities which are almost beyond imagination. Envision virtually everyone in the world having the same amount of energy at his or her fingertips as we currently enjoy, safely, cleanly, affordably. In fact, this is what people everywhere _are_ beginning to imagine, expect, and eventually, they _will_ have.

Energy determines the quality of life: transportation, people's productivity, public services in behalf of better health, pollution-free, prerequisite to attracting investors, creating markets, communications systems, reprocessing, conservation.

Assume the underdeveloped world's acceleration of demand for energy kicks in. It will. The ordinary projections of fuel needs and generation will have to be adjusted radically upward.

The opportunity issue should be framed in terms of full capacity to serve the new expectancy. Our goal should be nothing less than a world _rich_ in clean, sustainable power.

The pace at which science is currently readying us for the energy opportunities will shortly be found to be insufficient. We should be orchestrating now the resourcing of our quest to ensure the abundance of such fuels and means of power conversion to serve the expectation.

The energy opportunities and complexities are so substantial that were the major laboratories, including the National Energy Laboratories, not existent we would have to invent them. We would also have to invent the university laboratories. The private sector engineering laboratories have a dynamics unto themselves, and they will have to be expanded as they team up with their fellow laboratories.

If we only applied what we can learn from definable technology and economic roadmaps inside the United States it would be worthy of our efforts but the greater promise is to work the world. This proposal suggests that there is no limit to economic growth and social well being. The more we research alternatives the better we will be able to select new options of fuels and have the brightest outlook for the continuation of a substantial and more rapid growth in the availability and the use of clean, safe energy for generation after generation. One of the hidden values of instituting this program is that we will sooner, rather than later, stumble over more constructive surprises that nature still holds for us.

We can approach the idea either on the offense or the defense. Elsewhere in the world nations will be selecting their own aggressive strategies. To the extent that they proceed with second or third class solutions they and their neighbors will bear unwelcome ecological costs and their energy service will lag the new standards. Thus it is in our enlightened self-interest to develop and make commercially available new technologies as a purely defensive strategy.

On the positive side, the economic opportunity for American suppliers who will prosper by offering the best solution is substantial while the benefit to our worldwide customers is equally significant.

The multiplier effect of this effort is so favorable for wealth creation, investment generation, job creation and tax revenue sources as to merit it being selected as a national goal. There is an appropriate coordinating role for government.

The Task Force that first recommended corporatizing the major DOE laboratories no longer stands publicly alone in its advocacy. Others are awakening to its merits. For example, the National Petroleum Council (NPC) which represents the oil and gas industry, whose fuel products generate 2/3 of U.S. energy and which industry publicly acknowledges its increasing dependence for leadership on technology for environmentally sound operations and acceptable hydrocarbon fuels, concurs that the activities of the federal laboratories should be "privatized as appropriate."

The NPC believes that achievement of the necessary technological advancements is a strategic imperative for both the industry and the nation. They have already identified 35 technologies that are high priority whose likelihood of being achieved under business-as-usual scenarios is unlikely.

They, the private sector companies, are spending liberally for R&D (20 times the amount in private research and development compared to the good work in the labs). But, they recognize that the labs can play a more effective role in R&D, particularly if the Labs can tie in with industry in the definition of goals as well as the elimination of the barriers to collaboration. They recognize as was reported by the Galvin Task Force, excessive paperwork, red tape, inadequate timeliness, etc. that industry calls for the government to initiate simplified administrative procedures, minimizing paperwork and improving turnaround time in order to bring promising technology to practical application.

Supplement D

Restructuring the Federal Scientific Establishment
Future Missions and Governance for DOE National Labs

H.R. 2142 Schiff (Et al) "Laboratory Missions Act"	H.R. 1510 Roemer "Efficiency Improvement Act"	H.R. 1993 Tiahrt (Et al) "Abolishment of DOE"	H.R. 87 Bartlett (et al) "Laboratories Facilities Act of 1995
Missions: well defined and assigned National Security Stockpile stewardship Dismantlement Counter proliferation Verification Weaponry S and T Ensure Energy Supply Energy S and T Matter Instruments Facilities Environment R and D Collaboration with all others Governance Findings Inordinate compliance and management processes, administrative, support and oversight roles plus review groups including influence ceded to advisory boards E[illegible]ement of E.S.H. mixed. D[illegible] should not so enforce	Purpose: DOE not to be agency (for nondefense labs) to implement E.S.H. rules Purpose: Reduce employment at non-defense GOCO labs 1/3 in 10 years	Redesignate Energy Programs Resolution Agency Establish Energy Laboratory Facilities Comm. to consider all "options" but preserve traditional National Defense Privatize Federal Power Marketing Adm. Transfer/Disposal of Reserves Establish Defense Nuclear Programs Agency in DOD including: 3 DOE Labs Defense Nuclear Agency Defense Nuclear Facilities Safety Board Energy R&D limitations 25% reductions/year for 2 years including: Termination of Clean coal (all fossil energy and energy conservation (major cuts)) Energy conservation research (major cuts) and all terminated in 1999	Purpose: Establish (Study) Commission to recommend closure or reconfiguration of Labs
Analyses and Critique			
The objective is first rate, but we don't need "another study." Turn the Labs over to a Board of Trustees and the CEO of the Corporatized Organization who with the Labs involvement will refine the Missions and effect with the simplified support of the Congress, governance objectives implied and proposed in this Act.	I concur that DOE not implement E.S.H. rules and even would apply that restriction on their role re the Defense Labs. This focus on reducing employment on Labs is likely to be counter-productive. The focus should be on the whole federal system starting with Congressional policy and particularly DOE department personnel (beyond E.S.H.) which can in the aggregate be reduced 90+% re Laboratory affairs. These will save far more than the goal of this Act and preserve the potential for all the S & T that is judged valuable by an able Corporatized Board of Trustees.	Retain or rename DOE, privatize Marketing, and handle Reserves as you wish. But don't separate "Defense Labs" from the others or assign them to DOD. They already wisely have a healthy mix of missions that tie to other Labs. Don't presume to specify the exact savings of certain terminations and percent cutbacks at the Labs. Sound management practice questions simplistic formula solutions. This focus on reducing employment on Labs is likely to be counter-productive. The focus should be on the whole federal system starting with Congressional policy and particularly DOE department personnel (beyond E.S.H.) which can in the aggregate be reduced 90+% re Laboratory affairs. These will save far more than the goal of this Act and preserve the potential for all the S & T that is judged valuable by an able Corporatized Board of Trustees.	We don't need another study nor at this time a presumption of some closures. A solid experiment of corporatizing is far more promising of a productive Lab system and cost savings. Turn the Labs over to a Board of Trustees and the CEO of the Corporatized Organization who with the Labs involvement will refine the Missions and effect with the simplified support of the Congress, governance objectives implied and proposed in this Act. Eventually there could be some closure but would be the thoughtful result of the Trustees and Lab leaders basing proposals on new and better thinking about their entire efficient low cost S & T system.

Mr. SCHIFF. Thank you again for being here with us.

Mr. Bloch?

STATEMENT OF ERICH BLOCH, DISTINGUISHED FELLOW, COUNCIL ON COMPETITIVENESS

Mr. BLOCH. Thank you, Mr. Chairman.

The Council On Competitiveness appreciates the opportunity to testify today and explore with this Committee the future of one of the country's important national resources, namely, the DOE laboratories.

We commend the Committee for focusing on this very important and timely topic.

I will try to be very, very brief.

Let me just however remind you that the country's investment in all federal laboratories is very sizeable. Of the R&D budget of the U.S., $70 billion, the U.S. Government spends about one-third on federal laboratories.

In the opinion of the Council On Competitiveness, that's too big a portion of the federal R&D budget. The situation could become even worse if we reduce overall R&D spending while keeping that for government laboratories constant, thus increasing the percentage of the R&D budget that goes to laboratories.

The problem with the DOE laboratories is not with their intellectual capabilities, nor with their superb technological facilities, but with the entire DOE organization, its management style, its oppressive controls.

Much of the solution lies in reducing bureaucracy, regulations, micromanagement from the top, and reducing the size of the administrative work force, and therefore focusing better on the mission of the laboratories, their programs and their projects.

Let me address the questions in the legislation that is before you.

During the Cold War, the DOE laboratories, particularly the multi-program laboratories, had an overriding mission; weapons research, national security, and energy research.

To discharge their mission properly, the DOE laboratories have acquired a leading edge in critical sciences and technologies that underpin equally our industrial sectors, like material science and engineering, biological sciences, computer technology, to name just a few.

Because of their competence in these critical technology areas, the laboratories are uniquely capable of focusing on large, complex problems in science and technology that bring together many disciplines, complex and expensive equipment, modeling and experimentation methods.

This is important not only to the government but also to the universities and the manufacturing and service sectors of our economy.

The Chairman's proposed bill, HR 2142, addresses both the mission and role of the DOE laboratories. In particular, the Council commends the specific inclusion in Section 102 of academia and industry as users of basic research, instruments and facilities in emerging scientific fields.

We suggest that Section 101, item 5, acknowledge equally the mutually beneficial collaborative partnerships that have also been established with the private sector, in addition to those with other institutions in government and academia.

It took much effort and trust on both sides, industry and the laboratories, to bring us to a more productive level of partnering than what existed in the past, and I don't think we can ignore this progress because its results benefit all.

I want to state at the outset, when talking about the problems of the DOE national lab system, that the DOE lab system should not be looked at separately from DOE as a whole. The departmental laboratories are not the only areas that require your attention.

The DOE, itself, is the cause of many problems which must be addressed before or simultaneously with those of the laboratories.

Rather than repeating all the issues that many reports and committees have identified, let me generalize with two observations.

The first one is bureaucracies, whether in government, the private sector, or in academia—become the prime cause of their own demise over time.

What we are witnessing with DOE and the laboratories is the growth of a bureaucracy which continuously adds controls, complexity to the system, but which is never dismantled or streamlined.

The Galvin Report, using particularly crisp language, criticizes DOE for being over-sized, inefficient, and excessively managed. These practices delay the work of the laboratories and increase the costs unnecessarily, especially in fast-paced technical areas.

My second comment is that the DOE and its laboratories are faced with a problem that other institutions encounter when paradigms change: established at different times to accomplish specific missions, the laboratories are geared more to the Cold War era, which is behind us, than to the era of intense international economic competition that we face today and far into the future.

Programs were added to DOE for convenience sake and some have no connection as a mission of the laboratory or DOE.

If these observations have merit, then I would suggest some simple ground rules for streamlining the system.

The first one is the DOE and its laboratories need to be considered as a system.

Secondly, simplify the mission of DOE; move activities that are not fundamental to its mission to other agencies and I will give an example.

Thirdly, goals for downsizing must be clearly spelled out and a time frame mandated, measured in months and not years.

Fourth, Congress must refrain from becoming prescriptive in the mechanism of downsizing; instead, concentrate on policy, goal-setting and progress assessment.

And another point must be made. Not all 30 DOE laboratories should be treated the same. We must make a distinction between the nine multi-program laboratories, the four science laboratories, and the other 17 specialty laboratories.

All four bills under discussion today address in part many facts of streamlining the DOE and its laboratories. They do not, however, provide a vision of what the final result could be.

I would suggest the following:

First, make the DOE an independent agency. This eliminates many of the political impediments a cabinet department has to contend with.

An independent agency permits establishment also of a policy board that was recommended by the Galvin Committee similar to the NSF's National Science Board, composed of private citizens appointed by the Administration and confirmed by the Senate.

It would have the authority to shape policy and strategy and oversee enactment of the mission of the DOE labs.

Secondly, transfer the four science laboratories to the National Science Foundation. They have very little, if anything, to do with the main DOE mission, namely, energy. They have much to do with high energy physics and subatomic physics, both National Science Foundation missions.

These four laboratories are, for the most part, managed by university consortia anyway and serve university researchers.

Third, lead laboratories should be appointed for specific programs and activities that are geographically dispersed. HR 2142, which the Council supports in principle, addresses something very similar, but restricted to missions. This might be too global a concept.

The concept of lead laboratory can be important to promote a more coherent approach for more important programmatic research areas.

Fourth, the Council supports the establishment of a closing commission for the Energy laboratories, as expressed in HR 87 and HR 1993. This applies especially, but not exclusively, to the 17 laboratories that are neither multiprogram laboratories nor science laboratories.

Some of these labs have become outdated; most others were established for reasons that had little to do with national or technical imperatives. Furthermore, the commission could also focus on the regional offices, many of which are unnecessary and can be eliminated.

Fifth, clear goals for downsizing and a time line must be established. HR 1510 spells out some important goals. The Council is in full agreement with its intent and supports the concept of eliminating self-regulation, reducing management inefficiencies, and streamlining overhead costs.

There are, however, two additional points that must be made here.

(a) No distinction should be made between defense and non-defense laboratories. There is considerable unnecessary bureaucracy and inefficiencies in all of the laboratories.

(b) The time frame, as stated in Section 3 of HR 1510, is simply too long and will assure that nothing gets done. The 33-percent cut in staff is practical and necessary, but it should not take ten years to accomplish.

Similarly, the DOE-proposed 20-percent cut by 1998 has a similar problem.

So let me conclude then.

The DOE national laboratories represent the cutting edge of the federal lab system. The work done by these laboratories is a vital component to the continued well-being and growth of the United

States. Yet, the whole DOE organization requires a complete overhaul.

It's too bureaucratic, too expensive, and inhibits progress.

The proposal to turn the DOE into an independent agency, to transfer the four science labs to the NSF, and to create a closing commission to eliminate unnecessary and obsolete federal labs and regional offices will enhance the vital work of the laboratories and the balancing of the federal budget.

Thank you very much.

[The prepared statement of Mr. Bloch follows:]

Council on Competitiveness

TESTIMONY OF ERICH BLOCH

DISTINGUISHED FELLOW, COUNCIL ON COMPETITIVENESS

BEFORE THE HOUSE COMMITTEE ON SCIENCE

HOUSE SUBCOMMITTEES ON BASIC RESEARCH AND

ENERGY AND ENVIRONMENT

SEPTEMBER 7, 1995

1401 H Street, NW • Suite 650 • Washington, DC 20005
(202) 682-4292 • FAX (202) 682-5150

TESTIMONY OF ERICH BLOCH

DISTINGUISHED FELLOW, COUNCIL ON COMPETITIVENESS

BEFORE THE HOUSE COMMITTEE ON SCIENCE

SUBCOMMITTEES ON BASIC RESEARCH AND

ENERGY AND ENVIRONMENT

SEPTEMBER 7, 1995

I. Introduction.

My name is Erich Bloch and I am Distinguished Fellow at the Council on Competitiveness, a private-sector organization that represents a broad cross-section of American business, universities and organized labor. The Council works for changes that enhance the country's competitiveness.

Before joining the Council, I was director of the National Science Foundation and before that I was a corporate vice president at IBM. My experiences, therefore, span both the public and private sectors of our economy. My concern has been, and remains, the linkage between science and technology, our economic competitiveness and the need for cooperation in this area.

In addition, I have a great interest in and have had close relations with the National Laboratories going back to the 1960's when I was the manager of one of the key programs in IBM that designed and produced a state of the art Supercomputer for Los Alamos and Livermore. At present, I am a member of the outside advisory committees for Sandia, Oak Ridge, and the Pacific Northwest Laboratory, all multiprogram laboratories of the Department of Energy(DOE).

Over the last few years, I have become concerned with the roles, effectiveness and the future of government laboratories, with a particular interest in the laboratories associated with the DOE.

In September 1992, the Council published a report entitled *Industry as a Customer of the Federal Laboratories*. The report highlighted the following: federal lab directors should be given greater discretion in defining their programs and allocating budgets; they should be freed from excessive bureaucracy and should have more local autonomy; R&D and technical expertise in federal laboratories should be more accessible to civilian industry, and, therefore, industry and federal laboratories should partner and work closely in their efforts to promote technology transfer.

Today, in 1995, despite many positive changes and plans, the same comments are applicable. Aside from the Council's 1992 report, numerous other studies, such as the 1995 Galvin and Yergin reports, have been completed, but we are still waiting for definitive action.

To that end, the Council appreciates the opportunity to testify and explore with this Committee the future of one of the country's important national resources: the DOE laboratories. Discussion about the laboratories and their mission has become much more urgent, particularly in light of the deficit reductions and budget cuts proposed by the Congress. The Council, therefore, commends the Committee on Science for focussing on this very important and timely topic -- the future and effectiveness of our federal laboratories.

I would like to remind the Committee of one startling statistic -- from its $70 billion R&D budget, the U.S. government spends one third on federal laboratories. The opinion of the Council on Competitiveness is that this is too big a portion of federal R&D and represents too much of an effort going into government laboratories. The situation could become even worse if we reduce overall R&D spending, while keeping that for government laboratories constant, thus increasing federal laboratories' percentage of the R&D budget.

The problem resides not with the intellectual capabilities

of the DOE laboratories, nor with their superb technological facilities, but with the entire DOE organization, its management style and oppressive controls. Much of the solution lies with reducing bureaucracy, regulations, micro-management from the top, and overhead costs, while focussing better on the mission of the laboratories, their programs and projects. The human resources in the laboratories are excellent and cannot be allowed to atrophy because of the heavy hand of the Washington bureaucracy. In fact, they need to be stimulated and their knowledge utilized more fully through productive intercourse with the private sector.

II. Role and Mission of DOE National Laboratories.

During the Cold War, the DOE laboratories, particularly the multiprogram laboratories, had an overriding mission -- weapons research, national security, and energy.

To discharge their mission properly, the DOE laboratories have acquired a leading edge in critical sciences and technologies that underpin our industrial sectors. Examples abound: material science and engineering, biological sciences, and computer technology, to name the more obvious. That work and competence were overshadowed in the past by the national security aspect of their mission. Today, while missions in defense, energy, and environmental clean-up are still essential to the labs' existence, we need to utilize more effectively the competence, experience and unique facilities of the laboratories.

The laboratories' focus on large, complex problems in science and technology brings together many disciplines, complex and expensive equipment, and modeling and experimentation methods. This is important not only to the government and its missions, but also to the universities and U.S. companies that can employ the knowledge, capabilities and advancements in the manufacturing and service sectors of our economy.

The Chairman's proposed bill, H.R. 2142, addresses both the mission and role of the DOE laboratories in Title 1. In particular, the Council commends the specific inclusion in Section 102 of academia and industry as users of basic research, instruments and facilities in emerging scientific fields.

We suggest that Section 101, item 5 acknowledge the mutually beneficial collaborative partnerships that have also been established with the private sector, in addition to those with other institutions in government and academia. It took much effort and trust on both sides to bring us to a more productive level of partnering than that which existed in the past. We cannot ignore this progress because it results in benefits to all.

III. Problems with the DOE National Lab System.

Having briefly examined the role and mission of the DOE laboratories, it is necessary to look at their shortcomings in fulfilling these missions. More importantly, what must be realized is that the DOE lab system should not be looked at separately from the DOE as a whole. In other words, the departmental laboratories are not the only areas that require our attention. The DOE itself is the cause of many problems which must be addressed before, or simultaneously with, those of the laboratories.

Problems with the energy laboratories have been exposed in the areas of management, governance, and performance. Addressing the first concern, there is simply too much micro-management from the top, with pervasive bureaucracy and regulatory obstacles. Essentially, government bureaucracy, inside and outside the department, too often slows down the approval process and needlessly complicates both simple internal procedures and already complex industry-lab partnerships. These practices delay the work of the laboratories and increase costs unnecessarily in fast-paced technical areas.

Such bureaucratic inefficiencies and aberrations are well documented. The Galvin report, using particularly crisp language, criticizes the DOE and the laboratories it studied for being "oversized ...inefficient ...and excessively managed." However, the blame for this situation must be shared by the laboratories, the DOE, the contractors, as well as Congress.

Rather than repeating all the issues that many reports and committees have identified ad nauseam, let me generalize with two observations.

1. Bureaucracies, whether in government, the private sector or academia, become the prime cause of their own demise over time. What we are witnessing with the DOE and the laboratories is the growth of a bureaucracy which continually adds complexity to the system, but which is never dismantled or streamlined.

2. The DOE and its laboratories are faced with the problem that other institutions encounter when paradigms change: established at different times to accomplish specific missions, the laboratories are geared more to the Cold War era, which is behind us, than to the era of intense international economic competition that we face today and far into the future.

IV. Approaches.

If the Committee agrees with this analysis, then the remedy is obvious. It requires a top-down rethinking of the four bureaucracies involved, namely 1) the central departmental organization, 2) the field offices, which are anachronisms in today's age of decentralization and empowerment of individuals and groups, 3) the contractor bureaucracy, and 4) the lab organizations.

The ground rules for streamlining are self-evident, and are as follows:

1. The DOE and its laboratories need to be considered as a system. But there must also be a proper balance between laboratory independence and interdependence with the rest of the system.

2. Simplify the mission of DOE; move activities that are not fundamental to its mission to other agencies and give priority of streamlining to the DOE itself.

3. Goals for downsizing must be clearly spelled out and a time frame mandated -- measured in months, not years.

4. Congress must refrain from becoming excessively involved in the downsizing effort and, instead, concentrate on policy, goal setting and progress assessment.

Another point must be made. Not all 30 DOE laboratories should be treated the same. We must make a distinction between the nine multiprogram laboratories (Lawrence Livermore, Los Alamos, Sandia, Argonne, Brookhaven, Idaho, Oak Ridge, Lawrence

Berkeley and Pacific Northwest Laboratory), the four science laboratories (Princeton, Stanford Linear Accelerator Facility, CBAF, and the Fermi National Accelerator Laboratory), and the other 17 specialty laboratories that make up the DOE national lab system.

All four bills under discussion today address, in part, many facets of streamlining the DOE and its laboratories. They do not, however, provide a blueprint of what the final result should be. I would suggest the following approach:

First, make the DOE an independent agency. This eliminates many of the political impediments a cabinet department has to contend with. It also permits approaches to governance that today are not under consideration. For example, the tenure of the appointees could correspond to the time line of tasks, such as downsizing.

In addition to a new independent agency, the formation of a policy board, similar to the NSF's National Science Board, composed of private citizens appointed by the Administration and confirmed by the Senate, should be considered. It would have the authority to shape policy and strategy, and oversee enactment of the missions of the DOE labs. It could also provide the continuity for the implementation of a downsizing that Congress or the Administration, with their limited tenure, cannot guarantee.

Second, transfer the four science laboratories to the National Science Foundation. They have very little, if anything, to do with the main DOE mission, namely energy; they have much to do with high energy physics and subatomic physics, both National Science Foundation missions. These four laboratories are, for the most part, managed by university consortia and serve university researchers. The National Science Foundation provides a better environment and mission framework in which these laboratories could operate.

Third, lead laboratories should be designated to have responsibility for specific programs and activities that may be dispersed among many laboratories. H.R.2142, which the Council supports in principle, addresses the importance of mission assignment. However, this concept must be taken a step further. Giving oversight and overall control of a particular program to a designated DOE laboratory can be important to promoting core competencies within each DOE lab, while creating a more coherent and coordinated approach in each area of research.

For this process to be effective, several things need to occur: 1) each lab and its director need to have both technical and budgetary control over the assigned missions; 2) the DOE and Congress would have to utilize more bloc grants in place of a large number of small budget increments; 3) the time line for assigning missions should be shorter than the 18 months envisioned in the proposed bill, and the completion of the task should take less than ten years; and 4) there should be a closer examination of the need for excessive Federal Register publication before every step of the process.

Fourth, the Council supports the establishment of a closing commission for the Energy Laboratories, as expressed in H.R.87 and Title II of H.R.1993. This applies especially, but not exclusively, to the 17 laboratories that are neither science nor multiprogram laboratories. Some of these labs, established for specific purposes, have become out-dated and could be eliminated or merged with other federal laboratories; others were established for reasons that had little to do with national or technical imperatives. Furthermore, the commission could also focus on the regional offices, many of which are unnecessary and can be eliminated.

The Council believes that this is a practical way to deal with the streamlining of the federal laboratories. However, and again I repeat, the system must first be looked at as a whole. It must be streamlined in its entirety from the top-down. Until this is done, any closure or consolidation would be premature.

Laboratories cannot be cut first, followed by the Department; it must be the reverse.

Fifth, clear goals for downsizing and a time line must be established. H.R.1510 (the Roemer Bill) spells out some important goals. The Council is in full agreement with its intent and supports the concept of eliminating self regulation, reducing management inefficiencies, and streamlining overhead costs associated with the laboratories. There are two additional points that must be made here:

a) no distinction should be made between defense and non-defense laboratories. There is considerable, unnecessary bureaucracy and inefficiencies in all the DOE labs. What and how much to reduce should not be based on whether or not a program is part of a defense laboratory, but rather on the actual effectiveness and merits of a particular program.

b) the time frame, as stated in Section 3 of H.R. 1510, is simply too long and will assure that nothing gets done. This 33 percent cut in staff is practical and necessary, but should not and cannot take ten years to accomplish; similarly, the DOE-proposed 20 percent cut by 1998 has too long of a time frame. These time lines guarantee that no appreciable change will occur. They neither create the momentum that is needed, nor underline the urgency of the task.

V. Corporatization and Privatization.

Corporatization and privatization, as defined in the Galvin report, are desirable and intriguing ideas. However, they take time. The independent agency concept I have advanced here does not negate such possibilities. On the contrary, I believe this concept, accompanied by a top-down streamlining of the entire DOE system, can be a necessary step in that direction.

VI. Conclusions.

The DOE national laboratories represent the cutting edge of the federal laboratory system. The work done by these laboratories is a vital component to the continued well-being and growth of the United States. The laboratories constitute a wealth of technical talent, and some represent world-class facilities that do not exist in industry or elsewhere. The research that is performed can lead to new opportunities and advancements in science and technology, which, in turn, strengthen our leadership role in the world. We must preserve this national resource.

Yet, the whole DOE organization requires a complete overhaul. It is too bureaucratic, too expensive and too often blocks progress. My proposal to turn the DOE into an independent agency, to transfer the four science labs to the NSF, and to create a closing commission to eliminate unnecessary and obsolete federal labs and regional offices will help reduce management inefficiencies, overhead, redundant activities, and regulations so that the DOE labs can focus on their core missions.

Only a radical change, implemented within a short time frame, will result in the desired outcome. If accomplished, it will contribute to the advancement of technology and the balancing of the federal budget.

There is no mystery as to what the problem is. There is no lack of appropriate ideas that would improve the system and reduce its cost by large factors. Congress and the DOE must start on this difficult road now and face the tough choices and decisions that lay ahead.

Mr. SCHIFF. Thank you, Mr. Bloch.
Dr. Vest?

STATEMENT OF DR. CHARLES M. VEST, PRESIDENT, MASSACHUSETTS INSTITUTE OF TECHNOLOGY

Dr. VEST. Mr. Chairman, I appreciate the opportunity to participate in these hearings.

A balanced national R&D system includes four primary performers: research universities, industrial establishments, federal laboratories, and independent research institutions. Each has certain characteristics which must be thought about as the future of the Department of Energy laboratories is considered.

I will concentrate just on the first three of these organizations.

Universities combine the conduct of research with education and training of the next generation of scientists and engineers. This produces a double value for federal research dollars. The flow of students and postdoctoral researchers in and out of universities produces a vital intellectual environment for research and innovation that is continually renewed, and the structure has particularly strong capabilities for developing interdisciplinary work.

Universities have also successfully managed some of the large laboratories of the DOE.

In addition, several universities operate modest or small-scale laboratories on their campuses that are supported by the Department of Energy in the national interest.

Examples would include the Materials Research Laboratory at the University of Illinois, the Plasma Fusion Center and Laboratory for Nuclear Science at MIT.

In my view, the primary role of national laboratories should be to operate unique experimental facilities and programs that are of too large a scale, or are too costly to be maintained by individual research institutions outside the federal sector.

The DOE national laboratories are viewed by the scientific and technological community as doing a good job with large, complex projects scientifically, and there are important national missions that clearly are best met by DOE national laboratories.

Parenthetically, many believe that large scientific facilities should increasingly be internationalized. Our programs and laboratories will require fundamental and determined change if we are to move in that direction, largely because of the continuing inability of our federal government to make and adhere to agreements to fund large international partnerships.

Industry also has an important role to play in our R&D and innovation system of the country. Historically, large corporations contributed enormously to our underlying base of scientific and technological knowledge, but this is less true today.

During the last decade, our industrial R&D organizations have been transformed almost entirely. Most are now focused exclusively on issues of direct and known relevance to product lines and almost all their work is of a near-term nature.

These steps have generally been essential for economic competitiveness and indeed for corporate survival. Nonetheless, these changes are leading to a reduction in industrial input to the commonly-shared base of new scientific and technological information for the country.

This has implications for the future roles of universities and national laboratories.

Energy research, in my view, is essential to the future of the nation. The country has a long-term need to create new efficient sources of environmentally benign energy. Those nations that develop the new technologies will be the ones to produce and market them when they grow to be big businesses as population grows and industrialization proceeds around the world.

Thus, I believe the U.S. must maintain a varied portfolio of strong, long-range energy and environmental research. Both national laboratories and universities will be required to take part in an effective effort.

In closing, I would suggest three things. First, that DOE national laboratories do play an important role in the conduct of the nation's fundamental and energy research and that role will continue to be important, perhaps even increasingly important.

Second, the existence of the DOE national laboratories should be justified by their mission, which in turn should primarily be limited to functions that are clearly related to energy and that require large, complex, and long-lived facilities and organizations.

And third, when thought is given to downsizing or expansion or changing of missions of existing laboratories, merit-based competition, both within and without the system, should be introduced. This, in my view, is likely to lead to the establishment of more modest-scale laboratories and centers associated with universities and other performing organizations, as well as within the national laboratories.

Thank you very much for this opportunity.

[The prepared statement of Dr. Vest follows:]

Restructuring the Federal Scientific Establishment:
Future Missions and Governance for
The Department of Energy (DOE) National Laboratories

Joint Hearing of the Subcommittees on Basic Research
and Energy and Environment

September 7, 1995

Statement of Charles M. Vest

Mr. Chairman, members of the committees, I am Charles Vest, president of the Massachusetts Institute of Technology. I am a mechanical engineer by training and am a university administrator who is deeply concerned that the United States continue to lead the world in the quality of its scientific research and technological development. Thus I appreciate the opportunity to participate in this joint hearing. These committees are to be commended for participating in a thoughtful review of roles of the National Laboratories of the Department of Energy.

It is important that America rebalance and redirect both its intellectual resources and R&D infrastructure to match the new realities of the post Cold War world and the emerging era of intense global economic competition. Basic scientific research is an essential underpinning for our future competitiveness, and we eventually will need new and clean sources of energy if we are to maintain and improve our standard of living. Our long-term energy security, as well as our military security, must be provided for. The future of the DOE laboratories is an important matter in the context of these imperatives.

Others are far more qualified than I to address matters associated with the DOE role in the nation's weapons program and radioactive cleanup, so, with your permission, I will not address these two matters.

A balanced national R&D system includes four primary performers: research universities, industrial establishments, federal laboratories, and independent research institutions. Each has certain characteristics. I will concentrate on the first three types of organizations.

It seems to me that three questions must be considered in your deliberations and in related studies of the DOE Laboratories:

- Are research and development functions optimally distributed among these organizations?
- Are there functions that should be eliminated from one or more of these organizations?
- Are there important new functions that require new structures or new ways of organizing our efforts?

The search for optimal distribution of R&D functions and facilities is made both more difficult and more urgent by current and future funding constraints. Nonetheless, it is possible to identify and compare some key strengths and weaknesses of each type of performing organization.

First, the universities. America's research-intensive universities have a number of unique features and strengths. They combine the conduct of research with the education and training of the next generation of scientists and engineers. This produces a double value for federal research dollars. The flow of students and postdoctoral researchers in and out of universities produces a vital intellectual environment for research and innovation that is continually renewed. This flow of research-trained graduate students, and, increasingly, undergraduate students as well, also constitutes an important form of technology transfer. Finally, the structure, talent base, and ongoing dialogue within universities provide strong, inherent interdisciplinary capability that is increasingly important. Research universities are an asset that is essentially unique to the United States and which is the cornerstone of our R&D system.

Universities also have successfully managed large laboratories for the Department of Energy. Examples include the Lawrence Livermore Laboratory, the Los Alamos National Laboratory, and the Lawrence Berkeley Laboratory, managed by the University of California, the Argonne National Laboratory, managed by the University of Chicago, and Brookhaven National Laboratory, managed by a consortium of universities. In addition, and very relevant to this hearing, several universities operate modest or large scale laboratories on their campuses that are supported by DOE in the national interest. Examples include the Materials Research Laboratory at the University of Illinois, and the Plasma Fusion Center and the Laboratory for Nuclear Science at MIT. These laboratories have made many important research contributions and have been very cost effective.

Looking to the future, as new areas of science and technology require exploration, I recommend that the Department of Energy consider increasing the number of modest scale laboratories located on or near university campuses. These laboratories should pursue work in areas identified as having long term national importance relevant to the DOE mission, and they should be allocated through a merit-based competitive process. This distributed system, in my opinion, is likely to be more cost effective than increasing funding and redirecting the large national laboratories that have been developed for other tasks.

In my view, the primary role of national laboratories should be to operate unique experimental facilities that are of too large scale, or are too costly to be maintained by individual research institutions outside the federal sector.

The DOE national laboratories do a superb job of developing, operating and managing large-scale, complex, and well-focused experimental facilities and programs. They have displayed an ability to attract and hold together talented research and operating groups for long periods of time, providing needed continuity and quality of effort. The scientific and engineering communities view these laboratories and their management as doing a good job with large, complex projects. The nation needs this national laboratory structure to operate facilities and manage projects of magnitude and time scale that industry will not support, and that do not fit the capabilities and mission of individual universities. Simply put, there are important national missions that clearly are best met by the DOE laboratories.

When the DOE laboratories pursue their fundamental missions, they directly or indirectly develop both important fundamental knowledge and important technologies. These technologies are transferred to energy-related industry, and often to other industries as well. At their best, the large experimental facilities of the DOE laboratories establish effective university/industry/government partnerships as they serve the user community. Some smaller scale research, including single investigator programs, should be conducted in-house when it is directly related to the core mission of the laboratory. The national laboratories do this well, and it is necessary to maintain a first-rate scientific staff. Small research programs that are not directly related to a laboratory's core mission or facilities, however, should be awarded on a merit-based competitive basis to universities or other appropriate external organizations.

Parenthetically, it should be noted that many believe that large scientific facilities should increasingly be internationalized. Our programs and laboratories will require fundamental and determined change if we decide to move in this direction, largely because of the continuing inability of our federal government to make and adhere to agreements to fund large international partnerships.

It is interesting to note that the various DOE laboratories that perform basic scientific research such as Argonne, Brookhaven, Lawrence Berkeley, SLAC, etc. have a variety of management arrangements that have evolved both for historical reasons and by virtue of their mission. Thus there is a great deal of empirical evidence about cost effectiveness and productivity, which should be helpful in considering possible future changes. Whatever the mechanism, it is critically important to recognize the great importance of these facilities to the nation's quest for fundamental knowledge.

American industry has an important role to play in our R&D and innovation systems as well. They conduct most of the nation's technology development, providing coherence, focus, and responsiveness to market forces, in ways that neither national laboratories nor universities can or should. I must tell you, however, that the role of industry in this domain is in flux, and its future role is not entirely clear. Historically, our large corporations have contributed enormously to our underlying base of scientific knowledge, but this is much less true today.

During the last decade our industrial R&D organizations have been transformed almost entirely. Most are now focused exclusively on issues of direct and known relevance to their product line, and almost all work is of a near-term nature. The emphasis is on incremental improvement, decreasing product cycle times, minimizing time-to-market, and improving processes and quality. These steps have generally been essential for economic competitiveness and, indeed for corporate survival. Furthermore, in some ways industrial R&D has become more efficient for the companies, and important product and process advances have been made.

Nonetheless, these changes in industrial research laboratories are leading to a reduction in industrial input to the commonly shared base of new scientific and technological information. These changes appear to be profound, and, once fully implemented, will not readily be changed in the future. This has implications for the roles of universities and national laboratories because there is an increasing void in generic scientific and technological research having time horizons for commercial application of a decade or so. It is this area of research and development that often is a very important source of innovation, and is important in building our technical infrastructure.

Before concluding, I would like to comment on two important aspects of the decisions you face: technology transfer, and energy research.

Universities are increasingly effective in transferring technology to the private sector. The most important form of technology transfer occurs through the movement of well-educated people with skills and know-how. Universities, especially at the graduate level, educate men and women in a research-intensive environment. Most graduates then move into the industrial sector.

Universities also have become much more active in patenting inventions. For example, in 1992 they were awarded nearly 1500 patents, four times the number issued annually before the passage of the Bayh-Dole Act, which vests the ownership of intellectual property stemming from federally-sponsored research in the performing university. It is estimated that the private sector currently invests at least $5 billion per year in developing these university patents. These patents are conservatively estimated to result in about $17 billion per year in product sales, and to produce around 138,000 jobs. To give a somewhat parochial example: since 1980, over 70 active companies, employing some 1,600 people, have started up on the basis of MIT licensed technologies.

More recently, the DOE national laboratories have been encouraged to increase their technology transfer activities, and they have responded. This is a good idea, as long as the activities are clear and natural outgrowths of the laboratories' basic security and energy missions.

Energy research, in my view, is essential to the future of the nation. The country has a long-term need to create efficient sources of environmentally-benign energy. The needs for such new sources of energy are still more important for the world as a whole, and those nations that develop the new technologies will be the ones to produce and market them when they grow to be big businesses. The trend lines for world population growth and increasing energy demand as nations industrialize and progress are relatively clear. Global economic development will require at least a doubling of world energy output by 2050. If this is done with primitive technologies, particularly the burning of fossil fuels, dangerous environmental degradation will result. Although most of the growth of demand will be in what are now less-developed nations, the resulting environmental burdens will affect us all.

Thus I believe that the U.S. must maintain a varied portfolio of strong, long-range energy and environmental research. I would anticipate that both national laboratories and universities will be required to take part in an effective effort. Private energy companies do not invest much in long-range energy research. The trend is toward less R&D, and that which is conducted is increasingly near-term focused, just as in most other industries.

In closing, I would suggest that:

- DOE national laboratories play an important role in the conduct of the nation's fundamental and energy research. This role will continue to be important.

- The existence of the DOE national laboratories should be justified by their mission, which in turn should primarily be limited to functions that are clearly related to energy and that require large, complex, and long-lived facilities and organizations.

- When thought is given to downsizing, expanding, or changing the mission of existing laboratories, merit-based competition should be introduced. This is likely to lead to establishment of modest-scale laboratories or centers in universities or other performing organizations.

Thank you for the opportunity to express my opinions and to suggest items for your consideration as you study this important topic. I would be happy to respond to your questions.

Mr. SCHIFF. Thank you, Dr. Vest.
Mr. McCorkle?

STATEMENT OF SHERMAN MCCORKLE, PRESIDENT, TECHNOLOGY VENTURES, INC.

Mr. MCCORKLE. Thank you, Mr. Chairman. I appreciate the opportunity to present my views on these critical bills.

Technology Ventures Corporation is a company that was founded by Lockheed Martin Corporation.

My purpose today is to encourage, during your consideration of these bills, support for programs which facilitate the commercialization of dual use technologies originated within the Department of Energy laboratory structure.

The commercialization of these technologies advance our nation's ability to compete in the technological business world of today and tomorrow.

As for future missions of the DOE laboratories, I believe they should expand to include a greater contribution to the private sector by acting as a resource of people, facilities, equipment and technology that can be used to further national technological goals.

I should note that technology transfer is a term that does not adequately describe the commercialization of laboratory technology and has been mistakenly labeled as a form of corporate welfare which transfers technology out of the laboratories at government cost for a profit in the private sector.

This misperception assumes that technology is available off-the-shelf and for immediate use. This is not true, and we prefer to use the term "technology commercialization." Technologies need to mature and develop, or more precisely be developed before they are commercially viable. This development may be considered the process of commercialization.

Contrary to the view of corporate welfare, commercialization relies heavily on substantial investment from the private sector.

Technology Ventures was formed to facilitate the commercialization of technology developed at the national laboratories, primarily Sandia. To date, TVC has been a major contribution in the formation of seven new businesses built on leading edge technologies developed at Sandia Laboratory.

It has assisted in the expansion of eight businesses and in obtaining funding officers for over ten companies.

We have created and implemented a technology commercialization model that can be replicated throughout the Department's nationwide network of laboratories, and it has proven with a properly functioning conduit, core competencies and technical capabilities of the Department's laboratories can make a dual contribution, supporting both government and private sector needs while, at the same time, lessening the involvement and oversight of government.

I'd like to mention three quick examples.

Quantum Manufacturing is a technology which uses a rapid-fire, high-power pulsating electrical beam to harden the surfaces of metals, ceramics, plastics and other materials. This is a core competency with many applications, including tool and die industry, aircraft, automobile engines, medical implants, tools.

Prompted by such potential, TVC has worked with QMI over the past year, including a financial contribution to the project. The scientists were aided in developing a commercialization plan that created a business.

QMI recently reached an agreement on terms and conditions which could provide up to $4.125 million from private investors.

Another example is Silicon MicroDevices. It recently entered into a joint agreement with a major U.S. manufacturer to develop and bring to market a micro-mechanical drug delivery technology.

Again, this technology developed at Sandia is a micro-mechanical drug delivery system that administers a broad range of medications directly into the bloodstream.

This project is radically different from existing transdermal drug patches currently on the market.

Technology Ventures has provided Silicon MicroDevices with management assistance in the form of business formation and business plan consultation.

Lastly, Boissiere Engineering and Applied Robotics is a company that we have helped through the first phases of business formation, including the development of business plans, extensive classroom work on entrepreneurship, and the negotiation of licenses.

The technology focuses on telerobotics excavation systems for waste remediation applications.

There are many other examples of TV assisted business opportunities based on dual use technologies coming from Department of Energy laboratories, including software for virtual reality operating systems, advanced chemical processes for waste disposal at Los Alamos, and vertical cavity surface emitting lasers.

All these have formed companies in the past year.

We will continue to work towards a Congressional mandate that guides us, and we'll continue to support the Department of Energy in its efforts to commercialize technology and stimulate economic development by augmenting government resources.

In closing, we hope that in your consideration that the benefits to the private sector through technology commercialization are not lost.

[The prepared statement of Mr. McCorkle follows:]

Statement by
Sherman McCorkle
President
Technology Ventures Corporation

Before a Hearing of the
House Subcommittee on Basic Research
and
House Subcommittee on Energy and Environment

on the
"Department of Energy Laboratory Facilities Act of 1995"
"Department of Energy Laboratories Efficiency Improvement Act"
"Department of Energy Abolishment Act"
"Department of Energy Laboratory Missions Act"

Washington, D.C.

September 7, 1995

Mr. Chairman and Members of the Committee:

I am Sherman McCorkle, president of Technology Ventures Corporation, a company founded by Lockheed Martin Corporation. I appreciate the opportunity to present my views on several critical bills regarding the missions, governance, and role of the Department of Energy's (DOE) national laboratories in the context of the overall federal scientific establishment. My comments will generally address the DOE's Sandia National Laboratories, Los Alamos National Laboratory, Oak Ridge National Laboratory, Idaho National Engineering Laboratory and Lawrence Livermore National Laboratory.

Although I believe that my opinions are shared by many who feel as I do about the critical issues regarding the laboratories' future, the views I represent in this testimony are my own. In this regard, I speak from long involvement with the federal government. As former chairman of the Greater Albuquerque Chamber of Commerce in Albuquerque, New Mexico, and an active participant in a wide range of economic development initiatives in the State, I understand and appreciate the key role that the DOE's national laboratories play in the regional economy.

As a member of the Kirtland Task Force steering committee, a group that led the successful effort to keep Kirtland Air Force Base open during the 1995 Base Realignment and Closure process, I gained new insight into, and appreciation for, the difficult balancing act that government today performs in fulfilling its various missions within new budget restraints. Now, as president of an organization committed to commercialize technologies developed in our national laboratories and other government-supported facilities, I am aware of the enormous changes taking place in our government.

The bills under consideration, H.R. 87, H.R. 1510, H.R. 1993, and H.R. 2142 are wide-ranging. They vary in extreme from redefining the missions of the laboratories to abolishing the Department of Energy as we know it today. In general, they seek action which will streamline, realign, privatize, and improve the efficiency and reduce the cost of the DOE and its laboratories.

While I, as a citizen and a businessman, certainly cannot fault an objective to improve efficiency and reduce costs, I am concerned that these bills be written and implemented in a manner that recognizes the renowned technical and scientific leadership the DOE laboratories have provided for this nation and their unique role as stewards of our nuclear weapons stockpile. My purpose today is to encourage support of programs which facilitate the commercialization of dual-use technologies originated in the Department of Energy laboratory structure. The commercialization of these technologies advance our Nation's ability to compete in the technology business world of today and tomorrow. These dual-use technologies represent the seed of an entrepreneur's drive to create a technology business which 10 years from now might employ thousands of American workers.

I do support efforts that would allow the various laboratories to function more efficiently and more cost-effectively. For example, H.R. 2142, the "Department of Energy Laboratory Missions Act", proposes that DOE Laboratories be realigned according to clear-cut missions, determined by their unique core competencies that have been developed over the years. I support this bill because I support greater efficiencies in all matters of Federal government.

There may also be merit to some of the criticisms contained in the bill. For example, we at Technology Ventures Corporation have encountered frustrations trying to negotiate licenses for technologies in a timely fashion.

Core competencies have been developed during decades of research, both basic and applied. Because of this, the United States has played a major role in helping deter the repetition of global conflicts. It has also enjoyed a period of relative peace, during which it has become a world leader in science and technology. In the future, the laboratories will continue to contribute to the deterrence of war and will certainly continue to contribute to the technological leadership of the nation.

With regard to H.R. 1993, the "Department of Energy Abolishment Act", I believe that these committees need to consider the birthright of DOE's weapons laboratories. These organizations were established under the Atomic Energy Commission as the civilian keepers, the stewards, of our nuclear stockpile.

I urge caution in the closure of DOE facilities. They comprise the key element of our nation's scientific community, furthering basic research and playing a critical role in national security.

The "Department of Energy Laboratories Efficiency Improvement Act," H.R. 1510 aims to prohibit the Department from acting as the agency of implementation for certain regulations at non defense Laboratories. Where this prohibition would result in improved efficiency without detriment to the mission or core competencies of the laboratories, it seems a reasonable goal.

H.R. 87, called the "Department of Energy Laboratory Facilities Act of 1995", would form a commission that will seek, hear and determine recommendations on the closure, reconfiguration, and privatization of the Department's National Laboratories.

Regarding "privatization," we can see that some lessening of the burden of government is already being accomplished as the private sector takes on responsibilities for industrial and economic development based on technologies developed at the laboratories. I must emphasize that such commercialization doesn't replace the government-funded research in the laboratories. Rather, it enhances the value of the research by creating a "dual benefit." Government-sponsored research will continue to support the nation's defense needs, and we can rely on private sector demand to pull the technology into the broader economy at the expense of private investment. Thus, privatization of some functions may naturally occur under the heading of technology commercialization.

As we learned during the Base Realignment and Closure process, any cost-cutting effort needs to be closely examined to determine that it achieves the results intended, that it will indeed result in greater efficiency at a lower cost. Considerable investment -- in taxpayer ollars -- has gone into the laboratories. Simply reducing funding will not yield greater efficiencies. Rather, our efforts should be aimed at maximizing the return on that investment. This will lead to greater efficiencies and greater economies, while preserving the contribution of the national laboratories.

As for the future missions of the DOE laboratories, I believe they should continue to develop core competencies and technical capabilities that strategically position them to contribute to the scientific and technological well being of the nation. This should include a continuation of their current role in national security, and should expand to include a greater contribution to the private sector by acting as a resource of people, facilities, equipment and technology that can be used to further national technology goals.

Another mission is evolving, though it may not be a primary responsibility of the laboratories. It is the commercialization of the technologies that support the laboratories' primary missions. Whether this mission is undertaken by the private sector or government agencies, or a combination of both, I believe we must make it a top priority for the nation. The same technologies that benefit our national defense can and do find broad applications that will enhance our national economy, in terms of job growth and economic competitiveness.

There is also a growing awareness that all facets of government need to ensure the maximum return on the taxpayers' investment. This is true also for the DOE laboratories, which already provide a strong return on the taxpayers' "investment" by contributing to national defense and our nation's economy. However, other ways are emerging that can add value to the activity at the laboratories. Technology commercialization is one mechanism by which the return on investment in the laboratories can be maximized. We can use non-government mechanisms to commercialize technology developed in the laboratories to create jobs and wealth in the private sector.

I should note that "technology transfer" is a term that does not adequately describe the commercialization of laboratory technologies, and has been mistakenly labeled as a form of "corporate welfare" which transfers technology out of the laboratories at government cost for the profit of the private sector. This misperception assumes that the technology is available off-the-shelf for immediate use by the public sector. This is not true, and we prefer to use the term "technology commercialization." Technologies need to mature and develop, or more precisely, be developed before they are commercially viable. This development may be considered the process of commercialization. Technology transfer is only a result of the process. Contrary to the view of "corporate welfare," commercialization relies heavily on substantial investment from the private sector.

For example, to support the commercialization of laboratory-based technology, Lockheed Martin Corporation has committed approximately $10 million to fund nonprofit Technology Ventures Corporation and the construction of its building. This effort by the private sector has emerged as an effective non-government technology interface between the public and private sectors, supporting the commercialization of technologies developed with public funds.

Technology Ventures Corporation

Technology Ventures Corporation (TVC) is a nonprofit company founded in 1993 by Martin Marietta Corporation as part of its contract to manage and operate Sandia National Laboratories. Since the merger of Martin Marietta and the Lockheed Corporation, Technology Ventures Corporation continues under the auspices of the Lockheed Martin Corporation with headquarters in Albuquerque, New Mexico, in the Lockheed Martin Technology Center.

Mission

The mission of TVC is to facilitate the commercialization of technology developed by the national laboratories, primarily Sandia and Los Alamos, and the research universities in the region. TVC assists in the creation, expansion, retention, and relocation of technology based businesses. A primary focus of TVC is attracting risk investment money. TVC assists technology based companies by facilitating technology commercialization and coordinating management and business assistance.

Technology Ventures' mission supports a Congressional mandate, 15 US Code 3701(a)(1), which states that ". . . it is the continuing responsibility of the Federal Government to ensure the full use of the results of the Nation's federal investment in research and development. To this end the federal government shall strive where appropriate to transfer federally owned or originated technology to state and local governments and to the private sector."

Specific to the DOE, the 1989 Defense Authorization Act amended the Atomic Energy Act to establish technology transfer as a formal mission of the DOE. The 1989 National Competitiveness Technology Transfer Act requires the DOE to establish technology transfer as a mission at each of its contractor-operated laboratories.

Technology Ventures is an unique entity in the nation and in two years has proven the feasibility of commercializing technologies developed at the DOE's national laboratories. I believe that, because of its proven successes, TVC could become a model for developing commercialization efforts at other national laboratories.

The success of TVC underscores the opportunity to ensure the maximum return on the taxpayers' investment at Sandia National Laboratories and other research facilities, to create partnerships with private industry and other public agencies, and to contribute to the nation's scientific and technological leadership in the world market. It also emphasizes the importance of the DOE laboratories' contribution to the scientific and technical base of the nation.

Commercialization

TVC assists entrepreneurs in the formation of new businesses or expanding existing businesses, and in licensing their technologies. TVC support ranges from assisting in the development of business and strategic plans to identifying potential funding sources, as well as assisting in the development of legal, accounting and banking relationships necessary to business.

In short, Technology Ventures helps people with little to no business experience create a successful business around the technology they have developed.

Accomplishments

To date, TVC has been a major contributor in the formation of seven new businesses built on leading-edge technologies developed at Sandia National Laboratories. It has assisted in the expansion of eight businesses and in obtaining funding offers for 10 companies. In addition, licensing agreements have been signed or are being negotiated for nine companies.

Agreements totaling approximately $8 million have been reached between private sector investors and TVC assisted companies. More than 300 direct and indirect jobs have been created in the process. We believe this is an impressive record for a company in business for less than two years, with operational funding of only $1 million a year, but there is more than numbers to Technology Ventures' success. Technology Ventures has established itself as a recognized force in economic development. It has gained the trust and respect of the investment community, and has earned the cooperation of governmental bodies.

Of primary importance, TVC has provided a viable, successful channel for the commercialization of technologies developed at the laboratories, providing the public with a positive return on its investment in the laboratories.

The TVC Model

TVC has created and implemented a technology commercialization model that can be replicated throughout the Department's nationwide network of laboratories. It has proven that, with a properly functioning conduit such as Technology Ventures Corporation, the core competencies and technical capabilities of the Department's laboratories can make a dual contribution, supporting both government and private-sector needs, while at the same time lessening the involvement and oversight of government.

Investor Outreach

One of the greatest challenges facing TVC during its start-up period was to obtain qualified sources of financing for emerging companies who have no track record to lure investors. Investors historically have been very reluctant to deal with the laboratories, because of the controls imposed by the government. TVC is not a funding institution, and has been empowered, to date, by Lockheed Martin to grant only a total of $50,000 in seed-money grants to five promising companies.

Therefore, TVC 's challenge has been to establish itself as a critical link between technology and investment. TVC has developed an extensive network of potential financing sources in local, regional and national investment communities.

TVC created the New Mexico Equity Capital Symposium as one means of forging a link between the investment community and the emerging businesses of the labs. For a symposium, selected companies are groomed for presentation to an elite body of investors, including equity investors, venture capitalists and other financing sources. The two-day symposiums have been held twice, each time drawing scores of executives from some of the largest capital funds in the investment community. The symposiums have been a critical element in establishing credibility with investors and in securing funding offers for TVC's companies.

Company Selection

With a small staff and limited financial resources, TVC has recognized that it must direct its efforts to assisting those with the greatest potential for success. Consequently, it looks for technologies that may best be described as core technologies, those that can be used across a broad spectrum of industries and applications. This approach increases the potential impact on the economy. It also maximizes the opportunities for investors, creating a greater likelihood that funding will be found quickly. Consequently, TVC can increase the resources it allocates to each project.

This approach has yielded several noteworthy success stories including Quantum Manufacturing Inc., Silicon MicroDevices Inc. and Boissiere Engineering and Applied Robotics Inc.

Quantum Manufacturing Inc.

QMI recently reached agreement on the terms and conditions which can provide up to $4.125 million from private investors. The funding offer culminates five months of work by TVC staff with the two SNL scientists who developed the technology.

The technology uses a rapid-fire, high-power pulsing electrical beam to harden the surfaces of metals, ceramics, plastics and other materials. It enhances corrosion resistance and increases the lifetime of surfaces in hostile environments.

This is a core technology with many applications including the tool-and-die industry, aircraft manufacturing, automobile engines, medical implants and tools, and it can even be used on razor blades and cookware. It can be applied to high-value items, such as hardening an artificial joint used in hip replacements. Currently, such a joint may last 10 years before replacement. With this technology, it could last up to 30 years. It may have uses in the purification and pasteurization of food and it's environmentally friendly, because the process is chemical-free and creates no waste stream.

Prompted by such potential, TVC provided QMI free office space and related services, and also contributed $10,000 in seed funding to the project. The scientists were aided in developing a commercialization plan that created a business out of the technology. In addition, TVC helped them identify markets, map out a strategy that would attract investors and then introduced them to the investors themselves.

TVC's staff introduced the scientists to a dozen qualified investors, many of whom had attended the Technology Ventures' Equity

Capital Symposium in May of this year. The introductions resulted in four written offers from interested investors.

Silicon MicroDevices Inc.

Silicon MicroDevices Inc. recently entered a joint venture agreement with a major U.S. manufacturer to develop and bring to market a micro-mechanical drug delivery technology.

The technology, developed at Sandia National Laboratories, is a micro-mechanical drug delivery system that administers a broad range of medications directly into the bloodstream by overcoming the present barrier to nearly all such drug delivery, the human skin. The device delivers a drug directly and consistently into the vascular system without the drawbacks of current oral medication or syringe delivery systems. This product is radically different from existing transdermal drug patches currently on the market or under development, which use chemical or electrical methods to deliver only a small number of unique drugs through the outer layers of the skin.

Technology Ventures has provided Silicon MicroDevices with management assistance in the form of advice on company formation, business plan consultation and preparation for the first Equity Capital Symposium in October 1994.

Technology Ventures also provided a $10,000 seed-money grant in the Spring of 1995 to Silicon MicroDevices Inc.

Boissiere Engineering and Applied Robotics Inc.

Technology Ventures has assisted Boissiere Engineering and Applied Robotics (BEAR) through the first phases of business formation, including the development of business plans, classroom work on entrepreneurship and the negotiation of a license with Sandia National Laboratories for the technology on which the company is based, and also the negotiation of a technical assistance agreement with the laboratories. The company is currently in the marketing phase.

The technology focuses on telerobotics excavation systems for waste remediation applications. The technology was developed at SNL's Intelligent Systems and Robotics Center, and incorporates real-time graphic displays, graphic operator interfaces, computer control of onboard systems, model-based motion planning and sensor-controlled dynamic path controls.

Technology Ventures also contributed $10,000 in seed money to BEAR.

Additional examples of Technology Ventures-supported business opportunities, based upon dual-use technologies coming from Department of Energy laboratories, include: 1) software, that creates a virtual reality operating system; 2) advanced chemical processes for waste disposal; and 3) vertical cavity surface emitting lasers.

Future Strategies

Although Technology Ventures Corporation has achieved much in less than two years, we recognize that the future holds fresh challenges. As industry demands more and better technology, the importance of technology commercialization will grow, increasing the need for the services Technology Ventures provides. We must remain cost-effective and efficient, and we must continually provide an enhanced return on the taxpayers' investment in the technology developed at Sandia National Laboratories and other research facilities.

Therefore, Technology Ventures is already refining its project selection method to focus primarily on technologies and technologists that hold the most promise for commercialization and investment.

Technology Ventures will be able to increase the resources allocated to each project.

Funding emerging companies will continue to be a major challenge, and Technology Ventures will maintain and expand its risk capital resources. Equity Capital Symposiums will continue and every effort will be made to raise awareness that profitable technologies are emerging from DOE's laboratories and other facilities.

We believe that a major advantage can be gained by coordination with other Lockheed Martin organizations similarly dedicated to the commercialization of technology. This would give Technology Ventures' risk capital network exposure to technologies developed at other laboratories and federal installations, thus broadening the range and scope of opportunities for the investment community.

To conclude, Technology Ventures' impact can be expected to increase as it continues to build upon its past efforts. We will continue to work towards the Congressional mandate that guides us. We will continue to support the Department of Energy in its efforts to commercialize technology and stimulate economic development by augmenting government resources. This, we believe, will lessen the burden of government, and will help to maximize the return on the investment we have made in our national laboratories.

Respectfully submitted,

Sherman McCorkle
President
Technology Ventures Corporation

Mr. SCHIFF. Thank you, Mr. McCorkle.

Dr. Smith, before recognizing you, I have to say that I'm going to have to recess the hearing now so that I can cast a vote, but I'm going to ask all of the witnesses to kind of stay close to the table because Chairman Rohrabacher should be back any minute and will reconvene the hearing as soon as he gets back.

Mr. Galvin, I understand that you have to leave at 1:45. That's what I was informed. If that's necessary of course you're excused, and we appreciate your being here.

Well, good. I have some questions, and I'm glad you'll be able to stay a little longer.

Once again, thank you for indulging our schedule here, but I think you all understand the need to be sometimes in two places at once yourselves. We have that problem too.

We'll be in recess for just a few minutes.

[Recess.]

Mr. ROHRABACHER. I want to get as much done before Steve gets back, because now I've got the power.

[Laughter.]

Mr. ROHRABACHER. No, excuse me.

Dr. Smith, what we 'd like to do is proceed with your testimony and Steve will be, or Congressman Schiff will be returning momentarily, so you can proceed with your testimony.

Thank you very much.

STATEMENT OF DR. BRUCE L.R. SMITH, SENIOR STAFF, BROOKINGS INSTITUTION

Dr. SMITH. It's a great pleasure for me to be here, honor to be here with such distinguished colleagues and fellow witnesses. I wanted to establish my credentials as a very obedient witness by saying that I went over to the exhibit, as Chairman Schiff directed, as there's the proof right there.

So it's a very nice exhibit. I endorse it.

I think we should start out with the proposition that we don't really need to say here, but I think it is important to get up front here that we're not talking here about what is good for the labs, we're talking about what is good for the country. And we're not trying to invent ways to keep the labs going if there isn't the need, the national need that they serve.

So making that obvious point, but maybe it's important to put that on the record, it seems to me that there are a number of important issues that come out among which I think are the following.

What is the role of the labs in terms of the nation's R&D base, first.

Second is, what is the role of the lab in terms of economic development—broadly technology transfer—commercialization.

And thirdly, what is their role in the national security picture. I'd like to touch very glancingly on the first two points, a little bit more heavily on the third point, and then wind up, if I may, with some very brief comments on the four bills which are under consideration here this morning.

First, then, to shift the role of labs in the nation's research system, it is quite clear that the labs have played an important role over many years.

It's also quite clear that what is on the agenda today is what should be their role in the future.

And what are the national needs that they now serve and what is the nature and the need of the R&D base for the country.

I think here we have to again come back to essentials which you've touched on in your own remarks this morning, that there is overcapacity in our system.

Much, if not most, of that overcapacity is in the national labs, rather than in other parts of the system.

So I think we are facing some inevitable downsizing. This may seem a little churlish to our poor colleagues from the labs have been cutting their overheads and privatizing their this or that function, and they're facing a difficult situation.

But I think what we should do is encourage them in making the tough choices that they have because the country will be better off if we make those difficult decisions and not just grind everything down a little bit.

So I think this creates an opportunity where there may be new possibilities in cooperation with the university sector, for example.

One thinks here of the accelerator mode of producing tritium, if we do go down that route as a nation, that will be an occasion where there's some collaborative possibilities with the universities producing neutron sources for basic research and basic studies and advanced materials or bimolecular science.

On the other hand, we may simply have to defer big projects, downsize, weigh big projects against small-scale projects, and the whole system will have to adjust to this. If there's going to be fewer opportunities for advanced training of PhDs, post-docs, the universities will have to adapt to this.

So I think we're not saying that there isn't a role for the labs in a strong national R&D base, but I think this is a base that has become very expensive. It's expensive to maintain at its current levels, and it is very difficult to try to maintain it even more at even increasing levels.

So let me move on very quickly to the question of the labs in economic development, and there are witnesses here who are more knowledgeable than I am to speak to this issue, so I will not say too much.

However, I will not refrain from saying something.

And that is that I generally endorse the view expressed by the Galvin Report, and I won't read the quote that is in my written testimony, but it appears on page five of the Galvin Report, which expresses, I think it's fair to say, skepticism about whether there is a cornucopia of technology that is readily commercializable and the whole approach of a high-technology approach to economic development.

The Galvin Report states that there is not, in their view, in the view of this distinguished group of citizens, a vast kind of storehouse of technology which is ready to be commercialized, nor is the experience with CRADA's.

I think it's too early to judge us very definitively and authoritatively but we have spent something close to $750 million, $800 million on various CRADAs and the results to date, have been, I think it is fair to say, modest.

The last time I made a statement like this, someone jumped up and said, no, you must wait. How can you interrupt this great experiment in midstream?

Well, I think I'm probably persuaded that we shouldn't pull the plug on some of these important efforts at this time. Let's give them some more time to bear fruit.

But I think it is clear that there is not a new mission here of job creation, economic development in the form of these CRADAs, partnerships, what not. It just isn't there, and I think we are kidding ourselves if we suppose that it is.

Now let me move on to the point of the role of the labs in national security.

Is my time running out?

Mr. ROHRABACHER. Dr. Smith, your time has just about run out. But why don't you, if you could summarize that, that would be very helpful.

Dr. SMITH. Let me say very quickly that I think we need a nuclear deterrent, we need a science-space stockpile stewardship concept, but much as we've gone way too far under this rubric to justify things which are just not justifiable.

Things like the nuclear ignition facility is just, there's no conceivable rationale for that on science grounds, on energy grounds or on national security grounds.

We don't need many of the elaborate things that are proposed under it because we want to move this year to have a nuclear complete comprehensive test ban. And the more we push elaborate schemes to keep the labs going, the harder this will be to negotiate.

I think also that we should move toward a greater-user concept. The weapons labs should be directly administered by the Department of Defense. The Department of Defense is their customer.

There should be a transfer, whatever the status of the Department of Energy, the military themselves should decide how much and how big the weapons picture should be.

I'll forebear from my comments on the particular bills, but I did want to get in the proposition that I think we're somewhat going down the wrong tree, and that's just caught a mixed metaphor there, barking up the wrong something, by relying on the Bloch concept. I don't see that this is relevant.

But I thank you for the opportunity to present my views and I'm sorry for going over my time.

[The prepared statement of Dr. Smith follows:]

Testimony before the Subcommittee on Basic Research and Subcommittee on Energy of the Committee on Science, U.S. House of Representatives

September 7, 1995

Bruce L.R. Smith

The Brookings Institution

Washington, D.C.

Good morning, Mr. Chairmen and ladies and gentlemen. It is a great pleasure to appear today and discuss the challenging questions you have set before us. I am pleased to be included with such distinguished fellow witnesses. Let me say, first of all, that you and your colleagues on the Subcommittees on Basic Research and Energy are to be congratulated for tackling the tough issues concerning the future of the national laboratories. I hope that we will be able to provide some enlightening testimony to assist in your deliberations.

Among the critical issues that are before us today in my mind three broad concerns stand out: the role of the national labs in the nation's overall R&D effort, their role in economic development and technology transfer, and their contribution to national security in the post-Cold War era. I will touch glancingly on the first two broad concerns, but focus my attention here this morning to the third issue. I will comment on the four bills as they relate to the broad policy issues rather than attempting a detailed review of the merits of each bill. It goes without saying that the standard of judgment we should apply in addressing these issues is not what is good for the labs, but what is good for the country. The labs have made outstanding contributions to the nation's welfare and security in the past, but past contributions are not the issue today. Our task is to address whether, and how, and in what ways the labs can best serve current national needs.

The Labs and the Nation's Research Base

On the first issue, the role of the labs in the nation's overall science and technology effort, we must note that the labs have played an important role. Some of them have provided the facilities which, through the "user group" mode, have enabled university scientists and other scientists to carry out important areas of basic research. The labs have also been repositories of talent in applied fields of research, such as energy use and environmental quality, and they have been the employer of large numbers of scientists and engineers trained in the universities. A relatively stable division of labor for a long time prevailed among the universities, national labs and industrial research facilities. This relationship has been considerably shaken up in the post-Cold War era, with potential new areas of cooperation as well as conflict among the traditional research performers. All have faced a more somber fiscal outlook as the nation seeks to redefine its needs and reduce public expenditures.

Several of the bills, H.R. 1510 and H.R. 2142, seem to slight the civil science role of the labs by singling them out for personnel cuts. Employment at non-defense national labs would be reduced by as much as one-third over a ten year period, a step which would have serious effects on the supporting resources for the university scientists who use those facilities. H.R. 1993 also proposes extensive program cuts (along with abolishing the department and reducing it to an independent agency) but would exempt the DOE's General Science and Research activities from the most severe cutbacks. I do not find a compelling justification for directing cuts only toward civilian laboratories and activities in part because the defense labs also have non-defense functions which by this logic should be cut. This approach begs the question of whether current practices and staffing levels effectively serve the nation's changing defense needs. There is a case for reviewing all Department of Energy labs both civilian and defense-related, and at the same time for a more selective approach with respect to potential consolidation and cuts in the civilian labs themselves.

While I attach a high priority to the user group facilities for basic science, it is apparent that the nation has developed a very large and expensive scientific and technological enterprise during the Cold War which is increasingly difficult to support at current levels, let alone at increasing levels. Expensive large-scale science using national facilities will have to be weighed against smaller-scale research within university departments. We have chosen as a nation to support research within a mission agency framework, and as the missions of some agencies shrink, the R&D that they will be able to support will also shrink. This will have an impact across the whole research system, including the universities. But new forms of collaboration may be possible, such as an accelerator facility for the production of tritium that could also produce neutrons for basic studies of materials and biomolecules. In other cases, big projects may have to be deferred or canceled. To the extent that employment of scientists and engineers at national laboratories declines, the universities will correspondingly have to produce fewer scientists and engineers.

The Labs and Economic Development

On the issue of the labs' role in economic development there are other witnesses who are better able to comment than me. I will therefore limit myself to a few brief observations. In general I share the skeptical view expressed in the Galvin Report about an expansion of the laboratories' missions in the area of economic development. The Galvin Task Force found that "the laboratories are not now, nor will they become, cornucopias of relevant technology for a broad range of industries. A significant fraction of the laboratories' industrial competitiveness activities concern technologies which are of less than primary importance to their industrial collaborators and/or which these partners could obtain from other sources. There are only a relatively few instances in which the laboratories have technology that is vital to industry and that is uniquely available at the laboratories..." (Task Force of the Secretary of Energy Advisory Board on Alternative Futures for the Department of Energy National Laboratories, p. 45).

Industrial support for such technology transfer and economic activities is often influenced by the availability of government cost-sharing funds. Partnership arrangements with some firms, especially when they are large firms, may provoke strong opposition from other companies which are not part of the arrangement. Critics complain that government subsidies distort the market, create incentives for expensive "big technology" approaches to problems, or simply waste resources. The experience of the Department of Energy with cooperative

R&D agreements (CRADA's) between the labs and private firms to date does not permit a definitive evaluation of their effectiveness. There is probably a case to be made for allowing some partnership experiments to continue for a time to see if they produce useful results. But I would not look to consortia, CRADA's, and partnerships as having great promise for economic expansion, job generation or preservation, or some expanded mission for the Department of Energy's national labs.

The economic rationale has sometimes been advanced to help justify maintaining the labs at their present size, but a jobs argument does not add up to a convincing case for maintaining the labs in their present configurations and sizes. It may seem churlish to make this point when the labs are, in fact, presently engaged in a painful process of down-sizing, cutting overhead costs, privatizing support functions, and perhaps should be forgiven for grasping for any argument to cushion their slide toward a reduced role in the scheme of things. But I believe it is important to encourage the DOE and the laboratory leadership to continue to take strong steps in the right direction as difficult and painful as these steps might be.

The Labs and National Security

I would now like to turn to the difficult issue of the role of the national laboratories in the nation's changing defense needs. As with the questions of their contribution to the country's overall R&D base and their role in commercializing technology, the future role of the laboratories in the national security picture is an extremely difficult issue on which reasonable and well-informed people may differ. There is no question, in my view, that the nation will need to maintain a nuclear deterrent into the foreseeable future. As such, the reliability and safety of the nuclear stockpile is a necessity and is a vital role for the defense-oriented national laboratories. As there is a collapsing of functions back into the labs their role in some ways will increase in the future. One thinks, for example, of the closing of the Pinnellas special DOE-facility with some functions transferred to Sandia as illustrative of how the labs can acquire expanded roles. The closing of the Mound tritium factory may necessitate a wider lab role if the DOE were to decide on the accelerator route as the preferred means for tritium production. It is particularly important, I think, at a time when the nation is at peace and when there is no active looming national security threat for there to be forward thinking and anticipation of future needs. Of course, if the DOE were to be abolished as is envisaged under H.R. 1993 of if its regulatory functions were drastically curtailed, it would perforce return to a role akin to that of the pre-departmental days of the Energy Research and Development Administration(ERDA) and even before. This would be one future that we could imagine for the department, but perhaps is a topic somewhat beyond our immediate focus. The kind of research capacity that we are discussing now is suggested under the rubric of the "science-based stockpile stewardship" advocated by the DOE and the Defense Department.

In my view, the labs could play an expanded role in preventing the nonproliferation of nuclear weapons and to that end broaden their contacts with scientists and with defense labs in the former CIS countries. Having said this, I believe that there is some danger of stretching the science-based stockpile stewardship concept well beyond reasonable limits. We are being asked, under that concept, to justify measures that go considerably beyond what is needed in the national interest. The Nuclear Ignition Facility (NIF), to be located at Lawrence Livermore National Laboratory, is an apt illustration of the point. There is no reasonable, second-generation or otherwise, national security stockpile stewardship need to be served by the construction of this facility. The going in price is estimated to be some $1 billion, a sum that would very likely be exceeded in practice. The NIF's proposed giant laser is not needed to ensure the safety and reliability of the existing nuclear stockpile and the inertial confinement fusion concept as a potential source of energy is dubious. The Galvin Task Force, in its review of the nation's weapons design capabilities, came to the conclusion that Livermore should transfer its stockpile support to the other weapons laboratories over a five year period, a reasonable conclusion but one that has been ignored by the Department of Energy.

It is said that the reason why redundant capacities have been maintained is that a political bargain has been struck in which the national labs and the military services have agreed to back the Clinton administration's proposals for a comprehensive test ban (CTB) in return for commitment to maintain the labs at or near full funding. If such a bargain has been struck, it should be unstruck because it is not a good bargain for the country. There is no reason why the nation should be held hostage to a Cold War mentality, and an implicit threat of insubordination and political mischief-making, in order to pursue a goal that is clearly in the national interest. The reality is that there is overcapacity in the national labs in terms of the nation's realistic military needs. The sooner we get on with the task of an orderly and humane restructuring of the lab system (which is, after all, part of the logistical tail and not the war-fighting tooth of our military forces), the better off we will be. You might ask: what is the harm is taking out a little insurance and having excess nuclear capacity in the event of future need? The answer is that such capacities are very expensive, that serious observers agree that the stockpile is safe and reliable at present, that military planners do not want nuclear weapons and overwhelmingly opt for advanced conventional weapons, and that the nation has an overriding interest in preventing the spread of nuclear capabilities.

There is a paradox in our nuclear strength: the more we insist on an expansive definition of stockpile stewardship, the harder it will be to convince other nations that nuclear weapons are a costly albatross. The Russians have indicated informally that they cannot accept a comprehensive test ban because they lack our scientific capacities that make possible science-based stockpile stewardship. They indicate that they need continued testing up to 10 kilotons to ensure the safety and reliability of their stockpile. Clearly, while we cannot allow any nation to dictate U.S. policy on this or any other matter, we should properly be concerned at the prospect of any test ban without the participation of a major nuclear power. If we are to achieve the successful negotiation of a comprehensive test ban in the course of the next year--a goal strongly in the national interest--we must not undermine our negotiating posture by lumping under the stockpile stewardship concept a range of activities that give the appearance of a surreptitious attempt to evade either the spirit or the letter of the test ban. This is a matter of balancing reasonable, but partially conflicting, objectives. I am persuaded that the dual axis hydrodynamic test facility (DAHRT) is a valid part of the science-based stewardship approach, but the need to proceed further to a more elaborate three-dimensional test process to ensure the safety and reliability of the stockpile is more doubtful. Some countries already object to the whole idea of stockpile stewardship and claim that it is a subtle device to circumvent the treaty. We cannot satisfy everyone but let us give our negotiators every reasonable chance to secure a successful outcome.

The problems we are addressing are so difficult because they involve, as of course do all controversial and complex issues, a determination, first, of what is the right thing to do and, second, how to steer a practical course to achieve the desired end. I am not a politician, but I have a deep appreciation of the skills of compromise and conciliation which you as distinguished members of the two subcommittees will bring to the issues. I can see from the four bills we are discussing that you have struggled with a formula to achieve the right balance between compelling the executive branch to act and allowing them discretion to come up with an appropriate plan. The bills differ in the degree to which they would specify administrative actions and outcomes as against mandating a process by which the executive branch would reach decisions (with the Congress and its staff units playing various assigned roles and approving the recommendations). Without attempting a detailed analysis of each bill, let me make a few random comments for the committee's consideration.

First, as to H.R. 87, the bill proposes a somewhat unwieldy process for eventually reaching lab closure and/or reconfiguration. The Secretary of Energy is to "establish criteria" which will be a lengthy process and then will publish a list of proposed closures. The DOE Laboratory Facilities Commission to be established will then review the Secretary's recommendations and the Comptroller General will get into the act. The role of the Comptroller General could present separation-of-powers problems in constitutional terms but would in any event present practical problems as it re-does the work of the Department of Energy. The published criteria and the concurrent GAO review will present the Commission with a tangle of problems and numerous opportunities for legal and political challenges to its recommendations. The President comes into the process relatively late, as in the defense base closure process on which the proposed Commission is based, and can make recommendations for amendment which are sent back to the Commission and thence to the Congress. The Congress can only vote up or down on the whole package. We might ask why, if the Secretary of Energy could come up with a list of recommendations after one year, the Congress could not simply act right then and there on the recommendations without the further review processes.

The concept of the Commission shows up in all of the bills and has somewhat different proposed roles. I must note that I find the analogy to the defense base-closing commission somewhat problematical. The defense base -closing and reconfiguration commission has not, in my judgment, been a complete success. It has proved to be a laborious process, fraught with its own political problems, and probably has run its course and will not be renewed by the Congress for another round. At any rate, it is not an exact parallel for the DOE situation. The DOE labs are so diverse in mission and function that a common set of criteria for reviewing and assessing their activities will be difficult to achieve. I have written elsewhere on the uses and misuses of advisory commissions (Smith, The Advisers: Scientists in the Policy Process, Brookings, 1992) and I fear that we have here a case where the commission is asked to do either too much or too little. We cannot expect to lay the whole problem on the commission without any guidelines for choice, but if the guidelines are too precise and restrictive the commission would not be able to do anything creative or constructive. If the Department of Energy could truly lay out a plan for closing or reconfiguring the labs that had political support, it would not be necessary to have the device of the commission serving as cover. .

In the case of the defense bases, the Department of Defense knew which bases it wanted to close and the base closing commission helped provide the cover for taking the difficult steps (but even now many bases are in transition and a stretch-out phase with significant savings yet to be realized). The Department of Energy does not know or cannot decide which labs to close because it does not know or cannot decide which of its main missions— energy, defense, environmental cleanup, technology transfer, basic science--are most important and deserve the highest priority.

H.R. 2142 calls for and begins to lay out an extensive set of criteria to be be used in deciding which labs or programs to close or to consolidate. The criteria are reasonable and relevant, but laying out the criteria will not get one smoothly from the process of deliberation to the actual decisions. The problem is how to weigh the conflicting and often incommensurate values and reach a decision. The elaborateness of the criteria and their publication in the Federal Register in advance of the decisions may merely create opportunities for delay, stretching out the process, and legal challenge to the actions taken.

H.R. 1993 is a very detailed and carefully-thought out measure that would abolish the Department of Energy and substitutes an independent agency for the current department. Various functions are to be either privatized, reassigned to other departments, given to the new independent agency, or abolished. The bill, like the others,incorporates the notion of a commission to address the future role of the labs but differentiates the labs into several distinct categories. I cannot comment fully on this complex bill, but it appears on first reading that many of the DOE's functions will either be retained in the new independent agency or transferred to other agencies. If this is the case, one wonders if the gains are sufficient to outweigh the inevitable confusion, disarray, and wheel-spinning that accompanies a major organizational change. I sympathize with Congress's desire to resolve these issues through a major statute of this kind since the Department of Energy has had difficulty in producing a clear plan of action. However, the Congress may wish to consider as a first step the grant of reorganization powers to the Secretary of Energy, with Congress being asked to approve or disapprove the plans as a whole in a "fast-track" procedure or through a two-house legislative veto.

There are strong elements in common with the four bills. Each recognizes the need for major change, seeks to force more decisive action on the executive branch's part, and begins to define the goals that should guide policy. As such they contribute to informed debate on the future roles of the national laboratories which is very badly needed. They begin to lay the basis for considered action. I congratulate you for tackling this difficult problem as the nation moves to define its scientific and technological posture for the post-Cold War era. Thank you for the opportunity to offer some reflections on the measures under consideration here this morning.

Mr. ROHRABACHER. Dr. Smith, thank you very much.

What I'd like to do now is turn to our distinguished former Chairman of the Full Committee to begin the questioning.

Mr. Brown has been following this for many years and his experience is far beyond just any of us on this Committee.

So I think it's fitting that Congressman Brown begins this questioning of our expert witnesses.

Mr. BROWN. Thank you very much, Mr. Rohrabacher.

I am not going to belabor the points raised by the panelists, although I do want to express my appreciation to them for the very wise and balanced suggestions that they've made.

We seem to have a number of options here which need to be explored. On the one hand, we have heard suggestions that we could transfer some of the functions out of the Department of Energy and into other agencies or privatize them with some efficiency.

On the other hand, there has also been suggested by some, including Members of this Committee, that the Department of Energy could take over some of the functions now being performed in the Department of Commerce which is NIST, for example.

Basically, the programs aimed at enhancing cooperation with industry which the Department of Energy does very well.

Could I solicit from each of you your views as to whether it would be reasonable to add substantial functions to the Department of Energy while we are also considering downsizing it or transferring functions, as Mr. Bloch suggested in the case of the science labs into the National Science Foundation?

How do we make some sense out of these, what would appear to be opposing kinds of suggestions to improve the governance of the labs?

From all of you on that.

Mr. BLOCH. Let me start the conversation then.

I don't think that one should add to the DOE additional responsibilities, while we all are saying—and I think I've not heard anybody say something to the contrary—that the first order of business has to be the streamlining of that particular department.

And that's why I proposed to move things out which have nothing to do with the primary mission.

And the four science labs fall into that category.

Let me say right away, however, one needs to find a good place for it. One can't just move things out and let them hang that are important to continue.

And with regard to the science labs, I felt and I'm convinced that NSF is in a better position to handle that because of their existing mission.

That is not true about everything, however, that one wants to move out from there.

Mr. BROWN. I appreciate your views because of your own experience at NSF. You're in a position to evaluate that.

In the event that some of you were confused by this thought about moving other functions in, this is the thrust of one of the bills before us; to take some of the functions at Commerce and move them into Energy, just in case you weren't familiar with that.

Mr. ROHRABACHER. Does anyone else care to comment?

Dr. SMITH. I'll make a brief comment, and I'd like to affirm Chairman Rohrabacher praise to you, George, an old friend, and certainly one of the most knowledgeable people. I sat at your feet for many years, and I'm delighted to have a chance to testify here.

I think it depends on what function, I mean, what function you're trying to keep alive and to be served.

If it's a function that is in the country's interest, fine. But I doubt much, I sympathize with Congress' desire to find a formula to compel the Executive to do something, to do the right things, to set in motion a process there or to mandate certain changes on them, but I think looking at the Department and hearing some of the testimony this morning, it seemed that the Department was saying, yes, we agree the system is broke, but we don't want to change anything.

Yes, everything should be reformulated but everything's perfect.

I think I'd be a little skeptical about putting too much weight on that. I'd like to see the Energy Department go back more toward an ERDA concept where it is an R&D agency, the way it was before it became a Department.

Dr. VEST. It seems to me, sir, that where major facilities and laboratories belong should be governed by mission, and in a fairly narrow sense of that term. And that when programs need to be conducted that do not obviously fall one place or another, that the really important thing is to figure out how to introduce some level of real competition into the system so that it becomes optimized by different potential performers competing, both on the basis of merit, quality, and economics.

Mr. MCCORKLE. I believe one of the lessons that we learned during the base realignment and closure process is that any cost-cutting efforts need to be very closely examined to determine if you're going to achieve the desired result.

Frequently, moving chairs around the table, and moving missions from one agency to another does not provide for greater efficiency and does not maximize any return on investment.

Mr. BROWN. Well, I appreciate your responses. Of course, part of the reason for some of these suggestions stems from other factors, other than merely improving the efficiency of the DOE.

There is of course some thought that the Department of Commerce ought to be dismantled, and if it is, then you look for a place to put some of the functions you want to save. And to some degree, that's what's been happening here.

Or in some cases, there's a desire to create a new agency, such as the Department of Science, built on the framework of perhaps the DOE. I don't know.

So some of these suggestions stem from a broader agenda than merely how we make the best use of the resources and assets of the Department of Energy.

Dr. SMITH. Chairman Brown?

Mr. BROWN. Yes.

Dr. SMITH. Could I make one further short remark, an historical note?

I think it is interesting that if you look back at Vannevar Bush's report, one of the most significant things which is neglected in the analysis is that he doubted whether a mission agency approach was appropriate, and hence he favored a large Department of Science.

Now if, as you say, we are changing for wider reasons, and we've got a lot of R&D functions rattling around, the notion of a more centralized science department might make sense.

Bush's view of why he didn't like mission agencies running R&D is that they wouldn't have a long-run enough perspective, they would emphasize short-run operational considerations. I'm sure that's part of the problem why our colleagues from the labs don't want to be under the direct administration of Defense.

But I think that's an important—we have gone down the route of being a mission-oriented system for our supporting of R&D. That basic issue raised by Vannevar Bush is now back on the table.

Can you operate that way?

Mr. BROWN. I think that Mr. Bush found, from his own experience, how difficult it was to carry out that centralization that he was recommending, and in my opinion, after studying this for a couple of decades, I don't think it's any easier today than it was when Vannevar Bush tried to achieve it, and we might be guided by that.

Mr. ROHRABACHER. Thank you. Mr. Chairman, I would just like one minute before I yield to Mr. Schiff, and present this idea, or this concept.

There are, am I mistaken in the notion that if we were willing to spend twice as much money as we are spending today, there are many worthy science projects that could be used to justify the spending of that money, and vice versa? If we decide that we are going to have to spend less money, no matter how much if we go less, that money's going to be spent and it will then force people to set priorities among the many science projects that we could take on that are reasonable, and might benefit mankind and benefit our country?

So in this era when we have that, when the knowledge base is such that we could justify spending because there are many, many science projects, and justify spending this much or that much, isn't it better for us if we're trying to get people to set priorities and to basically restructure an institution, like the national labs, such as basically to set a price of what we're willing to pay?

And then let them determine what those projects are and what the organization structure will be?

Does that make any sense?

Mr. Galvin's shaking his head, so he should be the one who answers that first.

Mr. Galvin, why don't you, if you could, just comment on that?

Mr. GALVIN. Your statement answers itself, sir, the basic principles that you've just enunciated.

To me the issue here that I thought we were supposed to be talking about is the how-to and the what-to can be any size you want it to be, so you people can decide that.

My bias is always to spend more for science because I know we get something out of it, but I believe in that more than some people do.

So make it any size you want, but then let's seek the optimum way of achieving the best science result from that.

And I thought that was the purpose of this meeting.

I think we're frankly off on an awful lot of tangents here, sir.

Mr. ROHRABACHER. All right. Well, I've only been chairing just a little while.

[Laughter.]

Mr. SCHIFF. And see what you've done to this hearing.

Mr. ROHRABACHER. I so screwed up center field that nobody can play it. Right.

Anyway, I think I will yield to Mr. Schiff.

Mr. SCHIFF. Thank you, Mr. Chairman.

And since you raised the issue, I would like to say budgets will always exist. Budgets will always be a constraint. It's unavoidable.

I personally however would not like to have to be the one to make the decision about which of those R&D award-winning projects down the hall we really don't need and shouldn't be pursuing right now.

Mr. Bloch, if I may address you for a moment, sir?

In the political environment, and political environment I mean philosophical, I don't mean Republican and Democratic partisan politics, in the philosophical environment, many of the individuals who often praise the Council On Competitiveness and point to its recommendations in terms of the direction the country should go, are often times, not always, but often times the same individuals who object to government/industry partnerships and cooperation.

For this purpose, I'm referring to the national laboratories as government because they're government-sponsored programs.

And yet you spoke very highly of the concept of partnerships between industry and government, if I understood your testimony correctly.

I agree with you, but what about the concerns of those who say, and again, normally allies of the Council On Competitiveness, that government and industry were meant to stay as far away from each other as possible?

Mr. BLOCH. Well, I'm sure you're absolutely right. You can hear both views.

But let me reflect on that for a minute.

When we're talking about a partnership between the government agencies, laboratories, what-have-you, and the private sector, then I think one has to ask oneself: partnership at what level?

And first of all, there has to be participation, and by that one, I mean not just participation per se, but also economic financial participation on both sides, so that you get essentially a feeling and the recognition that both sides can benefit from it.

Secondly, it has to be at a level that does not distort the function of the government agency or the government laboratory and, at the same time, does not encroach on the industry responsibilities.

So it has to stay far away from the area of commercialization, the last few steps in the commercialization process. But I think you will find a lot of people that have changed their mind on that when you really focus them on the area of applied research or whatever you want to call it.

I hate to put a label on it because these labels get in our way. But in an area that is far removed from the marketplace, itself, on the one hand, and number two, on the other hand, however, is part of the mission of that particular agency, laboratory, university, whatever it might be. So if you are selective in your partnership, I think you will get a lot more consensus than if you just throw it open as a general kind of a subject.

Mr. SCHIFF. I understand the reservations that you have expressed about how these partnerships are put together, and I think they're well-stated. I'm merely making the observation that conceptually, the fact that at some level in some way, there is in fact a partnership between the government and private industry something you would support?

Mr. BLOCH. Absolutely.

Mr. SCHIFF. Mr. McCorkle, let me turn to you.

In terms of your having put together some of the beginning partnerships, do you believe, from what you have seen, that they have been mutually beneficial, not only to industry but to the government research at the government laboratories?

Mr. MCCORKLE. The short answer is yes.

I've only been involved in this for two years, but I believe that in the instances where we've been involved that clearly the patents and licensing agreements will be of substantial benefit to the government.

Mr. SCHIFF. As well as to industry?

Mr. MCCORKLE. As well as to industry.

Many of these technologies are core technologies which have very broad applications and tremendous potential.

Mr. SCHIFF. Mr. Galvin, if I may turn to you, sir, I have a couple of questions.

One is, you said almost cryptically, in looking at the four bills, that they all suggested, at least in some way, there'd be a reduction of employment at the national laboratories and you said that may be the wrong place to focus.

Where would be the right place to focus in terms of reduction of employment?

Mr. GALVIN. The Department of Energy personally unto itself. I would guess that all those people who could be censused, people who could be identified as having anything to do with the laboratory, you probably could reduce that by 90 to 95 percent.

Mr. SCHIFF. At the Department of Energy?

Mr. GALVIN. At the Department of Energy.

Remember, it's the system. That all the people that had to interface with those people, almost all of them are now reducible at the laboratories.

So right there would probably save your one-third, if you'd just approach that. You'd have to have a substitute to have a governance and that's where we suggest that you depoliticize the system. That word was used many times this morning as being possibly a potential, so depoliticize the system, turn it over to the private sector and the corporatization role, such as we have defined, such as I have defined and let a chief executive officer run this and give you tremendous results.

That's where I'd focus.

I think you can keep every bench engineer and scientist on the payroll if you want to. Maybe you don't want to, but I think you can afford to not cut any engineering and just cut overhead and save all the money that you want, from a budget standpoint, and you'll get way more science as a result of that.

Mr. SCHIFF. If I can just follow that for one more minute here.

Your emphasis on ccrporatization you've made very clear, not only here of course but in my personal meetings with you and your previous testimony, but as you heard earlier this morning, Chairman Walker referred to that proposal as the fundamental proposal of the Galvin Task Force.

I'm not negating its importance, but I didn't gather it was the fundamental recommendation of the Task Force. I'm not sure I could classify a fundamental recommendation.

Could you?

Mr. GALVIN. Yes. I think it is the most prominent recommendation we made, not just because it gathered a lot of attention, but I think it is the boldest suggestion of the group.

There are many other, there are over a hundred recommendations in the Task Force, and depending on one's point of view, each one of them may be among the first ten that anyone would select.

So I don't quarrel with the term fundamental. I think it's just the most prominent. I also think it's the most practical. I think it's the one that will achieve the greatest single monetary result and the greatest single efficiency result in terms of science.

But we concur on all the matters having to do with better roles and missions and all of those kinds of things. All, incidentally, couched in the fact we think the labs are superb. You'd have to reinvent them if they didn't exist, in order to achieve the science needs that the country's going to have.

But I would respectfully say it's right up there among the top couple.

Mr. SCHIFF. Thank you. I yield back, Mr. Chairman.

Mr. ROHRABACHER. Mr. Galvin, when you say corporatization, do you mean as similar to the Post Office corporatization?

Mr. GALVIN. I'm not capable of making that analogy, sir.

Corporatization means simply to us that the equity ownership of the property of the laboratories would be retained by the federal government, that the federal government would block-grant finance, and that then distinguishes what would be changed from being privatized. In other words, we will not have acquired yet, in this decade, the equity ownership of these laboratories, which incidentally can probably be accomplished in the year 2010 to 2020 if you'd like to aim for that.

And then it's corporatized in that you now separate it from your governance and from the Department governance in a new federally established corporation, of which you've done about 50 of them in the history of this Congress, and that corporation gets to operate essentially as a private institution with these other ownership and financing arrangements.

Dr. SMITH. Could I ask a question, Mr. Chairman?

Mr. ROHRABACHER. We would like to have a dialogue, so go right ahead.

Dr. SMITH. I hate to disagree with my distinguished colleague, Mr. Galvin, whose report is sort of the bible. Here it is right in my briefcase.

But to what purpose would the public sector continue to fund these 50 entities? What would they do?

If we need them less for national security or a somewhat smaller portion, what are they doing and for which we are continuing to fund them until the year 2020?

Mr. GALVIN. Well, first off, the national security responsibility will be ours for at least two score years, probably until the year 2030. That's the vestige of our having had the victory in the Cold War.

So about 25 percent of the budget for the laboratories will continue to be expended, probably over 30 to 40 years, just on issues that are the vestige of national security.

Mr. ROHRABACHER. But as you see corporatization, pardon me for interrupting you, do you see that percentage that you just mentioned as being mandated by Congress?

Mr. GALVIN. Yes, sir.

I do see a block grant financing by Congress for the next 30 to 40 years to whatever the entities are, in order to maintain the stockpile storageship, the non-proliferation, the looking at all the things having to do with atomic weapons and atomic vestiges for at least that period of time.

Now, that's an absolute fact, sir. You just can't avoid that responsibility.

Dr. SMITH. How are they going to be accountable to the user, the customer there, which is the military services, if they are sort of corporatized and they are outside of government. How are they going to do what the military wants?

Mr. GALVIN. Exactly the same reason that Lockheed can buy airplanes and Motorola can buy radar sets. Everything can be done better in this system if you vest by trust to the citizens of the country to do the job, versus presuming it has to be a government-owned entity.

Mr. ROHRABACHER. Mr. Galvin, there are some people—your report, of course, suggested that there's micromanagement, and then you also analyzed the cost in dealing with government involvement, but I think what Dr. Smith is bringing up is that there's a potential other risk, if you go the other direction, where you don't have as much guidance in the spending of public funds as we do today.

Mr. GALVIN. Well, that's certainly a point of view, sir. I happen to have greater trust in the citizens of this country than I think you people in federal government have. Why can't you trust us who are out there in the private sector as much as you trust yourselves?

Mr. ROHRABACHER. Boy, I'll tell you, if I trusted everybody out in the private sector, we'd be handing money, we'd have wheelbarrows full of money going down the hallways to all those special interest groups in the private sector.

Mr. GALVIN. I don't think so. I don't think so, sir.

I'm talking about a very responsible assignment to some 20 to 25 people, such as are sitting at this table, and I'll trust any one of all four of them, and some others like them to do an absolutely distinguished, honorable, professional job of serving you in a very much more efficient way than can be done by the bureaucracy that has been imposed from the top.

Let this thing come up from the bottom. Let the engineers define the roadmaps with universities, with the private sector, and you'll start to have the better definition of roles and missions, you'll have more efficient work done on the laboratory bench, you'll get far more results.

This is something that I've learned over 55 years. I don't know whether people that are in the Congress for two or three years can gain the appreciation of what can be done in institutional leadership.

Mr. ROHRABACHER. Well, let's move on, and Mr. Roemer, would you like to move into this discussion?

Mr. ROEMER. Sure. Let me, I'll come back to Mr. Galvin because I think he's onto some interesting questions for us as a Congress and particularly on what we're all about here, and that's how to, to get advice from this distinguished panel.

I'd like to go to Mr. Bloch, though, for some questions.

I appreciate some of your kind remarks about my legislation. However, one of the things you said was that the one-third cut in the personnel doesn't go far enough and it doesn't go fast enough.

What would your time line be with recommendations toward a cut in personnel and a time line and the accountability between Congress and the agencies, or the labs, in this case?

Mr. BLOCH. I'll comment on the time line.

I have built up organizations in industry and I've torn them down both. And my experience is that if you want to have an operation that is self-propelling after awhile, instead of just, you know, a mass edict from the top, you have to do it in an accelerated kind of way.

It develops its own dynamism after awhile.

And I think anything that takes five and ten years, I think it's out of the question that it will have any effect. There will be a hundred thousand reasons why it didn't happen. And some of them, by the way, are very good reasons, so it's not all excuses.

Mr. ROEMER. Well, we heard some of them this morning.

Mr. BLOCH. You will hear more, I'm sure.

And I would suggest that a downsizing has to happen in an 18-months kind of a time period, and not in a three-year, five-year and ten-year kind of a time period.

Otherwise, you will find out that it won't happen. Just the change in personnel alone will prevent it from happening.

Congress is here for two years, and then new people walk in. In the Administration, after four years, it is changing usually. Sometimes the people within the Administration faster.

Who is providing the continuity is really what I'm asking, and that's why I'm for accelerating the process.

And, by the way, it's not any more difficult if you do it on a faster time scale. These are all very difficult things to accomplish. I don't want to minimize it.

But I think by giving it too much time, you're not making the job any easier.

Mr. ROEMER. So you're saying eighteen months and you're saying within, to accomplish this, what are we using as the hammer on the anvil, so to speak? Is this just a budgetary recommendation? Is this a certain amount of the work force, a percentage, a goal?

What would you say should be the kind of vision for us to use?

Mr. BLOCH. I think you should give a broad goal, and not a very prescriptive, detailed kind of an instruction. And some of the things in the bill are highly prescriptive, and I think that is dangerous.

Give the Secretary the job of downsizing by X percent. You put the number X in, and then let her figure out how to do it, and give her a time scale. But don't give her 25 other things which she has to do at the same time that prevents her from doing the true and honest job.

Mr. ROEMER. Thank you, Mr. Bloch. I look forward to talking to you more about improving the bill.

Mr. Galvin, I first want to thank you for your time that you've put in on the recommendations. We appreciate it.

I noticed on the AP wire this morning that Motorola had decided to build a new plant in Virginia, and possibly employ up to 5,000 people at a cost of $3 billion to build a new line of semiconductors.

Certainly when you decide, as you did for years, and running so efficiently and so well the corporation, Motorola, there was accountability. There was a time frame, there was a budget that your managers had.

I'm just having a tough time understanding, and that's not to say I've decided how I come down on this corporatization, but how do we organize corporatization when we are elected officials?

We have a responsibility and an obligation to taxpayers. I happen to be a conservative Democrat that feels like we should balance the budget.

How do we make sure that these new corporations that are run by a CEO but are still responsible to the taxpayer are not all doing the same mission, are not all going out to build new semiconductors, or flat panel computer screens?

That some of them are taking some high risks that our national laboratories have done in the past, whether they be weapons research or energy production or solar technologies?

Some of these have come to fruition, some have not.

I guess my third question would be, in terms of liability, we seem to be saying to the CEO of the new national laboratory, you go ahead and do what you want to do and let's go bottom up with our engineers and our scientists, which may not be a bad idea, but then the liability is still with the government.

How do we work out and wrestle with some of these tough things?

All in the context of, when you said something at Motorola, it probably got done. If it didn't, somebody was probably gone underneath you as a manager.

When we say something in resolutions or in report language, it rarely gets done. If we say something in statutory language, most of the time it gets done.

Mr. GALVIN. Thank you for indicating that in institutions like ours, we do have accountability. I respectfully suggest this new corporation would have accountability.

Now there are many things that can be inveighed into this system that will give you confidence.

First, you will allocate funds in block form. Let's take national security stockpile storage, et al, et al. You may allocate, let's say you got a $4 billion budget for the laboratories, it was six, it probably can get finally down to four and keep all the science going.

You'll probably say, we'd like to have you allocate about a billion dollars each year to the stockpile stewardship responsibility.

We'd like to have you allocate about $800 million to environmental sciences.

A billion-one to energy sciences of one kind or another, et cetera. And there'll be a few tail end factors in there.

You will have an accounting from the management, and there can be an Arthur Andersen that attests to the accountability. You don't have to have GAO come in and do that. Our public accountants assure our stockholders that we have been good stewards of their funds.

And one of the things that hasn't been mentioned here, and there's no time to develop it, that when the laboratories finally embrace, and I think they are embracing, and the National Science Foundation further embraces, and the private sector is beginning to embrace the employment of roadmaps, technology roadmaps, which among other things are going to be a marvelous instrument for technology interchange and exchange.

You're going to have the most marvelous way of accounting for the fact that these institutions are doing something that is purposeful and achieving.

So institutionally, this is an easy thing for those of us that run our institutions to do. It's not that complex. We're doing it with as big an institution as you've got. You think this is big.

The ten labs that we looked at are comparatively small as far as my looking at institutional governance. So we can give you a marvelous hands-on accountability but without accounting for whether or not somebody overstepped a travel budget by $10,000 in the first quarter.

It's when you micromanage at all those kinds of goofy levels that you absolutely obfuscate an institution.

So think of the billion dollars. How are you doing on making sure we have stockpile stewardship? Have you accounted for your funds in an honorable way?

Incidentally, none of these outfits are going to go out and invest in the production of things. They have a science-based thing.

In the time we have here, sir, I can only say, institutionally this is not a difficult problem. If you give us enough time, we can show you how practical these things work out to be.

Mr. ROEMER. Let me just beg the Chairman's indulgence for one follow-up?

Mr. ROHRABACHER. Mr. Galvin only has a few more minutes with us, I believe, and what we'd like to do——

Mr. GALVIN. I'm at your service, sir, but please discipline yourself.

Mr. ROHRABACHER. Go right ahead.

[Laughter.]

Mr. ROEMER. I'll take the first part of your statement there, "I'm at your service," and I didn't hear the rest of it.

Let me just say this, Mr. Galvin, you and I had worked together, when I first got to Congress, on the Superconducting Supercollider.

I think Congress made a mistake in cancelling that project. I think you do too.

Now that's something that the private sector would not have done on its own.

Do we have assurances with some kind of a corporate model that the government will continue to be in these very risky areas with huge areas of liability and downsize, if we just give it the corporate model that you're talking about?

Mr. GALVIN. Again, I return to the excellent people that are already a part of this system, the ten lab directors and their peers.

Mr. ROEMER. But they don't have unlimited discretion now. They're going by a CEO's and a CFO's recommendations.

Mr. GALVIN. I refer to them on purpose because, sir, if you were to invite their leadership, a leader is someone who takes us elsewhere, invite their leadership of where we should go down this science roadmap, you would have the wisest direction of where to spend your funds.

And they do that in concert with those at the university level, the great scientists there. They do that in concert with the private sector. And we know how to sit 200 and 300 people around a table for a weekend and work out a roadmap of where we're going, not to discover the surprises of nature, but to send us in the right intellectual directions.

So you would have a far better probability of having worked on the things that will be useful to society if you take it out of these rooms and out of the Department of Energy building and put it out in the field.

Mr. ROEMER. Thank you, Mr. Galvin.

And I will discipline myself now, Mr. Chairman.

Mr. ROHRABACHER. I would like to invite, before we go to Mr. Tiahrt, any Member of the Committee who has a specific question to ask Mr. Galvin, because he does, is under some time restraint.

If you have a specific question that you'd like to ask Mr. Galvin at this time?

Ms. LOFGREN. I'll be real quick, because I did have a chance to talk to Mr. Galvin at the break.

I, as I said before, think that you're on the right track in terms of depoliticizing and debureaucratizing the management in governance, but I'm sorting for accountability models that will, understanding that taxpayers and voters, they want to know that they're getting their money's worth for whatever it is they are spending their money. And that's appropriate. There's certainly nothing wrong with that.

And yet they also understand, just like almost all the Members of this Committee, that we don't know the high energy physics details. I certainly don't and I doubt that I ever will.

And so I'm interested in your roadmap issue, your benchmark issue, and whether you have, and if you have not yet, whether you would sort through variations on the corporation theme, and maybe the corporation word is not exactly right because there aren't shareholders in the traditional sense. There wouldn't be votes of the shareholders.

But that would allow for reporting among agreed-upon benchmarks in advance so that the Congress, as the people's representative, would know that the lab directors and scientists in fact are moving in the direction that they decided?

I'm not disagreeing with what you're trying to do. I'm just trying to sort through various options we might have for governance and management that we could massage, and I guess the final question is, do any of the bills before this Committee really implement the recommendations in your report?

Mr. GALVIN. Starting with the last, I don't think any of the bills that are proposed are very germane to the issue of whether or not a corporatization, whatever it's called, phenomenon will occur.

So frankly, it's going to take a lot more time than the one or two minutes that you should allow me here, to talk about this accountability thing.

There are qualitative accountabilities that are far more valuable than the financial accountabilities.

As the Inspector General said earlier in our report, he said, Galvin, I don't understand physics. The only thing I understand is a transportation report, so that's my algorithm of whether or not the labs are being run right.

Folks, that's scandalous. That's the greatest waste of money in the world. That's what the people ought to be concerned about is that you people are making your associates spend money for things they shouldn't be spending it for. The engineers aren't wasting the money.

Ms. LOFGREN. Mr. Galvin, I couldn't agree with you more. I am not interested in process, focusing on processes. I think the public wants outcomes, and it's not the outcome of how many airplane tickets were taken. It's we just spent $6 billion on science, did the scientists work hard and was something discovered, and how do we get some handle that that's happening.

Mr. GALVIN. I respectfully suggest ma'am, that that is easy enough. Nothing is easy. But that's easy enough to do. It's happening in institutions like ours all the time. It's happened at SemiTech. We've had excellent qualitative reports of what has been accomplished, but nobody's worried about the little details of the things that we're working on here.

There could be superb accountability, way better accountability than you're getting now if you allow for the system to focus on the science results, measured against something that is benchmarkable. And although the idiom is much too shorthand for this, for what you want to have be a sophisticated answer, if we pivot off the managing of roadmaps, we will have the opportunity for the best accountability system you've ever had for science spending by the federal government.

Mr. ROHRABACHER. Is there another Member of the Committee that has a question, one specific question for Mr. Galvin?

Mr. OLVER. Mr. Chairman?

Mr. ROHRABACHER. Mr. Olver.

Mr. OLVER. My impression is we're about to lose Mr. Galvin so I would try to ask one thing there.

It is remarkable being a Member of Congress and having available the kind of testimony from the quality of people who we have here today, but it's also exceptionally difficult to maintain one's coherence in the process that we are going through.

And so let me just say one thing here.

We were here to talk about the management, or at least your particular major offering is in relation to the management of the DOE laboratories.

And you've indicated that there could be enormous efficiencies and cost savings coming from essentially creating world-class private sector corporate kind of an approach.

Now I don't know whether I'm creating a distinction that doesn't need to be made, but Mr. Vest had commented that in his view at least, the primary role of the national labs was to operate unique experimental facilities, too large-scale, too costly to be maintained by individual research institutions, which are the other groups, in a balanced research and development arrangement.

Your proposal for management then creates a corporate structure, yet it has been my impression that one of the things that has happened and created the imbalance over a period of time is that corporations, especially large corporations over a period of time, have been looking more and more toward a bottom line which is often a quarterly bottom line, not even a yearly or a three-year time frame, and that that has much reduced the R&D relationship of major corporations.

And I think if I might again go back to what Mr. Vest had said, it seems to me that that really lays out a difference between what the national labs are versus a corporation.

So I'm a little worried about the idea of putting us into that corporate mode, even though some savings are undoubtedly there.

And even more worried, I would say, that your proposal and coming out of the Task Force for that corporatization, as you have described it, and it's a little bit clearer to me now, is one that looks very like a mature corporation because it's very horizontal in its operation, and looks like a corporation, not those that are functioning most efficiently and most creatively in our operation now where they are relatively narrow and pretty well-focused on what they're trying to do, but maybe at the point where many large corporations are sort of diffusing and disintegrating almost.

So I'm a little worried that you create that kind of a very large corporation covering all of these laboratories that are left, recognizing that a number of people really say that there's over-capacity that suggests that we ought to be eliminating some of that.

Mr. ROHRABACHER. Mr. Galvin?

Mr. GALVIN. The culture of the leadership of major thinkers in the corporate world is very much oriented to desiring to support the long-term.

To the extent that this partnership, this collaboration between federal and private, is ordained with legislative intent and with block grants of funds, I think there would be a pure support for long-term spending for science in these laboratories.

Paradoxically, it makes it very comforting for industry to know that this class of putting technology on the shelf potential will take place.

With regard to structure, these laboratories do look very big to some viewers of the scene, but governing a horizontal institution of this kind with distinguished professionals such as exist, who are among themselves self-starters, and scientists are self-starters, as

Congressman Ehlers has spoken of, is all governable. We're learning now to govern these kinds of institutions so I don't think there is any great risk in terms of structure.

It certainly can't be any worse than what you've got now.

Mr. ROHRABACHER. Thank you, Mr. Galvin.

What we'll do for the Committee is we will keep this in session for another six or seven minutes, and finish up with a couple questions for Mr. Galvin.

Then we will break, we'll come back with the same panel, and finish up any other questions.

Mr. SCHIFF. Mr. Chairman, I just want to say for the record, the reason for these interruptions is the Congress is busy micromanaging the Defense Department right now.

[Laughter.]

Mr. ROHRABACHER. Mr. Baker?

Mr. BAKER. Thank you very much.

Mr. Galvin, over on your right.

Mr. GALVIN. Far right.

Mr. BAKER. Far right.

[Laughter.]

Mr. BAKER. If Motorola only looked to the next quarter, would it be investing $3 billion and creating jobs in chip manufacturing, or would you just seed that to Intel? And how much are you spending on research versus what you've spent before?

Mr. GALVIN. We spent approximately eight to nine percent of our total sales, which will be about $25 billion this year in sales, so something on the order of $2 billion.

Mr. BAKER. Two billion. Is that more or less than previously?

Mr. GALVIN. That's constantly increasing.

Mr. BAKER. I just wanted to reassure Mr. Olver that corporations aren't these greedy capitalists that we talk about in debate, but if they want to plan for the future, be they Hewlett-Packard, Compaq Computer, or Motorola, they're going to have to spend more and more on research, not less and less.

And I think if you look at Sandia, under the able stewardship of both AT&T and now Martin-Marietta, Rockwell, and others, you'll find some dedicated firms.

The idea we're going to have one firm control all labs, it would take billions in order to do that, and they wouldn't be willing to do it.

Get onto the important questions.

Instead of a lab closing panel, as Mr. Tiarht and my other good friend, Mr. Bartlett's misguided bills, shouldn't we have a lab or science management and accountability panel which would attempt to unscramble the egg and then put it back together?

And would you be willing to serve on such a panel?

Mr. GALVIN. That option, sir, would be a better one. I think Congressman Brown said it quite well. I think you've studied this thing enough. I mean, how fast a learners are you people? How slow are you at this thing?

[Laughter.]

Mr. GALVIN. I think you've got all the data to look at.

Mr. BAKER. The kids on this block have an attention span of three minutes, and also now we're drawn to vote.

I had the national highway bill up earlier, which is mark-up in another Committee meeting at the same time. We don't all get the same focus.

If we had the same dedication on redirecting our labs as Mr. Brown mentioned in his testimony, when Kennedy decided to go to the Moon, we probably wouldn't be 60 feet off the ground.

We haven't yet focused on this, and what I'm saying to you is I do think we need to draw all of these ideas together.

Mr. Bloch has great ideas about privatization, but he makes the broad sweep, we ought to cut 33 percent.

We're going to add, Mr. Bloch, 50 percent per person to the expenditure on Medicare and we're being attacked as making dastardly cuts which is going to wipe out health care for the elderly.

Does it sound like anywhere in this budget we're going to cut 33 percent?

Nowhere, not health, not welfare, not anywhere. So we have to bring all of these good ideas together and then become very realistic.

The leadership we need and the brains we need is sitting out at these panels, but we have to bring them all together.

My contention is that lab management is going to have to become leaders; they can't all just sit around and say we need more, we need more, and then compete for the dollars. They've got to decide what they're going to do.

If we said, as a panel, you folks, with Congress' support, that we want a missile defense stockpile stewardship, we want to defeat cancer and other health research problems, and we want nuclear power in the next generation so that France isn't the only one that has a NIF, an ignition facility, that France isn't the only one that has nuclear power, safe and clean, that America will join the twentieth century, would you not think that's a better idea?

How do we do it?

And you've got 20 seconds to tell us.

[Laughter.]

Mr. GALVIN. Proposed corporatization. Hold a hearing on that, and I think it would lead you to the answer.

Mr. ROHRABACHER. Mr. Tiahrt, you've got about two minutes before we break.

Mr. TIAHRT. All right, thank you for giving me the opportunity to speak behind Mr. Baker who is often misguided and misquoted me on my bill.

But we'll go on to another subject.

I think that earlier, Chairman Rohrabacher pointed out about how if we just trusted individuals that there'd be wheelbarrows of money rolling out of here.

And I think it might be illustrated, if there's a hundred dollar bill left in the street, you probably wouldn't get it back if you had lost it, because individuals have a tendency to take what they can and run with it.

But we have institutionally condoned the concept of competitiveness. We don't care whether Martin-Marietta spends its money wisely or McDonnell Douglas spends its money wisely because we allow them to compete for bids, and we therefore trust them to run their companies more effectively so that they can, because they're competing for the dollar that's going to be spent on aerospace, for example.

In your concept of a corporate model, where we block grant money to labs, would there still be an element of competition where we can not worry about them taking the money and run, but yet compete with each other and have the same confidence in this institutional concept that we've accepted for such a long time?

Mr. GALVIN. Invest in the chief executive officer and a small staff with some cognizance on the part of this trusted group of trustees, that they will generate a collaborative/competitive, I put a slash between the two of those things, they can co-exist, situation to where the labs that are not measuring up are not going to get the support from their management as to where the funds would be optimally allocated.

So, yes, there's plenty of opportunity for competition. In the private sector, we know how to compete within ourselves, with ourselves, as well as with our outside competitors.

Mr. ROHRABACHER. Mr. Galvin, thank you very much.

And if the panel could reconvene in probably about ten minutes—excuse me, there's going to be a second vote, so it would be 15 minutes from now.

And Mr. Galvin, thank you very much.

[Recess.]

Mr. ROHRABACHER [presiding]. For the panel, let me note that Mr. Bartlett is one of the Members of this Committee and also of course a Member of the House who is a scientist, and he's going to have to run off in about ten minutes.

So if we could pay him a bit of courtesy.

Mr. Bartlett?

Mr. BARTLETT. Thank you very much.

Let me add my apology to those that have already been made for our hectic schedule and the fact that we can't all be here all of the time.

Mr. Galvin I notice has gone. I wanted to make a comment on his comments about the Commission. This is not a commission to close laboratories, it is a commission to look at the laboratories to see what is best to do with the laboratories. And to characterize it as a laboratory closing commission, you know, really limits the scope of the commission.

One of you mentioned—I forget which one it was now—that in your view, the federal labs might well be limited to those kinds of activities that could not be supported elsewhere, very large facilities that accommodated a community of users. And that's, I think, an attractive argument to pursue further.

I just wanted to ask a question relative to that.

Are there large, multidisciplinary projects that even though no part of the project required facilities or equipment that couldn't be supported by individual universities or industries or whatever, is there an argument that you need large, government laboratories for large, multidisciplinary projects?

Dr. VEST. I believe you're referring, sir, to one of my comments so I might take at least a crack at that.

Mr. BARTLETT. Okay, thank you.

Dr. VEST. I did state, I believe, that it seemed to me that the primary role for national laboratories should be to maintain and operate facilities or programs which, due to their nature, their size, their complexity, their time scales, were not likely to fit well into other performing organizations, such as private companies responsible to stockholders or to universities and so forth.

So I did say both facility and program, although I must admit that I had primarily facility in mind.

I can imagine that we have areas in which national laboratories might get involved in things that are highly interdisciplinary, that fit particular government missions.

That certainly is the case in the defense establishment, for example, and even in the national security roles of the Department of Energy laboratories.

But at the risk of appearing to be somewhat self-serving, I do think that the university sector and, in some instances, the not-for-profit kinds of independent research organizations tend to be organizations that are particularly adept at highly interdisciplinary work, that bring together people from many disparate fields and tend to have a lot of continual renewal, at least in the case of universities, as students flow in and out.

So it's not clear to me that interdisciplinary nature, per se, is likely to be a primary motivation for a particular activity being funded through the mechanism of being a national laboratory.

Mr. BARTLETT. Thank you.

I have an observation to make from a personal experience. I would just ask each of you to very quickly indicate whether or not you would prioritize these environments as I have.

In any one lifetime, you obviously don't have the privilege of working in a great variety of places, but I've been in the scientific world and the engineering world and have about a hundred papers and about 20 patents, and I've worked in universities, I've worked for government, I've worked for large business, I've worked in small business areas, and if I was writing these in terms of environments that were most conducive to entrepreneurship and to creativity and to a free environment where you could pursue whether it was an engineering objective or a scientific objective, I would rate the university as number one, from personal experience. Small business would be number two. And surprisingly, I had better experiences in government laboratories than I did in large business.

And I was wondering if you have had collectively a variety of experiences.

When you're thinking about where a country puts its resources for R&D and research, you need to look at where you get the most mileage out of those resources.

From personal experience, I would rate them that way: universities, small business, government, and then large business. Large business in my personal experience being the least productive environment for doing new kinds of things.

What would be your personal experience?

Mr. BLOCH. Let me volunteer to answer your question.

I don't have much of a problem with your list, but I would want to say something about it. One has to be very careful that one doesn't fall into the trap where there is no room for all four, because all four are required.

Universities certainly would be the first on my list, primarily for one reason, not only that they provide an environment to do research but they do education at the same time. And without the two in conjunction with each other, you would have a hard time making up for that deficiency.

Small business certainly is an innovative kind of a process, but let me just remind you that small businesses become large companies if they are successful.

Mr. BARTLETT. If they're successful, right.

Mr. BLOCH. Okay. So we should keep that in mind.

The government laboratories in general, or DOE laboratories in particular, I think have a mission to play in this multidisciplinary big-project area that universities cannot afford to play in.

And let me give you an example maybe from the past. I'm not absolutely sure. It might still apply today.

The development of computer and information science, I think, was due to a large part to the work that went on not only in the university, but also in the federal in the government laboratories, especially DOE laboratories. And because of their capability of putting a very large installation together and dealing with very large problem, by the nature of what they were dealing with, as far as information science and computer science is what it is today. So one shouldn't disregard that.

And there are many more examples today, probably, that come to the surface.

Mr. BARTLETT. Thank you very much.

Just one final comment.

I think that it's productive to think of the subject we're addressing not as so much a problem but as an opportunity. As I said recently, the privilege of visiting a number of these laboratories and what a great variety of skills we have there, and it's a great challenge to decide how best to use these in the most efficient way for the national interest.

And so I like to think of this as a challenge rather than a problem.

Thank you all very much for your contribution. I'm sorry I have to run. Thank you very much.

Mr. SCHIFF [presiding]. Thank you, Mr. Bartlett.

Mr. Tiahrt, you're recognized for five minutes.

Mr. TIAHRT. Thank you, Mr. Chairman.

I think that we're going to be, you know, the question seems to be revolving around about closing labs, and that really wasn't the intent. I'm glad Congressman Bartlett kind of has contradicted to Mr. Baker. We're not trying to close labs necessarily here. What we're trying to do is to make sure that we get the most effective research done for the dollars we spend.

The question is not whether we're going to spend money on research and development or not. We are going to spend the money. The question is how much will actually be spent by engineers and scientists, and how much will be spent by overhead and excessive management and a redundant process.

So what we're trying to do I think, at least in a lot of the legislation we see, is come to a way of getting more research and development completed for the dollars that we expend, or an effectiveness that way.

Mr. Bloch mentions a couple of things that I think are interesting, giving to NSF four labs. That's something that I hadn't thought about before. I think it's interesting.

But also in the concept of where we're trying to downsize the Department of Energy as a whole, the bureaucracy, that it's not really effective to add more responsibilities to them at this point in time.

I think kind of in following with this, perhaps you could give me some ideas as why you think a separate, independent agency would be good to evaluate the laboratories. In the legislation that I've proposed, we have this energy laboratory facility committee that would go through and evaluate all the labs, establish some mission statements and try to take an independent look, and then come to Congress with a view.

And it also, I think another point that you brought up, was that a three-year or five-year or ten-year process is much too long. And I think you see this in many downsizes in the private sector. Once the decision is made, then go with it.

What the legislation that we have in HR 1993 says is that you've got 15 minutes to come up with a report—15 months, excuse me, to come up with a report.

[Laughter.]

Mr. TIAHRT. We cut it just a little quick there, didn't we?

Fifteen months to come up with a report, and then 18 months to get it facilitated.

So could you tell me just what is the benefits of, number one, of having an independent basis for decisionmaking?

And number two, again, reinforce this time line of a shorter time period?

Mr. BLOCH. Yes, I'll be glad to comment on both.

The independent agency I think opens up new avenues. First of all, it puts this continuity into the system and that this continuity could be used greatly to simplify the organization, to leave behind what is no longer necessary in that new environment.

Secondly, an independent agency frees you up from some of the political environment that a Cabinet agency is always subject to, regardless of what Administration you talk about.

Thirdly, you could think of making the Administrator or Director, whatever you want to call them, of an independent agency's tenure quite different from what it is today for the Secretary of Energy, which follows pretty much the Administration tenure.

Six years would not be out of the question. Maybe one can even go to seven or eight years.

And the projects that you're dealing with are of long-term duration, especially if you go to downsizing, that stretches out over a long period of time—who is going to be the conscience that this is going to go on year after year after year if people walk in and walk out of an agency?

And you could adjust that a lot better with regard to an independent agency.

Lastly, I think it allows you to put a board together, such as was proposed by Bob Galvin in his privatization proposal, that is made up of people that have the policy oversight over that particular agency, and I think that is something that you can do it within the present context of the Department of Energy.

What was mentioned this morning was an advisory board that is being put together right now. Well, an advisory board, you know what it is, you know, "I'll give you advice and you can take it or leave it", whereas if you had a policy board, an oversight board, there would be real demand on it that it formulates the right policies and that they are being executed.

So that's what I see the advantage of an independent agency to be.

With respect to the time line, I made the comment before, in answer to a question, that anything that stretches out that long over time, you're going to lose the impetus if you ever can gain it, whereas, if you put it into a short time frame, I think it will have its own dynamism that will propagate and propel the implementation of what you are trying to implement.

In one of the bills, and I don't know if it was yours or somebody else's, there was in the first year, a three percent reduction. Three percent doesn't mean a darn thing. Any manager can do with minus three percent. It doesn't take any effort at all.

But in order to really downsize in a significant kind of a way, you have to start the first year with a significant kind of a goal in mind. Otherwise, people are not going to take you seriously.

Mr. SCHIFF. The gentleman's time has expired. If the gentleman wants to do a follow up, he's recognized.

Mr. TIAHRT. Thank you, Mr. Chairman.

I just wanted to say you're right about—that wasn't my bill, the three percent. With attrition rates at about eight percent, I think you make a very good point, though.

Thank you, Mr. Chairman.

Mr. SCHIFF. Ms. Lofgren?

Ms. LOFGREN. I asked my questions earlier.

Mr. SCHIFF. In that case, I want to thank this panel, along with our previous witness, and thank you for your indulgence. We had to interrupt for various reasons, mostly to go over and vote.

We appreciate the contribution that you've made to this important debate and we thank you for being here.

With that, I'd like to call the next panel.

This panel includes Dr. Frederick Bernthal, who is President of Universities Research Association.

Dr. Albert Narath, who is President of the energy and Environment Sector of Lockheed Martin Corporation.

Dr. Douglas E. Olesen, President and CEO of Battelle Memorial Institute.

And Dr. C. Judson King, Interim Provost, University of California.

[Pause.]

Mr. SCHIFF. Let me welcome all the witnesses.

Let me first say that most Members are going to be tied up. There is a Members' briefing on Bosnia going on right now. However, as you've heard all day, the record is still being made and will still be distributed to all the Members of Congress in due course.

With that, I want to say to this panel, as I've said to previous panels, we do have your written statements. Without objection, they will be made a permanent part of this record, so I'd invite you to try to stay within about five minutes, if you can, for summary purposes of things you think that are most important.

And I'd like to begin with Dr. Bernthal, please.

STATEMENT OF DR. FREDERICK M. BERNTHAL, PRESIDENT, UNIVERSITIES RESEARCH ASSOCIATION, WASHINGTON, D.C

Dr. BERNTHAL. Thank you, Mr. Chairman.

It's a pleasure again to appear before this Committee. I've worked with you or various Members of it quite a lot in the past, most recently in 1994 as Deputy Director of the National Science Foundation.

I will be very brief knowing that the entire text of my testimony will go in the record.

The national laboratories that are the subject of this hearing are actually relatively few in number, and each has its singular character.

For some, such as Fermilab, for which Universities Research Association is responsible, the entire laboratory revolves around a major unique research facility used by scientists from all over the country.

Others, such as the Oak Ridge National Laboratory and Brookhaven National Laboratory, are broadly diversified in their programs and disciplinary thrust.

And still others, such as Los Alamos National Laboratory, entail major weapons R&D programs.

My point of going through this is simply to say that, in my judgment therefore, prescriptive, systemic solutions to this problem should be avoided. One size isn't going to fit all.

And with that in mind, I will just briefly go through a few recommendations.

First of all, I would say that to assure the vigor and productivity of the national laboratories, the historic partnership between this country's distinguished research universities and its national laboratories must be revitalized and substantially strengthened. This is consistent with a number of other comments to that effect we've heard today.

The motivation for this partnership may have changed, as the missions of the Atomic Energy Commission and its successor agencies evolved, but just as the laboratory/university partnership was essential to the nation in the decades immediately following World War II, it remains essential today if we're going to realize maximum return on this national laboratories investment.

Indeed, the research success of the various laboratories has long been directly correlated with the strength of those intellectual ties to the research universities.

Secondly, the Department of Energy national laboratories should evolve and become truly national research centers, available to serve a variety of customers in the federal government, in the states and, when appropriate, in industry.

HR 2142 defines clearly, succinctly, and in my judgment, at a sufficient level of detail, the mission and purpose of the national laboratories. The guiding principles set forth therein appear also to be in harmony, I should say, with the conclusions of the Galvin Task Force.

Beyond those guiding principles, I believe that the research objectives of the national laboratories should be determined by the marketplace of ideas and the needs of the country as defined by the myriad individual projects and programs of the various customers for that research and it should be limited only by the capabilities of the scientists and engineers themselves within the laboratories.

The size of the laboratories too should depend on their ability to deliver for their patrons who presumably will vote with their grants, contracts, and other agreements in favor of the best proposals and in favor of excellence of research product.

Thirdly, as part of the revitalized relationship between the laboratories and the nation's universities, a strong, new, corporate-style governing structure should be devised for DOE's major research laboratories.

The Department should establish in spirit and in fact, not just in name, the principle of the government-owned, contractor-operated laboratory in contrast to a system that, for all practical purposes, has become government owned and government operated.

With that principle as a starting point, I believe it's possible to achieve many of the advantages anticipated in the corporate-style laboratory governance recommended by Mr. Galvin and the product of the Task Force that he chaired.

Indeed, once one clearly delineates the responsibility and authority among DOE and its private-sector and university partners, the Department should be able to move beyond the prototype GOCO paradigm to realize many of the salutary governance objectives outlined in the Galvin Report.

I applaud DOE's recent movement in that direction as part of the Secretary's strategic realignment initiative.

That kind of transition could be substantially furthered at one or two laboratories on a pilot basis, laboratories which would be governed by a corporate-style board of directors composed of leaders of the nation's leading research universities and industries and responsible for the performance of the laboratory.

Research programs would be structured so that distinguished faculty from interested universities become full partners with their counterparts from the laboratories, and as appropriate, from industry, in the conception, in the proposal, and in the management of individual research programs within the laboratories.

My fourth and final point. When it comes to environmental—and this one will be brief—when it comes to environmental and occupational safety stewardship, Federal agencies should simply require their laboratories to comply with existing regulatory law, as any university or industrial research entity is already required to do.

Whatever arguments may once have rationalized the present arrangement, they've largely evaporated with the end of the Cold War.

No matter how federal support, in closing, no matter how federal support for the nation's research enterprise might be structured to achieve necessary efficiencies in this time of fiscal constraint, it's essential that the capabilities embodied in the DOE national laboratories continue to be engaged in that enterprise.

With many industries cutting back or eliminating in-house research in recent years, these laboratories assume added significance as sources of new knowledge for the national good.

As the exigencies of the Cold War have receded into history, it would be wasteful and short-sighted to permit the intellectual and capital investment the American people have made in these national laboratories over the last 50 years to be casually dissipated and I know that no one on this Committee intends that to happen.

Thank you very much, Mr. Chairman.

[The prepared statement of Dr. Bernthal follows:]

Testimony of
Dr. Frederick M. Bernthal
President, Universities Research Association
Washington, D.C.

House Science Committee
Subcommittees on Basic Research and on Energy and Environment
2318 Rayburn House Office Building
September 7, 1995

Chairman Schiff, Chairman Rohrabacher, it is a pleasure to return to testify before Members of this Committee, with whom I have worked closely over the years in a number of positions in government, most recently from 1990-94 as Deputy Director of the National Science Foundation.

I have never been an employee of the Department of Energy (DOE) or its predecessor agencies. But from five years on the staff of Senator Howard Baker, then as a Member of the Nuclear Regulatory Commission, as Assistant Secretary of State for Oceans, Environment and Science, and finally at the NSF, I had the opportunity to work with and observe the Department in many of its endeavors. And before I became sidetracked in Washington, my research as a professor at Michigan State University was for several years supported by DOE. My current post as president of a university consortium with management and operating (M&O) contract responsibility for DOE laboratories has afforded yet another perspective.

The organization I head, Universities Research Association Inc. (URA), is the DOE M&O contractor for the Fermi National Accelerator Laboratory (Fermilab), and for termination of the Superconducting Super Collider Project in the wake of its cancellation by Congress in 1993. My testimony today represents my own views, and not necessarily those of URA or its Trustees.

The charter we received for this hearing solicits comments on four pieces of legislation pending before Congress, particularly as those bills relate to the future of the DOE national laboratories. All four bills seek to assure a national laboratory system that will be as efficient and effective as it can be in serving the country, an objective I am sure we all share. While commenting on some specific elements of the proposed legislation, my testimony will also offer a more general view of, and some ideas on, the issues and problems these four bills seek to address.

I would like to begin by briefly recounting a little history of URA, not as an advertisement but because it has direct bearing on a key theme I want to stress today -- the essential role that the nation's universities have played in the development and achievements of the national laboratories.

In 1965, under the aegis of the National Academy of Sciences, 25 universities agreed to form a consortium with the following broad mandate:

> "...to acquire, plan, construct, and operate machines, laboratories, and other facilities, under contract with the Government of the United States or otherwise, for research, development and education in the physical and biological sciences...and to educate and train technical, research and student personnel in said sciences."

In the intervening years, URA has grown to comprise 80 universities and nearly all of the nation's leading research universities. The close laboratory-university partnership of DOE and URA at Fermilab continues to be highly productive, as it has been at other laboratories where that tradition exists.

The formation of URA in 1965 was certainly not the first time that the nation had turned to its distinguished universities for assistance in constructing and leading a research laboratory. We all know the important, indeed pivotal, service the University of California rendered through the National Laboratories at Los Alamos, Livermore and Berkeley. Argonne National Laboratory also traces its roots to that era, and to the leadership of the University of Chicago and Enrico Fermi.

Today, the most important single issue on the agenda of America's research enterprise may well be the future of these and their sister national laboratories in which this nation has invested and achieved so much. But despite the successes of the past, if current policies and trends continue I believe the national laboratories as a group will experience a slow, inexorable decline. The status quo is not an option -- not in the national laboratories and not in the universities -- and none of my comments should be understood to imply that major changes in laboratory governance, organization, and objectives are not possible and necessary.

The national laboratories of greatest significance in this regard are relatively few in number, and each has its singular character. For some, such as Fermilab, the entire laboratory revolves around a major, unique research facility used by scientists from all over the country. Others, such as the Oak Ridge National Laboratory and Brookhaven National Laboratory, are broadly diversified in their programs and disciplinary thrust. Still others, such as the Los Alamos National Laboratory, entail major weapons R&D programs. Prescriptive "systemic" solutions should therefore be avoided -- one size will not fit all. With that in mind, I have the following recommendations:

1) *To assure the vigor and productivity of the national laboratories, the historic partnership between the nation's distinguished research universities and its national laboratories must be revitalized and substantially strengthened.*

The motivation for this partnership may have changed as the missions of the Atomic Energy Commission and its successor agencies evolved from the Manhattan Project, through the cold war, the oil crises of the 1970's, and now into the post-cold-war era. But just as the laboratory-university partnership was essential to the nation in the decades immediately following World War II, it remains essential today if we are to realize maximum return on our national laboratories investment. Sustaining the vitality of these laboratories will require a robust intellectual partnership between the scientists and engineers at the laboratories and at the nation's other great centers of learning. Indeed, the research success of the various laboratories has long been directly correlated with the strength of their intellectual ties to the research universities.

The most remarkable "national laboratory" today is a virtual laboratory -- a network of research sites scattered across the country, encompassing the great research universities in which this country invested so heavily during the last half of this century. The centroid of America's research enterprise now resides in those universities, which have grown and matured to become the envy of the world. Ironically, however, the university research endeavor itself is now in troubled waters. It is confronted with a multi-billion-dollar requirement for modernizing research infrastructure, a problem recognized through the Reagan, Bush, and Clinton administrations, but one which, for obvious reasons, remains unresolved. In these circumstances, it is reasonable to ask whether the enormous investment the country has already made in research facilities at our national laboratories might offer a partial solution.

2) *The Department of Energy national laboratories should evolve to become truly national research centers, available to serve a variety of "customers" in the Federal government, the States, and when appropriate, in industry.*

H.R. 2142 defines clearly, succinctly, and at sufficient level of detail the mission and purpose of the national laboratories. The guiding principles set forth therein appear also to be in harmony with the conclusions of the Galvin Task Force.

Beyond such guiding principles, however, I believe that the research objectives of the national laboratories should be determined by the marketplace of ideas and the needs of the country, as defined by the myriad individual projects and programs of the various customers for that research, and limited only by the capabilities of the scientists and engineers within the laboratories. Laboratory "mission" in this context should not be confused with unusual cases of urgent national need (the Apollo project comes to mind) where rapid mobilization of resources, often with secondary regard to cost, has been driven from the highest levels of government.

The size of the laboratories too should depend on their ability to deliver for their patrons, who presumably will vote with their grants, contracts, and agreements in favor of the best proposals and for excellence of research product. To assist in setting collective policy directions for the laboratories, DOE has recently set up an internal Laboratory Operations Board, a helpful step that should clarify what DOE itself wants and expects from its laboratories.

Much as the National Science Foundation has demonstrated through its successful Engineering Research Centers and Science and Technology Centers, partnerships among researchers drawn from national laboratories, university faculty, and industry can provide exceedingly fertile ground for discovery, and for the technology that goes hand-in-hand with such discovery. With the continued decline of the major industrial laboratories in the U.S., such partnerships become a particularly important objective.

DOE's Cooperative Research and Development (CRADA) program was meant to establish research partnerships and arrangements between industry and the DOE laboratories. But the success of that or any similar program must be measured by the number of productive, working relationships that develop among the scientists and engineers actually doing the research -- by bridges built, across which people and information flow. Indeed, the traffic across those bridges is probably more important than the instant research project itself, because *people* are the mechanism for technology transfer -- people from different disciplines, with differing perspectives, working on common problems. As John Armstrong, former Vice President for Research at IBM, has put it, the best technology transfer vehicle is the moving van.

The Oak Ridge National Laboratory recently competed for and won $7.3 million for a center to develop technology for DNA analysis. Funded half by the National Institute of Standards and Technology and half by industry, this partnership with Perkin-Elmer Corporation, EG&G, Cornell University Medical College, the University of Minnesota, and Louisiana State University exemplifies a national laboratory promoting productive partnerships and serving a variety of customers: Federal, industry, and state.

3) As part of a revitalized relationship between the laboratories and the nation's universities, a strong new corporate-style governing structure should be devised for DOE's major research laboratories.

The Department should reestablish in spirit and in fact, not just in name, the principle of the Government-Owned, Contractor-Operated (GOCO) laboratory, in contrast to a system that has become, for all practical purposes, government-owned and government-operated. With this principle as a starting point, I believe it is possible to achieve many of the advantages anticipated in the corporate-style laboratory governance recommended by the Galvin Task Force. Indeed, after clearly delineating responsibility and authority among DOE and its private-sector and university partners, the Department should be able to move beyond the prototype GOCO paradigm to realize many of the salutary governance objectives outlined in the Galvin Report. I applaud DOE's recent movement in this direction, as part of Secretary O'Leary's Strategic Realignment Initiative.

This transition could be substantially furthered at one or two laboratories on a pilot basis. Those laboratories would be governed by a corporate-style board of directors, composed of leaders of the nation's research universities and industries, and responsible for the performance of the laboratory. Research programs would be structured so that distinguished faculty from interested universities become full partners with their counterparts from the laboratories, and as appropriate from industry, in the conception, proposal, and management of individual research programs within the laboratories. While this concept is not new, it also is not pervasive in the national laboratories today. The National Science Foundation's Engineering Research Centers and Science and Technology Centers mentioned earlier may offer a useful model in this context.

Where universities have a lead responsibility in the laboratory partnership, as I believe they should, they must bring a new sense of intellectual, as well as managerial, ownership and involvement. For its part, the Department should assess performance on the basis of results -- on the quality of research and scholarship, as judged by a strong peer review system, and on compliance with existing regulatory and other law. In short, the Department should be the tough auditor and the sophisticated customer, not the manager acting through a contractor surrogate.

The Committee has asked our opinion on "privatization" of the DOE laboratories. The term "privatization" seems to mean different things to different people. If it means selling the laboratories to the highest bidder, I believe that is a non-starter. It is not clear who would buy the laboratories in an era when industry seems to be systematically reducing in-house research of the type once carried out, for example, by the renowned Bell Laboratories. Indeed, the nation now increasingly relies on the Federal government, through the universities and the national laboratories, to carry out long-term and/or high-risk fundamental research. I believe the members of this Committee share my view of the important role the Federal government will continue to have as the dominant patron, in both senses of that word, in support of such research.

If, on the other hand, "privatization" means developing an augmented "corporatized" GOCO system, subject to the rigors of a different kind of marketplace where the laboratories compete to serve the various Federal, state, and industry customers for research -- that kind of "privatization" is appropriate. It would introduce by evolution a change that is likely to preserve the best the laboratories have to offer, without the disruption and mistakes that would likely arise from any ad-hoc group of women and men, however wise and capable, attempting to decide on issues of mission, downsizing, and consolidation in an R&D world that has the elite of our nation's private industry scrambling to keep up. In the end, the adaptive approach almost surely will make better choices, be more respectful of the many dedicated and talented scientists and engineers in our national laboratories, and when all is said and done, I would bet on it being faster and more efficient in achieving necessary change.

4) When it comes to environmental and occupational safety stewardship, Federal agencies should simply require their laboratories to comply with existing regulatory law, as any university or industrial research entity is already required to do.

This is an important objective of H.R. 2142, and of H.R. 1510 which makes clear, as I would, that the Department's research centers should here be distinguished from its so-called "production" and related facilities. In those latter facilities, the Department still struggles with special problems -- a difficult legacy of the cold war. But with regard to the national laboratories *per se*, DOE should be freed from a regulatory spiral that seems to have reached a point where the Department is required, in effect, to maintain its own Nuclear Regulatory Commission, its own Environmental Protection Agency, and its own Occupational Safety and Health Administration.

Whatever arguments may once have rationalized the present arrangement, they have largely evaporated with the end of the cold war. Normalizing regulatory oversight and requirements for the nation's research laboratories by placing that responsibility in the hands of the appropriate regulatory agencies almost certainly will result in more cost-effective operations.

It should be noted that DOE, again as part of the Secretary's Strategic Realignment effort, has taken important first steps in this direction, and I am pleased that the Fermi National Accelerator Laboratory recently became the pilot laboratory for development, with responsibility for implementation, of a simplified set of "necessary and sufficient" standards for environment, safety, and health.

To summarize: The spirit and intellectual vitality of the historic partnership between government and the university research community, of which URA has been representative and from which the nation has derived such great benefit, needs to be revitalized and nurtured throughout the national laboratory system.

No matter how Federal support for the nation's research enterprise might be structured to achieve necessary efficiencies in this time of fiscal constraint, it is essential that the capabilities embodied in the DOE national laboratories continue to be engaged in that enterprise. With many industries cutting back or eliminating in-house research in recent years, these laboratories assume added significance as sources of new knowledge for the national good. As the exigencies of the cold war recede into history, it would be wasteful and shortsighted to permit the intellectual and capital investment the American people have made in their national laboratories over the last 50 years to be casually dissipated.

In some cases, preserving expensive laboratory infrastructure is in itself a cost-effective objective, since leading-edge research increasingly requires concentrations of talent and facilities which often do not lend themselves to dispersal across our network of research universities. In other cases, merit-based competition within the research community can serve to streamline and rejuvenate operations to meet current national objectives. But research funding across all government agencies should now take into account the present and longer-term value of the human and capital investment in the DOE laboratories.

The mission of the DOE laboratories is sufficiently and appropriately defined in HR 2142. The mission definition set forth therein is a timely and necessary restatement of principles to guide the many and various programs and projects that the laboratories should pursue. To best fulfill that mission, the Department of Energy, by its patronage, should encourage partnerships among laboratory, university, and industry scientists and engineers for the proposal and management of specific research projects.

Finally, while the Department of Energy will likely remain the dominant patron of the DOE laboratories for the foreseeable future, the laboratories should nevertheless mature to become truly national in character, making their capabilities and resources widely available to other Federal agencies, to the states, and when appropriate, to industry. Accordingly, the mission, and the future, of any national laboratory should depend on its ability to achieve the diverse programmatic objectives of those customers.

I would be pleased to respond to any questions.

######

Mr. SCHIFF. Thank you, Dr. Bernthal.
Dr. Narath?

STATEMENT OF DR. ALBERT NARATH, PRESIDENT, ENERGY AND ENVIRONMENT SECTOR, LOCKHEED MARTIN CORPORATION

Dr. NARATH. Thank you, Mr. Chairman, for inviting me to testify before this Committee.

As you know, I have expressed my views before this Committee on earlier occasions, specifically back in March and June. Therefore, the statement that I've submitted for the record will probably come as no surprise to you.

I should also say that my views coincide extremely closely with those expressed so eloquently this morning by Deputy Secretary of Energy, Charles Curtis.

Since my views do coincide with his, I can be very brief in my oral remarks.

Let me just say that in studying the bills that are being considered here today, it seems very important to me that one distinguish very clearly between two sets of issues. And I divide these as follows:

There are, in the first place, a set of issues that relate to DOE's mission, and the roles that the laboratories should play in executing those missions or in supporting these missions. So these are mission-related issues.

There's another set of issues that I regard to be distinctly quite fundamentally different, and these have to do with management effectiveness and efficiency issues.

I firmly believe that the first set of these issues are clearly deserving of Congressional involvement and hopefully strong leadership.

I respectfully submit, however, that the second set, involving management issues, should, for the most part, be left to DOE, the laboratories and the responsible managing and operating contractors that deal with it, in response, of course, to Congressional guidance.

Here, I'm referring to items such as the relationship between DOE and its GOCO M&O contractors, the relationship between DOE and the laboratories, the manner in which laboratories are tasked, the manner in which overhead costs are controlled and hopefully reduced, the whole issue of right sizing of the laboratories to fit the missions that the Congress assigns to the Agency and, incidentally, the funding levels that are provided to perform those missions.

By this sort of reasoning, I arrive very quickly at a strong preference for HR 2142, the Department of Energy Laboratory Mission Act, and the only concern that I would express is in pushing towards a sharper, crisper definition of missions for the laboratories.

That we do not go so far as to narrowly confine each of the laboratories, because I think it's absolutely essential, as has been stated many times today, that the laboratories be able to take advantage of the multidisciplinary, multi-program or purpose nature, and here I'm now referring to the multi-program laboratories of the DOE.

I respectfully submit that the other bills, which are being discussed today, intrude excessively on management responsibilities that I believe belong to the Department of Energy.

And indeed, I'm pleased to say that the Department of Energy is taking rather bold steps towards solving management problems that have been identified by the Galvin Task Force and others before them.

These steps have been detailed earlier today by Charles Curtis and I don't think need to be repeated at this time.

I do want to comment very briefly on the corporatization proposal that Mr. Bob Galvin offered. I do so because I am on record as opposing that proposal.

And my reasons for that position appear in the statement that I've submitted today.

Let me just say that I admire the boldness of the proposal. It's very innovative. I dare say, if it could be implemented as set forth by Mr. Galvin, it would serve the intended purpose.

And if I could invent a world more ideal than the one we live in, I'm sure this would be the right way to go.

My fear is that the solution offered by Mr. Galvin may not be stable with respect to perturbations introduced by the reality of the world we live in.

For example, it's inconceivable to me that the sort of hands-off, block grant approach to funding the organization would be practical in today's world, nor do I think it would be easy within this corporate structure to achieve agreement as to which laboratory will do what and how the resources are to be divided.

I have experience in Bell Laboratories, following the divestiture of 1984, and I can tell you how difficult it is within a corporate structure that is in a state of transition to deal with those matters. Doing so itself requires a bureaucracy and I'm sure that the corporatization model offered in a very short time would rebuild a rather large bureaucracy in order to manage itself.

So I'm fearful that the solution offered may not be stable.

So I very much favor something that I think is more practical in the near term, and that is to fully implement and do so as quickly and vigorously as possible, the recommendations contained in Appendix B of the Galvin Report.

And again, I want to note that DOE is moving very rapidly in implementing these recommendations.

What are the imperatives then that we face? I think first and foremost, we need to reach consensus on core missions. Clearly, these missions involve national security, energy, environment, and basic science.

It seems to me while there's room to argue the relevant importance and appropriate funding levels, as far as the Federal role is concerned, it's difficult for me to understand how the federal government can disengage itself entirely from any one of these mission areas.

It may be true that the Cold War is over and it may require some rebalancing of resources, but each and every one of the mission areas I've mentioned is clearly in need of continued support.

At the same time, I would suggest that the Congress encourage DOE to continue to deal with its management-related challenges as expeditiously as possible, and in a way that meets the program direction set by the Congress.

The Congress of course does have the responsibility to provide the necessary oversight to make sure that DOE and its laboratories stay on track.

Ultimately, it seems to me, DOE's success will hinge on how effectively and efficiently the Department's multiprogram laboratories can function in support of the Department's missions.

I think there are four things absolutely essential:

That DOE continues to nurture a system of laboratories, and we've come a long way towards achieving that.

Here I'm talking about more effective coordination among the laboratories and improved collaboration.

Secondly, it's essential that we find ways to sustain and strengthen the scientific underpinnings.

Third, I'm a strong believer in the importance of carrying out mission-related private sector collaborations and partnerships.

It seems to me no institution, no organization, no system of anything today in the world of science and technology can do it all alone.

The world is full of innovative people and institutions, and the most effective organizations will be those that learn to interact strongly with others doing related work.

Ideas are flowing very rapidly and to isolate oneself from idea generation elsewhere, worldwide, would be detrimental.

I'm reminded that in our country, we have supported traditionally a system, an R&D system, consisting of Federal laboratories, universities and industrial labs.

People who worry about the behavior systems know that the action in systems occurs at the interfaces. Systems are most effective when the interfaces work harmoniously.

I would suggest there's no need for conflict between the universities and national labs in particular. They each have different responsibilities, different characteristics, different abilities, and they gain strength by working together.

And I would also very respectfully submit that while we all agree that there's much room for improvement in the way the laboratories are managed, and manage themselves, perhaps one ought to look at the same time at the efficiency with which the academic world manages itself.

I cannot believe that every research university in this country is equally effective. Not every university is an MIT.

The same of course applies to federally-funded laboratories.

And finally, it's very important that we are remindful of the importance of human resources. And above all, it's important that the national labs continue to provide the kind of environment that will allow them, in the future, to attract world class talent. Without that talent, the national labs will sink into mediocrity very quickly.

So let me just conclude by saying that I see a pressing need to reach agreement on DOE's missions and the level of support needed to accomplish these missions.

In the mean time, given adequate time and encouragement, I believe DOE will succeed in its management initiatives, but it will require much patience.

Experience in the private sector has shown that instant gratification as regards management improvements is seldom achieved.

And last but not least, let me say that Lockheed Martin, as a major contractor to the Department of Energy, is strongly committed to supporting the Department in the execution of its mission and its management improvement goals.

Thank you.

[The prepared statement of Dr. Narath follows:]

Statement of Albert Narath, President
Energy and Environment Sector
Lockheed Martin Corporation

United States House of Representatives
Committee on Science

Subcommittee on Basic Research
and
Subcommittee on Energy and Environment

Joint Hearing on the DOE National Laboratories

September 7, 1995

Statement of Albert Narath, President
Energy and Environment Sector, Lockheed Martin Corporation

United States House of Representatives
Committee on Science
Subcommittee on Basic Research
Subcommittee on Energy and Environment

Joint Hearing on the DOE National Laboratories
September 7, 1995

Introduction

Chairman Schiff, Chairman Rohrabacher, and distinguished members of the subcommittees, I am Al Narath, president of the Energy and Environment Sector of the Lockheed Martin Corporation. Lockheed Martin is well known as an electronics and aerospace defense contractor. It may not be quite so well known that Lockheed Martin is also a major managing and operating (M&O) contractor to the United States Department of Energy. We manage and operate three national laboratories for the Department — Oak Ridge National Laboratory, Idaho National Engineering Laboratory, and Sandia National Laboratories — as well as a number of other facilities. These responsibilities have given Lockheed Martin a perspective on DOE and its laboratories that you may find useful in your deliberations. They are consistent with views that I shared with you earlier this year: In March and in June I appeared before this committee representing Sandia National Laboratories, of which I was director from 1989 until last month.

Prior to my tenure as Sandia's director, I was, for five years, vice president of Government Systems at Bell Telephone Laboratories, with responsibility for all Bell Laboratories systems engineering and development for the federal government. For more than thirty years, I have been directly involved in the management of technical programs for DOE missions. During my career it has also been my privilege to chair several advisory committees for DOE and other agencies.

I believe my background in the management of research and development, in both the public and private sectors, provides me with a good basis from which to make informed comments on the legislation you are considering today. I am therefore pleased to offer candid views on issues for which you solicited my opinion.

The Issues Separate Into Two Classes

The four bills before your subcommittees offer different plans for achieving a strategic realignment of the DOE laboratory system. H.R. 1510, the "Department of Energy Laboratories Efficiency Improvement Act," would mandate a workforce reduction of one-third at the DOE laboratories within ten years. H.R. 87, the "Department of Energy Laboratory Facilities Act," would create a commission to review and modify (if it sees fit) recommendations by the Secretary of Energy for laboratory reconfiguration and closure. Title II of H.R. 1993, the "Department of Energy Abolishment Act," is similar to H.R. 87 in this regard, but it stipulates further that privatization may be considered as an option for the laboratories, in addition to reconfiguration or closure; and, as the bill's title implies, these actions would be taken as part of a larger plan to dismantle the Department of Energy altogether. Finally, H.R. 2142, the

"Department of Energy Laboratory Missions Act," would permit the Secretary to streamline the laboratory system in the context of a comprehensive analysis and reassignment of missions to facilities.

Let me state at the outset that these bills address two broad issues that, in my view, are best treated separately and in sequential order. The first issue concerns the question of DOE **missions** and the proper role of the national laboratories in supporting those missions. (A closely related question concerns the utilization of laboratory capabilities in addressing other national needs.) The second issue concerns DOE's **management efficiency and effectiveness**, including such items as laboratory tasking, overhead costs, and "rightsizing." It is difficult for me to understand how a sensible resolution of the management issues can be achieved before clarity with respect to mission-related issues is established. Furthermore, while the Congress has an unquestioned role in establishing DOE's missions and providing program funding to support those missions, its role in dealing with management issues is less clear. Decisions related to any downsizing and consolidation should be a DOE responsibility, in concert with its M&O contractors, and should be in response to Congressional authorizing and appropriation actions.

Realignment Should Be Based on Missions

The foregoing remarks are intended to provide the basis for my preference for the "Department of Energy Laboratory Missions Act," H.R. 2142. None of the other bills starts with missions, which must be the starting point if we are to end up with a laboratory system designed to satisfy government needs. The recent GAO report entitled, "Department of Energy: A Framework for Restructuring of DOE and Its Missions" (August 21, 1995), observes that "resolving internal issues without first evaluating and achieving consensus on missions is not the best approach to restructuring DOE" (p. 4). Yet three of the four bills before this committee today use that approach.

The GAO report goes on to criticize DOE for not reevaluating the validity of its existing missions, but this criticism is misdirected. It is you, the Congress, who — as a critically important stakeholder — must define, at least in general terms, the services you want this agency to perform. H.R. 2142 is the only bill that makes an attempt to explicitly define the core missions of DOE (Section 102).

If H.R. 2142 had gone further and made mission assignments to individual laboratories, it would have created a serious conflict with what I regard to be a DOE responsibility. But it wisely places the burden of making those decisions on the shoulders of the Secretary of Energy. It provides guidance to the Secretary on what criteria to consider when making laboratory mission assignments and proposals for streamlining. It sets a deadline for the Secretary to report those assignments and proposals to Congress. And it requires the Comptroller General to review and report on the DOE proposals. It is a tough bill.

The virtue of the procedure outlined in H.R. 2142 is that the Secretary of Energy is given the opportunity to succeed or fail based on the merits of his or her own initiatives and proposals. The common weakness of H.R. 87 and H.R. 1993 is that those bills tacitly assume that the Department cannot succeed and that therefore an independent Laboratory Facilities Commission must be created to review and modify DOE's plan. In my view, such a commission (if needed at all) should be chartered only after the Department has demonstrated failure in aligning its laboratory system with its mission responsibilities. This is not in evidence at this point. Indeed, the Department has taken bold steps in a first phase of strategic alignment. It should be permitted to proceed without the interference of an independent commission.

DOE Is Making Progress

We need to acknowledge the progress that the Department of Energy is already making on its own management initiative. Encouraging results have been achieved by DOE in just the last year in cutting costs and reforming programs. As I observe the actions DOE is taking, I have reason to believe the Department is prepared to make fundamental changes in how it conducts its affairs and how the laboratories are managed. Significantly, the Secretary has begun, with evident determination, to implement the actions outlined in Appendix B of the Galvin report, "Alternative Futures for the Department of Energy National Laboratories," by the Secretary of Energy's Task Force on Alternative Futures for the DOE National Laboratories.

The Department's Strategic Alignment initiative is an ambitious effort to achieve substantial operating efficiencies through restructuring and downsizing processes similar to those shown to be effective in the private sector. The changes that have been announced will cut costs by eliminating layers of management, eliminating or consolidating redundant organizations and field offices, integrating the energy R&D portfolio, curtailing support service contracts, and reducing total employment by more than one-quarter in both the federal and contractor work forces of the Department.

DOE is also making good progress in reforming its directives system. The Accelerated Directives Review Project, working with the DOE Directives Management Board, is going through DOE orders at a fast rate. The project is likely to achieve real success in reducing onerous and inefficient regulations. Bear in mind too that DOE may need the help of Congress in this effort. Often, actions by Congress stimulate over-reactions in the agency, particularly when Congress has been harshly critical of DOE's management. I would urge you to let DOE solve some of its own problems using generally accepted best business practices employed by the private sector. The report of the Secretary of Energy's Advisory Board Task Force on Strategic Energy Research and Development (the Yergin report) also endorses this approach.

In short, I cannot agree with those critics who assert that DOE is incapable of improving itself. The changes we are beginning to see belie this claim. To be sure, changes as bold as those being pursued by DOE require a span of several years to fully implement. Successful reengineering efforts in the private sector have typically required from five to seven years. Externally directed radical approaches are unlikely to achieve the desired outcome. I think it makes sense, for the time being at least, to let DOE continue to push its program of internal change.

At the same time, efforts are underway to reduce operational costs across the entire laboratory system. As directed by the Secretary of Energy, to the maximum extent possible, operational cost savings are focusing on improvements in administrative and business functions rather than on reductions in the laboratories' technical resources. The Galvin report identified over-administration of the laboratories as a serious problem that adds unnecessary overhead costs.[1] Standardization of laboratory management systems and centralization of some common administrative functions could realize substantial savings without cutting into the technical

---

[1] "Alternative Futures for the Department of Energy National Laboratories," Secretary of Energy Advisory Board, February 1995, p. 57.

muscle of the laboratories. I should add here that Lockheed Martin is strongly committed to the goals set by the Secretary of Energy and is intent on taking advantage of its extensive M&O responsibilities to achieve enhanced efficiency and effectiveness through improved laboratory coordination and process standardization.

One of the problems with the proposal contained in H.R. 1510 to cut employment by one-third in ten years is that the bill doesn't care where those savings come from, whether from administrative functions or technical programs. Another problem is that it presumes that national technical needs will be static; how else could it project with such confidence that the laboratories can achieve their missions in 2005 and beyond with one-third fewer employees? The truth is, no one knows with certainty what the technical needs of the government will be in ten years. Employment levels in the DOE laboratory system must be dictated by current and foreseeable mission requirements, not by a ten-year-old law.

A System of Multiprogram Laboratories Is Essential

I am generally supportive of H.R. 2142, but I do have some concerns. The bill calls for "well defined and assigned missions"[2] for the departmental laboratories, and it requires that specific mission assignments be made to each institution.[3] I fear this exercise may result in rigid and impenetrable barriers between the laboratories such that they cease to continue progress toward becoming an effective "System of Laboratories." The process of making mission assignments to the laboratories must not be overly detailed or proscriptive. Laboratory mission statements should not prevent DOE program managers and laboratory directors from configuring program work among different laboratories in ways that make technical sense.

Significant coordination and collaboration is already evident among the laboratories in support of the common technology base required for DOE missions. Such cooperation has always been true of the three defense programs laboratories, and it is increasingly true for all of the national laboratories. In particular, much collaboration occurs across the defense/energy boundary. Increasingly, the entire DOE laboratory community realizes that teamwork, collaboration, and strategic alliances are essential in this era of constrained resources.

Let me give you a specific example. Robotics technology is under active development at most of the DOE laboratories. This should not be surprising, because many DOE programs in defense, energy, and environment will employ robotics technology in some way. However, different laboratories emphasize different aspects of robotics engineering depending on their particular responsibilities. Oak Ridge National Laboratory has a very capable program for remote processing of nuclear materials with a human in the control loop. Sandia National Laboratories has a very capable program emphasizing automated intelligent systems to support the defense programs manufacturing needs. It turns out that both these facets of robotics are useful to multiple DOE sponsors, including the offices of Defense Programs, Nuclear Energy, and Environmental Restoration and Waste Management.

With DOE encouragement, the managers of the robotics programs at Oak Ridge and Sandia organized a collaborative program to support the general robotics needs of the Office of Environmental Restoration and Waste Management. The collaboration has benefited DOE

---

[2]Section 101 (7).

[3]Section 103 (a) (1)

customers and leveraged the capabilities of both laboratories. It is now expanding to include other DOE laboratories under a coordinated "virtual technology center" in robotics. Because of this collaboration, DOE may well have the strongest robotics R&D program in the world.

The integrated nature of the DOE laboratory system is evident in many other areas beyond robotics. The DOE Center of Excellence for the Synthesis and Processing of Advanced Materials brings together several complementary strengths in materials science R&D resident at twelve DOE laboratories. Other virtual technology centers exist in practice and are now being formalized. Plasma technologies, high-performance computing, advanced engineering design and manufacturing, environmentally conscious processes, and superconductive materials are all examples of the rapidly growing synergistic cooperation among laboratories within the DOE system.

It should be no surprise that several laboratories require the same or similar technical competencies as underpinnings for their missions, as illustrated by the robotics example I just described. The example also makes clear how important it is that the laboratories cooperate effectively with each other. By working toward, rather than against, a "System of Laboratories," the government can derive greatest advantage from the diversity of the DOE laboratories. The legislation you adopt should encourage concepts such as lead roles and distributed centers of excellence to produce inter-laboratory coordination in mission areas.

I am concerned that the mission assignment exercise required by H.R. 2142 could force DOE away from the multiprogram concept toward single-mission laboratories. The multiprogram, multidisciplinary environment is absolutely essential for excellence in most of DOE's missions (and that includes the defense mission). The synergy that exists in a multiprogram environment enhances mission performance. Consequently, we should expect more than one DOE laboratory to be involved in a given DOE mission.

The Need for Cross-Sector Collaboration

Collaboration between the DOE laboratories and other sectors, principally industry and universities, is increasingly essential for programmatic excellence. The old idea that the government's technical needs are so unique that they require a separate technology base is obsolete. The technology bases for government and commercial needs are rapidly converging. Cross-sector collaboration should not only be encouraged, it should be required, with emphasis on generic, precompetitive R&D on technical issues of mutual interest that can be useful for both government and industry.

H.R. 2142 is the only bill that explicitly permits departmental laboratories to establish collaborative relationships with entities in other sectors (Section 102). This is surprising because both the Galvin task force[4] and the GAO[5] endorse laboratory-industry collaboration that supports DOE mission work.

Many DOE missions, and particularly the nuclear-weapons program, can benefit substantially from working cooperatively with industry, as a result of the leverage provided by partners' in-kind contributions to joint projects, cost-free access to specific partner capabilities,

---

[4]"Alternative Futures for the Department of Energy National Laboratories," Secretary of Energy Advisory Board, February 1995, p. 7.

[5]"National Laboratories Need Clearer Missions and Better Management" GAO report, January 1995 Page 31.

the expanded reliability that results from partner-testing of components or materials, and the development and maintenance of commercial suppliers for DOE product needs.

One outstanding example of mutual benefit from joint R&D is the development, through collaboration with the private sector, of lead-free materials and processes for use in manufacturing. Health risks and environmental damage associated with lead-derived solders and fabrication processes that utilize lead have prompted efforts to curtail the use of such materials in the DOE weapons complex and as well as in private industry. Joint work by a DOE laboratory and industry evaluated commercial lead-free solders as well as a new alloy developed by DOE. The results of that collaboration are being widely adopted by industry and led directly to the application of lead-free solders in nuclear-weapon component manufacturing.

Other cooperative projects help ensure that critical DOE skills for weapons engineering and design remain up-to-par to meet future needs. The nuclear-weapon program is now in a phase where no new weapon development programs are in progress. Unless nuclear arsenals are abolished, new warheads must be designed and manufactured in the early part of the next century to replace aging warheads that will have exceeded their service lifetimes. Weapon engineering skills cannot be maintained through simulated design exercises alone. Engineers must work with real designs for real products to keep their skills sharp. Collaborative design of components for civilian or defense systems can provide useful experience. Moreover, the DOE laboratories must offer challenging, dual-benefit, scientific and engineering assignments if they are to recruit the best technical talent to support national security programs.

The Future Role of the DOE Laboratories

For all the criticism directed at DOE, the Department still maintains what are widely regarded collectively as the best scientific and engineering laboratories in the federal government. Over many years, a succession of commissions, blue-ribbon panels, and advisory boards have agreed on this point. Over sixty Nobel Prizes have been awarded to researchers who were funded by DOE or its predecessor agencies. DOE's nine multiprogram national laboratories have earned more than three hundred *R&D–100* awards, which acknowledge significant advances in technology. During the cold war, the defense programs laboratories designed, and to this day actively support, a nuclear-weapon stockpile that excels in military performance, reliability, safety, and control. During the 1970s and 1980s, it is documented[6] that the Department's energy R&D laboratories made advances that generated savings of many billions of dollars for industry and consumers and provided improved energy technologies for industry to exploit. The DOE laboratories are associated with thousands of discoveries and inventions that have proved useful in both defense and civilian applications and that have helped the United States sustain worldwide technological leadership. With such an exceptional record of accomplishment, it is reasonable to expect that the DOE national laboratories will continue to play an important role in federally funded R&D.

No other agency of the federal government performs the vertically integrated research and development that is such a distinguishing feature of the DOE laboratories. Many science and technology agencies manage R&D as a grant activity and perform very little in-house technical

---

[6] "The Role of Federal Research and Development in Advancing Energy Efficiency: A $50 Billion Contribution to the U.S. Economy," Howard Geller, Jeffrey P. Harris, Mark D Levine, Arthur H. Rosenfeld in *Annual Review of Energy*, Vol. 12, 1987. Jack M. Hollander, Ed., Annual Reviews, Inc., Palo Alto

work. Many others are devoted to narrow mission assignments and lack multidisciplinary breadth and depth. To my knowledge, the DOE laboratories are unusual if not unique in the federal R&D system because they perform the entire research, development, and product cycle, all the way from fundamental research to product design, development, and production support. This is absolutely the case for the defense programs laboratories, and it is largely true for the DOE energy laboratories as well (although some smaller laboratories concentrate on research alone). Vertical integration of the research and development cycle is a powerful strength of the DOE laboratory system, and it is not duplicated on the same scale anywhere else in the federal sector.

Finally, DOE's laboratories have distinguished themselves in the development and utilization of major scientific and engineering facilities that would be difficult to reproduce in a different setting. Today, most of these facilities are being operated as user facilities, providing unique capabilities to researchers drawn from industry, academia, and other government agencies.

Criteria for Future Missions

Future missions will evolve as national needs evolve. Unfortunately, reaching a national consensus on critical scientific and engineering needs that should receive federal R&D attention has been a slow and difficult process, at best. Many people hold the view that a free-market system, left to its own devices, will identify national needs and develop solutions to them without government involvement. This view fails to consider the influence of relative risks on those who make investment decisions in the private sector. As a general rule, private R&D is undertaken with the expectation that it will generate revenues in the not-too-distant future. Investment risks that do not reasonably assure future revenues within a fairly short time horizon are simply not within industry's means.

Useful and legitimate criteria can be stated for evaluating the appropriateness of federal R&D sponsorship in areas of national need. Some examples are:

1. The technical risks are too great or the benefits too diffuse for the private sector to assume financial risk (major user facilities fall into this category).
2. Enabling technologies do not yet exist.
3. A problem requires comprehensive evaluation and characterization before policy development can occur.
4. A problem possesses a high degree of complexity that cuts across government and industry boundaries.

There exist many areas of research of strategic importance to the nation for which the private sector cannot afford the expense or risk and for which the principal investigator model typical of academic research is not well suited. The Galvin report recognizes this role as a unique one for the DOE national laboratories:

> *We note that many of the least exploited investigative paths involve the need for extraordinarily sophisticated multidisciplinary teams using sophisticated instruments and tools. It is that role for which the national laboratories are uniquely qualified. It is the case for – the justification of – the existence of the DOE laboratories.*[7]

---

[7] "Alternative Futures for the Department of Energy National Laboratories," Secretary of Energy Advisory Board, February 1995, p. 3.

Research of strategic value to the nation includes such well-known efforts as the development of next-generation supercomputers and human genome mapping and sequencing. But a vast array of other strategic R&D is performed in less publicized areas, including materials science, superconductivity, photonics, computer science, and engineering disciplines such as advanced engineering design processes, agile manufacturing, and industrial ecology. Many of these efforts require large-scale, integrated programs that will ultimately benefit both the public and private sectors but are too generic for private investment.

Industry is also understandably reluctant to commit R&D funds when the very enabling technologies do not yet exist. This phenomenon is clearly observable in the area of hazardous waste management and site remediation. The problem represents a critical national need for both government and industry that by now should have stimulated a vital, aggressive commerce offering new technical solutions. Unfortunately, with a few notable exceptions, the solutions offered by industry to date have been disappointingly conventional. The fact is, for many classes of hazardous wastes, cost-effective treatment or containment technologies have not yet been demonstrated. Here is an obvious mission role for the DOE national laboratories in collaboration with industry.

The phenomena associated with the accumulation of carbon dioxide in the earth's atmosphere are worrisome. They may or may not represent a serious long-term hazard to global climatic and biological systems, but the U.S. Environmental Protection Agency and the National Academy of Sciences have urged action. Yet scientists do not command a fundamental understanding of the problem sufficient to permit the development of sound policy. This is clearly the sort of national problem that requires a government role. The U.S. Global Change Research Program coordinates the competencies of several agencies in a single, focused effort to characterize the problem, and DOE is part of that effort.

Finally, many emerging national needs are so complex that they cut across the usual boundaries separating government and industry domains. An obvious example is transportation. The national transportation infrastructure is so capital-intensive and comprises such vast public assets that it clearly must be a primary responsibility of government. But that responsibility cannot be performed without the intimate involvement of the transportation vehicle and energy supply industries. Technology and policy need intelligent coordination and long-term planning for the transportation infrastructure to evolve effectively. The DOE laboratories may have a legitimate role, in partnership with industry, in long-term public problems such as transportation.

Laboratory Governance

One of the remaining questions asked by the charter document for this hearing concerns laboratory governance: "Are there other governance structures, such as corporatization or privatization, which may better suit the future management of the DOE national laboratories?"

The Galvin Task Force makes a bold recommendation to convert the governance of the DOE laboratories to a new basis.[8] The Task Force believes that the GOCO (Government-Owned, Contractor-Operated) concept, the model on which the laboratories have operated for the last fifty years, has been irretrievably weakened through unrestrained growth in government micro-management, rule-making, and oversight, and they discount the Department's ability to revitalize

[8]Ibid., pp 53–61.

it. Only through de-federalization will the laboratories be able to operate with the efficiency and flexibility found in the private sector, in their view. To be more specific, the Galvin report proposes a "corporatization" governance for the DOE national laboratories, with the possible exception of the three defense programs laboratories (Chapter VII). It would create a not-for-profit R&D corporation with a board of trustees appointed to staggered terms by the President. Congress would provide multi-year block funding, and the corporation would allocate those funds to the laboratories. DOE would function as the government sponsor of both the corporation and the laboratories.

The rationale for such a radical change in governance is based on the belief that unless something is done to buffer the laboratories from the DOE bureaucracy, the inevitable tendency of bureaucrats to "micromanage" will continue to dominate. Moreover, having a board consisting 'primarily of distinguished scientists and engineers and experienced senior executives from U.S. industry"[9] would tend to insulate the laboratories from partisan politics, it is felt, and provide some measure of stability.

Such a clean-sheet-of-paper approach is well-intentioned and, in principle, offers some advantages. Nonetheless, as proposed, it does not seem to me either practical in the near term or necessarily sustainable over the long term, for the following reasons:

1. The principal weakness of this governance model is its elimination of a strong linkage between the laboratories and an agency of the executive branch. In the absence of such linkage, the ability of the laboratories (in the role of FFRDCs) to assist DOE in program planning and management would diminish greatly. As a result, the laboratories would likely lose their mission focus.
2. Changing the laboratories from GOCO to private or semi-private corporations would inevitably change the character of the laboratories in a way that is unpredictable, but probably detrimental. In the likely event that multi-year block funding is not provided, I worry that the laboratories would tend to become R&D job shops for small, discrete projects that lack the unifying initiative of a national mission. The critical mass for large, long-term, high-risk/high-consequence programs might be lost in the process.
3. At the same time, DOE's value-adding role would suffer. An "arms-length" relationship with the laboratories would encourage the Department, over time, to direct its funds elsewhere. If, in addition, the defense programs laboratories were moved to DoD or elsewhere, DOE would become an agency whose prime function would be to "pass-through" government funding. In either case, the separation between the energy research and defense programs laboratories is incompatible with DOE's concept of an integrated system of laboratories.
4. The Board of Trustees is unlikely to be effective in resource allocation and, more generally, in coordinating the R&D activities of the laboratory complex, unless it creates a bureaucracy of its own.
5. It is also most unlikely that the public would be supportive of the degree of independence from government oversight and control that is envisioned by the corporatization concept.

---

[9]Ibid., p. 55.

I believe a more practical approach to addressing the root problems identified in the Galvin report is to rejuvenate the GOCO relationship along the lines suggested by Appendix B of the report. The Laboratory Operating Board, recently created by DOE, incorporates many of the features of the Galvin model (distinguished leaders, staggered terms, and so forth). I believe this approach can achieve the benefits of the Galvin governance recommendations, provided it is embraced by senior managers throughout the DOE complex.

As stated earlier, I do not share the view that DOE is incapable of revitalizing the GOCO model. To be sure, it will be a challenging task for the Department and its M&O contractors to succeed in such an undertaking. In the last two years, however, I have seen significant progress in the Department that encourages me to believe that DOE is prepared to make necessary changes in how the laboratories are managed. For example, the Secretary has committed the Department to Total Quality Management as the operating paradigm. Significantly, the Department has begun to implement the actions outlined in Appendix B with energy and determination.

Many of the benefits of corporatizing the laboratory complex can be achieved by applying the quality management and reengineering tools used by industry. For example, some laboratories are reengineering their operating and administrative procedures to achieve greater efficiencies and cost savings. They are reviewing their business systems and site management practices and redesigning their information and communications infrastructures in order to automate and streamline business and management processes.

I advise great caution as you explore the pros and cons of corporatizing the DOE laboratories. With your support, I believe DOE's leadership can do much to restore the health and vigor of the GOCO model. Before embarking on a risky and uncertain new governance model, I would look for ways to accommodate the needs of tomorrow using a management approach that has been effective in the past.

Managing DOE's Nuclear-Weapons Program

Title V of H.R. 1993 proposes to move the DOE defense programs laboratories to an agency of the Department of Defense. I have a personal opinion on this proposal that is based on many years' experience with the nuclear-weapons program, and I feel it is important to express myself on this issue. (I know this hearing does not specifically address Title V of the bill, but my concern is great enough that I want to comment on it anyway.) Evidently this proposal is viewed favorably by many so-called "experts" both within and outside the government. I regard it as very unwise.

The dual-agency process for developing nuclear weapons has historically been regarded as a positive feature of the U.S. nuclear-weapons program. This arrangement permitted the military to specify requirements for nuclear weapons and delivery systems and gave the laboratories a somewhat independent role in developing weapons to meet those requirements. This independent role has allowed the civilian agency and its laboratories to be advocates of safety and other improvements, even when opposed by a reluctant military. In addition, the Annual Surety Report to the President requires approval from both DoD and DOE, providing checks and balances for surety vs. operational concerns.

Historically, the directors of the DOE nuclear-weapon design laboratories have been known to take positions on stockpile issues that were at odds with positions advocated by the military services. For example, in the early 1960s laboratory directors pushed for implementation of use-control devices on nuclear weapons in the face of adamant resistance by the services.[10] In 1990, I and the other directors of the DOE defense programs laboratories expressed concerns before Congress about the operational safety of the W69 short-range attack missile as then deployed. Our testimony brought into sharp focus the difficulties that can arise when safety considerations conflict with military utility. These examples illustrate that the requirement for dual-agency stewardship of nuclear weapons explicitly mandated by the Atomic Energy Act is embodied in the DOE nuclear-weapon laboratories.

It has been argued that a nuclear programs agency reporting to the Secretary of Defense can maintain a position of independence from the military services with respect to nuclear-weapon safety design and control issues. I am very skeptical of this argument. Crucial disagreements, such as trade-offs involving safety and performance in weapon design, will inevitably be appealed to the Secretary, who will have complete power to favor military performance considerations over safety and control issues and would most likely be under great pressure to do so. Papering over such concerns, as some critics have done, is a reckless disservice. The critics also seem to ignore the fact that the technical vitality of the nuclear-weapon laboratories is critically dependent on a diversity of mission responsibilities. It is unrealistic to assume that the Department of Defense could sustain the essential multiprogram format.

Former Secretary of Energy, Admiral James D. Watkins, captured the importance of agency independence with respect to stockpile stewardship in his 1989 Notice, "Setting the New DOE Course."[11] He said, "It is the proper moral and statutory obligation of the Department of Energy to be an advocate for safety and use control considerations with respect to nuclear weapons, just as military characteristics are the proper domain of the Department of Defense." Admiral Watkins, a former member of the Joint Chiefs of Staff, is intimately familiar with the nuclear-weapons business on both the DoD and DOE sides of that joint responsibility. I doubt that any other individual is more genuinely expert on this subject than he. I would like to refer you to Admiral Watkins' testimony before the Subcommittee on Energy and Power of the House Committee on Commerce on June 21, 1995, in which he cogently states the continuing need for separation of duties with respect to nuclear weapons, as originally envisioned by President Truman and the Congress.

The concept of separation of duties and joint agency responsibility for nuclear-weapon matters has earned the authoritative imprimatur of many advisory groups through the years. The 1985 President's Blue Ribbon Task Group on Nuclear Weapons Program Management concluded that "the advantages of the current arrangement include checks-and-balances for nuclear-weapon safety, security, and control." The ERDA transfer study explicitly stated that "safety, security, and performance features of nuclear weapons will be compromised in the absence of dual-agency judgments."[12] The Galvin task force "believes that there is much value at this time in maintaining an independent and technically expert organization to focus on nuclear stockpile issues and to continue to ensure that decisions regarding the safety, control, and

---

[10]See *Assuring Control of Nuclear Weapons: The Evolution of Permissive Action Links*, by Peter Stein and Peter Feaver. Center for Science and International Affairs, Harvard University, 1987.

[11]SEN-11-89, September 5, 1989.

[12]"Funding and Management Alternatives for ERDA Military Application and Restricted Data Functions," ERDA-97A, January 1967, p. 8.

stewardship of nuclear weapons are raised to the high policy level that they deserve."[13] Congress would be extremely ill-advised to repudiate this well-established concept.

Conclusion

Clearly, the DOE national laboratories need to become more efficient, but we should acknowledge the significant changes already initiated by DOE. The starting point for making any structural changes in the DOE laboratory system must be a clear understanding of the mandated missions and an objective projection of future funding trends. Congress should express itself on what general mission areas it expects DOE to perform. Laboratory mission assignments should be made by those who are directly responsible for managing the laboratory system, not by an independent facilities board that will have no continuing obligation for mission performance. If excess capacity exists, that fact should be determined by an analysis of the missions those laboratories are expected to perform. The nature of changes to the laboratory system should be determined by best business practices, not by an arbitrary prescription. Of the four bills under consideration by your subcommittees, only H.R. 2142 meets these criteria.

Any realignment of the DOE laboratory system should be carefully designed to preserve and strengthen the multiprogram laboratory model that is so essential for excellence in mission performance. Collaboration among laboratories and between the laboratory system and other sectors (industry and universities) is also essential in today's complex R&D environment. The GOCO (Government-Owned, Contractor-Operated) model of laboratory management should be revitalized and restored to its former vigor, as opposed to embarking on risky experiments in laboratory governance that could enervate these outstanding laboratories. Any change to the laboratory system should preserve the joint agency responsibility and accountability for nuclear weapons that has been a cornerstone of national nuclear policy since the Atomic Energy Act of 1954.

National technical needs and challenges will change and evolve, and so must the laboratories. But if we observe these principles as we make changes in the laboratory system, I believe the DOE national laboratories will continue to perform to the highest world standards of research and development in the decades ahead. Lockheed Martin is firmly committed to engage this challenge.

[13] "Alternative Futures for the Department of Energy National Laboratories," Secretary of Energy Advisory Board, February 1995, pp. 16–17.

Mr. SCHIFF. Thank you, Dr. Narath.
Dr. Olesen.

STATEMENT OF DR. DOUGLAS E. OLESEN, PRESIDENT AND CEO, BATTELLE MEMORIAL INSTITUTE

Dr. OLESEN. Thank you, Mr. Chairman. I appreciate the opportunity to appear before you today.

Although this hearing is certainly dealing with bills that are focused on the Department of Energy and the national laboratories, I believe we must think about these bills in the context of the total federal R&D investment and how this investment can generate maximum benefit for the nation.

In this regard, I think three principles are important.

Number one, federal R&D should focus on basic science and the science and technology needs of federal missions.

Two, commercially-oriented R&D should be the province of the private sector and public sector R&D output should be openly available to the private sector; and

Three, federal R&D should give priority to strengthening the academic roles of our universities and enhancing the technology position of industry.

And by this, I mean the federal government should give priority to universities and the private sector in selecting R&D providers.

Now let me turn to more specific comments concerning the Department of Energy and the national laboratories.

I concur with the Galvin Commission that DOE's core missions, as they've stated, are of high value to the nation and are appropriate federal roles.

The national laboratories are important assets in the nation's R&D enterprise, and have vital roles to play in supporting the Department in the pursuit of its missions.

It is important, however, that the missions of the laboratories be reexamined to achieve considerably more focus and specificity. This should also include the priorities for universities and the private sector, as R&D providers, which I mentioned earlier.

Improving the governance of the laboratories is required and can best be accomplished by utilizing a revitalized and performance-based, government-owned, contractor-operated management model.

We should expect rapid progress in improvement of productivity in the management of the laboratories.

Our own recent experience at the Pacific Northwest Laboratory demonstrates that costs can be reduced by more than 20 percent in a very short period of time.

I might add that we are achieving those results with the full cooperation of the Department of Energy.

This process, a mission focus and productivity improvement should precede any laboratory closure process.

Let me close by just two summary points.

DOE core missions are important to the nation, and the universities, private sector, and national laboratories all have roles to play.

And, two, we now have the knowledge and the experience to dramatically improve the governance of the national laboratories in a very short period of time.

Thank you.

[The prepared statement of Dr. Olesen follows:]

Written Testimony

of

Douglas E. Olesen
Chief Executive Officer
Battelle Memorial Institute

Comments on Legislation Regarding the DOE National Laboratories' Missions and Governance and their Role in the Overall Federal Scientific Establishment

Joint Hearing of the
Basic Research Subcommittee
and
Energy and Environment Subcommittee
of the House Committee on Science

September 7, 1995

Chairman Schiff, Chairman Rohrabacher and Members of the subcommittees, it is a pleasure to be here today to provide comments on behalf of Battelle Memorial Institute on a matter of importance to all of us. Battelle Memorial Institute, a not-for-profit research and development organization, carries out a wide array of research and development programs for industry and government customers. Today, we have nearly 8,000 people at locations throughout the world engaged in the entire spectrum of research and development. More importantly, for purposes of this hearing, Battelle is the management and operating contractor for one of the Department of Energy's national laboratories, the Pacific Northwest Laboratory in Richland, Washington.

The national laboratories have been a part of my professional life for almost thirty years. I spent the early part of my professional career as a member of the scientific staff at the Pacific Northwest Laboratory, and served as director from 1978 to 1983. I am currently chief executive officer of Battelle Memorial Institute. These roles have caused me to think long and hard about the missions that federally supported research and development must serve and about how best to conduct that research so as to provide the maximum benefit to the nation. Let me add that although I am here today to represent Battelle's views, the issues we're addressing are also of great interest to me as a private citizen, as I believe that a vigorous, effective, and properly directed federal research and development investment can contribute greatly to the long-term prosperity and security of our nation.

Let me begin at the foundation. The fundamental question we must answer is not how many national laboratories we need, or how they should be managed, or even whether DOE should continue its existence as a cabinet level agency. Rather, the first and most fundamental questions we must answer are "What missions should the federal research investment serve?" and "How should we conduct that research so as to provide maximum benefit to our nation?" As partial answer to these questions I'd like to articulate three principles:

- Government research and development investments should be directed towards basic science, and to the science and technology needs of government missions.

- Research and development that is primarily commercially oriented falls within the province of the private sector. However, the results from mission-oriented federal research and development investments should be readily available to the private sector.

- Federally funded research should be managed and conducted so as to provide the maximum possible benefit to the country by, first, strengthening the academic mission of our research universities and, second, enhancing the technology position of U.S. industry.

Let me stress that this third principle is not a call for large scale federal funding of commercially oriented research and development. Rather, it asserts that we should give appropriate consideration to the academic mission of our universities and to private companies in selecting the providers of basic science and mission directed research and development.

Let me outline the reasoning that has led me to this principle.

A steady supply of well-trained scientists and engineers available to industry, academia, and government is essential to our prosperity. It is the principle mission of our colleges and universities to provide an educated work force, including professionals trained in mathematics, science and engineering. Strong academic research programs are necessary to the training of technical professionals. Therefore, I believe that the government should give preference to supporting the academic mission of our universities in selecting research providers.

The conduct of government-funded research and development by U.S. industry builds technical capability and knowledge that enhances the nation's competitive position. Thus, where industry has the willingness and the capacity to perform, directing R&D to industrial providers as a second priority will both meet mission needs and provide the additional benefit of strengthening our economy.

How do these three principles apply to DOE and the national laboratories?

First we must ask the question as to whether DOE's core missions are both enduring and appropriate to the government. I concur with the conclusions of the Galvin task force that DOE's core missions in the areas of basic science, national security, the environment, and ensuring an affordable energy supply in the long term are both appropriate to government and of high value to the nation. I further concur with the Galvin task force that increasing economic productivity and enhancing the competitiveness of U.S. industry are not intrinsically government missions, and should not be a core mission of either DOE or the national laboratories.

What, then, should be the role of the national laboratories? In light of the second principle the primary research missions of the national laboratories should be those elements of government missions that are not more effectively conducted by our universities or by private industry. Further, the national laboratories should engage university collaborators and industrial partners to conduct their missions where practical and appropriate.

If we consider the relative strengths of our universities, private industry, and the national laboratories, I believe that we will find that each class of R&D providers has a clear role. The laboratories are uniquely suited to highly interdisciplinary, large or logistically complex, programs directed towards achieving well-defined, long-term public science or technology goals, or resulting in complex engineered systems or products that have modest commercial value . In contrast, research universities are organized and operated so as to most effectively conduct investigator-initiated research involving relatively few researchers working in a common or related discipline. Universities are highly suited to projects motivated by the scientific interests of the investigators, that do not require delivery of specified results on a fixed schedule. Industrial research capabilities are strongly focused on development of new commercial products and enhancements of existing products. This summary is, of course, an oversimplification, to which there are notable and very successful exceptions, but it offers useful general guidance.

When I examine DOE's core missions in light of these considerations, I conclude that there are substantial elements of those missions that are indeed most appropriate to the national laboratories. The development and operation of complex, one-of-a-kind scientific user facilities is a clear example. Technology development for the unique and daunting environmental management and remediation problems across the defense complex, stewardship for nuclear weapons technology, development of technical means to detect the potential proliferation of weapons of mass destruction, and the initial development of promising energy supply technologies that lie outside either the time scale or the technical and financial resources of the private sector also fall into this category.

In summary, it is clear to me that DOE's core missions are appropriate to the government and of high value to the nation, and that the national laboratories have unique and critical roles in the conduct of those missions. Given this foundation, we can effectively address the issues of governance and overall size of the DOE laboratories so forcefully posed by the Galvin task force report and other reviews of the Department of Energy, and towards which are directed the several pieces of legislation that are the subject of today's hearing.

Again, let me begin with two observations. The first, although perhaps obvious, and certainly broadly accepted by all of us who are addressing this issue today, may be a worthwhile reminder:

- You, as representatives of the public have the right to expect high productivity from, and cost-effective management of, the nation's investment in research and development. There is compelling evidence in the Galvin task force report and elsewhere that substantial improvement in the overall governance and productivity of the national laboratories is possible.

The second observation I believe is also broadly accepted, particularly by those of us with experience of major research institutions, either public or private:

- Impactful, high quality research institutions are built painstakingly over many years. The fragile culture of a first-rate R&D organization is difficult to replicate. Not one of the national laboratories could be recreated without very substantial investment over an extended period. Therefore, a decision to close or radically restructure one or more laboratories should be taken only after careful and complete deliberation.

Let me stress that in making this second point I am not asserting that each of the existing national laboratories should be retained in perpetuity at its present size, or even at all. All public institutions should indeed be subject to periodic review for both need and value as a matter of routine. Such changes in national needs as the dramatic change in national security requirements resulting from the end of the cold war should cause us to rethink our research and development infrastructure. I believe, however, that significant changes must be made thoughtfully.

Given these observations, I believe we have a clear strategy for responding to the fiscal constraints that at least partially motivate much of the legislation we're reviewing today. It is premature to embark on a rapid restructuring and downsizing of the national laboratories using, for instance, the military base closing mechanism. However, that should not stop us from realizing the rapid and significant cost savings that can be achieved through improved governance and management practices.

As described so well in the Galvin task force report, and by many who have testified before you on that report and related issues, over perhaps the last two decades we have built a governance system for the national laboratories that is very costly and actually hinders research productivity. In contrast to the technical assets of the national laboratories, this governance system is one institution that we should feel free to scrap rapidly without fear of adverse consequences!

I believe that our best alternative is to reaffirm the concept of the "Government-Owned, Contractor-Operated" or GOCO model and to incorporate the performance-based measures that are part of the DOE contract reform efforts. The government must play the role of the customer, determining what outcomes are to be achieved, providing the resources for those outcomes, selecting the most appropriate performer, and measuring progress towards the intended results. Management contractors for the laboratories would then be fully accountable for bringing best private sector practices to bear so as to achieve the specified outcomes rapidly and at reasonable cost. Note that in this model, and largely contrary to current practice, government does not specify either how the results are to be achieved, or what management systems and practices are to be used by the providers.

I will not rehash the many departures from the original GOCO model that have led us to the current situation; these are covered at length in the Galvin report and illustrated by the testimony of many who have appeared before you. However, as evidence of the practicality of my recommendation, I would like to share with you the results we are achieving at Pacific Northwest Laboratory. With the support and cooperation of the Department of Energy at both headquarters and field office levels, we are now demonstrating that very substantial savings -- projected to exceed 20% of total research costs by the time we are done -- can be achieved through introduction of best management and operational practices, and without damaging programs. We are achieving those savings via a top-to-bottom redesign of management systems and operations, modeled on a similar effort that we had previously carried out at our private laboratories in Columbus, Ohio. This effort has been carried out in full and active partnership with the management and staff of DOE's Richland field office, and may be a model that can be applied elsewhere in the laboratory system. I am convinced that by effecting similar improvements throughout the laboratory system Congress and DOE can achieve significant budget savings while improving research productivity, without being forced to reach premature and potentially damaging decisions on laboratory restructuring or closing.

As a final point on this issue of governance I'd like to stress that we all own the problems with the current management system. Congress, DOE, and we as management contractors have all had a role in creating the current unacceptable situation, and we must all accept responsibility to solve it.

Let me now turn to the final subject I'd like to address today. I strongly believe that a clear mission focus in each laboratory will improve the performance of the laboratories both individually and as a system. At Pacific Northwest Laboratory, we have recognized that we will be most effective if we give clear precedence to our core environmental science and technology mission. The scope of the laboratories' missions should be established and limited through clear recognition of the important roles of universities and private industry described earlier. It will also be important that sufficient flexibility remain to permit research and development output to easily flow between mission areas. Finally, to ensure continuing long-term value from our research and development investments, laboratories must be able to move to new public sector missions as required by the nation.

I'd like to end this portion of my testimony with a brief summary of the key points. DOE's core missions are both appropriate to the government and of high value to the nation. Along with university and industry providers the national laboratories do indeed have significant and appropriate roles in carrying out those missions. Significant cost savings can be realized through modifications to the original GOCO model. This will permit adoption of best private sector practices without compromising research programs. Finally, stronger mission focus for individual laboratories will enhance performance. In combination these factors of productivity and relevance provide an appropriate basis for determining the size of and need for individual laboratories.

Answers to Questions Posed by the Committee

1. *What is the future role of the DOE National Laboratories in the context of the overall Federally-funded scientific establishment?*

As a precursor to discussing the national laboratory role, I would like to reemphasize the need to recognize the priority which should be afforded university R&D funding to ensure a continuous flow of trained individuals into the work force. Similarly to the maximum extent possible, U.S. industry should be the R&D provider of choice to directly build the nation's competitive strength. As a third dimension, DOE laboratories represent a significant and in many respects irreplaceable component of the federal R&D capability. They are central to the success of DOE's core missions. Because of the technical capabilities in the laboratories, in some cases they may be the most appropriate R&D resource for elements of missions assigned to other agencies. In such cases their use should be encouraged. Finally, I would like to give particular emphasis to the user facility role which is a central element of the nation's R&D infrastructure, and which provides significant benefit to university science and industrial R&D.

2. *What should be the future missions of the DOE National Laboratories?*

As noted above, I concur with the Galvin task force that DOE's core missions of energy, environment, national security, and fundamental science are all enduring, appropriate to the government, and of high value to the nation. These missions should be the primary focus of the national laboratories in the intermediate term, with the scope of the missions determined by first recognizing the roles of universities and industry. Finally, it is important to recognize that national needs do evolve with time, and we should expect the missions of these preeminent technical institutions to evolve in response.

3. *Is there a need for size and personnel limits for the DOE National Laboratories?*

The "Government-Owned, Contractor-Operated" model came into existence in large measure to ensure that the Laboratories could apply best private sector human resource management practices, rather than being bound by the bureaucratic requirements that apply to the federal work force. Size and personnel limits are an example of exactly the kind of micromanagement that increases costs and reduces management flexibility to respond to changing government needs. Rather than attempting to regulate the size of the work force, the government should hold Laboratory management contractors accountable for achieving the scientific results and meeting the technology needs specified by the government. In meeting that accountability laboratory management will manage the work force through application of best private sector practices.

4. *Should there be consolidation or closure of the DOE National Laboratories? If so, should this occur after mission definition or concurrently?*

In keeping with the principles above, reconfiguration of the DOE National Laboratory system should be preceded by developing a clear understanding of national needs in the mission areas assigned to the Laboratories and should not be carried out hastily or capriciously. I further recommend that reconfiguration be preceded by the reform of governance recommended earlier in my testimony, and that the need for downsizing be pursued in light of the significant savings that can be achieved through adoption of best private sector management practices. In particular I recommend that we proceed with the following steps:

- Clear definition of the mission for each Laboratory in the context of the full spectrum of federal R&D needs and the roles of universities and industry, and

- Identification and realization of the savings to be derived from improved governance and management practices.

If in these steps it is found that there are facilities that are not relevant to national needs either because of lack of mission or weak technical capabilities, or that are insufficiently productive, then redirection or closure of such facilities is appropriate.

5. *Are there other governance structures, such as corporatization or privatization, which may better suit the future management of the DOE National Laboratories?*

To improve governance I recommend revitalization of the GOCO model as described in my testimony above. In contrast to the corporatization and privatization alternatives, we know from our own history that an appropriate

GOCO model, properly implemented, is highly effective in meeting government R&D needs productively and at a very high standard of performance. Moving first to an entirely new governance system or privatization would direct attention away from the necessary steps of mission focus and productivity improvement.

Mr. SCHIFF. Dr. King?

STATEMENT OF DR. C. JUDSON KING, INTERIM PROVOST, UNIVERSITY OF CALIFORNIA

Dr. KING. I'm pleased to be here, and I particularly appreciate the warmth of the welcome that I and the University of California have received in Washington.

As I landed last night, I heard everybody talking about Cal, which I'm sure was us.

[Laughter.]

Dr. KING. It is a pleasure to be here today to testify on behalf of our university about mechanisms for managing R&D at the DOE national labs.

As contractor operator of three of the laboratories, Lawrence Berkeley, Los Alamos, and Livermore, our university is perhaps uniquely qualified to point out some of the weaknesses in lab governance that need to be corrected, but also to underscore the many significant strengths of these laboratories, that for the good of the nation must be preserved.

In the interest of time, I will simply outline, point by point, the logical structure of my written testimony which you do have.

First, questions about how best to manage the DOE labs raise broader questions about how best to maintain U.S. capability to do first class science.

Second, we believe that the DOE national laboratories play a unique and essential role in the maintenance of that capability. They emphasize of course interdisciplinary teams and large facilities, and we do feel that they are non-duplicative of universities and industry which has its own place in research and development. They are complementary.

We do agree that the system which we use to manage that capability has broken down in ways that need to be fixed. But we believe that the way to do this is by maintaining the many strong points of the GOCO concept, but fixing what needs to be fixed.

We appreciate the Committee's efforts to clarify the place of the labs in the nation's science and technology system, and we stand ready to work with Congress and with the Department of Energy to reestablish a management environment with the labs in which the most creative science can continue to thrive.

Next, mission-driven multidisciplinary research, keyed to national needs and challenges, is the unique strength of the DOE national laboratories. That strength grows out of the lab's strong foundation in the fundamental sciences. It is a multi-dimensional capability that has developed over several decades.

It is a necessary foundation for the labs' defense programs. It has also created a multidisciplinary capability for addressing non-defense challenges, a good example being mapping the human genome. And that capability is unmatched in academic and corporate research departments.

So given that, it is the question of how best to manage this unique national resource that concerns us today.

The GOCO arrangement has provided scientists their usual measure of intellectual freedom and flexibility when compared to research laboratories owned and operated directly by the government.

In the case of the three U.C. labs, the university management has enabled the laboratories to attract and retain top flight scientists, has provided intellectual synergisms to the benefit of both the labs and the university, and in recent years has enabled us to bring to bear the collective wisdom of a distinguished President's Council on the National Laboratories for program evaluation and advice.

For a long time, the GOCO system has served the nation well. It played an essential role in winning the Cold War. Today, the system continues to deliver for the American people, providing a flexible, accessible and accountable scientific capability to respond to national needs.

The system we use to manage this capability has lately taken on too many of the trappings of a large bureaucracy. That is why we support a new management model that preserves the best features of the original GOCO model, and those are intellectual freedom and flexibility, but which ensures a much greater level of contractor responsibility, autonomy and accountability.

And I stress those three words as a group. They go together. Responsibility, autonomy and accountability.

We are pleased to note that some reforms in this direction have begun to take effect, although much more needs to be done.

At our labs, we are committed to maximizing our scientific and technical productivity while eliminating administrative waste.

The current University of California contracts pioneered the use, in the best and current business practices, including performance-based management and we stand willing to improve upon those further.

The University believes that reforms in the specific areas of environmental health and safety regulation must be carefully addressed and accomplished.

I am pleased to represent the University on the Advisory Committee on External Regulation of DOE Nuclear Activity. We await and hope and expect to support the Committee's final report, which should be issued later this year.

We believe that conclusions should not be reached nor actions taken before completion of that study.

We believe that the appropriate scales of the laboratories, in terms of budget and personnel, flow from their missions. We think that decisions about the size and scope of the national laboratories should be made after the missions have been evaluated and clearly defined.

Given our knowledge of the capabilities of the three U.C.-managed labs, we again welcome the opportunity to work with Congress and with the Department of Energy in the process of mission definition.

Budget should follow from mission and its associated priorities. Size follows from budget.

For these reasons, we do not support addressing size first.

More coordination and a clearer sense of mission among the laboratories is certainly desirable. However, as others have said, excessive differentiation or specialization of the various labs within the system would be detrimental to the overall effectiveness of the system.

What may look at first glance like duplication of research programs among labs may in fact represent the simultaneous investigation of different approaches to a single complex problem.

Too much consolidation would preclude the investigation of multiple promising paths and prevent the synergies that often occur because of the lab's multi-dimensionality.

In research, as well as in other investments, it is best to diversify one's portfolio.

The labs' flexibility and accessibility have kept them available to respond quickly to shifting national needs. Moreover, their scientific stature and independence has prevented the immense human resources of the laboratories from being raided haphazardly by those who would seek to employ them elsewhere.

What is needed now is a new partnership in which research for national missions is implemented by responsible and accountable contractors, institutions that are granted sufficient flexibility and autonomy to do an outstanding job.

In this fiscally-constrained era, it is especially important that we build upon and not take apart the unique investment that these laboratories represent. That investment has succeeded in protecting our democracy and substantially enhancing our quality of life throughout the second half of the 20th century.

More flexible and accountable management of that asset and consequently the assured maintenance in the United States of the environment required to nurture and sustain first class science is the best way to safeguard our capacity and to greet the new and exhilarating challenges that are sure to face us in the next century.

Mr. Chairman, that concludes my remarks.

[The prepared statement of Dr. King follows:]

Written Statement of
Dr. C. Judson King
Interim Provost, University of California

U.S. House of Representatives, Committee on Science, Joint Hearing of the Subcommittees on Basic Research and Energy and Environment on "Restructuring the Federal Scientific Establishment: The Department of Energy (DOE) National Laboratories"

Thursday, September 7, 1995
Rayburn House Office Building
Washington, D.C.

Introduction

Continued preeminence in science and technology is crucial for the United States, because it is the only guarantee we have that our nation's scientific capabilities will always be readily accessible to protect the peace, safeguard the health and enhance the economic welfare of the American people. The University of California believes that the DOE national laboratories have played -- and must continue to play -- a unique and essential role in the maintenance of that leadership capability. That is why we appreciate and strongly endorse the efforts of this Committee to clarify the place of these laboratories in the nation's science and technology infrastructure.

We concur, as well, with those -- some of whom serve as Members of this Committee and several others who have testified today -- who contend that the system that we use to manage that capability has broken down in ways that need to be fixed. The current system has increasingly deprived scientists at the labs of the unique benefits that the innovative government-owned contractor-operated system has provided so well -- flexibility and freedom from red tape. The

University of California stands ready to work with Congress and the Administration to reestablish a management environment at the labs in which the most creative science can thrive, an environment that prizes scientific innovation, intellectual independence and accomplishment, along with contractor accountability..

Background

The government-owned, contractor-operated approach to laboratory management began to evolve as a new institutional form during the Manhattan Project, when the Federal government asked the University of California to operate the secret laboratory site at Los Alamos. From its inception, the GOCO arrangement promised scientists an unusual measure of intellectual freedom and flexibility, allowing them to operate without the bureaucratic restrictions that can stifle creativity and impede innovation at scientific institutions owned and operated directly by the government.

Over the years, the resulting university-like environment helped the labs to attract and retain top-quality people. The laboratories have not only retained good links to science on university campuses, but also have been able to provide a critical service to academic researchers by providing access to their unique multidisciplinary research environment, as well as their state-of-the-art equipment and instrumentation. Moreover, because scientists at the national laboratories are accustomed to working on long-term projects characterized by high technical risk, their work has often attracted the interest of corporate R&D personnel whose privately-supported research efforts are constrained to focus on shorter-term product development.

For a long time, this system has served the nation well. It has enabled universities and companies to leverage the long-term investment made in the national laboratories by the American people to win the Cold War. It has facilitated interaction -- and therefore innovation -- across the different parts of the nation's science and technology infrastructure -- private industry, government, and academia.

Unfortunately, over the years, this once-flexible and dynamic system has taken on too many of the trappings of conventional government agency decision-making -- ironically, the very trappings that the GOCO arrangement is designed to replace. The line between oversight and implementation has blurred, and the system's effectiveness has become compromised by a proliferation of orders, directives, audits, and reviews.

As this nation embarks on the examination of its R&D system for a new century, it is the position of the University of California that a management model that preserves the best features of the original GOCO model but which ensures a much greater level of contractor responsibility, autonomy and accountability is needed to enable the national laboratories to fulfill their roles as efficient and cost-effective vehicles for carrying out high-caliber R&D in support of national missions. We are very pleased to note that both DOE, as evidenced by its current efforts to streamline and improve lab management, and the Congress, as evidenced by the legislation under consideration and these joint hearings in which we are participating today, agree that the system of lab governance needs to be reformed.

What is the future role of the DOE National Laboratories in the context of the overall Federally-funded scientific establishment?

The role of the DOE national laboratories should be to maintain an outstanding scientific capability which will be available at all times for the pursuit of compelling national missions as designated by Congress and the Department of Energy. The work of the laboratories should be mission-driven, keyed to national needs and issues, and focused on problems whose solutions require multidisciplinary expertise.

What should be the future missions of the DOE national laboratories?

Future missions should emphasize national needs whose potential solutions require a multi-program, multidisciplinary research and development capability. If a broad-based, state-of-the-art scientific and technological capability is maintained at the laboratories, then many different and emerging missions can be met and unanticipated challenges can be addressed.

One way to think about future missions is to think of national problems whose potential solutions possess features common to what economists call "public goods." A public good is a good from whose beneficial use no one can be excluded, one whose benefits are not diminished by anyone else's consumption of the good, and one whose benefits are essentially inexhaustible. Examples include national security (or, more specifically, an effective nuclear deterrent), energy efficiency, public health, and a clean environment.

Economists generally argue that the private sector, on its own, will not invest sufficiently in the development or production of public goods, as no company or inventor will be able to capture fully the economic returns to such investments. Where effective patent or intellectual property protection is not available or where the benefits of rapid development and dissemination are overwhelming and obvious (as, for example, in the case of the polio vaccine), the American solution has typically been to subsidize private-sector research, production and sometimes distribution of the good.

The missions outlined in HR2142 represent a thoughtful list that encompasses most, if not all of the missions that would be appropriate at this time in our nation's history. Certainly, not all of these missions are appropriate for every lab. But the list would provide a basis on which to analyze the capabilities, facilities, and expertise of each lab in order to define missions appropriate to it.

While the designation of missions is the joint responsibility of Congress and the Department of Energy, the University of California has extensive experience with and knowledge of the capabilities of the three UC - managed laboratories. The University of California realizes that we all need to work toward greater efficiencies, and at the UC - managed labs we are committed to maximizing our scientific and technological productivity while minimizing administrative waste. It is important to bear in mind, however, that the discovery of new knowledge and the solution of scientific challenges typically requires the simultaneous investigation of widely variant approaches and the ability to take advantage of unforseen results;

too much consolidation might slow the pace of scientific discovery and technological innovation and prevent the synergies that often occur because of the labs' multi-dimensional, multi-program nature.

Although we are not prepared at this time to endorse the specific idea of a laboratory facilities commission, as proposed in HR87, the University would welcome the opportunity to participate in any discussions concerning new laboratory missions and the appropriate use of specific laboratory facilities, in whatever forum Congress and the Department of Energy eventually choose to provide.

Is there a need for size and personnel limits for the DOE National Laboratories?

The appropriate scales for these laboratories flow from their mission(s), as designated by Congress and the Department of Energy. The missions outlined in HR2142 mark a useful step in this direction. There is probably, however, a minimum sufficient size for sustaining a first-class scientific capability to address national needs as they arise. Thus, while the objectives of HR1510 may be laudable, the University cannot endorse the proposed one-third reduction, which seems arbitrary and premature. Analyses could be conducted regarding the objectives stated in the bill, with identification of redundancies, inefficiencies, outdated facilities, etc. These analyses could lead eventually to reductions in size and personnel in the DOE national laboratories, but to an extent deemed appropriate after careful study -- and after the mission(s) of these laboratories (and the Department of Energy itself) have been more clearly defined through the appropriate process..

Should there be consolidation or closure of the DOE National Laboratories? If so, should this occur after mission definition, or concurrently?

Again, the University believes that any decisions about the size and scope of the national laboratories should be made only after their missions have been clearly defined. In addition, the missions of the DOE national laboratories are intricately linked to the mission(s) of the Department of Energy itself. Although we are not endorsing any specific recommendations to dismantle or even to restructure the Department of Energy, such as those proposed in HR1993, the University of California is pleased to participate in the overall process of delineating the effective institutional allocation of responsibilities for the nation's research and development enterprise.

As an integral part of that enterprise, the laboratory system would certainly benefit from more internal coordination. However, we must reemphasize our conviction that excessive consolidation or specialization within the system would be detrimental to the system's overall effectiveness. What looks at first glance like duplication of research programs among labs within a multi-lab system, may in fact represent the necessary investigation of widely variant approaches to the same problem. The assurance of mulitple, independent eyes scrutinizing each problem is one of the great strengths of this nation's decentralized R&D system; it makes possible what is, in fact, an intelligently conservative R&D investment strategy for the United

States, because it enables the nation to effectively spread its scientific and technological bets.

Are there other governance structures, such as corporatization or privatization, which may better suit the future management of the DOE National Laboratories?

It is the position of the University of California that a management model that preserves the best features of the original GOCO model but which ensures a much greater level of contractor responsibility, flexibility and accountability is needed to enable the national laboratories to fulfill their roles as cost-effective vehicles for carrying out high-caliber R&D in support of national missions. We are pleased to note that some reform along these lines has already begun to take effect, although much more needs to be done.

The new management approach should push beyond the classical GOCO arrangement to suit the fiscal and research environments of the 1990's, combining contractor flexibility -- essential when dealing with the management of a multidisciplinary research enterprise -- with enhanced contractor responsibility and accountability. Indeed the current University of California contracts are already written to take advantage of the best in current business practices, including performance-based management.

Concerning regulatory oversight, the University believes that reforms in the specific areas of environment, health and safety regulation -- the areas targeted in HR1510 -- must be carefully addressed and accomplished. The University is pleased to be participating in the work of the

Advisory Committee on External Regulation of Department of Energy Nuclear Safety, which has been appointed by the Secretary to address this complex set of issues. We await and hope to support the final report of the Committee, which is slated to be issued later this year.

In general, however, the flexibility inherent in the laboratories' management and operations contracts have kept the labs available to respond quickly to shifting national needs, as determined by the Congress and by successive Administrations. Because the contracts have created long-term, interactive partnerships between contractors and the government, there has been no need to enter into complex and inefficient contract negotiations every time the nation's public officials wished to assign the labs to work on an issue of urgent national concern. Thus, for more than five decades, the national laboratories have been able to create, nurture and safeguard for the American people an impressive array of scientific and technical capabilities.

A National Asset

The University of California would like to emphasize that the issues the Subcommittees are examining in these joint hearings have relevance far beyond the Department of Energy labs. Because the DOE has played a major role in the sponsorship and support of outstanding science in the United States, the changes we are discussing here today will likely impact the nation's entire scientific enterprise, far into the future. Questions about the role and purpose of the Department of Energy itself, as well as questions about how best to manage research and development at the DOE national labs, inevitably raise broader questions about what the United States needs to do to remain preeminent in science and technology in the 21st century.

The national laboratories play a unique and essential role in this nation's science and technology enterprise. They perform multidisciplinary, mission-driven research of a kind that is inappropriate or unsustainable at universities or private companies. The defense program labs, for example, are uniquely suited to the mission of addressing the long-range scientific and technological challenges inherent in keeping the world safe from nuclear catastrophe, a mission which draws on the expertise of scientists and engineers from a variety of disciplinary backgrounds, whether through their sustained efforts in non- and counter-proliferation, their efforts to implement science-based stockpile stewardship, or their attention to problems of hazardous waste disposition and environmental remediation.

Similarly, the multi-lab effort to chart the intricate geography of the Human Genome, an outgrowth of the laboratories' long-standing mission to understand the effects of radiation on the biological environment and human health, provides an essential navigational guide that can be used by researchers at universities and pharmaceutical companies to identify the genetic components of specific maladies.

In short, mission-driven research, keyed to national needs and challenges beyond the scope of university or private company efforts, is the unique strength of the national laboratories. That strength grows out of the laboratories' strong foundation in fundamental science, a capability that has developed over decades and one which must be sustained. The effective execution of national missions requires the existence of a first-class, multidisciplinary capability that can be applied to unforeseen scientific and technical challenges. Such a capability resides in the DOE national laboratories.

Thanks to their practical experience with a variety of scientific disciplines and advanced technologies, the national laboratories have been able to make significant and timely contributions in such diverse areas as environmental restoration and the discovery of new sources of energy supply, the development of new structural materials and of hardware and software advances for supercomputers, and the creation of novel techniques for sequencing the human genome.

The laboratories' scientific stature and independence have prevented the immense resources of the laboratories from being raided haphazardly. Moreover, the commitment of the laboratories to peer review, a commitment strengthened by their historical links to the University, provides another external mechanism of accountability, as well as added impetus internally to spur both integrity and scientific excellence in the research program.

Just as important, the commitment of these laboratories to quality and integrity, along with their unique multidisciplinary research environment, their unparalleled facilities and the strong tie to a leading university, make them one of this nation's most effective training grounds for the next generation of scientists.

Conclusion

In summary, the DOE national laboratories have proved to be a unique and irreplaceable national asset since the end of the Second World War. Nevertheless, the quality of that asset has been threatened in recent years because government officials, often with the best of intentions, have blurred the line between oversight and implementation. As a result, the laboratory system has taken on too many of the trappings of conventional government agency decision-making, a maze which is inimical to the flexible and innovative environment in which good science thrives.

What we need now is a new partnership, in which research for national missions established by Congress and the Administration is implemented by responsible and accountable contractors, according to best business practices, with sufficient flexibility and autonomy, and with a strong commitment to unbiased peer review. In this fiscally constrained era, it is especially important that we build upon -- rather than take apart -- the unique investment that these laboratories represent. This investment has succeeded in protecting our democracy and substantially enhancing our quality of life throughout the second half of the 20th century. More flexible and accountable management of that asset, and consequently the assured maintenance in the United States of the environment required to nurture and sustain world-class science, is the best way to safeguard our capacity to greet the new and exhilarating challenges that are sure to face us in the 21st.

Mr. SCHIFF. Thank you very much, Dr. King.

I'm going to be very brief, again we'll try to stay in the five-minute rule because we still have one more panel of course to hear from.

I want to say, first, Dr. King, my feelings are exactly with your statement that budget should follow mission. It is always true that budget is going to be limited. No one will have an unlimited budget, even though every agency would like to have some ideal like that.

So it's not a matter that somebody will get an unrestricted raid into the federal treasury. That will never happen.

But I think the basic approach, when we're trying to look at an operation like the national laboratories is to first look at what they ought to be doing, and how they should be doing it, and then try to build a budget as best we can around that.

I think that's the major difference between my bill and the other three bills that are offered here.

Second is I cannot say exactly what kind of legislation will move through the Congress. I also agree with you, Dr. King, that we should wait for the report from the Regulations Advisory Committee from the Department of Energy and see what they state, in my view, before we proceed with any legislation. And that's expected at the end of the year.

I want to say, though, that for the purpose of supposition, if we were to assume my bill were to pass as is, I'd be very grateful if the four of you would—not at this moment—but would reexamine the mission statement, as I wrote it, because it's not easy, as you know, to write a mission statement broad enough so that it doesn't leave out a potential important area of research, but at the same time, not so broad that it has no meaning, that would propose the labs be all things to all people, which we don't want to do either.

So at your convenience, perhaps you could let me know in a separate letter if there's any changes you would make in that.

Finally, I'd like to bring up one other issue, and that is the Deputy Secretary of Energy, I know you heard earlier, said that the Department was looking at various management reviews and that according to their own estimates, management reconfiguration of the laboratory might reduce national laboratory employment by ten percent or more.

However, most of the testimony I have heard has not looked at the employment level at the national laboratories as much as it's looked at the Department of Energy, employment levels at the Department of Energy, and what's driving them here.

In other words, Mr. Galvin said it pretty frankly, maybe we're looking at the wrong area here and where to downsize people.

In other words, the Department of Energy is causing this reexamination of management procedures which may result in a downsizing of the laboratory staff when who's looking at the Department of Energy?

And I'm going to ask a very frank question here. As contractors with the Department of Energy representing corporate entities or universities' desire to keep those contracts, are you in a position to argue back?

Are you in a position, if the Department of Energy says, well, we think this is a procedure in a laboratory you should cut out, eliminate some personnel, are you in a position to say, on whatever subject technically it might be: wait a minute, take a look at what you've got, what you're doing, and maybe the elimination should be under the Department of Energy.

I hope that's a reasonably clear question.

I don't have a specific example in mind, but the question is, do you have the freedom to argue back and say, no, we shouldn't cut the laboratory, the Department of Energy is the problem here, where you think that's the case.

Dr. Olesen?

Dr. OLESEN. Mr. Schiff, I would I guess answer that. In our particular case, we manage the Pacific Northwest Laboratory and we have, in the last nine months, been through a substantial reengineering process in which our staff reduction was in excess of 20 percent and our direct/indirect ratio went from one to one, to two to one.

And as I mentioned in my statement, we were able to do that with very solid cooperation from the Department of Energy by deciding what we could do more efficiently and more effectively and getting from the Department of Energy permission to do things differently.

And so I guess my answer to you is, I think at this point, the attitude within the Department is very receptive from a contractor's standpoint, to change and improvement and cost reduction.

Mr. SCHIFF. But my point is the opposite, Dr. Olesen. Are they pushing you to make reductions in areas where you might not think reductions are warranted?

Dr. OLESEN. I would have to say that ours was principally self-generated.

Mr. SCHIFF. Dr. Narath?

Dr. NARATH. I would agree with that answer. By and large, the target that the Secretary of Energy has set for reductions in staff at the laboratories and dollar savings were based on some rough estimate of what might be achievable by way of overhead reductions.

And I believe those numbers did come about following lengthy discussions with all or most of the contractors.

I should also say that the Department of Energy itself has set downsizing goals for itself, which are rather large. And these in turn came about through strong interactions with the laboratories.

If you'll recall, the Galvin Commission visited all of the laboratories, interacted with the lab directors, and out of those discussions and discussions with DOE, ultimately came rather strong recommendations, as concerns inefficiencies in the DOE management, following which the Secretary set out to set some very tough goals for DOE.

So DOE is doing its part. The laboratories are now being asked to get their act together and every laboratory currently, as you will hear I'm sure in the next panel, is hard at work to re-engineer their processes with the aim of saving dollars and reducing unnecessary staff.

I should also say that staffing should follow budgets. As budgets get squeezed, it's in the best interests of laboratory management to absorb that squeeze within overhead.

I mean, the motivation to cut overhead and not technical effort is enormous. So a little bit of squeezing of the budget and you will see most of that translated, at least initially, into cuts in overhead and PNL of course has taken a very vigorous position.

Mr. SCHIFF. Dr. Bernthal?

Dr. BERNTHAL. Let me just turn your question a little bit, Mr. Chairman, to note that what all of us have been asking today is how do you preserve the scientific and engineering competence within the laboratory, that programmatic part of the various laboratories.

And I must say that in that regard, there is a lot of support and many allies within the Department of Energy programmatic staff to do just that. There's great concern of course among us contractors, among the laboratories themselves, the directors of the laboratories, that the cuts not be made in the wrong places.

And I should say that we find a good deal of support on that score from the programmatic offices within the Department.

Mr. SCHIFF. Dr. King?

Dr. KING. I have just one thing to add and that is that from our point of view, the concept of partnership has arisen much more in recent years, a partnership between the Department of Energy and the contractor.

So things can be accomplished both by pushing on one another, but also by partnership. An example is some very effective meetings that the Department has had of contractor CEOs. These occur roughly quarterly.

Mr. SCHIFF. Before I recognize——

Mr. EHLERS. Would the gentleman yield?

Mr. SCHIFF. I yield to the gentleman from Michigan.

Mr. EHLERS. Thank you, Mr. Chairman.

I just wanted to add to your question, which I think is an excellent one, another point that is often missed, and even in the discussion today, it's been assumed somehow that administrators administer and scientists do research.

In my comments this morning, I commented on some of the difficulties that I've seen develop, and one of the major ones is that more and more scientists are being asked to do administrative work as part of their duty.

And that, I think, has been a very deleterious factor in the research effort of the nation.

I've just seen this where a principal scientist may spend half of his or her time doing routine administrative tasks, just because they are imposed on him or her by either the lab administration or the DOE.

So I think we have to be aware that that's a major part of the problem and the squeeze we're talking about may get rid of some of the administrative overhead but we also have to address the problem of scientists spending a lot of their time doing administration.

Thank you.

Mr. SCHIFF. I thank the gentleman for your comment on that.

I just want to say, before recognizing Chairman Rohrabacher, that my question was not intended to be hostile to the DOE. As I indicated at the beginning of the hearing, I am an opponent of those who think they can dissolve the DOE and simply transfer those responsibilities effectively elsewhere.

I just wanted to make sure that as we talk about examining management problems and looking for more efficiency, and therefore for more savings, that there was the ability of a two-way street here. That as the DOE looked at the national laboratories, the national laboratories and the contractors have the opportunity, which you are assuring me they do, to just look back at the DOE and how they are presenting themselves, all in the same process.

Mr. Rohrabacher?

Mr. ROHRABACHER. Do any of you think that we can just sort of give the money out and let all the decisions be made out there and we don't have to worry about the decisions after that?

Go right ahead.

Dr. NARATH. No, I don't think that's so at all. I mean, clearly, the Congress has a very important oversight responsibility. You need to ask what value is returned for the investment you make.

All we're asking is that we be given the opportunity to decide how best to manage.

Because if you set arbitrary goals, you may get the wrong result.

Mr. ROHRABACHER. This wasn't aimed at you, actually.

Dr. NARATH. I understand.

Mr. Ehlers I thought made a wonderful point.

One way you can reduce overhead or appear to be reducing overhead, you could fire your administrative staff and let the scientific staff do the administrative work.

On paper, it will appear as if you've done wonders in regard to overhead, but you better look at the technical productivity.

So it's the net effect that's achieved, and I maintain to do that most effectively requires somebody inside the organization who really knows something, and by the way, has experienced somewhere as to how to go about improving productivity.

Mr. ROHRABACHER. Well, I used to work for a newspaper and I was a writer, and I can tell you that I'm not a very good manager when it comes to managing newspapers, but I consider myself a fairly decent writer. And I have to believe that the creative process in your arena is probably about the same.

And I imagine there are some people who are, you know, renowned in science that are also great managers, but I think management is not necessarily going hand in hand with that particular knowledge base of science.

However, you know, I'm not going to ask you more questions. Bill had a good idea. I maybe don't want to express it here, but I thought it was a good idea. And I yield to Mr. Baker.

Mr. BAKER. I think some of the frustration we have is quantifying science.

We took the Committee to the lab and Mr. Rohrabacher was there and Chairman Walker and a number of other Members on both sides of the aisle, and we watched them break down the genes, the zillions and zillions of genes and what each function does and where a disease is likely to be carried or malformation is likely to be carried.

How do you quantify that?

And that's what we're really struggling with.

If we could solve cancer, it would be worth billions in future costs, but in order to achieve that, we can't quantify effective cost spending on the billions it's going to take to defeat cancer.

But we have to do that. And my idea was to place the Galvin Commission, and we're talking about the leaders of each field, whether it's Intel and the pentium chip, and Galvin and his company, Genentech and the gene splicing, put leaders of industry together with the lab managers and the university people, along with the Department of Energy, and say what should the management structure be so that your reporting to Congress reflects peer-related science.

Is this worth chasing?

Can we really split something the size of a grain of salt with 192 lasers and come up with the measurement of the stockpile or the new nuclear power?

Is this worth a billion dollars?

Is it worth so much chasing gene splicing in order to cure cancer?

And have the scientists report back to some kind of a measurement board.

The problem we've been faced with so far is that somebody from industry comes in with a CRADA, cooperative research agreement, comes to the lab and says, we'd like to go to the moon, and everybody dies and breaks out laughing, but it's worth it because scientists don't care. I mean, they want to look at things like that. So it only costs a billion dollars. Kick it up to the Department of Energy.

They go into a fit. How are we going to quantify that? How are we going to put this in terms that Congress will understand and ratify?

And so it takes two years. By that time, they've gone to France and France has already done it.

And so then when Congress gets it, we want to micromanage too. So we want to tell the Department of Energy, you're too big and fat because you spend all your time trying to analyze CRADAs that come to you from off-the-wall scientists.

So how do we create a structure where the taxpayer knows that his money's being well-spent, that we are on the chase of energy independence, we are going to cure cancer, and we, as a government, are going to participate with the leading firms in America to do it.

How can we create such an entity?

Remembering that the focus here in this Committee is about three minutes at a time. The bell will ring, we will leave, the fundraiser is tonight, the party with Lockheed is next door. You're showing us all of the great inventions of the last twenty years at the labs. We're stretched thinner than a rubber band.

How do we focus on this in order to create the correct management tool to allow us to measure and therefore have the confidence that we can defeat science if we make the investment?

Can anyone address that?

Go ahead and start, Dr. Narath.

Dr. NARATH. Let's see, first of all, perhaps we ought to spend more time looking retrospectively, rather than prospectively.

One big advantage of the GOCO system is that once you've developed a trusting relationship with a contractor, based on past performance, you can probably place your money on future results. We spend an awful lot of time trying to sell things that might happen in the future, and in the process, have a tendency to exaggerate and overstate in order to sell.

Why don't we spend more time looking at what institutions have actually accomplished in the past, and then place some trust in them that they will do equally well in the future, knowing that if they don't, perhaps they will cease to receive generous support.

In that regard, I sound very much like Mr. Galvin.

Mr. BAKER. But Mr. Galvin's report stated that the CRADA proposition, the partnerships between business and government, were not well-focused, not well-defined.

Dr. NARATH. I don't totally agree, and I can only speak for the institution that—let's see, once upon a time, I was a lab director. I think it was two or three weeks ago. A lot of things have happened since then.

But if I look back over my tenure as lab director, sure you can find CRADAs that may, you know, have been sort of on the fringes, but in the main, the CRADAs were strongly focused in Sandia's mission areas, and I can show that they were relevant and added to the laboratory, and I think, in most cases, added something to the partner who, by the way, put upward of 70 percent of the cash.

Mr. BAKER. Well, are you saying, then, that we don't need to change the management of the current laboratories?

Mr. SCHIFF. I need to interrupt for a moment. Mr. Rohrabacher's time has expired, but I'm prepared to, if the gentleman just wants to continue with this line, I'm prepared to recognize the gentleman for his own five minutes this time, and then recognize Mr. Brown.

Mr. BAKER. I'll take the five minutes then to try and elicit from your four, is there a better mousetrap to manage the scarce resources of science dollars, noting that we may not get a return for five, ten, fifteen, twenty years?

Dr. NARATH. Well, let me just say one thing and then I'll turn it over to my colleagues.

We've already stated that we've identified opportunity for significant improvements in productivity. I take that as a given.

Some labs have gone further in that direction than others, but we're all moving towards becoming more productive.

Once the decision has been made to entrust us with dollars to achieve certain goals, I think—I know we will become more efficient in reaching these goals.

But how to make the decisions up front as to what is worth supporting at one level——

Mr. BAKER. But how can we become—let's examine your statement.

You feel in the future you can become more efficient.

How?

Do you think the structure that working our way up through the Department of Energy back down to the laboratories, back over to

Congress, chasing the dollars, auditing, do you think this is efficient?

Dr. NARATH. No. Look, there are a lot of things that need to be changed.

In the first place, there is need to improve the administration of the laboratories. By the time DOE gets done reducing its work force, the federal work force by some 30 percent or whatever is targeted, you'll see a lot of changes.

Laboratories are hard at work to reduce their overhead in response.

We will become more effective. If we don't, you will no longer support us. It's just that simple. And by the way, there will be fewer dollars available. We all recognize that.

Mr. BAKER. Well, we had one of the folks here earlier, a person from one of the foundations, Eric Bloch, who said we ought to cut science research 33 percent.

I don't agree, but we have to justify to the taxpaying public that as we freeze and slow down the growth of spending, we can get a return for that money, whether it's a scientific return or a monetary return.

And I don't think we have the measurement devices now to prove it.

Mr. SCHIFF. Okay.

Dr. KING. The question is really one of how to assess something that is in the future, rather than the present or the past, and something that has risk associated with it in that the very nature of research means you don't know what you will end up with at the time that you started.

So how best to do this, and to recognize also the fact that scientific research is complex and not everybody understands the elements of it that well.

I think the best method we have come up with is one of peer review and that is something that can't be built into the contractor mechanism and the choice of contractors.

I did mention during my testimony, our President's Council on the National Laboratories, which is a group of quite distinguished people drawn from around the country from many different walks of life, whose service with us is designed to evaluate the worth, the likelihood, the risk, or lack of risk, associated with research.

I think that's about the best we can do.

I would also mention, for this purpose, that there are people within universities and elsewhere who make quantitative studies of the return on investment for research.

This is one of the things that Michael Boskin does at Stanford now.

A man named Edwin Mansfield at the University of Pennsylvania has done it for some years.

David Mowry at the University of California Berkeley gets into this area.

And the studies are different from one another but they generally come out showing that the research dollar has around a 20 to 30 percent return on investment, recognizing the fact that some of it leads nowhere but some of it leads to very important places.

Mr. SCHIFF. Dr. Bernthal, I think you wanted to get in on this one?

Dr. BERNTHAL. Yes.

I wanted to make clear, at least in my own mind, it seems to me that nobody has argued, at least I've not heard many people arguing and I don't think the intent—if I may speak for my former boss, by the way—of Eric Bloch's comment, was to suggest that science should be cut, whatever the number was, 30 percent. That's not quite the same statement certainly as what Bob Galvin was saying, and I think all of us agree that the science programs, the engineering research programs that have been carried out in the national laboratory system by and large have passed a very high standard of peer review that's carried out in a variety of ways.

It seems to me that Mr. Galvin has outlined, in some detail, in the report of his Task Force and again here today, where he perceives the difficulty as being, and that is in the administrative structure that attaches to the carrying out of that research.

Now, you may be asking a related question, and that is, how do you make judgments across disciplinary lines?

And that is a more difficult question and one that Phil Griffiths, for example, chaired a panel at the National Academy of Sciences some time back, that tried to come to grips with that issue.

There's a very high standard of peer review when you are within a certain disciplinary arena, but most scientists are reluctant to, and find it very difficult to decide between human genome research on the one hand, and particle physics on the other hand.

That's something the scientific community itself, I would say, has not fully come to grips with, and it's an extremely difficult problem for obvious reasons.

There are very few people who are expert in enough different fields to do that.

I don't know whether that was the thrust and intent of your question.

Mr. BAKER. No, I'm trying to cast a little urgency out here. We have a stack of bills——

Mr. SCHIFF. I have to say that the gentleman's time has expired again. However, if the gentleman would briefly——

Mr. BAKER. I'll conclude. I'll conclude, and I'd like to ask Mr. Olesen to finish his remarks too. He was not allowed to jump in here.

But we have a stack of bills here, everything from shutting down the Department of Energy to shutting down some of the labs.

And we sit here saying, well everything's all right, there's no problems. In the meantime, we're going to balance the budget. Where do you do that?

You take the next billion dollar scientific program has no constituency, has no base, and we trim it. And I don't think that's the correct solution.

So I'm asking you, can we get together, the scientific and business community and the university community, and figure out a better line and staff management organization so that the taxpayer will have confidence his dollar's being well spent in science.

If we can hear from Dr. Olesen, I'll conclude?

Dr. OLESEN. Thank you, Mr. Baker.

I guess I would like to refer back to some of the comments that Mr. Galvin made in the previous panel in which he focused very hard on the issues of micromanagement which originate in Congressional legislation, and I think what that does to us in so much of our systems is it focuses on process and why we're doing things and how we're doing things, and a tremendous amount of the energy in the R&D system now is utilized to just work processes.

And if we could get into a management system which the Congress is much more focused on what we want to do and how much we're willing to spend on it, and then the rest of the organization was allowed to use best industrial practices to manage it, I believe then the conversation would turn to just the subjects that you are concerned about, how much did we spend in each area.

And I would also submit that the private sector makes those decisions everyday with very large amounts of money, determining whether to go in one field or another, or to go to two at the same time.

And so I think the processes are there in the private sector to do what you want to do, but our energy is unavailable to do that, as long as we are in this micromanagement climate.

Mr. BAKER. Thank you.

Mr. SCHIFF. Mr. Brown, you're recognized for such time as you may wish to consume.

Mr. BROWN. Thank you very much, Mr. Chairman.

May I say that I've enjoyed the interchange very much. It's a part of a process I guess which you would call a learning process for Members of Congress. And sometimes it doesn't appear to be all that fruitful but it generally ends up creating a more enlightened Member of Congress, which is always to be hoped for, you know.

The question of how we downsize, how we determine the desirable budget, how we, I think Dr. King mentioned how to maintain the U.S. capability to do first-class science, are extremely provocative questions, which we don't have answers to, and we don't even know how to measure them.

One of the great benefits that scientists have is their output is generally non-quantifiable despite the efforts of economists to demonstrate that it has a remarkable beneficial effect on the economy.

And so you have these anomalous situations where you may, we'll say, change the ratio of direct to indirect costs, which means that say your principal investigator will have less support staff. Obviously, he will be doing more of the support work. It will look like you're saving money, but it may actually be costing you money because he has less time to spend on the work that he presumably is best qualified to do, which is scientific investigation, or just thinking about abstract problems, he'll have less time to do that because he'll be spending more time in filling out paperwork.

Now that's one side of the coin.

The other side is your overhead may be the type represented by the DOE's Washington office which is creating problems for investigators out in the laboratories, for managers out in the laboratories. And by reducing the Washington overhead, and their regulatory role, you may be enhancing the time and ability of investigators to do more creative work out in the labs.

Now how do you distinguish between the two kinds of reductions in overhead or support staff or whatever you want to call it.

I don't know the answer to that, but you've certainly helped my thinking in terms of trying to understand that a little bit better.

Now, I don't want to make this into a monologue. I've been working for years trying to see if there are metrics you can determine how science contributes to the quality of life of society. I don't have the answer yet.

We're talking here about science budgets that may go up or down by as much as—well, down by at least a third. Nobody's suggesting that they go up very much at this point.

How do we determine whether this is good or bad for the society?

Is it an impossible question?

Is it possible to determine what the answer is?

Can we take the reduction all out of non-scientific overhead or support? What is the direction that we should follow?

Now in some general way, I have come to believe that science contributes to the overall quality of life. And the quality of life can be measured, although the metrics aren't very good.

And that an advancing society will have an advancing number of people of a creative type, such as scientists. It also includes artists and others who contribute to the quality of life.

If you decide to take a scientific budget that's going downhill over the next five years by 30 percent or 40 percent, what does that mean to your ability to support increasing numbers of scientifically trained people? Is there a relationship here?

Or how does it comport with what our competitor nations are doing?

Now, Dr. Narath, you were with Bell for a long time, Bell Labs, which decided to cut out their research function.

Did that affect the quality of life of the nation?

It apparently affected Bell's bottom line positively.

What does that mean in terms of the desirability of supporting the research that Bell Labs did?

Dr. NARATH. I've always felt that probably the most effective national laboratory that ever existed was then called Bell Telephone Labs. I mean, as you well know, it had a very protected status.

The ratepayers paid, you know, what the system said was needed, and was a small fraction of the total, and the people had a great deal of freedom.

But that laboratory did have a mission focus: ten percent in basic research, 90 percent in applied work and engineering development. It was a really superb example of how science and technology interact for human welfare.

Of course, all of that changed with divestiture and it was owned by a corporation that had to worry about the next quarter's bottom line, and a lot of things changed.

It's confused, however, by the fact that technology also caused changes, because many of the topics that the laboratory got out of were topics that were simply not as current anymore.

I mean, things began moving towards the software side and away from hardware issues. So to what extent AT&T Bell Labs today has reacted to the reality of now working in a competitive field, and to what extent it's simply a reflection of how science and technology have changed in terms of their priorities, I'm not smart enough to know. It's just very complicated.

It's not as simple as saying that Bell Labs got out of research. And I'm with you. I don't know how whatever happened impacted the quality of life.

I'm with you in believing that science is important. I believe a society that is advancing should probably be able to afford an increasing fraction of its gross national product investments in science, the arts, and so on.

But what is the right level? I don't know.

Mr. BROWN. Yes.

Dr. Bernthal?

Dr. BERNTHAL. I'm just worried that this sounds too equivocal here today. Quite aside from what science may do for the soul and perhaps in some respects can even be categorized with the arts, for example, there have been legitimate attempts, and Dr. King has outlined the authors, or mentioned the authors of some of those attempts, there have been legitimate attempts to try and work out the societal benefits and returns to society of government (I'm sure industry, as well) investment in research and development.

And I know of no study (to be conservative) here that suggests less than double-digit returns, as I'm sure all the members of this panel know.

But it seems to me we ought to stipulate that for the record, that it's up to you gentlemen in the Congress to decide how much money there is ultimately, but I think we should say, for the record, very clearly, that all the evidence is that the returns are very large when the country invests in science and technology.

Mr. BROWN. I'm familiar with those studies and cite them all the time myself when I'm trying to influence constituents or other Members of Congress. But I don't have a great deal of confidence in the direct applicability of those studies to present-day budgeting.

Most of them are based upon an analysis over generational periods, for example. And just as Bell Labs could decide that their bottom line in terms of profits would probably be improved if they shed the cost of the laboratory or the Bell System, so the Congress may decide that in order to meet the higher goal of a balanced budget, we can shed all of our investments in R&D over a period.

The basic decision comes down however to an ordering of priorities. What is the political priority of investing in R&D as compared with not cutting Medicare another X percent.

That's what makes the Congressional priority process work. It has nothing to do with the quality or contribution of science when you get right down to it. And we rarely think in terms of our overall government investments in science and give it a priority as compared with, say, investments in defense or social programs or anything else.

It's a very sticky situation, and the more we understand the complexity of it, the better we will probably do.

I would like to pursue this for a couple of days but I doubt if it would be appropriate to do that.

So let me close with a comment to Dr. King.

How long have you been associated with the management of the laboratories at the University of California?

Dr. KING. Well, that doesn't have a simple answer.

I've been at the University of California for about 32 years at this point, and most of that on the Berkeley campus. And so that gave me a very strong tie to the Lawrence Berkeley Laboratory.

I held administrative positions on the Berkeley campus, which also gave me a close administrative tie with the national laboratories, and it was one year ago, plus two months at this point, that I moved into the position of Vice Provost of Research of the University of California, and had the direct programmatic concern and responsibility with the labs.

Mr. BROWN. Well, obviously, you cannot be blamed for the mistakes of the University in the management of the labs in prior years, then, and you can take credit for the improvements that have been made. And I hope you will do that.

But I was very critical of the failure of the University to exercise what I thought was prudent management for a number of years. And I saw them, improperly of course, as sitting there collecting a fee and doing very little to justify it.

Now that's changed considerably because of circumstances which you are well aware of, and we're moving toward a management system which will put the University in the loop in terms of responsibility, accountability, and what was the other thing that you mentioned?

Dr. KING. Flexibility.

Mr. BROWN. Flexibility.

And I hope that will continue.

The only point in raising it is every management system consists of many parts, and all of them can be improved at any time. And this is what we need to encourage with the Department of Energy labs at the present time, and I hope you'll continue to seek improvement there.

Dr. KING. I appreciate your comments and they are well-taken. There has been a step up in the University's management process and function with regard to the laboratories in recent years.

But with regard to the past, I think it would be also fair to point out that we are a public institution and, as such, thoroughly on display, all of our warts, outside and inside the body.

And it may be that we do not have more warts, or have not had more warts than others, but just that they've been more visible because of that structure.

Mr. SCHIFF. Strange as it may seem, we have some understanding of being on public display.

[Laughter.]

Mr. SCHIFF. With that, let me thank this panel and for your indulgence in waiting to testify and for your cooperation and for your forthright testimony before us today.

We thank you very much, and I'm now going to call the next panel.

Our final panel, and someone has to be the first panel and someone has to be the last panel, and it's not a judgment of credentials, I want to assure everybody.

Is we have Dr. Charles F. Gay, who is the Director of the National Renewable Energy Laboratory.

Dr. Siegfried S. Hecker, who is Director of the Los Alamos National Laboratory.

Dr. Alan Schriesheim, who is Director of the Argonne National Laboratory.

Dr. C. Bruce Tarter, Director of the Lawrence Livermore Laboratory.

Dr. Alvin W. Trivelpiece, Director of Oak Ridge National Laboratory.

And Dr. John C. Crawford, Executive Vice President of Sandia National Laboratories.

Gentlemen, welcome, and I'll wait a moment while you all get situated there.

[Pause.]

Mr. SCHIFF. Okay. Gentlemen, welcome. I know that you have, or I believe that all of you, or almost all of you certainly have testified frequently before Congress, so you know our procedures.

Without objection, your written statements are all made part of the record.

I would welcome a very brief summary from each of you on any point or points that you think it imperative to make in addition to your written statements, because I'd like to proceed directly to some questions based upon all the testimony you've heard today.

But with that, you are free to proceed as you deem best. And we'll begin with you, Dr. Gay.

STATEMENT OF DR. CHARLES F. GAY, DIRECTOR, NATIONAL RENEWABLE ENERGY LABORATORY

Dr. GAY. Thank you, Mr. Chairman.

I'll be very brief.

I wanted to comment on one of the remarks that were in Deputy Secretary Charles Curtis' testimony, in his written testimony, where he states that what observers of the laboratories actually are looking for is confidence that the Department is allocating taxpayer funds in the most cost-effective way to accomplish its missions.

And a lot of the thinking that is in my written testimony derives from that same style of thinking because it's a strong, simple statement that I think will resonate with the investment manager, which is Congress, and the actual investors, who are our taxpayers.

The basic thrust of the comments in my written testimony are that I agree that improvements in the DOE national lab system should be and can be addressed in a comprehensive and objective manner.

And that the appropriate sequence of how best to look at the role of the national laboratories can be stated in five easy pieces here.

The first one is that we agree on a clear statement of the mission of the laboratory system, and I want to emphasize system. A lot of what we've discussed here has been related specifically to perhaps unique geographic sites or individual centers.

The labs are a system that together work very well and which together can continue to improve the way that they operate in concordance with each other.

That the statements of these missions relate to the priority research tasks that are undertaken, especially directed to maintain a technology edge for U.S. industry's growth.

And that the aggregate resources that we make available to the labs and their missions come from the allocation of funding that is done over a meaningful time period, not just on an annual basis, but because of the nature of R&D, that time frame be looked at over a longer time horizon.

The second point is that as part of this process of looking at the system, we assess the core competencies that we have in hand today so that we can build around those capabilities and continue to maintain those capabilities while we develop the execution of the current missions and the definition of our future activities.

The third point I'd like to make is that I believe it would be an excellent idea to define and to assign specific missions to what I characterize as centers of excellence.

These centers of excellence don't necessarily have to be a specific laboratory site, but perhaps be focused on a specific site for purposes of accountability and that the laboratories work together to put forward the proposals for what the government needs to have in the long haul.

A lot of this also requires the elimination of inappropriate or unnecessary redundancy. What we are doing at the National Renewable Energy Lab, as my colleagues from the other labs are doing, is well underway to emulate, within our laboratories, the same cost cutting restructuring, re-engineering efforts that the Department of Energy has been pursuing.

We've estimated that from the total $235 million program that we pursue, we can save between 33 and 45 million dollars a year, and we will be finished with that process of making those changes in the next four months.

Fourthly, that it's appropriate to define and review the governance structure with an emphasis on how we can maintain those operating efficiency opportunities that are well underway now.

The Department and its field offices have been extremely supportive of allowing us to pioneer the adoption of best business practices in the way that we handle procurement in contracting.

I've only been at the lab for seven months. Prior to this, I've been in industry for the last 20 years. And a lot of the changes that are possible in the laboratories are the same kinds of processes and the same kinds of measures that have been followed by industry for well over the last ten years.

And the fifth point is that I believe that we should examine and define the laboratory management structure that best provides the most effective oversight and guidance to the labs without unnecessary constraints, and allows the labs to put forward proposals for what ought to be done that could be reviewed by a board or an oversight committee that Congress appoints, or that Congress may delegate to the Department in order to assure that the money is being properly targeted.

I believe that this Committee and its Subcommittees should consider how Congressional deliberations on restructuring DOE might best be integrated with the improvements and the processes that the DOE already has underway.

Thank you very much.

[The prepared statement of Dr. Gay follows:]

Testimony of Dr. Charles F. Gay

Director
National Renewable Energy Laboratory

Before the
U.S. House of Representatives
Committee on Science

Subcommittee on Basic Research
and
Subcommittee on Energy and Environment

Joint Hearing on

Restructuring the Federal Scientific Establishment:
Future Missions and Governance for
the U.S. Department of Energy (DOE) National Laboratories

Comments on H.R. 2142, H.R. 87, H.R. 1510 and H.R. 1993 Title II
and on Questions Posed in the Hearing Charter

September 7, 1995

Introduction — Improving a Key National Resource in Difficult Times

I fully support DOE's national laboratory realignment activities, which are aimed at making the laboratories more effective and efficient in meeting our national needs.

This Committee has before it several legislative proposals for reviewing and, as appropriate, restructuring the U.S. Department of Energy (DOE) national laboratory system. Some of these proposals parallel activities already under way or completed as a result of DOE-initiated realignment activities led by the Secretary of Energy. I fully support efforts launched and implemented by DOE to review current operations of the DOE laboratory system with the objective of better serving our nation. Based on my present position and my twenty years of industrial experience, my comments on the primary thrust of the Bills, as I understand them, are aimed at offering insights into how the DOE national laboratory system, which already contributes significantly to our national needs, might most effectively and efficiently be re-engineered to deliver even more.

The DOE laboratory system is a key resource for assuring sustainable energy supplies into the future.

The DOE laboratory system is a key national resource that serves a broad range of strategic research needs and is essential to the continued security, prosperity, and well-being of the nation. Under the leadership of DOE and its predecessor agencies, the laboratory system has served us well in developing weapons to keep the peace, in addressing the environmental challenges of nuclear weapons and nuclear power, in improving the efficiency of existing large-scale energy technologies, and in exploring the new energy technologies necessary to ensure a diverse, sustainable energy supply for the nation's future.

Budgetary constraints mandate that the DOE laboratory system be re-engineered to assure that high quality research is performed within available funds.

These are difficult and dynamic times, however, and it is appropriate that Congress ask, through its oversight role, how the DOE laboratory system might best be realigned and re-engineered to meet the challenges ahead. Such an effort could complement the work already performed under the leadership of the Secretary of Energy and can result in the implementation of significant improvements in the laboratory system. This must be done both to increase the nation's return on its investment and to ensure that high-priority research and development missions of the labs are accomplished within the funding available in these times of severe budget constraints.

A comprehensive strategic plan is needed to define laboratory missions and to allocate resources to accomplish these missions.

I believe that the necessary changes and improvements can be implemented within the basic framework that exists today. A comprehensive strategic plan detailing the current missions of the integrated DOE laboratory system and of the individual laboratories is essential for agreement on defining the work to be done and how responsibilities are to be divided. A methodical assessment of the core competencies of each individual laboratory can help to best decide the distribution of responsibility and resources for fulfilling our missions.

DOE has begun this process

Defining specific, distinct missions—and allocating resources based on the prioritization of the missions—will create an environment that promotes both increased accountability and maximum productivity. DOE has begun this process, and proposals before this Committee might contribute to the process proceeding in an objective and orderly fashion.

The DOE laboratories can be effectively staffed and operated within realistic financial constraints.

It is essential that we not lose sight of the laboratories' value nor of their leveraging role now and in the next century. The DOE national laboratory system is a key resource that can be operated within the financial constraints imposed by current fiscal reality while helping to meet the critical needs of the country for long-term energy, national security, and economic prosperity.

Comments on the Questions Posed in the Hearing Charter

1. What is the future role of the DOE national laboratories?

The DOE laboratories' focus has been on R&D beyond the scope or resources of industry and universities

The DOE national laboratory system serves a critically important and definitively distinct role in the nation's overall effort to advance science and technology. In general, the laboratories' focus has been on long-term, exploratory, and national security research and development tasks that are beyond the scope or resources of industry and universities.

There must be an appropriate division of responsibilities and complementary roles for the DOE laboratories, universities and industry.

Based on my experience, and at the risk of oversimplifying the technology development process and the interplay of its various contributors, one can craft a framework of distinct and complementary roles for government laboratories, universities, and industry in the nation's overall federally funded scientific and technical endeavors. To maximize the nation's return on its investment in science and technology, there must be a recognition of the appropriate division of responsibilities among the national laboratories, industrial research institutions, and research universities. I believe a reasonable emphasis and categorization of responsibilities—one which recognizes the ebb and flow of progress resulting in periodic activity overlap—would proceed along the following lines:

> Universities should address fundamental sciences and engineering and focus on educating skilled scientists and engineers;
>
> National laboratories should address mid- to long-term exploratory and developmental research tasks that promise to substantially promote the national interest, and on providing large multi-user research tools that are beyond the reach of private industry;
>
> Industrial research institutions should address applied research and development with the express aim of advancing new technologies to the marketplace.

NREL has extensive interaction and numerous partnerships with universities and industry.

At the National Renewable Energy Laboratory (NREL), we operate in this framework by entering into partnerships with universities and industry. We have a total of 380 such partners in 44 states. A large number of our industry contracts are cost shared and more than 77 percent of all industrial work is with small business. Our 36 cooperative research and development agreement partners average a cost-share contribution of 75%, which substantially leverages federal funding.

Federal investment is clearly suited to fundamental and long-term R&D that assures a safe and secure energy supply.

The basic research and the long-term research and development programs of the national labs are necessary to ensure that the nation continues to have a safe and secure energy supply, and therefore clearly deserving of federal investment. The DOE laboratory system is well positioned to conduct the mid- to long-term, high-risk, resource-intensive research and development that is needed to develop large-scale energy sources that are beyond the capabilities of individual businesses or do not provide a sufficient return on the investment horizon of these companies. The nation would be ill-served by a significant reduction in the DOE laboratory system that would impair our ability to undertake and complete programs aimed at development of such energy sources.

2. What should be the future missions of the DOE national laboratories?

DOE laboratories contribute to national security, energy supply continuity, environmental quality and industrial competitiveness.

a. At present the DOE laboratories are actively engaged in a wide spectrum of science and technology endeavors deemed to be in the national interest. These activities include nuclear and "star wars type" weaponry, environmental restoration and waste management, multi-user research tools for basic and applied sciences, and energy research and technology development.

DOE leadership seeks to synergistically combine research and other work in these diverse fields with the aim of contributing to national security, ensuring a more secure energy supply, and enhancing both environmental quality and industrial competitiveness. The activities of the DOE national laboratories support the critical federal role of anticipating and helping to meet the nation's longer term needs.

I believe government does and can continue to provide a foundation upon which America can build.

Although, my area of expertise is in the field of energy technology—specifically renewable energy technologies, I view federally funded energy research in the context of the overall role of government. The basic purpose of government is, I believe, to provide a foundation upon which America can build and sustain its industry, its jobs and its competitive edge in the global economy. Individual Americans build on this foundation and they excel based on education, merit, initiative and hard work. American businesses build on this foundation and they succeed based on innovation, investment, and prudent risk-taking.

Stable energy supply requires diverse energy sources.

A key cornerstone of America's foundation and its industrial strength is safe, reliable, low-cost energy. The continuing stability of America's energy supply requires a diverse portfolio of viable energy sources. The development and maintenance of this portfolio requires a balance between incremental, near-term improvements in existing energy sources and innovative, longer term exploration of new energy resources and technologies that minimize damage to the environment.

Federal funding of energy R&D is necessary to assure the progress in development of energy sources that industry is unable or unwilling to fund.

Continued federal funding of energy research is essential for ensuring the timely development of new and improved energy sources and for maintaining the ability of U.S. industry to compete effectively in today's global marketplace. American business alone has not been willing—possibly because of near term profit challenges—to fund the necessary long-term, high-risk investments.

I strongly support the Galvin and Yergin Task Force recommendations that a diversified portfolio of energy sources requires continued allocation of federal R&D funding.

I believe it is also prudent for the nation to have a balanced energy research program that both leverages and facilitates near-term improvements and promotes promising long-term innovations. I therefore strongly support the Galvin and Yergin Task Forces' recommendations that a diversified portfolio of national investment in conservation, energy efficiency, enhanced oil and gas recovery, and renewable energy be given highest priority in allocating federal energy-supply research funds.

Renewable energy R&D and industrial competitiveness require continued federal support.

Renewable energy technologies are important to America's long-term national security, economic competitiveness, and quality of life. Renewables offer a workable alternative to the geopolitical uncertainties of imported fuels, the environmental unknowns that threaten long-term use of America's fossil fuel supplies, and the financial and security questions that plague nuclear power. Competitiveness in and future development of renewable energy technologies require continuing federal support if the nation is to realize the ultimate benefits that can now be attained as a result of the substantial progress we have achieved to date.

The National Renewable Energy Laboratory (NREL) has responsibility for doing the research necessary to put renewable energy technologies to work for America. NREL's mission statement is clear:

> *Lead the nation toward a sustainable energy future by developing renewable energy technologies, improving energy efficiency, advancing related science and engineering, and facilitating commercialization.*

NREL's work is directed at renewable energy R&D and involves collaboration with universities and industry.

NREL's work is directed at accelerating the maturation of viable renewable energy technologies (wind energy, photovoltaics, biomass conversion, etc.) and energy efficiency technologies from the early stages of research and development to the point of commercialization. NREL works with its industry and university collaborators to do the research, development, and experimental production tasks necessary to advance renewable energy technologies to widespread use. As a technology moves closer to commercialization, industry assumes a proportionately greater responsibility for defining and funding its development. NREL only takes on projects that are related to its primary mission.

In accomplishing its mission, NREL also works with other national laboratories, the venture capital community and small business enterprises. Examples of these activities include:

To better accomplish our mission, NREL is looking beyond the horizon for new ways for the geographically dispersed national laboratories to work together to meet the needs of America. We have already taken the first steps to form strategic alliances with the renewable energy industrial community, our sister laboratories, the venture capital community and small business enterprises to better fulfill the spirit of our responsibility to American taxpayers. Examples of these activities include:

The First NREL Enterprise Growth Forum

> The First NREL Enterprise Growth Forum, held in Washington, D.C., in July, in which the investment community and small businesses were brought together. The result was a dialogue that had not previously existed and the genesis of a new role for successful laboratory facilitation of business relationships and access to new financial resources that will lead to job creation in the field of renewable energy and energy efficiency.

The national New Energy Incubator Network

The national New Energy Incubator Network for select urban and rural areas, for which NREL is developing programs to use the lab's facilities and proven expertise in renewable energy and energy efficiency technologies to ensure the survivability of small technology firms. This initiative differs from existing business incubators. Our approach is national in scope, it is focused on renewable energy and energy efficiency and it provides access to our broad range of capabilities all across the country. Companies in our highly focused incubator network will find it easier to access the information and expertise required for successful entry into the highly competitive global energy marketplace.

State and Local activities including the "New Mexico Initiative"

NREL has taken steps to address state and local government needs, while simultaneously connecting with local community efforts to assist small and mid-size firms working to bring new products and services to the national and international marketplaces. We are working in partnership with DOE's Office of Energy Efficiency and Renewable Energy and the National Association of State Energy Offices in this effort. One recent example is the "New Mexico Initiative," signed on August 23 of this year, in which NREL and Sandia National Laboratories participated in the formation of a public and private partnership aimed at saving taxpayers millions of dollars by conserving important energy and water resources, while creating jobs for the local community.

The "Sun-Lab" Initiative in partnership with Sandia National Laboratory

NREL and Sandia National Laboratories have recently created a new paradigm for cooperation with the formation of a unified "virtual" laboratory called Sun-Lab. This prototype initiative is built around the cost-effective employee empowerment approach being adopted by industry, best described as "self-directed" work teams. Employees from our two laboratories are responsible for defining a strategic operating plan, which needs approval by a "Board of Directors" composed of higher-level management at both laboratories and the DOE. The result has been streamlined management and administration, clear accountability, ease of collaboration with industry and greatly improved motivation and efficiency. We are presently evaluating the possibilities for expanding this initial success to a wider array of collaboratives. The synergies of cross-laboratory teamwork will mean less duplication of effort, new opportunities for enhancing U.S. competitiveness and a sum which is vastly greater than the individual parts.

A clearly defined mission is essential to efficiently and effectively operating each DOE national laboratory.

b. A clearly defined mission is essential to efficiently and effectively operating a competitive research laboratory. There was a time when economic circumstances were such that industry could afford to fund large, captive laboratories investigating a wide array of basic and applied sciences. The mandate at some of these industrial facilities seemed no less broad than to perform interesting science that was arguably, though perhaps distantly, related to the company's present or future business interests.

Today, domestic and international competition requires a closer focus on the value of industrial research and development to the immediate specific needs and advantage of the funding company or group of companies. This focus on added value has caused American business to better define the mission of its industrial laboratories in order to ensure a competitive return on its research investment.

Clearly defined missions are equally essential to efficiently and effectively operating the DOE national laboratory system. The array of activities presently under way at the laboratories is in part a reflection of the many tasks the labs were assigned during the difficult Cold War period. Under today's changed circumstances, each laboratory should develop and follow a succinct statement of its specific mission within the evolving mission of the Department of Energy.

DOE's responsibility is to assure that the missions of the individual national laboratories are complementary and workable in attaining a stable and secure energy supply.

DOE, with its overall stewardship and accountability responsibilities, must ensure that the missions of the individual national laboratories are complementary and workable, and that these integrated missions address the nation's interests including its need for a stable, secure, diverse, cost-effective energy supply. A limited degree of complementary overlap in individual laboratory missions may be advantageous in order to ensure adequate resources and a multiplicity of innovative approaches to critical tasks. However, excessive redundancy and excess capacity—whatever the underlying reason—is wasteful and should not be supported.

I strongly advocate concentrating resources at individual centers of excellence, such as NREL which was established by Congress to meet our evolving energy concerns.

I strongly advocate concentrating resources at individual centers of excellence. Given a prudent diversity in government-funded research in energy technologies, it is imperative that sufficient funds are concentrated at individual laboratories to operate technology-specific centers of excellence. NREL was established (initially as the Solar Energy Research Institute) by Congress to meet the energy concerns of the 1970's and is now America's center of excellence in renewable energy and energy efficiency technologies. As such, NREL depends on receipt of sufficient resources to continue to fulfill its mission and to preserve the critical mass that it has created and is continuing to evolve in the development of alternative energy. The accomplishments have been significant and quantifiable. For example:

> The cost of wind-generated electricity has dropped from 30 cents per kilowatt-hour in 1980 to about 5 cents per kilowatt-hour today.
>
> The cost of ethanol from biomass has been cut threefold in the same period to $1.20 per gallon.
>
> The decline in the cost of photovoltaic solar cell electric power has been dramatic - from $15 per kilowatt hour in 1975 to less than 30 cents per kilowatt-hour today.

The roadmap exists to continue this progression of success. As another indicator of quality and performance, over the recent five-year period NREL has been awarded nearly 2.5 Research and Development Magazine R&D 100 awards per 100 technical staff employees. In addition, a customer survey performed this year revealed that nearly two-thirds of our industrial partners reported that NREL services or research products resulted in increased sales or substantial cost savings for their businesses. Finally, during its brief history, NREL has spawned 27 start-up companies. Many of these companies, like our industrial business partners are well positioned to capture export sales. Global energy demand, arising mainly from developing economies, is expected to grow by about 40 percent in the next 15 years.

3 & 4. Is there a need for size and personnel limits for the DOE national laboratories?

Should there be consolidation or closure of the labs?

Although laboratory staffing can be reduced, critical mass and core competencies must be retained in the highest priority research areas.

Given the nation's limited financial resources, it is appropriate that the DOE laboratory system is asked to contribute by re-engineering operations. It is possible to reduce staffing at DOE laboratories without materially harming the priority elements of mission performance, provided that a critical mass is retained in the highest priority research areas, and provided the governance of the laboratories is also reduced to a level consistent with the need to assure sound financial stewardship of the federal investment.

An objective assessment of laboratory core competencies is critical in rationally defining laboratory missions.

The first steps in considering the future purpose and structure of the DOE laboratory system are to agree on laboratory missions and priority technology tasks and to objectively assess laboratory-specific core competencies. Agreement on mission and priority technology tasks is essential in successfully concentrating available resources on the leveraging of technology tasks. An objective assessment of core competencies is critical in laying the foundation for an efficient and rational definition of lab missions. Once technology priorities and core competencies are delineated, one can objectively allocate responsibilities and resources. The Galvin and Yergin Task Forces, which were established at the request of the

Secretary of Energy, have provided useful guidance on energy research priorities.

Under DOE leadership, NREL is implementing innovative initiatives within its NREL 2000 project to increase operational efficiency and facilitate better business practices.

Under DOE's leadership, the laboratories are already working to improve efficiency and effectiveness. NREL, for example, is implementing innovative initiatives to increase its operational efficiency and to better facilitate business enterprises in exploiting the technologies that are being developed. These improvements represent NREL's proactive response to the DOE-led initiatives to meet the nation's science needs within emerging federal funding constraints. We have named our re-engineering project *NREL 2000*. Our general strategy for improving the lab's internal effectiveness is to streamline and simplify our organization and its operations by incorporating a set of tools which parallel those found in modern business. A tabular arrangement of the results expected for the Fiscal Year beginning next month are listed according to the tracking categories requested by DOE.

Estimated Savings for the National Renewable Energy Laboratory Based on NREL 2000 Re-engineering

NREL 2000 re-engineering will result in total estimated savings of $14-20 million.

Category	Approach	FY96 Estimated Savings, $ million
Projected savings resulting from decreased DOE oversight	Utilize prudent business oversight practices, instead of detailed compliance measures.	$2-3
Projected savings resulting from using best commercial business procurement practices	Replace cumbersome federal compliance practices with best business practices in procurement and subcontracting	$5-7
Savings that result from intra-laboratory restructuring	Incorporate best business organization and work planning practices to more closely align subcontract performance and operational efficiency to NREL's R&D objectives	$7-10
Total Estimated Savings		**$14-20**

One of the additional metrics that NREL will use to measure its progress in maximizing the allocation of resources to research and development is the ratio of science and technology personnel to support staff. Our current index is about 1.9 : 1. We will endeavor to maintain or increase this ratio, while FY 1996 budget reductions require significant staffing reductions beyond the laboratory-initiated improvements already underway, since March of this year.

Congress and the Administration should focus on key resource allocation and oversight and not specific details of laboratory size and personnel limits.

Decisions regarding what technology research tasks should receive priority and on how much money can be spent in aggregate on securing the nation's energy supply will be more fruitful than unstructured discussions of size and personnel limits for the DOE laboratory system. Setting energy research priorities and total funding levels is in the national interest. Debating specific details of individual laboratory operations and staffing numbers obscures the key resource allocation and oversight issues that should be the first priorities of Congress and the Administration.

Individual laboratories should be allowed to exercise best technical judgment and to use best business management practices in meeting mission objectives within budget.

Within a framework of budgetary guidelines and research priorities, DOE can restructure the laboratory system to maximize its cost-effectiveness, operational efficiency and science output. Within the defined organizational and mission structures, individual laboratories should then be given the flexibility to exercise their best technical judgement and to use best business management practices to meet their mission objectives within budget. This flexibility should include responsibility for determining the optimal allocation of resources to individual research areas.

I believe that an independent, nonpartisan commission can effectively assist in the restructuring of the DOE laboratory system.

I believe that the task of restructuring the DOE laboratory system may benefit from the creation of an independent, nonpartisan commission to recommend an integrated framework. The wide-ranging and long-lasting impacts of significant changes in the nation's energy research labs make it critical that the process not be subject to political considerations or pressures.

5. What governance structure might best suit management of the DOE national labs?

DOE, consistent with its oversight and accountability roles, should delegate maximum authority and responsibility to laboratory management.

The DOE laboratory system governance structure is less important than operating principles and missions. One of the central operating principles for DOE should be to delegate maximum authority and responsibility to individual laboratory management, consistent with legitimate matters of national security, prudent fiscal oversight and accountability.

The existing DOE laboratory management structure is replete with micro-management

As the Galvin report indicates, and the Secretary of Energy has agreed, the existing laboratory management structure is replete with micro-management and multi-layered checks, balances, and secrecy necessary and suitable only for the most sophisticated weapons work. The Secretary of Energy is already taking action to implement the Galvin recommendations and we expect to see significant improvements as a result of her actions.

Privatized facilities will not attract sufficient funding to effectively fulfill national missions.

It is important to emphasize that federal funding will be required by the DOE laboratory system. As stated earlier, federally funded laboratories focus on technology tasks of national importance that are beyond or outside the capabilities of universities and industry. Therefore, it is not reasonable to expect that privatized facilities focusing on issues of national concern will be able to attract sufficient private funding to effectively fulfill their national missions.

6. Summary of comments on the questions in the hearing charter

Improving the DOE national laboratory system involves the following steps:

Improvements to the DOE national laboratory system should be addressed in a comprehensive and objective manner outside of the annual appropriation process and the ongoing discussions of the role and structure of the Department of Energy. The appropriate sequence of steps in determining how to best do this is:

Establish clear missions, priority research tasks and funding

1. Agree on clear statements of the missions of the DOE laboratory system, of the priority research tasks to be undertaken, and on the aggregate resources available to fund these activities during a meaningful time period.

Assess core competencies

2. Assess the core competencies of the individual laboratories.

Assign specific missions

3. Define and assign specific missions to the individual laboratories. Eliminate inappropriate or unnecessary redundancy and excess capacity.

Review and redefine governance structure

4. Define and review governance structure with an emphasis on operations efficiency and delegated responsibility.

Define the best DOE oversight and laboratory management structure

5. Examine and define the laboratory management structure that best provides the most effective oversight and guidance to the labs without unnecessary management constraints and costs.

Congressional deliberations on restructuring the national laboratory system should be integrated with initiatives already undertaken by DOE

The Secretary of Energy has numerous initiatives under way to address these issues. I believe that this Committee and its Subcommittees should consider how Congressional deliberations on restructuring the DOE laboratory system might best be integrated with the improvement initiatives already under way at DOE.

Comments on the Legislative Proposals

<u>H.R. 2142</u> (Schiff and others), "Department of Energy Laboratory Missions Act"

NREL agrees with the basic thrust of H.R. 2142

NREL is in agreement with the basic thrust of H.R. 2142, namely, that DOE laboratories should have well-defined missions and that the missions of the labs should be organized so as to fulfill the needs of the nation and to avoid unnecessary duplication. This bill provides a good starting point for better defining laboratory missions.

H.R. 2142 should also emphasize DOE's role in securing our nation's energy sources and supplies

As drafted, HR 2142 appears to emphasize only two of DOE's important roles, namely its role in design, development, production, and maintenance of nuclear weapons and its role in nonproliferation of nuclear weapons. I recommend that the bill also emphasize DOE's multifaceted role in securing our nation's present and future energy sources and supplies.

My specific recommendations are:

- On page 1, change "establishing missions" to "clarifying missions" in the preamble to better reflect the key issues, namely that:

  1. some laboratories have specific and well-defined missions,
  2. other laboratories may not have current, well-defined missions; and
  3. better definition and coordination of laboratory missions is needed to eliminate wasteful duplication and inefficiency.

- On page 3, lines 1 and 2 [101 (1)], change "scientific and technological" to "scientific, technological, economic, and environmental" to better capture the broad value to the nation of the research programs in the labs.

- On page 3, line 16 [101 (4)], change "achievement of national technology goals" to "technological foundation upon which America's public and private interests can build" to better embody the role of government in providing a firm foundation for individual and collective enterprise, rather than mandating technology specifics.

- On page 5, line 19 [102 (1)], acknowledge the importance of stable energy supplies in avoiding international conflict by adding a new subpart (1) (D) to Section 102 as follows:

> "(D) To reduce the threat of armed conflict and economic disruption, by assuring stable, domestic energy supplies."

- On page 5, lines 21 and 22 [102 (2)], delete "generic." The use of "generic" might be misconstrued to conflict with the use of cooperative research and development agreements to transfer specific commercially promising technologies to American industry.

- On page 6, line 24 [102], delete "with an emphasis on long-term, high-risk research" in order to not inappropriately and inaccurately limit the scope of the contributions of the laboratories. Long-term, high-risk research is in many cases a candidate for federal investments in technology development; however, as drafted, the scope of activities would be unworkably and inappropriately narrow.

H.R.2142 should also address government funding for:

- ***Basic science and engineering research***
- ***Long-term efforts to develop new energy sources***

The emphasis on long-term, high-risk research might be modified to include the following areas for which, we believe, government-funded research is both necessary and appropriate:

1. Fundamental research

Basic science and engineering research in materials, processes, and structures.

2. Long-term research and development

Unlike private business which must increasingly focus on near-term return, government is charged with the well-being of both its present and future citizens and institutions. Hence, government is able to consider and must support the longer term planning horizons necessary to develop significant new energy sources.

R&D activities requiring major investments

3. Activities requiring major investment

Some research and development activities require major investments in complex equipment and highly skilled workers beyond the reach of any corporation given the risk-adjusted expense and benefits.

Fundamental and high-risk research that is critical, but is underfunded by industry

4. Activities involving national interests but no near-term individual competitive advantage

Fundamental and high-risk research that is critical for collective industrial progress but that does not provide a clear basis for individual competitive advantage and is underfunded by industry in today's competitive business environment.

A well-reasoned and comprehensive balance of research endeavors in these four arenas is, I believe, clearly appropriate. Restriction to any one arena or sub-arena risks the nation being left with no qualified entity to fulfill these tasks.

- On page 7, at line 24, subparts (A) & (B), underscore the importance of DOE proactively implementing the guidance of the Galvin Task Force to focus on high priorities and to increase Departmental operational efficiency by rounding out the considerations that the Secretary shall consider in developing criteria for setting lab missions. Insert two new subparts between existing subparts A and B as follows:

> "the importance of diversified investment in a balanced energy research program that includes leveraging near-term improvements and promising long-term innovations that minimize harmful environmental effects. These include conservation, energy efficiency, enhanced oil and gas recovery, and renewable energy as high-priority research areas;
>
> the value of focusing specific missions at established Centers of Excellence;

H.R. 87 (Bartlett and others), "Department of Energy Laboratory Facilities Act"
H.R. 1993 (Tiahrt and others), Title II, "Department of Energy Abolishment Act"

Resources should be focused on high priority tasks.

Although I do not believe that our nation has a surplus of national laboratories, I am of the opinion that any unnecessary or unproductive redundancies that may exist should be eliminated and that our nation's fiscal constraints require that available resources be focused on achieving high priority tasks.

In general, I support the formation of an independent commission to make recommendations on reconfiguring and streamlining the DOE laboratory system.

In general, I support the formation of an independent commission to review and make recommendations on how the DOE laboratory system could best be reconfigured and streamlined. A commission, as provided by these bills, offers a mechanism for objectively preparing recommendations based on mission priorities and operational efficiency, while remaining essentially independent of the strong political forces that can surface in the development of such recommendations.

Both bills, as presently drafted, are too narrowly focused. They should seek to facilitate the clear definition of laboratory missions; evaluate prioritization of laboratory work; assess whether current missions are being effectively accomplished; identify unnecessary overlap and application; ascertain whether any laboratories should be consolidated, reduced in size or scope, reconfigured or closed; and determine appropriate staffing levels for individual laboratories.

However, I believe that both bills, as presently drafted, are too narrowly focused on the reconfiguration, closure, or privatization of DOE national laboratories, rather than on undertaking a comprehensive review of these laboratories and their future missions and roles. Therefore, I believe that these bills should be merged to produce a single omnibus bill, that would incorporate the following purposes to assure that the proposed National Laboratory Commission would have sufficient authority to develop comprehensive recommendations on the future missions and roles of the national laboratories:

- Review, validate and make recommendations on missions for the national laboratories

- Review and evaluate DOE's process for prioritizing and assigning research work to the various laboratories

- Determine whether presently assigned missions are being accomplished in an effective manner

- Identify unnecessary overlap and duplication among DOE laboratories and between DOE national laboratories and other government, or private, laboratories

- Ascertain whether any national laboratories should be consolidated, reduced in size and scope, reconfigured, privatized, or closed

- Determine appropriate minimum staffing levels for individual laboratories and a timetable for reaching these levels.

H.R. 2142's core mission provisions could provide appropriate guidance to a commission.

Furthermore, I believe that the core mission provisions contained in H.R. 2142, if modified as discussed above, would provide appropriate Congressional guidance to a Laboratory Review Commission in carrying out the purposes outlined above.

Such a commission should review and evaluate all pertinent recent studies

Finally, I believe that such a Commission should review and evaluate all pertinent recent studies concerning the DOE laboratories, including the Galvin and Yergin reports, the Secretary of Energy's Strategic Realignment Initiative and the General Accounting Office report.

The definition of missions for the DOE laboratory system and for each individual laboratory is essential

The definition and implementation of specific, distinct missions for the DOE laboratory system and for each individual laboratory is essential in objectively prioritizing and allocating resources. To underscore this point, I recommend that the end of H.R. 87, Section 3, Part (a) (1) on page 8, line 7 be changed to read,

> "...under this paragraph. In developing the criteria, the Secretary shall develop and apply a clear framework of specific missions and priority technology development tasks for the DOE laboratory system and for individual laboratories. This mission framework shall be combined with an objective assessment of existing core competencies and resources as the primary basis for defining the criteria to be used for making recommendations on closure or reconfiguration of departmental laboratories.

> In developing the criteria, the Secretary shall also consider..."

Similarly, I recommend that H.R. 1993, Title II, Section 202, item (a)(4) on page 17, Line 21 be changed to read,

> "(4) give its highest priority to developing and applying a clear framework of specific missions and priority energy technology development tasks for the DOE laboratory system and for individual laboratories; for using this mission framework combined with an objective assessment of existing core competencies and resources as the primary basis for defining the criteria to be used for making recommendations on closure or reconfiguration of departmental laboratories; and for ensuring that the activities of each such laboratory are focused on its mission or missions; "

The DOE national laboratories have yielded—and will continue to yield—technology advances that industry can commercialize.

The national laboratories have yielded—and will continue to yield—technology advances that can be commercialized by U.S. industry to the benefit of the nation. Therefore, I recommend that a new subpart (G) be added to H.R. 87, Section 3, Part (a) (1) on page 9, line 3 as follows:

> "(G) the potential for fostering private-sector business growth."

with suitable grammatical and punctuation changes in subparts (E) and (F).

Similarly, in H.R. 1993, Title II, Section 202 I recommend adding a new subpart (a)(11) on page 18 as follows:

> "(11) consider the potential for fostering private-sector business growth; and"

with suitable changes in present subparts (10) and (11).

H.R. 1510 (Roemer and others), "Department of Energy Laboratories Efficiency Improvement Act"

NREL supports elimination of self-regulation at DOE laboratories

NREL fully supports elimination of self-regulation at DOE laboratories. Given adequate attention to information and materials security concerns, the efficiency benefits of eliminating self-regulation should not be limited to the non-defense laboratories.

Mandated reductions in laboratory staff will not increase operational efficiency.

Mandated reductions in laboratory staff are not, in my experience, an efficient way to increase the operational efficiency of the DOE laboratory system. HR 1510 as drafted does not incorporate any consideration of mission and goals. The current draft equates "efficiency improvement" with "personnel reductions" in a "downsizing for downsizing's sake" manner which has proven counterproductive in the private sector. Laboratory staffing levels should remain a dependent function of the critical drivers in laboratory management, namely: research priorities, mission, core competencies, available funding, and personnel productivity.

Careful attention should be given to maintaining America's science infrastructure, and not relying on the availability of foreign facilities.

Subpart (b) (2) of Section 3 on page 3, line 3 concerning closing of U.S. facilities that duplicate facilities in foreign countries should be reconsidered. Careful attention should be given to the importance of maintaining America's science infrastructure, including facilities as well as to the geopolitical reality that foreign governments may not always provide U.S. scientists with "access" to their facilities.

The nation's needs are better served by concentrating resources at individual centers of excellence.

Consideration should also be given to how subpart (b) (3) of Section 3 on page 3, line 10 might be modified to clarify that the objective is to realize the advantages of concentrating resources in well-targeted centers of excellence. As drafted, the subpart can be misinterpreted to mean that "bigger is better" in concentrating activities at a few large facilities. In my opinion, the nation's needs in energy research and development can also be effectively accomplished by concentrating resources at smaller, focused, individual centers of excellence.

Mr. SCHIFF. Thank you, Dr. Gay.
Dr. Hecker?

STATEMENT OF DR. SIEGFRIED S. HECKER, DIRECTOR, LOS ALAMOS NATIONAL LABORATORY

Dr. HECKER. Thank you, Mr. Chairman.

I won't try to summarize my statement.

I simply want to make a couple of points that were brought up during the course of the day.

The first one is, this morning there were several references to the end of the Cold War, the need for reconfiguration, and the unacceptability of the status quo, leaving the impression that somehow we, the labs, are out there not having realized yet that the Cold War has really ended.

And I just want to make sure that I go on record for indicating that is indeed not the case. And in fact, I have daily reminders of that.

Last week, I just had a large group of people come back from the Russian Los Alamos, and that is where we're over there working hand-in-hand with them on scientific experiments on working with them how to control their nuclear materials. That's certainly very different than what we were doing five years ago.

In fact, the compelling mission for our laboratory has changed significantly in that five year time frame. Instead of developing new nuclear weapons, what I'd like to say that we do today is to help reduce the global nuclear danger and that is not only take care of stockpile stewardship, as was discussed this morning, but also worry about how to remanufacture weapons, what to do about non-proliferation, counter-proliferation.

How do we solve the nation's and the world's plutonium problem, that is, the management of plutonium?

And how do we handle the legacy of the nuclear waste and clean up associated with 50 years of production?

That, to me, is a very compelling central mission for these laboratories.

And as Mr. Galvin said, that defense mission is going to be here for many decades to come.

And what we are out to do is to help save the Department and the government a significant amount of money over all the defense programs and in the environmental cleanup expenditures and not just in how much you can reduce the budgets at the laboratory. I think that's the way that we'll need to be judged.

So even though that's our compelling mission though, what I'd like to say is don't constrain us too tightly because the way these laboratories work, for instance, in our case, for our mission, we have to understand plutonium. To understand plutonium, you have to understand what the electrons do, not only the nuclear.

To understand the electrons, you have to understand magnetism and superconductivity.

Out of that then comes the sort of breakthrough that we announced earlier this year in superconductivity technology.

To do weapons work, we have to know how to compute.

To do computing, then you have to worry about hardware and software.

Out of that come the sort of inventions that you saw next door in one of our fiber optic links as to how to hook computers together for the next generation of supercomputing.

So I don't think there's much of an issue of these laboratories having a core central compelling mission. It's there, it's changed significantly. I think what we have to do is do a better job to make sure that message gets across.

The second message is the one on this whole issue of cost effectiveness and much as Dr. Gay has just pointed out, all of us are working on that issue to be able to ascertain and to be able to show you that we are using the taxpayers' money wisely.

And, again, let me tell you, our world has changed. I'm in the process right now of taking a thousand people out of the ten thousand people labor force at Los Alamos, to help reduce the overhead and administrative burden at Los Alamos in the spirit of gaining greater productivity.

And we're not doing that over the next five years or the next ten years, we're doing it over the next couple of months time frame.

So those are the main messages that I wanted to comment on.

We have a compelling mission, we are worried about getting the taxpayer the most for their money and their investment.

Thank you.

[The prepared statement of Dr. Hecker follows:]

TESTIMONY OF SIEGFRIED S. HECKER

DIRECTOR
LOS ALAMOS NATIONAL LABORATORY

HEARING
of the

SUBCOMMITTEES ON BASIC RESEARCH AND
ENERGY AND ENVIRONMENT

COMMITTEE ON SCIENCE
UNITED STATES HOUSE OF REPRESENTATIVES

SEPTEMBER 7, 1995

Introductory Remarks

Thank you for the opportunity to provide a statement for the record of this hearing on Future Missions and Governance for the Department of Energy National Laboratories.

My comments are organized around the five questions asked by the subcommittee chairmen. In addition I have specifically addressed the legislation in H.R. 2142, H.R. 1993, H.R. 87 and H.R. 1510.

There are three principal points that I would like to stress today.

1. I strongly support the importance of defining missions for the DOE laboratories. At Los Alamos, our core mission for the post-Cold War era is *reducing the global nuclear danger*, which includes stewardship of the enduring nuclear weapons stockpile, stemming the spread of nuclear weapons, dealing with the global nuclear materials problem, and finding solutions to the nuclear waste and environmental legacies of 50 years of weapons production. This compelling mission, combined with a continued focus on fundamental science and selective contributions in civilian R&D will allow us to make salient contributions to important national problems.

2. In addition to a compelling mission, it is imperative that the laboratories demonstrate cost effective operations to the American taxpayers. At Los Alamos, we are implementing a workforce productivity project that will allow us to make the kind of productivity improvements made in the private sector and called for in the Galvin Task Force Report. To achieve dramatic reductions in our overhead functions we will need strong support from the Department of Energy to change the current oversight and administrative burden. I am encouraged by the Department's response to date.

3. I do not favor establishing additional commissions or conducting more studies of the laboratories, nor do I endorse arbitrary size reductions. I suggest we follow the path outlined in H.R. 2142 to define the missions of the laboratories and then size them accordingly. In addition, I believe that abolishing the parent agency, the Department of Energy, is not a good idea. For over 50 years, the Department and its predecessor agencies have demonstrated an ability to run some of the finest scientific laboratories in the world capable of solving important national problems. Moving the laboratories to other agencies without defining what their missions are and ensuring that their new home have an equally strong track record would jeopardize the ability of the laboratories to contribute to solving important national problems in the future.

1. What is the future role of the DOE National Laboratories in the context of the overall Federally-funded scientific establishment?

Over the past 50 years the DOE laboratories have helped to end World War II, preserve global peace through nuclear deterrence, and develop and apply scientific knowledge to important national civilian problems. After the end of the Cold War and as a result of major international changes brought about by the emergence of a global economy, technology has become the most important driver for economic growth -- which, in turn, affects our military security and our social infrastructure. I believe that three crucial research functions continue to be best performed by the DOE laboratories -- nuclear weapons defined broadly, energy and environment, and a sharing of the fundamental research mission with other federal agencies.

As we look to the future, not only is technology the key driver, but government must remain a major sponsor for the development of science and technology and for the diffusion of technology. In retrospect, defining the proper government role for science and technology during the Cold War was easy because a formidable adversary provided the rationale by having defense requirements drive technological needs. Today, there is little consensus on what the proper government role should be -- yet that role will be crucial to the future of our nation.

The nation's current technology portfolio is rich, thanks to the supportive role of the Federal government for 50 years and the international market dominance that U.S. industry enjoyed for several decades following World War II, which allowed the nation to develop some of finest public and private research institutions in the world. Unfortunately, current Federal and industrial trends threaten the long-term strength of that portfolio. The changing nature of defense requirements and the substantial cuts in the defense budget are dramatically decreasing the benefits of Federal defense R&D investments to civilian and commercial endeavors. At the same time, global economic pressures encourage industry to focus its R&D much more closely on product realization and on closely integrating research with manufacturing.

While some U.S. firms have reaped the benefits of such strategies and many have dramatically improved their market position in a cut-throat international environment, the implications for the long-term economic health of these companies and the nation remain unclear. As one indication, corporate investment in long-term research aimed at creating new knowledge and potential technological breakthroughs is in serious decline. Industrial research giants have actually reduced their overall R&D budgets -- by 33 percent since 1992 in IBM's case. Others such as AT&T Bell Laboratories are reducing research in the physical sciences while focusing more on information science. In addition, universities and federal laboratories are being admonished to be more relevant. I am concerned that the current trends will cause a severe technology pipeline problem resulting in a shortage of new ideas and technological breakthroughs in the future.

I believe the international competitive pressures on U.S. industry will not allow individual firms to emphasize longer-term, high-risk research in the foreseeable future. Currently, industry funds approximately 60 percent of the total R&D in the United States, while performing 72 percent of the R&D and employing just over 80 percent of all R&D scientists and engineers (from NSF Report 95-304, *National Patterns of R&D Resources: 1994*). Given the short-term focus of industry today, it is crucial that the government continues to support mid-to-long-term research that provides the necessary scientific underpinnings for civilian and commercial endeavors. Universities will continue to emphasize more fundamental research which fits well with their educational mission. In areas such as biotechnology and computers, such research is readily adapted to the marketplace, allowing universities to make significant economic contributions through their research and their personnel. But, government support of only basic research will not put the nation in a competitive position to apply that knowledge to solve key civilian problems and to provide the technology base for internationally competitive industries in the future.

The Federal laboratories fill an important niche in the nation's scientific enterprise. Their R&D fulfills the immediate needs of the Federal government and contributes to the national scientific and technological infrastructure. They also provide a vital part of the scientific infrastructure for academic and industrial R&D, for example through collaborative agreements and access to user research facilities. Their research applications extend beyond those of universities because the Federal government is itself a customer for a broad range of technologies. Yet, the laboratories do not produce goods to compete with industry. Approximately $25 billion, about one-third of all Federal R&D, is spent at the 700-plus Federal laboratories. Most of these laboratories perform very applied functions for their Federal agencies. Aside from the rather specialized laboratories of the National Institutes of Health, only approximately 25 of those remaining are major research laboratories, with many of these being within the Department of Energy.

Over the past 50 years, the DOE laboratories have maintained a focus on science while performing mission-driven research for the Department of Energy and its predecessors. The total R&D budget of the DOE laboratories is approximately $6 billion. These laboratories have excelled in research on problems that require a strong science base, a multidisciplinary approach, team work, special facilities, and, often, problems that are large in scale. Some of the laboratories also bring a vertical integration of research capabilities to such problems and all bring an attitude of public service. The future of the laboratories must be closely linked to compelling national missions. The laboratories must also become part of a strong research network with universities and industry to help solve pressing national or international problems and to keep the United States competitive in the international marketplace.

2. What should be the future missions of the DOE National Laboratories?

I applaud the focus on laboratory missions in H.R. 2142. Without compelling missions addressing identifiable national needs, the laboratories will atrophy. Without a focus on science, the laboratories will lose their flexibility and resilience to respond to changing national priorities. In spite of the end of the Cold War, national security missions remain paramount. First, defense is clearly within the purview of the Federal government and second, technological leadership is of the utmost importance. However, the reduction in international military tensions should allow the Federal government to tackle many of the key civilian problems that are not addressed well by the private sector alone. H.R. 2142 recognizes the need for the DOE laboratories to contribute in such areas as energy supply, environmental science and technology, and fundamental science.

I support these mission areas and I would like to add that it is often the interplay among technical areas that is critical for progress. More specifically, I see the principal civilian mission area for the DOE laboratories to be the integration of energy concerns and environmental issues, which cannot be isolated from the economic impacts. Therefore, successful conduct of this mission requires a close collaboration between the laboratories and industry. A strong focus on fundamental research is required to ensure the best technology is applied to the government missions. In addition, the DOE laboratories have historically provided the next generation of large, complex user research facilities for the nation's scientific community in areas such as particle and nuclear physics, materials research, biosciences and chemistry.

Mission assignment for the individual laboratories should reflect their scientific and technical core competencies as well as the ability of the laboratory to satisfy specific customer requirements. I would like to caution that the missions of the laboratories not be too narrowly constrained because breakthroughs are often made at the intersection of scientific areas or through the application of a scientific approach from one mission area to the problems of another mission area. In addition, leveraging the scientific capabilities to several missions (serving several customers) can be a very cost effective way of fulfilling the government's needs and retaining core competencies at the laboratories. For example, complex computer simulation and modeling analyses developed at Los Alamos for Department of Defense military force deployment have allowed us to introduce the revolutionary approach of microsimulation to transportation problems in a very timely and cost-effective manner for the Department of Transportation. Similarly, the interdisciplinary science capabilities developed for defense missions, especially in computational science and lasers, at Los Alamos and Livermore allowed these laboratories to be major proponents and contributors in the Human Genome Project.

To underscore this point, let me briefly describe how we view our mission at Los Alamos (a longer description is provided in the appendix). Over the past 52 years our compelling mission evolved from developing the first atomic bomb during the Manhattan Project to providing nuclear weapons technology for deterrence during the Cold War. We accomplished both successfully. Today, the Cold War cycle of nuclear weapons development and deployment has ended and our central mission must reflect the incredible global events of the past six years.

Our vision of the laboratory's role for the next decade or two is embodied in our mission theme of *reducing the global nuclear danger*. This mission includes stewardship of the nation's enduring nuclear stockpile with full responsibility for the safety, security and reliability of the weapons without underground nuclear testing; integrating R&D with enhanced surveillance and the remanufacturing of weapons as defined by national requirements; keeping nuclear weapons out of the wrong hands or countering them if they do fall into such hands; and dealing effectively with the legacy of 50 years of nuclear weapons production -- which includes the awesome problem of stabilizing, securing, storing and disposing of many hundreds of tons of weapons-usable nuclear materials, disposing of nuclear waste and cleaning up the environmental legacy.

This mission is every bit as challenging as anything we have done in the past couple of decades. The three DOE defense laboratories are the principal, and in some cases the only, institutions with the capability and the charter to tackle these problems. To perform this mission as effectively as possible, we must continue to strengthen our scientific foundations and core technical competencies. This will require a close relationship with universities to stay close to the best science and it will require close collaboration with industry to integrate research and new manufacturing technology. In turn, the capabilities developed for this mission will allow us to stay at the forefront of many areas of science which we can apply to some of the complex civilian problems facing the nation. Cooperative R&D partnerships with industry have proven to be an especially effective mechanism for supporting our government mission, while concurrently stretching the time and risk horizon of industry's R&D programs.

The laboratory's mission then is on one hand tightly focused on the theme of reducing the nuclear danger, while on the other hand sufficiently flexible to allow us to combine with the best of universities and industry to contribute in civilian areas while supporting our defense mission. I believe that this multiprogram nature of the laboratory is key to serving the nation as well in the next 50 years as we have over the past 50.

3. Is there a need for size and personnel limits for the DOE National Laboratories?

Size must follow function. It is critical that the mission question be addressed expeditiously by the Department of Energy for all of its laboratories to the satisfaction of Congress. Only then, can the right size of the laboratory complex be determined, from which will follow the right size for the individual laboratories. I believe that Congress should not decide on the size of the laboratories. Congress will naturally be involved in the mission issue through the bills that are before this committee now and through the annual budget process.

For example, in the nuclear weapons and environmental programs areas, with clear requirements from the Administration and the Congress, the Department of Energy is in the best position to decide how to get the work done. In the past few years it has become quite clear that the DOE must shift its nuclear weapons program from one that was capacity driven to one that is capability driven. Without the constant cycle of new weapons development and deployment and without underground nuclear testing, the laboratories will have to take a more science-based approach to nuclear weapons stewardship, develop more scientific approaches to weapons surveillance and become stewards of many of the manufacturing technologies. Therefore, the role of the three DOE defense laboratories will actually increase in the next few years in spite of a much smaller DOE defense programs budget compared to five years ago.

Having said all of this, let me add that the laboratories must decrease the size of their overhead functions. The Galvin Task Force challenged the DOE and the laboratories to dramatically change the oversight and governance of the laboratories to allow them to achieve the level of productivity increases achieved in private industry resulting from modern quality management approaches.

We at Los Alamos are rising to that challenge with our Workforce Productivity Project aimed at increasing the scientific and technical productivity of the laboratory. We recognize that we must be accountable to the American taxpayer by providing cost-effective R&D. We have targeted a decrease of approximately $60 million in our overhead functions for this coming year, with additional $30 million scheduled for fiscal year 1997. We have learned from the experience of many private firms that we must not only take out overhead functions, but also people. Therefore, we are in the process of taking close to 1000 people out of our workforce in the next couple of months. Most of these will come out of the overhead or support functions at the laboratory. Let me emphasize my earlier comment that size must follow function. This effort is not simply a downsizing. It is an initiative to make us more productive. We will increase the ratio of people doing technical work compared to the people it takes to support that work. We are on track to increase that ratio by 15 percent this coming year, and an additional 20 percent the following year.

Naturally, a workforce reduction of this magnitude can be devastating for the local communities, especially in northern New Mexico where the Los Alamos National Laboratory represents directly and indirectly over one-third of the jobs in three of the biggest counties. I want to thank Congress for the provisions of Section 3161 of the 1995 Defense Authorization Act which allowed us to offer educational incentives to affected employees and for the DOE to offer community assistance. We have received excellent cooperation from the DOE in administering a voluntary separation program to mitigate the effects of these cuts. I would also like to encourage your committee to reconsider support of the science education programs contained in the various DOE bills that encourage the laboratories to work with local communities to encourage an interest in science and math education. These programs are critical in cultivating the scientifically competent workforce that we will need in the future.

4. Should there be consolidation or closure of the DOE National Laboratories? If so, should this occur after mission definition or concurrently?

Considerations of consolidation and closure of laboratories must also follow the definition of functions. Major changes should only be made in conjunction with specific definitions of the missions of the DOE laboratories.

For example, many suggestions have been made for consolidation of the functions of the three DOE defense laboratories in light of the end of the Cold War. In fact, the Galvin Task Force made specific recommendations to transfer some of the nuclear weapons functions from the Lawrence Livermore National Laboratory to the other two laboratories. However, subsequent developments including concerns about the robustness of stockpile stewardship from the Joint Chiefs of Staff and President Clinton's decision to seek a zero-yield comprehensive test ban treaty make it clear that this would not be a prudent course of action. In fact, the challenge of stockpile stewardship for the indefinite future in an era of no nuclear testing and no new cycle of weapons replacements is as difficult as any we have faced in decades. These concerns must now be carefully folded into considerations of further consolidation. I should add that Los Alamos and Livermore have already jointly consolidated many of their functions to reflect changing priorities and significantly reduced budgets.

Similar considerations are in order for the civilian DOE laboratories. Let me again stress the issue of leverage and synergism of defense and civilian missions. It would be devastating for the defense laboratories and harmful to the nation if the defense laboratories lost their civilian R&D programs because of a consolidation edict. Our core technical competencies and the approach we take to problem solving allow us to make very special contributions to civilian problems. Likewise, some of the civilian laboratories are making important contributions to the national security arena because of their core technical competencies. This represents an effective way of leveraging the Federal R&D investment.

5. Are there other governance structures, such as corporatization or privatization, which may better suit the future management of the DOE National Laboratories?

Personally, I believe that the GOCO (government-owned, contractor-operated) system of governance devised for the Manhattan Project during World War II was innovative and enlightened. Unfortunately, as noted in the Galvin Task Force Report, it has eroded dramatically over time. I would prefer that we rebuild this system based on the same fundamental principles, but reflecting the realities of today's administrative world. It will be absolutely imperative that strong, independent and respected research institutions -- best represented by the nation's research universities -- play the predominant role in operating the laboratories. Without the contractor's appreciation for world-class research, the laboratories will lose their focus on science. Without that science, they will lose what has made the DOE laboratory system so successful in achieving its missions over the past 50 years.

The Galvin Task Force was sufficiently pessimistic about fixing the GOCO system that it recommended a corporatization scheme to insulate the laboratories from what it considered the overly prescriptive nature of government oversight. I view corporatization as an interesting notion for that reason, but I have not been able to devise a scheme that would work within the current government structure. Hence, I have turned my energies to fixing the GOCO system within the Department of Energy. I am encouraged that DOE officials, from Secretary O'Leary down to the field office managers, have taken the concerns of the Galvin Task Force seriously and that they are working with us to decrease the bureaucracy and increase our productivity. As I mentioned above, we have initiated an ambitious workforce productivity project at Los Alamos with encouragement from the DOE. We are applying some of the best quality practices we have learned from the private sector. Although we can learn much from the private sector, I do not believe that the nature of our government missions allow us to be "privatized."

I would also like to address the proposal for taking the DOE defense laboratories out of the DOE and having them report to the Department of Defense. I strongly oppose such a move for several reasons. First, the 1946 Atomic Energy Act deliberately placed atomic weapon development and stewardship under control of a civilian agency not within the military chain of control. This separation of powers has served the nation well for many years and is equally compelling today. I personally feel that I can discharge my duties to ensure that the nuclear weapons stockpile is safe, secure and reliable with greater independence outside of the DoD structure.

Second, as I pointed out before, the overriding challenge today of reducing the nuclear danger is much broader than stockpile stewardship. The nonproliferation issues, the control and disposition of nuclear materials, and the problems of nuclear waste disposition and environmental cleanup should not be separated from the stockpile stewardship functions. Yet, the Pentagon has rather little interest or experience in some of these areas.

Third, many issues concerning nuclear weapons and civilian nuclear power are strongly intertwined. I have mentioned the problems of managing an inventory of hundreds of tons of nuclear materials. We must recognize that the civilian plutonium inventory is already five times as large as the weapons plutonium inventory of the United States and Russia combined, and it is growing rapidly. Separation of civilian and defense nuclear problems into different Federal agencies would represent a step backward in what already is a major international problem area.

Fourth, the future nuclear mission will require the best scientific talent the nation has to offer. Placing the DOE defense laboratories into the custody of the Department of Defense (even under civilian leadership) will most likely break the synergistic bond that these laboratories have developed over the years between their defense and civilian missions, as well as hurt our ability to recruit the best and the brightest scientists. In the end, losing the affiliation with a separate civilian Federal agency will not provide the type of scientific leadership for nuclear weapons stewardship that this nation needs.

I find these objections to be serious obstacles to a transfer of the laboratories to the DoD. It is interesting to note that Secretary of Defense, Dr. William Perry, has also gone on record as opposing such a move.

Specific comments on legislation:

H.R. 2412: Department of Energy Laboratory Missions Act.

I want to thank Congressman Schiff for crafting this very thoughtful legislation. It goes right to the heart of the issue -- establishing missions for the Department of Energy laboratories. As I indicated in my remarks, a compelling national mission is a necessity for each laboratory. The bill calls for core missions for the DOE labs in four important national areas: national security, energy, fundamental research and environmental science and technology. I strongly support these as the right general mission areas for the laboratories. I wish to add a few specific comments.

In national security, H.R. 2142 lays out the significant challenges that remain in the post-Cold War era. I am encouraged by the inclusion of fighting the spread of all weapons of mass destruction including chemical and biological agents. The laboratories' technical expertise can help with problems such as biological agent detection. I am also pleased to see conventional weapons technology and intelligence assessments specifically included. I would only add specific reference to the daunting challenge of managing the nuclear materials legacy of the Cold War. The laboratories must play a significant role in developing and deploying technologies to stabilize, secure, store and dispose of plutonium and other weapons-usable materials. The challenge is even more daunting in the states of the former Soviet Union. The laboratories should be encouraged to continue their path-breaking work in helping to secure the Russian nuclear materials inventory. I should also note that the fate of civilian plutonium is inextricably intertwined with national security considerations. Hence, the laboratories can play a significant role in helping to think through and develop technologies for the entire nuclear fuel cycle.

The civilian mission focus in H.R. 2142 is very good. I want to underscore the interrelationship between energy, environment and the economy. These issues cannot be considered in isolation. Because the potential effects of energy options and environmental considerations on the economy are significant, it will be crucial to work in partnership with American industry in these areas. I am very pleased to see the strong focus on fundamental research in H.R. 2142, both as it underpins the civilian technologies and to keep the United States preeminent in all fields of science.

I believe that Sec. 101 (6) encouraging collaboration in partnerships among the DOE laboratories, other Federal agencies, academe and industry is a very important recognition of what it will take to have the DOE laboratories continue to be leading players in the nation's science and technology enterprise in the future. I was especially pleased to see the encouragement of working with private industry through cooperative research and development agreements. Over the past few years, the laboratories have not only demonstrated that this is an effective way of ensuring the government the maximum return of the taxpayer's investment by partnering with industry in hundreds of collaborations, but we have found that the benefits that accrue back to the government missions through what we learn from industry are truly substantial. Hence, we are well under way of demonstrating the efficacy of this government - private sector partnering experiment. I appreciate the encouragement provided in H.R. 2142.

In assigning the missions of the laboratories, I would like to see Congress give the Department of Energy maximum flexibility within the overall guidelines of the legislation with the minimum of bureaucracy. This would allow the DOE to look at the laboratories as a system of laboratories, but recognizing that it is a system of quite different individual institutions. I would also caution, as I did in my earlier remarks, not to push the DOE to define the missions too narrowly because of the synergism and leverage of multiple missions, particularly the interplay of defense and civilian missions.

I want to add a final comment on streamlining. The mission assignments will help to streamline the departmental laboratory system. In addition, the laboratories are each working on reducing the overhead burden in their operations. I described the Los Alamos Workforce Productivity Project above to show how we will significantly streamline our own laboratory and produce more science and technology for the taxpayer's investment.

H.R. 1993: Department of Energy Abolishment Act.

I have considerable difficulty with Title I of this legislation -- the abolishment of the Department of Energy. I believe that the Department of Energy and its predecessor agencies have served a most valuable function for the nation over the past 52 years. Recent commemorations of the Trinity Test and the end of the war with Japan have reminded us of the crucial role played by the Department's laboratories during the war and in the ensuing Cold War. Similarly, the contributions to the advancement of science by the Department's laboratories are recognized throughout the world. I believe that three crucial research functions continue to exist in the post-Cold War world that are best performed by the Department's laboratories: the nuclear weapons mission defined broadly, the civilian missions in energy and environment, and sharing a fundamental research mission with other Federal agencies.

I do not see this bill providing a proper home or environment in which these functions can be performed if the DOE is summarily abolished. In my remarks, I noted that our new nuclear mission is *reducing the global nuclear danger*. This mission involves not only stewardship of the nuclear stockpile, but also nonproliferation, the nuclear materials and nuclear waste legacy, and the environmental cleanup legacy. These issues are all closely related through fundamental technological challenges that are not easily tackled by any single Federal agency, and they would suffer considerably by being split up among several agencies. I have already provided my assessment of the problems associated with moving the defense functions of the DOE to the Department of Defense.

Similarly, the DOE laboratories have very special contributions to make in the civilian government mission areas of energy and the environment. These two areas are closely linked and both must be underpinned by solid fundamental scientific research to offer long-term solutions to key national problems. Splitting these up into other Federal agencies is a step backward. Privatizing these functions will jeopardize proper national solutions to these complex problems that do not lend themselves to strictly market-driven solutions.

Our nation is experiencing fundamental changes in its science and technology enterprise. Doing away with an agency that has been the home to some of the finest science and technology laboratories in the world and ones that still have compelling national missions without offering concrete alternatives does not appear to me to be a step in the right direction.

Most of my comments on Title I also apply to Title II. I do not see the need for yet another commission on the laboratories. I believe that it is time that the policy makers decided on a group of missions for the DOE and charge the Department with assigning these responsibilities to the laboratories as appropriate. I much prefer H.R. 2142 which calls for such mission assignments and for the streamlining of the laboratories to meet the challenges of the future. Such a process should size the laboratories according to what the Federal needs are and should result in cutting any unproductive redundancies that may exist.

H.R. 87: Department of Energy Laboratory Facilities Act of 1995.

I concur with the intent of the legislation to make the DOE laboratory system more cost effective. However, my comments are similar to those for H.R. 1993. I do not see how one can effectively consider closure or reconfiguration of the DOE laboratories without first defining the necessary functions and assigning the appropriate missions to the Department laboratories. I prefer to follow the process outlined in H.R. 2142 to define these missions and then streamline the laboratories to achieve those missions.

H.R. 1510: Department of Energy Laboratories Efficiency Improvement Act.

The issue of self-regulation of the Department of Energy with respect to its laboratories is critical to public support for departmental activities and has important ramifications on the cost effectiveness of the laboratories. The Galvin Task Force pointed out that the current system of oversight is cumbersome and inefficient. The DOE has taken these recommendations very seriously and established the *Advisory Committee on External Regulations of Department of Energy Nuclear Safety*, comprised of national experts in matters of safety, health and environment, as well as a range of important stakeholders. We have met with this committee to discuss the pros and cons of external oversight for the myriad of operations at the laboratory. I suggest that we wait for the recommendations of this committee before taking any actions.

I should add that I do not understand why the departmental defense laboratories should be excluded from consideration of external oversight. I do not believe that our defense mission would preclude the advisability of some external oversight functions. We believe that one of the most important aspects that must be considered is a mechanism for cutting the layers of oversight currently in the system. This problem exists for all DOE laboratories, regardless of mission.

On the issue of personnel reductions in Sec. 3, I strongly believe that this legislation is not the right way to size the laboratories. I again stress that size must follow function. H.R. 2142 provides a proper mechanism for assigning function through mission assignments. Once that is complete, the proper size of the laboratories should follow.

Concluding Remarks

I am very pleased with the focus of defining missions for the DOE laboratories in H.R. 2142. Compelling national missions exist for the laboratories in the nuclear weapons arena and in the civilian energy and environmental technologies areas. These missions combined with a focus on fundamental science can continue to serve this nation well as it transitions to the post-Cold War era. I believe that these laboratories will be effectively woven into the fabric of this nation's science and technology establishment by building on the strong networks they have developed with academe and U.S. industry.

APPENDIX

A. THE LOS ALAMOS MISSION: REDUCING THE NUCLEAR DANGER

At Los Alamos we believe that a compelling mission is essential to our future if we are to be successful in applying science and technology to the service of the nation. Our central mission has evolved since developing the first atomic bomb during the Manhattan Project and developing nuclear weapons for deterrence during the Cold War. We accomplished both successfully. Today — gratefully — the Cold War cycle of nuclear weapons development and deployment has ended and our central mission must reflect the incredible global events of the past six years. Our mission statement, ***"Reducing the Nuclear Danger,"*** was developed over two years ago and reflects the vision we had at the time of our role in the changing world. As a result of the deliberations of the Galvin Task Force on Alternative Futures for the Department of Energy Laboratories and our own strategic planning process, we set about to focus that mission statement more clearly, and to emphasize how the different components work together. The result is summarized by the following diagram.

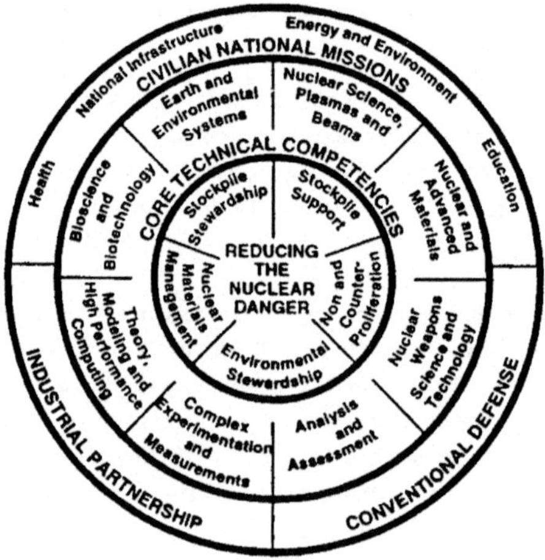

As shown in the diagram, *Reducing the Nuclear Danger* is the core mission of the Laboratory. There are five elements of that principal mission.

Reducing the nuclear danger calls for nuclear weapons *stockpile stewardship* — keeping those weapons that the nation needs safe, secure and reliable. Stewardship has actually become more challenging in a world in which the nuclear weapons will remain in the stockpile long beyond their originally designed lifetimes and one with no nuclear testing. Stockpile stewardship must now be based on more exacting science instead of verification by nuclear tests. Stockpile stewardship also requires that the nation retains the capability to respond to a variety of uncertain futures.

Reducing the nuclear danger involves *stockpile support* — providing the capabilities ranging from dismantlement to reconstituting manufacturing if some of the weapons need to be remanufactured in the future. The United States must keep its weapons safe, secure and reliable, and it must be able to retain its confidence in these weapons. Much of the stockpile surveillance, dismantlement, and manufacturing technological expertise will eventually reside only at the laboratories.

Reducing the nuclear danger involves *nuclear materials management* — assuring the availability or safe disposition of plutonium, highly-enriched uranium and tritium. It is currently projected that a new supply of tritium will be needed around the year 2010. No need for new plutonium or uranium is anticipated; rather, the principal concern is one of safe disposition. Currently, many hundreds of tons of these materials exist not only in returned warheads, but also as production scrap, residues, or nuclear waste, as well as in spent fuel from civilian power reactors. We are particularly concerned about the disposition of these materials in the former Soviet Union where these weapons-grade materials represent a significant proliferation danger.

Reducing the nuclear danger will require *the development of effective non-proliferation and counter-proliferation technologies*. We must keep nuclear weapons, nuclear materials and nuclear weapons knowledge out of the wrong hands. The proliferation threat poses the most significant risk to our national security today. Controlling nuclear proliferation means controlling nuclear materials. The defense laboratories are applying their skills to develop technologies for nonproliferation (keeping the materials out of the wrong hands) and counterproliferation (responding to the proliferation threat).

Finally, *reducing the nuclear danger* also requires that we *clean up the legacy of 50 years of weapons production*. As the global military threat recedes it is imperative that we turn our attention and technical talents to remediating the environmental problems in the defense complexes of the United States and the former Soviet Union.

Reducing the nuclear danger will be a compelling central mission for Los Alamos for the foreseeable future. This mission is supported by eight core competencies:

- nuclear and advanced materials;

- nuclear weapons science and technology;
- nuclear science, plasmas and beams;
- analysis and assessment;
- complex experimentation and measurements;
- theory, modeling, and high-performance computing;
- bioscience and biotechnology; and
- earth and environmental systems.

We have developed these competencies in response to national needs and we will be able to satisfy those needs in the future only if we maintain the health and vigor of our scientific competencies in these areas. We also must maintain these competencies in order to fulfill our core defense mission. However, we recognize that because of funding constraints, the nuclear weapons program alone cannot support these competencies adequately. In order to maintain the ability to perform our core mission, we must compete for programs in other areas that can help support these competencies. The key to our future success will be the extent to which we are able to maintain the multiprogram nature of our Laboratory and the synergy that supports defense as well as other national needs.

These core competencies in turn provide the basis for us to participate in civilian national missions, conventional defense R&D, and industrial partnerships. Work in these areas serves important national needs while providing critical support to our core mission by strengthening and maintaining our core competencies. These activities are essential to the future well-being of the Laboratory. They enable us to recruit and retain some of our best scientists and engineers, personnel who are then available to the weapons program for our core mission. These activities also contribute in an essential way to the character of the laboratory — they ensure that we are well connected to the academic and industrial worlds.

While our location was chosen for its isolation in 1943, in today's world of electronic communication and air travel, we are hardly isolated. At Los Alamos, our staff is drawn from the best scientists and engineers from across the nation. Collaboration with university faculty is absolutely essential to participation in the world's most demanding research community and maintenance of the highest standards of knowledge. We typically have affiliate or guest scientist agreements with more than 1,000 faculty members from universities across the nation and around the world. This includes several hundred faculty members who visit the Laboratory each year for seminars and workshops. We also involve students and postdoctoral fellows in the Laboratory's programs. It is not unusual in a typical year to have 400 postdoctoral fellows and 1500 students working at the Laboratory.

Interactions and partnerships with industry also help. Los Alamos can learn "best business practices" through industrial interactions. Where the best science and technology reside outside of Los Alamos, interactions with appropriate partners enable us to obtain the right technology to solve our mission problems. We find industrial interest in many of our key technologies, and we can leverage this interest to help support our competencies. Selected industrial interactions also help the Laboratory to provide a stimulating research environment that allows us to attract and retain world-class research talent.

The result of interactions with academe and industry can be seen in the quality of the research done at the Laboratory. The successful and substantial accomplishments of the Laboratory over the years, including development of the nuclear deterrent, the construction and operation of large-scale user facilities, and the continuing stream of recognized advances in fundamental and applied science, serve as validation of the quality of the research done at the laboratories. These developments often flow from civilian research to defense applications and back again. The Manhattan project was built on the foundation of civilian nuclear physics research at universities and it in turn led to the flowering of basic research in the structure of matter in the post-WW-II era. Knowledge of accelerator design from the nuclear and high-energy physics programs in turn supported the Strategic Defense Initiative and the possibility of accelerator production of tritium. The Laboratory has shown again and again the ability to develop new capabilities in order to execute programs and projects to meet national needs. The DOE laboratories have the ability, unmet by any other institutions, to respond substantively to complex, long-term, cross cutting issues of national importance.

Thus ***"Reducing the Nuclear Danger"*** is an effective shorthand for our mission, but it requires an understanding of the competencies required to fulfill that mission and how they will be supported. The Laboratory's identity and international recognition rests upon its performance in satisfying national needs in science and technology. Our future mission must encourage sustaining this recognition.

B. DEFENSE AND CIVILIAN MISSIONS

A COMPELLING MISSION

Our central mission evolved from developing the first atomic bomb during the Manhattan Project to developing nuclear weapons for deterrence during the Cold War. We accomplished both successfully. Today, the Cold War cycle of nuclear weapons development and deployment has ended, and so our central mission must reflect the incredible global events of the past six years. In conjunction with the Department of Energy we define our primary mission as providing the technical foundation to *reduce the global nuclear danger* to ensure a more secure future for our nation.

STOCKPILE STEWARDSHIP AND MANAGEMENT

A central and vital component of *reducing the global nuclear danger* is nuclear weapons *stockpile stewardship*—keeping those weapons that the nation needs safe, secure, and reliable. Stockpile stewardship also requires that the nation retains the capability to respond to a variety of uncertain futures. *Reducing the nuclear danger* will also require *stockpile management*—providing the capabilities ranging from dismantlement to reconstituting manufacturing if some weapons need to be remanufactured in the future. Much of the stockpile surveillance, dismantlement, and manufacturing technological expertise will eventually reside only at the laboratories. An overview of our vision of nuclear weapons stewardship is attached to this testimony as an appendix.

Los Alamos has historically been a major contributor to national security through its role in developing and assuring the United States nuclear deterrent. We continue that role today, through active stewardship of the weapons systems that will remain in the enduring stockpile and those that are in the process of dismantlement. We are performing pit surveillance for the stockpile. We are developing boost gas technology for implementation on the Trident I warhead and as the tritium storage technology of choice for much of the enduring stockpile. We are on track for our nonnuclear manufacturing responsibilities in neutron tube target loading and detonator production and surveillance and are working toward a demonstrated remanufacturing capability for a limited number of stockpile pits. Finally, we are archiving existing design, engineering, and test data on enduring weapons systems. Each of these activities is a part of our overall role in the Department's stockpile stewardship and management programs.

The stockpile is now being drawn down, but the recently completed Nuclear Posture Review concluded that nuclear deterrence remains central to the security of the United States and that we must hedge by maintaining capability. With the many changes of the last several years, the weapons laboratories' role has evolved to a new and in many ways more technically demanding challenge. They must provide for stewardship of the stockpile without nuclear testing as weapons age beyond their design lifetime, and they must provide a smaller, more economical, and environmentally responsible capability for fabrication and replacement of weapon components. We have been pleased to work jointly with the Department and Dr. Reis in developing a vision of how such an enterprise could look in the year 2010, and in beginning to turn it into a rational plan for the evolution of the nation's nuclear complex. This vision joins a capability-based deterrence with a right-sized capacity for weapon component manufacture and replacement, at an ultimate real saving to the taxpayer compared to continued reliance on remnants of the Cold War infrastructure.

This enterprise centers on the stockpile stewardship and stockpile management programs. We must have the intellectual capital and technical tools that we will rely on to accurately evaluate and revalidate the performance, safety, and reliability of stockpile weapons, and when necessary judge that an aging weapon or weapon component needs to be repaired or replaced. This same set of expertise and tools must be able to certify that such a repaired or replacement weapon will itself be safe and provide the expected performance. This is the challenge facing the science-based stockpile stewardship program, which provides the science and technology for evaluation and judgments on the efficacy of the enduring stockpile. Under a comprehensive test ban and stringent international nonproliferation regime, these judgments and evaluations must in the future be based on science-based understanding rather than the dramatic and clear validation obtained from a nuclear test. We have, of course, always relied on science and excellence in our scientific expertise as the foundation of our nuclear weapons activities. To answer the challenge now posed to us, however, we must improve our understanding and modeling, and this requires improvements in both our computational and experimental science capabilities. This in turn requires the funding and institutional vitality necessary to keep excellent, experienced people.

The stockpile management component of the enterprise is the fabrication, maintenance, and materials management counterpart of the Stockpile Stewardship Program. This program has responsibility for the many limited-life components that must be periodically replaced, for the management and production of tritium, and for fabrication of the components, as necessary, of nuclear weapons. A key part of these responsibilities is the technology for processing and fabrication of plutonium parts for weapon primaries, which historically had been manufactured at Rocky Flats.

Together, science-based stockpile stewardship and stockpile management will link science, materials, and manufacturing, and the surveillance of stockpile weapons to provide for assurance in the safety and capability of our deterrent. Science-based stewardship will develop the capability for confidence in the stockpile in the absence of a nuclear testing program. Stockpile management will assure the physical capability to maintain and replenish weapon components and systems. The Department has undertaken to prepare a programmatic environmental impact statement on stockpile stewardship and management.

The United States' nuclear stockpile is presently judged to be safe and reliable. However, problems with safety, performance, or reliability have historically been observed and will continue to occur. Weapons change due to material degradation, corrosion, and other factors. Cracks and voids can develop in components. Helium impurities from radioactive decay will build up in plutonium. To illustrate why proper stockpile stewardship and stockpile management are such an important issue for national security, we can look to some of our historical experience. Of the weapon types introduced since 1970, nearly one-half used post-development nuclear testing to verify, resolve, or fix problems. Also since 1970, several thousand stockpile weapons underwent major modifications or were hastened toward retirement because of safety or performance concerns. These kinds of problems have been observed in weapons designed by both design laboratories. A particularly clear example, because it involved an unexpected aging phenomenon, was the now-retired warhead for the Poseidon SLBM. The high-explosive in this warhead was discovered to be decomposing prematurely and had to be replaced lest the weapon become inoperable. Because certain materials had become commercially unavailable since the original development program, other modifications were required in addition to changing the high-explosive formulation. Nuclear tests helped ensure that these modifications did not compromise the weapon's performance. This experience also illustrates the concern that identical remanufacturing cannot necessarily be assured and that expert evaluation is needed. In the absence of nuclear testing, the certification of such changes will indeed be a technical challenge requiring a strong base of scientific expertise.

Tritium Supply

Tritium supply is a critical issue for the nuclear weapon stockpile because it decays at 5.5% per year and is required for our weapons to operate. The DOE has been in the process of developing a replacement capability since the tritium production reactors at Savannah River were shut down in 1988. To support the projected stockpile level called for in the Nuclear Posture Review, the DOE must have a new operational tritium supply by the year 2011. The requirement date could be moved to as early as 2005 if DoD requirements change. Although new production reactors have been considered, another option, accelerator production of tritium (APT) is under study. The APT option proposed by Los Alamos has become very attractive because of its flexibility to meet reduced tritium requirements at a low capital cost and at the same time maintain the option of increased production, should that be necessary. In addition, APT can be on-line in the year 2005, if required.

The APT project is a national effort begun in FY 1992 with Los Alamos, Brookhaven, and Sandia. Industrial participation from FY 1992-1995 was obtained by competitive bid selection of Bechtel, Grumman, General Atomics, Maxwell Balboa, Babcock and Wilcox, Westinghouse, and Merrick. The design developed and documented by the Laboratories and industry has undergone extensive examination by top scientific and engineering panels over the past few months. APT is, in words taken from the 1995 JASON Review "... a viable option for meeting US needs for tritium production." Principal advantages of the APT system include its high flexibility to meet demand; very low environmental safety and health impact, because there is no fissile material in the system; and greater public acceptance compared to a reactor.

On March 1, 1995, the DOE released a draft Programmatic Environmental Impact Statement on Tritium Supply and Recycle, and will issue a Record of Decision on the technology of choice by November, 1995. There are five potential sites for tritium production: Savannah River, Oak Ridge, Pantex, Idaho National Engineering Laboratory, and the Nevada Test Site. Site selection will be made later in the context of the DOE plan for the entire weapons complex.

Los Alamos' Role

Los Alamos is ready to serve the nation as a key part of the Department of Energy's vision of capability-based deterrence. *Of the seven systems that will remain in the U.S. nuclear arsenal after the turn of the century, Los Alamos designed and engineered five.* Continuing responsibility for these nuclear weapon systems is a core responsibility of the Laboratory. In addition, many of the key capabilities required for both stockpile stewardship and stockpile management are either principally or uniquely located at Los Alamos.

The absence of the large, capacity-based enterprise in the future places challenging new requirements on the Laboratories, especially Los Alamos, to assure the availability of components needed to maintain that stockpile. One of the responsibilities related to this goal is to demonstrate the ability to produce small quantities of war-reserve components for the existing stockpile. The importance of this demonstration is underlined by the reality that capabilities to produce certain nuclear and nonnuclear components have been shut down or are in the process of planned consolidation. Los Alamos will apply the strengths of its research and development to many of the requirements for the manufacture of materials and components for the enduring stockpile. Manufacturing and certification of components at Los Alamos will be done differently than previously in the complex, but will maintain the same exacting quality standards found in components produced earlier. The difference in Los Alamos' approach to manufacturing lies primarily in three areas: First, manufacturing and research and development activities will be integrated in a seamless fashion that will promote the manufacturing of high-quality, certified components in a cost-effective manner. Second, this integration will provide the means to maintain critical Laboratory skills and expertise while conserving existing resources. Third, manufacturing activities will build on our experiences and partnerships with industry.

These differences are illustrated by a recent manufacturing activity in Los Alamos' Detonation Systems Group. This group received the mission of detonator manufacturing in the DOE's Non-Nuclear Reconfiguration initiative and is tasked with demonstrating manufacturing capability in January 1996. Recently, though, this group was assigned responsibility for producing actuator simulants, not detonators but related electrical devices used to verify aspects of weapon reliability. The simulants were required and produced on an accelerated schedule with only four weeks for fabrication, and with limited funds, yet they were manufactured with the formality and demonstrable quality of a level appropriate for a DOE "diamond-stamped" product. This success confirms the key elements mentioned above—seamless integration of research and development and manufacturing using crucial skills available in the Laboratory.

This integration of research and development and manufacturing capability at Los Alamos is a tribute to effective partnerships formed within the Laboratory and with the DOE's Albuquerque Field Office. This partnership enabled Los Alamos to use quality methods and techniques learned from private-sector companies, Motorola and Milliken, to produce these components with controls appropriate to stockpile items, but at a dramatically reduced cost. It is precisely this type of effort that will allow Los Alamos to help maintain the stockpile and retain critical expertise, all at reduced cost to the taxpayer.

Integrating manufacturing capability with R&D tools and expertise is a powerful concept that extends beyond "diamond-stamped" detonator production. Today the R&D and fabrication capabilities of the laboratories are in some cases the only operational means for manufacturing replacement components or supporting any needed stockpile reliability or surety improvements. The details of future manufacturing configurations will be determined in late 1996, following the Stockpile Stewardship and Management Programmatic Environmental Impact Statement. Los Alamos has plutonium component fabrication capabilities, the nation's only full-service plutonium facility, which can support limited remanufacturing for a smaller stockpile. Our detonator production, tritium processing, and beryllium fabrication facilities assignments support non-nuclear consolidation. Los Alamos' uranium, salt, and high explosive R&D facilities and infrastructure could, with modest added facility investment, meet many of the future component needs of the stockpile As part of the Advanced Design and Production Technologies (ADaPT) initiative, Los Alamos will also be developing technologies and manufacturing processes to reduce costs and waste and enhance the efficiency of future fabrication of many of these components.

The extensive plutonium research and fabrication capabilities of Los Alamos are essentially unique in the United States. In recent years, Los Alamos has taken on the critical responsibility of surveillance of the plutonium "pits" from stockpiled weapons primaries, and we are pleased to report that these surveillance operations are proceeding successfully. Recently we have begun to recognize that stockpile-focused, science-based stewardship calls for a new and more integrated relationship between fundamental science, computational simulation, and surveillance. In this new relationship, science and simulation will teach us to be more insightful and clever in our surveillance measurements to detect and anticipate problems, as well as being used to interpret surveillance results to evaluate the current and future status of a weapon system. This enhanced surveillance paradigm is essential if we are to determine the proper and sufficient means by which to repair, or otherwise respond to, stockpile issues that could compromise safety, reliability, or performance. This is a lot like the close relationship between clinical medicine and biomedical research. The combination of Los Alamos' research capabilities with its many specialized facilities for plutonium, uranium, high-explosives, and other weapons materials provides an excellent opportunity to grow this kind of synergistic relationship. In fact there is a close parallel between integrated manufacturing that takes advantage of a close interaction between component manufacture and R&D, and enhanced surveillance that creates a close coupling between the scientific base and individual stockpile weapons.

One of the most important challenges in science-based stockpile stewardship is that of developing the computational methods and tools that we will need to accurately evaluate whether the aging stockpile needs repair and to certify any remanufactured or replacement weapons. Los Alamos has been a leader in the development of high-performance computing and in exploiting massively-parallel computer technology for three-dimensional weapons safety analysis and other complex applications. In addition to the core computational activities supporting our stewardship responsibilities, our participation in the Accelerated

Strategic Computing Initiative (ASCI) will ensure that the needs of these crucial applications are met by enabling a significant enhancement of the physical and numerical models and by accelerating the development of the relevant technologies to be delivered by the vendor community.

Computational simulations are only as good as the science and physical models that they apply. Validation of modern computer codes against the underground test data archive is essential but far from sufficient. The understanding that we will need for accurate evaluation in the absence of nuclear testing will also require data from a suite of experimental facilities such as the Dual Axis Radiographic Hydrotest Facility (DARHT), the Los Alamos Manuel Lujan Jr. Neutron Science Center (LANSCE), and the Atlas pulsed-power facility, each of which addresses important issues in stockpile performance and reliability.

Hydrodynamic tests—high-explosive-driven experiments for studying primary implosions—constitute the most important aboveground, nonnuclear testing capability for nuclear weapons. They allow an integral test of our prediction of these implosions and address the most important issues for the stockpile, the functionality and safety of the primary. The current X-ray radiographic facilities in the United States are insufficient for the kinds of evaluation we will have to make in the absence of nuclear testing. DARHT was initiated to provide the necessary capability in radiographic quality together with a second, simultaneous view from another direction, which will enable three-dimensional imaging so necessary to predictions of nuclear safety and reliability. The construction of DARHT has been halted by court action pending completion by the DOE of an Environmental Impact Statement (EIS) including consideration of alternatives, and the issuance of a Record of Decision. We believe that the enhanced hydrotest capabilities DARHT is designed to provide remain a vital component of the suite of tools necessary to maintain confidence in the nuclear stockpile.

LANSCE, for its part, will provide an opportunity to employ the unique penetrating capability of neutrons to study various materials science issues, including many related to aging. Materials issues can be exceedingly important for predicting compression in supercritical weapon assemblies and for inferring nuclear reactivity in the absence of direct nuclear testing. Neutron resonance radiography will also shed light on high-explosive behavior. Neutron radiography of weapon components, including primaries and secondaries, is an important emerging capability in our long-term plans to assess the effects of aging in the enduring stockpile.

LANSCE will also provide critical data in the area of applied nuclear physics. Recertifications of designs will depend on careful analysis of past data in order to properly attribute performance effects to constituent physical processes. Finally, LANSCE will offer the opportunity to refine our detailed models of the fission process itself. These effects may prove significant in explaining performance-related phenomenology, details that are required in building truly predictive simulation tools.

Much of weapon science depends on detailed study of hydrodynamic or radiation physics, often at higher energy densities than can be readily obtained in high-explosive experiments. The proposed Atlas facility is a twenty-five-million ampere pulsed-power capacitor bank that will enable us to study phenomena associated with both weapon primaries and secondaries with centimeter-scale experimental configurations, at temperatures and pressures high enough to partially ionize the materials. Its unique capabilities will be important for our evaluation of a number of issues related to the aging stockpile, such as the effect of narrow cracks on the implosion and performance of weapon components. We have demonstrated the extremely precise hydrodynamic implosions necessary on the smaller Pegasus facility which is already in use for weapons science experiments within its operational parameters.

Atlas, DARHT, and LANSCE were endorsed by the recent JASON report on science-based stockpile stewardship, and the Department has proposed Atlas for a FY 1996 start. DARHT, LANSCE, and continued experimentation were also explicitly recognized by the Galvin Task Force as needed for stockpile stewardship. These three critical facilities represent the capital improvements needed for science-based stockpile stewardship.

The upgrade to LANSCE, now under way, will also benefit the weapons program directly through its contribution to APT. Los Alamos has been chosen by the DOE to lead the national effort in APT design and development, and LANSCE will play an important role in demonstrating APT technology. If APT is selected as the technology of choice, industry will be brought into the project by competitive bid as early as possible in FY 1996 to participate in the technology demonstrations and to lead the plant design and subsequent construction efforts.

Los Alamos is ideally positioned to lead the national APT effort, having high-power accelerator design and operating experience, high-power beam target design expertise, and a strong nuclear physics and engineering base. In addition, specialized facilities exist in which to assemble and test APT components without costly and time-consuming civil construction. Although the APT design is based on existing technology and well established principles, some technology development to determine the most cost-effective, reliable system is needed. Work to be conducted at Los Alamos over the next four years includes effort in three main areas: 1) construction and operation of an engineering model of the first sections of the APT accelerator to demonstrate performance, reliability and operability; 2) demonstration of the tritium production efficiency at LANSCE using the existing accelerator facilities; and 3) further studies of the materials that will be used to construct APT target systems at equivalent beam power densities using the 800-kilowatt beam from LANSCE. I urge the Committee's support for this important technology demonstration effort.

Nuclear Materials Management and Disposition

Reducing the nuclear danger will require *nuclear materials management*—assuring the availability or safe disposition of plutonium, highly-enriched uranium and tritium. It is currently projected that a new supply of tritium will be needed by the year 2011. This issue was discussed above under stockpile management. No need for new plutonium or uranium is anticipated in the foreseeable future. The principal concern is one of safe disposition. Currently, many hundreds of tons of these materials exist not only in returned warheads, but also as production scrap, residues, or nuclear waste. We are particularly concerned about the disposition of these materials in the former Soviet Union where these weapons-grade materials represent a significant proliferation danger.

A major challenge lies with the responsible management of nuclear materials, especially plutonium. Reduction of the nuclear weapon stockpile, together with the subsequent dismantlement of weapons and the facilities that formerly produced them, has left the nation with growing and degrading inventories and decreasing capability to address the problem. At Los Alamos, we have the expertise, facilities, and most importantly, the broad global perspective needed to effectively address this issue.

The driver for nuclear materials management in the United States comes primarily from concern for public and worker health and safety and risk to the environment. The Department of Energy has recently completed a study of the vulnerabilities associated with the deteriorating conditions of plutonium storage across its facilities and has undertaken a program to address shortcomings and assure safe and secure storage pending decisions on ultimate disposition. This important vulnerability study was initiated in part as a result of early efforts by Los Alamos to identify and analyze problems involving plutonium storage containers. Los Alamos researchers were then called upon to train the vulnerability assessment team in relevant material properties and hazards related to plutonium processing and storage. Los Alamos has also taken the lead in stabilizing its own inventories as well as in developing and demonstrating technologies that can be applied to remediate nuclear material vulnerabilities across the complex.

At the Rocky Flats Plant that formerly produced all of the plutonium pits for the nuclear arsenal but is now destined for closure and restoration, 12.9 metric tons of plutonium inventories exist in a spectrum of undesirable material forms that have been largely untouched since production operations were suspended at the site in June 1989. Because of its weapons stewardship role, Los Alamos has the personnel and facilities to help stabilize and secure the plutonium residues at Rocky Flats. The capabilities that we maintain for our weapons stewardship role are also available to DOE to characterize and stabilize plutonium-containing materials at other sites. We consider this effort to be one of the most urgent in the entire DOE complex. In fact, our people have advised and aided Rocky Flats management for a number of years. In the past couple of years, the direct involvement of Laboratory personnel has greatly enhanced assay, examination, and stabilization capabilities that will allow for rapid analysis and reduction of potential hazards at the site.

For example, portable radiography equipment from Los Alamos was used to interrogate a drum of high-plutonium-assay residues that had been mislabeled at the time it was placed in storage. This drum could not be moved because of a suspicion that the material in the drum was so highly pyrophoric that it could ignite and burn spontaneously. The radiography equipment demonstrated that this was not the case and the drum could be moved. Los Alamos employees are currently working with the site contractor personnel to design and assemble real-time radiography equipment of their own.

Some of these materials are in solutions that are starting to leak out of their containment and present a significant risk that needs to be addressed at Rocky Flats. In recent experiments, Los Alamos has used its expertise and facilities to demonstrate that the liquid stabilization approach first proposed would not meet the established criteria and has developed and experimentally demonstrated an alternate approach that meets all the criteria and has been embraced by Rocky Flats. The procedures are being developed and the personnel are being trained at Los Alamos to expedite implementation of this liquid stabilization process at Rocky Flats.

The nation can further leverage its investment in Los Alamos plutonium processing capabilities for the solution of DOE's pressing plutonium problems, including stabilization and storage of plutonium-bearing materials. Los Alamos has recently demonstrated several technologies that purify and efficiently partition nuclear materials from other waste thereby reducing radioactive waste generation, cost, and risk. For example, we have demonstrated technologies for separating plutonium-containing salts, a big concern at Rocky Flats, from bulk waste. This technology can save hundreds of millions of dollars compared to planned direct disposal in repositories and can have wide applicability across the complex.

In another example, we are examining the possibility of fabricating processing lines in mobile or transportable assemblies. If successful, this approach could minimize transportation risk by moving laboratories for stabilizing residues to sites within the weapons complex, eliminating the need for expensive construction of processing facilities and personnel training at other sites. This approach would provide an optimum method for exporting stabilization technologies to Russia.

Los Alamos is enthusiastic about applying its extensive expertise and special facilities to other key tasks at Rocky Flats and around the DOE complex. At Rocky Flats we are also working on nuclear criticality safety, safe storage standards for metals and oxides, stabilization of other residues, and in support of the environmental restoration program at the site.

The types of plutonium problems we face in the United States at Rocky Flats, Hanford, and Savannah River sites are compounded in Russia by additional concern for the security of the nuclear materials. I will discuss below what Los Alamos is doing to help combat the proliferation concerns in the states of the former Soviet Union by introducing western nuclear materials protection, control, and accountability standards and practices.

In addition to concerns over military plutonium, the amount of civilian plutonium from nuclear reactors around the world is already several times greater than the military stockpiles of the United States and Russia—and it continues to grow. Most nations view this plutonium as an energy source for their future generations, and they are not about to dispose of it without extracting useful energy. This places an additional burden on the United States to work with the international community to find a long-term solution to the plutonium problem. First, we must stabilize materials such as those at Rocky Flats and similar materials in Russia. Then, we must secure these materials, store them under an international safeguard regime, and develop suitable techniques for disposing of the materials and their waste.

Los Alamos is also investigating new technologies for ultimate disposition of plutonium, such as the development of mixed oxide fuels for partial burning in reactors, and accelerator based transmutation technologies for complete destruction of plutonium. Several of these technologies may also address the larger problem of plutonium in commercial power reactor spent fuel. This is the kind of challenge that laboratories like Los Alamos can help to tackle.

PROLIFERATION CHALLENGES

Reducing the nuclear danger will require *the development of effective nonproliferation and counter-proliferation technologies*. We must keep nuclear weapons, nuclear materials and nuclear weapons knowledge out of the wrong hands. The threat of proliferation of weapons of mass destruction poses the most significant risk to our national security today. The defense laboratories are applying their skills to develop technologies for nonproliferation (keeping the materials out of the wrong hands) and counterproliferation (responding to the proliferation threat), and we are working with our former adversaries in Russia to prevent diffusion of nuclear materials and expertise.

Russian Nuclear Weapons

One of the principal proliferation challenges is that related to the nuclear weapons and weapons expertise of the former Soviet Union. The national laboratories are actively engaged with our counterparts in Russia to prevent the diffusion of weapons, materials, and scientists to countries that would represent a proliferation risk. Our interactions with the Russian institutes have two objectives:

- Stabilization of weapons expertise. Russian weapons scientists are an extremely valuable asset to a potential proliferator. By working with these scientists and directing their attention to peaceful, yet scientifically challenging problems, we reduce the likelihood of their emigration or their working for a rogue nation.
- Stabilization of weapons and weapons-capable materials. The shortest routes to proliferation are to obtain a complete weapon, critical weapon components, or materials. We are assisting the Russians to develop and apply technologies and systems to help prevent such a diversion.

Los Alamos is engaged in what are called laboratory-to-laboratory collaborations with Russian nuclear weapons and nuclear energy institutes. These collaborations are aimed at jump-starting work on the two above-mentioned objectives. These collaborations are able to advance productively while more formal government-to-government deliberations are proceeding.

We see these laboratory-to-laboratory efforts complementing those of our governments. The scientific relationships that have been developed with our Russian counterparts have allowed us to make significant and rapid progress. Let me highlight just two examples.

Scientific Exchanges: The first joint scientific experiment involving the nuclear weapons laboratories of the United States and Russia (Los Alamos and Arzamas-16) was performed in September, 1993. This has been followed by five others in several areas of basic science. Many publications have resulted, and the interaction receives broad and frequent coverage in the Russian press, helping to blunt concerns over U.S. motives for working in Russia. A number of Russia's core weapons people are now working almost full time on these projects, with the expectation that they will soon be supported to do scientific work, rather than weapons design,.by the Russian government.

Materials Protection, Control, and Accountability: Trust developed during the scientific exchanges enabled Los Alamos to put into place and lead a program in nuclear materials control that now involves five other U.S. laboratories and ten key Russian nuclear institutes. Contracts were signed within four weeks of funding, and the first major demonstrations occurred within six months. The Russians now want to move faster and further than our funding will allow, a contrast to other programs in this area.

Recently, at Arzamas-16, a demonstration of equipment and methods for safeguarding nuclear materials was completed. The demonstration was designed for Russian facilities such as those for nuclear weapons disassembly and storage of highly enriched uranium and plutonium. The best of United States and Russian equipment and methods were employed in this work. The demonstration was also designed to give the operators of Russian facilities hands-on experience and familiarity with improved materials protection, control, and accountability methods, which would then be introduced into their operating facilities. These methods are now to be deployed throughout the Russian nuclear weapons complex.

The DOE nonproliferation and arms control program is funded at $76.8M in FY 1995. In FY 1996 the DOE request of $162M represents an $85M increase to capitalize on major opportunities created by the lab-to-lab programs for control of Russian nuclear materials and scientific exchanges. Based on the success of the laboratory-to-laboratory program in the last two years, we are now poised to make a major contribution to the safety and stability of Russian weapons, materials, and expertise. This is exciting and important work that I hope will receive the support of this Committee.

Verification and Control Technology

Technology: With negotiations underway on a comprehensive nuclear test ban treaty, we face new challenges in verification technology. Our concerns with nuclear testing are no longer focused solely toward the former Soviet Union, but toward the much more complex threat of nuclear tests that could occur in any medium and in any part of the world. The challenge of discriminating among signals that could arise from natural phenomena as well as from nuclear tests of unidentified origin is an extremely difficult one. We are responding to it by studying a suite of monitoring technologies—seismic, acoustic, radiochemical, and electromagnetic as well as satellite-based observation. Meanwhile, to deter proliferation at an even earlier stage, Los Alamos and other laboratories cooperate in the DOE's proliferation detection technology program. This program supports advanced technologies such as laser monitoring of atmospheric emissions, multispectral thermal imaging of suspect areas, and effluent monitoring (soil, water, and air) to detect the presence of potential proliferation activity. Still other contributions to nonproliferation and anti-terrorist efforts come from programs in emergency response, export control, and intelligence analysis. With increasingly huge amounts of proliferation-related data, the unparalleled Los Alamos computing capability will be increasingly important for information integration and management.

Analysis: The intelligence program element provides a mechanism to engage the DOE laboratories in the analysis of foreign nuclear weapon capabilities and trends. For example, estimates of the Chinese nuclear program have been most helpful to national-level decision makers. An evolving activity that has received recent notoriety is the illicit transfers of special nuclear materials. The DOE intelligence unit is engaging the national laboratories in helping to assess potential sources, suppliers, recipients and networks. In this era of widespread information regarding nuclear technologies, including weapons, the laboratories also help in assessing potential proliferation pathways and interdiction options.

For over thirty years the DOE national laboratory and United States Air Force joint effort has produced a highly successful and cost-effective, satellite-based verification program. Another example is technical support to the International Atomic Energy Agency (IAEA); Los Alamos has been the most consistent and productive supplier of new safeguards technology to IAEA safeguards inspectors monitoring nuclear power facilities for the past twenty-five years. The weapons laboratories provided experts and technology during the Iraq and North Korea crises—to the UN Special Commission in the case of Iraq and to the State Department during the confrontation with North Korea over its nuclear weapon program. Because they draw on the same suite of technical skills, the strong synergism between stewardship and nonproliferation activities must be continued at Los Alamos.

Satellites: Our small satellite program has been very successful in demonstrating the viability of a new approach that allows the design, construction, and launch of satellites using advanced technologies for arms control and verification activities on very short time schedules compared to conventional satellite launch schedules. This program is another good example of how we approach our work. The design and purpose of the program is verification, but the satellites produce information of interest to the astrophysics research community as well.

Counterproliferation

Counterproliferation efforts must focus on threats posed by chemical and biological weapons as well as nuclear weapons. Counterproliferation activities include detecting the spread of such weapons; deterring it through incentives and force; responding with appropriate military and diplomatic tools; and protecting U.S. citizens, property, and interests worldwide. The Department of Defense is defining the scope of counterproliferation efforts and is integrating its efforts with those of other agencies. Los Alamos has responded to the new counterproliferation initiative by establishing a dedicated counterproliferation office and by expanding its participation in a number of emergency response programs. The new effort at Los Alamos is built around the Nuclear Emergency Search Team (NEST) and Accident Response Group (ARG) programs, both of which are funded by DOE. These teams address the potential need to find and secure nuclear weapons and nuclear materials in unusual circumstances. NEST/ARG-related skills will be expanded to address chemical and biological threats. Thus, the expanded counterproliferation program at Los Alamos will be closely coupled to the existing nonproliferation program.

In support of counterforce options in counterproliferation, we are applying modeling capabilities and techniques developed in our conventional munitions programs to analyze the lethality of fragmentation and hit-to-kill warheads against various threats, including canister munitions that may contain chemical or biological agents. The demonstration of multimode warhead munitions to drastically reduce logistics and strike-planning burdens is also being pursued. These lethal mechanisms are optimized for a wide spectrum of targets from a single warhead package.

THE ENVIRONMENTAL LEGACY

Reducing the nuclear danger also will require that we *clean up the legacy of 50 years of weapons production.* As the global military threat recedes, it is imperative that we turn our attention and technical talents to remediating the environmental problems in the defense complexes of the United States and the former Soviet Union.

Los Alamos is applying its multidisciplinary staff and dedicated resources to areas of concern including waste minimization, characterization and remediation (including treatment, disposal, and storage), environmental restoration, waste management, and pollution prevention. DOE possesses a number of legacy wastes (hazardous, high- and low-level radioactive, transuranic, and mixed) that are complicated and often heterogeneous in nature. These waste types pose a significant treatment and management challenge. Industry faces similar problems. For example, waste from nuclear medical procedures shares many of the characteristics of mixed waste.

The Galvin Task Force pointed out the opportunity to apply new science and technology to applications in environmental remediation. A larger fraction of the environmental restoration program budget should be allocated to research and development activities. There are many new areas of technology which, if developed further, could yield benefits both in cost and in reduced hazards to the public and the environment compared to current technologies.

Waste management science must evolve to bring under control the large volume of waste and contaminated material that come from restoration and decontamination and decommissioning activities. The following table shows just three areas in which Los Alamos is developing technologies that have application to a number of sites in the DOE complex.

DOE Needs	Los Alamos Technology Areas	Applicable Sites	Industry Partners
Low-level radioactive contamination from soils	Magnetic separation	Savannah River, Nevada Test Site, Rocky Flats Plant, Hanford, Idaho National Engineering Laboratory, and military armor penetrator firing ranges.	AWC Lockheed CRADA established with Los Alamos
Effluent wastes, volatile organic compounds (VOCs), nonarid site VOCs, hazardous-solvent-contaminated machining oils, incinerator/thermal unit off-gas, arid site VOCs, vapor-plume VOCs, solvents, explosives & munitions secondary treatment	Silent discharge plasmas	Savannah River, Rocky Flats Plant, Hanford, Los Alamos National Laboratory, Department of Defense, Electric Power Research Institute (EPRI)	EG&G, General Electric, and Westinghouse
Separation of radioactive constituents and organics from high-level defense waste	Chemical separations	Savannah River, Hanford, Rocky Flats Plant, and Los Alamos National Laboratory	Grumman, GE, TRW, IBM, General Atomics, McDonnell Douglas, and Westinghouse

Conventional Defense

In 1985, the President's Blue Ribbon Task Group on Nuclear Weapons Program Management headed by Judge William Clark concluded that the DOE defense laboratories (Los Alamos, Sandia, and Livermore) should be tasked to serve some of the research and development needs of the Department of Defense in nonnuclear areas. Such work would concurrently benefit the laboratories' competencies for their nuclear weapons requirements. Ten years later, the three DOE defense laboratories have demonstrated the wisdom of Judge Clark's recommendation with many contributions to DoD requirements, especially under the auspices of the joint DoD/DOE munitions program.

As the DoD restructures and consolidates its research and development enterprise today, the Blue Ribbon Task Group's recommendation is more applicable than ever. The DOE defense laboratories can support the DoD laboratories and help extend the shrinking defense science and technology base of the United States. The science and technology base developed for our nuclear and past conventional defense activities are a resource to address the emerging threats of the 21st Century. Use of these capabilities by the DoD is an effective way to leverage the investments made in the nuclear weapons program for conventional defense. In turn, conventional defense programs at Los Alamos are a vital part of the Laboratory's portfolio, supporting and strongly complementing its nuclear national security missions. These programs are also a major contributor to our defense science and technology base.

We have organized our defense technologies portfolio based on technology and programmatic platforms to best support new DoD initiatives while meeting current commitments. We are building strategic partnerships with the military services and service laboratories, industry, and academia to support science and technology efforts.

Conventional Weapons Technology

Conventional weapons technology includes the Non-Nuclear Munitions Memorandum of Understanding, technology programs and projects in high-explosives, conventional weapons, lethality, and survivability for DoD applications. The joint munitions program supported by both DOE and DoD has been very successful. It was funded at $24 million in FY 1995, and is scheduled for the same level for FY 1996; this is a program that provides significant leverage and could easily be increased.

One example of this work is the armoring of C-141 aircraft. Based on the capabilities developed in our Armor/Anti-armor program, we were able to design and produce modular kits to retrofit C-141 aircraft with cockpit armor. Five complete sets were fielded within eight weeks to protect the crews and critical systems of these aircraft as they flew peacekeeping missions in Bosnia. Other examples include new classes of insensitive high-explosives that are far less vulnerable to detonation in accident conditions; the development of new processes for the safe, environmentally sound demilitarization of energetic materials; and new, smart, adaptable warheads for multiple target sets.

Biological Warfare Agent Detection

The Desert Storm campaign clearly identified the inability of U.S. and Allied forces to effectively detect and identify biological-warfare (BW) agents as a critical military deficiency. Because of the low level of technology required to manufacture BW agents, and the relative ease with which they may be employed, our military forces could easily be confronted with the potentially catastrophic effects produced by these agents. Los Alamos was selected by DoD to pursue the development of innovative technologies for BW agent detection and identification. Drawing on our interdisciplinary skills in lasers, optics, information technologies, and engineering design, a light detection and ranging (lidar) system, designated the XM-94 by the Army, was designed, built, and tested by Los Alamos in a period of five months in 1993. The XM-94 is an order of magnitude smaller in size and weight and has substantially improved operational characteristics, compared to an earlier prototype BW agent detection lidar quickly fielded by Los Alamos during Desert Storm. As part of the DoD Counterproliferation Support Program, Los Alamos will build two military-engineered-and-qualified advanced prototypes based on the XM-94 concept, and transfer the technology to industry for production.

In a closely related activity, Los Alamos has also been tapped by the Army to exploit its expertise in sensors and biotechnology to develop a miniature flow cytometer (a technology that Los Alamos pioneered) for its Biological Integrated Detection System, which provides point detection and rapid identification of BW agents at forward deployment locations. Compared to current, off-the-shelf flow cytometers, the mini-system will represent a significant reduction in system volume, weight, and power requirements; operate in a semiautomatic detection and identification mode; and be designed and engineered for the military environment. This will bring the military's capability significantly closer to its goal of near-real-time, positive BW agent identification. Production beyond the initial test articles will also be transferred to an Army-selected industrial contractor.

Modeling and Simulation

Advanced modeling and simulation capability will allow the our military to "practice" an actual engagement scenario while varying tactics and weapons to determine an optimum approach that minimizes casualties and collateral damage, as well as providing a structured approach to procurement decisions and the evaluation of life-cycle costs.

Simulation is defined as macroscopic systems modeling for requirements, prototyping, procurement, test and evaluation, operations, and training, including man-in-the-loop scenarios. The full utilization of high-performance computing for modeling needs of the defense community, for simulation of agile manufacturing and process control, and for analysis of complex systems involves the use of scalable workstation resources linked effectively with high-performance computers.

Significant results with the 1024-node Connection Machine 5, vectorized codes on Cray machines, and connection to a network funded by the Advanced Research and Projects Agency and the National Science Foundation will enable Los Alamos to make major contributions to the modeling and simulation of defense problems. The object-oriented modeling of systems for global and theater missile defense, corps engagements, and satellite architectures has shown great utility for many defense simulation applications and can provide a framework for modeling advanced technology concepts and evaluating acquisition strategies.

Beams and Sensors

Los Alamos work encompasses particle, laser, and microwave beams and active and passive sensors. The primary emphasis in laser technology at Los Alamos in the near future will be on laser systems that provide frequency-agile sources, both continuously and discretely tunable, for defense-related applications such as biological warfare agent detection, missile defenses, lidar systems, countermeasures, and antisensor devices.

Recent advances in electronics, electrooptics, and computers are facilitating the development of highly capable, compact, active and passive sensors that support a wide variety of DoD applications, such as the use of lidar technology to detect biological agents and theater ballistic missiles and the use of passive threat-warning systems to detect spacecraft, aircraft, and land vehicles. Space environmental sensors and novel low-light level and multispectral imaging sensors developed for nonproliferation and counterproliferation missions are also applicable to DoD needs.

Advanced Concepts

Advanced concept technologies encompass a broad range of projects. Advanced materials for specific applications could be developed that have unique properties such as strong absorption of specific frequencies of electromagnetic radiation. Hypervelocity interceptor missile technologies could enable boost-phase interception of theater ballistic missiles. Other technologies include capabilities and systems that support peacekeeping, low-intensity conflicts, and special missions, those that provide the military and policymakers with flexible options; and novel energy storage systems and beam sources.

Summary

In the past, the DoD put considerable reliance and investment in its science and technology base to provide top-flight weapons systems to our armed forces. Examples include stealth technology, precision-guided munitions, and global positioning systems. With reductions in defense budgets and increasing demands for operational readiness, this investment in the future is at risk.

Moreover, recent changes in DoD procurement practices and restrictive interpretation of authorization and appropriations language have had a negative effect on the DoD's and the Services' ability to leverage and access the science and technology expertise resident in the DOE defense laboratories. We would advocate new approaches to incorporating the DOE defense laboratories in the DoD science and technology base to ensure the provision of innovative solutions for the future force structure and to help maintain the technological superiority of our defense.

DEFENSE MISSION SUMMARY

Los Alamos is well positioned to serve the nation in this new world. Of the seven nuclear systems that will remain in the U.S. nuclear arsenal after the turn of the century, Los Alamos designed and engineered five. However, the scientific challenge of ensuring the stockpile beyond its design lifetime and doing it without nuclear testing is greater than was the challenge of designing new weapons. At Los Alamos, we have the most complete set of facilities to help support the stockpile of tomorrow. We have a history of technical accomplishments and facilities to help manage the nuclear materials, and we have turned our considerable expertise in chemistry, engineering, and life sciences to addressing the daunting problems of the environmental legacy of the production complex. We are working closely with Livermore and Sandia laboratories to provide the nation with the best technologies to prevent and respond to the proliferation of weapons of mass destruction. We have made significant progress in developing a cooperative working relationship with its counterpart laboratories in Russia to address worldwide proliferation concerns.

So, *reducing the nuclear danger* will be a compelling central mission for Los Alamos for the foreseeable future. This mission will require that we keep excellent, experienced people committed to these challenges and that we maintain and modernize our facilities. We must also maintain excellence in several core technical competencies that cannot be supported entirely by our core mission activities. Programs in civilian science and technology, whether directly funded or performed in partnership with industry or universities, help maintain the competencies needed by our core defense mission areas while at the same time contributing to broader national goals.

II. CIVILIAN SCIENCE AND TECHNOLOGY

For this Laboratory to perform its defense missions, the strength and reputation of its scientific and technical capabilities must be maintained. The challenge of assuring a safe and secure nuclear deterrent, particularly in the absence of nuclear testing, requires a diverse scientific and technical environment. In a stringent budget climate this entails access to skills and technologies beyond those that can be supported solely for the national security mission. Civilian research programs now supported by other Department of Energy offices such as the Office of Energy Research, as well as work for other federal agencies, and partnerships with industry, help support necessary defense capabilities. Further, maintenance of the quality of the Laboratory's work requires that the Laboratory's scientists be integrated into the broader scientific and technical community. The multiprogram nature of our Laboratory must be maintained if we are to continue to perform, much less excel, in our defense mission.

I view work in civilian research and development as being vitally important to the Laboratory. *First*, there are direct benefits to working in these areas that accrue to the Laboratory. The intellectual challenges brought by civilian research and development often provide the necessary dynamics for development of technology for mission applications. A *second* reason for the essential character of civilian research and development is the need for the Laboratory to continue to attract the best scientists and engineers. Work in these fields helps provide the level of challenge needed to recruit a world-class staff. I am concerned that we may find it difficult to maintain the competencies necessary for the performance of our core defense mission if that mission is interpreted too narrowly. Civilian research is therefore a strong supporting component to the defense mission of the Laboratory.

BASIC RESEARCH

Basic research has long been a central feature of work at Los Alamos. It has served to inspire young scientists to come to Los Alamos, and it has helped retain some of our most productive senior people. A healthy basic research program also helps keep a focus on science and enhances the reputation of the institution for excellence. Basic research, exemplified by the first detection of the neutrino by a Los Alamos team in 1956 and our recent research on the mass of the neutrino, is essential to our defense mission. Research in materials using spallation neutrons at the Los Alamos Manuel Lujan Jr. Neutron Science Center (LANSCE) will support the defense mission as well, leading to greater understanding of stockpile stewardship issues, new means for tritium production, and perhaps to new ways to rid the nation and the world of long-lived radioactive wastes.

The laboratory provides a base of support for many projects in basic research that have direct applicability to our defense mission. Work in theoretical astrophysics has long had close ties to our weapons design capability. Research in the synthesis of novel materials; the interaction between radiation, both nuclear and electromagnetic, and materials; and in the properties of materials under extremes of pressure and temperature has produced direct benefits to our core mission.

One of the most synergistic facilities at the Laboratory for the last 25 years has been the Clinton P. Anderson Los Alamos Meson Physics Facility (LAMPF). As a national user facility, it brings scientists from all over the world to Los Alamos to perform experiments and interact with our staff, and sometimes join us as employees. The cross-fertilization that comes from interacting with these visitors is part of what keeps the Laboratory a vital and exciting place.

Neutron scattering is a basic tool for probing the structure and dynamics of condensed matter systems and is complementary to more conventional X-ray diffraction, microscopy, magnetic resonance, and structural probes. The use of neutrons as a probe in biological and materials science is growing worldwide, and the importance of neutron beam research facilities has been established by high level review committees, each stressing that existing United States reactors for neutron research are now over 20 years old and that new sources are urgently needed. When the LAMPF accelerator came on-line in 1972, it became a new source of neutrons for research, an activity enhanced again by LANSCE, which started operating from the LAMPF beam in 1985.

Basic research at LANSCE covers a wide range of topics in condensed matter physics, materials science, chemistry, structural biology, geology, and engineering. Static structure and atomic and magnetic fluctuations are probed in a variety of systems ranging from high-temperature superconductors to macromolecules that control muscle contraction. Scientists at LANSCE have concentrated over the past few years in developing techniques in scientific areas to which neutron scattering has not been applied in the past. As a result, the facility has a number of unique capabilities, including diffraction measurements at high pressure, neutron reflection studies of liquid surfaces, and studies of materials under shear. Neutron radiography has been demonstrated, and this can provide an important non-destructive evaluation technique for nuclear assemblies with microscopic resolution and unique isotopic selectivity.

With the medium-energy nuclear physics national user program ending at LAMPF after FY 1995, neutron research will become the focal activity for the high-power accelerator facility and will become an important element of the Laboratory's stockpile stewardship program. The $35M LANSCE Upgrade project, currently funded and underway for Phase I, will improve facility availability with a goal of running eight months per year at 85% reliability. Better access to LANSCE will be important to the institutional vitality of the Laboratory, as more scientists from around the world use its facilities and increase contact and collaborations between Los Alamos scientists and their peers from government, universities, and industries.

The DOE's plan to build the Advanced Neutron Source (ANS) reactor at Oak Ridge National Laboratory is shown terminated in the FY 1996 President's Budget because of cost. The identified alternative is an *accelerator-driven spallation neutron source*, such as that pioneered at LANSCE and the Argonne National Laboratory Intense Pulsed Neutron Source. However, LANSCE and its sister facility at Argonne are oversubscribed and underpowered with respect to future user demand. The Neutron Scattering Society of America, through its Pulsed Spallation Source Committee (PSSC) hosted by Lawrence Berkeley Laboratory, has laid out a roadmap for spallation neutron source development which relies on facilities and expertise at Los Alamos and Argonne national laboratories.

LANSCE can also become a higher-power operational prototype. The 1-MW accelerator provides the only beam near this power level in the United States for target development. For the research community, the prototype facility would be a source of neutrons that is at least equivalent to the reactor at the National Institute of Standards and Technology, and in some cases better than the world's best neutron research reactor, the 57-MW reactor in Grenoble, France. This test bed is projected to cost in the $50-100 M range and will serve the community well for 10-15 years until the next generation source (5-10-MW range) is on-line. The PSSC recommended the High Power Spallation Testbed at Los Alamos as an important component of the U.S. spallation neutron roadmap and is likely to ratify this decision even with the cancellation of the ANS. Thus the United States can, for a modest investment, develop a facility at Los Alamos that is equivalent to the best neutron source in the world until the major next-generation neutron facility is designed and built, a source that will have both defense and non-defense applications.

ENERGY AND ENVIRONMENT

The Laboratory's capabilities in long-term interdisciplinary research and development, nurtured by our defense mission, can also be applied to other civilian research and development needs, thereby leveraging both investments. I discussed our work for the DoD above as examples of mutual benefit to important national needs that in turn support our core nuclear weapons mission. The same is true for programs in energy and environment. In a broader view, energy security is also an integral part of national security; the potential for economic disruption that dependence on foreign sources implies has been demonstrated more than once.

Per-capita demand for energy can be expected to continue to increase worldwide. While there may be no immediate needs for new energy sources in the United States, development of high-efficiency, low-polluting sources should be pursued more vigorously. The form, value, and efficient use of energy in applications is as important as new capacity; therefore a systems approach to energy production and use needs to be taken. These activities can help sustain the developing world and make our own industry more efficient and cost-effective. More effective energy technologies and integration of raw materials issues with product design and recycling considerations will also work to increase the effectiveness of our industrial base.

These issues are too complex and interwoven to expect industry to find solutions by themselves. Many promising technologies are sufficiently speculative that their development poses too high a risk for any industrial segment. The benefits from such work, however, accrue to the public, not individual firms. Success in these areas therefore requires a strong partnership between the federal government and industry, using all the technological resources the nation has to offer. Work at Los Alamos in a number of areas contributes both to new source exploration and the efficient use of energy.

An early example of this approach was the establishment in FY 1988 of the Superconductivity Technology Centers (STCs) at Los Alamos, Argonne, and Oak Ridge national laboratories. The centers' specific mission is to form partnerships with U.S. industry to expedite the development of high temperature superconductor (HTSC) technology with commercial feasibility. These partnerships are industry driven (that is, they are based on research and development projects of joint interest to a company and the Laboratory) with industry bearing the full cost of its participation. The partnership concept benefits both government and industrial research and development programs and focuses on the timely introduction of practical HTSC devices into the commercial marketplace. The emphasis in developing these partnerships is on power applications of HTSCs, although the Laboratory does respond to strong industry interest in collaboration on electronics applications. Industry's positive response is expected to lead to an expansion of the STC program with increased DOE funding. The Laboratory uses its center as a model for industry/national laboratory partnering by extending the concept to other important strategic technologies.

The Laboratory also participates in the Natural Gas and Oil Technology Partnership program, which encourages the domestic natural gas and oil industry to use the scientific and engineering resources of the DOE laboratories to acquire new technologies for improved domestic natural gas and oil recovery. The domestic industry guides the research and development efforts proposed as part of this initiative. Costs of partnership projects are shared with industry collaborators.

The Advanced Computing Technology Initiative (ACTI), which is a major collaboration with the nine multipurpose national laboratories and U.S. industry, primarily the major gas and oil producers, aims to apply the high-performance computing capabilities at the national laboratories to assist in oil and gas explorations, reservoir performance simulation, and other extraction activities. I discuss this program further when I discuss how our scientists work with industry.

A greater emphasis on fundamental environmental research and development is also needed. Examples in which the Laboratory has demonstrated capabilities include

- Instrumentation, applied information processing, and monitoring technologies and integration.

- **Global atmospheric and climate modeling and measurements; e.g., the understanding of the effect of greenhouse gases.**
- Risk assessment considerations and methodologies.
- Modeling of complex industrial and demographic systems, e.g., transportation systems.
- Modeling and simulation of energy and environmental recovery processes.

In the past year Los Alamos has become one of the preeminent institutions in computer modeling of the earth's oceans. The original task was to make changes necessary to run a few ocean-circulation codes efficiently on the massively parallel supercomputers at the Laboratory's Advanced Computing Laboratory. Los Alamos scientists did much more. They made such substantial improvements to the numerical methods and physics that these codes now are ranked as the best in the world. This happened because of the legacy of the nuclear weapons design program. The years of experience with large fluid-dynamic computer codes and the large numbers of scientists expert in fluid flow and nonlinear dynamics, numerical methods, and computer science that the weapons design program has supported were easily able to make rapid strides in this non-weapons effort.

Today the Lab is running the most highly resolved ocean simulation (6-10 mile grid) with complete topography (continental margins, islands, and subsurface topography). Details of ocean circulation compare well with satellite observations. The Arctic Ocean is being included for the first time with sea ice physics. Two different codes are being worked representing two different numerical approaches. Plans are being made to couple one of these codes to a very powerful global atmospheric code offering the possibility of the best coupled ocean/atmosphere simulations of the climate. The use of these coupled models to study the effects of energy development in the Third World, for example the use of soft coal as a primary energy resource in China as it develops its economy, ties directly to our fundamental energy mission.

Similar results have come from the weapons program in the area of global atmospheric studies. In the mid-1980s, Laboratory scientists responded to requests for a substantial study of the so-called "nuclear winter" scenario. Much work was being done around the country on this subject, but none of it was conclusive. Los Alamos scientists made substantial modifications to a global atmospheric code originally developed at the NSF-funded National Center for Atmospheric Research. In about 18 months, working with atmospheric scientists from NASA's Ames Research Center, they were able to make fully 3D simulations of the response of the earth's atmosphere to massive loading of black smoke and soot. Their analysis showed the major mechanisms that would come into play, and at the special National Academy of Sciences meeting in Washington DC, Los Alamos scientists were the only ones able to show such results. A few years later this capability was used again to make predictions—a task done in only two weeks—of the effects on global climate from the burning of the Kuwaiti oil fields.

Recent measurements and demonstrations conducted by Los Alamos in collaboration with a variety of other organizations have shown that lidar technology, developed by the Laboratory for verification activities, can be a powerful tool for measuring air quality associated with vehicle emissions. Experimental campaigns conducted in Mexico City, Mexico; Barcelona, Spain; and Albuquerque, New Mexico, have located sources of pollution, tracked the movement of aerosols, and located mixing-layer boundaries as a function of time and traffic conditions.

In a somewhat different category, natural disasters cost the United States over one trillion dollars annually. The ability to base real-time decisions on event simulations would significantly reduce the destruction of property and the loss of life. By combining predictive models with adaptive systems that enable the extraction of information from large, often noisy, low-confidence data; understanding the limits of predictability driven by the inherent sources of uncertainty; and by creating an environment that accelerates model building to ensure agile responses to developing conditions, Los Alamos could develop the capabilities to predict the rapidly unfolding future, provide guidance to manage emergencies, and develop strategies to optimize remediation efforts. This grand challenge computing problem would be tractable only at an institution like Los Alamos, where the high performance computing hardware is joined with extensive software, data analysis, modeling, and scientific expertise.

Challenges like these, as with our work in basic research, contribute significantly to the nation, thereby leveraging the nation's investment in the Laboratory, and help to support the science and technology base needed to succeed in our defense mission.

Work for Other Federal Agencies and Industry

In addition to the DOE's own programs, work for other federal agencies and industry, whatever the mechanism, also maintains and strengthens Laboratory capabilities which are required for the performance of its core defense mission while contributing to other national needs.

Work for other federal agencies and industry represents the principal application of the Laboratory's core competence and varied capabilities to national needs in a broader context and to a broader customer base. At the same time, the Laboratory must maintain its mission orientation and not become a "job shop" for industry or for other federal agencies.

The Department must recognize that part of its mission is the facilitation of the use of its laboratories by other federal agencies and by industry. The Department has a trustee responsibility to preserve the competence of the Laboratory as a *national* resource and should not impede the broader use of Laboratory facilities and expertise through the imposition of arbitrary taxes and added factors.

Department of Transportation: We are supporting the Department of Transportation under the Intermodal Surface Transportation Efficiency Act of 1991 in several ways. We are partners with the State of New Mexico, local universities, and Sandia National Laboratory in the New Mexico Alliance for Transportation Research. This alliance brings the research and development capabilities of the Laboratory to bear on infrastructure issues.

Los Alamos is also being funded by the Federal Highway Administration to develop new modeling and analysis capabilities for transportation system planning. We have developed a systematic approach based on principles of dynamic analysis rather than the traditional functional decomposition of transport systems. The Transportation analysis simulation system (TRANSIMS) architecture uses what is appropriate from the traditional process, while developing new and more powerful methods employing modern and newly emerging computing technologies, software technologies, simulation techniques, and analytical methods for complex dynamical systems.

The most important new capabilities offered by TRANSIMS are the integration of congestion and incident effects analysis, detailed air quality impact analysis, and intermodal systems analysis. A significant difference between TRANSIMS and traditional methods is the incorporation of regional scale traffic microsimulation. Vehicle emissions data produced by the microsimulation is collected for mobile emissions source analyses and verification against atmospheric measurements.

National Institutes of Health: The multidisciplinary nature of the Laboratory and its strong capabilities in physical science and large-scale computing enable its scientists to conduct biological and environmental research programs not possible at academic institutions. The National Institutes of Health have drawn on these capabilities to establish at Los Alamos a number of programs including the National Flow Cytometry and Sorting Research Resource, which makes advanced flow-cytometric instrumentation available to the biomedical research community; the National Stable Isotope Resource, which develops new and efficient methods of incorporating stable isotopes into compounds of immediate use in biomedical research; the Genome Sequence Database, which contributes to an understanding of the role of genes and chromosomes in disease; and the human immunodeficiency virus/autoimmune deficiency syndrome (HIV/AIDS) database, which collects and distributes deoxyribonucleic acid (DNA) sequences and determines phylogenetic relationships.

The National Institutes of Health programs nicely complement the Human Genome Project which is funded jointly by DOE and the National Institutes of Health. Los Alamos has just finished a high-resolution map of chromosome 16 as one of the principal responsibilities of its DOE Center for Human Genome Studies work.

TIES TO INDUSTRY

Industrial interactions continue to be a key contributor to the scientific vitality of Los Alamos National Laboratory. I view working with industry not as an option but as a business necessity. To carry out our mission of nuclear weapons stockpile stewardship and stockpile management, we will increasingly have to integrate manufacturing and maintenance with research and development. We must learn the best practices of American industry which has made great strides in concurrent engineering and quality manufacturing in the past decade. In addition, we find a great deal of commonality with American industry in technology development—this is especially evident in areas such as high-performance computing, modeling, and simulation; advanced materials and processing; advanced sensors; environmentally-conscious manufacturing; optoelectronics; and chemical processing.

The Laboratory's collaboration with American industry has increased dramatically over the past five years. We can credit this increase to the 1989 National Competitiveness and Technology Transfer Act (NCTTA) and the Congressionally supported DOE Defense Programs Technology Transfer Initiative (TTI). The 1989 NCTTA provided the vehicle for effective interactions, the Cooperative research and development agreement (CRADA). The DOE TTI program provided the financial support for cost-sharing, collaborative research and development with industry where direct benefit could be demonstrated for DOE Defense Programs as well as for industry. The NCTTA provided sufficiently attractive intellectual property rights to the private sector to make cost sharing interesting to industry. In fact, these arrangements, and the dual benefits that accrue, encouraged the laboratories and industry to collaborate across a broader spectrum of defense programs, not necessarily limited to the TTI program.

At Los Alamos, we have just signed our 166th CRADA; our CRADA contracts now have a total multiyear value in excess of $385 million. The interest from industry continues to outpace our funding levels by factors of eight to ten. Just as importantly, we are finding enormous excitement among the Laboratory's technical staff for working with industry. We find that by selecting the technology and the industrial partner carefully, we can not only maintain, but enhance, the core technical competencies required for our defense mission. Furthermore, we have several cases where collaboration with industry in an area closely related to defense technologies allowed us to keep critical scientists and engineers in the weapons program.

Let me provide a few examples, to highlight both their contribution to our DP mission and their impact on U.S. industry:

We developed a new acoustic technique called resonant ultrasound spectroscopy at Los Alamos to evaluate material properties of high-temperature superconductors. That technology has now been further developed through licenses and CRADAs into commercial gear usable for a wide range of characterization.

One company is now selling non-destructive testing instruments for applications ranging from improved ball bearing characterization (critical in predicting and improving lifetimes of rotating systems) to improved ceramic oxygen sensors for a major U.S. car company. These same acoustic technologies are now also being used for characterization of weapon pits at one of the Department's facilities. We anticipate that such improved acoustic technologies will be a key contributor to the requalification of weapon components to minimize the need for future production.

The Los Alamos technology base in geophysics and computational modeling has been applied to improved characterization of underground oil and gas reservoirs through improved collection and interpretation of seismic signals and better characterization of the permeability of the underground rock formations. We've further improved this industry's capabilities through work with a major oil field service company to significantly improve the use of well-logging tools. In this latter effort, we applied a class of radiation transport computer codes ("Monte Carlo transport"), developed at Los Alamos to predict the interaction of radiation with materials (important in nuclear weapons design), to improve the accuracy of well logging. Through well-logging, the structure of geologic strata outside the oil well casing can be measured and potentially oil-bearing formations localized. The Director of Research for Schlumberger Doll Research noted that "...the improvements will ultimately provide crucial capabilities required to develop new and improved logging tools and more accurate measurement interpretation, which translates into more economic recovery of oil and gas." Our defense mission also benefits directly from the improvements made in the computational physics capabilities and the development of improved user-friendly interfaces for the many Los Alamos applications of radiation transport codes, most of which have weapons applications.

With Amoco Oil Company, we expanded an important defense mission research area, the study of turbulent interpenetrating material flows, and improved our ability to simulate these flows more accurately with massively parallel computers. Amoco, for its part, is now able to design more efficient processing systems for residual oil and heavy crude. Through the new Advanced Computing Technology Initiative (ACTI), we will further expand the development of these approaches. For the industry, this can mean improved recovery by better relating seismic measurements and simulations to the parameters of each reservoir and well hole. ACTI projects also contribute to explosives technology, the speed of simulation codes, and database development. Department missions benefit from improved use of seismic signals to interpret underground disturbances, including clandestine nuclear detonations, and better tools for determining the safety of radioactive waste storage.

With General Motors we have had the opportunity to develop a novel idea for surface treatment of materials based on an invention at the University of Wisconsin. Surfaces of materials such as gears or dies are treated in a plasma generated with equipment that the Laboratory was able to bring together from its fusion research, weapons program, and strategic defense research. This Plasma Source Ion Implantation CRADA with General Motors promises to improve hardness and wear of industrial materials in an environmentally benign process, while concurrently opening up the possibility of improving materials for enhanced nuclear weapons safety and for decontaminating surfaces of nuclear process equipment at sites such as Rocky Flats.

Much has been said about having the DOE laboratories contribute to the competitiveness of American industry. The Galvin Task Force report cautioned that the laboratories should stay within their mission areas in forming partnerships with industry. Our experience over the past few years, drawn principally from the DOE TTI program where dual benefit to defense programs was built in at the planning stage, is that Los Alamos does indeed have much to offer to American industry. However, the real story is just how much the Laboratory has benefited from these partnerships. We have carefully examined our 150 CRADAs and found that all of the TTI CRADAs, which constitute the bulk of the 150, have direct benefits to our defense programs, with most of them greatly contributing to the core competencies required for our core mission of reducing the global nuclear danger.

Over the next few years we see the laboratories integrating their R&D in nuclear weapons stockpile stewardship with manufacturing. To be able to offer the nation the ability to manufacture whatever will be required in the future without having a large and expensive production complex in a standby mode, we will have to develop agile manufacturing techniques similar to those American industry is developing to stay competitive in a global market place. In the future, small numbers of a variety of remanufactured weapons and/or components will likely be needed, and this will require a highly flexible manufacturing capability with the highest quality assurance standards. Hence, we see future cooperation with industry becoming more focused on providing benefits for the nuclear weapons program. In some cases, we can work cooperatively with U.S. industries to develop manufacturing capabilities that will not only enable future weapon component manufacturing, but also advance the state-of-the-art in the manufacturing sciences crucial to U.S. industry. We have found the CRADA mechanism and the TTI funding channel a very useful way to encourage this truly mutually beneficial arrangement. I encourage the Committee to continue its support of this effort.

III. A FINAL REMARK

Los Alamos has served the nation for fifty-two years. We are prepared to face the new challenges of a different era. Thank you for your thoughtful consideration of the vital issues facing the laboratory.

Mr. SCHIFF. Thank you, Dr. Hecker.
Dr. Schriesheim?

STATEMENT OF DR. ALAN SCHRIESHEIM, DIRECTOR, ARGONNE NATIONAL LABORATORY

Dr. SCHRIESHEIM. Thank you, Mr. Chairman.

I too will not go over the written testimony in any detail.

But listening today, there are just a few comments I might make, I would like to make.

There are three issues when you boil all of the issues down, I believe.

One is the rationale for the existence of the laboratories, the second is the governance of the laboratories, and the third is the efficiency with which the laboratories do what they do.

I would make one comment on the rationale for the laboratories, listening all day to what people have to say about the rationale for their existence.

One that I feel strongly about has to do with this issue of the development of intellectual capability around the world. We often talk about competition, financial competition around the world, but there's a global technological competition.

We no longer have a lock on brains in this country. Everyone agrees to that.

But we should not ourselves go about dismantling the intellectual capability that we have.

When I go around the world to the different countries that I visit, I don't visit their financial institutions, I visit their technological institutions.

They are jealous of what we have constructed in this country. They know our national labs very well, and a number of the countries, the developing countries in fact are developing their own version of the national laboratories that we have in this country.

And I hope we don't go the way of what Ed David, the former science advisor, says we're doing in American industry, and that is dumbing-down the country by dumbing-down the national laboratory system.

So I, you know, we can talk about the specifics a lot but in order for us to continue to compete technologically, I believe there is a rationale for the existence of the laboratories.

Now with respect to the governance, I'm not sure I can add much to the discussion on the governance. I can tell you what I don't think would be effective, and that is the privatization of the laboratories.

Not very long ago, I was in England and I visited Harwell. I've been to Harwell many times in my career. Harwell was, at one point, the equivalent of Oak Ridge or Argonne, a multi-program laboratory, that high-risk, long-range, had very talented people, and has now been converted to privatization, and I'm careful to use that word. It's a little more than a technical service arm of British industry.

If that's the way we want to go, we can certainly do it, but I don't think that's an effective way to go. I'm not talking about corporatization, that's a different issue, but I'm talking about privatization.

So in governance, I know what I don't like. A number of these other schemes we can continue to——

Now in terms of efficiency, as the Chief Executive Officer of a laboratory, it was my other laboratory directors here, certainly each one of us attempts to operate as efficiently as possible within our own constraints.

We do a zero-based budget every year of our indirect operation. Our indirect costs have not increased in the past three years, even with the rise in all of these external issues.

We've almost finished the construction of the largest major facility in the non-weapons DOE facilities and that's certainly on budget, and it will be done in less time than had been predicted to be done.

So in terms of the effectiveness or the efficiency of the system, I would like to echo something that I think, Mr. Chairman, you said.

And that, we have to be careful about numbers because the labs, in their multi-program activities, can not be just judged on one particular number.

If you take a look at computing within the lab, you have one person doing computing. You don't have five people supporting that one person.

On the other hand, if you're running an around the clock facility, you need a lot of people supporting one professional person.

So these numbers have to be looked at carefully.

Thank you, Mr. Chairman.

[The prepared statement of Dr. Schriesheim follows:]

Written Testimony
of
Alan Schriesheim, Director
Argonne National Laboratory

Before the
Subcommittee on Basic Research
and the
Subcommittee on Energy and Environment
of the
Committee on Science
U.S. House of Representatives

September 7, 1995

Introduction

Mr. Chairman and Members of the Subcommittees, I am Alan Schriesheim, Director of Argonne National Laboratory. Argonne conducts its work at two sites. One with about 4,000 employees is located near Chicago, Illinois; the other with about 800 employees is near Idaho Falls, Idaho. I am pleased to have this opportunity to comment on issues that have decisive importance to the future missions and programs of the Department of Energy national laboratories. I shall also address questions presented in the hearing charter.

Laboratory Missions

The mission of the Department of Energy is clearly stated in its strategic plan. We endorse this plan and recognize that our principal mission is to support DOE in carrying out its plan.

We were pleased that recent studies by the Galvin Task Force and the Yergin Task Force reaffirmed DOE's mission. The Galvin Task Force generally supported DOE's core missions in the areas of energy, environment, national security, and fundamental science. Like the Task Force, we believe there is a compelling agenda of important work to be carried out in these traditional DOE mission areas. The Yergin Task Force, which reviewed DOE's energy R&D portfolio, concluded that "the federal government should continue to provide leadership, focus, and substantial financial support for energy R&D."

One of the most important missions for DOE laboratories is the design, construction, and operation of user research facilities. At Argonne, such facilities range in size from multi-million dollar electron microscopes to the nearly $500 million Advanced Photon Source (APS), which we are now commissioning for operation in FY 1996. We also operate the Argonne Tandem-Linac Accelerator System (ATLAS), a heavy-ion accelerator. The world's first accelerator based on superconducting radio-technology, ATLAS can now accelerate ions -- from hydrogen (mass 1) to uranium (mass 238) -- for research to understand nuclear structure and properties. Argonne also operates the Intense Pulsed Neutron Source (IPNS), where university, laboratory and industrial scientists have pioneered the application of neutron diffraction techniques to industrially important materials, such as advanced metal-ceramic composites.

Researchers from outside the Laboratory use Argonne's facilities each year in numbers roughly proportional to the capital investment: scores of users at our electron microscopes, hundreds at ATLAS and IPNS, and a few thousand at the APS, when it is fully functioning. If we look across the laboratory system, we find that user facilities supported by DOE's Office of Energy Research represent an investment of over $10 billion and serve roughly 15 thousand scientists each year.

We concur with the recommendation of the Galvin and Yergin Task Forces that DOE improve the coordination of its basic sciences program with its energy technology programs. Both studies also recommended greater coordination of DOE and industry research and development efforts. On this point, there appears to be some confusion. Several reviews of the task force reports have interpreted their recommendations that DOE concentrate on long-term research to imply less DOE laboratory involvement with industry. Closer readings indicate that both task forces urge DOE and its laboratories, at least in the core mission areas, to develop even closer ties with industry. I fully agree with these recommendations.

Working closely with industry has become a way of doing business in technology development at Argonne. Congress enabled this new emphasis by enacting the Bayh-Dole Act (1986) and the National Competitiveness Technology Transfer Act of 1989. This legislation allows the Laboratory to enter into cooperative R&D partnerships with U.S. industry, based on cost-shared research and negotiated property rights. We find that this new way of working with industry is becoming exceptionally productive.

Counting agreements with industry only begins to tell the story, but it is the best "leading indicator" that we have. Over the past four years, Argonne has negotiated more than 330 partnerships with industry, including 111 cooperative R&D agreements (CRADAs) representing a total investment of $106 million, plus 68 high-temperature superconductivity agreements for a $26 million total investment. About half of these partnerships are with small businesses. Time does not allow me to continue the story, for example to the more than 50 licenses and options to intellectual property that we have negotiated under the new partnership framework, or the new companies that have been formed on the basis of Argonne inventions. Suffice it to say that industry's confidence in the Laboratory as a business partner has increased markedly over the last four years, and the effectiveness of our technology transfer has increased as a result.

Strategic Alignment, Downsizing, and Overhead Cost Reduction

Over the past two years DOE has undertaken many management initiatives and improvements to create a Department of Energy that works better and costs less. Management actions include development of a strategic plan, the Strategic Alignment and Downsizing Initiative, the Galvin and Yergin reviews, contract reform, and a management improvement roadmap to implement the recommendations of the Galvin Task Force.

Through its Strategic Alignment and Downsizing Initiative, the Department has committed to achieving $1.7 billion in organizational cost savings over five years. The Department is achieving these savings by eliminating organizational redundancies, streamlining processes, and reducing overhead expenses. DOE plans to cut its workforce by 3,800, or 27 percent, within five years.

For their part, the laboratories are committed to reducing their overhead costs by $1.4 billion over five years. Each has either instituted a new program or strengthened an existing program to reduce overhead costs.

At Argonne, we plan and budget our overhead and support operations under a rigorous management process. Based on a modified zero-based budgetary system, the process engages all levels of the organization, from first-level supervisors in support operations to top management. We regard it a major achievement that Argonne managed to hold its indirect rate constant during the FY 1992 to FY 1994 period, when, in response to new DOE requirements, the Laboratory rapidly expanded its activities in environment, safety and health and in conduct of operations. In FY 1995 we managed to reduce our indirect rate from 26% to 24%. This was achieved through significant delayering and realignment within our support organizations, where we increased productivity, broadened spans of control, and generally exploited cost-reduction opportunities wherever they were found.

We plan further overhead cost reductions in FY 1996. Five months ago I established the Director's Cost Savings Committee. This committee, which I personally chair, is examining opportunities for additional cost reductions through re-engineering business functions, outsourcing, and early retirement programs.

We are encouraged in these efforts by the new performance-based contract that the University of Chicago and DOE recently signed for the operation of Argonne. A product of DOE's contract reform initiative, the contract gives the Laboratory more management flexibility in such areas as personnel policies and salary decisions. In return, the Laboratory has agreed to reduce total compensation costs by a specified amount every year for the next four years. If we are successful in meeting these targets, a large part of each year's compensation, overhead, and other savings will be available to fund an incentive award program for Laboratory employees.

Let me conclude my comments on organizational alignment and cost reduction with a few general observations. First, as I have already indicated, Argonne management has long regarded overhead cost control as a top management priority. The immediate reason is simple. The funds we receive from DOE and other sponsors are provided only for research and development. There is no separate funding for operating support services, which the Laboratory must finance by "taxing" the R&D funding. This process automatically makes every research program manager at Argonne a champion for overhead cost reduction. To the research manager, from principal investigator to the associate laboratory director, the longer-term benefits of overhead cost reduction are clear. They make us more cost-competitive with our sister laboratories and with other R&D performers. In the short run, the benefits are even clearer: every overhead dollar saved is a research dollar earned!

Thus, we and our sister laboratories have always been motivated to save on overhead costs. What is new about the present situation is that DOE has offered the laboratories unprecedented opportunities to work jointly with the Department to reduce costs. We hope that these joint hearings before key subcommittees of the House Committee on Science signal a further opportunity, to work with Congress to eliminate the root causes of much of DOE's micromanagment of its laboratories.

Elimination of Self-Regulation

Moving from self-regulation of its laboratories to direct external regulation by EPA, OSHA, and NRC is one of the most important steps that DOE could take to improve the governance and streamline the oversight of its laboratories. Such external regulation should substitute for DOE self-regulation, not add to it. It will not be feasible to shift regulatory functions for all operations at all laboratories to other federal agencies. But for most operations this approach is entirely feasible. At Argonne, I believe it would be straightforward to identify and isolate those few operations where continued DOE regulatory oversight would be necessary. We would be happy to serve as a test bed for such an approach.

Mr. SCHIFF. Thank you, Dr. Schriesheim.

Dr. Tarter.

STATEMENT OF DR. C. BRUCE TARTER, DIRECTOR, UNIVERSITY OF CALIFORNIA LAWRENCE LIVERMORE NATIONAL LABORATORY

Dr. TARTER. Thank you very much, Mr. Chairman.

I will try to hold your request to be very brief.

I have two comments in each of the areas of mission, and then something on the order of maintenance or the management part.

I would like to echo a theme which Dr. Hecker alluded to in the opening part of his comment. That I think in the national security area, which is not the specific area of this Committee but it's a major mission for DOE, in my own mind, I think that is one of the striking examples of extraordinary success within the Department and its laboratories in the past year to year and a half.

I think the new stockpile stewardship and management program represents an extraordinary transformation. It has changed beyond that which is characteristic of the government over many years. That has been done in the period of about a year to a year and a half.

My own model and my own view of the way DOE (or whatever governing body of the missions for the laboratories), and I think your bill, and I think there's general consensus on the broad missions, a similar thing can and should happen in each of those major areas, whether they be cleanup or energy R&D.

And I think one of the most powerful suggestions Bob Galvin has made is adopting the roadmap philosophy for each of those major mission areas.

I think we've done that in national security. I think it's well on its way in some of the subfields. I think that's my approach to mission, is to build on success, not to worry about micromanaging the interstices of difficulties.

And I think we have success models well beyond that which I've commented on in the written testimony.

I think as each of the others has so far commented, there are two aspects to reducing the indirect costs or the overhead costs, or whatever you want to call that stuff that isn't work.

And I think one of those, I think Deputy Secretary Curtis described, both in his written testimony and the verbal testimony, all the things going on at DOE.

I think almost everyone at this table is certainly encouraged by them, and I think it's too early to report, but I think we're participating with great enthusiasm to each of the joint reductions in administrative overhead from DOE, either locally or centrally.

As I think each of the others indicated, each of our laboratories is engaged in a major activity.

Let me give you one anecdote about the one at Livermore.

Like everyone else, we are going to try to overhaul and completely re-engineer our own processes. My particular way of doing this has been to charter a Task Force. That's what one does, right? charter Task Forces?

But I, like some of the others, have picked a half-a-dozen of the senior people in the laboratory whose normal jobs is to do work.

And I have said, go out and address every indirect part of the laboratory for all the things of value. Is this currently smart? Is it a legacy? All the questions you would ask if you put everything on the table.

But the other thing I said to them is, anybody can cut cost. Anybody can find a way to slash. What I want out of you is a clever way to re-engineer and to rethink the world, where the product that you have in mind is a better effective laboratory, not simply a system where I have listed twelve ways to cut costs.

And I think that is the trick whether you're doing it within a laboratory, within the Agency, or even from the Congressional perspective.

And I think several of you in your comments during the day have tried to get at that, and I think Chairman Walker said it well this morning. This is something we have to do right.

And so in the laboratory it's not easy. It won't be easy in DOE, and I hope we all will get it right.

Thank you very much.

[The prepared statement of Dr. Tarter follows:]

FUTURE MISSIONS AND GOVERNANCE FOR THE DEPARTMENT OF ENERGY NATIONAL LABORATORIES

Joint Hearing of the Subcommittees on Basic Research
and Energy and Environment
Committee on Science
U.S. House of Representatives

September 7, 1995

C. Bruce Tarter, Director
University of California
Lawrence Livermore National Laboratory

INTRODUCTION

I am the Director of the Lawrence Livermore National Laboratory (LLNL). We were founded in 1952 as a nuclear weapons laboratory, and national security continues to be our principal mission. In addition, we have major programs in energy, environment, and biosciences.

I appreciate this opportunity to present my views on Future Missions and Governance for the Department of Energy National Laboratories. My comments are focused on the five questions asked by the subcommittees and on the four pending pieces of legislation before the House of Representatives.

Since the end of the Cold War there has been intense re-examination of the role of the federal government in scientific research and development (R&D). There have been studies of the Department of Defense laboratories and engineering research centers, the NASA system of Laboratories and Centers, the Environmental Protection Agency, and the Department of Energy (DOE) and its laboratories (by both the Galvin Task Force and the U.S. General Accounting Office). Broadly speaking, all of these assessments have produced two general recommendations: clarify and revitalize the core missions, and dramatically reduce the administrative and bureaucratic apparatus that oversees the actual work that takes place.

I believe the Department of Energy and its laboratories have initiated significant actions that are very responsive to these two recommendations. I will speak to each in turn.

Mission of the DOE National Laboratories

The core mission areas of the DOE national laboratories are clear: national security, energy, environmental science and technology, and underpinning fields of basic science. The Department, its laboratories, the Galvin Task Force, and the authors of H.R.2142, which concisely states the core missions of DOE laboratories in Section 102, are in agreement on this point. What is at issue is how these broad mission responsibilities translate into strategic program goals within the Department and technical programs to be executed at the national laboratories and other research facilities.

Mission Definition and Program Integration

In the area of national security, the Department and its three defense laboratories (Livermore, Los Alamos, and Sandia) have responded to President Clinton's challenge and developed a dramatically revised program to provide for the stewardship and management of the nuclear weapons stockpile in the absence of nuclear testing. This program builds on the technical strengths and unique facilities of each of the laboratories, and provides for efficient interaction with the production facilities as we transition to the requirements of the post-Cold War world. Similarly, in the areas of nonproliferation and arms control, the Department and five of its laboratories are pursuing an integrated effort to deal with a range of issues from the worldwide control of nuclear materials to technology development for arms control verification, nonproliferation monitoring, and counter-proliferation.

In the area of basic science, the Department has an unparalleled set of large scientific user facilities that provide an extraordinary resource to university, industrial, and federal researchers across a broad range of scientific disciplines.

Two more contentious areas are environmental clean-up, and some aspects of civilian R&D, particularly energy research. In both areas, the Department and the laboratories could benefit from better-articulated goals and roadmaps, and such efforts are underway. Dealing with the environmental legacy of fifty years of nuclear weapons production raises so many jurisdictional and legal issues that it is difficult to use a science- and risk-based assessment to set priorities. However, in the long term, this is the only approach that can produce cost-effective and workable solutions. I believe the Department and the laboratories are beginning to make progress on this task, but it will require patience, as well as advice and support, from both the executive and legislative branches of government to make major inroads on this very difficult problem. In my view—and that of the Yergin Task Force—there also is an important role for the federal government in long-term energy research. The size and character of that effort is under discussion and development.

In short, I believe the overall missions of the Department of Energy in national security, environmental clean-up, basic sciences, and long-term energy research address clear national needs, and in the majority of areas I think the Department has a clear strategy. In others it needs more work and some redefinition, but this is a matter for debate and iteration, not a rationale for wholesale rethinking of a programmatic structure whose aims are sound. Activities to refine goals and missions are consistent with language in H.R.2142, and the legislation could provide a formal framework for continuation of these efforts, and a means by which Congress could monitor the process and progress we make.

Mission Specificity at the Laboratories

Each major DOE laboratory clearly needs to have a defining purpose, whether it be in national security, the running of a major scientific user facility, or a coherent set of responsibilities in energy and environment. However, one of the great strengths of the laboratories is their extraordinary array of scientific talent, and efforts to rigidly compartmentalize their activities into narrow areas will lower the quality of both the staff and its output. Science and technology are opportunistic, and the country will be best-served by enhancing a focus on core missions without creating bureaucratic barriers to other activities.

Sizing Technical Programs at the National Laboratories

I have concerns about laboratory-sizing legislation that is overly prescriptive and mandates specific reductions. In my judgment, the laboratories will "size" themselves correctly as the mission and program definitions are refined, and as the management requirements are restructured. Streamlining should result from elimination of non-value-added administrative activities and from *better integration* by DOE of the programmatic efforts at the laboratories *rather than greater differentiation* in the broad mission responsibilities. Of the proposed legislation, H.R.2142 offers the most workable means for achieving that objective.

Administration and Operations at the DOE National Laboratories

Streamlining Administrative Functions at the National Laboratories

The administrative and operational viscosity within the Department was thoroughly described in the report of the Galvin Task Force. Since that time the Department has initiated a number of actions and projects aimed at a sweeping reform of the existing bureaucratic system. The goals are laudable: a strong movement toward external regulation (what's good enough for the rest of the country ought to be good enough for the Department and its laboratories), the adoption of "best business practices" as a way of carrying out business-like activities, a major reduction in bureaucracy and the number of bureaucrats, and a general test for all administrative and operational activities that they produce some clear "value-added" to a skeptical observer. I am very encouraged by the progress to date in some of these areas, but I think it is too early to make a full assessment of the overall impact.

Initiatives and Activities at LLNL

Livermore is aggressively responding to the need for reductions in bureaucracy. First, we are enthusiastically seeking opportunities to join with DOE and other oversight bodies to eliminate non-value-added regulation and management. We are pushing for performance-based assessment, for pilot projects to decrease the frequency and scope of reviews, and for as rapid and extensive a conversion to external standards as can be achieved. Within the Laboratory, we have chartered a high-level, cross-cutting task force whose job is to re-examine all of our internal practices to see which ones add value, which ones can be done in a more cost-effective way, and which ones ought to be changed entirely. This group's principal charter is to a develop a set of recommendations to make the Laboratory cost-competitive, less bureaucratic, and more efficient in executing its primary scientific and technical missions. We expect to achieve a much higher ratio of scientific to administrative effort, but the precise numbers will depend both on the task force's analysis and DOE's ability to reduce excessive requirements. I am confident that this task force and our subsequent actions will produce a long-needed overhaul in the internal way the Laboratory does its job.

Governance of the DOE National Laboratories

A second aspect of administration and operations is the role of the contractor in overseeing the work of the laboratories. As I will comment in more detail later in this testimony, I think the University of California has provided excellent oversight of Livermore, Los Alamos, and Berkeley during the past decades. The current contract added a much stronger management role for the University, and it also introduced performance measures as a way of evaluating the activities of the laboratories. On balance the new contract has been quite successful. It pioneered the whole concept of performance-based management within DOE, and in many ways this contract has paved the way for other recent contractual actions taken by DOE. I believe the basic government-owned, contractor-operated (GOCO) laboratory arrangement has been so successful that every effort should be made to retain and improve it. It has produced some of the most outstanding laboratories in the world—including NASA's Jet Propulsion Laboratory run by Cal Tech as well as the DOE laboratories—and in my mind combines the best features of federally-sponsored research with the independence provided by the contractor.

In summary, I am encouraged by progress to date in reducing the scope and extent of administrative and operational oversight and regulation, but it's too early for a full report card. The efforts underway are in the right direction, the contractors are pursuing similar approaches, and the laboratories are zealously engaged in cost-cutting initiatives. If this combined approach can succeed, we will have a streamlined, effective system that should provide the framework in which outstanding science and technology can flourish.

MISSION OF THE DOE NATIONAL LABORATORIES

Four bills pending before the House (H.R.87, H.R.1510, H.R.1993, and H.R.2142) deal either implicitly or explicitly with the issue of mission definition for the DOE national laboratories for the purpose of downsizing or streamlining the DOE laboratory complex.

A motivation behind these legislative efforts to establish more precise laboratory mission definitions is a perception that there is considerable overlap of responsibilities among the DOE laboratories and that the laboratories have been inappropriately diversifying their activities beyond their traditional responsibilities. Some of these concerns were expressed earlier this year in the Galvin Task Force report, *Alternative Futures for the Department of Energy National Laboratories*, and the GAO report, *National Laboratories Need Clearer Missions and Better Management*. More recently, the Yergin Task Force noted that "Energy R&D programs that are presently dispersed through different DOE laboratories should be reorganized and consolidated around defined strategic research foci (e.g., centers of excellence)..."

Undoubtedly, opportunities exist for improved programmatic integration within DOE to more effectively manage distributed responsibilities among laboratories. Nevertheless, in an overall sense, the missions of the Department and the laboratories are clear. The DOE's mission areas include national security, energy, environmental science and technology, and underpinning fields of basic science. Section 102 of H.R.2142 concisely restates these core missions of the Department.

The DOE national laboratories' principal mission is to carry out R&D activities in support of the Department's core missions, where, according to the Galvin Task Force, "there remains a compelling agenda of important work to be performed." The laboratories' capabilities are needed and most effectively utilized when:

- The national interest is at stake.
- The best science and technology are required.
- Large and complex research facilities are needed.
- Expertise in a variety of disciplines must be integrated.
- The technical risk is high, with the potential of very high rewards.
- A sustained long-term commitment is needed.
- The job will not be accomplished if the national laboratories don't do it.

Each of the DOE national laboratories needs a clear defining purpose, whether it be in national security, the running of a major scientific user facility, or a coherent set of responsibilities in energy and environment. In our case, the defining purpose is national security, and the core competencies and special facilities at the Laboratory align with that purpose. LLNL is a multiprogram laboratory because of the breadth of these core capabilities, which include nuclear science and technology, lasers and electro-optics, computer simulation of complex systems, advanced sensors and instrumentation, biotechnology, and advanced process and manufacturing technology. Each capability is necessary for and supportive of our national security work. Their integration provides us with an extraordinary array of scientific talent that can effectively and efficiently be brought to bear on a wide range of problems.

It follows that mission definition for a multiprogram laboratory, such as Livermore, must be broad—and seemingly in conflict with a goal of more precise differentiation among the mission elements assigned to the various laboratories. We believe that there is no real conflict. It is at the program definition level that distinctions are more readily apparent. Rather than greater differentiation in broad mission responsibilities, what is needed is better integration by DOE of the programmatic efforts at the laboratories. To illustrate this point, consider as an example our important responsibility to ensure the safety, security and reliability of the U.S. nuclear weapons stockpile and associated activities at the three DOE defense laboratories.

Mission Definition and Program Integration: Successes and Pitfalls to Avoid

Two years ago President Clinton challenged the nuclear establishment to "explore other means of maintaining our confidence in the safety, the reliability and the performance of our own weapons" under a Comprehensive Test Ban Treaty. Since then we have been working with the

DOE Assistant Secretary for Defense Programs, who has led the Department, the national security laboratories, and other sites in the weapons complex in developing a long-term plan for post-Cold War stewardship of the nuclear weapons stockpile.

DOE's Stockpile Stewardship and Management Program envisions a much smaller overall complex, operating in a more integrated fashion and drawing on the unique strengths of each site. It is a coordinated plan to manage the defense laboratories as a "diversified research system" similar to the manner recommended in the GAO report, *National Laboratories Need Clearer Missions and Better Management*.

Much consolidation has already occurred to achieve a leaner national nuclear weapons program, and one focused on stockpile stewardship rather than new design and testing. We have eliminated unnecessarily redundant facilities and capabilities among the laboratories. Livermore's core nuclear weapons program is a factor of two smaller than it was at the end of the Cold War. As a leaner element of the integrated program, we have sharpened our focus. We have preserved the core competencies necessary to support our broad national security mission and we attend to LLNL-developed weapons in the stockpile or being dismantled. We also operate special user facilities that provide unique capabilities to the national program. These include the High Explosives Applications Facility, the Nova laser, the Flash X-Ray Facility at Site 300 for hydrodynamic testing, and the Superblock complex for special nuclear materials research and engineering testing.

The Stockpile Stewardship and Management Program is an example where the process of mission definition and program integration—involving the Department and its laboratories—is working well. And there are many other success stories, such as the arms control and nonproliferation program at DOE, which is an integrated five-laboratory effort, the Human Genome Project being pursued at Livermore, Los Alamos, and Berkeley, and the B-factory being built by SLAC, Berkeley, and Livermore. In each case there is clear program leadership from a single office within DOE, a goal and a roadmap to achieve it are delineated, and distribution of responsibilities among several laboratories and collaborating universities and industry—including lead-institution designation for program subelements where warranted.

In other mission areas where the Department's strategic goals (and roadmaps to achieve them) continue to evolve, we are assisting the Department in refining both its goals and the Laboratory's mission definition to support those goals. The Yergin Task Force report suggests that energy R&D is a case where the programs at the laboratories could be better focused, and, as I have noted, environmental clean-up of the DOE nuclear weapons complex would benefit from use of scientific risk-based assessments to set priorities and from environmental technology development at the laboratories to reduce costs. These activities to refine goals and missions are consistent with language in H.R.2142 that specifies a procedure by which the Secretary of Energy is to make proposals for laboratory mission assignments. H.R.2142 could provide a formal framework for continuation of these efforts, and a means by which Congress could monitor the process and progress we make.

It is important that the process followed to improve mission definition and integrate programs avoids certain pitfalls:

- Mission definition which excessively constrains unique capabilities to integrate disparate technologies. As noted in their report, "The [Galvin] Task Force recognizes that there are important and practical limitations on how narrow one can be in delineating missions for multi-program laboratories which exhibit vast breadth both in technical expertise and programmatic activities, and whose uniqueness in large degree derives from an ability to support complex, multi-disciplinary R&D activities."

  I believe that the most distinguishing feature of LLNL is the continually-demonstrated ability of our workforce to integrate the capabilities embodied in our core competencies and special facilities to solve complex technical problems. We work mission-driven issues from concept formulation through to engineering development and/or transfer to the private sector. Matrix management and our multidisciplinary project-team approach foster integration of basic research and applied R&D efforts at the Laboratory and combine core competencies in a way that stimulates innovative problem-solving.

  Our mission-driven activities have always been focused on delivering "products" of national importance. We have delivered, for example, fully tested nuclear weapon designs, the Nova laser, the AVLIS system, several generations of magnetic fusion facilities, world-class precision machining capabilities, and the sensor systems for the Clementine moon mapping satellite. Rigid compartmentalization of missions among the laboratories would restrict our ability to apply Livermore's extraordinary capabilities to such a wide range of national needs.

- Mission definition that stifles innovation and effective application of special expertise to new and important problems. A narrowing of laboratory mission definition invariably will lead to a narrowing of opportunities for innovative spin-offs. For example, if our responsibilities were limited to defense applications, many dual-use opportunities that have had far-reaching impact might have been missed. Multidisciplinary national security work at the Laboratory has led to numerous scientific and technical innovations that have been in news this year—

- a micropower impulse radar technology developed for inertial confinement fusion experiments, which may lead to a revolutionary new generation of "smarter" consumer products,
- development of aerogels that might cut the cost of contaminated water treatment and water purification by a factor of 10,
- discovery of dark matter in the galaxy,
- demonstration of the use of harmless micro-organisms to clean up solvent-contaminated groundwater for environmental restoration,
- development of a means for detecting flaws in roadways and bridges with minimal disruption of traffic flow, and
- the test firing of an ultra-short-pulse 100-trillion-watt laser opening up a new regime of physics to be explored.

- Technical program micromanagement. Division of responsibilities among laboratories is a simpler—but much less efficient—management tool than integration of the capabilities within the laboratories. It also tends to lead to the kind of micromanagement that plagues administrative areas.

Sizing Technical Programs at the National Laboratories

Mission definition for each of the DOE national laboratories affects future decisions about the long-term size and configuration of the laboratory complex. The four aforementioned bills pending before the House (H.R.87, H.R.1510, H.R.1993, and H.R.2142) deal with these decisions in different ways. H.R.1510 is the most prescriptive of the bills, requiring a reduction in workforce by one-third at the nondefense laboratories. H.R.87 and H.R.1993 each establish a "Laboratory Facilities Commission" and a process for deciding whether or not to reconfigure, privatize, or close laboratories or some their facilities. (H.R.1993 also abolishes the Department of Energy.) In H.R.2142, the Secretary of Energy is required to assign missions to laboratories and to streamline them, if necessary.

The thrust of these bills is that clearer definition of laboratory missions will help identify unnecessary redundancies in capabilities, facilities and/or effort, which will enable streamlining of programs at the laboratories without undue impact on the Department's most important missions. The costs to taxpayers would be expected to be lower and the savings could help balance the budget.

The principle is valid and as I have described, has already been put into practice in the formulation of Defense Programs' stockpile stewardship and management program. The lead and shared responsibilities of three defense laboratories are being clarified, and the laboratories' programs are being sized accordingly. We are committed to achieving major reductions in our costs of doing business.

However, I have concerns about laboratory-sizing legislation that is overly prescriptive and mandates specific reductions (as in Sec.3.(a) of H.R.1510 and Sec.601 of H.R.1993). In my judgment, the laboratories will "size" themselves correctly as the mission and program definitions are refined, and as the management requirements are restructured. For example, only a few years ago, the LLNL employee level was approximately 15% greater than the present 7300.

In the longer-run, each laboratory should be held accountable for nurturing its core strengths, for focusing on its major mission, and for avoiding "job shopping" activities. At the same time, innovative and effective application of the special expertise of the labs to appropriate new and important problems should be rewarded.

Principally, streamlining should result from elimination of non-value-added administrative activities and from *better integration* by DOE of the programmatic efforts at the laboratories *rather than greater differentiation* in the broad mission responsibilities assigned to the multiprogram laboratories. Of the proposed legislation, H.R.2142 offers the most workable means for achieving that objective. We question the usefulness of other proposals in pending legislation for overly prescriptive mission assignment to the laboratories and their sizing.

STREAMLINING THE DOE NATIONAL LABORATORIES

Streamlining Administrative Functions at the National Laboratories

Considerable cost savings may be realized by further streamlining of administrative functions at the laboratories through a revamping of the system of oversight and DOE regulations. The Galvin Task Force posited that 20 to 50 percent would be saved if the laboratories were "corporatized" as they recommended. The Yergin Task Force recommended that the Department develop a plan "that will reduce total energy R&D cost by 15 percent, accomplished over a one-year period, without reducing funds going directly to scientists and engineers actually engaged in research. These cuts will be directed at administrative, compliance, and other overhead costs."

Top DOE management is strongly committed to reforming the way the Department manages its laboratories. However, problems that have led to wasteful bureaucratic redundancies in Laboratory operations and management will take time to rectify. In addition to their efforts in strategic planning and strategic alignment, and the task forces and advisory committees they have formed, DOE has initiated steps to improve its management of the laboratories. Some actions include efforts to:

- implement an entirely new "commercial best practices" procurement system for the contractors;
- reduce the burden imposed by excessively frequent DOE requirement-driven audits and appraisals through new initiatives such as the Business Management Pilot Oversight project;
- reform the DOE system of orders and directives that dictate DOE-mandated requirements; and their implementation; and
- work toward better ES&H performance at the laboratories at lower cost, including charting a path toward external regulation.

We encourage Congress to support these initiatives and monitor these activities through periodic reports on progress and achievements. I am very encouraged by the progress to date in some of these areas—most notably in the area of procurement and, to a lesser extent in the area of oversight (audits and appraisals). However, it is too early to make a full assessment of the impact of DOE's initiatives. Our perspective of some of the most important of the Department's actions is as follows:

- Reform of procurement practices. Within the last six months, DOE has embarked on a major revision of the framework it requires our procurement activities to follow. We are moving away from an inefficient and bureaucratic "federal norm" model toward widespread adoption of best commercial practices. The relaxation in our need to follow strict federal procurement processes, such as those historically required by the Federal Acquisition Regulations (FARs) and the DOE Acquisition Regulations (DEARs), will significantly reduce costs, cycle times, and the excessive documentation normally associated with federal procurements. Our ability to benchmark our procurement program against commercial best practices has already produced sizable cost savings in the low-dollar procurements through the use of such tools as purchasing cards. As we and the other laboratories develop new commercially-based procedures to effect the high-dollar procurements, additional cost savings and efficiency gains will be realized.

- Reform of management oversight (audits and appraisals). Bureaucratic redundancy in the management of the Laboratory stems from two distinct major sources: excessive oversight and excessive regulation. Oversight pertains to the audits and appraisals conducted at the Laboratory each year, which number in the 100's. In the area of business practices, we are reviewed by the DOE, our DOE Operations Office (Oakland), and UC, in additional to our internal appraisals. In the area of ES&H, we are also reviewed by DOE/EH, cognizant DOE program offices, and State agencies (CalEPA) and other Federal agencies. Until recently, too little effort has been made to coordinate these activities, which has resulted in multiple appraisals and audits of the same function. DOE has undertaken Pilot Oversight Programs to reduce the number of on-site visits through better coordination of oversight activities.

— *In business management.* The Business Management Pilot Oversight project was instituted in April for a one-year trial period. It seeks to evaluate the feasibility of establishing a single comprehensive annual review of contractor performance based on measured performance and results—as opposed to numerous audits and reviews throughout the year. The oversight is to be conducted on a results-oriented performance basis and will rely substantially, but not exclusively, on laboratory self-assessments.

We view the Business Management Pilot Oversight as a very positive step that complements the performance-based management contract established by UC and DOE in 1992. In fact, the methods devised in Appendix F of the UC contract—including procedures, schedules, self-assessments, and performance measures—have provided a model to help design the agency-wide pilot process. Both LLNL and UC look at this project as a way to strengthen their partnership with DOE and to improve operational performance and lower administrative and support costs.

— *In ES&H.* We are also working on a similar Pilot Oversight project with Defense Programs to coordinate programmatic ES&H reviews. As in the business management case, the plan is to have all on-site review activity conducted once a year during a scheduled two-week period. The reviews conducted by the Office of the Assistant Secretary for Environment, Health and Safety, however, will continue to be independent.

- Reform of DOE orders. There is widespread agreement that the DOE's system of directives—including Policies, Orders, Notices, Manuals and Rules—is not working as an effective management tool. The Department has set as a goal the complete overhaul of the system. At a minimum, we expect the Department to eliminate redundancy and overlap among Orders, Orders that are process-oriented (how-to-do) rather than outcome-oriented, and excessive requirements which do not balance costs vs. risks.

The DOE is already able to point to a substantial reduction in the number of Orders. However, although they are doing a good job eliminating redundant Orders, the results to date generally have not yet substantially reduced non-value-added requirements or our costs. We intend to work constructively with the Department to make these efforts succeed. We recognize that there is a commitment by top management for reform, that there is a need within the Department for reform to meet the cost and personnel reductions identified in their Strategic Alignment Initiative, and that it will take some time to undo the damage inflicted by years of overly compliance-oriented bureaucracy.

External Regulation of the DOE National Laboratories

Two of the four proposed bills explicitly address elimination of self-regulation by the Department of Energy. In general, we are favorably disposed to the concept of external regulation of the laboratories because of the inordinate bureaucratic burden that self-regulation by the Department has imposed on us. Self-regulation, in principle, could have been more efficient than external regulation, but that is far from the case now. There may be no other way to remedy the situation than to take steps toward external regulation, which could provide real cost savings. Oversight consistently and sensibly based on external standards and regulations would help remove existing bureaucratic redundancies and provide more stability and cost certainty to laboratory activities. It could also boost public confidence in the safe operation of our facilities.

The Department recognizes that its system of directives to manage ES&H at the laboratories is not working properly and is taking steps to revamp the system. DOE is taking three actions in parallel:

- Reform of the DOE system of directives applying to ES&H to remove redundancies and to make them results-oriented rather than process-oriented. As I have noted, the DOE initiative to reform its ES&H Orders has yet to have a major positive impact on operations at the Laboratory. Almost all of the requirements in the old ES&H Orders have been maintained in the new Orders or have been moved to new DOE Implementation Guidance or Standards which spell out the Department's expectations. While the number of pages of Orders is being reduced, the number of pages of Guidance and Standards is increasing rapidly.

In addition, DOE is requiring DOE-approved Implementation Plans by contractors that are descriptions of methods the contractor will use to meet requirements in the new Orders. We anticipate that we will have to justify equivalency of any deviations in our Implementation Plans from DOE's Guidance and Standards. Other regulatory agencies do not require *a priori* approved implementation plans to describe methods for meeting requirements, except in cases where a significant violation has been found. Further reduction of the regulatory load is needed.

- Change in the DOE orders to make the regulatory activities that which is "Necessary and Sufficient" according to the specifics of the facility and its operations. The concept is to adopt a "Graded Approach" to regulations rather than "one size fits all." Regulations should balance risks and costs dictated by site specifics. One needs to analyze the work being performed and the hazards involved to develop a set of "Necessary and Sufficient" standards based on objective technical measures. This set would include all legally mandated standards and would likely include National Consensus standards used by the private sector. It would then be the responsibility of local managers to devise procedures—integrated into operations for cost efficiency—to meet those standards.

  LLNL is participating in a pilot project to develop "Necessary and Sufficient" standards for dealing with radiological wastes, and we believe that substantial improvements in efficiency may follow. The lessons learned by DOE in this and other pilot projects will affect the pace of widespread implementation of "Necessary and Sufficient" standards to substitute for the Department's Orders and Implementation Guidance and Standards.

- Examination of efficacy and feasibility of moving to external regulation by the Advisory Committee on External Regulation of Department of Energy Nuclear Safety (the Ahearne Committee). The Ahearne Committee, which was appointed to help the DOE to "chart a path toward external regulation," is expected to provide the Secretary a set of recommendations by the end of the year. While hearing widespread support for a move to external regulation, the Committee is concerned about the transition process (which facilities are to move to which regulations when) and the need for clear definition of the responsibilities and accountability of line managers. We expect their recommendations to have a strong impact on the transition process whether external regulation happens as a result of Congressional legislation or as a follow-on to the Committee's report to the Secretary.

External regulation will help lower our costs and streamline management functions only if it is a *substitute* for DOE regulation rather than an *addition*. Of course there are a few areas where no body of external regulations exist (e.g., nuclear explosives safety), but this list should not become expansive to other areas simply because DOE operations are greater in magnitude at a specific DOE contractor site than those at private industry facilities. And, in areas where a "Necessary and Sufficient" analysis indicates that existing external regulations are not sufficient, they should be augmented rather than replaced by DOE orders. Finally, external regulations will require a new approach by DOE to overseeing its contractors. If DOE continues appraisals that duplicate those of the regulatory agencies or fails to coordinate appraisals, as has been the past practice, cost-saving opportunities will be lost.

"Streamlining" Initiatives at Lawrence Livermore National Laboratory

In addition to our enthusiastic participation with DOE and other oversight bodies in efforts such as the Pilot Oversight projects, we have been taking steps at LLNL to improve our internal management of programs and to streamline administrative functions. Four prominent activities include:

- Programmatic alignment and strategic planning at LLNL. In June 1994, we published *Framing the Laboratory's Future: A Vision for Lawrence Livermore National Laboratory*. This vision statement was the first formal step in laying out our strategic vision for the future of the Laboratory. Since then we have better aligned Laboratory Programs with the organization of DOE so that we can be more responsive to our principal customer, and the Programs have developed mission statements and strategic plans.

- Implementation of Appendix F of the DOE-UC contract. We have worked closely with the University and the Department to help make the performance-based management system built into the DOE-UC contract a success. Appendix F in the contract contains more than 130 specific performance measures that must be attained in Science & Technology and Operations & Administration. We have agreed to be held accountable to achieve specified results, and both LLNL's and UC's management are evaluated on how well the Laboratory performs against jointly agreed upon standards. This past year, the "scores" assigned in each separate category by UC and DOE are almost indistinguishable—indicating that the system is working—and LLNL was rated "excellent" (or "exceeds expectations") for both Science & Technology and Operations & Administration.

- Cost accountability at LLNL. We are restructuring the Laboratory to meet new and future programmatic and business goals. As a first step, this past year we changed the way we budget and account for distributed and indirect costs. The intent was to provide additional consistency in the distribution of costs across activities, to make costs more visible, and to closely tie the distributed/indirect costs back to all programs on a causal-beneficial basis. The new approach is helping managers make more informed business decisions based on true costs, thereby allowing appropriate sizing of activities.

- The Cost Cutting Initiative Task Force. In July 1995, we established a Task Force to review LLNL programmatic and institutional operations to see which ones add value, which ones can be done in a more cost-effective way, and which ones ought to be changed entirely. The Task Force is made up of seven senior Laboratory managers who will work full-time on this effort for the next four to six months. They have been directed to consider "everything on the table," to challenge current methods, and to accept reasonable risks. With strong senior management support and involvement, the Task Force is to find ways to achieve a much higher ratio of scientific to administrative effort, recognizing that the precise numbers will depend on their analysis and DOE's ability to reduce non-value-added oversight and regulations. Their goal is to manage down operational costs to make the Laboratory cost-competitive, less bureaucratic, and more efficient in executing its primary scientific and technical missions. The Task Force is to provide recommendations that can impact FY96 operations and associated budgets.

GOVERNANCE OF THE DOE NATIONAL LABORATORIES

Mission definition for the departmental laboratories, their proper sizing, their oversight by the Department, and the DOE regulations they must abide by are issues which I have just discussed. Here I wish to focus on two governance issues: Livermore's future as a GOCO laboratory and consideration of the transfer of LLNL to the Department of Defense (DoD). Sec.504 of H.R.1993 provides for the transfer to an Under Secretary in DoD of all "national security functions of the Department, including defense, nonproliferation, and defense-related environmental management programs." This is to include "oversight of the defense and nondefense functions and budgets" at the three DOE defense laboratories.

LLNL's Future as a GOCO Laboratory

As I have said, the governance problems that have led to bureaucratic redundancies in laboratory operations and management will take time to rectify despite top DOE management's strong commitment to reform. We believe that continuation of our relationship with University of California as a government-owned, contractor-operated (GOCO) laboratory provides us our best opportunity to preserve scientific excellence and to deal with these governance problems.

- Our connection with the University of California (UC) is important to us. UC has been the contractor for our Laboratory as well as those at Los Alamos and Berkeley since our beginning. This arrangement has provided great benefit to the Laboratory and the nation. It has been a major factor in attracting and maintaining the quality of our workforce, it has provided an atmosphere in which independent views and technical honesty are treated as core values, and it has led to an array of scientific and technical associations that would have otherwise not been achievable.

  The University's connection with DOE is both historic and very forward looking. Leading up to the most recent management and operating (M&O) contract renewal in 1992, both organizations saw the need to restructure the contract. During the negotiations, UC proposed a new approach—a Performance-Based Management System, which focuses on results achieved and demands greater contractor accountability. It was an innovative breakthrough for a government contract and, in hindsight, probably became a benchmark for the contract reform movement and efforts to reform DOE's governance of its laboratories. The preamble of the contract expresses the desire of both parties "to provide for significantly expanded and enhanced University management oversight of the Laboratory which will enable the DOE to lessen its oversight presence at the Laboratory."

- We need to re-energize the GOCO concept, with enhanced contractor accountability. The performance-based management concept embodied in the UC contract provides a basis for important steps being taken by the Department to revitalize the GOCO concept. The contract balances scientific program flexibility with management accountability. DOE defines required results ("what") and the contractor employs the most effective methods ("how"). The contract provides clear performance objectives, metrics for measuring performance, incentives for improved performance, and means for resolving issues through facilitated communications. It also strengthens UC's oversight and accountability.

On balance, the contract is working well, and it has been useful as a model for subsequent M&O contracts negotiated by DOE with other contractors. The contract defines schedules, self-assessments, and performance measure for contractor accountability in Science and Technology and in Business Management. It provides the baseline, nationwide, for performance measurement systems in the DOE Business Management Pilot Oversight project. This is an important start, but much more needs to be accomplished.

My strong governance preference is for the best possible rendering of Appendix B of the Galvin Task Force report. That Appendix spells out in detail the changes required for successful revitalization of the GOCO arrangement. We must bring the series of reforms initiated by the Department to fruition. As I have suggested, Congress should monitor these activities to ensure that necessary improvements take place within a reasonable period of time.

- The Laboratory Operations Board being established by DOE can help. DOE management, in consultation with the laboratory directors, took the step of creating a DOE Laboratory Operations Board (LOB) to help address the many governance issues that have been identified. The Board, co-chaired by senior managers from DOE and private industry, will play a major role in the Department by addressing issues such as mission allocation, rightsizing laboratories, cost containment, and elimination of excessive oversight functions and regulatory requirements. We expect the LOB will assist in the revitalization of the GOCO concept by monitoring the progress achieved in reaching the goals set out in Appendix B of the Galvin Task Force report.

In summary, I believe the best model for the future is a revitalized GOCO system of national laboratories, based on the concept of performance-based management by the M&O contractors and the principles contained in Appendix B of the Galvin Task Force report. The GOCO arrangement has had many decades of great success, it produced the finest set of government-sponsored laboratories in the world, and I believe it is worth trying to recapture most of its original principles with enhanced contractor accountability.

Potential Department of Defense Management of DOE National Security Laboratories

The idea of transferring DOE's defense work to the Department of Defense has been studied and rejected numerous times since the passage of the Atomic Energy Act. The concept is still viewed unfavorably by both the Secretary of

Energy and the Secretary of Defense. In letters to Congress dated 29 March 1995, Secretary of Defense William Perry stated: "Over the past 50 years, there has been a clear and distinct separation of the nuclear weapons-related roles and responsibilities of the Department of Defense and the Department of Energy (and its predecessor agencies). This dual-agency approach has served the nation well by creating institutional checks and balances that are vital for meeting the performance, safety, and reliability requirements of the nuclear arsenal. With the new technical challenges of providing stewardship of the stockpile in the absence of underground testing, this is not a time to be fundamentally restructuring the management of these activities."

I concur with Secretary Perry's analysis and believe that transfer of LLNL's functions and budgets to an Under Secretary of Defense for Defense Nuclear Programs is not in the nation's best interests. In my view, proponents of DOE dismantlement and transfer of the Department's nuclear security functions to DoD have not make a persuasive case that significant cost savings result. I also do not see the merit in transferring DOE's unique environmental management problems to an agency with no comparable experience dealing with radiological wastes or mixed radiological and toxic wastes. They would be burdened with the same technological and legal constraints.

Most importantly to us, the transfer likely would weaken our Laboratory and devalue our important contribution to nuclear security. Let me elaborate.

- Transfer of DOE nuclear security functions to the DoD would eliminate an important set of checks and balances. As Secretary Perry has said, the dual-agency process established in the U.S. for developing nuclear weapons has served the nation well. In this arrangement, the DoD is responsible for specifying the military requirements for nuclear weapons and their delivery systems, and the DOE laboratories independently are responsible for developing weapons to meet the military's requirements. The laboratories have served as advocates of improved safety and surety features in weapons, some of which have had negative impact on cost or operational effectiveness. In the early 1960's, the laboratories took the initiative in pushing for inclusion of use control devices on nuclear weapons and we have worked continually to improve safety features on weapons, including enhanced fire resistance, use of insensitive high explosives, and incorporation of modern electrical system safety.

  The independence of our views continues to be important as we move into a situation where we must certify the performance of an aging stockpile without the use of underground nuclear testing. In the words of the President, stockpile stewardship "will now be tied to a new certification procedure" which includes participation by the three nuclear laboratories and the DoD. Now is not the time to alter an important set of checks and balances by confining crucial technical judgments and decisions that affect national security within one executive Department.

- Transfer of LLNL to DoD likely would weaken the multiprogram, multidisciplinary strengths of the Laboratory and negatively impact our national security efforts. Moving the Laboratory to DoD would separate our activities from other science research. Our nondefense scientific programs would become detached from their prime sponsor, I believe to the detriment of their long-term health. We would have increased difficulty maintaining the core competencies and supporting multipurpose special facilities necessary for our national security work, but increasingly reliant on support funding from multiple sources. We would also stand to lose opportunities to "spin-off" or "spin-on" dual-benefit technologies that have both defense and nondefense applications. Our nuclear weapons work currently benefits from our other R&D efforts, some in partnership with industry and universities. Finally, to attract young scientists, the Laboratory profits from having a rich mixture of military and civilian work and both basic and applied R&D activities. For stockpile stewardship to succeed, we need the best scientific talent the nation has to offer.

Moreover, I would be concerned about the impact of abolishment of the DOE on the nation's overall scientific and technical base. The Galvin Task Force concluded that "there remains a compelling agenda of important work to be performed [at the national laboratories] in their traditional missions," which include (in addition to national security) energy, environmental science and technology, and underpinning fields of basic science. In the energy area, the Yergin Task Force identified the critical importance of federally-supported R&D to meet future energy needs. In environmental science and technology, we need to develop advanced technologies for environmental cleanup that make more affordable dealing with the wastes of 50 years of nuclear weapons production. In basic science, DOE is one of the nation's top supporters of fundamental research across a broad range of disciplines, helping to ensure world leadership in scientific endeavors that contribute to U.S. national security and economic well-being.

SUMMARY REMARKS

As a multiprogram laboratory with defining responsibilities in national security, LLNL has continually demonstrated an ability to integrate the capabilities embodied in its core competencies and special facilities to solve complex technical problems of national importance. We have succeeded because of our focus on problem-solving, and by exploiting opportunities that utilize and reinforce our special strengths. Laboratory personnel organize into multidisciplinary teams to pursue mission-driven issues from concept formulation to product delivery. Our products have included fully-tested nuclear weapon designs, the Nova laser, the AVLIS system, several generations of magnetic fusion facilities, world-class precision machining capabilities, and the sensor systems for the Clementine satellite. Innovative advances in science and technology at the Laboratory on a smaller scale have also had far-reaching impact.

In these particularly cost-conscious times, we are working to deliver even more per dollar invested in our Laboratory in two ways:

- First, we are working with DOE program offices to help them develop strategic visions, goals, and roadmaps, such as the effort by Defense Programs to develop the Stockpile Stewardship and Management Plan. The plan envisions a much smaller weapons complex, operating in a more integrated fashion and drawing on the unique strengths of each site. The result is a focused, leaner—yet robust—nuclear weapons technology program at Livermore with lead responsibilities in selected areas and shared responsibilities in others. It is important that other such DOE program planning efforts lead to better integration of the R&D efforts of the laboratories rather than greater differentiation in the broad mission responsibilities assigned to the multiprogram laboratories.

- Second, we are working to eliminate wasteful bureaucratic management practices, stemming largely from excessive oversight functions and excessive DOE regulations. This is a nest of problems which were years in the making and will take time to fix. We believe that the best approach entails revitalization of the GOCO concept, with performance-based management by the DOE M&O contractors and actions taken to reduce bureaucratic administrative functions, such as those suggested in Appendix B of the Galvin Task Force report.

As strategic goals and missions are refined, and as management requirements are restructured, the DOE laboratories will meet the nation's vital needs with even greater effectiveness and efficiency.

Mr. SCHIFF. Thank you, Dr. Tarter.

Dr. Trivelpiece.

STATEMENT OF DR. ALVIN W. TRIVELPIECE, DIRECTOR, OAK RIDGE NATIONAL LABORATORY

Dr. TRIVELPIECE. Thank you, Mr. Chairman.

It's sort of hard, at the end of the day, to think of anything new to say. But what struck me as a possibility here is several times during the day, people have said things, either from the Committee's point of view, or the witness' point of view, that was sufficiently humorous that the audience here laughed.

That's quite appropriate.

What doesn't seem to be appropriate, however, is breaking out into applause occasionally when you hear something you like.

And there were several times today that I would like to have broken out into applause.

Most of them occurred during the time that Deputy Secretary Curtis was testifying. I think he was right on the mark. I thought his enthusiastic support of your bill, as contrasted with the others, is right on the mark, and I want to align myself very closely with that because I believe that your approach at least has the elements of being able to bring about the effective changes that are necessary.

One of the things that has troubled me in these hearings, and I've participated in several of them, including your field hearing in Oak Ridge, is there seems to be a lack of recognition of the distinction between money and the manner in which we receive it.

We are not funded as institutions. We do not get a large chunk of money which is given to us for the purpose of operating the institutions we're responsible for.

Therefore, when somebody says cut the lab's budget by ten percent, I really don't mechanically know what to do, because what I receive are funds from lots of programs, from various Assistant Secretaries, from other agencies of the federal government. I wouldn't know where to send the check back to if I were able to cut the costs, but I do know that by cutting costs, I improve the effectiveness and the efficiency of the institution.

I'm highly desirous of doing that, and I would cheer or applaud my colleagues when they talk about how they would like to reduce their overhead costs.

We have the highest natural motivation to want to reduce the costs, but we get help in areas which makes it difficult for us to do so, and the so-called "phantom overhead" which has been discussed in various forms here today, that is, you are given instructions on something to do, but you are not given the resources with which to do it.

It's also called unfunded mandates in other corners. That's been a major growth of reduction of efficiency that we have. And to the extent that can be rooted out, I think that would be wonderful.

And the processes that the Department has started and that your legislation would promote I think are in the right direction, but it is essential that it not be done in a way where somebody says, cut ten percent, because we don't have the means to do that, and that just creates additional frustration.

If you want to stop a program, fine, stop the program and we will be out the money that program reflects the reduction of. But as long as the program is there, I believe that we ought to be able to compete. And if we can compete in a manner in which our excellence is superior to the excellence of any other institution, including that of competing among each other, then that ought to be the institution that is funded to do the work.

I believe very strongly that excellence ought to be one of the hallmarks of these activities, and I felt that it was in fact mentioned too infrequently today.

Thank you.

[The prepared statement of Dr. Trivelpiece follows:]

Proposed Testimony of

Alvin W. Trivelpiece
Director
OAK RIDGE NATIONAL LABORATORY

Restructuring the Federal Scientific Establishment: Future Missions and Governance for The Department of Energy (DOE) National Laboratories H.R. 87, H.R. 1510, H.R. 1993 (Title II), and H. R. 2142

before the

COMMITTEE ON SCIENCE
JOINT HEARING
SUBCOMMITTEE ON BASIC RESEARCH
AND
SUBCOMMITTEE ON ENERGY & ENVIRONMENT
U.S. HOUSE OF REPRESENTATIVES

September 7, 1995

OAK RIDGE NATIONAL LABORATORY
Oak Ridge, Tennessee 37831
Managed by
Lockheed Martin Energy Systems, Inc.
for the
U.S. Department of Energy
under Contract No. DE-AC05-84OR21400

Mr. Chairmen and Members of the Subcommittees, I am pleased to have the opportunity to testify before this Committee to present my views on the restructuring the federal scientific establishment regarding the future missions and governance for the Department of Energy (DOE) National Laboratories. In particular, I will focus my remarks on several bills: H.R. 2142, the "Department of Energy Laboratory Missions Act"; H.R. 87, the "Department of Energy Laboratory Facilities Act"; H.R. 1510, the "Department of Energy Laboratories Efficiency Improvement Act"; and H.R. 1993, Title II, the "Department of Energy Abolishment Act." I have solicited opinions from the directors of some of the other Department of Energy national laboratories not represented here today. I have also discussed elements of my testimony with several colleagues at the Oak Ridge National Laboratory (ORNL), and with several individuals in the Lockheed Martin Corporation. Even so, the viewpoints in this testimony are my own.

I have had the good fortune to visit research institutions in many countries, and I have had the opportunity to meet with delegations visiting the United States from other countries. It is my impression that most of these countries envy our system of national laboratories. In many cases they have set up institutions that are similar to ours. Therefore, I find it perplexing to learn that there are recommendations to establish a version of the Defense Base Closing Commission to decide which of our national laboratories should be closed. There are major differences between research laboratories and military bases. Although base closing may be painful and economically disruptive in a particular location, if the need arises, the bases can be reopened. Or, the military function they performed can be completely restored, even though it may be at another site. With research labs, this is a little different. The processes that bring together a productive group of scientists and engineers into a multiprogram activity are not so well understood. It may take years to get a productive group going and only a few minutes to kill it. And major experimental facilities are not so easily dismantled and reassembled as munitions and materiel.

The call to close one or more of the national laboratories is also disturbing because the private sector in the United States has decreased its investment in research. Like many of my colleagues, I am distressed that several large industrial firms have significantly weakened their long-term commitments to R & D in the course of downsizing and realignment. Bell Labs and IBM are the most recent to come to mind. Philip A. Griffiths, the director of Princeton's Institute for Advanced Study, points out in an August 16, 1995, article in the Wall Street Journal that the most productive years of IBM and AT&T Bell Laboratories occurred when these companies dominated their industries. This has changed and research is now viewed as a "variable overhead expense." That is, research is now viewed as a portion of overhead rationed to the need to produce earnings for investors. It would be difficult to re-create a research institution of the scope and excellence of Bell Labs here in the United States. It is my understanding that as a condition of doing business in both Singapore and China, AT&T is setting up research institutions like Bell Labs in those countries. This pattern worries me. I hope that it worries you also.

On what should be a more encouraging note, the national laboratories are widely recognized by industry as a unique resource. Partnerships that span the range from basic research through applied programs to technology development have resulted in new processes and products that help U.S. industries to compete in the global marketplace.

However, suggestions have been made that corporate America should entirely fund the research it needs for its benefit and survival. Taking advantage of the resources of the national laboratories has been derided as "corporate welfare." The leveraging of scarce research dollars through cost-shared partnerships strikes me as eminently sensible. Thanks to the Department of Energy technology transfer programs, ORNL researchers now participate in 212 cooperative research and development agreements. That is, agreements have become commonplace in which the corporations have made a substantial contribution.

In addition to partnerships with industry, the national laboratories work with one another, with other Federal agencies, with universities, and with researchers from other nations. In a recent survey we found that over 70 percent of ORNL's publications in scientific journals are jointly authored with another institution. This fraction has grown dramatically over the last decade and it demonstrates how much we have changed over the past few years.

This change is not always recognized by external groups such as those convened recently to study the DOE national laboratories, their governance, or their research direction. These include the Galvin Task Force on Alternative Futures for the DOE National Laboratories, the Yergin Task Force on Strategic Energy R&D, and the President's Committee of Advisors on Science and Technology panel on fusion energy. Some of these groups have said that the labs must change - that they should be more open and bring in industry and have more interactions with universities. Well, we have changed, a lot. At ORNL we now have more than 4000 guest scientists and engineers per year. About one third of them are from industrial organizations. We aren't saturated with visitors, but it is clear that another doubling would be tough to accommodate. All of this change has occurred in the last ten years or so. Most of the activities that have led to this change started over ten years ago. It's sometimes frustrating that there is so little recognition of how much we have changed in the past few years.

But, leaving my frustrations aside, there is another aspect to this openness and collaboration that needs to be considered. Having guest scientists and engineers visit is one thing, but working closely with them on collaborative projects is another effort that must increasingly become the norm as the competition for increasingly scarce funding continues. The experience at ORNL is similar to that at other DOE national laboratories, all of which have shown a great interest in collaboration.

In that light I would like to address the stated purpose of several of the bills: to produce cuts in the budgets of the laboratories. If the present round of budget considerations is going to reduce the support for research, then I believe that the Administration and the Congress should agree on what programs or projects are going to be continued and which are going to be eliminated, rather than asking which institutions should be affected. If a given program reduction results in reductions at a national laboratory or university, so be it. The institution(s) best able to perform the program should either be assigned to do the work or allowed to propose to compete for it. Making a decision to close a facility that is best qualified to do a particular project, and then deciding to expand that particular project makes no sense at all.

As an example of how program cuts affect a laboratory, consider the decision to stop work on one version of a new production reactor. This programmatic decision resulted in a $14 million reduction of work at ORNL, and my job was to make the necessary changes at ORNL to accommodate this reduction. If, on the other hand, I had been given the instruction to reduce programs at ORNL by $14 million I would not have known how to do that within the law. The appropriated funds for the various projects at ORNL have been apportioned to the Laboratory, and the work should be performed in accordance with the appropriation language that permits their expenditure. We are not allowed to spend them for some purpose other than that for which they were appropriated. So if I am instructed to reduce the activities at ORNL by some percentage, I don't have a basis for deciding which of the programs I am supposed to reduce or stop. Across the board cuts appear to present a simple solution, but the delays in progress and limitations on staffing and equipment that they impose do not necessarily result in a well-managed program.

Two of the bills, H.R. 1510 and H. R. 2142, contain language regarding external regulation of DOE laboratories. Secretary O'Leary has appointed the Ahearne Task Force on External Regulation of DOE Nuclear Safety. The members of this Task Force are examining the current practice of self-regulation of the Department. I anticipate that efficiencies will accrue to the laboratories from this effort and from the Department's pilot programs focusing on Environment, Safety, and Health and Business Management. These reflect the Department's commitment to reduction of operational costs and improved efficiencies with concern to the health and safety of its workers, the public, and the environment.

This has been an outstanding year for ORNL in the recognition achieved by its researchers. A Nobel Prize was won by Clifford Shull for his work on neutron scattering at ORNL. It is interesting to note that eight previous Nobel Prizes have had their foundation in Shull's work. I'm pleased that he has now been accorded this honor. Liane B. Russell, of ORNL's Biology Division, received the Enrico Fermi Award for her contributions to genetics and radiation biology. Gerard M. Ludtka received an E. O. Lawrence Award for his work in materials technology. Gerald D. Mahan in his dual capacity as ORNL/University of Tennessee at Knoxville Distinguished Scientist, became the most recent ORNL staff member to be elected a member of the National Academy of Sciences. I am elated that ORNL achievements were awarded five R&D 100 Awards in the 1995 competition bringing our total to 79. It is similarly impressive that the

Department of Energy is far and away the leader among federal agencies in the history of this competition.

These honors and awards reinforce my belief that the DOE national laboratories are an essential component of the national science and technology infrastructure. The scientific discoveries and technological innovation that underpin our nation's economic competitiveness and social well-being are produced by this infrastructure which is based on a foundation of academic, industrial, and federal laboratory research and development. These institutions play complementary roles in serving the national interest. Basic research initiated by individual investigators has been the academic model. Industry focuses on short-term, product-driven research and development. Federal laboratories have addressed complex, applied interdisciplinary science and technology issues as well as work in the fundamental sciences.

The DOE national laboratories play a unique role in this national science and technology infrastructure. Their ability to conduct large-scale, long-term, integrated research projects has produced a remarkable set of contributions, ranging from fundamental scientific discoveries to commercial products, that have improved national security, economic productivity, human health, and environmental conditions. The success of the national laboratories in applying science and technology to national challenges derives in part from a special organizational structure that supports long-term, high-risk, problem-focused research and development particularly on a larger scale than most universities can manage. Successful projects have been characterized by interdisciplinary integration of science and engineering, focused project management, defined cost and time schedules, and relevant delivery of solutions to problems. The report of the Task Force on Alternative Futures for the Department of Energy National Laboratories (the Galvin Task Force) notes, "One of the great strengths of the multiprogram laboratories derives from the diversity of technical expertise that can be brought to bear from within these laboratories on specific scientific and technical challenges."

There is much debate within the national laboratories on how to uniquely identify ourselves. Certainly at a level of a one paragraph summary, nearly all of the national laboratories look alike. This is because of the mission of the Department of Energy: "The Department of Energy, in partnership with our customers, is entrusted to contribute to the welfare of the Nation by providing the technical information and scientific and educational foundation for technology, policy, and institutional leadership necessary to achieve efficiency in energy use, diversity in energy sources, a more productive and competitive economy, improved environmental quality, and a secure national defense." Individually, the national laboratories pursue complementary and interlocking programs as directed by the Department of Energy program managers. I am confident that with the management initiatives now underway in the Department of Energy, significant benefits in increased operational efficiency and effectiveness will accrue to the national laboratories.

Mr. SCHIFF. Thank you, Dr. Trivelpiece.

Dr. Crawford, am I correct that this might be your debut?

Dr. CRAWFORD. That's correct, sir.

Mr. SCHIFF. Before Congress.

Well, you can see that your colleagues have all survived.

Dr. CRAWFORD. They've all survived.

Mr. SCHIFF. This far in the afternoon, I hope you'll take that as a good sign.

Dr. CRAWFORD. I do. They've also said a lot of things, and I tend to agree with them.

STATEMENT OF DR. JOHN C. CRAWFORD, DEPUTY DIRECTOR, SANDIA NATIONAL LABORATORIES

Dr. CRAWFORD. I would like to just make a couple of quick remarks.

And that is that the laboratories have an important and enduring mission, to serve the nation and to serve the national agenda.

It seems that our strategic challenge is, how do we maintain our technical competence and our technical capabilities in the face of very tightly constrained resources?

Two things I would like to emphasize that I believe will enable us to do this is, first of all, to retain and enhance the multiprogram, multidisciplinary environment of the laboratories.

This is an incredibly important part of managing and developing a vital laboratory.

Our core competencies draw strength from each and every program that we support.

It is no longer possible to support the appropriate set of core competencies from a single program.

Second, and maybe even more important: many of the advances that we see in today's world come from the intersection of these various programs.

Those intersections are very fruitful as far as research advances and research opportunities.

And the third, it produces a laboratory that challenges the best of our people and allows us to pursue the agenda that is important to the nation.

The second major piece that I would hold up is the ability to form strategic partnerships. And I include in those partnerships the universities, the private sector, and the other laboratories.

At Sandia, it is actually impossible to carry out our mission without partnerships—without partnerships with the private sector, without partnerships with the other laboratories and universities.

In the defense business, the national security, it is not possible in today's condition of constrained resources to develop and design the components necessary for nuclear defense and have unique, captive capability to produce them. We must depend on the industry.

That means we must design, we must conceive the components and the processes necessary that are consistent with industrial practice.

So in our future, it appears to us that industrial partnerships are an essential part of us completing our mission.

Which leads me to my final point, that I believe the legislation that seeks to crystallize and better define our mission as a first step towards reorientation is the right way to go. That I believe mission ought to drive our funding, and funding ought to drive our size and management capability.

Thank you very much, sir.

[The prepared statement of Dr. Crawford follows:]

Statement of John C. Crawford, Deputy Director
Sandia National Laboratories

United States House of Representatives
Committee on Science
Subcommittee on Basic Research
Subcommittee on Energy and Environment

Joint Hearing on the DOE National Laboratories
September 7, 1995

Introduction

Chairman Schiff, Chairman Rohrabacher, and distinguished members of the subcommittees, I am John Crawford, deputy director of Sandia National Laboratories, a multiprogram laboratory of the United States Department of Energy. I thank you for this opportunity to appear before your subcommittees; I send the regrets of the laboratory director, Paul Robinson, who is in Europe and therefore could not attend. I welcome this opportunity to comment on the four bills[1] before your subcommittees that would affect the missions, size, and structure of the DOE laboratory system. I will comment on the proposals contained in these bills in the context of Sandia's future responsibilities and strategic needs.

Sandia National Laboratories is managed by Sandia Corporation, a Lockheed Martin Company. The laboratory performs scientific and engineering research as well as product design and development for U.S. government needs in defense, energy, environment, and the basic sciences necessary to support these missions. Our record of technical innovations and integration to provide system solutions to important national problems is unrivaled.

Sandia has a central role to play in DOE's national security missions, particularly in maintaining confidence in the safety, security, control, and reliability of the nuclear weapon stockpile and providing an efficient production complex for the smaller stockpile of the future. We also develop technology to support the verification of arms reduction agreements and to assist our nation's policy of limiting the proliferation of weapons of mass destruction. These national security responsibilities are formidable and enduring and we take them very seriously.

As important as this work is, we recognize that the federal budget is under great pressure and that we must perform this mission more efficiently. Our challenge is strategic: How do we maintain the technical competencies (staff, facilities, and knowledge) required for our DOE missions as budgetary resources become more constrained? Our approach to dealing with this

---

[1]H.R. 2142, "Department of Energy Laboratory Missions Act"; H.R 87, "Department of Energy Laboratory Facilities Act"; H R. 1510, "Department of Energy Laboratories Efficiency Improvement Act"; and H.R. 1993, Title II, "Department of Energy Abolishment Act".

problem is based on two strategic principles: multiprogram management and synergistic partnerships.

Multiprogram Management

A strong commitment to a common set of core technical competencies serving the needs of, and supported by, a diversity of several major national programs is a crucial strategy for Sandia. The Laboratories' ability to sustain its core competencies has been made difficult over the past several years by declining funding for nuclear weapon research and development. This is critical to our support of DOE's national security mission, as well as DOE's missions in energy, environment, and the basic sciences, and it will continue to be critical as resources become more constrained.

A world-class base of scientific and technological excellence has always been essential for meeting the extreme requirements placed on nuclear weapons, especially in regard to weapon safety, security, and reliability. The science and technology needs that characterize DOE's nuclear weapon mission are extremely broad, covering most of the physical sciences and engineering disciplines recognized today, as well as the computational and modeling technologies required for modern scientific investigation. These technical capabilities overlap those required for DOE missions in energy and environment.

Sandia's core competencies derive from a matrix of scientific and integrated technological initiatives that are most generally described by the term, "science-based engineering." Our scientific research is focused on materials, microelectronics and photonics, computational and information sciences, and engineering sciences such as robotics. Sandia's principal integrated technologies—advanced manufacturing technology, electronics technology, advanced information technology, and pulsed power technology—are rooted in our scientific foundations and apply directly to our DOE mission applications. We commonly refer to these as "strategic initiatives," because they are technologies of vital importance to the success of DOE's missions in the future. These four initiatives are producing revolutionary advances in technology that will in turn revolutionize the ways we perform all of our missions.

In my view, the multiprogram, multidisciplinary environment is essential for excellence in Sandia's national security, energy, and environmental missions. The synergy that exists in the multiprogram laboratory environment enhances mission performance in all areas. This committee should be careful to preserve the multiprogram concept for national laboratories. As currently written, some of the bills under consideration before this committee today run the danger of seriously weakening the multiprogram laboratories.

Synergistic Partnerships

Another critically important element of Sandia's strategy is a strong commitment to R&D partnerships with industry, universities, and other federal laboratories. These relationships are entirely compatible with the recommendations of the report of the Secretary of Energy's Task Force on Alternative Futures for the DOE National Laboratories (the Galvin report), which endorses collaboration in areas germane to DOE missions.

Sandia's success in establishing large numbers of mutually beneficial relationships with the private sector is in large measure a consequence of its competencies being well aligned with the technical interests of the private sector and universities. For example, manufacturing support technologies are central to Sandia's mission for DOE's office of Defense Programs and constitute a large fraction of our technology base. The future operating environment of the DOE nuclear weapons production complex will require greater manufacturing agility and cost-effectiveness. The DOE Defense Programs laboratories cannot achieve these goals in isolation from the nation's manufacturing community.

Sandia's strategic initiative in advanced manufacturing technology derives from its long-standing responsibility for engineering design of DOE non-nuclear components. This initiative vigorously supports DOE's strategic requirement for Advanced Design and Production Technologies (ADAPT), an important element of the DOE Defense Programs strategic plan. The investment in the ADAPT initiative will result in a nuclear weapons complex that will be able to safely, efficiently, and cost-effectively repair, requalify, or renew weapons and components in the enduring stockpile as they age. This capability will, in turn, provide an affordable, safe, secure, and reliable nuclear deterrent. The goals of ADAPT are to enable an affordable design and production capability for DOE in the long term and to continuously support stockpile assurance activities. A key ingredient of this effort is collaboration with industry.

The necessity for industrial collaboration is also clearly evident in the electronics arena. DOE's requirements for many electronic devices cannot be met with commercial electronic products. Sandia is unique among the national laboratories in having design and production oversight responsibility for all electronic components in DOE nuclear weapon systems. To meet its mission requirements, Sandia has developed a broad-based competency in electronics, from the fundamental science of semiconducting materials to device design and manufacturing processes. We can only maintain this capability in partnership with industry, and our program collaborates intensely with the semiconductor industry and universities through consortia and other arrangements. We are setting a goal of obtaining nearly 90% of our future weapon parts from industrial suppliers (The level was 50% during the Cold War).

One way in which we interact with industry is through team pursuit of industry-generated technology road maps such as those prepared by the Semiconductor Industry Association and the Optoelectronics Industry Development Association. In addition, we provide a direct mechanism for applying university research to manufacturable electronics products and processes.

In the next room is a DOE display of R&D 100 Awards. Sandia, which has long been a strong competitor in this prestigious competition, is displaying information about a capability that has won this award for three consecutive years, our expertise in electronics quality and reliability. Sandia's Electronics Quality/Reliability Center is a DOE/Defense Programs-driven industrial collaboration that proves the value — and necessity – of such synergistic partnerships. The nuclear weapons mission of DOE requires electronics of extremely high reliability, which has presented a unique challenge in science and engineering. Reliability is also a universal need of the private electronics industry. This Center has worked with over 100 private industry partners in 26 states, and has applied the results of its Cooperative R&D Agreements (CRADAs) back into its nuclear weapons mission. For example, we developed with Schlumberger an expert system for diagnosing failures in integrated circuits. We have now used this system to assist in diagnosing failures in the integrated circuits used in nuclear weapons.

In 1995, this Center received an R&D100 award for a patent pending technique that can locate a break in any one of the millions of microscopic connections on an integrated circuit in minutes. Previous techniques could take days or weeks with consequent high costs. Originally developed to analyze a problem related to our defense mission, this technique now has been licensed to electronics manufacturers, and diagnostic test equipment manufacturers are making instruments dedicated to this technique.

CRADAs with interested industrial participants yield significant benefits to the nuclear weapons program and help reduce the cost of this research to DOE. Sandia's Electronic Quality/Reliability Center has entered into ten CRADAs with manufacturers of integrated circuits (ICs) or related equipment or software. CRADA partners include Intel, National Semiconductor, LSI Logic, Advanced Micro Devices, Philips, Analog Devices, Schlumberger, Hewlett Packard, Honeywell, and Micron. These partnerships are rooted in the reliability needs of Defense Programs and have produced significant benefits to DOE.

A similar example can be found in the area of robotics, where Sandia is working with a professional association and industry and university partners to develop strategic plans for partnering on areas of common underlying science and technology.

The Galvin Task Force report judged the appropriateness of collaborative R&D based on whether the collaborating industry is within or outside traditional DOE mission areas. However, it seems to me that a more appropriate criterion is whether the technology (not the industry) falls within or outside the core technical competencies required for DOE missions. From a DOE perspective, a key factor in developing relationships, with the private sector, with universities, and with other federal agencies, should be the potential contribution of the collaboration to advancing mission-critical technologies.

For example, the tire industry may seem to have little in common with DOE missions. However, improving an engineering tool for solving structural mechanics problems common to both tire design and the design of certain nuclear weapon components should be an appropriate field for collaborative R&D. In fact, Sandia has been collaborating with Goodyear Tire and Rubber Company on such a problem. The company has benefited from access to modeling and simulation codes and experimental techniques developed in the weapons program; DOE has benefited from substantial improvements in those codes resulting from the industrial interaction. The improved computer codes will be used to solve weapon component design problems that previously were intractable.

Strategic Realignment of the DOE Laboratory System

One of the questions listed in the charter for this hearing asks, "Will there be the need for consolidation or closure of the DOE national laboratories?" In my view, it is entirely possible that some sort of realignment of the DOE laboratories may be necessary. However, the extent and form of such changes should be driven by mission requirements and best business practices. It seems unwise to prescribe an explicit size and personnel limitation, as H.R. 1510 would mandate. Sandia's size (as well as that of the other labs) has always been set by the programs it is funded to perform by its government customers. It expands or contracts as needed to fill these customer's needs. It also seems unwise to make closure recommendations (as would be required by H.R. 87 and H.R. 1993, Title II) before missions have been mapped to resources and facilities.

H.R. 2142 has the virtue of letting mission requirements drive realignment decisions. After mission assignments have been made, based on the mission assignment and streamlining criteria outlined in Section 103 (a), a logical basis will exist for the Secretary to make proposals for streamlining the DOE laboratory system.

I have two cautionary notes regarding HR2142. I worry that, as missions are defined for the laboratories, a trend toward finer and finer differentiation among missions might eventually move the multiprogram laboratory system in the direction of very narrowly defined, single-mission laboratories. I will reiterate the point I made earlier in this statement that, as a general rule (with some exceptions) multiprogram laboratories are technically stronger research institutions than those laboratories that lack multiprogrammatic synergy. This is particularly true for laboratories that are responsible for designing end-products. The mission sets for the DOE laboratories may overlap extensively; but this condition should not be regarded as evidence of duplication so long as programs are managed within the laboratory system as a whole.

A second concern with HR2142 is with the last paragraph in Section 105. As I've stated, Sandia whole-heartedly believes that partnerships with the private sector, with universities, and with other federal agencies are essential for our missions. However, as written the bill limits such partnerships to "nonproprietary and unclassified information." In many cases, the DOE labs work on classified projects with and for the Department of Defense and other federal entities; we also have occasion to, through the CRADA process, engage in the exchange of proprietary information. Thus, we would request the deletion of the phrase "nonproprietary and unclassified information."

Enforcement of Environmental, Safety, and Health Requirements

Another of the questions listed in the charter for this hearing concerns the desirability of eliminating self-regulation of environmental, safety, and health requirements by DOE. Both H.R. 2142 and H.R. 1510 call for this action.

I would like to clarify any misunderstanding that may exist concerning DOE's authority for self-regulation under current law. The DOE laboratories have no exemption from standard regulatory requirements concerning occupational safety and health and environmental requirements for industrial or commercial operations. The laboratories are already regulated by federal, state, and local agencies responsible for environmental, safety, and health enforcement. They are routinely audited by such agencies for compliance with a variety of federal, state, and local laws and regulations.

The only issue is that of self-regulation of DOE-owned nuclear facility operations. Self-regulation has been regarded as appropriate in this case because many of DOE's nuclear facilities are unique. The special understanding and experience required to properly oversee the health and safety issues and the environmental integrity associated with heterogeneous R&D, special tests, and low-production-volume environments is found only in DOE.

If the regulation of DOE nuclear operations were to be transferred to another agency, the major concern would be the imposition of prescriptive, detailed, procedural regulations on a non-routine, highly fluid research and development environment. Under DOE regulation, there is an opportunity to develop and utilize higher-level performance objectives and operational standards that are both necessary and sufficient to ensure safe, effective operations.

The Advisory Committee on External Regulation of DOE Nuclear Safety has heard testimony from DOE management, the laboratories, many stakeholder organizations, and representatives of organizations in the private sector regulated by agencies other than DOE. Sandia believes that the regulation of DOE nuclear safety should remain the responsibility of DOE, provided regulatory reforms now underway in the department prove successful.

We also noted to the Advisory Committee that the DOE labs are presently performing at a superior level of safety with respect to accidents, injuries, and deaths compared to industry as s whole. As long as this level of safety is maintained (at reasonable cost) why change the ES&H requirements.

Laboratory Governance

The hearing charter also asks whether "other governance structures, such as corporatization or privatization" might better suit the future management of the DOE national laboratories.

The Galvin report proposes a *corporatization* model. I suppose corporatization could offer some advantages, such as greater autonomy, a wider variety of customers, and a more market-oriented approach to R&D. Whether or not these characteristics are appropriate for federal R&D is perhaps debatable. In my view, I cannot envision the corporatization model as either appropriate or useful for DOE's Defense Program laboratories. And indeed, the Galvin report acknowledges that the three Defense Program laboratories should probably be excepted from the corporatization movement. In any case, any experiment in corporatization should be carefully thought out and implemented on a limited, trial basis.

I believe a more practical approach to addressing the root problems identified in the Galvin report would be to rejuvenate the GOCO relationship along the lines suggested by Appendix B of the report. We would note that an important rationale for the creation of GOCO's was to provide the benefits of "best-business practices" of the private sector to government efforts. Many of the benefits of corporatizing the laboratory complex can be achieved by applying the quality management and reengineering tools pioneered in industry by the existing GOCO's. For example, at Sandia we are reengineering our operating and administrative procedures to achieve greater cost-effectiveness. We are examining several categories of laboratory processes and making basic changes. We are looking closely at our business systems, site management practices, and operational safety and health practices. We are also redesigning our information and communications infrastructure so that many business and management processes can be automated or streamlined. DOE's Strategic Alignment initiative applies total quality tools and best business practices in a similar way to achieve efficiencies in the department's operations.

In summary, I would advise great caution as you explore the pros and cons of corporatizing the DOE laboratories. With your support, I believe DOE's leadership can do much to restore the health and vigor of the GOCO model.

The Future Role of the DOE National Laboratories

The future role of the DOE national laboratories must be tied to the future needs of U.S. government R&D. H.R. 2142 identifies four core mission areas of the Department of Energy that I believe have enduring importance for our nation. Those missions are (1) national security, including both the nuclear weapons role and the nonproliferation and arms control responsibility; (2) enhancing our nation's energy supply posture through long-term, high-risk R&D that is precompetitive and generic; (3) basic research to advance our understanding of energy and matter and to explore emerging scientific fields; (4) environmental R&D and technology development to reduce the environmental impacts of energy use and production and to cope with hazardous and radioactive wastes.

These mission areas represent major national challenges. Any one or all of these missions could be abolished as a responsibility of the Department of Energy, but the national challenges will not go away. I believe these challenges require the best technical leadership obtainable. In all the criticism that has been leveled at DOE and its laboratories, the quality of their technical work has never been at issue. The Department of Energy still maintains what are widely regarded collectively as the best scientific and engineering laboratories in the federal government, perhaps even the world. The hundreds of R&D 100 awards, some of which are on display in the next room, and the many other prizes garnered by DOE are evidence to this fact. I believe the DOE national laboratories will endure, with changes, because formidable technical challenges that threaten our national well-being will persist.

This committee and Congress as a whole should be prudent about the changes in structure, management, and configuration that it will require of the DOE laboratories. A national laboratory is more than a collection of facilities and people with technical skills. The creative synergy of a multiprogram laboratory environment is established over time and is the result of relationships among technical core competencies that are exercised for the benefit of sponsors' programs. Those competencies may be difficult to reconstruct in another environment or at another time. Consequently, I urge you to exercise a degree of caution as you consider proposals for changing or restructuring the DOE laboratories.

One possible future for the DOE Defense Programs laboratories especially worries me. At least one proposal has been made to transfer those laboratories out of DOE and place them in the Department of Defense (H.R. 1993, Title V). I believe such action could be detrimental to the prudent stewardship of the nation's nuclear weapon responsibility. The dual-agency responsibility for nuclear weapons that Congress created when it passed the Atomic Energy Act many years ago still makes sense today. The Defense Programs laboratories within the Department of Energy are an independent voice—an independent conscience—for the safety, control, and reliability of the weapons in our nuclear arsenal. This independence has served the nation well, and it is serving it well today.

Conclusion

It is clear that some sort of strategic realignment in the DOE laboratory system will occur. It is important, however, that those changes be driven by program and mission requirements and best business practices rather than by predefined percentage targets or externally prescribed models of reorganization. Two principles are especially important to keep in mind when considering strategic changes in the DOE laboratory system. The first is the importance of the multiprogram model of R&D management, which adds synergy and depth to the R&D environment. The second is the imperative of collaboration and strategic partnerships with R&D entities in industry and academia as well as with other national laboratories.

In addition, I urge your subcommittees to consider the unique role of the DOE laboratories in the federal R&D system. No other set of agency laboratories in the federal government succeeds so well in integrating the spectrum of research, development, design, and production support as is routinely done in the DOE laboratories. Our record of technical innovations and integration to provide system solutions to important national problems is unrivaled. This is a unique attribute that you should seek to enhance, rather than diminish, as you ponder options for the DOE laboratory system.

Mr. SCHIFF. Thank you, Dr. Crawford, and welcome.

You can now and at any future time say you've testified before Congress.

Dr. CRAWFORD. Thank you.

Mr. SCHIFF. I'm not sure whether that's an asset but you can put it in your resume.

Well, I gather if this panel voted on the bills, my bill would do pretty well. I'm pleased to hear that.

I want to make a couple of observations about my bill.

The first is, I'm going to ask each of you, at your convenience, to do what I asked the previous panel to do, and that is, not at this moment, but in the near future to reexamine the list of missions that I've proposed in my bill.

I'm concerned that it's very difficult not to be too narrow and that it's very difficult not to be too broad.

And so I would really appreciate a tight review of it to see maybe if we're one or the other, and this is how it ought to be changed.

I want to say that since this is a hearing on the bills, that there's two matters that I'm not sure I have spelled out correctly in the bill and I may have to rewrite.

One is when I say that the labs would be empowered to work with non-federal agencies, I mean the private sector as well. It simply did not mean non-federal government agencies, and I'll look to spell that out since I'm in agreement.

And I was pleased to receive Dr. Bloch's testimony from the Council On Competitiveness in support of partnerships with industry under certain guidelines certainly, but he did not take the position of there ought to be this artificial separation between the two, which I personally regard as a concept that no longer fits the present world economy.

Also, I want to make it clear, because I've been asked a couple of times, that when my bill, if it were to go into effect, when it directs the Secretary of Energy to specifically designate which laboratories have which responsibilities, it was not my intention to have each laboratory with one mission.

I think that there can be justification for duplication.

First of all, a subject like environmental cleanup can be so broad that it means many different things, and it really isn't duplicative to have more than one laboratory working on it.

Second, a more specific subject, like improved mileage from gasoline, might have more than one approach. So once again, there could be a justification for duplication.

I'm only saying that if there is duplication, it should be recognized and justified by the Department of Energy, not that it can't exist. And it's on my head to review my own bill that way, but I want to make that clear for the record.

With that, I'm going to hold the balance of my time for questions and recognize other Members for questions right now, beginning with my co-Chairman of these hearings, Chairman Rohrabacher.

Mr. ROHRABACHER. We actually have spoken before because we've had hearings before where you testified. I've probably been asked the same question that I asked then, which is, rather than reducing the amount of money available to finance your operations, would it not be better to close the operation of the least effective laboratory?

And you can just give me a very brief answer all the way down the line.

Dr. GAY. I think that there are a variety of ways of financing laboratories. Traditionally, we've relied on the flow through DOE from Congress and the taxpayer.

I think that in addition to this traditional mechanism, there are new mechanisms that we could be creative about, and Galvin's comments about corporatization tend to point us in the direction of the ways that we can look for additional sources of funding.

So while there may be a need to look at missions and scope and whether or not we have a critical mass or not to maintain core competency, I think that thought also ought to be given to the laboratories to look at new and innovative ways of helping fund the on-going effort to maintain that critical mass.

And we can look at a broader range of opportunity than we have in the past.

Mr. ROHRABACHER. Let me summarize then. What you're saying then, if there's going to be a shortfall, rather than going for a closing, we can actually come up with more creative means of maintaining a certain level of funding that rather than closing up a lab and maintaining current funding.

Is that what you're saying?

Dr. GAY. Yes. We need enough time to be able to make that kind of a transition because we're talking about a transformation of the way that labs operate in total. But that we can begin now moving in a more aggressive way to do that.

Mr. ROHRABACHER. I'm not saying that a decision has been made that even I could point to and say, all right, the decision's been made, we're going in this direction.

But earlier we heard testimony and I agreed with that testimony, that we need to make a decision and we need to do whatever we're going to do and get it over with so people can get on with their business and quit having people spend all their time talking about what they're going to do, and get on with doing it.

So we'll see.

Dr. Hecker?

Dr. HECKER. Thank you, Mr. Chairman.

I'd like to answer at two levels, one from a mission standpoint. By all means, don't treat us all the same and cut us across the board. Decide what you want done, who can do it best, fund those that can do it, and don't fund those that can't.

And I think it's been said several times. The mission comes, that determines the functions, that should determine the size, and that shouldn't be across the board.

From an administrative standpoint, what Mr. Galvin pointed out, because of the way things have evolved, all of our institutions can effect administrative cost savings in conjunction with the Department of Energy changing its governance.

And from that standpoint, I think we can all do that across the board, once we settle on the missions and what we need to do.

Mr. ROHRABACHER. Thank you very much.

Dr. SCHRIESHEIM. Well, missions determine survival, and once the missions are worked out, it could well be possible that there would be some decisions made on a closing, if that's your question.

You know, if the question is to make an arbitrary decision instantaneously, you know, we'll close whatever it is. There's 17 labs, we'll close three, before an investigation of the missions and an assignment of the missions is concerned. That I don't think is the right way to go.

Dr. TARTER. Again, I think Dr. Trivelpiece said it quite well in his statement. You don't fund laboratories, you fund programs. And so if a program is funded at a level that doesn't support the laboratories that did it, then I think you could ask the Department to make a decision at some point that laboratory or that set of laboratories, that would be an efficient way to manage.

But I think you do have to decide the program first and then ask whoever is running the set of labs to make their decision about how to execute the program.

Dr. TRIVELPIECE. You're getting down almost to the level of decision that an individual scientist or engineer doing research has to make, and each of us sitting here at the table have been practicing scientists at one time or another, engineers.

And so you come up against a situation in which the program, no matter how much you want to continue doing it, or how much you believe in it personally or would like to dedicate your efforts to it, the funding to pursue it simply isn't there, and you go find something else to do.

It's very painful, very difficult.

Now if you sort of elevate that to an institutional level, when I was Director of Energy Research, Dr. Bernt Matias, who is a professor at the University of California at San Diego, died, and his death was somewhat of a blow to part of the national science activities in that he was the expert on high temperature superconductivity.

I was highly motivated to want to keep a high temperature superconductivity program alive in the United States. That subject, the subject had become passe. There wasn't anybody in the country that wanted money to work on that.

Physics department professors didn't want to do it. All of a sudden, Mr. Mueller and Bednorz figured out there was high temperature superconductivity. Suddenly, there was not enough money in the budgets I had available to me to feed all the hungry robins that wanted to work in that field.

It suddenly overnight became very fashionable. Fortunately, there was enough resources in the Department and people at the laboratories that the United States very quickly mounted a very substantial program that led to a great deal of results in high temperature superconductivity.

That's the right way for it to occur.

If you had arbitrarily said, well, put a lot of money into superconductivity, it wouldn't have worked. At the point that everybody worked on it, it would have been foolish to say, I want to cut the superconductivity program. There's a certain natural ebb and flow that the science or engineering itself dictates, and that the Congress and the Administration need to be sensitive to managing in a way that optimizes that to best benefit.

Dr. CRAWFORD. Well, I certainly agree that programs must be considered separately and the laboratory's survival must be dependent on how effectively they support those programs.

So it's a matter of mission, programs, and your judgment and the DOE's judgment about our effectiveness in supporting those programs.

Mr. ROHRABACHER. All right, well thank you very much, and thank you, Mr. Chairman.

Mr. SCHIFF. Thank you, Mr. Chairman.

Mr. Bartlett, recognized for five minutes.

Mr. BARTLETT. Thank you very much.

I was just sitting here thinking, having spent a fair part of my life in scientific and engineering areas, as to what would be the best way to proceed.

And I was thinking about two things. One is funding and where money comes from, and now most of your money comes, I guess through the Congress and appropriations from the Congress.

Of course, the Congress has no money until it's taken from somebody's paycheck or taken from the profits of an industry, and so I like to emphasize that there's no such thing as federal dollars. They are all dollars that came from somebody's paycheck and came from the profits of some industry.

So there are ways that money could come to the laboratories rather than going through government, through the bureaucracy of government.

Another thing that I was thinking about was the interplay, and I know some of you are intimately associated with universities, I worked in a university and I've worked for large business, small business, and worked for government.

And clearly, for the things that can be productively done in the university, you get more mileage for your dollar, and I say that very kindly. That's because of all the slave labor we have in the universities in the form of graduate students.

And I spent several years being one of those very willing slave laborers in the university.

And I was wondering about a future for our laboratories, which are really a national treasure, that would involve more diversity in funding and perhaps more association with universities because of the synergism that would occur because of the increased productivity you get from a few dollars because of the kinds of, my youngest son, we have ten children, the youngest son is just starting graduate school in chemical engineering and he spends probably 16 hours a day in front of his computer.

You know, that's the kind of a commitment that you don't get, you don't have many people in your laboratories working 16 hours a day without pay because they're challenged and they love to do it.

I was wondering what your thoughts were about looking for a future to the laboratories that had a diversity of funding and more association with universities?

Dr. HECKER. If I may start that.

From Los Alamos, we've always had of course a very close association with the University of California because it's our parent organization.

But in fact, even with that, we actually have set out the three laboratories run by the University of California to try to get an even more synergistic relationship with the nine campuses of the University of California system for precisely the reasons that you indicate.

If you want to do science and stay at the forefront, you must work closely with the research universities. As I said we do that. We even hope to make that better.

I do want to take issue, and I must say that on behalf of those folks who are back at Los Alamos working 16 hour days right now, that's not just for graduate students. People who are able to pursue the things that they really want to do put in whatever time it takes. And the enthusiasm for their research stays long after the slave labor of graduate school.

So the real key is whether you can match the institution's interest with the personal interest to get that sort of productivity out.

Just one last comment on the diversity of funding sources. We're here principally for the U.S. government to do a mission for the United States. Government. I think personally it would not be a good idea if we got a substantial amount of our funding from the private sector.

I think the sort of relationships we've developed through collaborative R&D agreements are precisely right, and that they help to stretch the time and risk horizon of industry while, at the same time, doing significant benefit for our government missions.

Mr. BARTLETT. Just one comment, and I understand your concern about a diversity of funding.

If you are here for the benefit of the government, then one could argue, as was done in a previous panel, that the only thing the national laboratories should be doing are those things which could not reasonably be done anywhere else, or would not reasonably be done anywhere else.

And this, you know, gets back to very large facilities that no one else could afford singly.

I think, for instance, of a consortium, an organization run by a consortium of universities, the National Radio Astronomy Observatory, down at Green Bank in West Virginia. This is something that no university could do. Nobody could do it except government. It's now run by a consortium of universities.

But this is a role, Abraham Lincoln said the government should only do for its citizens what they cannot do for themselves. And I think that's maybe not a bad principle to apply to our national laboratories.

I think of them more as being an asset to our country, rather than to our government. You may think those are the same thing, but sometimes I think the government does not properly reflect the needs of the country.

Dr. HECKER. Again, if I may just respond very quickly, because when it was said before, I didn't agree with the statement that a prime mission would be to run large user research facilities.

Our prime mission at my laboratory, at least, is a defense mission, and I would say that's indeed one that only the government can do.

And then, in addition to that, however, with the government's appropriate leveraging, we could also make contributions in energy and environment where neither industry nor university may be exactly the right place.

And so I would broaden what you heard before, from large user research institutions to several other things, and certainly national defense is at the forefront of that.

Mr. BARTLETT. My time is up. But I would agree completely.

And if you look at Article I, Section 8 of the Constitution, defense is one of the relatively few things that the federal government constitutionally is permitted to be involved in. We've kind of stretched the Constitution a bit, and I hope we let it relax a bit.

Thank you very much, Mr. Chairman.

Mr. SCHIFF. Thank you, Mr. Bartlett.

Mr. Baker, you're recognized for five minutes.

Mr. BAKER. With all due respect to the Chairman, would it not be better, rather than prescribed functions or missions to the laboratories, to design a management structure from DOE down that sets relevant priorities and allows you to make the decisions on what missions you are, and to allow the lab directors to work together to set those missions?

Start anywhere, but we've got to hurry. I only have five minutes.

Dr. TRIVELPIECE. We do that to some extent.

Mr. SCHIFF. Much of which went away with that question, I can assure you.

Dr. TRIVELPIECE. There is a process by which individual scientists at the laboratories do prepare, in effect, proposals. These proposals are rolled up into the Department, they become part of the Department's internal budget review process. That process leads to a vetting. That vetting is then interacted with the Office of Management and Budget.

Mr. BAKER. And sometimes the scientist at the bottom lives long enough to see it come back.

Dr. TRIVELPIECE. No, it comes back fairly rapidly. I think to that extent that there are programs, there are people who get things funded in a given year, and there is a minor amount of flexibility that permits us to start new things with the interaction of our program managers in Washington.

I think they do a fairly responsible job in most cases in trying to listen to what it is that needs to be done, and try to make appropriate decisions between programmatic elements.

It isn't perfect, but it's not bad.

Mr. BAKER. Anyone else have a thought on that?

John?

Dr. CRAWFORD. I actually believe that establishing national priorities and establishing missions isn't all that different a concept. That establishing national priorities is the first step to defining a mission.

And then once you have national priorities defined, an iterative process or a discussion process with the labs and among the labs can define missions to support those priorities.

So I think what you've stated is indeed the first step to defining well-described missions for the laboratories to build their work around.

Mr. BAKER. What I'm afraid of, and I'll tell you why I asked the question, is that we'll go back to this earlier theory a year ago, that we prescribe one lab to be a green lab and one lab to be a defense lab.

I want to see the cross pollination of all the scientists at all of the labs. But we have to become more efficient, just like the phone company and IBM and the Bank of America have all downsized their fat, middle management. We have to do the same, but it has to be done by the people themselves.

That's why I'm asking the question.

And if we begin to prescribe, you're going to see a green lab and a defense lab, and a mess.

Go ahead.

Dr. GAY. I think this is a process of successive approximation here.

On the one end, there's a general guidance framework, and on the other end, from the laboratories, we should be putting forward proposals of what we believe will fit within that framework, so that there is something to react to and to progressively improve upon in defining the goals and the missions.

And what Congress can do is to reward laboratories for their teaming together to put forward those kinds of proposals that would be responsive to the general construct of what the priorities ought to be and the execution of that. And more importantly, the feedback in terms of measuring.

We say we're going to deliver X in a certain time period, and if we don't deliver X in that certain time period, we understand the consequences that are associated with that, and we are held accountable for those consequences.

It's that give and take that I'd like to see.

Mr. BAKER. All right.

Anyone else?

Let me ask—Bruce, go ahead.

Dr. TARTER. I'd just make a short comment, Bill.

I think, you know, I think the system of labs, and it isn't yet a system but the collection of laboratories has actually done a fairly good job over the past two or three years, moving along the direction which you've indicated, at least in a number of the areas.

I think we have a long way to go, but I think there has been real progress in taking on collaborative projects in which the laboratories are central elements in deciding how best to accomplish a particular piece of work.

So I think there's been some progress, and I think you heard from all of us about the administrative and how to get some of that out. But I think we've made real progress in the areas of beginning to act more like a system.

Mr. BAKER. Okay, last question.

Can we improve our royalty system so that we can give back some of what we invent and it eventually winds its way to the private sector into a science fund so that there'll be more money for research for future generations?

Dr. TRIVELPIECE. In about 1980, I think it was, and a lot of us have patents from work we've done at laboratories. You get a buck and that's it, forget it. That is not a very well-incentivized system.

Since then, as a result of a number of changes that have taken place, now in most circumstances, the inventor can get something, the laboratory can get something, the contractor can get something, and the government gets something. And of course if it turns out to be a highly successful, commercial venture, to the extent there are taxes paid on it, then the government gets something by virtue of that.

It's, like a lot of these systems, it's certainly not perfect, but it is substantially better than it was ten or 15 years ago.

Dr. GAY. I think there's a lot more powerful opportunities than just depending upon royalties as a cash flow source that we could use to create a venture fund.

I may have understood your question a little bit differently in terms of how can we take alternative funding sources, such as royalty streams, and make use of those to continue to fund our ongoing efforts.

If, for example, laboratories could take equity positions in spinoffs and startups that emerge from the laboratory initiated activities, we would have a much greater return on investment than we would see simply waiting for royalties which tend to be a relatively small, or sometimes patents are simply used as trading stamps in order to practice art in a certain field.

Mr. BAKER. My time is up.

I'd like to congratulate my two representatives on this panel.

And, Mr. Chairman, you've stolen one of them. And I congratulate you. He's moving to New Mexico to upgrade his congressional representation. The money is the side.

Mr. SCHIFF. Well, something about California's loss, I think.

Mr. Fawell, you're recognized for five minutes.

Mr. FAWELL. Thank you.

My congratulations to you folks lasting it out. It's been a long day.

And I have not had the privilege of listening to a great deal of the testimony.

Dr. Schriesheim and I, I think, arrived, you arrived at Argonne shortly before I arrived in Congress, back around '84, '85. And you'll forgive me but it seems that to a degree, deja vu all over again. These little crises have come and gone, and the desires to find missions and programs and are they synonymous? I'm not sure if they are. But it seems to me that while I agree that labs are a national treasure and I think most highly of them, they've grown more like little topsy, it seems to me, than by any plans.

Programs beget programs and they beget more programs, and then of course we have an awful lot of lobbying in Congress by people who are extremely jealous about their particular areas.

So I'm not quite sure how much we can, in reality, change all of that.

I have, in reviewing some of the Galvin Report, statements, though it seems to me what we're really talking about is the management system, and I'm sure that's been talked about over and over again today.

Just quoting the Galvin Report, where it states the management system is broken and should be replaced with a bold alternative, the Task Force is quoted as saying, calling for a blank sheet of paper approach, the rethinking of the labs because they were so encrusted with irrelevant tradition and procedures that only hampered their operation.

Pretty strong language.

I would like, I suppose you've all been asked, well, is that fair criticism?

And he goes on to say, also, cautioned the labs against going too far afield in technology transfer efforts, and instead to focus on their primary mission of energy development and waste cleanup, etcetera.

Are those fair criticisms?

Dr. TRIVELPIECE. I think this comment by Mr. Galvin's been misunderstood, and I think Dr. Schriesheim has referred to this already, but the issue in part has to do with the comment about Harwell, and I think that's, if Dr. Schriesheim would like to repeat what he said before I think is in fact the appropriate thing. Do not allow the laboratories to become the handmaidens of industry.

Mr. FAWELL. What about this statement though about management. I'm no proponent for privatization, but there is an awfully strong indictment of management. Now whether it's of DOE necessarily or of the labs is another question too, but it's, we all talk about efficiency, better administration, and all that, and it can be lightly said, but what new mold shaking alternatives do we have to meet this type of criticism?

Dr. SCHRIESHEIM. I guess there are two questions in that one.

One, is it true that the labs are, I can't remember the exact statement, are encrusted with inappropriate management, I guess.

And the second is, what are the bold alternatives.

Mr. FAWELL. Encrusted with irrelevant tradition and procedures that only hamper their operation.

Dr. SCHRIESHEIM. I think I won't get in hot water if I refer back to Charlie Curtis' testimony this morning, when I believe he agreed essentially that if I could say the old DOE, sort of an old DOE and a new DOE, that the old DOE is certainly, there are a number of inefficient practices that were highlighted in the Galvin Report in Appendix B.

There were a large, Appendix B is a proscription for dealing with these encrustations.

And I don't know. I certainly can't speak for every lab director at the table but I believe that they would all agree that their costs, laboratory costs are higher than they should be pre-this operating on Appendix B.

DOE is operating on Appendix B, the labs are operating on Appendix B. And assuming again, as Charlie Curtis said, he cannot make a promise that the system will deal with every one of those Appendix B items, but assuming that they do, then there's an opportunity for operating the lab system more efficiently, DOE and the lab system more efficiently.

Now the second part of your question has to do with a bold initiative to develop an entirely new management structure. I think that's the thrust of the question.

Mr. FAWELL. I wouldn't assume, as far as I am concerned, that necessarily has to include privatization or corporatization.

Dr. SCHRIESHEIM. And what Al pointed out, Dr. Trivelpiece pointed out was a statement that I had made, that in my wanderings around the international scene, the one institution which we know very well, Harwell in England, similar to Oak Ridge and Argonne in the past, high, great infrastructure, terrific people, has degraded itself and become a privatized technical service operation for a lot of British industry. And if that's the way it was meant to be, that's what happened.

And I hope, as a director of a national lab, that's far from that, that we do not go in that direction.

With respect to corporatization, I frankly don't quite know what to say about that. It hasn't really been fleshed out, so I don't know quite what to say about it in terms of examining it.

Bold, new directions, I guess I'm a conservative scientist. Breakthroughs don't happen often. A bold, new management structure, I don't know.

But my vast experience, it depends on people, provided one doesn't put in a structure where one size fits all, good people take poor structures and do good things with them. Good people take poor programs and do great things with poor programs.

Poor people take great programs and foul them up. Poor people take great management systems and do terrible things with them.

So if DOE can attract great people, if we can attract great people, if Congress can attract great people, and we don't put in a one-size-fits-all, I think that the chances are that we'll do great things together.

Mr. SCHIFF. I don't like to interrupt when it's being so profound.

The gentleman's time has expired, but if witnesses want to further answer?

Dr. Hecker, I believe you indicated?

Dr. HECKER. Yes, I would.

Since I've said it to this Committee before, the last time we met, I said it that time, that I thought Mr. Galvin was right. He came to this job as being Mr. Quality USA, and from what he saw, he concluded this was not a way to run a productive organization.

And I agree with that. I think today Mr. Curtis agreed with that.

And initially, that system of governance which was really put in place 52 years ago was bold and innovative; but it has eroded over the years and has become broken, and it needs to be fixed now.

The question is what bold things one does now. I agree with Al's comment about the corporatization proposal, but let me tell you, the things that I'm doing, at least right now at Los Alamos, are bold. They are things that I would not have dared to do a year ago. And I'm depending on the Department of Energy to come through with its part of the deal of helping to fix the governance in the spirit that Mr. Curtis said earlier today.

Mr. FAWELL. Fine. Thank you very much, gentlemen.

Mr. SCHIFF. Anyone else want to further respond?

Dr. Crawford?

Dr. CRAWFORD. I might just add that things are not static. I think things are changing.

DOE has started its realignment process and as they realign their own organizations, it has impact on the laboratories.

And the instance I was going to cite is that we do watch the number of audits that we get at the laboratory, and for the past few years, we've been literally inundated with audits.

That has indeed begun to drop, the number of audits at the laboratory. And my sense is the environment of those audits is also changing to one that's more constructive.

So there are some changes starting to happen which enable us then to run our laboratories a bit better.

Mr. SCHIFF. Okay, thank you very much, Mr. Fawell.

I'd just like to say two things before concluding the hearing.

The first is, I meant to say it before, but it echoed what I know Dr. Schriesheim and I think several of you said.

I'm very concerned about this term that's been thrown around all through this hearing that the Cold War is over, in the sense that I think it's been used.

It is true that the situation we had of a direct confrontation between the United States and NATO allies versus the Soviet Union and the Soviet Bloc that's behind us, so it's true that we're looking at a new geopolitical environment.

But I think that term is being used to suggest that all of our problems have gone away. You know, gee, we can just dismantle all these structures we've put together.

I think that's a tremendous mistake. I think even on the military side, if you consider the fact that the defense laboratories were set up to give us nuclear deterrence, we now have a situation where proliferation makes certain countries that we would have laughed at in this context at being nuclear threats, as being very much potentially nuclear threats, or threats with other weapons of mass destruction.

So I just want to say I do agree the Cold War is over. It's an obvious fact. I don't agree with I think the implication from that is that everyone can just declare victory and go home. I wish that were the case.

I want to say one other word, and I think all the witnesses here would know this but add it especially for Dr. Crawford.

I don't know if you know how significant a hearing this was today in this sense. I've been at many hearings where the only Members of Congress at the hearing were the Chair and the senior Member from the minority party.

Now that is no offense at my own institution of the Congress. As indicated, a record is being made. The record is distributed to all the Members of Congress. They have staff that are watching and taking notes, so the information gets out really regardless of how many Members of Congress happen to be in the room.

However, despite the fact that this, and our first week back from a rather long recess, we are competing not only with everything getting started from the Defense Department appropriations bill on the floor to a live military action situation in the Balkans, despite all that competition, there were quite a number of members here throughout this hearing, including the Chairman and senior minority party Member of the Full Committee.

And what I think that indicates is the interest in the Science Committee and the Congress in this subject. And so I just want you to know that we don't treat lightly inviting the level of witnesses we've had here today away from their other duties, yourselves as laboratory directors, and the witnesses you saw before you.

But I think you can see that the Congress is at the point of feeling that we need to take some action and move in a direction here. There's a great deal of interest in that, and it's expressed personally by Members being here.

And so I want to assure you that the time you've spent I know being here again I think has been well spent because I think there's every likelihood that important decisions will be made in the near future.

With that, I want to thank all of the witnesses from beginning to end, who testified here today, and declare that the hearing is adjourned.

[Whereupon, at 5:30 p.m., Thursday, September 7, 1995, the hearing was concluded, and the Committee recessed, subject to call of the Chair.]

[The following material was received for the record:]

AMERICAN ASSOCIATION OF ENGINEERING SOCIETIES

Statement

of the

The Engineers' Public Policy Council of the
American Association of Engineering Societies

to the

Subcommittees on Basic Research and Energy and Environment
House Committee on Science

on the

<u>Future Missions and Governance for</u>
<u>The Department of Energy National Laboratories</u>
(H.R.2142, H.R.87, H.R.1993 - Title II)

September 7, 1995

1111 NINETEENTH STREET, N.W. • SUITE 608 • WASHINGTON, D.C. 20036-3690
(202) 296-2237 • (202) 296-1151 (FAX)

INTRODUCTION
The Engineers Public Policy Council of American Association of Engineering Societies (AAES) endorses the objectives of H.R.2142, the "Department of Energy Laboratory Missions Act." AAES is a professional organization dedicated to coordinating the collective efforts of over 800,000 members to advance the knowledge, understanding and practice of engineering.

While federal investment in basic and applied research and development is critical to the technological advances that sustain our economic prosperity and military strength, AAES supports efforts to evaluate objectively the full range of federal R&D funding to maximize return on taxpayer investment. The research capabilities of the Department of Energy laboratories are a cornerstone of the federal R&D enterprise that must remain strong, even in tight times. The diversity and depth of talent of almost 60,000 scientists, engineers and technicians working in multidisciplinary teams is extraordinary, and the sophisticated tools and instruments and unique user facilities are among the best in the world.

Certainly, post Cold War changes in the nation's defense requirements, increasing global competition, and budgetary constraints demand that DOE optimize its considerable but shrinking budget to maintain this science and engineering capability on which the nation relies. This growing challenge reinforces the continuing need for DOE to better define and coordinate missions for its laboratories. We believe the effective assignment of clear missions focusing on individual and collective lab strengths may be the key to facilitating solutions to many ongoing problems within the DOE laboratory structure.

Recent studies by the General Accounting Office (GAO) and DOE's Galvin Task Force maintain that inefficiencies within the lab system result from costly and ineffective management by DOE, including burdensome administrative requirements, excessive auditing and oversight reviews, and balkanization of DOE program offices. It follows that efforts to achieve cost savings and strengthen performance should begin with administrative reform, while reducing adverse impact on research and facilities. The assignment of coherent lab missions should form the basis for increasing cross-lab interaction, coordination between labs and DOE headquarters, integration of program areas, management changes and, if necessary, facility and program consolidation and closure.

CLOSURE COMMISSION
Although we understand the desire to reduce the deficit and the frustration over numerous reports calling on DOE to address excess capacity and ongoing inefficiencies within its lab complex, separate bills sponsored by Reps. Bartlett (H.R.87) and Tiarht (H.R.1993) to establish an independent commission to close and reconfigure labs seem premature. Examination of lab reconfiguration or closure must be preceded by a comprehensive and current analysis of the distinguishing core competencies of the labs, and the subsequent assignment of specific missions to each lab based on how core competencies coincide with national needs. Until this critical challenge is met, informed decisions on closure options will be difficult if not impossible given the current absence of a coherent departmental strategy and clear missions against which to measure the costs and benefits of major restructuring of the labs.

In our judgement, DOE should be required to compare core competencies, set clear missions and achieve cost savings through efficiencies and streamlining based on such mission assignment, and then consider closure possibilities. While Mr. Bartlett's bill is preferable to Mr. Tiahrt's in that it allows DOE to propose its own criteria for reconfiguration and closure (including a comment period under DOE's purview), we believe the best approach is that adopted by Chairman Schiff under H.R.2142. H.R.2142 sets out core mission areas, requires DOE to propose criteria for assigning missions (including public comment), and leaves initial decisions on streamlining to the Department, rather than to another commission. DOE is currently addressing many problems set out in the Galvin report, but must do considerably more. We also suggest that other agencies be encouraged to evaluate laboratories under their purview. Closure options should not be limited to DOE, but include all 730 federal labs.

MISSIONS

A. FOR LAB COMPLEX

We endorse the general mission areas described in H.R.2142, including national security, energy supply and efficiency, and minimizing environmental impacts of energy use. These core missions are consistent with legislation reported by the committee last year and reinforced by the Galvin Task Force report in February.

The Galvin report makes a renewed and compelling case for advancing a comprehensive national energy agenda that focuses on enhancing the long-term supply and efficient use of energy, which is clearly a primary mission of the labs. We applaud the emphasis in H.R.2142 on R&D furthering generic, precompetitive technologies in high risk areas - which have the potential to benefit a wide range of companies - and the support for collaborative partnerships with industry and academia within mission areas. Such partnerships should further departmental missions and stimulate innovation in the private sector. Under the environmental mission, we recommend that R&D on more efficient utilization of energy be included explicitly in order to advance environmental technologies and pollution prevention. This mission area was clearly articulated in the Galvin report and also suggested in the GAO study.

We are pleased that H.R. 2142 gives appropriate attention to basic research and the unique role of DOE's user facilities. Such cutting edge research and capabilities are imperative and must be sustained. We emphasize, however, that basic research is a fundamental and permanent underpinning to the other mission areas, rather than a separate mission, which the Galvin report acknowledges. Evaluating missions through performance criteria and measurable goals will be complicated if basic research is treated as a separate mission because the nature and timing of breakthroughs can not be set out in advance or measured against strict criteria.

The core missions of defense, energy and minimizing environmental impacts should be set out in an over-arching mission statement for the laboratory complex, including general R&D priority areas under each core mission consistent with national needs. The mission statement should emphasize the importance of integrating basic and applied research. The role of basic research as an integral part of furthering core mission areas must be made explicit. Similarly, technology partnerships should not be a separate mission but integrated within mission areas and viewed as an essential component and/or outgrowth of mission related R&D. Other important goals such as cross-lab interaction, cross-program coordination, and cooperation with state and other federal agencies, universities and industry to minimize duplication and enhance collaboration should be included in the mission statement as they involve the laboratory complex as a whole.

B. FOR EACH LABORATORY

As important as a coherent mission statement for the lab complex is the assignment of clear and specific missions to each lab consistent with the over-arching mission statement. The generic nature and uncertainty of lab missions is a long-standing problem that breeds underutilization of talent and resources and undercuts the effectiveness of the complex. Part of the problem is that rather than setting out core areas of expertise, labs generally list **all** activity areas or technical competencies, keeping their options open in various fields to protect funding. Even worse, DOE distributes lab work program by program, without significant attention to comparative strengths within the system. Barely distinguishable missions are the unfortunate result. (Naturally, this is more of a problem for the multiprogram labs than it is for DOE's single program labs and facilities).

We believe considerations for setting criteria for mission assignment and streamlining under Section 103 should reflect the need to describe and compare distinguishing core competencies of all departmental labs. Until it is clear which labs do what better than others, missions will likely continue to be too dispersed. It makes little sense to assign broad missions under which all lab competencies can fit. Overlapping competencies within the system must be addressed, and while some duplication is necessary, only core competencies that further specific lab missions should be maintained.

At the same time, missions should not be unnecessarily restrictive so as to fence off important core competencies. Lab directors must have the flexibility to pursue innovative research and new capabilities within or perhaps at the margins of focused lab missions. The real challenge in assigning missions will be balancing the strength of the multi-attribute character of the national labs against the need for a better strategic focus in tight fiscal times. The idea is to capture the primary focus of the labs by measuring core competencies against the over-arching mission statement for the complex, then assign lab missions and defined goals within those missions against which performance can be assessed. Such an effort will help labs operate better as a system and may facilitate the pursuit of the "lead lab" concept under which one lab coordinates all lab contributions within a specific mission area. Another option is for two to three labs to form a virtual "center of excellence" to secure a critical mass of expertise within a priority area. Both concepts were identified in the Galvin report and should be explored.

CLOSING REMARKS

Few disagree that DOE's laboratory complex has excess capacity. Thus, while we believe a commission designed to close labs is premature, H.R.2142 should be strengthened by encouraging DOE to consider reconfiguration and/or closure of labs as part of its final report. It is essential, however, that mission assignment for each lab and administrative changes based on these assignments precede such considerations. Finally, under Section 104 of H.R.2142, DOE is given 4 years from the time its report is transmitted to assign missions and implement streamlining. Considering the corresponding recommendations of many studies and that DOE is making strides in addressing problems through its Laboratory Operating Board and other mechanisms, **much** quicker action should be expected. The future performance of the labs hinges on a steadfast commitment by DOE and Congress to focus lab strengths at a time when DOE's budget is projected to decline steadily over the next five years.

**TESTIMONY OF JOSEPH A. DEAR
ASSISTANT SECRETARY
FOR OCCUPATIONAL SAFETY AND HEALTH
UNITED STATES DEPARTMENT OF LABOR
Submitted to the
SUBCOMMITTEE ON BASIC RESEARCH
AND
SUBCOMMITTEE ON ENERGY AND ENVIRONMENT
COMMITTEE ON SCIENCE
UNITED STATES HOUSE OF REPRESENTATIVES**

SEPTEMBER 6, 1995

I am pleased to have the opportunity to comment on two bills that have come before the Subcommittees for consideration: H.R. 2142, the "Department of Energy Laboratory Missions Act," and H.R. 1510, the "Department of Energy Laboratory Efficiency Improvement Act." These bills would shift the responsibility for enforcing safety and health regulations at certain Government-Owned, Contractor-Operated (GOCO) laboratories from the Department of Energy (DOE) to the Occupational Safety and Health Administration (OSHA).

As requested by the Subcommittees, OSHA has analyzed these bills to determine their impact on the agency and what resources would be needed in order to carry out the additional responsibilities the proposed legislation would place on OSHA. We have also considered the jurisdictional issues raised by the bills and whether any statutory changes would be necessary in order for Federal OSHA to assume responsibility for safety and health enforcement at GOCO laboratories.

Before I address the issues the Subcommittees asked me to discuss concerning the proposed legislation, I will briefly provide you with background information concerning the history of DOE-OSHA GOCO-related activity and general information about OSHA's mission and current resources.

HISTORY OF DOE-OSHA GOCO-RELATED ACTIVITY

In 1990, in response to DOE's request for assistance, OSHA conducted an evaluation of DOE's occupational safety and health programs for its GOCO facilities. The purpose of the evaluation was to provide DOE with a blueprint for strengthening these programs. OSHA found that although top management at DOE had made it clear that safety and health should be among the Department's highest priorities, that concern was not being reflected in the resource allocation and planning decisions of DOE and GOCO managers.

OSHA recommended that DOE take a number of actions, including the establishment of an independent oversight capability in the Office of Environment, Safety and Health (ES&H), increased safety and health staffing for both ES&H and the operations offices, and the strengthening of line responsibility for safety and health. Other recommendations included: developing more effective incentives for GOCOs to comply with safety and health regulations; improving training and technical support capabilities; requiring GOCOs to assign higher priority to safety and health programs; strengthening employee involvement; and improving the handling of employee complaints. OSHA offered to provide assistance to DOE in three major areas: improving DOE's technical information and training capabilities; strengthening DOE's independent oversight; and continued OSHA evaluation for a period of two to three years.

DOE accepted OSHA's recommendations and has implemented many of them; however, shortcomings still exist in some GOCOs' safety and health programs. In 1993, DOE announced its interest in transferring the safety and health oversight function to an external agency. Since then, OSHA and ES&H have been cooperating to exchange technical information, in order for each agency to familiarize itself with the other's policies and programs.

OSHA'S MISSION AND RESOURCES

OSHA is a relatively small agency with a total of 2,300 employees, approximately 1,000 of whom are inspectors. Since the late 1970's, OSHA's appropriation, adjusted for inflation, has remained virtually flat, and the number of authorized personnel has dropped 15 percent, from 2,717 in 1977 to 2,317 in 1995. Yet the number of establishments covered by OSHA has increased by 40 percent during that same time period, from 4.4 million to 6.2 million, and the number of covered workers has risen from 65 million to 93 million.

OSHA's authorizing legislation permits States to operate their own occupational safety and health programs, with Federal OSHA's approval. Currently, 23 States and two Territories operate their own plans, and receive up to 50 percent of their funding from Federal OSHA. They have a total of about 1,000 State-plan safety and health inspectors. Even if these inspectors are taken into account, the ratio of safety and health inspectors to worksites in this country is one to 3,100. At last year's rate of inspection, it would take the combined Federal and State safety and health inspection workforce 62 years to inspect every establishment.

PROPOSED LEGISLATION

Now I will address H.R. 2142 and H.R. 1510. Each bill includes a section titled "Elimination of Self-Regulation". However, the language of the sections is not consistent, and OSHA is unable to completely determine the specific intent of each bill regarding implementation and enforcement of safety and health rules and regulations at DOE facilities.

Under H.R. 2142, DOE would continue to "implement" safety and health rules and regulations at GOCO laboratories, but would not be the agency that enforces such rules. H.R. 1510, on the other hand, would appear to eliminate DOE's implementation **and** enforcement responsibilities. H.R. 1510 does not actually mention enforcement except in the title. It simply states that

DOE "shall not be the agency of implementation" of safety and health rules.

Neither bill specifies which agency would develop future safety and health regulations for DOE laboratories or whether OSHA would enforce its own safety and health regulations in the laboratories, or DOE's rules. H.R. 1510 also differs from H.R. 2142 by providing for the retention of DOE responsibility for safety and health for three defense laboratories -- Lawrence Livermore, Los Alamos, and Sandia.

It is unclear in both of the proposed bills whether OSHA would be given responsibility only for the 26 national DOE laboratories, or whether the intent is for OSHA to cover all 56 DOE GOCO sites not already being covered by OSHA. Section 5 of H.R. 1510 states that "the term departmental laboratory means a Federal laboratory, or any other laboratory or facility designated by the Secretary of Energy, operated by or on behalf of the Department of Energy." Section 2 of H.R. 2142 contains the same definition. This definition appears to allow the Secretary of Energy to designate any or all GOCO facilities as "departmental laboratories". Regardless of whether it is Congress' intent to transfer responsibility for just the 26 facilities currently classified as laboratories by DOE, or for all DOE GOCOs, there would be serious resource implications for OSHA.

Resource Implications

In any proposal which would add to OSHA's responsibilities, resource implications must be considered. One factor to be considered is the possibility that OSHA's budget will be significantly smaller in FY 1996. Legislation passed by the House in July would reduce our appropriation from $312,500,000 to about $264,000,000, an overall cut of 15.5 percent. The enforcement function would be cut by 33 percent, which would severely impact our inspection program. OSHA is in no position to take on enforcement responsibility for 26-56 complex GOCO facilities absent sufficient resources to ensure that safety and health protection is not further diluted at sites for which OSHA currently has responsibility, and that the current level of protection at GOCOs is maintained. Transferring responsibility without sufficient resources would convey the false impression to the public and to GOCO employees that their right to a safe and healthful workplace is being protected, when in fact it is not.

Another consideration is the need for additional resources to train inspectors. OSHA does not currently have the expertise to effectively enforce safety and health rules at the DOE GOCO laboratories, many of which have unique processes and hazards not found in private sector workplaces. For example, many sites have large amounts of mixed hazardous waste containing both toxic chemicals and radioactive materials. The materials are uncharacterized and some stem from the country's war years.

Other facilities use high-energy research equipment, such as linear accelerators, that produces tremendous amounts of heat and use large amounts of electricity. This equipment produces very high electrical and magnetic fields. Significant resources would be needed to train OSHA inspectors to deal with these hazards.

DOE-DOL Activities

OSHA and DOE are involved in several joint activities dealing with enforcement at DOE facilities. OSHA and DOE have discussed and conceptualized two projects that would help the agencies quantify the personnel and other resource needs associated with the transfer of enforcement responsibilities. The two agencies are also participating on an advisory committee investigating external regulation of DOE's nuclear facilities.

The first project is a pilot wherein OSHA would take over enforcement at one GOCO to test the application of OSHA enforcement methods at DOE facilities. The pilot would be limited in duration and would involve a location where the OSHA Area Office has staff available to conduct enforcement activities at the site. Several issues remain to be worked out.

The second project, agreed to in a Memorandum of Understanding on June 17, is a $500,000 study (funded by DOE) that will determine the best methods and the resource requirements for transferring DOE facilities for purposes of OSHA enforcement. This study will run approximately six months once started. Critical issues which will be explored include: current DOE compliance with OSHA regulations; additional resources necessary for OSHA to assume jurisdiction; incentives toward occupational safety and health-related improvements at these facilities; an examination of lessons learned from OSHA Special Emphasis Programs and existing DOE external enforcement activities; and the development of a transition schedule for OSHA if it were to assume enforcement authority over working conditions at DOE GOCO facilities. DOE and OSHA are in the process of procuring a contractor to carry out this study.

In addition to the two projects, DOE and OSHA are participating on the Department of Energy Advisory Committee on External Regulation, which was formed by Secretary of Energy O'Leary in January. The Committee's purpose is to develop recommendations concerning whether and how DOE's nuclear facilities should be externally regulated in all areas, including worker and public safety and health, environmental protection, and nuclear safety. The Committee has been meeting since March and its co-chairs issued an interim report in August, a copy of which was provided to you by DOE. The Committee's final report is due by the close of the year.

OSHA strongly believes that we should wait until the pilot project and the study are complete and the Advisory Committee's final report is issued before developing estimates of the resources required for transfer of safety and health enforcement responsibility.

Statutory Issues

Legislation to provide for OSHA coverage of DOE-administered national laboratories must take into account a variety of jurisdictional issues which arise from the unique legal status of these facilities. Section 4(b)(1) of the Occupational Safety and Health Act (OSH Act) specifies that OSHA coverage does not apply to working conditions for which other Federal agencies have issued regulations, or to conditions for which State agencies have promulgated regulations under Section 274 of the Atomic Energy Act of 1954, as amended. Therefore, it would be necessary to exempt the departmental laboratories from Section 4(b)(1) of the OSH Act, in order for OSHA to assume coverage.

Moreover, Section 3(5) of the OSH Act excludes from the definition of a covered employer the United States and any State or political subdivision of a State. Because certain of these laboratories are operated by State university personnel, an exemption from Section 3(5) would have to be provided.

Finally, although certain of the facilities covered by the proposed legislation are located in States which administer Federally-approved State OSHA programs, enforcement of safety and health requirements in Federal facilities must, under current law, be carried out exclusively by the Federal government unless Congress explicitly authorizes State regulation. OSHA recommends that Federal jurisdiction be maintained in the DOE laboratories, provided the Congress authorizes the necessary exemption from Section 3(5) of the OSH Act (in order to ensure Federal OSHA coverage for all GOCO personnel).

Importance of Maintaining an Internal Management System

As the Subcommittees consider legislation to externalize safety and health oversight at DOE facilities, OSHA urges you to keep the following key points in mind:

- An internal management system with clearly defined responsibilities and accountability is essential to worker safety and health protection. Management commitment, worker participation, and a focus on finding and fixing serious hazards and measuring results are the basic elements of the system.

- While external regulation can provide incentives and sanctions that encourage the development and operation of an internal management system, it cannot replace or supplant such a system.

- In any case, OSHA oversight alone would not be an adequate substitute for the level of worker protection currently afforded by the presence of on-site GOCO safety and health professionals. Thus, any legislation should ensure that

GOCO facilities are required to maintain an appropriate level of safety and health staffing.

I hope that my testimony proves helpful to the Subcommittees as they consider the implications of H.R. 2142 and H.R. 1510. My staff is available to discuss these issues with you as you consider the proposed legislation.

National Renewable Energy Laboratory

1617 Cole Boulevard
Golden Colorado 80401-3393
(303) 275-3000

H.admin.om/subcommittee

September 22, 1995

Honorable Steven H. Schiff
Chairman, Subcommittee on Basic Research
U.S. House of Representatives
Suite 2320 Rayburn House Office Building
Washington, DC 20515-6301

Dear Congressman Schiff:

I am writing today in response to your request for commentary on how H.R. 2142, the "Department of Energy Laboratory Missions Act," might be further enhanced. As you know, I commented on H.R. 2142 in a letter to Mason Wiggins in July and again in early September at the joint hearing on restructuring the DOE national laboratories. In this letter I have synthesized my earlier comments with recent thoughts on how the effectiveness and efficiency of the DOE national laboratories might be improved through a better definition of missions.

Let me begin by endorsing the guiding principles of DOE's "Management Improvement Roadmap". Paraphrasing from the written statement of DOE Deputy Secretary Charles Curtis submitted for the September 7 Hearings, the five Principles capturing the objectives of the Roadmap are:

1. Create a more productive, mission-focused, and cost-effective Department and Laboratory system;

2. Adopt best business practices throughout the system;

3. Require performance-based, results-oriented accountability;

4. Achieve credible regulation and oversight;

5. Shift the balance of focus at the laboratories away from process compliance and toward mission success and results.

I believe that a sixth Principle is essential in assuring that the DOE National Labs fulfill their full potential, namely:

The Honorable Steven Schiff
September 25, 1995
Page 2

6. Target the missions of the Laboratory system on those science and technology tasks of national importance for which no other credible or sufficiently reliable path of accomplishment exists.

In my view H.R. 2142 will be most effective if it combines the essence of Principles 1, 3, 5 and 6, namely that:

i. Laboratories should focus on complementary and well-defined missions,

ii. DOE should assure that the integration of the individual Laboratory missions addresses the key science and technology missions of the Lab system,

iii. Lab missions must be appropriately targeted at tasks deserving of Federal funding, and

iv. The limited resources available must be focused on the highest priority research and development missions.

This will require a comprehensive strategic plan detailing the specific missions of the integrated DOE Laboratory system and of the individual Laboratories. A methodical and objective assessment of the core competencies of each individual Laboratory will be necessary to best decide the distribution of responsibility and resources for fulfilling the missions. The definition of specific, distinct missions and allocation of resources based on the prioritization of the missions will create an environment of proper accountability and productivity. A limited degree of overlap in individual Laboratory missions may be advantageous in assuring adequate resources and a multiplicity of innovative approaches to critical tasks; however, excessive redundancy and excess capacity is wasteful and unacceptable. I strongly support concentrating resources at individual Centers of Excellence.

I believe that Federal science and technology funding is best targeted in five general areas:

i. Fundamental Research

Basic science and engineering research in materials, processes and structures, including for example compound semiconductor crystal formation, the physics and chemistry of nanoparticles, and human genome mapping.

i.i Long-term Research and Development

Exploratory research and development aimed at providing the technological foundations for future commercial implementation, including for example the underlying waste treatment and containment technologies needed for hazardous waste management and site remediation.

iii. Activities Possessing Great Complexity and/or Requiring Major Investments

Research and development activities of great complexity and/or requiring major investments in specialized equipment and highly-skilled workers beyond the reach of the private sector given the risk-adjusted costs and benefits. This includes such endeavors as space exploration, terrestrial transportation infrastructure, and large-scale testing of biofuels production processes.

iv. National Interests Without a Clear Basis for Individual Competitive Advantage

Fundamental and high-risk research that is critical for collective national industrial progress but that does not provide private industry with a clear basis for individual competitive advantage. This includes tasks for which the technical risks are too great or the benefits too diffuse for private sector investment. Examples are next-generation supercomputers, full-scale wind turbine testing, and multi-lateral advanced technology implementation programs.

v. Science and Technology of Public Policy Issues

Scientific research and technology development directed at providing a scientific basis for public policy debates, including for example global climate change research aimed at quantifying the impacts of "greenhouse" emissions.

A reasoned and reasonable balance of research endeavors in these five arenas is appropriate.

With regards to task prioritization in energy research, I strongly support the Galvin Task Force's recommendations that a diversified portfolio of national investment in conservation, energy efficiency, enhanced fossil oil and gas recovery, and renewable energy be given highest priority in allocating Federal energy supply research funds.

My specific recommendations on H.R. 2142 are:

1. On page 1, change "establishing missions" to "clarifying missions" in the preamble to more accurate reflect the existing situation, namely that:

   a. some Laboratories already have specific and well-defined missions,
   b. other Laboratories have only ill-defined and/or disjointed missions; and
   c. better definition and coordination of Laboratory missions is needed to eliminate wasteful duplication and inefficiency.

2. On page 3, line 1&2, change "scientific and technological" to "scientific, technological, economic and environmental" to better capture the broad value to the nation of the research programs in the Labs.

3. On page 3, line 16, change "achievement of national technology goals" to "technological foundation upon which America's public and private interests can build" to better embody the role of government in providing a firm foundation for individual and collective enterprise, rather than mandating technology specifics. Technology specifics are better left to the competitive marketplace.

4. On page 5, line 19, acknowledge the importance of stable energy supplies by inserting a new subpart (1) (D) in Section 102 as follows:

   "(D) To contribute to the nation's security, prosperity and well-being by undertaking research and development necessary to assure diverse, sustainable energy supplies."

5. On page 5, line 21&22, delete "generic". The use of "generic" might be misconstrued to conflict with the use of Cooperative Research and Development Agreements (CRADA's) to transfer specific commercially-promising technologies to American industry.

The Honorable Steven Schiff
September 25, 1995
Page 5

6. On page 5, line 24, delete "with an emphasis on long-term, high-risk research" in order to not overly limit the scope of the contributions of the Laboratories. A reasoned and reasonable balance of research endeavors in the five arenas outlined above is appropriate. Restriction to any one arena or sub-arena risks the nation being left with no qualified entity to fulfill tasks of critical national importance.

7. On page 7, lines 24, subparts (A) & (B), underscore the importance of the DOE pro-actively implementing the guidance of Galvin Task Force to focus on high priorities and to increase Departmental operational efficiency by rounding out the considerations that the Secretary shall consider in developing criteria for setting Lab missions. Insert two new subparts A' and A" between existing subparts A and B as follows:

   "(A') the importance of a diversified investment in a balanced energy research program that includes leveraging near-term improvements and promising long-term innovations, including conservation, energy efficiency, enhanced fossil oil and gas recovery, and renewable energy as high priority research areas;

   (A") the value of focusing specific missions at established Centers of Excellence;"

I appreciate this opportunity to share my thoughts on how H.R. 2142 might best achieve its goal of defining missions to improve the efficiency and effectiveness of the DOE National Laboratory system. I would welcome any additional questions or comments that you might have.

Sincerely,

Charles F. Gay

Dr. Charles F. Gay
Director

cc B. Marshall
B. Noun
C. Riordan

STATEMENT SUBMITTED

BY

CHAIRMAN SHIRLEY ANN JACKSON

UNITED STATES NUCLEAR REGULATORY COMMISSION

TO THE

SUBCOMMITTEE ON BASIC RESEARCH

AND THE

SUBCOMMITTEE ON ENERGY AND ENVIRONMENT

COMMITTEE ON SCIENCE

UNITED STATES HOUSE OF REPRESENTATIVES

CONCERNING

H.R. 2142 - "DEPARTMENT OF ENERGY LABORATORY MISSIONS ACT"

AND

H.R 1510 - "DEPARTMENT OF ENERGY LABORATORIES EFFICIENCY IMPROVEMENT ACT"

SUBMITTED: SEPTEMBER 7, 1995

The Nuclear Regulatory Commission ("NRC" or "Commission") is pleased to present its views on H.R. 2142, the "Department of Energy Laboratory Missions Act" and H.R. 1510, the "Department of Energy Laboratories Efficiency Improvement Act." In particular, you have asked for our thoughts on what statutory changes and resources would be necessary if Congress were to transfer a portion of the Department of Energy's regulatory responsibilities for Federal environmental, safety, and health rules to the Commission.

As you know, H.R. 2142 and H.R. 1510 are directed toward streamlining and defining the future missions of the National Laboratories of the Department of Energy (DOE). However, both bills are also designed to provide for external health, safety and environmental regulation of the Department's National Laboratories.

While the NRC is not necessarily seeking expansion of its statutory jurisdiction to encompass the National Laboratories, the NRC will fulfill the missions which Congress assigns to it. Also, the NRC already endeavors to respond to the requests of the Executive Branch for assistance in its areas of expertise on a case-by-case basis. Expansion of NRC authority to encompass the National Laboratories would raise numerous issues which we will discuss in this testimony.

We recognize that recent and on-going reviews of DOE facilities either have or will provide important analyses for consideration of external regulation of the National Laboratories. These studies include: "National Laboratories Need Clearer Missions and Better Management," Report to the Secretary of Energy, U.S. General Accounting Office, January, 1995; and, "Alternative Futures for the Department of Energy National Laboratories," Secretary of Energy Advisory Board, Task Force on Alternative Futures for the Department of Energy National Laboratories, February, 1995. We anticipate that valuable insights will also be provided in the report of the Advisory Committee on External Regulation of DOE Nuclear Safety which expects to conclude its work later this year.

We believe that an evaluation of the proposed transfers of regulatory authority, including detailed answers to your questions, depends upon our obtaining a full understanding of the nature and scope of the facilities that would fall under NRC jurisdiction and the degree of licensing or regulatory oversight contemplated by the Congress. However, we can identify a number of the factors and issues that we believe have an important bearing on the overall logical framework for evaluation of the matter of external regulation as well as the need for statutory changes and resources that would flow from such consideration.

First, the Commission supports preservation of the long-standing principle of separation of regulation of civilian uses of nuclear energy vis-a-vis national security-related uses. General adherence to this principle maintains the distinction between the commercial nuclear sector and national security needs. In addition, the NRC's carefully-developed regulatory framework and philosophy for protection of public health and safety in connection with civilian applications of nuclear energy would appear to differ from the framework and philosophy that may apply to national security uses, since the latter could involve a balancing of national security requirements against public health and safety. For instance, it would appear to be particularly inappropriate for the NRC to regulate the portion of DOE's program for research, development, manufacture, testing, or dismantlement of nuclear weapons since regulatory priorities might conflict with national defense requirements.

In this regard, we note that Section 2 of H.R. 1510 expressly excepts Departmental defense laboratories (defined in section 5(d) as Lawrence Livermore National Laboratory, the Los Alamos National Laboratory, and the Sandia National Laboratories) from the proposed transfer of regulatory responsibility from DOE to other Federal and state agencies. However, H.R. 2412 does not appear to provide a similar exception. Because some of the laboratories may perform both defense and civilian-related activities, it may be difficult to establish a bright line between the two types of activities that would facilitate NRC regulation.

Also, for facilities or components of facilities that are in a decommissioning mode, Congress would need to consider whether the benefits of external regulatory oversight of the DOE facilities would be commensurate with the costs that would be incurred. Moreover, while the nature of the environmental conditions at the laboratories are being evaluated and funding mechanisms to pay for mitigation are under development, the abrupt application of NRC regulations might be challenging for all involved.

The level of licensing or regulatory oversight that the Congress would contemplate needs to be considered. As currently written, it would appear that the full force of the licensing requirements of the Atomic Energy Act would come into play. When Congress gave the NRC the task of regulating the gaseous diffusion plants of the DOE, it recognized special challenges associated with imposing a new regulatory scheme on facilities that had been built and operated under a different regulatory scheme. In response to the new responsibility, the NRC developed a new process of certification utilizing newly-established NRC regulations. This will entail NRC approval of a DOE plan for achieving compliance with the new NRC regulations, in lieu of regular licensing under the Atomic Energy Act.

Another aspect for the Congress to consider is the scope of NRC jurisdiction to clarify whether NRC's regulatory authority would contain materials and facilities currently regulated under the Atomic Energy Act or would extend beyond NRC's currently existing regulatory base. If the Congress decided to expand NRC's regulatory authority, then it is reasonable to expect it would be a challenging task for DOE to develop an appropriate program to meet new NRC requirements. Also, in the event of expansion of NRC's regulatory jurisdiction, the NRC would need to reassess whether it possessed relevant expertise applicable to the additional responsibilities associated with regulation of all the facilities which would be subject to NRC regulation. It is possible that a major agency reorganization would be required. Both the activities by the DOE and NRC would take time and thus legislation should consider an appropriate transition period to phase in these new regulatory responsibilities.

Sufficient funding for the assumption of new duties would be essential to prevent a dilution of the already diminishing resources which the NRC has for the protection of public health and safety in its regulation of the civilian nuclear industry. Moreover, since the NRC is an approximately 100% fee recovery agency, it would be inappropriate to burden commercial NRC licensees and their customers with the cost of regulating the National Laboratories. Thus, if the NRC were given such additional responsibilities, there would be a need to either amend section 161w. to permit NRC to collect fees from DOE for licensing, inspection and other regulatory activities associated with the agency's new statutory responsibilities, or to identify some other funding mechanism.

Another consideration is the potential for organizational conflict of interest issues if NRC were given regulatory authority over the laboratories. Currently, a substantial amount of the research and technical contracts to support NRC regulatory efforts is conducted by the National Laboratories. Questions could arise under section 170A. of the Atomic Energy Act as to whether the NRC could continue to utilize the laboratories since we normally do not obtain research or technical support from the communities we regulate due to potential conflicts. Congress would need to consider carefully the implications of the proposed legislation for NRC's programs, and changes to section 170A. would be essential.

In summary, the resolution of the issues we have raised should be considered in order to estimate the resources that would be required to implement any proposed legislation in this area. Regulation of the National Laboratories would be a significant undertaking. We conclude that a major change in NRC's regulatory jurisdiction would likely involve the need for additional resources and agency expertise to meet these expanded regulatory responsibilities.

The Commission would be pleased to work further with the Committee on this important legislation.

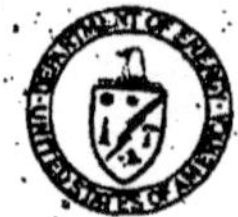

Department of Energy
Washington, DC 20585

June 29, 1995

The Honorable George E. Brown, Jr.
Ranking Minority Member
Committee on Science
U.S. House of Representatives
Washington, DC 20515

Dear Congressman Brown:

Thank you for your letter of June 27, requesting comparative budget information with regard to H.R. 1816, the Department of Energy Research and Development Authorization Act of 1995. In response to your request, accompanying this letter are the following tables:

- By laboratory, a comparison of the Department's R&D programs as
  - appropriated in FY 1995;
  - expected if the Doyle Substitute to H.R. 1816 were enacted;
  - expected if the Subcommittee bill were enacted; and
  - as expected if the Full Committee bill were enacted into law.
- Comparisons of the four proposals broken down by funding level for all DOE budget accounts within the jurisdiction of the House Committee on Science.
- Comparisons of the impact of the four proposals on Departmental programs relevant to the State of California.

As you recommended, the nonbinding Committee report language was not used to develop these tables.

Please let me know if there is additional information which the Department can provide which will assist in the House consideration of H.R. 1816. I can be reached at 586-4171.

Sincerely,

Joseph F. Vivona
Chief Financial Officer

Enclosures (3)

Impact of Final House Science Committee Action at
Department of Energy
Comparison between Proposals
(dollars in thousands)

	FY 1995 Adjusted Approp.	Walker Cut %	FY 1996 Mark (Walker)	Rohrabacher Cut %	FY 1996 Mark (Rohrabacher)	Doyle Cut %	FY 1996 Mark (Doyle)
Solar and Renewables							
Solar Programs	292,182	-48%	153,009	-57%	126,519	-10%	263,000
Geothermal	37,807	-46%	20,345	-54%	17,464	-21%	30,000
Hydrogen	9,616	160%	25,000	160%	25,000	160%	25,000
Other Solar and Renewables	84,768	-56%	37,097	-59%	34,658	-30%	59,400
Total, Solar and Renewables	424,373	-45%	235,451	-52%	203,641	-11%	377,400
Fossil Energy							
Coal	154,393	-68%	49,955	-68%	49,955	-26%	114,900
Oil	81,706	-47%	43,234	-50%	41,234	-0%	81,700
Gas	116,273	-49%	59,829	-50%	57,829	0%	116,300
Program Direction	72,263	-37%	45,535	-55%	32,192	-11%	64,000
Other Fossil	33,530	-33%	22,397	-32%	22,757	-36%	21,400
Total, Fossil Energy	458,167	-52%	220,950	-55%	203,967	-13%	398,300
Energy Efficiency							
Buildings	115,636	-52%	55,074	-65%	40,107	-46%	62,700
Industrial	135,193	-59%	55,110	-62%	51,116	-10%	121,700
Transportation	206,257	-46%	112,123	-48%	106,731	-10%	185,700
Utility	8,756	-100%	—	-100%	—	-100%	—
Other Energy Efficiency	48,701	-84%	7,813	-84%	7,813	-11%	43,400
Total, Energy Efficiency	514,543	-55%	230,120	-60%	205,767	-20%	413,500
Nuclear Energy							
Nuclear Energy R&D	199,146	-14%	170,895	-39%	120,988	-19%	161,000
Other	89,198	12%	99,553	12%	99,553	7%	95,100
Total, Nuclear Energy	288,344	-6%	270,448	-24%	220,541	-11%	256,100
Energy Research							
Biological & Environmental Research	436,641	-15%	369,645	-18%	358,136	-2%	429,500
Fusion	368,421	-31%	254,144	-38%	229,144	-25%	275,000
Basic Energy Sciences	733,940	13%	827,981	4%	765,852	4%	761,000
Laboratory Technology Transfer	56,900	-100%	—	-100%	—	-30%	40,000
University & Science Education	69,572	-100%	—	-100%	—	-71%	20,000
Other	108,379	-34%	71,621	-37%	68,091	-47%	57,100
High Energy Physics	642,129	6%	680,137	5%	674,137	4%	665,000
Nuclear Physics	331,502	-4%	316,873	-12%	290,110	-3%	321,100
Total, Energy Research	2,747,484	-8%	2,520,401	-13%	2,385,470	-7%	2,568,700
ES&H & Civilian Waste R&D	144,612	-11%	128,433	-12%	127,291	0%	144,600
Environmental Management	731,649	-12%	644,197	-13%	638,323	-12%	642,000
Clean Coal Technology	37,121	-100%	—	-100%	—	-100%	—
Total, Science Jurisdiction	5,346,293	-21%	4,250,000	-25%	3,985,000	-10%	4,800,600

Estimated Impact of Final House Science Committee Action at:
Oak Ridge National Laboratory
Comparison between Proposals
(dollars in thousands)

	FY 1995 Estimated Oblig.	Walker Cut %	FY 1996 Estimate (Walker)*	Rohrabacher Cut %	FY 1996 Est. (Rohrabacher)*	Doyle Cut %	FY 1996 Estimate (Doyle)*
Solar and Renewables							
Solar Programs	4,630	-48%	2,425	-57%	2,005	-10%	4,168
Geothermal	—	-46%	—	-54%	—	-21%	—
Hydrogen	200	160%	520	160%	520	160%	520
Other Solar and Renewables	13,150	-56%	5,755	-59%	5,376	-30%	9,215
Total, Solar and Renewables	17,980	-52%	8,700	-56%	7,901	-23%	13,903
Fossil Energy							
Coal	6,534	-68%	2,114	-68%	2,114	-26%	4,863
Oil	—	-47%	—	-50%	—	-0%	—
Gas	—	-49%	—	-50%	—	0%	—
Program Direction	—	-37%	—	-55%	—	-11%	—
Other Fossil	—	-33%	—	-32%	—	-36%	—
Total, Fossil Energy	6,534	-68%	2,114	-68%	2,114	-26%	4,863
Energy Efficiency							
Buildings	14,300	-52%	6,811	-65%	4,960	-46%	7,754
Industrial	15,684	-59%	6,393	-62%	5,930	-10%	14,119
Transportation	35,334	-46%	19,208	-48%	18,284	-10%	31,812
Utility	1,000	-100%	—	-100%	—	-100%	—
Other Energy Efficiency	550	-84%	88	-84%	88	-11%	490
Total, Energy Efficiency	66,868	-51%	32,500	-56%	29,262	-19%	54,175
Nuclear Energy							
Nuclear Energy R&D	7,394	-14%	6,345	-39%	4,492	-19%	5,978
Other	4,612	12%	5,147	12%	5,147	7%	4,917
Total, Nuclear Energy	12,006	-4%	11,492	-20%	9,639	-9%	10,895
Energy Research							
Biological & Environmental Researc.	21,913	-15%	18,551	-18%	17,973	-2%	21,555
Fusion	28,726	-31%	19,816	-38%	17,866	-25%	21,442
Basic Energy Sciences	80,581	13%	90,906	4%	84,085	4%	83,552
Laboratory Technology Transfer	9,664	-100%	—	-100%	—	-30%	6,794
University & Science Education	1,507	-100%	—	-100%	—	-71%	433
Other	35,454	-34%	23,429	-37%	22,275	-47%	18,679
High Energy Physics	290	6%	307	5%	304	4%	300
Nuclear Physics	11,639	-4%	11,125	-12%	10,186	-3%	11,274
Total, Energy Research	189,774	-14%	164,134	-20%	152,689	-14%	164,029
ES&H & Civilian Waste R&D	7,048	-11%	6,259	-12%	6,204	-0%	7,047
Environmental Management	105,904	-12%	93,246	-13%	92,395	-12%	92,928
Clean Coal Technology	—	-100%	—	-100%	—	-100%	—
Total, Science Jurisdiction	406,114	-22%	318,445	-26%	300,204	-14%	347,840

* Note: This table assumes that this laboratory is cut in each detail line above by the same percentage as DOE as a whole. The percentages on the total lines are calculated based upon the sum of the cuts in the detail lines. Depending on how the split of work at the lab within any total compares with the split in the DOE as a whole, the percentage cut at the lab on a total line may vary from the overall DOE percentage cut, and from cuts at any other lab.

Solar and Renewables							
Solar Programs	—	-48%	—	-57%	—	-10%	—
Geothermal	—	-46%	—	-54%	—	-21%	—
Hydrogen	—	160%	—	160%	—	160%	—
Other Solar and Renewables	4,350	-56%	1,904	-59%	1,779	-30%	3,048
Total, Solar and Renewables	4,350	-56%	1,904	-59%	1,779	-30%	3,048
Fossil Energy							
Coal	2,116	-68%	685	-68%	685	-26%	1,575
Oil	1,449	-47%	767	-50%	731	-0%	1,449
Gas	600	-49%	309	-50%	298	0%	600
Program Direction	—	-37%	—	-55%	—	-11%	—
Other Fossil	—	-33%	—	-32%	—	-36%	—
Total, Fossil Energy	4,165	-58%	1,761	-59%	1,714	-13%	3,624
Energy Efficiency							
Buildings	5	-52%	2	-65%	2	-46%	3
Industrial	9,486	-59%	3,867	-62%	3,587	-10%	8,539
Transportation	6,964	-46%	3,786	-48%	3,604	-10%	6,270
Utility	—	-100%	—	-100%	—	-100%	—
Other Energy Efficiency	400	-84%	64	-84%	64	-11%	356
Total, Energy Efficiency	16,855	-54%	7,719	-57%	7,257	-10%	15,168
Nuclear Energy							
Nuclear Energy R&D	30,435	-14%	26,117	-39%	18,490	-19%	24,605
Other	—	12%	—	12%	—	7%	—
Total, Nuclear Energy	30,435	-14%	26,117	-39%	18,490	-19%	24,605
Energy Research							
Biological & Environmental Research	18,440	-15%	15,611	-18%	15,125	-2%	18,138
Fusion	6,992	-31%	4,823	-38%	4,349	-25%	5,219
Basic Energy Sciences	183,382	13%	206,879	4%	191,356	4%	190,143
Laboratory Technology Transfer	8,476	-100%	—	-100%	—	-30%	5,959
University & Science Education	4,742	-100%	—	-100%	—	-71%	1,363
Other	6,595	-34%	4,358	-37%	4,143	-47%	3,475
High Energy Physics	8,550	6%	9,056	5%	8,976	4%	8,855
Nuclear Physics	15,131	-4%	14,463	-12%	13,242	-3%	14,656
Total, Energy Research	252,308	1%	255,190	-6%	237,191	-2%	247,808
ES&H & Civilian Waste R&D	3,212	-11%	2,853	-12%	2,827	-0%	3,212
Environmental Management	25,544	-12%	22,491	-13%	22,284	-12%	22,414
Clean Coal Technology	—	-100%	—	-100%	—	-100%	—
Total, Science Jurisdiction	336,869	-6%	318,035	-13%	291,544	-5%	319,879

* Note: This table assumes that this laboratory is cut in each detail line above by the same percentage as DOE as a whole. The percentages on the total lines are calculated based upon the sum of the cuts in the detail lines. Depending on how the split of work at the lab within any total compares with the split in the DOE as a whole, the percentage cut at the lab on a total line may vary from the overall DOE percentage cut, and from cuts at any other lab.

Estimated Impact of Final House Science Committee Action at

Sandia National Laboratory

Comparison between Proposals
(dollars in thousands)

	FY 1995 Estimated Oblig.	Walker Cut %	FY 1996 Estimate (Walker)*	Rohrabacher Cut %	FY 1996 Est. (Rohrabacher)*	Doyle Cut %	FY 1996 Estimate (Doyle)*
Solar and Renewables							
Solar Programs	33,356	-48%	17,468	-57%	14,444	-10%	30,02[illegible]
Geothermal	7,000	-46%	3,767	-54%	3,233	-21%	5,5[illegible]
Hydrogen	1,500	160%	3,900	160%	3,900	160%	3,900
Other Solar and Renewables	6,732	-56%	2,946	-59%	2,752	-30%	4,717
Total, Solar and Renewables	48,588	-42%	28,081	-50%	24,329	-9%	44,197
Fossil Energy							
Coal	2,504	-68%	810	-68%	810	-26%	1,863
Oil	7,000	-47%	3,704	-50%	3,533	-0%	6,999
Gas	—	-49%	—	-50%	—	0%	—
Program Direction	—	-37%	—	-55%	—	-11%	—
Other Fossil	—	-33%	—	-32%	—	-36%	—
Total, Fossil Energy	9,504	-53%	4,514	-54%	4,343	-7%	8,862
Energy Efficiency							
Buildings	50	-52%	24	-65%	17	-46%	27
Industrial	2,919	-59%	1,190	-62%	1,104	-10%	2,628
Transportation	2,377	-46%	1,292	-48%	1,230	-10%	2,140
Utility	—	-100%	—	-100%	—	-100%	—
Other Energy Efficiency	—	-84%	—	-84%	—	-11%	—
Total, Energy Efficiency	5,346	-53%	2,506	-56%	2,351	-10%	4,795
Nuclear Energy							
Nuclear Energy R&D	3,220	-14%	2,763	-39%	1,956	-19%	2,608
Other	7,600	12%	8,482	12%	8,482	7%	8,103
Total, Nuclear Energy	10,820	4%	11,245	-4%	10,438	-1%	10,706
Energy Research							
Biological & Environmental Research	1,335	-15%	1,130	-18%	1,095	-2%	1,313
Fusion	8,437	-31%	5,820	-38%	5,247	-25%	6,298
Basic Energy Sciences	22,816	13%	25,739	4%	23,808	4%	23,657
Laboratory Technology Transfer	—	-100%	—	-100%	—	-30%	—
University & Science Education	695	-100%	—	-100%	—	-71%	200
Other	—	-34%	—	-37%	—	-47%	—
High Energy Physics	—	6%	—	5%	—	4%	—
Nuclear Physics	—	-4%	—	-12%	—	-3%	—
Total, Energy Research	33,283	-2%	32,689	-9%	30,150	-5%	31,468
ES&H & Civilian Waste R&D	350	-11%	311	-12%	308	-0%	350
Environmental Management	—	-12%	—	-13%	—	-12%	—
Clean Coal Technology	—	-100%	—	-100%	—	-100%	—
Total, Science Jurisdiction	107,891	-26%	79,346	-33%	71,919	-7%	100,378

* Note: This table assumes that this laboratory is cut in each detail line above by the same percentage as DOE as a whole. The percentages on the total lines are calculated based upon the sum of the cuts in the detail lines. Depending on how the split of work at the lab within any total compares with the split in the DOE as a whole, the percentage cut at the lab on a total line may vary from the overall DOE percentage cut, and from cuts at any other lab.

Estimated Impact of Final House Science Committee Action at

Lawrence Livermore National Laboratory

Comparison between Proposals
(dollars in thousands)

	FY 1995 Estimated Oblig.	Walker Cut %	FY 1996 Estimate (Walker)*	Rohrabacher Cut %	FY 1996 Est. (Rohrabacher)*	Doyle Cut %	FY 1996 Estimate (Doyle)*
Solar and Renewables							
Solar Programs	—	-48%	—	-57%	—	-10%	—
Geothermal	—	-46%	—	-54%	—	-21%	—
Hydrogen	1,000	160%	2,600	160%	2,600	160%	2,600
Other Solar and Renewables	—	-56%	—	-59%	—	-30%	—
Total, Solar and Renewables	1,000	160%	2,600	160%	2,600	160%	2,600
Fossil Energy							
Coal	220	-68%	71	-68%	71	-26%	164
Oil	350	-47%	185	-50%	177	-0%	350
Gas	150	-49%	77	-50%	75	0%	150
Program Direction	—	-37%	—	-55%	—	-11%	—
Other Fossil	—	-33%	—	-32%	—	-36%	—
Total, Fossil Energy	720	-54%	333	-55%	323	-8%	664
Energy Efficiency							
Buildings	9	-52%	2	-65%	2	-46%	3
Industrial	335	-59%	137	-62%	127	-10%	302
Transportation	295	-46%	160	-48%	153	-10%	266
Utility	—	-100%	—	-100%	—	-100%	—
Other Energy Efficiency	—	-84%	—	-84%	—	-11%	—
Total, Energy Efficiency	635	-53%	299	-56%	282	-10%	571
Nuclear Energy							
Nuclear Energy R&D	—	-14%	—	-39%	—	-19%	—
Other	—	12%	—	12%	—	7%	—
Total, Nuclear Energy	—	—	—	—	—	—	—
Energy Research							
Biological & Environmental Research	20,616	-15%	17,453	-18%	16,909	-2%	20,279
Fusion	27,400	-31%	18,901	-38%	17,042	-25%	20,452
Basic Energy Sciences	42,531	13%	47,981	4%	44,380	4%	44,099
Laboratory Technology Transfer	—	-100%	—	-100%	—	-30%	—
University & Science Education	1,000	-100%	—	-100%	—	-71%	287
Other	—	-34%	—	-37%	—	-47%	—
High Energy Physics	2,677	6%	2,835	5%	2,810	4%	2,772
Nuclear Physics	724	-4%	692	-12%	634	-3%	701
Total, Energy Research	94,948	-7%	87,862	-14%	81,775	-7%	88,590
ES&H & Civilian Waste R&D	1,130	-11%	1,004	-12%	995	-0%	1,130
Environmental Management	—	-12%	—	-13%	—	-12%	—
Clean Coal Technology	—	-100%	—	-100%	—	-100%	—
Total, Science Jurisdiction	98,433	-6%	92,098	-13%	85,975	-5%	93,555

* Note: This table assumes that this laboratory is cut in each detail line above by the same percentage as DOE as a whole. The percentages on the total lines are calculated based upon the sum of the cuts in the detail lines. Depending on how the split of work at the lab within any total compares with the split in the DOE as a whole, the percentage cut at the lab on a total line may vary from the overall DOE percentage cut, and from cuts at any other lab.

Estimated Impact of Final House Science Committee Action at

Los Alamos National Laboratory

Comparison between Proposals
(dollars in thousands)

	FY 1995 Estimated Oblig.	Walker Cut %	FY 1996 Estimate (Walker)*	Rohrabacher Cut %	FY 1996 Est. (Rohrabacher)*	Doyle Cut %	FY 1996 Estimate (Doyle)*
Solar and Renewables							
Solar Programs	100	-48%	52	-57%	43	-10%	90
Geothermal	1,400	-46%	753	-54%	647	-21%	1,111
Hydrogen	350	160%	910	160%	910	160%	910
Other Solar and Renewables	3,900	-56%	1,707	-59%	1,595	-30%	2,733
Total, Solar and Renewables	5,750	-40%	3,422	-44%	3,195	-16%	4,844
Fossil Energy							
Coal	—	-68%	—	-68%	—	-26%	—
Oil	265	-47%	140	-50%	134	-0%	265
Gas	300	-49%	154	-50%	149	0%	300
Program Direction	—	-37%	—	-55%	—	-11%	—
Other Fossil	—	-33%	—	-32%	—	-36%	—
Total, Fossil Energy	565	-48%	294	-50%	283	—	565
Energy Efficiency							
Buildings	5	-52%	2	-65%	2	-46%	3
Industrial	4,246	-59%	1,731	-62%	1,605	-10%	3,822
Transportation	2,800	-46%	1,522	-48%	1,449	-10%	2,521
Utility	—	-100%	—	-100%	—	-100%	—
Other Energy Efficiency	—	-84%	—	-84%	—	-11%	—
Total, Energy Efficiency	7,051	-54%	3,255	-57%	3,056	-10%	6,346
Nuclear Energy							
Nuclear Energy R&D	12,735	-14%	10,928	-39%	7,737	-19%	10,296
Other	1,200	12%	1,339	12%	1,339	7%	1,279
Total, Nuclear Energy	13,935	-12%	12,267	-35%	9,076	-17%	11,575
Energy Research							
Biological & Environmental Research	23,384	-15%	19,796	-18%	19,180	-2%	23,002
Fusion	6,196	-31%	4,274	-38%	3,854	-25%	4,625
Basic Energy Sciences	22,298	13%	25,155	4%	23,268	4%	23,120
Laboratory Technology Transfer	—	-100%	—	-100%	—	-30%	—
University & Science Education	1,208	-100%	—	-100%	—	-71%	347
Other	—	-34%	—	-37%	—	-47%	—
High Energy Physics	775	6%	821	5%	814	4%	803
Nuclear Physics	39,398	-4%	37,659	-12%	34,479	-3%	38,162
Total, Energy Research	93,259	-6%	87,705	-13%	81,595	-3%	90,059
ES&H & Civilian Waste R&D	2,557	-11%	2,271	-12%	2,251	-0%	2,557
Environmental Management	1,611	-12%	1,418	-13%	1,406	-12%	1,414
Clean Coal Technology	—	-100%	—	-100%	—	-100%	—
Total, Science Jurisdiction	124,728	-11%	110,632	-19%	100,862	-6%	117,360

* Note: This table assumes that this laboratory is cut in each detail line above by the same percentage as DOE as a whole. The percentages on the total lines are calculated based upon the sum of the cuts in the detail lines. Depending on how the split of work at the lab within any total compares with the split in the DOE as a whole, the percentage cut at the lab on a total line may vary from the overall DOE percentage cut, and from cuts at any other lab.

Estimated Impact of Final House Science Committee Action at:
Lawrence Berkeley National Laboratory
Comparison between Proposals
(dollars in thousands)

	FY 1995 Estimated Oblig.	Walker Cut %	FY 1996 Estimate (Walker)*	Rohrabacher Cut %	FY 1996 Est. (Rohrabacher)*	Doyle Cut %	FY 1996 Estimate (Doyle)*
Solar and Renewables							
Solar Programs	—	-48%	—	-57%	—	-10%	—
Geothermal	—	-46%	—	-54%	—	-21%	—
Hydrogen	—	160%	—	160%	—	160%	—
Other Solar and Renewables	250	-56%	109	-59%	102	-30%	175
Total, Solar and Renewables	250	-56%	109	-59%	102	-30%	175
Fossil Energy							
Coal	560	-68%	181	-68%	181	-26%	417
Oil	650	-47%	344	-50%	328	-0%	650
Gas	551	-49%	284	-50%	274	0%	551
Program Direction	—	-37%	—	-55%	—	-11%	—
Other Fossil	—	-33%	—	-32%	—	-36%	—
Total, Fossil Energy	1,761	-54%	809	-56%	783	-8%	1,618
Energy Efficiency							
Buildings	15,650	-52%	7,454	-65%	5,428	-46%	8,486
Industrial	799	-59%	326	-62%	302	-10%	719
Transportation	2,525	-46%	1,373	-48%	1,307	-10%	2,273
Utility	1,100	-100%	—	-100%	—	-100%	—
Other Energy Efficiency	100	-84%	16	-84%	16	-11%	89
Total, Energy Efficiency	20,174	-55%	9,169	-65%	7,053	-43%	11,567
Nuclear Energy							
Nuclear Energy R&D	—	-14%	—	-39%	—	-19%	—
Other	—	12%	—	12%	—	7%	—
Total, Nuclear Energy	—	—	—	—	—	—	—
Energy Research							
Biological & Environmental Research	44,564	-15%	37,726	-18%	36,552	-2%	43,835
Fusion	6,205	-31%	4,280	-38%	3,859	-25%	4,632
Basic Energy Sciences	56,573	13%	63,822	4%	59,033	4%	58,639
Laboratory Technology Transfer	8,626	-100%	—	-100%	—	-30%	6,064
University & Science Education	2,554	-100%	—	-100%	—	-71%	734
Other	6,043	-34%	3,993	-37%	3,797	-47%	3,184
High Energy Physics	24,538	6%	25,990	5%	25,761	4%	25,412
Nuclear Physics	25,108	-4%	24,000	-12%	21,973	-3%	24,320
Total, Energy Research	174,211	-8%	159,811	-13%	150,973	-4%	166,840
ES&H & Civilian Waste R&D	2,707	-11%	2,404	-12%	2,383	-0%	2,707
Environmental Management	13,902	-12%	12,240	-13%	12,129	-12%	12,199
Clean Coal Technology	—	-100%	—	-100%	—	-100%	—
Total, Science Jurisdiction	213,005	-13%	184,542	-19%	173,425	-8%	195,106

* Note: This table assumes that this laboratory is cut in each detail line above by the same percentage as DOE as a whole. The percentages on the total lines are calculated based upon the sum of the cuts in the detail lines. Depending on how the split of work at the lab within any total compares with the split in the DOE as a whole, the percentage cut at the lab on a total line may vary from the overall DOE percentage cut, and from cuts at any other lab.

Estimated Impact of Final House Science Committee Action at

Argonne National Laboratory — West

Comparison between Proposals
(dollars in thousands)

	FY 1995 Estimated Oblig.	Walker Cut %	FY 1996 Estimate (Walker)*	Rohrabacher Cut %	FY 1996 Est. (Rohrabacher)*	Doyle Cut %	FY 1996 Estimate (Doyle)*
Solar and Renewables							
Solar Programs	—	-48%	—	-57%	—	-10%	—
Geothermal	—	-46%	—	-54%	—	-21%	—
Hydrogen	—	160%	—	160%	—	160%	—
Other Solar and Renewables	—	-56%	—	-59%	—	-30%	—
Total, Solar and Renewables	—	—	—	—	—	—	—
Fossil Energy							
Coal	—	-68%	—	-68%	—	-26%	—
Oil	—	-47%	—	-50%	—	-0%	—
Gas	—	-49%	—	-50%	—	0%	—
Program Direction	—	-37%	—	-55%	—	-11%	—
Other Fossil	—	-33%	—	-32%	—	-36%	—
Total, Fossil Energy	—	—	—	—	—	—	—
Energy Efficiency							
Buildings	—	-52%	—	-65%	—	-46%	—
Industrial	—	-59%	—	-62%	—	-10%	—
Transportation	—	-46%	—	-48%	—	-10%	—
Utility	—	-100%	—	-100%	—	-100%	—
Other Energy Efficiency	—	-84%	—	-84%	—	-11%	—
Total, Energy Efficiency	—	—	—	—	—	—	—
Nuclear Energy							
Nuclear Energy R&D	7,527	-14%	6,459	-39%	4,573	-19%	6,085
Other	66,471	12%	74,188	12%	74,188	7%	70,869
Total, Nuclear Energy	73,998	9%	80,647	6%	78,761	4%	76,954
Energy Research							
Biological & Environmental Research	—	-15%	—	-18%	—	-2%	—
Fusion	—	-31%	—	-38%	—	-25%	—
Basic Energy Sciences	—	13%	—	4%	—	4%	—
Laboratory Technology Transfer	—	-100%	—	-100%	—	-30%	—
University & Science Education	—	-100%	—	-100%	—	-71%	—
Other	—	-34%	—	-37%	—	-47%	—
High Energy Physics	—	6%	—	5%	—	4%	—
Nuclear Physics	—	-4%	—	-12%	—	-3%	—
Total, Energy Research	—	—	—	—	—	—	—
ES&H & Civilian Waste R&D	—	-11%	—	-12%	—	-0%	—
Environmental Management	4,463	-12%	3,930	-13%	3,894	-12%	3,916
Clean Coal Technology	—	-100%	—	-100%	—	-100%	—
Total, Science Jurisdiction	78,461	8%	84,577	5%	82,655	3%	80,870

* Note: This table assumes that this laboratory is cut in each detail line above by the same percentage as DOE as a whole. The percentages on the total lines are calculated based upon the sum of the cuts in the detail lines. Depending on how the split of work at the lab within any total compares with the split in the DOE as a whole, the percentage cut at the lab on a total line may vary from the overall DOE percentage cut, and from cuts at any other lab.

Estimated Impact of Final House Science Committee Action at:

Idaho National Engineering Laboratory

Comparison between Proposals
(dollars in thousands)

	FY 1995 Estimated Oblig.	Walker Cut %	FY 1996 Estimate (Walker)*	Rohrabacher Cut %	FY 1996 Est. (Rohrabacher)*	Doyle Cut %	FY 1996 Estimate (Doyle)*
Solar and Renewables							
Solar Programs	—	-48%	—	-57%	—	-10%	—
Geothermal	4,500	-46%	2,422	-54%	2,079	-21%	3,571
Hydrogen	—	160%	—	160%	—	160%	—
Other Solar and Renewables	450	-56%	197	-59%	184	-30%	315
Total, Solar and Renewables	4,950	-47%	2,619	-54%	2,263	-21%	3,886
Fossil Energy							
Coal	1,040	-68%	336	-68%	336	-26%	774
Oil	327	-47%	173	-50%	165	-0%	327
Gas	320	-49%	165	-50%	159	0%	320
Program Direction	—	-37%	—	-55%	—	-11%	—
Other Fossil	—	-33%	—	-32%	—	-36%	—
Total, Fossil Energy	1,687	-60%	674	-61%	660	-16%	1,421
Energy Efficiency							
Buildings	5	-52%	2	-65%	2	-46%	3
Industrial	3,424	-59%	1,396	-62%	1,295	-10%	3,082
Transportation	3,318	-46%	1,804	-48%	1,717	-10%	2,987
Utility	—	-100%	—	-100%	—	-100%	—
Other Energy Efficiency	—	-84%	—	-84%	—	-11%	—
Total, Energy Efficiency	6,747	-53%	3,202	-55%	3,014	-10%	6,072
Nuclear Energy							
Nuclear Energy R&D	8,040	-14%	6,899	-39%	4,885	-19%	6,500
Other	1,620	12%	1,808	12%	1,808	7%	1,727
Total, Nuclear Energy	9,660	-10%	8,707	-31%	6,693	-15%	8,227
Energy Research							
Biological & Environmental Research	3,110	-15%	2,633	-18%	2,551	-2%	3,059
Fusion	3,180	-31%	2,194	-38%	1,978	-25%	2,374
Basic Energy Sciences	2,816	13%	3,177	4%	2,938	4%	2,920
Laboratory Technology Transfer	745	-100%	—	-100%	—	-30%	524
University & Science Education	3,000	-100%	—	-100%	—	-71%	862
Other	—	-34%	—	-37%	—	-47%	—
High Energy Physics	—	6%	—	5%	—	4%	—
Nuclear Physics	—	-4%	—	-12%	—	-3%	—
Total, Energy Research	12,851	-38%	8,004	-42%	7,467	-24%	9,739
ES&H & Civilian Waste R&D	3,855	-11%	3,424	-12%	3,393	-0%	3,855
Environmental Management	12,953	-12%	11,405	-13%	11,301	-12%	11,366
Clean Coal Technology	—	-100%	—	-100%	—	-100%	—
Total, Science Jurisdiction	52,703	-28%	38,035	-34%	34,791	-15%	44,566

* Note: This table assumes that this laboratory is cut in each detail line above by the same percentage as DOE as a whole. The percentages on the total lines are calculated based upon the sum of the cuts in the detail lines. Depending on how the split of work at the lab within any total compares with the split in the DOE as a whole, the percentage cut at the lab on a total line may vary from the overall DOE percentage cut, and from cuts at any other lab.

Estimated Impact of Final House Science Committee Action at
Brookhaven National Laboratory
Comparison between Proposals
(dollars in thousands)

	FY 1995 Estimated Oblig.	Walker Cut %	FY 1996 Estimate (Walker)*	Rohrabacher Cut %	FY 1996 Est. (Rohrabacher)*	Doyle Cut %	FY 1996 Estimate (Doyle)*
Solar and Renewables							
Solar Programs	400	-48%	209	-57%	173	-10%	360
Geothermal	—	-46%	—	-54%	—	-21%	—
Hydrogen	100	160%	260	160%	260	160%	260
Other Solar and Renewables	625	-56%	274	-59%	256	-30%	438
Total, Solar and Renewables	1,125	-34%	743	-39%	689	-6%	1,058
Fossil Energy							
Coal	258	-68%	83	-68%	83	-26%	192
Oil	825	-47%	437	-50%	416	-0%	825
Gas	—	-49%	—	-50%	—	0%	—
Program Direction	—	-37%	—	-55%	—	-11%	—
Other Fossil	—	-33%	—	-32%	—	-36%	—
Total, Fossil Energy	1,083	-52%	520	-54%	499	-6%	1,017
Energy Efficiency							
Buildings	1,285	-52%	612	-65%	446	-46%	697
Industrial	—	-59%	—	-62%	—	-10%	—
Transportation	500	-46%	272	-48%	259	-10%	450
Utility	—	-100%	—	-100%	—	-100%	—
Other Energy Efficiency	—	-84%	—	-84%	—	-11%	—
Total, Energy Efficiency	1,785	-50%	884	-61%	705	-36%	1,147
Nuclear Energy							
Nuclear Energy R&D	150	-14%	129	-39%	91	-19%	121
Other	250	12%	279	12%	279	7%	267
Total, Nuclear Energy	400	2%	408	-8%	370	-3%	388
Energy Research							
Biological & Environmental Research	28,367	-15%	24,015	-18%	23,267	-2%	27,903
Fusion	83	-31%	57	-38%	52	-25%	62
Basic Energy Sciences	73,372	13%	82,773	4%	76,562	4%	76,077
Laboratory Technology Transfer	7,920	-100%	—	-100%	—	-30%	5,568
University & Science Education	2,394	-100%	—	-100%	—	-71%	688
Other	7,837	-34%	5,179	-37%	4,924	-47%	4,129
High Energy Physics	74,335	6%	78,735	5%	78,040	4%	76,983
Nuclear Physics	96,445	-4%	92,189	-12%	84,403	-3%	93,419
Total, Energy Research	290,753	-3%	282,948	-8%	267,248	-2%	284,829
ES&H & Civilian Waste R&D	1,874	-11%	1,664	-12%	1,650	-0%	1,874
Environmental Management	24,602	-12%	21,661	-13%	21,464	-12%	21,588
Clean Coal Technology	—	-100%	—	-100%	—	-100%	—
Total, Science Jurisdiction	321,622	-4%	308,828	-9%	292,625	-3%	311,901

* Note: This table assumes that this laboratory is cut in each detail line above by the same percentage as DOE as a whole. The percentages on the total lines are calculated based upon the sum of the cuts in the detail lines. Depending on how the split of work at the lab within any total compares with the split in the DOE as a whole, the percentage cut at the lab on a total line may vary from the overall DOE percentage cut, and from cuts at any other lab.

Solar and Renewables							
Solar Programs	300	-48%	157	-57%	130	-10%	270
Geothermal	—	-46%	—	-54%	—	-21%	—
Hydrogen	—	160%	—	160%	—	160%	—
Other Solar and Renewables	950	-56%	416	-59%	388	-30%	666
Total, Solar and Renewables	1,250	-54%	573	-59%	518	-25%	936
Fossil Energy							
Coal	1,075	-68%	348	-68%	348	-26%	800
Oil	—	-47%	—	-50%	—	-0%	—
Gas	398	-49%	205	-50%	198	0%	398
Program Direction	—	-37%	—	-55%	—	-11%	—
Other Fossil	—	-33%	—	-32%	—	-36%	—
Total, Fossil Energy	1,473	-62%	553	-63%	546	-19%	1,198
Energy Efficiency							
Buildings	10,493	-52%	4,998	-65%	3,639	-46%	5,690
Industrial	3,660	-59%	1,492	-62%	1,384	-10%	3,295
Transportation	475	-46%	258	-48%	246	-10%	428
Utility	300	-100%	—	-100%	—	-100%	—
Other Energy Efficiency	375	-84%	60	-84%	60	-11%	334
Total, Energy Efficiency	15,303	-56%	6,808	-65%	5,329	-36%	9,747
Nuclear Energy							
Nuclear Energy R&D	350	-14%	300	-39%	213	-19%	283
Other	—	12%	—	12%	—	7%	—
Total, Nuclear Energy	350	-14%	300	-39%	213	-19%	283
Energy Research							
Biological & Environmental Research	82,712	-15%	70,021	-18%	67,841	-2%	81,359
Fusion	3,230	-31%	2,228	-38%	2,009	-25%	2,411
Basic Energy Sciences	11,949	13%	13,480	4%	12,469	4%	12,390
Laboratory Technology Transfer	7,712	-100%	—	-100%	—	-30%	5,421
University & Science Education	870	-100%	—	-100%	—	-71%	250
Other	3,744	-34%	2,474	-37%	2,352	-47%	1,973
High Energy Physics	45	6%	48	5%	47	4%	47
Nuclear Physics	—	-4%	—	-12%	—	-3%	—
Total, Energy Research	110,262	-20%	88,251	-23%	84,718	-6%	103,851
ES&H & Civilian Waste R&D	17,847	-11%	15,850	-12%	15,709	-0%	17,846
Environmental Management	—	-12%	—	-13%	—	-12%	—
Clean Coal Technology	—	-100%	—	-100%	—	-100%	—
Total, Science Jurisdiction	146,485	-23%	112,335	-27%	107,032	-9%	133,861

• Note: This table assumes that this laboratory is cut in each detail line above by the same percentage as DOE as a whole. The percentages on the total lines are calculated based upon the sum of the cuts in the detail lines. Depending on how the split of work at the lab within any total compares with the split in the DOE as a whole, the percentage cut at the lab on a total line may vary from the overall DOE percentage cut, and from cuts at any other lab.

Estimated Impact of Final House Science Committee Action at:
National Renewable Energy Laboratory
Comparison between Proposals
(dollars in thousands)

	FY 1995 Estimated Oblig.	Walker Cut %	FY 1996 Estimate (Walker)*	Rohrabacher Cut %	FY 1996 Est. (Rohrabacher)*	Doyle Cut %	FY 1996 Estimate (Doyle)*
Solar and Renewables							
Solar Programs	155,810	-48%	81,594	-57%	67,468	-10%	140,249
Geothermal	580	-46%	312	-54%	268	-21%	460
Hydrogen	2,200	160%	5,720	160%	5,720	160%	5,720
Other Solar and Renewables	750	-56%	328	-59%	307	-30%	526
Total, Solar and Renewables	159,340	-45%	87,954	-54%	73,763	-8%	146,954
Fossil Energy							
Coal	348	-68%	113	-68%	113	-26%	259
Oil	—	-47%	—	-50%	—	-0%	—
Gas	—	-49%	—	-50%	—	0%	—
Program Direction	—	-37%	—	-55%	—	-11%	—
Other Fossil	—	-33%	—	-32%	—	-36%	—
Total, Fossil Energy	348	-68%	113	-68%	113	-26%	259
Energy Efficiency							
Buildings	12,775	-52%	6,084	-65%	4,431	-46%	6,927
Industrial	10,290	-59%	4,195	-62%	3,891	-10%	9,263
Transportation	46,178	-46%	25,103	-48%	23,896	-10%	41,576
Utility	1,300	-100%	—	-100%	—	-100%	—
Other Energy Efficiency	250	-84%	40	-84%	40	-11%	223
Total, Energy Efficiency	70,793	-50%	35,422	-54%	32,258	-18%	57,989
Nuclear Energy							
Nuclear Energy R&D	—	-14%	—	-39%	—	-19%	—
Other	—	12%	—	12%	—	7%	—
Total, Nuclear Energy	—	—	—	—	—	—	—
Energy Research							
Biological & Environmental Research	—	-15%	—	-18%	—	-2%	—
Fusion	—	-31%	—	-38%	—	-25%	—
Basic Energy Sciences	4,603	13%	5,193	4%	4,802	.4%	4,773
Laboratory Technology Transfer	—	-100%	—	-100%	—	-30%	—
University & Science Education	150	-100%	—	-100%	—	-71%	43
Other	—	-34%	—	-37%	—	-47%	—
High Energy Physics	—	6%	—	5%	—	4%	—
Nuclear Physics	—	-4%	—	-12%	—	-3%	—
Total, Energy Research	4,753	9%	5,193	1%	4,803	1%	4,816
ES&H & Civilian Waste R&D	—	-11%	—	-12%	—	-0%	—
Environmental Management	—	-12%	—	-13%	—	-12%	—
Clean Coal Technology	—	-100%	—	-100%	—	-100%	—
Total, Science Jurisdiction	235,234	-45%	128,682	-53%	110,937	-11%	210,018

* Note: This table assumes that this laboratory is cut in each detail line above by the same percentage as DOE as a whole. The percentages on the total lines are calculated based upon the sum of the cuts in the detail lines. Depending on how the split of work at the lab within any total compares with the split in the DOE as a whole, the percentage cut at the lab on a total line may vary from the overall DOE percentage cut, and from cuts at any other lab.

Estimated Impact of Final House Science Committee Action in:

California

Comparison between Proposals
(dollars in thousands)

	FY 1995 Estimated Oblig.	Walker Cut %	FY 1996 Estimate (Walker)*	Rohrabacher Cut %	FY 1996 Est. (Rohrabacher)*	Doyle Cut %	FY 1996 Estimate (Doyle)*
Solar and Renewables							
Solar Programs	—	-48%	—	-57%	—	-10%	—
Geothermal	—	-46%	—	-54%	—	-21%	—
Hydrogen	1,000	160%	2,600	160%	2,600	160%	2,600
Other Solar and Renewables	7,519	-56%	3,291	-59%	3,074	-30%	5,269
Total, Solar and Renewables	8,519	-31%	5,891	-33%	5,674	-8%	7,869
Fossil Energy							
Coal	3,463	-68%	1,120	-68%	1,120	-26%	2,577
Oil	2,670	-47%	1,413	-50%	1,347	-0%	2,670
Gas	852	-49%	438	-50%	424	0%	852
Program Direction	—	-37%	—	-55%	—	-11%	—
Other Fossil	—	-33%	—	-32%	—	-36%	—
Total, Fossil Energy	6,985	-57%	2,971	-59%	2,891	-13%	6,099
Energy Efficiency							
Buildings	16,055	-52%	7,647	-65%	5,568	-46%	8,705
Industrial	11,335	-59%	4,621	-62%	4,286	-10%	10,204
Transportation	2,820	-46%	1,533	-48%	1,459	-10%	2,539
Utility	1,100	-100%	—	-100%	—	-100%	—
Other Energy Efficiency	100	-84%	16	-84%	16	-11%	89
Total, Energy Efficiency	31,410	-56%	13,817	-64%	11,329	-31%	21,537
Nuclear Energy							
Nuclear Energy R&D	41,944	-14%	35,994	-39%	25,482	-19%	33,910
Other	—	12%	—	12%	—	7%	—
Total, Nuclear Energy	41,944	-14%	35,994	-39%	25,482	-19%	33,910
Energy Research							
Biological & Environmental Research	99,723	-15%	84,422	-18%	81,794	-2%	98,092
Fusion	103,371	-31%	71,307	-38%	64,293	-25%	77,159
Basic Energy Sciences	140,825	13%	158,869	4%	146,948	4%	146,017
Laboratory Technology Transfer	9,166	-100%	—	-100%	—	-30%	6,444
University & Science Education	3,674	-100%	—	-100%	—	-71%	1,056
Other	6,887	-34%	4,551	-37%	4,327	-47%	3,628
High Energy Physics	202,950	6%	214,963	5%	213,066	4%	210,179
Nuclear Physics	28,504	-4%	27,246	-12%	24,945	-3%	27,610
Total, Energy Research	595,100	-6%	561,358	-10%	535,373	-4%	570,185
ES&H & Civilian Waste R&D	9,570	-11%	8,499	-12%	8,424	-0%	9,569
Environmental Management	37,139	-12%	32,700	-13%	32,402	-12%	32,588
Clean Coal Technology	—	-100%	—	-100%	—	-100%	—
Total, Science Jurisdiction	730,667	-10%	661,230	-15%	621,575	-7%	681,757

* Note: This table assumes that this state is cut in each detail line above by the same percentage as DOE as a whole. The percentages on the total lines are calculated based upon the sum of the cuts in the detail lines. Depending on how the split of work in the state within any total compares with the split in the DOE as a whole, the percentage cut in the state on a total line may vary from the overall DOE percentage cut, and from cuts in any other state.

Printed in Great Britain
by Amazon

83949209R00386